48: *American Poets, 1880-1945,* Second Series, edited by Peter Quartermain (1986)

49: *American Literary Publishing Houses, 1638-1899,* 2 parts, edited by Peter Dzwonkoski (1986)

50: *Afro-American Writers Before the Harlem Renaissance,* edited by Trudier Harris (1986)

51: *Afro-American Writers from the Harlem Renaissance to 1940,* edited by Trudier Harris (1987)

52: *American Writers for Children Since 1960: Fiction,* edited by Glenn E. Estes (1986)

53: *Canadian Writers Since 1960,* First Series, edited by W. H. New (1986)

54: *American Poets, 1880-1945,* Third Series, 2 parts, edited by Peter Quartermain (1987)

55: *Victorian Prose Writers Before 1867,* edited by William B. Thesing (1987)

56: *German Fiction Writers, 1914-1945,* edited by James Hardin (1987)

57: *Victorian Prose Writers After 1867,* edited by William B. Thesing (1987)

58: *Jacobean and Caroline Dramatists,* edited by Fredson Bowers (1987)

59: *American Literary Critics and Scholars, 1800-1850,* edited by John W. Rathbun and Monica M. Grecu (1987)

60: *Canadian Writers Since 1960,* Second Series, edited by W. H. New (1987)

61: *American Writers for Children Since 1960: Poets, Illustrators, and Nonfiction Authors,* edited by Glenn E. Estes (1987)

62: *Elizabethan Dramatists,* edited by Fredson Bowers (1987)

63: *Modern American Critics, 1920-1955,* edited by Gregory S. Jay (1988)

64: *American Literary Critics and Scholars, 1850-1880,* edited by John W. Rathbun and Monica M. Grecu (1988)

65: *French Novelists, 1900-1930,* edited by Catharine Savage Brosman (1988)

66: *German Fiction Writers, 1885-1913,* 2 parts, edited by James Hardin (1988)

67: *Modern American Critics Since 1955,* edited by Gregory S. Jay (1988)

68: *Canadian Writers, 1920-1959,* First Series, edited by W. H. New (1988)

69: *Contemporary German Fiction Writers,* First Series, edited by Wolfgang D. Elfe and James Hardin (1988)

70: *British Mystery Writers, 1860-1919,* edited by Bernard Benstock and Thomas F. Staley (1988)

71: *American Literary Critics and Scholars, 1880-1900,* edited by John W. Rathbun and Monica M. Grecu (1988)

72: *French Novelists, 1930-1960,* edited by Catharine Savage Brosman (1988)

73: *American Magazine Journalists, 1741-1850,* edited by Sam G. Riley (1988)

Documentary Series

1: *Sherwood Anderson, Willa Cather, John Dos Passos, Theodore Dreiser, F. Scott Fitzgerald, Ernest Hemingway, Sinclair Lewis,* edited by Margaret A. Van Antwerp (1982)

2: *James Gould Cozzens, James T. Farrell, William Faulkner, John O'Hara, John Steinbeck, Thomas Wolfe, Richard Wright,* edited by Margaret A. Van Antwerp (1982)

3: *Saul Bellow, Jack Kerouac, Norman Mailer, Vladimir Nabokov, John Updike, Kurt Vonnegut,* edited by Mary Bruccoli (1983)

4: *Tennessee Williams,* edited by Margaret A. Van Antwerp and Sally Johns (1984)

5: *American Transcendentalists,* edited by Joel Myerson (1988)

Yearbooks

1980, edited by Karen L. Rood, Jean W. Ross, and Richard Ziegfeld (1981)

1981, edited by Karen L. Rood, Jean W. Ross, and Richard Ziegfeld (1982)

1982, edited by Richard Ziegfeld; associate editors: Jean W. Ross and Lynne C. Zeigler (1983)

1983, edited by Mary Bruccoli and Jean W. Ross; associate editor: Richard Ziegfeld (1984)

1984, edited by Jean W. Ross (1985)

1985, edited by Jean W. Ross (1986)

1986, edited by J. M. Brook (1987)

1987, edited by J. M. Brook (1988)

Concise Series

The New Consciousness, 1941-1968 (1987)

Colonization to the American Renaissance, 1640-1865 (1988)

Realism, Naturalism, and Local Color, 1865-1917 (1988)

Dictionary of Literary Biography • Volume Seventy-three

American Magazine Journalists, 1741-1850

Dictionary of Literary Biography • Volume Seventy-three

American Magazine Journalists, 1741-1850

Edited by
Sam G. Riley
Virginia Polytechnic Institute and State University

A Bruccoli Clark Layman Book
Gale Research Inc. • Book Tower • Detroit, Michigan 48226

Manufactured by Edwards Brothers, Inc.
Ann Arbor, Michigan
Printed in the United States of America

Library of Congress Cataloging-in-Publication Data

American magazine journalists, 1741-1850/edited by Sam G. Riley.
    p. cm.—(Dictionary of literary biography; v. 73)
"A Bruccoli Clark Layman book."
Includes index.
ISBN 0-8103-4551-X
    1. Journalists—United States—Biography. I. Riley, Sam G. II. Series.
PN4871.A47 1988
070'.92'2—dc19
[B]   88-17586
                                                          CIP

To Janie B. and Sam G. Riley, Jr.

wonderful parents, who, like a good reference book, are
a font of knowledge and are virtually always right

Contents

Plan of the Series ix

Foreword xi

Acknowledgments xv

Park Benjamin (1809-1864) 3
  Edward Sumter

Andrew Bradford (1686-1742) 11
  Carol Sue Humphrey

William Bradford III (1719-1791) 17
  Patricia Bradley

Charles Brockden Brown (1771-1810) 21
  Mark J. Schaefermeyer

Orestes A. Brownson (1803-1876) 29
  Sam G. Riley

Joseph Tinker Buckingham (1779-1861)
  and Edwin Buckingham (1810-1833) 38
  James Boylan

William Evans Burton (1804-1860) 43
  Jacqueline Steck

Mathew Carey (1760-1839) 50
  James N. Green

Stephen Cullen Carpenter (birthdate
  unknown-1820?) 67
  David E. Matchen

Lewis Gaylord Clark (1808-1873) 72
  Kathleen Kearney Keeshen

Joseph Dennie (1768-1812) 76
  James S. Featherston

Ralph Waldo Emerson (1803-1882) 85
  Donald R. Avery

Timothy Flint (1780-1840) 93
  Elizabeth M. Fraas

Benjamin Franklin (1706-1790) 101
  Alf Pratte

Sarah Margaret Fuller, Marchesa D'Ossoli
  (1810-1850) 112
  Nora Baker

William Davis Gallagher (1808-1894) 124
  John Nerone

William Gibbons (birth and death
  dates unknown) 130
  Ada Van Gastel

Caroline H. Gilman (1794-1888) 133
  Maurine H. Beasley

Louis A. Godey (1804-1878) 139
  Edward H. Sewell, Jr.

Samuel Griswold Goodrich (Peter Parley)
  (1793-1860) 146
  Judith Serrin

George Rex Graham (1813-1894) 153
  Alf Pratte

Sarah Josepha Hale (1788-1879) 159
  Edward H. Sewell, Jr.

James Hall (1793-1868) 168
  Elizabeth M. Fraas

Henry William Herbert (Frank Forester)
  (1807-1858) 175
  Mary S. Mander

William Gibbes Hunt (1791-1833) 184
  William E. Huntzicker

John Inman (1805-1850) 192
  Sam G. Riley

Washington Irving (1783-1859) 197
  Jacqueline Steck

Caroline M. Kirkland (1801-1864) 207
  Ada Van Gastel

Hugh Swinton Legaré (1797-1843) 217
  Edward L. Tucker

George Pope Morris (1802-1864) 221
  Jean Folkerts

Thomas Paine (1737-1809) 225
  James Glen Stovall

Edgar Allan Poe (1809-1849) 235
  John A. Lent

William Carey Richards (1818-1892) 252
  Ernest C. Hynds

George Ripley (1802-1880) 258
  Lloyd E. Chiasson

Lydia H. Sigourney (1791-1865) 264
  Dorothy A. Bowles

William Gilmore Simms (1806-1870) 275
  James Everett Kibler, Jr.

John Stuart Skinner (1788-1851) 293
  Jack W. Berryman

Contents

Ann Sophia Stephens (1810-1886) 299
   Sam G. Riley

Thomas Swords (1763-1843)
   and James Swords (?-1844) 306
   June N. Adamson

Isaiah Thomas (1750-1831) 310
   Terry Hynes

John Reuben Thompson (1823-1873) 327
   George Green Shackelford

Tobias Watkins (1780-1855) 331
   June N. Adamson

Noah Webster (1758-1843) 335
   Lloyd E. Chiasson

Daniel K. Whitaker (1801-1881) 342
   Patt Foster Roberson

Nathaniel Parker Willis (1806-1867) 349
   John J. Pauly

Frances Wright (1795-1852) 357
   Earl L. Conn

Checklist of Further Readings 363

Contributors 367

Cumulative Index 371

Plan of the Series

. . . Almost the most prodigious asset of a country, and perhaps its most precious possession, is its native literary product—when that product is fine and noble and enduring.

Mark Twain*

The advisory board, the editors, and the publisher of the *Dictionary of Literary Biography* are joined in endorsing Mark Twain's declaration. The literature of a nation provides an inexhaustible resource of permanent worth. We intend to make literature and its creators better understood and more accessible to students and the reading public, while satisfying the standards of teachers and scholars.

To meet these requirements, *literary biography* has been construed in terms of the author's achievement. The most important thing about a writer is his writing. Accordingly, the entries in *DLB* are career biographies, tracing the development of the author's canon and the evolution of his reputation.

The purpose of *DLB* is not only to provide reliable information in a convenient format but also to place the figures in the larger perspective of literary history and to offer appraisals of their accomplishments by qualified scholars.

The publication plan for *DLB* resulted from two years of preparation. The project was proposed to Bruccoli Clark by Frederick G. Ruffner, president of the Gale Research Company, in November 1975. After specimen entries were prepared and typeset, an advisory board was formed to refine the entry format and develop the series rationale. In meetings held during 1976, the publisher, series editors, and advisory board approved the scheme for a comprehensive biographical dictionary of persons who contributed to North American literature. Editorial work on the first volume began in January 1977, and it was published in 1978. In order to make *DLB* more than a reference tool and to compile volumes that individually have claim to status as literary history, it was decided to organize volumes by topic, period, or genre. Each of these freestanding volumes provides a biographical-bibliographical guide and overview for a particular area of literature. We are convinced that this organization—as opposed to a single alphabet method—constitutes a valuable innovation in the presentation of reference material. The volume plan necessarily requires many decisions for the placement and treatment of authors who might properly be included in two or three volumes. In some instances a major figure will be included in separate volumes, but with different entries emphasizing the aspect of his career appropriate to each volume. Ernest Hemingway, for example, is represented in *American Writers in Paris, 1920-1939* by an entry focusing on his expatriate apprenticeship; he is also in *American Novelists, 1910-1945* with an entry surveying his entire career. Each volume includes a cumulative index of subject authors and articles. Comprehensive indexes to the entire series are planned.

With volume ten in 1982 it was decided to enlarge the scope of *DLB*. By the end of 1986 twenty-one volumes treating British literature had been published, and volumes for Commonwealth and Modern European literature were in progress. The series has been further augmented by the *DLB Yearbooks* (since 1981) which update published entries and add new entries to keep the *DLB* current with contemporary activity. There have also been *DLB Documentary Series* volumes which provide biographical and critical source materials for figures whose work is judged to have particular interest for students. One of these companion volumes is entirely devoted to Tennessee Williams.

We define literature as the *intellectual commerce of a nation:* not merely as belles lettres but as that ample and complex process by which ideas are generated, shaped, and transmitted. *DLB* entries are not limited to "creative writers" but extend to other figures who in their time and in their way influenced the mind of a people. Thus the series encompasses historians, journalists, publishers, and screenwriters. By this means readers of *DLB* may be aided to perceive litera-

*From an unpublished section of Mark Twain's autobiography, copyright © by the Mark Twain Company.

ture not as cult scripture in the keeping of intellectual high priests but firmly positioned at the center of a nation's life.

DLB includes the major writers appropriate to each volume and those standing in the ranks immediately behind them. Scholarly and critical counsel has been sought in deciding which minor figures to include and how full their entries should be. Wherever possible, useful references are made to figures who do not warrant separate entries.

Each *DLB* volume has a volume editor responsible for planning the volume, selecting the figures for inclusion, and assigning the entries. Volume editors are also responsible for preparing, where appropriate, appendices surveying the major periodicals and literary and intellectual movements for their volumes, as well as lists of further readings. Work on the series as a whole is coordinated at the Bruccoli Clark Layman editorial center in Columbia, South Carolina, where the editorial staff is responsible for accuracy of the published volumes.

One feature that distinguishes *DLB* is the illustration policy—its concern with the iconography of literature. Just as an author is influenced by his surroundings, so is the reader's understanding of the author enhanced by a knowledge of his environment. Therefore *DLB* volumes include not only drawings, paintings, and photographs of authors, often depicting them at various stages in their careers, but also illustrations of their families and places where they lived. Title pages are regularly reproduced in facsimile along with dust jackets for modern authors. The dust jackets are a special feature of *DLB* because they often document better than anything else the way in which an author's work was perceived in its own time. Specimens of the writers' manuscripts are included when feasible.

Samuel Johnson rightly decreed that "The chief glory of every people arises from its authors." The purpose of the *Dictionary of Literary Biography* is to compile literary history in the surest way available to us—by accurate and comprehensive treatment of the lives and work of those who contributed to it.

The *DLB* Advisory Board

Foreword

This volume of the *Dictionary of Literary Biography* is the first in a series of three volumes devoted to magazine editors and publishers from 1741 to 1950. This volume treats magazine journalists who were active from 1741-1850; subsequent volumes cover the periods 1850-1900 and 1900-1950. Only editors and publishers of periodicals having substantial literary content have been included. Excluded were magazine journalists who worked with specialized, nonliterary magazines, such as most business magazines, newsmagazines, and agricultural periodicals.

The first American magazines were received indifferently by colonial readers. The earliest, Andrew Bradford's *American Magazine*, lasted for but three monthly issues in 1741. The second, Benjamin Franklin's *General Magazine*, did little better, publishing for six months in that same year. The third, the *Boston Weekly Magazine* of 1743, was similarly short-lived, lasting for three issues. Throughout the 1700s, according to the calculations of magazine historian Frank Luther Mott, the average life of an American magazine was only eighteen months.

By the mid-1700s most Americans were too busy taking care of their basic needs to devote much time to reading, and even if they had the time, they were unable to afford the cost of a magazine subscription. By the same token there were few writers in colonial America who were adept at providing copy for the magazines attempted on this side of the Atlantic. Most early magazines were filled largely with "selected" material taken without payment from books, newspapers, and other magazines, most of which were English.

Early editors and publishers were also hampered by distribution problems—bad roads and uneven postal service. Given a small population spread thinly over a huge geographic area, getting magazines to subscribers was no easy matter, a factor that served to keep the circulation of even the most successful eighteenth-century magazines to about fifteen hundred copies. These problems were exacerbated by the fact that the raw materials of publishing—presses, type, ink, and paper—had to be imported at considerable cost, and that magazines of this period contained only a tiny amount of advertising.

Still, a quest for cultural independence from England, paradoxically coupled with a desire to emulate the success of English periodicals, led a fair number of enterprising Americans to venture into the highly risky magazine business. Some of the best efforts of the 1700s were Boston's *American Magazine and Historical Chronicle* (1743-1745); Philadelphia's *American Magazine and Monthly Chronicle* (1757-1758); the *Royal American Magazine* of Boston (1774-1775); Newark's *United States Magazine* (1779); New York's *American Magazine* (1787), *Columbian Magazine* (1787-1792), and *New York Magazine* (1790-1797); Philadelphia's *American Museum* (1787-1792); and the *Massachusetts Magazine* of Boston (1789-1796).

Obviously, the primary magazine publishing centers in eighteenth-century America were Philadelphia, Boston, and New York. Unless one counts the *North Carolina Magazine, or Useful Intelligencer* (1764-1765), which was part magazine, part newspaper, the earliest journal south of Philadelphia was the *Free Universal Magazine* (1793) published in Baltimore, a city that thereafter made rapid gains in publishing and accounted for five more eighteenth-century titles. The only other southern city to achieve any importance in early magazine publishing was Charleston, South Carolina, home to three fledgling journals before 1800. To the west, the first magazine city was Lexington, Kentucky, though no titles were published there until just after the turn of the century.

As the years passed, editors found it somewhat easier to obtain original copy. Though items were often identified as original, most pieces were run without credit to the author or signed only with initials or a pen name. The practice of anonymity in eighteenth- and nineteenth-century periodicals can be attributed partly to a residual Puritan belief that art and literature should be their own reward; partly to the notion that writing was not an altogether respectable occupation for genteel folk; partly to the selfish, if often necessary position of the editor-publisher—that if their writers remained unknown to the reading public, they could not command much compensation for their writings. In addition, magazine proprietors often rationalized their policy of running copy unsigned by arguing that such a practice presented the work of new, unknown writers on equal footing with that of more famous contributors. In some cases, publishing contributors' names would have been an embarrassment to the editor, who frequently had to write most of an issue's original copy himself.

Most early American magazines can safely be described as "miscellanies"; they usually had a generous measure of political content, entirely natural in such politically charged times. Later, especially after the War of 1812, "literary miscellanies," magazines whose editors wished to popularize belles lettres, emerged. Also in the decade from 1810 to 1820 appeared what writer Neal Edgar has called "special miscellanies," magazines that attempted to direct their still rather general content at identifiable groups—members of specific organizations, women interested in fashion, those who still had a keen interest in the English heritage, and the like.

It is important to keep in mind that the magazines of this early period were basically elitist—published by and for the American "aristocracy." Subscribers were more accurately supporters than customers. Their writers were educated business and professional people or clergy who wrote for pleasure, not for profit. A feeling of noblesse oblige pervades much early magazine copy, the writers' polished, gentlemanly prose and verse, replete with classical allusions, often reflecting on the civic virtue of the higher orders of society. One also detects a considerable "literary patriotism," a desire to stimulate a new American literature.

On the whole, magazine copy of the late 1700s and early 1800s tends to be far less frivolous than its present-day equivalent, usually employing the essay style popularized still earlier in England by Joseph Addison and Sir Richard Steele. It was not until the 1840s, the era of Jacksonian democracy, that the hold of elitism began to relax. Fiction occupied little space in America's earliest magazines, though verse, both reprinted and original, was plentiful. Some of the most memorable magazine poetry was satirical, most of the worst, sentimental.

In 1800 only a dozen American magazines were being published, yet in the two decades that followed, the total increased to well over one hundred. During the proliferation of magazine publishing, fiction increased in popularity, and homegrown verse took a back seat to the works of English poets, especially Sir Walter Scott and

Lord Byron. Still, the first two decades of the nineteenth century exhibited a strong nationalistic expression. Increasing the quantity and quality of the literary output was hampered by the overriding importance of commerce and politics to most educated citizens and by the almost complete absence of full-time, professional writers. In various cities small literary societies lent their support to the efforts of the era's magazines. Prominent examples were Boston's Anthology Club, New York's Friendly Club, Baltimore's Delphian Club, and Philadelphia's Tuesday Club. Despite these efforts, the larger share of the period's prose remained ponderous and the verse less than memorable. Articles were still run unsigned, and a few periodicals, including the *Christian Spectator* (1819-1838), *Atlantic Magazine* (1824-1825), and the *North American Review* (1815-1939/1940) began compensating their contributors, often at a dollar a page. In this period of highly personalized publishing, when the titles of editor and publisher were often held by the same person and profits were insignificant, editors normally worked without payment.

During the early 1800s magazines were limited to local circulation, if not always to a local outlook. Though it could boast such important titles as the *North American Review* and the *Monthly Anthology* (1803-1811), Boston's overall growth and its importance as a magazine center had fallen behind the pace set by Philadelphia and New York. Philadelphia had begun in the 1800s as the nation's leader where magazines were concerned, but New York's burgeoning growth in population and commerce gradually helped it overcome Philadelphia's preeminence.

Baltimore became a lively magazine city in the early 1800s, with its excellent prototype news periodical *Niles' Weekly Register* (1811-1849), which some would classify as a newspaper; the highly successful *American Farmer* (1819-1897); the dignified *Portico* (1816-1818); the sprightly *Observer* (1806-1807); and its several early humor magazines. In the South, Charleston was home to the *Traiteur* (1795-1796), *Weekly Museum* (1797-1798), and *Monthly Register, Magazine, and Review of the United States* (1805-1807). In the West, Lexington, Kentucky, with its *Western Review and Miscellaneous Magazine* (1819-1821) and *Western Luminary* (1824-1835) and Cincinnati with its *Cincinnati Literary Gazette* (1824-1825) and *Western Quarterly Reporter of Medical, Surgical, and Natural Sciences* (1822-1823) were most important.

The 1830s and 1840s were a time of unprecedented magazine growth. By Mott's reckoning, the total number of magazines being published in 1850 was six hundred, a sixfold increase in twenty-five years. Of the general monthlies of this period, those that stand out are *Graham's Magazine* (1840-1858) of Philadelphia, the *New England Magazine* (1831-1835) of Boston, and two New York arrivals, the *Knickerbocker Magazine* (1833-1865) and *Sartain's Union Magazine* (1847-1852), which later was moved to Philadelphia.

Sarah Josepha Hale's *Ladies' Magazine* (1828-1836) of Boston was the first really successful women's magazine, but it was the next such periodical she edited, *Godey's Lady's Book* of Philadelphia, that really epitomizes the genre. Running a combination of excellent material by the best writers, alongside more average fare, and also hand-colored fashion plates, by 1850 *Godey's Lady's Book* reached the largest circulation attained by any American magazine to that time, roughly forty thousand. Probably the best of *Godey's* many imitators was *Peterson's Ladies' National Magazine* (1842-1849), also of Philadelphia.

The *New York Mirror* (1823-1857) and *Saturday Evening Post* (1821-1969) are examples of the many literary weeklies that were popular in this period, and in a similar but distinct category were *Brother Jonathan* (1839-1845) and *New World* (1840-1845), both of New York, that used enormous page sizes to feed their readers heavy doses of popular fiction, including some complete novels. The popular culture of the time was also contributed to by cheap magazines devoted to education of a sort: New York's *Magazine of Useful and Entertaining Knowledge* (1830-1831) and Boston's *American Magazine of Useful and Entertaining Knowledge* (1834-1837), for instance. In addition to the somber quarterly reviews–the *North American Review*, *American Quarterly Review* (1827-1837), *New York Review* (1837-1842), and *Boston Quarterly Review* (1838-1842)–the *Dial* (1840-1844) allowed Margaret Fuller and Ralph Waldo Emerson to show literary America a new kind of quarterly, a journal that combined opinion and belles lettres.

By 1850 New York's population was vastly larger than that of any other U.S. city, and its lead in periodical publishing was greater than ever. Due to the combined efforts of Henry Wadsworth Longfellow, James Russell Lowell, Ralph Waldo Emerson, Henry David Thoreau, Nathaniel Hawthorne, and Oliver Wendell Holmes, Boston's influence in periodical litera-

ture had outstripped that of Philadelphia. To the south Baltimore continued to be an important magazine city, with such entries as the short-lived *Emerald* (1828), the *Baltimore Monument* (1836-1839), and the *Spirit of the XIX Century* (1842-1843). Further south, Charleston's William Gilmore Simms was the dominant figure in pre-Civil War periodical work, editing such literary magazines as the *Southern Literary Gazette* (1828-1829), the *Magnolia* (1840-1843), the *Southern Quarterly Review* (1842-1857), and the *Southern and Western Magazine and Review* (1845). In the West, Cincinnati had achieved new prominence with such literary periodicals as the *Western Monthly Review* (1827-1830) and *Western Monthly Magazine* (1833-1837). Louisville, St. Louis, and Columbus also gained in importance, as to a lesser degree did Pittsburgh, Chicago, and Indianapolis.

With the heavy attention being given to New World literary efforts, this period was marked by acrimonious rivalry between American and English writers. Much space was occupied in U.S. magazines by replies to the charges leveled at American cultural life by Charles Dickens, Harriet Martineau, Frances Trollope, and Frederick Marryat. All the same, this animosity did not prevent the continuing practice of pirating English writers, especially in such periodicals as the *Eclectic Magazine* (1844-1907) of New York and *Littell's Living Age* (1844-1941) of Boston. (One should hasten to add that the English periodicals did their share of pirating the works of the best writers in the United States, as well.) Part of the reason was that quality American fiction was still sparse. Despite the fine work of Edgar Allan Poe, Washington Irving, and Hawthorne, the short story was not yet a well-defined literary genre, and much short fiction by Americans, especially in the women's magazines, was cloyingly sentimental and moralistic. But that was about to change, due in large part to the increasing professionalism of magazine publishing. The 1840s marked the emergence of a few individuals designated "magazinists," men and women who made their living by writing for, and sometimes editing, magazines. Nathaniel Parker Willis was perhaps the first, followed by Poe, Park Benjamin, Simms, Lydia Sigourney, Ann Stephens, and others. By 1850 the popular magazines, especially women's magazines and the literary weeklies, had begun giving bylines. A few leaders, notably *Graham's, Godey's, Sartain's,* and the *Knickerbocker,* had begun paying at least their better-known contributors. By 1850 a far greater variety of periodical reading was being published. The magazine business had not yet become "the magazine industry," but with the advent of better and more regular payment to contributors, a new class of magazine specialists emerged, promoting professional editorial standards and encouraging the development of American authorship.

—Sam G. Riley

Acknowledgments

This book was produced by Bruccoli Clark Layman, Inc. Karen L. Rood is senior editor for the *Dictionary of Literary Biography* series. Ellen Rosenberg Kovner and J. M. Brook were the in-house editors.

Production coordinator is Kimberly Casey. Art supervisor is Cheryl Crombie. Copyediting supervisor is Joan M. Prince. Typesetting supervisor is Kathleen M. Flanagan. Laura Ingram and Michael D. Senecal are editorial associates. The production staff includes Rowena Betts, Charles D. Brower, Joseph Matthew Bruccoli, Patricia Coate, Mary Colborn, Holly Deal, Mary S. Dye, Sarah A. Estes, Cynthia Hallman, Judith K. Ingle, Maria Ling, Warren McInnis, Kathy S. Merlette, Sheri Neal, Virginia Smith, and Jack Turner. Jean W. Ross is permissions editor. Joseph Caldwell, photography editor, and Penney Haughton did photographic copy work for the volume.

Walter W. Ross and Rhonda Marshall did the library research with the assistance of the reference staff at the Thomas Cooper Library of the University of South Carolina: Daniel Boice, Cathy Eckman, Gary Geer, Cathie Gottlieb, David L. Haggard, Jens Holley, Dennis Isbell, Jackie Kinder, Marcia Martin, Jean Rhyne, Beverly Steele, Ellen Tillett, Carol Tobin, and Virginia Weathers.

Dictionary of Literary Biography • Volume Seventy-three

American Magazine Journalists, 1741-1850

Dictionary of Literary Biography

Park Benjamin

(14 August 1809-12 September 1864)

Edward Sumter

See also the Benjamin entries in *DLB 3: Antebellum Writers in New York and the South*, and *DLB 59: American Literary Critics and Scholars*.

MAJOR POSITIONS HELD: Editor, *New-England Magazine* (1834-1835), *American Monthly Magazine* (1835-1838), *New-Yorker* (1838), *Brother Jonathan* (1839), *New World* (1839-1844).

SELECTED BOOKS: *A Poem on the Meditation of Nature, Spoken September 26th, 1832, Before the Association of the Alumni of Washington College* (Hartford: F. J. Huntington, 1832);
The Harbinger: A May-Gift, by Benjamin, Oliver Wendell Holmes, and John D. Sargent (Boston: Carter, Hendee, 1833);
Poetry: A Satire, Pronounced Before the Mercantile Library Association at Its Twenty Second Anniversary (New York: J. Winchester, 1842);
Infatuation: A Poem Spoken Before the Mercantile Library Association of Boston October 9, 1844 (Boston: W. D. Ticknor, 1844);
True Patriotism: An Address Spoken at the Presbyterian Church, Geneva, N.Y., on the Fourth of July, 1851 (Geneva, N.Y.: I. & S. H. Parker, 1851);
Poems of Park Benjamin, edited by Merle M. Hoover (New York: Columbia University Press, 1948).

PLAY PRODUCTION: *The Fiscal Agent*, New York, Park Theatre, 28 February 1842.

OTHER: Alexander Dumas, *The Three Guardsmen*, translated by Benjamin (Baltimore: Tay-

Park Benjamin (photograph by Mathew Brady; courtesy of the Library of Congress)

lor, Wilde, 1846; revised edition, New York & Baltimore: William Taylor, 1846).

PERIODICAL PUBLICATIONS: "American Criticism," *New-Yorker*, 7 (6 April 1839): 45;

"Reflections After the Manner of Rochefoucauld," *New-Yorker*, 8 (28 September 1839): 17-18;

"Valedictory," *New-Yorker*, 8 (19 October 1839): 77;

"Ralph Waldo Emerson," *New World* (29 February 1840);

"James Fenimore Cooper," *New World* (21 March 1840);

"Hints on Criticism," *New World* (28 March 1840);

"Mr. Hoffman's Romance," *New World* (11 July 1840);

"Once More Unto the Breach," *New World* (29 August 1840);

"The Old School House," *New World* (3 April 1841).

In the three decades preceding the Civil War, America experienced an era of reform movements: woman's rights, temperance, public education, Sunday schools, utopian communities, and the abolition of slavery, all of which had vociferous advocates. It seemed as if Americans had come of age and wanted to investigate new ideas for a better life. The new movements found a public voice in the newspapers, magazines, and books that were brought within the reach of many Americans by the adoption of the steam press. Led by such newspaper publishers as James Gordon Bennett and Horace Greeley, the penny press emerged with innovations in newsgathering and illustrating. At this starting point of modern journalism the precursor of today's magazines began to develop, although they were sometimes disguised as literary newspapers. The goal of these periodicals was to popularize good literature, and one man who became a symbol of this goal was Park Benjamin.

Poet, editor, lecturer, Benjamin has been treated unevenly by journalism historians, although Benjamin himself might have agreed with all the assessments. He was labeled the "father of cheap literature in the United States" by early commentator Frederic Hudson. This label derived both from the fact that the periodicals were mass-produced inexpensively, and authors, even such popular ones as John Greenleaf Whittier and Walt Whitman, received little payment for their published material; a writer of such stature as Charles Dickens was paid mainly in praise. Critic John Tebbel denounced Benjamin as a money-grabbing literary pirate; since the editor was not constrained by modern copyright laws, he often helped himself to literature published

elsewhere. Such practices were the fashion of the day, however, and as noted historian Frank Luther Mott points out, Benjamin was responsible for bringing the *New-England Magazine* to its greatest prominence. In a period of twelve years (1834-1845) he published more than a hundred poems, edited six magazines, and popularized such authors as Dickens with a huge American audience. Later he edited the *New World*, an important literary newspaper that eventually disintegrated financially because of new postal laws, fierce competition, and new copyright agreements. Benjamin left editing at that juncture to become a lecturer.

Benjamin was born into an old New England family, residing at the time of his birth in Demerara, British Guiana. The future editor was named for his father, a wealthy, adventurous ship's captain who was lost at sea when Park was fifteen. His mother was Mary Judith Gall Benjamin, a planter's daughter. A tropical disease, contracted when Park was three, left him so lame that he was required to use crutches for life. At six the youngster was sent to Norwich, Connecticut, where he lived with an aunt until his family relocated in New Haven.

In the course of preparing for a career in law, Benjamin befriended such architects of nineteenth-century American literature as Oliver Wendell Holmes, Henry Wadsworth Longfellow, Nathaniel Hawthorne, and Edgar Allan Poe. In 1833, after completing courses at Harvard and Yale, Benjamin signaled his divorce from law by collaborating with Holmes and John D. Sargent in publishing a book of poems, *The Harbinger: A May-Gift*. Although Benjamin's poetry is virtually unknown today, his sentimental verse about departed dear ones, disappointed love, and the beauty of nature were printed in almost all the contemporary literary publications, from *Godey's Lady's Book* to the *Broadway Journal*.

Benjamin had tried his hand at editing before he entered law school, but his *Norwich Spectator* had only survived ten issues in the winter of 1829-1830. He then planned to publish a series of popular books, the texts of which he expected to pirate, in the practice of the day. The only book to materialize in this manner was Thomas Carlyle's *Life of Schiller*. In the year after *The Harbinger* appeared, Benjamin became editor of the *New-England Magazine*, recently purchased from Joseph Buckingham by Sargent and Samuel G. Howe. Although this periodical had a relatively short life, Mott considers it to have been the

THE
NEW-ENGLAND MAGAZINE.

APRIL, 1835.

ORIGINAL PAPERS.

YOUNG GOODMAN BROWN.

BY THE AUTHOR OF 'THE GRAY CHAMPION.'

YOUNG goodman Brown came forth, at sunset, into the street of Salem village, but put his head back, after crossing the threshold, to exchange a parting kiss with his young wife. And Faith, as the wife was aptly named, thrust her own pretty head into the street, letting the wind play with the pink ribbons of her cap, while she called to goodman Brown.

'Dearest heart,' whispered she, softly and rather sadly, when her lips were close to his ear, 'pr'ythee, put off your journey until sunrise, and sleep in your own bed to-night. A lone woman is troubled with such dreams and such thoughts, that she's afeard of herself, sometimes. Pray, tarry with me this night, dear husband, of all nights in the year!'

'My love and my Faith,' replied young goodman Brown, 'of all nights in the year, this one night must I tarry away from thee. My journey, as thou callest it, forth and back again, must needs be done 'twixt now and sunrise. What, my sweet, pretty wife, dost thou doubt me already, and we but three months married!'

'Then, God bless you!' said Faith, with the pink ribbons, 'and may you find all well, when you come back.'

'Amen!' cried goodman Brown. 'Say thy prayers, dear Faith, and go to bed at dusk, and no harm will come to thee.'

So they parted; and the young man pursued his way, until, being about to turn the corner by the meeting-house, he looked back, and saw the head of Faith still peeping after him, with a melancholy air, in spite of her pink ribbons.

'Poor little Faith!' thought he, for his heart smote him. 'What a wretch am I, to leave her on such an errand! She

VOL. VIII.   32

First page for one of the seventeen tales Nathaniel Hawthorne contributed to Benjamin's first magazine

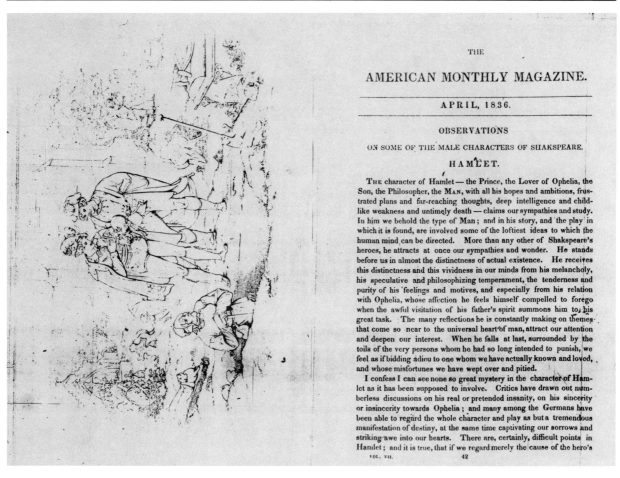

Engraving and first page from an issue of Benjamin's second magazine

most important general magazine in New England before the *Atlantic Monthly* began publication in 1857. The list of its contributors reads like a literary roll of honor and includes the work of writers such as Longfellow, Whittier, Edward Everett, and Noah Webster.

Within two months of joining the *New-England Magazine*, Benjamin found himself to be the sole owner; Howe and Sargent withdrew from the venture, finding it unprofitable. In his role as editor Benjamin wrote reviews and criticism. Merle M. Hoover, Benjamin's biographer, said he was "caustic and cutting in his comments," a practice that left him "in continual controversy, and he enjoyed nothing better." He never lowered his standards for excellence, and his goal was to build a better literature for America. Although he tried to maintain a high literary quality, Benjamin found the public unattracted to the journal, and the magazine went out of business. Nathaniel Hawthorne, then an unknown author, was dismayed when the periodical disap-

peared; Park had published Hawthorne's work in nearly every issue.

The *New-England Magazine* merged with the *New York American Monthly*. Benjamin stayed in Boston and shared editorial duties with Charles Fenno Hoffman, who was in New York. The *American Monthly* was beginning to compete successfully with its long-established rival, the *Knickerbocker*, and Benjamin boosted this movement by contributing the works of established New England writers such as Holmes, as well as up-and-coming ones, such as Hawthorne.

Nearly seven months after the merger, on the night of 13 July 1836, the *American Monthly* printing plant burned to the ground with the issue that was on the press. This misfortune, followed shortly by the panic and depression of 1837, brought Benjamin to the edge of financial ruin. During this time his two sisters, with whom he was sharing a home in Boston, married. Mary Elizabeth wed New England literary historian John Lothrop Motley, and Susan Margaret married Motley's close friend Joseph L. Stackpole.

THE NEW WORLD.

PARK BENJAMIN,
EDITOR.

J. WINCHESTER
PUBLISHER

"No pent-up Utica contracts our powers; for the whole boundless continent is ours."

EXTRA SERIES.	OFFICE 30 ANN-STREET.	NUMBER 34
VOL. II....No. 10.	NEW-YORK, NOVEMBER, 1842.	PRICE 12½ CENTS.

Original Temperance Novel.

Entered according to Act of Congress, in the year 1842,
BY J. WINCHESTER,
In the Clerk's Office of the Southern District of New York.

FRANKLIN EVANS;

OR

THE INEBRIATE.

A TALE OF THE TIMES.

BY WALTER WHITMAN

INTRODUCTORY.

THE story I am going to tell you, reader, will be somewhat aside from the ordinary track of the novelist. It will not abound, either with profound reflections, or sentimental remarks. Yet its moral—for I flatter myself it has one, and one which it were well to engrave on the heart of each person who scans its pages—will be taught by its own incidents, and the current of the narrative.

Whatever of romance there may be—I leave it to any who have, in the course of their every-day walks, heard the histories of intemperate men, whether the events of the tale, strange as some of them may appear, have not had their counterpart in real life. If you who live in the city should go out among your neighbors and investigate what is being transacted there, you might come to behold things far more improbable. In fact, the following chapters contain but the account of a young man, thrown by circumstances amid the vortex of dissipation—a country youth, who came to our great emporium to seek his fortune—and what befell him there. So it is a plain story; yet as the grandest truths are sometimes plain enough to enter into the minds of children—it may be that the delineation I shall give will do benefit, and that educated men and women may not find the hour they spend in its perusal, altogether wasted.

And I would ask your belief when I assert that, what you are going to read is not a work of fiction, as the term is used. I narrate occurrences that have had a far more substantial existence, than in my fancy. There will be those who, as their eyes turn past line after line, will have their memories carried to matters which they have heard of before, or taken a part in themselves, and which, they know, are real.

Can I hope, that my story will do good? I entertain that hope issued in the cheap and popular form you see, and wafted by every mail to all parts of this vast republic; the facilities which its publisher possesses, giving him the power of diffusing it more widely than any other establishment in the United States; the mighty and deep public opinion which, as a tide bears a ship upon its bosom, ever welcomes anything favorable to the Temperance Reform; its being written for the mass, though the writer hopes, not without some claim upon the approval of the more fastidious; and, as much as anything else, the fact that it is as a pioneer in this department of literature—all these will give "THE INEBRIATE," I feel confident, a more than ordinary share of patronage.

For youth, what can be more invaluable? It teaches sobriety, that virtue which every mother and father prays nightly, may be resident in the characters of their sons. It wars against Intemperance, that evil spirit which has levelled so many fair human forms before its horrible advances. Without being presumptuous, I would remind those who believe in the wholesome doctrines of abstinence, how the earlier teachers of piety used parables and fables, as the fit instruments whereby they might convey to men the beauty of the system they professed. In the resemblance, how reasonable it is to suppose that you can impress a lesson upon him whom you would influence to sobriety, in no better way than letting him read such a story as this.

It is usual for writers, upon presenting their works to the public, to bespeak indulgence for faults and deficiences. I am but too well aware that the critical eye will see some such in the following pages; yet my book is not written for the critics, but for THE PEOPLE; and while I think it best to leave it to the reader's own decision whether I have succeeded, I cannot help remarking, that I have the fullest confidence in the verdict's being favorable.

And, to conclude, may I hope that he who purchases this volume, will give to its author, and to its publisher also, the credit of being influenced not altogether by views of the profit to come from it? Whatever of those views may enter into our minds, we are not without a strong desire that the principles here inculcated will strike deep, and grow again, and bring forth good fruit. A prudent, sober, and temperate course of life cannot be too strongly taught to old and young; to the young, because the future years are before them—to the old, because it is their business to prepare for death. And though, as before remarked, the writer has abstained from thrusting the moral upon the reader, by dry and abstract disquisitions—preferring the more pleasant and quite as profitable method of letting the reader draw it himself from the occurrences—it is hoped that the New and Popular Reform now in the course of progress over the land, will find no trifling help from a "TALE OF THE TIMES."

First page for Benjamin's best-known "extra," Walt Whitman's first separately published work and his only novel

With his magazines and money gone, his home life disintegrated, Benjamin headed for bachelor quarters in New York. There he sought a new editorial opportunity, which he found almost at once.

New York Tribune editor Horace Greeley took Benjamin under his wing, and the New Englander became one of the journalists to be nurtured by the editor in a group that included the founder of the *New York Times*, Henry J. Raymond, the *Sun's* editor, Charles A. Dana, the onetime editor of the *Dial*, Margaret Fuller, and European correspondent Karl Marx. In 1838 Greeley appointed Benjamin literary editor of the *New-Yorker*, which competed with Nathaniel Parker Willis's *New-York Mirror*. These magazines were about the same size as today's news magazines, although only one or two pages of news crept in among the poetry, prose, and sheet music that crowded each issue, along with wood or steel engravings to enliven the written word. There was little or no advertising.

Under Greeley, Benjamin quickly educated himself. Greeley was able to make frequent trips to Albany to consult with political partners Thurlow Weed and William H. Seward. He would leave Benjamin completely in charge of the *New-Yorker*. One year later Benjamin was adept enough at publishing to help start the mammoth *Brother Jonathan*. This new literary newspaper, named for the cartoon ancestor of "Uncle Sam," was a symbol of the American belief that bigger is better. The giant newspaper was designed for Sunday reading when people had leisure for literature and, perhaps, the inclination to unfold this paper monster. The flatbed steam presses at that time printed a four- or eight-page paper roughly equivalent to the newspaper page dimensions of today. A giant newspaper was possible by printing a single, large page in place of the customary newspaper's two or four pages. A large woodcut, the size of a modern poster, often covered the front page or the immense centerfold. Once in the 1840s, for example, the *Brother Jonathan* front page featured a huge equestrian picture of Zachary Taylor that promoted the general's presidential candidacy. Other newspapers disputed the claim made by *Brother Jonathan* to be the "biggest." In Boston the *Universal Yankee Nation* masthead boasted "The Largest Newspaper in All Creation"; it required two people to unfold the four pages to its dimensions of over three by five feet.

Late in 1839 after a quarrel with the publisher of *Brother Jonathan*, James G. Wilson, Benjamin and Wilson's editor Rufus Wilmot Griswold founded the *New World*. In the next five years Park Benjamin earned his magazine editing reputation. Edgar Allan Poe, who also edited several magazines, claimed that Benjamin was an editor second to none.

The *New World* was a newspaper in appearance and a magazine in content. And it was the literary content that brought instant success to the *New World*. Authors included Poe, Dickens, Longfellow, Whitman, William Gilmore Simms, Washington Irving, Captain Marryat, Charles Lamb, and William Cullen Bryant. Within a year the *New World* was reduced in size to an attractive quarto edition and became even more popular.

Benjamin turned his focus on his *New World* "extras." He printed pirated work of authors such as Alexander Dumas and Honoré de Balzac. These "extras" were immediately copied by his competition. Dickens's "American Notes" appeared almost simultaneously in the *New World* and in its competitor, *Brother Jonathan*.

Park Benjamin enjoyed his popularity, but he did not abandon his characteristically caustic criticism. He kept up a continuous flow of barbs aimed at *Brother Jonathan*, and Benjamin was one of the first to enter the New York newspaper "moral" war against James Gordon Bennett's sensationalism in the *Herald*. Of course editors' wars dated back to the bitterness and jealousies of the 1790s, the "dark ages of journalism," and as late as the twentieth century, editors shot each other for printing contrary opinions. However, no one was shot in this war protesting Bennett's excesses. Nor was there much investigation into the morality of literary pirating or the newsgathering methods practiced by those who threw the stones against Bennett's *Herald*. But Bennett could take abuse and returned the favor, especially by tormenting Benjamin as the "Black Dwarf."

Park Benjamin, who personifies the American Victorian combative editor, did not restrict his literary arrows to journalists. He joined friend Horace Greeley in that editor's seemingly endless libel suits brought by James Fenimore Cooper. The *New World* leaped into the fray, charging that Cooper had pandered to European prejudices by demeaning America and Americans. Cooper promptly sued and, as usual, won. Greeley and Benjamin paid. As political pressure mounted to enforce copyright laws, the *New World* began to fade. Benjamin resigned as editor

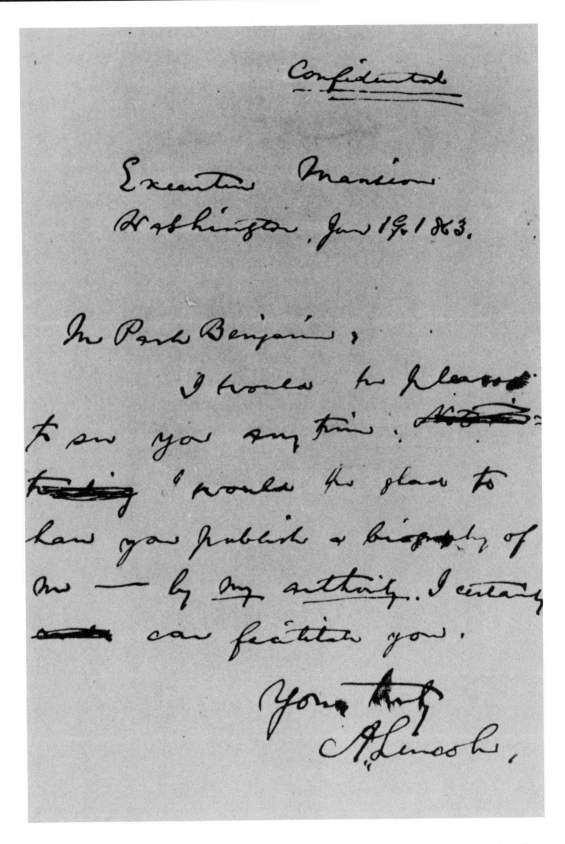

Letter authorizing Benjamin to write a biography of Abraham Lincoln (Park Benjamin Collection, Butler Library, Columbia University)

in March 1844, when new postal regulations threatened to increase expenses.

Benjamin never regained editorial prominence. He tried many publishing ventures, but none succeeded. Early in 1846 he edited *Western Continent* in Baltimore but returned to New York by mid year. The following year his *American Mail* was launched and rapidly sank. His final magazine attempt came just before the Civil War with the enormous *Constellation*. The monster lived only for a few issues. In 1848 Benjamin's mother burned to death in those days of voluminous skirts and open fireplaces, and on 8 May 1848, the editor-poet married Mary Brower Western, sixteen years his junior. They eventually had eight children. Shortly after his marriage the former poet and editor became a popular lecturer, a career pattern duplicated later by Dickens and Mark Twain. On 19 June 1863 Abraham Lincoln authorized Benjamin to write his biography. Park Benjamin died the next year never having started the project.

Unknown today as a poet, Benjamin is remembered as a competent lecturer, who often shared the platform with popular speakers such as Henry Ward Beecher and Horace Greeley. As a militant critic and editor, his judgment enhanced the periodicals he touched. He made substantial progress toward popularizing literature through the medium that has become our modern magazine.

Biography:

Merle M. Hoover, *Park Benjamin, Poet & Editor* (New York: Columbia University Press, 1948).

References:

William Harlan Hale, *Horace Greeley, Voice of the People* (New York: Harper, 1950), pp. 20, 29, 49, 64, 91;

Merle M. Hoover, *Genealogy of Park Benjamin* (New York: Columbia University Press, 1948);

Hoover, *Poems of Park Benjamin* (New York: Columbia University Press, 1948);

Frederic Hudson, *Journalism in the United States from 1690 to 1872* (New York: Haskell House, 1968), pp. 457, 459, 462, 524, 589;

Lurton D. Ingersoll, *The Life of Horace Greeley, Founder of the N.Y. Tribune* (New York: Beedman Publishers, 1974), pp. 119-121, 361;

Samuel Longfellow, *Life of Henry Wadsworth Longfellow* (Boston: Ticknor, 1886);

Frank Luther Mott, *A History of American Magazines*, 5 volumes (Cambridge: Oxford University Press, 1938-1968), I: 599-603;

James Parton, *The Life of Horace Greeley* (Boston: Osgood, 1872), p. 139;

John Tebbel, *The American Magazine: A Compact History* (New York: Hawthorn Books, 1969), pp. 53-54.

Papers:

The Park Benjamin Collection at Columbia University Library contains books, letters, a collection of poems, and magazines edited by him.

Andrew Bradford

(1686-24 November 1742)

Carol Sue Humphrey
Oklahoma Baptist University

See also the Bradford entry in *DLB 43: American Newspaper Journalists, 1690-1872.*

MAJOR POSITIONS HELD: Printer, founder, and editor, *American Weekly Mercury* (1719-1742); printer, *American Magazine, or A Monthly View of the Political State of the British Colonies* (1741).

A member of one of the most prolific printing dynasties in American history, Andrew Bradford founded in 1719 the first newspaper in the Middle Colonies, the *American Weekly Mercury*, and in 1741 the first colonial magazine, the *American Magazine, or A Monthly View of the Political State of the British Colonies*. Although rarely remembered for anything he himself wrote for these periodicals, Bradford was one of the most capable and successful printers prior to 1800.

Andrew Bradford, born in Philadelphia in about 1686, was the older son of William and Elizabeth Sowle Bradford of London. The Bradford and Sowle families had been printers in England, and Andrew's father, William, had brought his trade to Philadelphia in 1685. Following a disagreement with his major customers, the Quaker leaders, William Bradford moved his family to New York City in 1693. Andrew spent the rest of his minority in New York, learning the printing trade in his father's office. He became a freeman of the city in 1709 at the age of twenty-three. He remained in New York for several years, apparently working in his father's shop as a journeyman printer. He moved to Philadelphia sometime in 1712 or 1713.

Bradford had no competition during the first ten years of his printing career in Philadelphia and obtained the business of both the government and the Quakers. In 1713 he published for the government the laws of the province passed during that year, *Acts and Laws of the Province of Pennsylvania, October 14th, 1712 to March 27, 1713*. His work for the Quakers consisted primarily of pamphlets and sermons.

For the first ten years he was in Philadelphia, Bradford was the sole printer in the four-colony area of Pennsylvania, Maryland, Delaware, and New Jersey. He therefore acquired a sizable number of printing jobs. In 1714 he published a complete set of the provincial laws for the government. He also published *The Laws of the Province of Maryland* (1718) and a speech by Governor Burnet for the Colony of New Jersey in 1723. Nongovernmental projects consisted primarily of books and pamphlets on a variety of subjects. A mainstay of the American eighteenth-century printing trade was the yearly almanac, and over the years Bradford published several, including almanacs compiled by Jacob Taylor, Titan Leeds, and John Jerman.

Bradford was married twice, first to Dorcas Boels, who died in or around 1740, then to Cornelia Smith of New York City. Bradford adopted the son of his brother William II. William III, whom Andrew took into partnership for one year, later became known as the "patriot-printer of 1776" for his contributions to the American Revolution.

Andrew Bradford's major business was printing, but he also engaged in many other money-making ventures. For almost ten years, from 1728 to 1738, he served as Philadelphia's postmaster. He ran a general store in conjunction with his printing establishment; the store's wares included books, molasses, cloth, and stationery. Bradford also became a partner in the Durham Iron Company, one of the first such establishments in the American colonies.

Bradford's varied interests established him soundly as a member of Philadelphia society. Having become a freeman of the city in 1717, he was elected a member of the city council in 1727. He held this post until his death in 1742. He also served as a vestryman of Christ Church. Bradford invested in real estate, including several lots in the city and several hundred acres in the surrounding countryside.

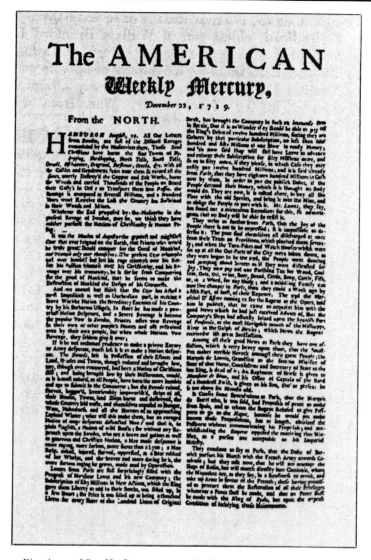

First issue of Bradford's newspaper, the first printed in Philadelphia

On 22 December 1719 Bradford's printing office launched what was to become one of the most important endeavors of his career: the *American Weekly Mercury,* a newspaper that would run for more than twenty-six years, missing only one issue, which was in the week following Bradford's death. One of the better colonial news sheets, the *Mercury* seems to have had a wide circulation throughout the colonies and carried a respectable number of advertisements. Bradford's handling of news, both foreign and domestic, generally proved reliable and trustworthy.

The *Mercury* was similar to other newspapers that appeared in the 1700s; however, there were several differences. Bradford's paper was often more outspoken than its competitors, which sometimes caused the printer some problems. On several occasions Bradford used the pages of his newspaper to criticize government authorities and their activities. For example, in 1722 the *Mercury* carried several pieces concerning the state of Pennsylvania's economy. One of the essays was followed by the statement: "Our General Assembly are now sitting, and we have great expectations from them, at this juncture, that they will find some effectual remedy to revive the dying credit of this Province, and restore us to our former happy circumstances." The Provincial Council immediately summoned Bradford to explain why he had published this apparent criticism. Bradford explained that a journeyman in his employ had inserted the paragraph. The council accepted this explanation, reprimanding Bradford and ordering him not to print anything else concerning the provincial government without acquiring official permission first.

First page of Bradford's prospectus for his
American Magazine

Bradford again faced official ire for a publication in 1729. The annual election provided the occasion. A series of essays entitled the "Busy-Body" had urged people to take an active role in the election in order to ensure that capable leaders were chosen. The governor and council perceived some of these essays as attacks on their performances as public officials. They ordered Bradford's imprisonment, and he apparently went to jail without complaint, conducting his business from his cell. Although arrested, Bradford was never tried in this case, and he was freed. The furor apparently died quietly without any official settlement.

The second difference between the *American Weekly Mercury* and other colonial news sheets resulted from Bradford's greater interest in local events than that exhibited by his rivals. Detailed reports of fires and accidents appeared regularly; crime news received some notice. Accounts of public executions proved popular, and Bradford often published a complete transcript of the condemned felon's last speech. Bradford's interest in local happenings sometimes produced stories with comical features. On 28 September 1721 the *Mercury* reported:

> Several Bears were seen Yesterday near this Place, and one killed at German-Town, and another near Derby. Last Night a very large Bear, being spied by two Amazons, as he was eating his last Supper of Acorns up a tree, they calling some Inhabitants of this Place to their Assistance, he was soon fetch'd down from thence, and entirely dispatched by em [*sic*]. Afterwards finding no more Sport with Bears, they quarrel'd with one another for the Body as madly as the Centaurs upon a like Occasion. The following Lines were writ in Praise of the Notable Heroine, who spied him first and attended him to his Execution.

> "Fair P–, sure 'twas wisely, bravely done,
> To shew thy self a modern Amazon,
> Unus'd to hunt, or draw the strenuous Bow,
> To poise the Lance, or fatal Dart to throw;
> Yet Atalanta's Courage shone in thee,
> That durst approach the monster-bearing Tree:
> For R–r's arm you mark'd the destin'd Prey
> Nor fearful turn'd your Virgin Face away,
> And merited with him the Honour of the Day."

Bradford advertised his plans for the first colonial magazine in the 6 November 1740 issue of the *American Weekly Mercury*. The *American Magazine* debuted on 13 February 1741. Only three issues were printed. Bradford's plunge into the new field embroiled him in a serious public argument with his major competitor, Benjamin Franklin.

Bradford's announcement of 6 November 1740 undercut Franklin's own plans to publish a magazine. In fact, Bradford's editor, John Webbe, had been first approached by Franklin to undertake the same job for him. During the next several months Franklin's *Pennsylvania Gazette* and Bradford's *American Weekly Mercury* exchanged barbs concerning the magazine proposals. Franklin declared that he and Webbe had reached an agreement, but Webbe went to Brad-

The AMERICAN MAGAZINE

OR

A MONTHLY VIEW OF

The Political State

OF THE BRITISH COLONIES:

For FEBRUARY, 1740-1.

(To be Continued Monthly)

Containing,

I. Continuation of the REMARKS on the MARYLAND Government.
II. PROCEEDINGS in the Assembly of that Province.
III. PROCEEDINGS of the Assembly of PENNSYLVANIA, in Relation to the inlisting of Servants.
IV. PROCEEDINGS of the Assembly of NEW-YORK, re-

specting the King's Instructions to make Provisions for the Troops, directed to be raised there.
V. An ACCOUNT of the SPEECHES in Assembly of his Excellency the Governor of NEW-JERSEY.
VI. The PRESENT STATE of the WAR.
VII. The AFFAIRS of EUROPE.

PHILADELPHIA: Printed and Sold by ANDREW BRADFORD:
(Price One Shilling *Pennsylvania* Currency, or Eight Pence *Sterling*.)

Second issue of the first American magazine

Magazine for public consumption just three days prior to the first appearance of Franklin's *General Magazine and Historical Chronicle*.

The contents of the *American Magazine* proved to be fairly typical of well-established magazines in Great Britain. In general, British journals functioned as extensions of newspapers, containing news summaries, essays, and poetry. Bradford and Webbe modeled their production after such successful publications. They included brief accounts of the war between France and England, as well as essays on a variety of topics such as paper money, the dangers of "popery," and the religion of the Indians. Overall they achieved their goal of mimicking their British models.

Bradford and Webbe also desired to extend the scope of their periodical. In the original plan they "propos'd to publish Monthly, An Account of the publick Affairs transacted in His Majesty's Colonies, as well on the Continent of America as in the West India Islands: Under this Head," they continued,

will be comprehended, the Speeches of several Governors, the Addresses and Answers of the Assemblies, their Votes, Resolutions and Debates. So that this Part of the Work will contain Journals of the most important Proceedings of each particular Assembly. Moreover, at the End of every Session, we shall give an Extract of the Laws therein passed, with the Reasons on which they were founded, the Grievances intended to be remedied by them, and the Benefits expected from them.

Furthermore, Bradford and Webbe intended their magazine to be "an Attempt to Erect, on Neutral Principles, A Publick Theatre in the Center of the British Empire in America, on which the most remarkable Transactions of each Government may be impartially represented, and fairly exhibited to the View of all His Majesty's Subjects, whether at Home or abroad, who are disposed to be Spectators." They clearly desired to use the *American Magazine* as a political forum for their readers.

Bradford and Webbe were most successful in their efforts to cover colonial politics. The three issues that appeared in 1741 contained a variety of political items consisting of reports on the activities of the colonial assemblies of New Jersey, Pennsylvania, Maryland, and New York. There were several political essays concerning the problems in Maryland's constitution, slurs by Jonathan Swift directed at Pennsylvania, and conflicts

ford in hopes of a better financial arrangement. Webbe replied that he and Franklin had not reached a settlement and that his arrangement with Bradford was perfectly legitimate. Bradford himself said little on the matter directly, although he opened the pages of the *Mercury* for Webbe to respond to Franklin's accusations.

It is difficult to judge who was telling the truth. Webbe clearly discussed the possibility of a magazine with both Franklin and Bradford, but whether he broke an understanding with Franklin when he reached an agreement with Bradford is not proven. Franklin expressed considerable anger because of Bradford's plans to compete with him in this new business venture, but he did not prove that Webbe had betrayed him.

Both Bradford and Franklin worked diligently to get their respective magazines published first. Bradford produced the *American*

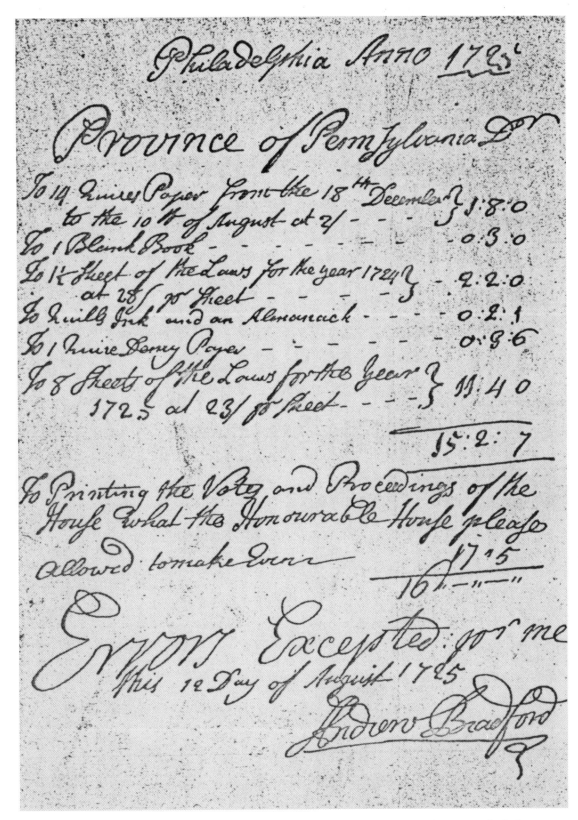

Bradford's bill to the Province of Pennsylvania for his services as a government printer (Horatio G. Jones,
Andrew Bradford, 1869)

between the governor and assembly of New Jersey.

Attempts to produce something new and different proved futile, for Philadelphia was not ready to support any journalistic effort beyond the scope of newspapers. Bradford's magazine lasted only three months, while Franklin's effort died after six issues. However, failure to survive does not mean Bradford's effort should be relegated to oblivion. Bradford was a successful printer when he embarked on the magazine venture. His willingness to risk a foray into an untried field deserves recognition.

Overshadowed though he was by his brilliant rival Benjamin Franklin, Andrew Bradford not only published the first colonial American magazine but also the first newspaper in the Middle Colonies, which, in marked contrast to most of the short-lived papers of that era, lasted for twenty-six years. These accomplishments, coupled with his printing and importing of books, pamphlets, and other matter, made Bradford a significant force in colonial printing and publishing.

Biographies:

John William Wallace, *An Address Delivered at the Celebration by the New York Historical Society, May 20, 1863, of the Two Hundredth Birth Day of Mr. William Bradford, Who Introduced the Art of Printing into the Middle Colonies of British America* (Albany, N.Y.: J. Munsell, 1863);

Horatio G. Jones, *Andrew Bradford, Founder of the Newspaper Press in the Middle States of America* (Philadelphia: King & Baird, Printers, 1869; New York: Arno, 1970);

Henry Darrach, *Bradford Family, 1660-1906* (Philadelphia, 1906);

Anna J. De Armond, *Andrew Bradford: Colonial Journalist* (Newark, Del., 1949).

References:

Henry L. Bullen, "The Bradford Family of Printers," *Americana Collector,* 1 (February 1926): 164-170;

John T. Faris, "The Story of Three Bradfords, Colonial Publishers and Printers," in his *The Romance of Forgotten Men* (New York & London: Harper, 1928), pp. 34-62;

Charles R. Hildeburn, *A Century of Printing: The Issues of the Press in Pennsylvania, 1685-1784,* 2 volumes (Philadelphia: Press of Matlack & Harvey, 1885-1886), I: 9, 47, 294; II: 88, 92;

James M. Lee, *History of American Journalism* (Boston & New York: Houghton Mifflin, 1917), pp. 31-33;

Douglas C. McMurtrie, *A History of Printing in the United States,* 2 volumes (New York: Bowker, 1936), II: 7-9, 14-16;

Isaiah Thomas, *The History of Printing in America,* second edition, 2 volumes (Albany, N.Y.: Joel Munsell, printer, 1874), I: 208-229;

Lawrence C. Wroth, *The Colonial Printer* (Charlottesville: University Press of Virginia, 1964).

Papers:

Files of the *American Weekly Mercury* and the *American Magazine* may be found at the American Antiquarian Society; the Philadelphia Library Company; the Historical Society of Pennsylvania, Philadelphia; the New York Historical Society; the New York Public Library; and the Library of Congress. The Bradford family manuscripts and papers are held by the Historical Society of Pennsylvania.

William Bradford III

(19 January 1719-25 September 1791)

Patricia Bradley
Temple University

See also the Bradford entry in *DLB 43: American Newspaper Journalists, 1690-1872.*

MAJOR POSITIONS HELD: Founder, publisher, and editor, *Weekly Advertiser, or Philadelphia Journal*, renamed *Pennsylvania Journal, or Weekly Advertiser* in 1742 (1742-1793); publisher, *American Magazine, or Monthly Chronicle for the British Colonies* (1757-1758); publisher, *American Magazine* (1769-1769).

BOOKS: *Books Just Imported from London, and to Be Sold by William Bradford, at His Shop, Adjoining the London Coffee-House in Market Street* (Philadelphia: Printed by William Bradford, 1755);

Catalogue of Books Just Imported from London, and to Be Sold by William Bradford, at the London Coffee-House, Philadelphia. Wholesale and Retaile. With Good Allowance to Those That Take a Quantity (Philadelphia: Printed by William Bradford, 1760?);

Imported in the Last Vessels from London, and to Be Sold by William and Thomas Bradford, Printers, Booksellers, and Stationers, at Their Bookstore in Market-Street, Adjoining the London Coffee-House; or by Thomas Bradford, at His House in Second-Street, One Door from Arch-Street, . . . A Large and Neat Assortment of Books and Stationary [sic] (Philadelphia: Printed by W. & T. Bradford, 1769);

Catalogue of Books Just Imported from London, and to Be Sold by W. Bradford (Philadelphia: Printed by William Bradford, 1788).

William Bradford is most often remembered as the "patriot printer of '76" because of his contributions to the cause as editor and publisher of the *Pennsylvania Journal, or Weekly Advertiser* and his military service during the American Revolution. Bradford also occupies a niche in the history of magazine journalism. As publisher of the *American Magazine, or Monthly Chronicle for the British Colonies,* and later of a second *American Mag-*

William Bradford III (Gale International Portrait Gallery)

azine, Bradford encouraged the growth of national unity, provided a forum for the recognition of native talent, and contributed to the intellectual life of the colonies.

Bradford was born in Hanover Square, New York City, the son of Sytje Santvoort and William Bradford II. He was the grandson of William Bradford I, who had established the second press in America after arriving in Pennsylvania as part of William Penn's expedition. The eldest Bradford subsequently moved his press to New York as the result of a major rift with the ruling Quaker hierarchy. The rift marked an ongoing dynamic between the Society of Friends and the Bradford family.

17

Although William was born in New York, he was reared by his Philadelphia uncle, Andrew Sowle Bradford, who had established the first newspaper in the Middle Colonies, the *American Weekly Mercury*. Andrew and his first wife, Dorcas, who were childless, adopted the young William as an infant and, according to family notes, raised him in "the lap of affection and indulgence." This life-style came to an end in 1740 when Andrew married Cornelia Smith following the death of his first wife. Cornelia Bradford wished the young Bradford to marry her niece. When he refused, she "imbibed a settled prejudice against him," says Bradford's contemporary Isaiah Thomas. According to family history the partnership that Bradford had entered into with his uncle in 1739 was dissolved the following year at Cornelia's insistence. When Andrew died in 1742 William did not share in the estate, and the *American Mercury*, on which William had learned the printing trade, became the property of Cornelia Bradford, who continued its publication under her own name. An early historian recorded her as a woman "whose extravagance before her death" demolished what was left of William's inheritance.

Following the family disagreement William spent the year 1741 in England, reconnecting with his English relatives and establishing business contacts. He returned to the colonies in 1742 and, possibly with some underwriting from his English great-aunt Tace Sowle Rayton, founded his own newspaper in Philadelphia in December in competition with the *Mercury*.

Thus, like many other colonial printers, Bradford set about building his newspaper and printing business from scratch. But perhaps because of his early upbringing, Bradford, unlike other colonial printers, appeared to align himself with the middle class of his city. While many colonial printers seldom strayed from the interests of the tradesmen class, Bradford mixed with Philadelphia's elite as a member of at least two social clubs. His marriage to Rachel Budd in 1742 was considered a prestigious one. Bradford did not establish newspapers in other places, a common practice for the colonial printer, and his business enterprises outside the printing office were not related to publishing. In 1754 he established in Philadelphia the London Coffee House, which became a center of merchant and, later, revolutionary activity, as Bradford became involved in the patriot cause as a member of the Sons of Liberty. Bradford and a partner established a marine insurance business in 1762.

Bradford and his wife had six living children. The oldest son, Thomas, became his father's partner in the *Pennsylvania Journal* in 1766, when, homesick and ill during his second year at college, he wrote letters begging to come home. The second son, William, however, graduated from Princeton in the same class with James Madison, who continued to be a family friend. William IV went on to become United States attorney general in the Washington administration and a member of the Pennsylvania Supreme Court. Of the Bradford children, only Thomas remained connected with the printing business and, like his father, became a respected member of Philadelphia society and an active member of the Presbyterian Church. He was well known for his work on behalf of prison reform.

Bradford's middle-class values aligned him with the "Society of Gentlemen," who helped conduct the editorial functions of his first magazine, the *American Magazine, or Monthly Chronicle for the British Colonies*, which was published in 1757 and 1758. Certainly the magazine represented many of his own views. Despite his Quaker antecedents, Bradford was a proponent of military preparedness. He became lieutenant of a volunteer militia company as early as 1748 when Philadelphia shipping was threatened by war. He was recognized as a strong Presbyterian, known for his lack of sympathy for Quaker positions. His business interests aligned him to the merchant class, and his encouragement of his children's education suggests he may have had an appreciation for the belles lettres, history, and natural science that appeared in the magazine. On another level his personal history, entailing the loss of his own parents, the security provided by his adoptive parents, and the loss again of his uncle, suggests he may have been particularly amenable to a growing nationalism that put its faith in its own present accomplishments rather than the dubious security offered by the mother country.

For sake of clarity it should be noted that the earliest *American Magazine* was published in Philadelphia in 1741 by William's uncle, Andrew Bradford; the second magazine of this title was published in Boston from 1743 to 1746 by Rogers and Fowle. The third *American Magazine*—the one presently under consideration—was William's first. His second, the fourth *American Magazine*, appeared in 1769. Finally a fifth and last eighteenth-century magazine to bear this title was edited

18

from 1787 to 1788 in New York City by Noah Webster.

Bradford's *American Magazine* came about as a result of the French and Indian War and was strongly pro-British in its support of a military victory against France. That pro-British agenda was clear in the woodcut that headed the front page of each issue–an Indian leaning upon his gun centered between two figures representing the English and French nations. The plainly dressed Englishman, as the bearer of Protestantism and the fruits of hard work, is posed reading from the Bible with a roll of cloth under his arm. The Frenchman, extravagantly, even foppishly dressed, offers the Indian a tomahawk and a bag of gold.

Despite its war-connected origins, the magazine indicated ambitions beyond a wartime polemic. The war, having focused attention on the American colonies, according to the introductory remarks in the first issue, provided the opportunity of informing readers of events in all of the colonies "not confined to the affairs of a few particular ones." Moreover, the magazine was to seek its audience not only at home but also in Great Britain and in Ireland, particularly among readers who had previously dismissed colonial matters as "of inferior or secondary consideration."

From its inception the *American Magazine* was designed as flag bearer for the colonies, emphasizing their unified rather than disparate histories and seeking international acknowledgment and influence. The magazine's emphasis was thus on the current state of American affairs, a theme illustrated by a series of essays bearing the grandiose title "History of North America" but which chose 1749 as its starting date. Bradford's magazine gave particular attention to the accomplishments of the colonists. Francis Hopkinson's poetry was first published in its pages, as was the first public notice of the paintings of Benjamin West. In something of an investigative article the *American Magazine* charged that Philadelphian Thomas Godfrey, Sr., not the English captain whose name it bore, was the rightful inventor of the "Hadley Quadrant," a navigational instrument.

Although such articles were meant to foster American nationalism, the magazine firmly reflected the issues of its time. Edited for its entire run by William Smith, provost of the College of Philadelphia (now the University of Pennsylvania), the magazine called for a Pennsylvania militia, suggested Quakers whose consciences would not allow them to bear arms resign from posts of public protection, and supported the interests of the Pennsylvania proprietors against those of the Quaker-controlled Assembly.

The promilitary, anti-French stance of the magazine cast American Indians as a people whose values differed vastly from those of the colonists. Native Americans were portrayed as "descendants of murdering Cain," whose cruelty and barbarity would likely be unleashed by French encouragement. The magazine did not appear to hold strong hope that Christianity would materially change the practices of the American Indian, given the relentless detail of the writer's descriptions of Indian cruelty. Similarly, the editor issued no call for a change in the status of slaves. The Golden Rule, which was a founding principle of Quaker opposition to slavery, was interpreted by one essayist to mean the slaveholder should be as tolerant to his slaves as if he were a slave himself, a certain narrowing of the Quaker interpretation of the biblical injunction.

The *American Magazine* ceased publication in 1758 after one year, not for lack of support–it had an estimated thousand subscribers–but because William Smith, who had been arrested and sentenced for libel during the course of the year, sailed for England upon his release.

Bradford published, in 1769, a second *American Magazine,* which appeared without a frontispiece or motto. It was printed in the shop of William and Thomas Bradford. The periodical was a result of the formation of the American Philosophical Society in 1769, in a merger of two previous organizations. Edited by Lewis Nicola, a member of the society, the magazine became a showcase and archive for the society's papers. The emphasis of the second magazine was on inventions, natural history, and science, unlike the original, which focused on literature and essays. The Bradfords' growing anti-British stance may have been an influence in one of the few poems to appear, "The Choice," which is little more than a propaganda piece dedicated to the boycott of British goods.

More and more, Bradford was demonstrating unswerving support for the patriot cause. He was an uncompromising opponent of the Stamp Act, and the *Pennsylvania Journal* appeared in a tombstone makeup to express his opposition. He was a member of the Sons of Liberty, a signer of the Non-Importation Resolutions of 1765, and an early advocate of a continental congress.

When the first Congress met in Philadelphia, the Bradfords were named its official printers.

Bradford's military involvement began in 1775. Following the publication of the Declaration of Independence, at fifty-six, he joined the patriot army as a major and rose to the rank of colonel, fighting in the battles of Trenton and Princeton. He retired from active service after the British evacuated Philadelphia in mid 1778.

Publication of the *Pennsylvania Journal* had been suspended during the British occupation of Philadelphia. When the newspaper resumed publication in 1778, it was entirely in Thomas's hands. Although Bradford's health was damaged as a result of his wartime service, he lived until 1791. He is buried in Philadelphia.

Biographies:

John William Wallace, *An Address Delivered at the Celebration by the New York Historical Society, May 20, 1863, of the Two Hundredth Birth Day of Mr. William Bradford, Who Introduced the Art of Printing into the Middle Colonies of British America* (Albany, N.Y.: J. Munsell, 1863);

Wallace, *An Old Philadelphian. Colonel William Bradford, the Patriot Printer of 1776. Sketches of his life* (Philadelphia: Sherman, 1884);

Henry Darrach, *Bradford Family, 1660-1906* (Philadelphia, 1906).

References:

Carl and Jessica Bridenbaugh, *Rebels and Gentlemen, Philadelphia in the Age of Franklin* (New York: Reynal & Hitchcock, 1942);

Horatio Gates Jones, *An address delivered at the annual meeting of the Historical Society of Pennsylvania, February 9th, 1869* (Philadelphia: King & Baird, printers, 1869; New York: Arno/ *New York Times*, 1970);

Frank Luther Mott, *A History of American Magazines*, 5 volumes (Cambridge: Oxford University Press, 1938-1968), I: 25, 80-82;

Peter J. Parker, "The Philadelphia Printer: A Study of an Eighteenth-Century Businessman," *Business History Review*, 40 (January 1966): 25-48;

Lyon N. Richardson, *A History of Early American Magazines 1741-1789* (New York: Nelson, 1931);

Albert H. Smyth, *The Philadelphia Magazines and their Contributors 1741-1850* (Philadelphia: Lindsay, 1892);

Frederick D. Stone, "How the Landing of Tea was Opposed in Philadelphia By Colonel William Bradford and Others in 1773," *Pennsylvania Magazine of History and Biography*, 15 (Fall 1891): 385-393;

Isaiah Thomas, *History of Printing in America*, volume 2, edited by Marcus McCorison (New York: Weathervane, 1970).

Papers:

The Bradford Manuscripts and Papers are located at the Historical Society of Pennsylvania, in Philadelphia.

Charles Brockden Brown
(17 January 1771-22 February 1810)

Mark J. Schaefermeyer
Virginia Polytechnic Institute and State University

See also the Brown entries in *DLB 37: American Writers of the Early Republic* and *DLB 59: American Literary Critics and Scholars, 1800-1850.*

MAJOR POSITIONS HELD: Editor, *Monthly Magazine, and American Review* (1799-1800), renamed *American Review, and Literary Journal* (1801-1802), *Literary Magazine, and American Register* (1803-1807), *American Register, or General Repository of History, Politics, and Science* (1807-1809).

BOOKS: *Alcuin: A Dialogue* (New York: Printed by T. & J. Swords, 1798);
Wieland; or, The Transformation. An American Tale (New York: Printed by T. & J. Swords for H. Caritat, 1798; London: H. Colburn, 1811);
Ormond; or, the Secret Witness (New York: Printed by G. Forman for H. Caritat, 1799; London: William Lane, 1800);
Arthur Mervyn; or, Memoirs of the Year 1793, part 1 (Philadelphia: Printed & published by H. Maxwell, 1799); part 2 (New York: Printed & sold by George F. Hopkins, 1800); parts 1 and 2 (London: Lane & Newman, 1803);
Edgar Huntly; or, Memoirs of a Sleep-Walker, 3 volumes (Philadelphia: Printed by H. Maxwell, 1799; London: Lane & Newman, 1803);
Clara Howard; In a Series of Letters (Philadelphia: Printed by H. Maxwell & published by Asbury Dickins, 1801); republished as *Philip Stanley; or, The Enthusiasm of Love*, 2 volumes (London: Printed at the Minerva Press for Lane, Newman, 1807);
Jane Talbot, A Novel (Philadelphia: John Conrad/Baltimore: M. & J. Conrad/Washington, D.C.: Rapin, Conrad, 1801; London: Lane, Newman, 1804);
An Address to the Government of the United States, on the Cession of Louisiana to the French; and on the Late Breach of Treaty by the Spaniards: Including the Translation of a Memorial, on the War of St. Domingo, and Cession of the Mississippi to France. Drawn up by a French Counsellor of

Charles Brockden Brown, circa 1798 (portrait by James Sharples; courtesy of the Worcester Art Museum, Worcester, Massachusetts)

State (Philadelphia: John Conrad/Baltimore: M. & J. Conrad/Washington, D.C.: Rapin, Conrad, 1803);
Monroe's Embassy; or, The Conduct of the Government in Relation to Our Claims to the Navigation of the Missisippi [sic], *Considered* (Philadelphia: Printed by H. Maxwell & published by John Conrad, 1803);
An Address to the Congress of the United States on the Utility and Justice of Restrictions upon Foreign Commerce . . . (Philadelphia: Printed by John Binns & published by C. & A. Conrad, 1809);
Carwin, the Biloquist, and Other American Tales and Pieces, 3 volumes (London: Henry Colburn, 1822);

The Rhapsodist and Other Uncollected Writings of Charles Brockden Brown, edited by Harry R. Warfel (New York: Scholars' Facsimiles & Reprints, 1943);

Memoirs of Stephen Calvert, edited by Hans Borchers (Frankfurt am Main, Bern & Las Vegas: Lang, 1978).

Collections: *The Novels of Charles Brockden Brown,* 7 volumes (Boston: Published by S. G. Goodrich, 1827);

The Novels and Related Works of Charles Brockden Brown: Bicentennial Edition, 6 volumes, edited by Sidney J. Krause, S. W. Reid, and Donald A. Ringe (Kent, Ohio: Kent State University Press, 1977-1986).

OTHER: C. F. Volney, *A View of the Soil and Climate of the United States of America: With Supplementary Remarks upon Florida; on the French Colonies on the Mississippi and Ohio, and in Canada; and on the Aboriginal Tribes of America,* translated by Brown (Philadelphia: Printed by T. & G. Palmer & published by John Conrad, 1804);

"A Sketch of the Life and Character of John Blair Linn," in *Valerian, A Narrative Poem,* by John Blair Linn (Philadelphia: Printed by T. & G. Palmer, 1805), pp. iii-xxiv.

PERIODICAL PUBLICATIONS:
NONFICTION

"Preface," *American Review, and Literary Journal,* 1 (July 1801): iii-vi;

"Remarks on Reading," *Literary Magazine, and American Review,* 5 (March 1806): 163-168.

FICTION

"Dialogues of the Living," *Monthly Magazine, and American Review,* 1 (April 1799): 19-21;

"Thessalonica: A Roman Story," *Monthly Magazine, and American Review,* 1 (May 1799): 99-117;

"Portrait of an Emigrant: Extracted from a Letter," *Monthly Magazine, and American Review,* 1 (June 1799): 161-164;

"Memoirs of Stephen Calvert," *Monthly Magazine, and American Review,* 1 (June-September 1799); 2 (January 1800); 2 (April-June 1800);

"A Lesson on Concealment; or, Memoirs of Mary Selwyn," *Monthly Magazine, and American Review,* 2 (March 1800): 174-207;

"The Trials of Arden," *Monthly Magazine, and American Review,* 3 (July 1800): 19-36;

"The Editors' [sic] Address to the Public," *Literary Magazine, and American Register,* 1 (October 1803): 3-6;

"History of Philip Dellwyn," *Literary Magazine, and American Register,* 1 (November 1803-February 1804);

"Devotion: An Epistle," *American Register, or General Repository of History, Politics, and Science,* 3 (1808): 567-578.

Often referred to as America's first important novelist, Charles Brockden Brown might also be considered the father of American literature and criticism. Although he had no one integrated theory, Brown recognized the importance of mastering the belletristic tradition that had made European literature superior. At a time when, in his own words, "our population is increased, our national independence secured, and our governments established, and we are relieved from the necessities of colonists and emigrants, there is reason to expect more attention to polite literature and science," Brown fostered a national literature through his pursuits as publisher, editor, novelist, annalist, and geographer. He sought to provide critical magazines as vehicles for American writers to present their poetry, prose, criticism, and ideas. In the preface to volume 1 of the *American Review, and Literary Journal,* Brown argued that "[G]enius in composition, like genius in every other art, must be aided by culture, nourished by patronage, and supplied with leisure and materials. The genius of the poet, orator, and historian, cannot be exercised with vigour and effect, without suitable encouragement, any more than that of the artist and mechanic." At a time when he had largely given up his own career as a novelist, Brown committed himself to encouraging other writers of the fledgling republic.

Born in Philadelphia on 17 January 1771, Charles Brockden Brown was the fifth son of Elijah and Mary Armitt Brown. According to his biographer William Dunlap, Brown was somewhat frail and, rather than engage in physical sports, he cultivated an early fondness for reading books. Between the ages of eleven and sixteen, Brown attended Robert Proud's Quaker Latin School, where he learned the rudiments of Latin and Greek and showed an affinity for geography. When Brown left Proud's school, he wrote a number of essays in verse and prose and sketched plans for three epic poems concerning Columbus, Pizarro, and Cortez. Eschewing a college education, he chose the legal profession and apprenticed in the office of Alexander Wilcox, a prominent lawyer in Philadelphia.

After each day of copying standard legal documents or of studying Blackstone, Brown often would spend his evenings composing and transcribing letters, recording the day's events and his thoughts, and copying his friends' letters into his journal–all with an eye toward improving his thinking and writing. A member of the Belles Lettres Club, a literary society established by John Davidson, Brown served as the club's president and recorded his judgment on questions debated before the society. He was, reported a friend, a "model of the dry, grave, and judicial style of argument."

In 1789 Brown wrote a series of essays as "The Rhapsodist" which were published in the *Universal Asylum, and Columbian Magazine.* In the first Brown alludes to his future as a writer and reveals his Quaker upbringing. While affirming to his readers that they can always expect the truth from him, Brown asserts his desire to amuse and instruct his readers, saying, "In short he [the Rhapsodist] will write as he speaks, and converse with his reader not as an author, but as a man."

Eventually literature, not law, became the primary focus of his life. In 1792, shortly after his twenty-first birthday, Brown gave up his job with Wilcox and set his sights on becoming a writer, much to the dismay of family and friends.

In 1794, through his friend Elihu Hubbard Smith, he became acquainted with William Dunlap and the members of the New York literary circle known as the Friendly Club. In Dunlap and Smith, Brown found a kinship that influenced his desire to succeed in his career as an author. However, while they had the fortitude to finish projects, Brown would start with an idea, develop it for a time, and then abandon it for lack of interest. This inability to complete work served only to push Brown further into "that profound abyss of ignominy and debasement" into which, he said, he was "sunk by [his] own reflections." Over the next two years Brown was apparently hard at work, for he had very little contact with his friends. At one point he shared part of a manuscript for a novel with Smith but abandoned this project in early 1796.

In September 1796 Brown moved to New York in hopes of being more productive and refreshed in his writing; he was also able to keep in closer contact with Smith, Dunlap, and other members of the Friendly Club, though he only occasionally attended their meetings. During this time he produced "Sketches of a History of Carsol" and the beginning of "Sketches of the History of the Carrils and Ormes" (both reprinted in volume 1 of Dunlap's biography). Each of these fictional essays reflects Brown's interest in history, but neither is well-organized; they rarely venture beyond historical summary and generalization and contain no dialogue.

Back at home in Philadelphia following March 1797, Brown went into virtual seclusion, maintaining little contact with the New York contingent. However, in August he forwarded to Smith the initial two parts of *Alcuin,* a dialogue on the rights of women. Dunlap was particularly pleased with the writing and philosophical accuracy contained within; Smith was so eager to see his friend succeed, he published the essay in April 1798. (The third and fourth parts remained unprinted until Dunlap included them in the biography of Brown.)

The publication of *Alcuin,* coupled with the appearance of "The Man at Home" and "Original Letters," both in serial form in the *Weekly Magazine,* heralded the arrival of a small measure of success. Though *Alcuin* was received rather coldly, the publication of his shorter prose pieces likely gave Brown just enough confidence to continue writing. He focused his attention on completing *Wieland* (1798) and on a plan for a new magazine. Despite the increased circulation of his work, however, the previous six years had left their mark on his health and on his understanding of the literary profession. An essay on "Authorship" in the October 1803 issue of *Literary Magazine, and American Register* alludes to Brown's situation during those years.

> But authorship, as a mere trade, seems to be held in very little estimation. There is no other *tradesman,* to whom the epithet *poor,* is more usually applied. A *poor author* is a phrase so often employed, that the two words have almost coalesced into one. The latter, if used alone, signifies merely a man who writes and publishes; but if *poor* be prefixed, it clearly indicates a writer by trade.... Any thing that gives a permanent revenue, however scanty the sum, or laborious the service, is deemed preferable to authorship....

Even though he was to publish six more novels in the span of four years, Brown never seemed to experience any sense of achievement with his novel-writing and would later abandon fiction.

Prior to Brown's arrival in New York Elihu Smith had suggested a magazine in which the

Page from an outline for Wieland *(Historical Society of Pennsylvania)*

Friendly Club's membership might publish their writings. After Smith died in September 1798, all of his associates in the club urged Brown to coordinate publication of the new magazine; the new periodical was realized in memory of their friend.

In April 1799 Brown took on the editorship of the *Monthly Magazine, and American Review* with the hope of appealing to the literate class as a whole. Although he had hoped to address a wide range of topics, including politics, he found it most expeditious to limit the journal to literary and scientific subjects. He used the periodical to publish his own work, as well. The issues of volume 1 contain, for example, Brown's "Memoirs of Stephen Calvert," a fragment of *Edgar Huntly,* portions of "Walstein's School of History," and other essays. While Brown was assured by his literary "Friends" that they would supply him with a wealth of material, he soon found that he had overestimated their ability to produce. This was a problem that continued to plague Brown's role as editor in subsequent magazines.

The *Monthly Magazine* ran only through three volumes of six issues each. Each issue included a section called "Original Communications." Its topics ranged from hair powder to penal law reformation, from shaving to standards of measure. Selected material, another feature, collected information from other sources on topics similar to those in "Original Communications." "American Review" regularly showcased reviews of books, sermons, orations, and poetry, and a poetry section featured both original and selected pieces.

Late in 1800 the thin population of the nation, coupled with problems of distribution, a shortage of contributors, and increasing cost, necessitated a change in the original plan for the magazine. Following the completion of the third volume, the magazine went to a quarterly publication schedule and was renamed the *American Review, and Literary Journal.*

With the change in title came a marked change in focus. Each issue began with the "Review," and Brown took pains to set forth a specific stance on the practice of criticism as pertaining to the nation's young authors. In the preface to the first issue (July 1801), Brown argued that a good critic "possessed of liberality and candour, and a just view of the end of writing, as well as a sense of the imperfection of all human skill and capacity" cannot fail to satisfy both the reading public and the author of the work reviewed. As in the *Monthly Magazine,*

Brown desired to keep the reviews from reflecting any prejudice: "Though not indifferent in the great questions of politics, which are so often discussed, and which at present agitate the world, they [the reviewers] hope to be above the influence of that *party-spirit,* which engenders so many unworthy and selfish passions, and whose views are limited by personal, local and temporary considerations." *American Review* lasted for two years; publication ceased in the fall of 1802.

In the months before Brown began editorship of yet another monthly publication, the *Literary Magazine, and American Register,* he was by no means idle. Always busy on the sociopolitical front, Brown authored *An Address to the Government of the United States, on the Cession of Louisiana to the French* (1803), which caused controversy. Harry R. Warfel argues that the entire episode explains why Brown turned away from fiction. "It is not difficult to understand why a man, anxious to teach lessons through books to his countrymen, yielded ambition in imaginative literature when factual writing was rewarded with the headiest kind of vituperation and praise." Brown wrote three other political pamphlets before he died and continued to exhibit a sound understanding of politics, economics, and international affairs.

In September 1803 Brown began editing the *Literary Magazine, and American Register* for John Conrad. As in the previous magazines Brown sought to enlighten the American public. According to David Lee Clark, the periodical, devoted exclusively to literature, resembled the best British journals and was the "most imposing magazine that America yet had seen." At the time it appeared it was the only monthly periodical available in the new nation. In the editor's address to the public, Brown expressed his reluctance to rely on himself and his own talents. Rather he intended to assemble America's writers and their works to present in *Literary Magazine.* And while he admitted that many magazines had failed in America already, he believed they had done so at the fault of the publishers or editors, particularly those who "have commonly either changed their principles, remitted their zeal, or voluntarily relinquished their trade or, last of all, and like other men, have died." Of particular importance, because it shows the ethical foundation of his editorial stance as well as reflecting his personal theory of a periodical's function, Brown made a promise to his readers:

As, in the conduct of this work, a supreme regard will be paid to the interests of religion and
morality, he [the editor] will scrupulously guard
against all that dishonours or impairs that principle. Everything that savours of indelicacy or li-
centiousness will be rigorously proscribed. His
poetical pieces may be dull, but they shall, at
least, be free from voluptuousness or sensuality,
and his prose, whether seconded or not by genius and knowledge, shall scrupulously aim at
the promotion of public and private virtue.

Finally Brown noted that there was no other
monthly publication in America; he only hoped
that the public at large would be willing to take a
new "visitor" into their homes once a month.

Unfortunately those who had promised to
provide contents for the new venture were often
remiss in sending material to the editor. In the
April 1804 issue Brown reminded his friends of
their promises to contribute. "The literary fraternity of New York, friends of the editor, and of
the editor's friends, are respectfully saluted, and
requested not to be unmindful, in the midst of
their professional engagements, of their promises." Later that summer, in a letter to his future
brother-in-law, the poet John Blair Linn, Brown
complained of having been forced to compose virtually all of the original material in the June
1804 issue.

In these later years Brown was often a vic-
tim of his poor health and trying circumstances.
Though his marriage to Elizabeth Linn, on 19 November 1804, brought companionship and a family of three sons and one daughter, he had gone
against his parents' wishes and married outside
the Quaker faith, a situation which continued to
cause him stress. Later the Browns experienced a
series of familial tragedies. His sister and brother
both died in 1807; Elizabeth's father died in
early 1808. Brown took a journey for his health
in early 1807, but his consumptive coughing
seemed to get worse with each fresh attack.

Brown's connection with the *Literary Magazine* lasted for five years, until he decided in 1807
to begin the *American Register, or General Repository of History, Politics, and Science*—essentially a continuation of the statistical portions of *Literary
Magazine*. In his preface Brown indicated his
need to publish a work "unattempted" in America. An objective and scrutinized "history of American affairs and foreign transactions" was "absolutely necessary to be known by those who
would be acquainted, not with the municipal law
but the political conditions of their own country."

Included in the five semiannual volumes he edited were a review of American literature for
1806 and 1807, a chronology and analysis of
events on both sides of the Atlantic, abstracts of
laws and public acts, memorable occurrences, British and American scientific intelligence, American and foreign state papers, an American
register of deaths, and selected poetry.

Brown's concern for providing his fellow citizens with historical, political, and geographical information about the world around them was
further demonstrated in his plan for a two-
volume "System of General Geography." According to one biographer this manuscript, which was
to encompass a topographical, statistical, and descriptive survey of the United States (volume 1)
and the rest of the world (volume 2), was lost before publication.

In November 1809 Brown experienced a violent pain in his side—he never left his bed after
that. On 22 February 1810 he died from advanced tuberculosis.

Brown desired to create a national literature
which would fortify the place of new American authors in the world of belles lettres. No doubt
many of the magazine issues which he edited
might never have gone to press without the ware-
house of fiction and nonfiction he wrote. While
most of the critical commentary on Brown is focused on his novels and the debate over his place
in early American literature, it can be argued
that his nonfiction writing and his various roles
as editor should have been given more importance in his biography.

The magazines Brown edited were highly re-
flective of his personal concerns. Essays on the fan-
tastic motifs of mesmerism, somnambulism, and
mysticism often found their way into the reports
on "scientific intelligence." Under "strange occurrences" were published stories of boulders and
fireballs which had been seen to drop from the
sky. Particularly prevalent in *American Review, and
Literary Journal* were critiques of orations and sermons. In keeping with fashionable notions of critical practice, numerous articles were published on
taste and the picturesque. Occasionally an article
would appear that pronounced upon the benefits
of reading and learning or assessed the then-
current state of American literature. In unsigned
essays Brown even wrote about novel writing.
His own studies of Milton and Cicero likely
prompted the critical analyses, which appeared in
the reviews, of both authors.

THE

LITERARY MAGAZINE,

AND

AMERICAN REGISTER.

No. I.]   SATURDAY, OCTOBER 1, 1803.   [Vol. I.

THE EDITORS' ADDRESS TO THE PUBLIC.

IT is usual for one who presents the public with a periodical work like the present, to introduce himself to the notice of his readers by some sort of preface or address. I take up the pen in conformity to this custom, but am quite at a loss for topics suitable to so interesting an occasion. I cannot expatiate on the variety of my knowledge, the brilliancy of my wit, the versatility of my talents. To none of these do I lay any claim, and though this variety, brilliancy of solidity, are necessary ingredients in a work of this kind, I trust merely to the zeal and liberality of my friends to supply me with them. I have them not myself, but doubt not of the good offices of those who possess them, and shall think myself entitled to no small praise, if I am able to collect into one focal spot the rays of a great number of luminaries. They also may be very unequal to each other in lustre, and some of them may be little better than twinkling and feeble stars, of the hundredth magnitude; but what is wanting in individual splendor, will be made up by the union of all their beams into one. My province shall be *to hold the mirror up* so as to resemble all their influence within its verge, and reflect them on the public in such manner as to warm and enlighten.

As I possess nothing but zeal, I can promise to exert nothing else; but my consolation is, that, aided by that powerful spirit, many have accomplished things much more arduous than that which I propose to myself.

Many are the works of this kind which have risen and fallen in America, and many of them have enjoyed but a brief existence. This circumstance has always at first sight, given me some uneasiness; but when I come more soberly to meditate upon it, my courage revives, and I discover no reason for my doubts. Many works have actually been reared and sustained by the curiosity and favour of the public. They have ultimately declined or fallen, it is true; but why? From no abatement of the public curiosity,

First page of Brown's statement of purpose for the magazine he edited from 1803 until 1807

Whatever Brown's role in the formation of a national literature for the United States, whatever difficulties he was known to have had in completing his early literary projects, whatever criticism can be leveled against his style or inability to appeal to wide audiences, Charles Brockden Brown can be said to have cared deeply about his craft, both philosophically and practically.

Bibliographies:
Robert E. Hemenway and Dean H. Keller, "Charles Brockden Brown, America's First Important Novelist: A Check List of Biography and Criticism," *Papers of the Bibliographical Society of America*, 60 (1966): 349-362;
Sydney J. Krause, with assistance of Jane Nieset, "A Census of the Works of Charles Brockden Brown," *Serif*, 3, no. 4 (1966): 27-55;
Paul Witherington, "Charles Brockden Brown: A Bibliographical Essay," *Early American Literature*, 9 (Fall 1974): 164-187;
Charles E. Bennett, "The Charles Brockden Brown Canon," Ph.D. dissertation, University of North Carolina at Chapel Hill, 1974;
Bennett, "The Letters of Charles Brockden Brown: An Annotated Census," *Resources for American Literary Study*, 6 (1976): 164-190;
Patricia Parker, *Charles Brockden Brown: A Reference Guide* (Boston: G. K. Hall, 1980);
Charles A. Carpenter, "Selective Bibliography of Writings about Charles Brockden Brown," in *Critical Essays on Charles Brockden Brown*, edited by Bernard Rosenthal (Boston: G. K. Hall, 1981), pp. 224-239.

Biographies:
William Dunlap, *The Life of Charles Brockden Brown: Together With Selections from the Rarest of His Printed Works, from His Original Letters, and from His Manuscripts Before Unpublished*, 2 volumes (Philadelphia: James P. Parke, 1815);
William Hickling Prescott, "Memoir of Charles Brockden Brown, the American Novelist," in *The Library of American Biography*, first series, edited by Jared Sparks (Boston: Hilliard, Gray, 1834), I: 117-180; republished in Prescott's *Biographical and Critical Miscellanies* (New York: Harper, 1845), pp. 1-56;
Harry R. Warfel, *Charles Brockden Brown, American Gothic Novelist* (Gainesville: University of Florida Press, 1949);
David Lee Clark, *Charles Brockden Brown, Pioneer Voice of America* (Durham: Duke University Press, 1952);
Paul Allen, *The Life of Charles Brockden Brown: A Facsimile Reproduction*, edited by Charles E. Bennett (Delmar, N.Y.: Scholars' Facsimiles and Reprints, 1975); also published as *The Late Charles Brockden Brown*, edited by Robert E. Hemenway and Joseph Katz (Columbia, S.C.: Faust, 1976).

References:
Alan Axelrod, *Charles Brockden Brown: An American Tale* (Austin: University of Texas Press, 1983);
Maurice J. Bennett, "Charles Brockden Brown's Ambivalence Toward Art and Imagination," *Essays in Literature*, 10 (Spring 1983): 55-69;
Warner B. Berthoff, "Charles Brockden Brown's Historical 'Sketches': A Consideration," *American Literature*, 28 (May 1956): 147-154;
Robert A. Ferguson, "Literature and Vocation in the Early Republic: The Example of Charles Brockden Brown," *Modern Philology*, 78 (November 1980): 139-152;
Ernest Marchand, "The Literary Opinions of Charles Brockden Brown," *Studies in Philology*, 31 (October 1934): 541-566;
Bernard Rosenthal, ed., *Critical Essays on Charles Brockden Brown* (Boston: G. K. Hall, 1981).

Papers:
Holdings of Brown manuscript material may be found at the University of Texas at Austin, the University of Virginia, the Historical Society of Pennsylvania in Philadelphia, and Bowdoin College.

Orestes A. Brownson

(16 September 1803-17 April 1876)

Sam G. Riley
Virginia Polytechnic Institute and State University

See also the Brownson entries in *DLB 1: The American Renaissance in New England* and *DLB 59: American Literary Critics and Scholars, 1800-1850.*

MAJOR POSITIONS HELD: Editor, *Gospel Advocate and Impartial Investigator* (1828-1829), *Genesee Republican and Herald of Reform* (1829-1830); editor and publisher, *Philanthropist* (1831-1832); editor, *Boston Reformer* (1836-1837); editor and publisher, *Boston Quarterly Review*, merged with *United States Magazine and Democratic Review* (1838-1842), *Brownson's Quarterly Review* (1844-1864, 1873-1875).

BOOKS: *An Address, on the Fifty-fifth Anniversary of American Independence Delivered at Ovid, Seneca Co. N. Y. July 4, 1831* (Ithaca: S. S. Chatterton, 1831);

An Address on Intemperance, Delivered in Walpole, N. H. February 26, 1833 (Keene, N.H.: J. & J. Prentiss, 1833);

An Address, Delivered at Dedham, on the Fifty-eighth Anniversary of American Independence, July 4, 1834 (Dedham, Mass.: H. Mann, 1834);

A Sermon Delivered to the Young People of the First Congregational Society in Canton, on Sunday, May 24th, 1835 (Dedham, Mass.: H. Mann, 1835);

New Views of Christianity, Society, and the Church (Boston: James Munroe, 1836);

A Discourse on the Wants of the Times, Delivered in Lyceum Hall, Hanover Street, Boston, Sunday, May 29, 1836 (Boston: James Munroe, 1836);

Babylon is Falling. A Discourse Preached in the Masonic Temple, to the Society for Christian Union and Progress, on Sunday Morning, May 28, 1837 (Boston: I. R. Butts, 1837);

An Address Delivered on Popular Education, Delivered in Winnisimmet Village, on Sunday Evening, July 23, 1837 (Boston: Putnam, 1837);

An Oration Delivered Before the United Brothers Society of Brown University, at Providence, R. I., Sep-

Orestes A. Brownson (courtesy of the Museum of Fine Arts, Boston)

tember 3, 1839 (Cambridge, Mass.: Metcalf, Torry & Ballou, 1839);

Brownson's Defence. Defence of the Article on the Laboring Classes (Boston: Benjamin H. Greene, 1840);

Charles Elwood: or the Infidel Converted (Boston: Little, Brown, 1840; London: Chapman Brothers, 1845);

The Labouring Classes, an Article from the Boston Quarterly Review (Boston: Benjamin H. Greene, 1840);

An Oration before the Democracy of Worcester and Vicinity, Delivered at Worcester, Mass., July 4, 1840 (Boston: E. Littlefield/Worcester: M. D. Phillips, 1840);

Oration of Orestes A. Brownson, Delivered at Washington Hall, July 5th, 1841 (New York: G. Washington Dixon, 1841);

The Policy to be Pursued Hereafter by the Friends of the Constitution, and of Equal Rights (Boston: Benjamin H. Greene, 1841);

A Review of Mr. Parker's Discourse on the Transient and Permanent in Christianity (Boston: Benjamin H. Greene, 1841);

Constitutional Government (Boston: Benjamin H. Greene, 1842);

The Mediatorial Life of Jesus. A Letter to Rev. William Ellery Channing, D.D. (Boston: Little, Brown, 1842);

An Oration on the Scholar's Mission (Boston: Benjamin H. Greene, 1843);

Social Reform. An Address before the Society of the Mystical Seven in the Wesleyan University, Middletown, Conn. August 7, 1844 (Boston: Waite, Peirce, 1844);

A Review of the Sermon by Dr. Potts, on the Dangers of Jesuit Instruction, Preached at the Second Presbyterian Church, St. Louis, on the 25th September, 1845 (St. Louis: "News-Letter" Publication Office, 1846);

Essays and Reviews Chiefly on Theology, Politics, and Socialism (New York, Boston & Montreal: D. & J. Sadlier, 1852);

An Oration on Liberal Studies, Delivered before the Philomathian Society, of Mount Saint Mary's College, MD., June 29th, 1853 (Baltimore: Hedian & O'Brien, 1853);

The Spirit-Rapper; an Autobiography (Boston: Little, Brown/London: Charles Dolman, 1854);

The Convert: or, Leaves from My Experience (New York: D. & J. Sadlier, 1857; New York: Edward Dunigan, 1857);

The War for the Union. Speech by Dr. O. A. Brownson. How the War Should Be Prosecuted. The Duty of the Government and the Duty of the Citizen (New York: George F. Nesbitt, 1862);

The American Republic: Its Constitution, Tendencies, and Destiny (New York: P. O'Shea, 1865);

Conversations on Liberalism and the Church (New York: D. & J. Sadlier/Boston & Montreal: P. H. Brady, 1870);

An Essay in Refutation of Atheism, edited by Henry F. Brownson (Detroit: Thorndike, Nourse, 1882);

The Two Brothers; or Why are You a Protestant?, edited by Henry F. Brownson (Detroit: H. F. Brownson, 1888);

Uncle Jack and His Nephew; or Conversations of an Old Fogy with a Young American, edited by Henry F. Brownson (Detroit: H. F. Brownson, 1888).

Collections: *The Work of Orestes A. Brownson*, edited by Henry F. Brownson, 20 volumes: volumes 1-19 (Detroit: Thorndike, Nourse, 1882-1887); volume 20 (Detroit: Henry F. Brownson, 1887);

Essays on Modern Popular Literature, edited by Henry F. Brownson (Detroit: Henry F. Brownson, 1888);

Literary, Scientific, and Political Views of Orestes A. Brownson, edited by Henry F. Brownson (New York: Benziger, 1893);

Watchwords from Dr. Brownson, selected and edited by D. J. Scannell O'Neill (Techny, Ill.: Society of the Divine Word, 1910);

The Brownson Reader, edited by Arvan S. Ryan (New York: P. J. Kenedy, 1955);

Orestes Brownson: Selected Essays, edited by Russell Kirk (Chicago: Regnery, 1955).

New Englander Orestes Brownson was, above all else, a man of "-isms." In his long career as writer and editor, his religious beliefs changed frequently, taking him from Congregationalism and Presbyterianism to Universalism, Unitarianism, Transcendentalism, and, finally, Roman Catholicism. His writing and editing, which ranged widely over theology, philosophy, politics, sociology, economics, and literary criticism, brought his intellect to bear on such far-ranging "-isms" as deism, Hobbism and agnosticism, sansculottism and Chartism, Jacobinism, Nativism, and know-nothingism. His was a life of the intellect, and his concern was not with individuals or with things, but with large ideas, such as libertarianism vs. authoritarianism, spiritualism vs. temporalism, utopian socialism vs. capitalism, and political absolutism vs. political pluralism. How he dealt with all these "-isms" was most prominently displayed in two quarterly reviews he edited and published, the *Boston Quarterly Review* (1838-1842) and *Brownson's Quarterly Review* (1844-1864, 1873-1875), and in his more important books.

Orestes Augustus Brownson was born on 16 September 1803, the son of Vermonter Sylvester A. Brownson and Relief Metcalf Brownson, formerly of New Hampshire. Orestes' interest in religion began in his early boyhood after the death of his father. Relief Brownson, impoverished after her husband's attack of pneumonia and sudden death, was forced to send Orestes at age six to board with an elderly farm couple near Stockbridge, Vermont. The lonely boy turned to God as a substitute for the earthly father he no longer had and in later years reported that he had read the King James Bible through by age eight and had memorized much of it by fourteen.

In 1816, the year when winter came to Vermont in summer and crops were killed, the Brownsons were forced to move to Saratoga County, New York. Here Orestes spent perhaps a year at Ballston Academy, learning some Greek and Latin, and in the community of Ballston Spa, Orestes apprenticed himself to printer James Comstock, eventually reaching the level of journeyman printer. His search for religious truth led him to join the Presbyterian church. Later he taught school in the village of Stillwater, a position he lost after parting company with Presbyterianism, which he came to find overly negative, bigoted, and uncharitable in its somber Calvinism. For a time Brownson took the position that no church had the right to consider that it spoke for Christ.

Under the influence of Hosea Ballou, Brownson was attracted to the more positive, liberal approach of the Universalists, whose beliefs were directed to a God of love, not the more intimidating fire-and-brimstone God of the Presbyterians. In 1824 Brownson moved to the Detroit area, where he again taught school, this time at Springwells, Illinois. He contracted malaria and was ill for the better part of 1825. During his convalescence he decided to become a Universalist minister; at age twenty-two he was ordained as such and preached in this capacity for three years in New Hampshire, Vermont, and New York. In 1828 he began to write for the nation's most influential Universalist periodical, the semimonthly *Gospel Advocate and Impartial Investigator* of Ithaca, New York. Brownson became editor after a few months. Reflecting on the Universalist belief in salvation of all men by an all-loving God, Brownson concluded that such lax beliefs would undermine morality. In the Bible he came to find far more questions than answers, and his very belief in God was shaken.

His writing became more social and political than theological, and his editorship of the *Gospel Advocate* lasted only a year. Now more or less an agnostic, Brownson returned to New York and taught school at the town of Elbridge. He met and on 19 June 1827 married Sally Healy, with whom he eventually had eight children. In 1829 Brownson formally broke with the Universalists and came under the influence of three humanitar-

ian social reformers: Robert Owen, William Godwin, and Frances Wright. He collaborated with Owen and Wright as a corresponding editor of their *Free Enquirer,* a New York City weekly that was the successor to the better-known *New Harmony Gazette* that Owen and Wright had edited in Indiana. With his fellow Free Enquirers, Brownson helped organize and promote the Workingmen's party in New York and in 1829 became editor of the *Genesee Republican and Herald of Reform,* published at Leroy, New York. The radical issues of socialistic agrarianism, a redistribution of land and state guardianship of all children, soon split the Workingmen's party and rendered it ineffectual.

In the fall of 1830 Brownson split with the Free Enquirers. Returning to religion, he set himself up in Ithaca as an independent minister and continued his tortured inner search for religious truth and the means of social reform. He built a reputation as an orator and at Walpole, New Hampshire, in 1831, founded and edited his own weekly journal, the *Philanthropist.* Nonpayment by subscribers forced him to discontinue this journal in June 1832.

Temporarily depressed by his lack of success and failure to find the answers he sought, Brownson turned to Unitarianism and later in 1832 became the Unitarian minister in Walpole. Here he improved his grasp of the classical languages and, in addition, acquired a reading knowledge of French, Italian, Spanish, and German. He delivered frequent addresses around New England, a few of which were printed in pamphlet form, and he contributed to two Unitarian periodicals, the *Unitarian* and the *Christian Register.*

In 1834 Brownson took a new pulpit at Canton, Massachusetts. The educational and spiritual improvement of the working class became his primary interest. In 1836 a long friendship began when Henry David Thoreau, then a Harvard student, stayed for six weeks at Brownson's home in Canton to be evaluated as to his fitness for teaching.

By 1836 Brownson was ready to play on a bigger stage. He moved to the Boston area and launched his socioreligious Society for Christian Union and Progress, by which he hoped to find a proper mix of the spiritual and the material. Catholicism, he believed, had overplayed spiritualism, then Protestantism had degraded itself by excessive materialism. Brownson looked for a middle road and in an attempt to gain converts wrote *New Views of Christianity, Society, and the*

BROWNSON'S

QUARTERLY REVIEW.

JANUARY, 1844.

—◆—

Art. I. — Introduction. — *The Boston Quarterly Review.* — *Greeting to Old Friends.* — *Design of the Work.* — *Change of Views.* — *Eclecticism.* — *Saint-Simonism.* — *German Philosophy.* — *Philosophy of Life.* — *Theology.* — *The Church.* — *Law of Continuity.* — *Ultraists.* — *Conservatism.* — *Constitutionalism.* — *Moral and Religious Appeals.*

At the close of the volume for 1842, I was induced to merge the Boston Quarterly Review, which I had conducted for five years, in the Democratic Review, published at New-York, on condition of becoming a free and independent contributor to its pages for two years. But the character of my contributions having proved unacceptable to a portion of its ultra-democratic subscribers, and having, in consequence, occasioned its proprietors a serious pecuniary loss, the conductor has signified to me, that it would be desirable for my connexion with the Democratic Review to cease before the termination of the original agreement. This leaves me free to publish a new journal of my own, and renders it, in fact, necessary, if I would continue my communications with the public. I have no fault to find with the conductor of the Democratic Review, Mr. O'Sullivan, — a gentleman for whom I have a very

VOL. I. NO. I.   1

First issue of the periodical Brownson started after severing ties with the United States Magazine and Democratic Review

Church (1836). Although several of his addresses and a sermon had been published, *New Views* was Brownson's first book-length publication. The optimism of both the society and the book is revealed in the society's motto: "Paradise on earth is before us." In his attempts to Christianize the labor movement, Brownson aroused the distrust, or at least the suspicion, of both rich and poor, and even the Boston clergy viewed his efforts unfavorably. While contending with these obstacles to the success of his "church of the future," Brownson edited the *Boston Reformer*, a newspaper that gave his unorthodox views a wider audience than they otherwise would have enjoyed. He proclaimed himself not a radical, but more nearly a conservative. The readers of the *Reformer* complained that Brownson was orienting it too much toward religion, not enough toward politics.

Meanwhile, Brownson established a warm friendship with historian and prominent Democrat George Bancroft, who led Brownson into the sphere of partisan politics. When Van Buren was elected president in 1836, Bancroft was made collector of the port of Boston and in turn gave Brownson the stewardship of the United States Marine Hospital, which paid a yearly salary of sixteen hundred dollars, freeing him from financial cares.

The editorship of the *Reformer* was relinquished in favor of a new, more dignified forum for Brownson's thoughts, the *Boston Quarterly Review*, in which he had full freedom to discuss anything that interested him. The first issue appeared in December 1837, and in it he declared his intention to keep his new quarterly free of allegiance to party, class, or doctrine, and to make it an unfettered vehicle of the search for truth. Each issue would contain six essays, plus literary notices. Many of the essays were run unsigned, though some of Brownson's own were signed "The Editor." The greater part of the copy in this *Quarterly Review* came from Brownson's own pen, though essays also appeared by such contributors as Bancroft, Margaret Fuller, George Ripley, W. H. Channing, Albert Brisbane, Alexander Everett, Sarah Whitman, and Elizabeth Peabody. Circulation quickly reached a thousand, which Brownson found gratifying. Brownson used the critical essays he wrote for his new review to explore the relationship of church and state, presenting democracy as the political manifestation of Christianity and speaking out against elitism.

It was at this time that Brownson began forming a vague, uneasy alliance with the other Boston intellectuals who came together in 1836 as the Transcendental Club. Reacting to the old Puritanism, the Transcendentalists believed that truth existed in another dimension, and that man was capable of divining the truth through intuition. Brownson was far too independent-minded to subscribe to all the Transcendentalists' beliefs, but when they began to discuss founding a journal of their own, he suggested that it might be merged into his *Quarterly Review*. The idea was rejected, and the club later published the *Dial* (1840-1844).

The July 1840 issue of the *Boston Quarterly Review* contained Brownson's most controversial essay to date, "The Laboring Classes." It began as a review of Thomas Carlyle's pamphlet on Chartism, a discussion of the plight of England's labor class. Brownson took the position that labor and capital were enemies, not partners in economic life. He compared the dual system of labor in the United States, slave labor in the South and wage labor in the North, and declared that despite his general disapproval of slavery, he found it the better of the two systems. In the economic depression that lasted from 1837 into the 1840s, he had seen dramatic evidence that America's new merchant class had fared infinitely better than her wage laborers. Drastic changes were called for, he wrote, adding that little help for the poor could be expected from the church. He drew a line between Christianity as he believed it to have been taught by Christ and the sacrosanct orthodoxy and hierarchy of established churches in the United States. He went so far as to call for an end to preaching as a profession, then suggested, just as radically, that hereditary descent of private property be abolished so that when a man died his property would go entirely to the state.

One can well imagine the storm of protest that followed this article. Brownson was called a traitor to the Democratic party, and Van Buren attributed partly to Brownson his defeat in the November presidential election. Other critics accused Brownson of calling for the abolition of Christianity, which he later denied, but in doing so added that the church should be absorbed by the state.

Some writers have portrayed Brownson as a founder and resident of the utopian Brook Farm Institute, founded by his friend and fellow reformer George Ripley in 1841 on a 192-acre

Brownson, circa 1870

tract in West Roxbury near Boston. Though he sympathized with Ripley's aims, he had little faith in the experiment's success and was not a Brook Farm resident himself, though he did send his son Orestes to live there. The elder Brownson, like Ralph Waldo Emerson, Bronson Alcott, and Margaret Fuller, was only a visitor, along with several thousand curiosity seekers who went there more or less as tourists. In a letter to Emerson dated 9 November 1842, Brownson affirmed that he had given up on utopian schemes of social reform. Around this same time the circulation of the *Quarterly Review* had fallen off badly, and Brownson decided to accept an offer to write for the New York-based *United States Magazine and Democratic Review,* a successful, dignified political journal. Accordingly, Brownson's *Boston Quarterly Review* was merged with that magazine in November 1842.

Brownson's association with the *Democratic Review* was not a happy one. His ponderous es-

says on "Schmucher's Psychology" and "Synthetic Philosophy" were far too heavy for a popular magazine. Furthermore, Brownson began to express doubts in the ability of the people to make wise use of democracy. Such sentiments also failed to please the readers of the *Democratic Review,* yet Brownson continued to write for them through most of 1843. Also, in 1843 his growing conservatism surfaced in a series of articles on "The Mission of Jesus" in a new weekly, the *Christian World.*

In January 1844 Brownson revived his quarterly, this time titling it *Brownson's Quarterly Review.* It was much like his earlier review in that most of the copy he wrote himself. The content, however, was even more theological than before, especially following his conversion to Roman Catholicism in October of the same year. Many pages were devoted to trying to detail for his readers the tortuous path he had followed in search of true faith. He also used its pages to promote the presidential candidacy of his favorite states- man, South Carolina's John C. Calhoun. He de- fended Calhoun's states' rights doctrine, an unusual position for a northern editor in the 1840s. Under the tutelage of Bishop John Fitzpatrick, Brownson plunged into a detailed study of Catholicism. He wrote as he learned, quickly becoming the most outspoken Catholic apologist in the nation at a time when Catholi- cism was under severe and bigoted attack in many parts of the country.

At forty-two, the six-foot-two-inch Brown- son sported a full beard to go with his leonine mass of graying hair and was a formidable figure as he did battle for his new beliefs. His battles were ordinarily verbal, of course, though on one occasion he was pushed to the level of physical vio- lence by a Charleston, South Carolina, man named Hoover who loudly accused him of being a traitor to his country and to Protestantism. The editor warned Hoover that if he continued his abuse Brownson would throw the man over the room's stovepipe. The man continued, and the hulking Brownson made good his promise.

Brownson used his new *Review* to discuss the proper sphere of woman, the shortcomings of Transcendentalism, the essentially religious basis of truth and worth in works of literature, and other weighty issues, but his primary thrust was an examination of the various schools of theol- ogy within the Catholic church. His appeals for making the U.S. church more American and less Irish plus his criticism of parochial schools made him as controversial within his new church as with- out. He produced a novel in 1854, *The Spirit- Rapper; an Autobiography*, a gloomy work on mesmerism, good and evil, and world reform. In 1855 Brownson escaped Bishop Fitzpatrick's influ- ence by moving his family and his *Review* to the New York area. In 1857 he produced his real auto- biography, *The Convert: or, Leaves from My Experi- ence*, largely an examination of his long path to Catholicism. Frequent lecture tours netted him enough money to provide for his family and to continue his *Review*. While his lectures were bring- ing converts to the church, Brownson's increasing liberalism engaged him in many a serious wran- gle with the Catholic hierarchy.

Prior to the beginning of the Civil War, Brownson's position was that the U.S. govern- ment had no right to demand that slavery be abol- ished in the southern states, but after the shooting began, he spoke in favor of emancipa- tion and became a Lincoln supporter. Brownson

was nominated for Congress in 1862 by the Repub- lican party of New Jersey but was defeated. Later he split with Lincoln, backed John Charles Fre- mont in the 1864 presidential race, but in the end voted for Lincoln. Brownson's son Henry was wounded at Chancellorsville in 1863, and Brownson's brother William was killed in a Ne- vada stagecoach accident in July 1864. Then in Au- gust of 1864 his son Edward, known as Ned, died in battle at Ream's Station, Virginia. On top of these personal losses, the war had cut the sub- scription list for his *Review* in half, and nonpay- ment by subscribers had cost him seventeen thousand dollars. With regret he discontinued his *Quarterly Review*.

At this low point in Brownson's fortunes, prominent New York Catholics arranged an annu- ity of two thousand dollars a year for him, which provided him the opportunity to work on his most important book, *The American Republic: Its Constitution, Tendencies, and Destiny*, which ap- peared in 1865. It was an in-depth examination of America's unique place in the political move- ments of Western civilization and Judeo-Christian religious tradition. Now older and afflicted with gout, Brownson again swung back toward conser- vatism and from 1865 to 1873 wrote, sometimes anonymously, for the Catholic magazines *Ave Maria* and *Catholic World*.

On 19 April 1872 Brownson's wife, Sally, died. Her last wish was that he might revive *Brownson's Quarterly Review*. Though old and gout- ridden, he complied, resuming publication in Jan- uary 1873. He received much encouragement from Catholic officialdom and launched an at- tack on what he considered the pseudoscience of the age, new ways of thinking that had earlier been given credence by Charles Darwin's *On the Origin of Species* (1859). He also lashed out at what he saw as the "mannish" tendencies of popu- lar women writers of the day. The last number of his *Review* was issued in October 1875, after which he moved to Detroit to live with his son Henry and family. On 17 April 1876, at seventy- two, he died and was buried in Detroit's Mt. Elliot Cemetery. Ten years later his body was moved to a crypt in Notre Dame University's Sa- cred Heart Chapel.

Brownson is a hard man to sum up, at least for anyone who lives in today's world of specializa- tion. Through all his innumerable changes of opinion, orientation, and religious affiliation, his considerable intellect was directed to the widest range of issues. Among all the company of editors and publishers of American periodicals, he was one of the most profound and complex, as well as one of the most mercurial. He was a well-known man in his own time in America, England, and France, but he is accorded little space in current history books, with the exception of histories of the Roman Catholic faith. In retrospect Brownson's remarkably frequent changes in outlook and opinion suggest that he thought too much, or that he took stands before having thought them out sufficiently. Still, his writing–the lyrical, the logical, and the philosophical–was forceful and as deep as it was prolific. He was a man who was never afraid to speak his mind.

Letters:

Daniel Ramon Barnes, "An Edition of the Early Letters of Orestes Brownson," Ph.D. dissertation, University of Kentucky, 1970;

The Brownson-Hecker Correspondence, edited by Joseph F. Gower and Richard M. Leliaert (Notre Dame: University of Notre Dame Press, 1979).

Biographies:

Henry F. Brownson, *Orestes A. Brownson's Early Life: from 1803 to 1844* (Detroit: H. F. Brownson, 1898);

Brownson, *Orestes A. Brownson's Middle Life: from 1845 to 1855* (Detroit: H. F. Brownson, 1899);

Brownson, *Orestes A. Brownson's Latter Life: from 1855 to 1876* (Detroit: H. F. Brownson, 1900);

Arthur M. Schlesinger, Jr., *Orestes A. Brownson: A Pilgrim's Progress* (Boston: Little, Brown, 1939);

Theodore Maynard, *Orestes Brownson: Yankee, Radical, Catholic* (New York: Macmillan, 1943);

Thomas R. Ryan, *Orestes A. Brownson: A Definitive Biography* (Huntington, Ind.: Our Sunday Visitor, Inc., 1976).

References:

Daniel R. Barnes, "Brownson and Newman: The Controversy Re-examined," *Emerson Society Quarterly*, no. 50 (First Quarter 1968): 9-20;

Kenneth W. Cameron, "Thoreau and Orestes Brownson," *Emerson Society Quarterly*, 51 (Second Quarter 1968): 53-74;

A. R. Caponigri, "Brownson and Emerson: Nature and History," *New England Quarterly*, 18 (September 1945): 368-390;

Paul R. Conroy, "Orestes A. Brownson: American Political Philosopher," Ph.D. dissertation, St. Louis University, 1937;

Thomas I. Cook and Arnaud B. Leavelle, "Orestes Brownson's *The American Republic*," *Review of Politics*, 4 (January 1942): 77-90; 4 (April 1942): 173-193;

Sister M. Felicia Corrigan, *Some Social Principles of Orestes A. Brownson* (Washington, D.C.: Catholic University of America Press, 1939);

Bertin Farrell, *Orestes Brownson's Approach to the Problem of God* (Washington, D.C.: Catholic University of America Press, 1950);

M. A. Fitzsimmons, "Brownson's Search for the Kingdom of God: The Social Thought of an American Radical," *Review of Politics*, 16 (January 1954): 22-36;

Leonard Gilhooley, *Contradiction and Dilemma: Orestes Brownson and the American Idea* (New York: Fordham University Press, 1972);

Carroll Hollis, "The Literary Criticism of Orestes Brownson," Ph.D. dissertation, University of Michigan, 1954;

Carl Krummel, "Catholicism, Americanism, Democracy, and Orestes Brownson," *American Quarterly*, 6 (Spring 1954): 19-31;

Arthur I. Ladu, "Political Ideas of Orestes A. Brownson, Transcendentalist," *Philological Quarterly*, 12 (July 1933): 280-289;

Americo D. Lapati, *Orestes A. Brownson* (New York: Twayne, 1965);

Vincent A. Lapomarda, "Orestes Augustus Brownson: A 19th Century View of Blacks in American Society," *Mid-America*, 18 (July 1971): 160-169;

George Parsons Lathrop, "Orestes Brownson," *Atlantic Monthly*, 77 (May 1896): 770-780;

Hugh Marshall, *Orestes Brownson and the American Republic* (Washington, D.C.: Catholic University of America Press, 1971);

Thomas T. McAvoy, "Orestes A. Brownson and American History," *Catholic Historical Review*, 40 (October 1954): 257-268;

Virgil G. Michel, "Brownson's Political Philosophy and Today," *American Catholic Quarterly Review*, 44 (October 1919): 193-202;

Robert E. Moffit, "Metaphysics and Constitutionalism: The Political Theory of Orestes Brownson," Ph.D. dissertation, University of Arizona, 1975;

Vincent J. Moran, "The Relation of Brownson to the Philosophy of Kant," Ph. D. dissertation, University of Toronto, 1954;

Frank Luther Mott, *A History of American Magazines,* 5 volumes (Cambridge, Mass.: Harvard University Press, 1938-1968), I: 685-691;

John Reidl, "The Life and Philosophy of Orestes Brownson," Ph.D. dissertation, Marquette University, 1930;

George Ripley, "Brownson's Writings," *Dial,* 1 (July 1840): 22-46;

Lawrence Roemer, *Brownson on Democracy and the Trend Toward Socialism* (New York: Philosophical Library, 1953);

Alvan S. Ryan, "Orestes Brownson: The Critique of Transcendentalism," in *American Classics Reconsidered, A Christian Appraisal,* edited by Harold C. Gardiner (New York: Scribners, 1958), pp. 98-120;

Thomas R. Ryan, *The Sailor's Snug Harbor: Studies in Brownson's Thought* (Westminster, Md.: Newman Press, 1952);

Arthur M. Schlesinger, Jr., "Orestes Brownson, An American Marxist Before Marx," *Sewanee Review,* 47 (July-September 1939): 317-323;

Chester A. Soleta, "The Literary Criticism of O. A. Brownson," *Review of Politics,* 16 (July 1954): 334-351;

Peter J. Stanlis, "America Is Hard To See," *University Bookman,* 13 (Spring 1973): 52-60;

Per Sveino, *Orestes A. Brownson's Road to Catholicism* (New York: Humanities Press, 1970).

Papers:
The major collection of Orestes A. Brownson papers is held by the University of Notre Dame Archives, which produced a nineteen-roll microfilm copy of letters by Brownson, drafts of essays and books by Brownson, letters to or about Brownson, and newspaper clippings concerning him. Besides the University of Notre Dame collection, other Brownson manuscripts exist in the Archives of the Paulist Fathers, St. Paul's Church, New York City; Library of Congress; Harvard University Libraries; Birmingham Oratory, Birmingham, England; and Pius XII Memorial Library, St. Louis, Missouri.

Joseph Tinker Buckingham

(21 December 1779-11 April 1861)

and

Edwin Buckingham

(26 June 1810-18 May 1833)

James Boylan
University of Massachusetts–Amherst

MAJOR POSITIONS HELD: Joseph Tinker Buckingham, editor, *Polyanthos* (1806-1807, 1812-1814); editor, *New-England Galaxy* (1817-1828); editor, *Boston Courier* (1824-1848); coeditor, editor, *New-England Magazine* (1831-1834). Edwin Buckingham, coeditor, *New-England Magazine* (1831-1833).

BOOKS by Joseph Tinker Buckingham: *Trial: Commonwealth v. J. T. Buckingham, on an Indictment for a Libel* (Boston: New-England Galaxy, 1822);
Specimens of Newspaper Literature: with Personal Memoirs, Anecdotes, and Reminiscences, 2 volumes (Boston: C. C. Little and J. Brown, 1850);
Personal Memoirs and Recollections of Editorial Life, 2 volumes (Boston: Ticknor, Reed, and Fields, 1852).

Joseph Tinker Buckingham was one of the New England breed of poor, self-educated young printers who lifted themselves to eminence in journalism. Like Benjamin Franklin before him and Horace Greeley after, Buckingham learned language and the arts at the printer's case, sought his fortune in the city, and ultimately shed his apron to become an editor and writer–in Buckingham's case, a controversialist of distinct ferocity. He founded a successful newspaper, the *Boston Courier*, but is better remembered for his role in creating three periodicals: the *Polyanthos* (1806-1807, 1812-1814), which pioneered in portrait illustration and musical criticism; the *New-England Galaxy*, a weekly that he edited from 1817 to 1828, frequently fending off libel suits; and the *New-England Magazine*, a general monthly that he edited with his talented son, Edwin, whose life ended at the age of twenty-two. The last has been called a prototype of the *Atlantic Monthly*, founded a quarter of a century

later, and of the genteel nineteenth-century literary magazine.

The elder Buckingham's childhood was spent in the depths of poverty. He was born in Windham, Connecticut, to Nehemiah Tinker, a shoemaker, and Mary Huntington Tinker. He was baptized Joseph Buckingham because of a request by a relative, evidently of that name; he officially took the name of Joseph Tinker Buckingham in 1804. When he was three his father died bankrupt, and the family of ten children was dispersed; he was sent to live and work at the farm of a kindly elderly couple. As early as the age of thirteen, a visit to a printer's shop persuaded him of his vocation, and at sixteen he became an apprentice in a shop in New Hampshire. He found the hazing and drinking there distasteful and moved on to learn his trade at a newspaper shop in Greenfield, Massachusetts.

Much as Franklin migrated to Philadelphia and Greeley left Vermont for New York, Buckingham gravitated toward Boston, cultural capital of New England, where he arrived in February 1800. Within weeks he was hired by Thomas and Andrews, an establishment of the eminent editor-printer Isaiah Thomas and reputedly the largest in America at that time. In 1804, only twenty-four years old, Buckingham contracted to manage Thomas and Andrews for five years. This rise in status did not enrich him, but it permitted him to marry and start a family. In 1805 he married Melinda Alvord of Greenfield; over the next twenty-five years they had thirteen children. Stimulated by the intellectual and cultural atmosphere of the city, he found himself longing to make his mark in letters as well as business.

His first step in that direction was the founding of the *Polyanthos* ("many-flowered"), a monthly review, at the end of 1805. As editor, Buckingham prided himself on printing in each issue a portrait engraving of an eminent New Englander, the first such series in America, he claimed. But he also named himself the theater and music critic, and it was in this role that he became known for his outspokenness. His most memorable encounter in this period was with David Poe and his wife, Elizabeth Arnold, actors (and, later, parents of Edgar Allan Poe). Elizabeth Poe was playing a character called "Little Pickle," and Buckingham wrote that she had been "a very *green Little Pickle*." Poe sought out Buckingham and threatened, as Buckingham said, to "chastise my impertinence," but had to leave without doing so. Of his theater criticisms in this period, Buckingham observed mildly: "Some of them are severe, but I am not aware that any were unjust."

Prosperity did not come to the *Polyanthos* or to Buckingham, and he suspended it after twenty months. He revived it in 1812, and it lasted two more years, again with no commercial success. In 1809 he published a short-lived political periodical, the *Ordeal*, which was designed to serve as a vehicle for Benjamin Pollard, known to Buckingham as "a warm politician of the federal school," who served as editor. But the subscriptions did not cover the printing costs, and after six issues the *Ordeal* ended.

Nor did the printing business provide more than a sparse living for Buckingham and his growing family. A deal in which he acquired Thomas and Andrews turned sour, and he was lucky to escape bankruptcy. He turned for a time to school-teaching, fared no better, and returned to printing in 1816 as a shop overseer but really "nothing more than a journeyman," almost where he had started sixteen years before. He later recalled these years as laden with "embarrassments, deprivations, and physical and mental suffering."

In 1817 Buckingham finally had a change of fortune. While publishing two minor religious periodicals to order, he formulated a proposal for a weekly of "literary and miscellaneous character." Samuel Knapp, a lawyer recently arrived in Boston, liked the idea and suggested that such a magazine could gain circulation by including a Masonic section, to be edited by Knapp. Buckingham issued a prospectus for the *New-England Galaxy and Masonic Magazine*, and a first issue—printed with secondhand type on an old press—appeared, dated 10 October 1817. The enterprise was shaky, backed by no capital whatsoever. Indeed, Buckingham declined to take the price of a full year's subscription from the first potential subscriber.

Filled with the pessimism born of experience, Buckingham was surprised to have the magazine survive, in great part because of the initial response of the region's Masonic community. But the weekly continued even after Knapp wearied, in less than a year, of editing Masonic news, and *Masonic Magazine* was dropped from the title in 1820. It remained under Buckingham's direction until 1828, when he sold it to new owners who continued it six years more.

The *New-England Galaxy* gave Buckingham the critic a new vehicle, and he was soon ruffling feathers again. He remarked of the magazine's first turbulent year: "The freedom of remark which had been indulged had excited some angry feelings." One of his early targets was Joseph Lancaster, an English lecturer on education, whom he considered a "quack of the first order."

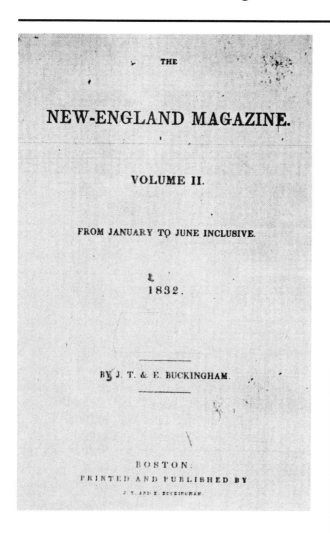

ADVERTISEMENT.

In presenting this second volume of the New-England Magazine, the pledge given at the commencement of the work is redeemed. It was an experiment of quite uncertain result; but we promised to give it a year's probation. The year has expired, and the event, if it have not brought the realization of our hopes, has not disappointed our expectations. The circulation of the Magazine has increased monthly. It is yet far from being a source of pecuniary profit; but the experiment thus far encourages us to enter on another year, with no less of hope and with more of confidence.

It was originally intended to embellish the magazine with a series of Portraits. This intention it has been impossible to fulfil. There is some difficulty in procuring original likenesses, and more in obtaining correct copies of originals. The fastidiousness of individuals in two or three instances has frustrated our design. But with all these discouragements, the design will not be abandoned. We make no *promises*, the fulfilment of which depends upon the whims and caprices of others. A reliance on our own resources is the only basis of any pledge we may offer to the public.

We tender our acknowledgements to many friends, for gratuitous assistance, and solicit a continuance of their kindness.

Jos. T. Buckingham.
Edwin Buckingham.

Boston, June 1, 1832.

Title page and advertisement celebrating a successful first year of the Buckinghams' magazine

Buckingham attracted further censure for printing criticism of the famed actor Edmund Kean.

Buckingham's fearless, even reckless, practices led inevitably to the trial court. In the *New-England Galaxy* for 10 October 1822, he published an anonymous letter charging that the Reverend John N. Maffit, a touring Methodist preacher, had conducted himself improperly with female converts. Since libel was a crime prosecuted by the state, and truth had never been accepted in Massachusetts as a defense, Buckingham was in danger of being jailed. But the judge, Josiah Quincy, invoking the Bill of Rights, permitted testimony on the truth of the charges, and Buckingham was acquitted, to wild applause in the courtroom. Buckingham's published account of the trial sold twelve thousand copies, and ultimately the defense of truth was written into state law. Buckingham reflected years later: "The trial was the most important incident in my somewhat rough and stormy life."

Despite the frivolousness of the cases that brought him into court (he was fined one hundred dollars for libeling the Russian consul, who had been lampooned in the *Galaxy*), Buckingham was also a serious critic who contributed substantially to the formation of musical tastes in Boston. Although his phrasing was sharp—he referred, for example, to one singer's voice as being as "inflexible as the tone of a mail-carrier's trumpet"—he had consistent and firm views of excellence. A modern musicologist, Nicholas Tawa, surveying Buckingham's work in the *New-England Quarterly*, has concluded: "Buckingham wrote about music economically, colorfully, and efficaciously. His was the voice of authority to many Bostonians."

In 1824 he founded the *Boston Courier*, a daily newspaper designed to support the Whig party. When he went to Washington in the winter of 1827-1828 to write about and lobby for a Whig tariff, the newspaper was left in charge of his eldest son, Joseph. But the father already had his eye on Edwin, his favorite, younger son. Edwin left the Boston English High School in 1824, at the age of fourteen, to take up his father's trade. Three years later he and one associate were given charge of the *New-England Galaxy* during his father's absence, and he promptly redesigned the typography. After the *Galaxy* was sold, Edwin moved to the editorial side of the *Courier*, where he underwent a thorough apprenticeship—a tour as Washington correspondent, a trip through the West and South, and the chance to write major local stories. At the end of his training, in 1831, his father named him joint editor of the *Courier*.

Already Edwin was seriously ill with tuberculosis, which his father believed he had contracted on cold night-rides home from covering a murder trial in Salem. But Edwin persisted in planning the project that was to leave his mark as an editor. His father wrote after Edwin's death:

> The *New-England Magazine* was the offspring and the property of EDWIN BUCKINGHAM. In projecting the work, the idea of making money was no part of the consideration. The elder of the editors had previously had sufficient experience in the publication of literary periodicals to enable him to feel how uncertain and delusive are all calculations of that sort. The other was just passing that point in age where the law sets up a distinction between the man and the minor,—ardent, ambitious, active . . .

The periodical that began publication in July 1831 was, according to the magazine historian Frank Luther Mott, possibly "the most important general magazine published in New England before the birth of the *Atlantic Monthly*." Edwin was able to attract as contributors the cream of New England letters: Henry Wadsworth Longfellow, Oliver Wendell Holmes, Richard Hildreth, Edward Everett, John Greenleaf Whittier, and Noah Webster. The *New-England Magazine* broke with the pattern of "long and elaborate essays in the form of reviews" and offered instead a menu of readable poems, sketches, and stories of literary merit, creating a pattern that persisted through the nineteenth century. Finally, it offered the unusual inducement, for that day, of payment of a dollar a page.

Edwin Buckingham's illness grew worse during the magazine's first year, and in October 1832 he sailed to Smyrna, in Asia Minor, hoping for a cure. By spring he knew he was failing and boarded a boat for home, only to die five days out of Boston; he was buried at sea. His father wrote a restrained memorial in the July issue of the magazine: "He, for whom the Magazine has existed, is no more. Brief as its term has been, it has yet outlived its parent."

Despite his grief, the elder Buckingham carried on the editorship of the magazine by himself. He later declared: "Of all the literary enterprises I had undertaken, this was the most trying." Without the aid of his son he found himself oppressed by having to write the tedious

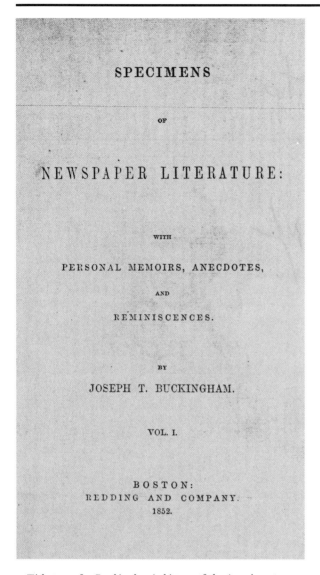

SPECIMENS

OF

NEWSPAPER LITERATURE:

WITH

PERSONAL MEMOIRS, ANECDOTES,

AND

REMINISCENCES.

BY

JOSEPH T. BUCKINGHAM.

VOL. I.

BOSTON:
REDDING AND COMPANY.
1852.

Title page for Buckingham's history of the American press

"Monthly Record," to read manuscripts, and to deal with the complaints of rejected writers. Still, he was a success in carrying out Edwin's hopes. The *New York Mirror* paid the senior Buckingham's editorship this tribute: "The course of this periodical has been not unlike that of a river, increasing in depth, breadth, power, and beauty as it advances from the source. . . . " Finally, after the fortieth issue, that of November 1834, Buckingham yielded ownership to two Bostonians, Samuel G. Howe and John O. Sargent. They named a talented young editor, Park Benjamin, to see the *New-England Magazine* through what proved to be its final year.

Buckingham did not return to magazine editing. He continued to edit the *Boston Courier*

boldly and belligerently until 1848, when he resigned rather than oppose the Whig presidential candidate publicly. Nearly seventy, he turned to the mellower occupation of writing books. His two-volume *Specimens of Newspaper Literature* (1850) was a history of the American press in the spirit of Isaiah Thomas's 1810 *History of Printing in America,* to which he acknowledged his debt. Two years later appeared the two volumes of his *Personal Memoirs and Recollections of Editorial Life* (1852), which constitute not only the fullest account of the three magazines with which he was associated, but are a valuable source for the history of American printing.

He died one day before the start of the Civil War, a man particularly associated with the era then closing, in which journalists made their mark by strident opinion rather than reportage. On balance historians have noted his career less for all the harsh words he wrote than for his modest, fatherly assistance in helping his son start the *New-England Magazine.*

References:

Allison Busterbaum, "The New England Magazine," in *American Literary Magazines,* edited by Edward E. Chielens (New York: Greenwood Press, 1986), pp. 269-271;

George Willis Cooke, "The First 'New England Magazine' and Its Editor," *The New England Magazine,* new series 16 (March 1897): 103-117;

Merle M. Hoover, *Park Benjamin: Poet & Editor* (New York: Columbia University Press, 1948);

Frederic Hudson, *Journalism in the United States from 1690 to 1872* (New York: Harper, 1873);

Frank Luther Mott, *A History of American Magazines,* 5 volumes (Cambridge, Mass.: Harvard University Press, 1938-1968), I: 125, 127, 169, 224-225, 599-601;

Rollo G. Silver, *The American Printer 1787-1825* (Charlottesville: University Press of Virginia, 1967);

Nicholas Tawa, "Buckingham's Musical Commentaries in Boston," *New England Quarterly,* 51 (September 1978): 333-347;

Tawa, "Musical Criticism and the Terrible Mr. Buckingham," *New-England Galaxy* [Sturbridge, Mass.], 20 (Summer 1978): 3-11.

William Evans Burton

(24 September 1804-10 February 1860)

Jacqueline Steck
Temple University

MAJOR POSITION HELD: Editor, *Gentleman's Magazine* (1837-1840).

BOOKS: *Ellen Wareham, the Wife of Two Husbands, A Domestic Drama in Two Acts* (London: Lacy, 1833);
The Ladies' Man, A Farce in One Act, Taken from the French (Philadelphia: Carey & Hart, 1835);
The Court Fool; or, A King's Amusement, A Tragic Drama in Three Acts, from the French (New York, 1837);
The Yankee Among the Mermaids, and Other Waggeries and Vagaries (Philadelphia: Peterson, 1843);
The Baronet's Daughter. And The Secret Cell (Boston: Williams, 1845);
St. Vallier's Curse; or, The King's Fool (Providence, 1852).

OTHER: *Burton's Comic Songster, A Collection of Original and Popular Songs,* edited by Burton (Philadelphia: James Kay, Jun. & Brother; Pittsburgh: John I. Kay, 1837);
The Literary Souvenir, 2 volumes (Philadelphia: Carey & Hart, 1838, 1840);
The Cyclopaedia of Wit and Humor; Containing Choice and Characteristic Selections from the Writings of the Most Eminent Humorists of America, Ireland, Scotland, and England, 2 volumes, edited by Burton (New York, London: Appleton, 1858).

William Evans Burton (photograph by Mathew Brady; courtesy of the Library of Congress)

William Evans Burton's reputation as a magazine writer, editor, and publisher has been overshadowed by his great success as an actor, playwright, and theater manager, and by his notoriously stormy relationship with Edgar Allan Poe, who was for a year his coeditor on the *Gentleman's Magazine.* Scholars interested in American literature and journalism in that period judge his talents to have been minor.

William Burton was born in London on 24 September 1804. His father, William George Burton, was a printer with some literary pretensions, having had one significant religious work published. He believed his son was destined for the church and provided him a classical education at St. Paul's School. However, the senior Burton died when William was only eighteen, and the boy had to withdraw from school to take over his father's print shop. He aspired to be an author and publisher and tried vainly at this early age to start a monthly magazine. In the course of his unsuccessful efforts, he met a variety of people, including many theater folk, and a whole new and exciting world opened up to him. He was drawn to the glamor and excitement of the drama, the mystique of the theater where it was performed, and the magnetism of its performers. He began to perform in amateur theatricals. His professional acting career began in 1831 at London's Pavilion Theater, where he played Hamlet. Throughout his life he was drawn to the great figures of Shakespearean tragedy, only to learn that his gifts lay in playing comedy.

In 1834 he set out for the United States in response to an offer from the Arch Street Theater in Philadelphia. On 18 July 1834 he married an actress named Caroline Glessing of London. He had previously been married for a very brief period to an English actress, but little is known about his first wife.

The city to which the young actor came was a flourishing center of journalism and literature. Three years after his arrival in the States he realized his early ambition–to found and edit a magazine, which he titled the *Gentleman's Magazine.* Charles Alexander, publisher of the weekly *Alexander's Messenger,* published Burton's periodical as well.

The name of the publication changed several times during its life of three and a half years. According to magazine historian Frank Luther Mott, it was called the *Gentleman's Magazine* in 1837 and 1838 and from July to December 1840. In January and February 1839 it was known as the *Gentleman's Magazine and Monthly American Review.* From March to December 1839 the name appears as *Burton's Gentleman's Magazine.* Then from January to June 1840 it was *Burton's Magazine and American Monthly Review.* In December 1840 *Graham's Magazine* also appears as a partial title.

Alexander remained as publisher until February 1839. Burton took over from March 1839 to November 1840, at which time the magazine was purchased by George R. Graham, editor and owner of the *Casket,* a popular miscellany that Graham had purchased in May 1839. *Graham's* was the name of the publication resulting from the merger.

Philadelphia's magazine scene was clearly enlivened by the new entry. The first issue of the *Gentleman's Magazine* appeared in July. The handsome periodical was well printed, beautifully, though sparsely illustrated, and full of reprints and original stories, articles, poems, and even a song printed with full notation. An engraved frontispiece uses symbols calculated to appeal to the male reading public of the era: the Declaration of Independence unrolling, topped by an Ameri-

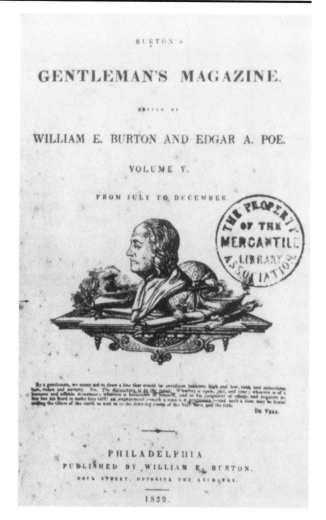

Title page for the first volume of Burton's magazine that listed Edgar Allan Poe as an editor (courtesy of the Maryland Historical Society)

can eagle; panels depicting archery, hunting, and other sports; carriages, militia, a library.

The table of contents runs to four pages, and the selections are eclectic. There is a confident preface, written by Burton, addressed "To Our Friends." "We feel no hesitation," he writes, "in submitting our work to the acumen of the critical few, because we have been encouraged by the countenance of the liberal many; and we honestly avow that we entertain the comfortable belief that success is the best criterion of merit." Adding that he expected the publication to show improvement each month, he declared himself resolved not to relax until he had made the *Gentleman's Magazine* worthy of "a place upon the parlor table of every Gentleman in the United States."

In a statement, "To Our Friends," written at the end of the magazine's first volume for the bound edition, Burton, the transplanted Englishman, ingratiates himself to his readers by remarking: "There are some persons who imagine that European reputation is necessary to the establishment of a literary fame upon this side of the Atlantic–we are happy to inform these noodles, who confess their inability to think for themselves" that some original material from early issues of *Gentleman's Magazine* had been pirated and republished in England, in turn recopied by other American magazines, and mistakenly praised as the work of superior English writers.

The writing is fairly typical of the period. The humor is heavy-handed and coy, the narratives overlong and melodramatic, more emotionally appealing than intellectually stimulating. "My Vagabond Days–An Autobiographical Delineation" by Robert Sullivan tells of his Dickensian childhood and features menacing villains called The Smasher and The Skulker. It is maudlin and lengthy, but since its kind of story appears in most subsequent issues, it must have pleased the readers.

A feature that would continue in the magazine was contributed by Burton himself. Called "Experiences of a Modern Philosopher," it was more like the *New Yorker*'s later "Talk of the Town" with unconnected paragraphs of narration and comment, generally entertaining, sometimes obviously intended to be satirical or inspirational. Comments on the drinking of wine, seduction, lemonade, second helpings of soup, and the joy of cigars enliven the pithy paragraphs with which Burton entertained his readers. Modern day readers will probably find the material unfunny and labored, although they provide a view of life in the early nineteenth century sometimes not found in formal history.

"Leaves from a Life in London" is the title of another continuing Burton contribution. His "The Convict and His Wife," in the maiden number, is a tragic story, treated melodramatically. Perhaps his readers enjoyed other people's miseries, because Burton repeatedly wrote gloomy stories about the seamy side of London.

Burton was a heavy contributor to his own pages in early volumes; usually these contributions were tales: "The Ladies in Black," "The Secret Cell," "The Excommunicated," "The Autobiography of a Proud Man," "The Man in the Big Boots."

Early issues offered light fare as well: "A Scene at the Theater," an extract from a book; much poetry, often by highly-respected writers;

an article on the great Paganini, illustrated by four engravings; a song, "Kathleen Mavourneen"; reviews, headed "Cosmogonical Squintings"; translations of stories from several languages; a marvelously titled article, "Philadelphia in the Dog Days–An Incoherency"; "Field Sports and Manly Pastimes"; a story on the many breeds of dogs, accompanied by beautiful drawings. There were stories in dialect, obviously intended to be humorous.

The magazine also carried a continuing saga of a French minister of police named Vidocq. Literary historians believe this story may have been the first to feature a detective and his exploits. It is also thought to have been an influence on Edgar Allan Poe's mystery stories.

In the second volume (the monthly was published in two volumes yearly) appears "The Anniversary Register and Monthly Calendar of American Chronology," a compilation of important historical events that had occurred on each day of the month, from the 1500s to the year of issue. In his preface to the second bound volume Burton calls this calendar "a novel feature in the history of magazines"; it continued to appear monthly through December 1838.

Burton's own contributions to volume 2 still included tales, such as "The Cork Leg," from a story told him in France, and "The Land Pirates," but in this volume he began contributing personal experience sketches: "A Day on Lake Erie"; "My First Performance," an account of how he first became "stage-struck, thesbian bitten" [sic] as the Spanish conqueror Pizarro; and "My First Cousin and My First Kiss." Also in this volume Burton printed the words and notation to a comic song he had written, "The Way the Money Goes." Its first verse began: "We find throughout this earthly ball/The one thing needful governs all./By tag-rag, tip-top, dunces, scholars,/There's nothing done without the dollars."

In the third and fourth volumes Burton's own contributions became less frequent. These volumes were heavy with the poetry of Catherine H. Waterman and Thomas Dunn English, tales by William Landor, and articles by a professor, Joseph Holt Ingraham, and Capt. Frederick Marryat. In the final two volumes of the magazine, before its sale to another publisher, Burton was once again more prolific, mainly supplying tales.

A major change came in the magazine's history when Edgar Allan Poe was hired. Although he was widely respected as a literary figure, Poe

Covers for the issue of Burton's Magazine *that contains the first installment of Poe's unfinished serial "The Journal of Julius Rodman"*

had become a figure of some controversy just before he signed on with Burton to coedit the *Gentleman's Magazine.* Working as a textbook editor, he was charged with plagiarism, which caused him some temporary embarrassment and inconvenience. He had free-lanced as a magazine writer, too, but was bringing in very little money. In this shaky position, he began negotiating with Burton, and his name first appeared on the masthead of the July 1839 issue of volume 5. But the Burton-Poe relationship was brief and troubled.

In January 1840 the *Gentleman's Magazine* began serial publication of Poe's "The Journal of Julius Rodman, Being an Account of the First Passage across the Rocky Mountains of North America ever Achieved by Civilized Man." While Burton seems to have admired Poe's work, he apparently deplored his temperament. Both men were overly sensitive, critical, and egotistical.

Their correspondence reveals continuing disagreements over matters both personal and professional. For both men, however, the partnership was a matter of expediency. When Poe joined the magazine staff, the coeditors disagreed at once in their perceptions of journalism. Poe regarded it as a literary profession; Burton saw it as an avocation. Poe had wanted to found a superior literary journal; finding the *Gentleman's Magazine* to fall short of this ideal, he treated it with something like contempt. He privately referred to Burton as "a buffoon and a felon."

Poe once wrote a review of a juvenile adventure story in which he described the story as a "miserable mental inanity, a positive baldness of thought ... a feeble childishness of manner which would be unpardonable in any school boy of decent pretensions." In a letter to Poe, Burton tried to steer him away from such vituperation in

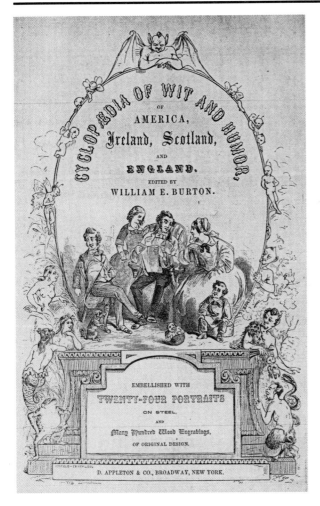

Engraved title page for Burton's 1858 compendium

his reviews. "I have been as severely handled in the world as you can possibly have been, but my sufferings have not tinged my mind with a melancholy hue, nor do I allow my views of my fellow creatures to be jaundiced by the fogs of my own creation. You must rouse your energies and conquer the insidious attacks of the foul fiend, care. We shall agree very well, but you must get rid of your avowed ill-feelings towards your brother authors. . . . Several of my friends, hearing of our connexion, have warned me of your uncalled for [sic] severity in criticism. . . . I wish particularly to deal leniently with the faults of genius. . . . "

All the reviews in that July 1839 edition were written by Poe, but he did not regard the contributors' efforts any more admiringly than he did the magazine. In fact he wrote to a friend, Philip Pendleton Cooke, "Do not think of subscribing. . . . The criticisms are not worth your notice. I pay no attention to them—for there are two of us. It is not pleasant to be taxed with the twaddle

of other people or to let other people be taxed with ours. Therefore, for the present I remain upon my oars, merely penning an occasional paragraph without care." Despite his protestations about his own patience and good humor in reviewing, Burton himself was often acerbic, even when analyzing the work of close friends and associates.

The two disagreed over how much analysis there should be in their critical essays. Poe sometimes spent pages analyzing florid dedications and grammatical constructions. Burton deplored this attention to minutiae, preferring the expediency of scathing denunciations. Some critics found Burton's work lacking sufficient insight, provoking Burton to describe literary analysis as akin to pulling to pieces "a beautiful moss rose in order to point out its botanical characteristics" (*Burton's Gentleman's Magazine*, January 1839).

Poe attempted to enlarge the scope of the magazine by using his reviews as a starting point for essays on the psychology of creativity. He explored the theories of literary criticism in lengthy articles, wrote about the nature of literature, the role of the romantic school of writing, the American response to contemporary literature and criticism, the duties of men of literary talent, and the value of originality. As this kind of analysis increased, his reviews became less vicious, but the change did not please Burton. They quarreled often on personal relationship as well as literary judgment; the break between them came in May 1840. The immediate cause was an argument over money.

Burton wrote to Poe, who owed him a substantial sum. Poe responded angrily, disputing the amount. He charged that Burton "bullied" him and was furious that some articles he had written were rejected by Burton. Also he had heard that Burton had spoken of him disrespectfully, and he was angry that Burton had advertised the *Gentleman's Magazine* for sale without consulting him. He had heard, too, he wrote, that Burton had said that Poe was frequently drunk. In June Poe resigned. Burton then turned down a half dozen critiques that Poe had written.

By this time Burton was weary of his literary avocation and sold the magazine to George R. Graham, editor and owner of the *Casket*. The seventh and final volume of *Gentleman's Magazine* contained two of Burton's tales. The last number, December 1840, was also the first number of *Graham's*. It contained Poe's "The Man of the Crowd."

Burton's home at 174 Hudson Street in New York City

It was the end of Burton's career in journalism. He continued with his stage work in Philadelphia until 1848 when he moved to New York. For the next eight years he was the acknowledged leader in American theater. Outstanding actors of the day vied for places in his companies. The repertoire included Burton's beloved Shakespeare but also contemporary works. He managed the Chambers Street Theater until its closing in September 1856, and he then opened the Metropolitan Theater, which later became the Winter Garden. He not only managed the theaters, but he produced, acted, and directed in them. The man who opened as Hamlet closed as Falstaff, a role for which he was internationally famous.

His last performance as an actor was in Canada in December 1859. On the journey north, he was trapped aboard a train in a blizzard and returned from the trip exhausted. Less than two months later on 10 February 1860, he died at his New York City home of an enlarged heart. He was buried in Greenwood Cemetery and was survived by his wife and three daughters. His major legacy was his huge library with its impressive collection of Shakespeare.

Burton's home at 174 Hudson Street was connected by a gallery to a three-story building beside it that housed his collection of some sixteen thousand books, art works, and various relics. With the ample income from his highly successful acting career, Burton had collected Shakespeareana, incunabula, first editions of English poetry from the 1500s and 1600s, old dictionaries, books about America, old magazines and reviews, and literary oddities. Burton also kept a country house at Glen Cove, Long Island.

His literary output was small and not particularly distinguished. Several of his works were for the theater: *Ellen Wareham* (1833); "The Toodles"; an adaptation of R. J. Raymond's "The Farmer's Daughter of the Severn Side"; and *The Court Fool* (1837). Then there was *Burton's Comic Songster* (1837), a collection of popular songs edited by Burton. He contributed a series of articles on the theater called "The Actor's Alloquy" to the *Knickerbocker Magazine* and in 1838 and in 1840 edited an annual entitled *Literary Souvenirs.*

Mott's assessment of the *Gentleman's Magazine* is that it "was not a great periodical." He sees its primary importance in its one-year connection with Poe, but he concedes that it must be commended for being "entertaining without baseness."

To a less critical reader, it provides a fascinating look at life in Philadelphia as seen through the eyes of a sophisticated, good-natured man of the theater. It offers an eclectic sampler of the literary tastes of an early-nineteenth-century audience.

When it was sold to George Graham in 1840 for thirty-five hundred dollars, it delivered thirty-five hundred subscribers to him. They had been entertained, diverted, provoked, informed, and occasionally inspired by the magazine that belonged on every gentleman's parlor table.

Biographies:

William L. Keese, *William E. Burton, Actor, Author and Manager* (New York: Putnam's, 1885);

"Wm. E. Burton," *Publications of the Dunlap Society,* 14, 1891.

References:

Robert D. Jacobs, *Poe: Journalist and Critic* (Baton Rouge: Louisiana State University Press, 1969): pp. 215-248;

Frank Luther Mott, *A History of American Magazines,* 5 volumes (Cambridge, Mass.: Harvard University Press, 1938-1968), I: 343, 587, 609, 673-676.

Papers:

Harvard University holds Burton's diary and a list of plays that were in his library.

Mathew Carey

(28 January 1760-16 September 1839)

James N. Green
Library Company of Philadelphia

See also the Carey entry in *DLB 37: American Writers of the Early Republic.*

MAJOR POSITIONS HELD: Editor and copublisher, *Columbian Magazine; or Monthly Miscellany* (1786-1787); publisher, *American Museum, or Repository of Ancient and Modern Fugitive Pieces*, renamed *American Museum, or, Universal Magazine* (1787-1792); publisher, *Thespian Monitor, and Dramatick Miscellany* (1809); publisher, *Philadelphia Journal of the Medical and Physical Sciences* (1820-1822); editor, *Political Economist* (1824).

SELECTED BOOKS: *The Urgent Necessity of an immediate Repeal of the whole Penal Code candidly considered* (Dublin, 1779);
The Plagi-Scurriliad: A Hudibrastic Poem. Dedicated to Col. Eleazer Oswald (Philadelphia: Printed & sold by the author, 1786);
Desultory Account of the Yellow Fever, Prevalent in Philadelphia, and of the Present State of the City (Philadelphia, 1793);
A Short Account of the Malignant Fever, Lately Prevalent in Philadelphia: With a Statement of the Proceedings That Took Place on the Subject in Different Parts of the United States (Philadelphia: Printed by the author, 1793; revised, 1794; London: Printed for J. Johnson, 1794);
Observations on Dr. Rush's Enquiry into the Origin of the late Epidemic Fever in Philadelphia (Philadelphia: From the press of the author, 1793);
A Short Account of Algiers, and of Its Several Wars against Spain, France, England, Holland, Venice, and Other Powers of Europe, from the Usurpation of Barbarossa and the Invasion of the Emperor Charles V. to the Present Time; with a Concise View of the Origin of the Rupture between Algiers and the United States (Philadelphia: Printed by J. Parker for M. Carey, 1794);
Address of M. Carey to the Public. Philadelphia, April 4, 1794. The Industry Used in Circulating a

Mathew Carey (courtesy of the Library of Congress)

Libel Against Me, Signed Argus . . . (Philadelphia: Printed by Mathew Carey, 1794);
Address to the House of Representatives of the United States, on Lord Grenville's Treaty (Philadelphia: Printed by Samuel Harrison Smith for Mathew Carey, 1796);
Fragment, Addressed to the Sons and Daughters of Humanity, as a Citizen of the World (Philadelphia: Printed by Lang & Ustick for Mathew Carey, 1796);
Miscellaneous Trifles in Prose (Philadelphia: Printed by Lang & Ustick for the author, 1796);

50

A Plumb Pudding for the Humane, Chaste, Valiant, Enlightened Peter Porcupine (Philadelphia: Printed for the author, 1799);

The Porcupiniad. A Hudibrastic Poem . . . , canto 1 (Philadelphia: Printed for & sold by the author, 1799; improved edition, 1799); cantos 2-3 (Philadelphia: Printed for & sold by the author, 1799);

Desultory Reflections, Excited by the Recent Calamitous Fate of John Fullerton. Addressed to Those Who Frequent the Theatre (Philadelphia: Printed by R. Carr for the author, 1802);

Cursory Reflections on the System of Taxation Established in the City of Philadelphia; With a Brief Sketch of Its Unequal and Unjust Operation (Philadelphia: Published by the author, 1806);

Desultory Reflections on the Ruinous Consequences of a Non-Renewal of the Charter of the Bank of the United States (Washington, 1810);

Nine Letters to Dr. Adam Seybert, Representative in Congress for the City of Philadelphia, On the Subject of the Renewal of the Charter of the Bank of the United States (Philadelphia: Published by the author, 1810); enlarged as *Letters to Dr. Adam Seybert . . .* (Philadelphia: Published by the author, 1811);

Examinations of the Pretensions of New England to Commercial Pre-Eminence . . . (Philadelphia: Printed for M. Carey, 1814);

A Calm Address to the People of the Eastern States, on the Subject of the Representation of Slaves; Representation in the Senate; and the Hostility to Commerce ascribed to the Southern States (Philadelphia: Published by M. Carey, 1814);

The Olive Branch; or, Faults on both sides, Federal and Democratic. A Serious Appeal on the Necessity of Mutual Forgiveness & Harmony, to Save Our Common Country from Ruin (Philadelphia: Published by M. Carey, 1814; enlarged, 1815; enlarged again, 2 volumes, 1815; enlarged again, 1815; enlarged again, Philadelphia: M. Carey & Son, 1817);

Reflections on the Consequences of the Refusal of the Banks to Receive in Deposit Southern and Western Bank Notes (Philadelphia, 1815);

Essays on Banking (Philadelphia: Published by the author, 1816);

Reflections on the Present System of Banking, in the City of Philadelphia (Philadelphia: The author, 1817);

Appendix to the Eighth Edition of the Olive Branch; or, Faults on Both Sides, Federal and Democrat (Philadelphia: Printed & published by M. Carey & Son, 1817);

Vindiciae Hibernicae: Or, Ireland Vindicated: An Attempt to Develop and Expose a Few of the Multifarious Errors and Falsehoods Respecting Ireland, in the Histories of May, Temple, Whitelock, Borlase, Rushworth, Clarendon, Cox, Carte, Leland, Warner, Macauley, Hume, and Others: Particularly in the Legendary Tales of the Conspiracy and Pretended Massacre of 1641 (Philadelphia: Published by M. Carey & Son, 1819);

Three Letters on the Present Calamitous State of Affairs. Addressed to J. M. Garnett, Esq. President of the Fredericksburg Agricultural Society (Philadelphia: M. Carey & Son, 1820);

A View of the Ruinous Consequences of a Dependence on Foreign Markets for the Sale of the Great Staples of this Nation, Flour, Cotton, and Tobacco . . . (Philadelphia: M. Carey, 1820);

The New Olive Branch: or, An Attempt to Establish an Identity of Interest between Agriculture, Manufactures, and Commerce (Philadelphia: M. Carey & Son, 1820);

Address to the Farmers of the United States, on the Ruinous Consequences to Their Vital Interests of the Existing Policy of this Country (Philadelphia: M. Carey & Son, 1821);

An Address to William Tudor, Esq., Author of letters on the Eastern States. Intended to prove the Calumny and Slander of his Remarks on the Olive Branch (Philadelphia: M. Carey & Son, 1821);

Strictures on Mr. Cambreling's Work, Entitled, An Examination of the New Tariff, as Neckar (N.p., 1821);

Essays on Political Economy; or, the most Certain Means of Promoting the Wealth, Power, Resources, and Happiness of Nations: Applied Particularly to the United States (Philadelphia: H. C. Carey & I. Lea, 1822);

An Appeal to Common Sense and Common Justice; or, Irrefragable Facts Opposed to Plausible Theories: Intended to Prove the Extreme Injustice, as Well as the Utter Impolicy, of the Existing Tariff (Philadelphia: H. C. Carey & I. Lea, 1822);

Hamilton, series 1-12 (Philadelphia, 1822-1826);

Desultory Facts, and Observations, Illustrative of the Past and Present Situation and Future Prospects of the United States: Embracing a View of the Causes of the Late Bankruptcies in Boston (Philadelphia: H. C. Carey & I. Lea, 1822); revised as *Facts and Observations, Illustrative of the Past and Present Situation and Future Prospects of the United States . . .* (Philadelphia: H. C. Carey & I. Lea, 1822);

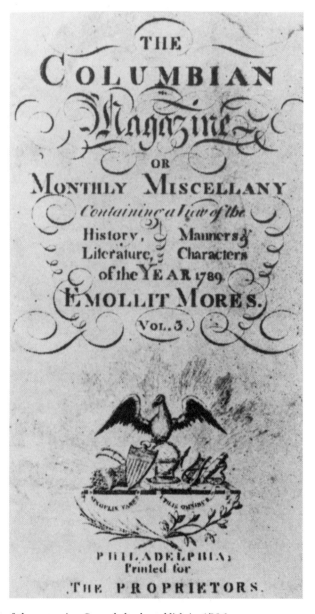

Frontispiece and engraved title page for volume 3 of the magazine Carey helped establish in 1786

A Desultory Examination of the Reply of the Rev. W. V. Harold to a Catholic Layman's Rejoinder . . . (Philadelphia: H. C. Carey & I. Lea, 1822);

The Crisis: A Solemn Appeal to the President, the Senate and the House of Representatives and the Citizens of the United States, on the Destructive Tendency of the Present Policy of this Country, on Its Agriculture, Manufactures, Commerce, and Finances (Philadelphia: H. C. Carey & I. Lea, 1823);

Sketch of the Irish Code, Entitled "Laws to Prevent the Growth of Popery:" But Really Intended, and With Successful Effect, to Degrade, Debase, and Enslave the Roman Catholics of Ireland, and to Divest Them of Their Estates . . . (Philadelphia: H. C. Carey & I. Lea, 1823);

A Warning Voice to the Cotton and Tobacco Planters, Farmers, Merchants of the United States, on the Pernicious Consequences to Their Respective Interests of the Existing Policy of the Country (Philadelphia: H. C. Carey & I. Lea, 1824);

Examination of a Tract on the Alteration of the Tariff, written by Thomas Cooper, M.D. (Philadelphia: Printed for H. C. Carey & I. Lea, 1824);

Twenty-one Golden Rules to Depress Agriculture, Impede the Progress of Manufactures, Paralize Commerce, Impair National Resources, Produce a Constant Fluctuation in the Value of Every Species of Property, and Blight and Blast the Bounties of Nature . . . (Philadelphia: H. C. Carey & I. Lea, 1824);

Fifty-One Substantial Reasons Against Any Modification Whatever of the Existing Tariff . . . (Philadelphia: H. C. Carey & I. Lea, 1824);

Address Delivered before the Philadelphia Society for Promoting Agriculture . . . (Philadelphia: Printed by J. R. A. Skerrett, 1824; revised, 1824);

Exhibit of the Shocking Oppression and Injustice Suffered for Sixteen Months by John Randel, Jun., Esq., Contractor for the Eastern Section of the Chesapeake and Delaware Canal . . . (Philadelphia, 1825);

Colbert, series 1-3 (Philadelphia, 1826-1827);

Reflections on the Proposed Plan for Establishing a College in Philadelphia (Philadelphia, 1826);

Reflections on the Subject of Emigration from Europe, with a View to Settlement in the United States . . . (Philadelphia, 1826);

Essays tending to prove the Ruinous Effects of the Policy of the United States on Three Classes, Farmers, Planters and Merchants, as Hamilton (Philadelphia: Printed by J. R. A. Skerrett, 1826);

A Roland for an Oliver. Letters on Religious Persecution: Proving That Most Heinous of Crimes, Has Not Been Peculiar to Roman Catholics . . . (Philadelphia: Dornin, 1826);

Slave Labor Employed in Manufactures, as Hamilton (Philadelphia, 1827);

A Common Sense Address to the Citizens of the Southern States, as Hamilton (Philadelphia, 1828); enlarged as *Common Sense Addresses to the Citizens of the Southern States* (Philadelphia: Printed by Clark & Raser, 1829; enlarged again, 1829);

Emigration from Ireland and Immigration into the United States, as Hamilton (Philadelphia, 1828);

Auto biographical Sketches, In a Series of Letters Addressed to a Friend . . . (Philadelphia: Printed by J. Clarke, 1829);

African Colonization, as Hamilton (Philadelphia, 1829);

The Protecting System, as Hamilton (Philadelphia, 1829);

Essay on Railroads, as Hamilton (Philadelphia, 1830);

Miscellaneous Essays . . . (Philadelphia: Carey & Hart, 1830);

The New Olive Branch. A Solemn Warning on the Banks of the Rubicon, nos. 1-12, as Hamilton (Philadelphia, 1830);

Prospects on and beyond the Rubicon, as Hamilton (Philadelphia, 1830);

Address to the Wealthy of the Land, Ladies as Well as Gentlemen, on the Character, Conduct, Situation, and Prospects, of Those Whose Sole Dependence for Subsistence, is on the Labour of Their Hands (Philadelphia: Printed by W. F. Geddes, 1831); republished as *Appeal to the Wealthy of the Land* . . . (Philadelphia: Printed by L. Johnson, 1833);

The New Olive Branch: Addressed to the Citizens of South Carolina, new series, nos. 1-13, as Hamilton (Philadelphia, 1831);

Brief View of the System of Internal Improvements of the State of Pennsylvania; Containing a Glance at Its Rise, Progress, Retardation,–The Difficulties It Underwent,–Its Present State,–and Its Future Prospects (Philadelphia: Printed by Lydia R. Bailey, 1831);

A Plea for the Poor, nos. 1-3, as Hanway (Philadelphia, 1831-1832);

Letters on the Colonization Society; with a view of its probable Results (Philadelphia: Young, 1832);

Reflections on the Causes that Led to the Formation of the Colonization Society: With a View of Its Proba-

ble Results ... (Philadelphia: Printed by W. F. Geddes, 1832);

The Olive Branch. No. III. Or, An Inquiry Whether Any Arrangement is Practicable between the Friends and Opposers of the Protecting System ... (Philadelphia: Printed by Clark & Raser, 1832);

The Crisis. An Appeal to the Good Sense of the Nation, against the Spirit of Resistance and Dissolution of the Union (Philadelphia: Printed by William F. Geddes, 1832; corrected edition, 1832);

The Dissolution of the Union. A Sober Address to All Those Who Have any Interest in the Welfare, the Power, the Glory, or the Happiness of the United States ..., as Hamilton (Philadelphia: Printed by J. Bioren, 1832);

Essay on the Dissolution of the Union, Second Part ..., as Hamilton (Philadelphia: Printed by L. Johnson, 1832);

The Tocsin: A Solemn Warning against the Dangerous Doctrine of Nullification ..., as Hamilton (Philadelphia, 1832);

The Olive Branch, No. IV, as Hamilton (N.p., 1832);

Prospects beyond the Rubicon ..., as Hamilton (Philadelphia, 1833);

Prospects beyond the Rubicon ..., second series, as Hamilton (Philadelphia, 1833);

Collectanea: Displaying the Rise and Progress of the Tariff System of the United States. Also, the Rise, Progress, and Final Triumph of Nullification ... (Philadelphia: Printed by T. B. Town, 1833; improved edition, 1833);

The Olive Branch Once More, nos. 1-4 (Philadelphia, 1833);

Outline of a System of National Currency; and Substitute for a Bank of the United States, as Colbert (New York: Printed by W. Pearson, 1834);

To the Editor of the New England Magazine (Philadelphia, 1835); republished as *Mathew Carey Autobiography* (Brooklyn: Research Classics, 1942);

Female Wages and Female Oppression (Philadelphia, 1835);

Philosophy of Common Sense. Practical Rules for the Promotion of Domestic Happiness ... (Philadelphia, 1838; improved edition, Philadelphia: Lea & Blanchard, 1838);

The Querist, An Humble Imitation of a work under a similar title published by the celebrated Berkeley, Bishop of Cloyne (Philadelphia, 1839).

OTHER: *Debates and Proceedings of the General Assembly of Pennsylvania. On the Memorials Praying a Repeal or Suspension of the Law Annulling the Charter of the Bank,* edited by Carey (Philadelphia, 1786);

Select Poems, on various occasions chiefly American, edited by Carey (Philadelphia: Printed by Mathew Carey, 1787);

The Beauties of Poetry, British and American ..., edited by Carey (Philadelphia: From the press of M. Carey, 1791);

Carey's American Atlas, compiled by Carey (Philadelphia: Engraved for, and published by Mathew Carey, 1795);

The American Remembrancer; Or, an Impartial Collection of Essays, Resolves, Speeches, &c. Relative, or Having Affinity to the Treaty with Great Britain, 3 volumes, nos. 1-12, edited by Carey (Philadelphia: Printed by Henry Tuckniss for Mathew Carey, 1795-1796);

Select Pamphlets, 3 volumes, pamphlets by Carey and others, collected by Carey (Philadelphia: Published by Mathew Carey, 1796);

Carey's American Pocket Atlas, compiled by Carey (Philadelphia: Printed for Mathew Carey by Lang & Ustick, 1796);

Carey's General Atlas, compiled by Carey (Philadelphia: Published by Mathew Carey, 1796; improved and enlarged, 1814);

The Columbian Spelling and Reading Book, edited by Carey (Philadelphia: Printed for Mathew Carey, 1798);

The Columbian Reading Book or Historical Preceptor: A Collection of Authentic Histories, Anecdotes, Characters, &c. &c. Calculated to Incite in Young Minds a Love of Virtue from Its Intrinsic Beauty and a Hatred of Vice from Its Disgusting Deformity, edited by Carey (Philadelphia: Printed for Mathew Carey, 1799);

The School of Wisdom: or, American Monitor, edited by Carey (Philadelphia, 1800);

Catalogue of the Library of M. Carey, Philadelphia, edited by Carey (Philadelphia: Skerrett, 1822).

An influential editor and publisher in the years following the founding of the American Republic, Mathew Carey helped to shape public opinion on the subjects of national unity, economic development, and literature. From an obscure beginning in Philadelphia in 1785, Carey's publishing business grew to become the largest in the United States in the first quarter of the nineteenth century. For twenty years he was the leading publisher of the quarto family Bible, and he was a pioneer in the effort to organize a national distribution system for books.

The publishing venture which first brought Carey to national attention was a monthly magazine, the *American Museum, or Repository of Ancient and Modern Fugitive Pieces*. Running from 1787 to 1792, it was the most highly esteemed and widely read American magazine of its time. It came to share with the *Columbian Magazine; or Monthly Miscellany* (which Carey had helped to found in 1786) the honor of being the longest-lived and most successful magazine in the country up to that time. After 1792 Carey's magazine and publishing ventures were few, but his prodigious output as a writer kept him in a position to mold American politics and literature.

Mathew Carey was born in Dublin on 28 January 1760, the son of Christopher and Mary Sherridan Carey. His father was a baker who had risen to the middle classes by hard work and a lucrative contract with the British navy. Mathew was given an excellent primary education, but though he loved to read he was not an outstanding student. Carey limped all his life because as an infant his foot was injured when a nurse dropped him. As a boy he felt vulnerable to the taunts of others, and he developed a bad temper. He became intensely idealistic as a young man and had radical interests and pro-American sympathies. In 1775, at age fifteen, he was apprenticed to Thomas McDonnel, bookseller and publisher of the radical pro-American and anti-British *Hibernian Journal*.

In November 1779 Carey wrote his first pamphlet, *The Urgent Necessity of an immediate Repeal of the whole Penal Code candidly considered*. Dublin then was in a state of tension provoked by the Volunteers, forty thousand citizens, ostensibly armed to repel a French invasion, but actually armed to force the English into reforming the laws governing Ireland. Carey's pamphlet was not particularly inflammatory, but while it was still in the press he printed a handbill to advertise it, "To the Roman Catholics of Ireland," which used alarming language. In the Irish Parliament the advertisement was offered as proof of the treasonous intentions of the Volunteers, and a penal reform bill which had had a good chance of passing was defeated. The Catholics offered a reward for the discovery of the author and announced their intention to prosecute. When Carey confessed to his astonished father that he was the author, he was spirited off to Paris. In France his pro-American reputation procured him introduc-

tions to Benjamin Franklin, who put him to work at his press in Passy, and to the young Marquis de Lafayette. These acquaintances would later prove to be useful. He also worked awhile for the printer Didot *le jeune*.

By the end of 1780 the threat of a prosecution against Carey had faded, and he returned from exile. He worked from 1781 to 1783 as an editor of the *Freeman's Journal*, the organ of the Volunteer movement. Then in October 1783 he established his own *Volunteer's Journal*, which soon became the most outspoken antigovernment newspaper in Ireland. It flirted more and more boldly with sedition until the issue of 5 April 1784 crossed the line with a cartoon depicting the hanging of Irish Parliament Member John Foster, alias Jack the Blood-Sucker, as a traitor for his role in the defeat of a protective tariff bill. Foster ordered Carey's arrest. Friends rallied to his support, and debate over his case was prolonged until the adjournment of Parliament made it no longer possible to hold him. But Foster was also suing for libel, and, feeling he would not escape again, Carey fled the country on 7 September 1784 on the ship *America*, bound for Philadelphia. Legend has it that he was smuggled on board dressed as a woman.

Carey landed in Philadelphia on 1 November with about a dozen guineas in his pocket. The Marquis de Lafayette, who happened to be passing through town, heard that Carey had just arrived and wrote him a note inviting him to call. Carey spoke of his ambition to start a newspaper in Philadelphia. The next morning the Marquis sent a letter enclosing four hundred dollars, and later he wrote a letter commending Carey to George Washington. Carey never forgot that Lafayette had launched him in America, and forty years later, when the Marquis returned impoverished to America, Carey persuaded him to accept a return of the loan.

Carey announced the inaugural issue of the *Pennsylvania Evening Herald* and then–cart before horse–set out to secure a press and type. He counted on buying a used press which was coming up at auction, but at the sale Col. Eleazer Oswald, editor of the *Independent Gazetteer*, fearing competition and disliking foreigners, kept raising the bid until Carey had to pay almost the cost of a new press, a third of his capital.

The first issue of the *Pennsylvania Evening Herald* appeared on 25 January 1785, less than three months after Carey had stepped off the boat. He was trying to break into a market al-

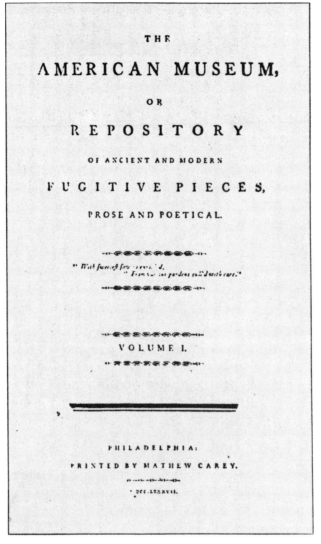

THE

AMERICAN MUSEUM,

OR

REPOSITORY

OF ANCIENT AND MODERN

FUGITIVE PIECES,

PROSE AND POETICAL.

VOLUME I.

PHILADELPHIA:

PRINTED BY MATHEW CAREY.

Title page for volume 1 of Carey's eclectic blend of literature and political polemic

ready crowded with newspapers, and at first the response was poor. The newspaper's anti-English and pro-Irish tone made its appeal less than universal. Then at the end of the summer Carey began publishing exact transcripts of debates in the state's General Assembly which he took down in shorthand from the visitors' gallery. Though this practice was known in England, it was new to America. Circulation soared.

In the fall of 1785 Eleazer Oswald began to attack Carey viciously in his *Gazetteer,* ridiculing the Irish in general and Carey and his lameness in particular. Carey replied in kind in his own newspaper. The quarrel spread in January 1786 when Carey published in pamphlet form an astonishingly bitter and insulting satire on Oswald called *The Plagi-Scurriliad: A Hudibrastic Poem.* Oswald challenged Carey to a duel. The colonel was

a marksman, while Carey could scarcely fire a pistol. Carey missed his target altogether and was struck in the thigh of his game leg. Due to his neglectful care of it his leg took fifteen months to heal and worsened his limp.

As the wound healed Carey began to yearn for something that would give him wider scope than a local newspaper. For a time he toyed with the idea of returning to Ireland, since he was no longer in danger of prosecution. In the end his growing affection for America and his love of the freedom it offered induced him to stay. There was one particular opportunity which he was well qualified to fill. In Ireland he had been accustomed to writing and printing for a national audience. In America there was not a single national periodical publication. If he were to publish a magazine which would address a national audience, which would appeal to the spirit of liberty and patriotism that was alive in the nation, and which would help unify culturally the not-so-United States, the potential audience would be huge and the competition nil. He could make his fortune by it while also gaining a platform for his idealistic republican views.

On 2 August 1786 an advertisement appeared in Carey's newspaper for a new publication, the *Columbian Magazine*, to be edited by Carey in partnership with William Spotswood (also a partner in the *Herald*), the booksellers Thomas Seddon and Charles Cist, and the engraver James Trenchard. The first issue appeared in September. It was an imitation of the most successful English magazine, the *Gentleman's Magazine* (begun 1731) and *its* imitators, such as the *London Magazine*. The contributions the new magazine received were mainly literary essays, historical notes, and poems; most were printed unsigned. The issues also carried weather observations, some foreign and domestic news reprinted from newspapers, and extracts reprinted from books about America. Each forty-eight-page monthly issue had two fine copperplate illustrations by American engravers and artists. A subscription cost a modest twenty shillings a year. Carey wrote much of the material in the first issue, including a remarkable piece of prognostication in which the narrator dreams he is transported to the year 1850 and hears news of American military victories, booming settlements on the Mississippi, canals to the Ohio and across Panama, the resettlement of blacks in Africa, the publication of a history of America "in 10 vols. folio, adorned with 200 copperplates," and other signs of cultural progress and enlightenment.

The magazine was moderately successful from the first, but Carey could not get his partners to promote it as vigorously as he wished, so the profits looked as if they would not be worth his while when divided by five. Though it was advertised as being for sale by booksellers in New York and in a few southern towns, the partners were evidently not working hard enough to build up subscriptions in New England or country areas. The absence of political issues in the magazine also may have been the result of the "discordant views" of the partners. Carey's quarrels with his partners grew increasingly bitter.

On 13 January 1787 Carey announced that as of 10 February he was withdrawing from the newspaper partnership in order to publish "a new periodical work, (on a plan hitherto unes-

sayed in this country) of which the title will be *The American Museum, Or, repository of ancient and modern fugitive pieces, prose and poetical.*" It was to be an imitation of another English periodical, *Remembrancer; or, impartial repository of public events,* published from 1775 to 1784 by John Almon, the London bookseller who published innumerable pamphlets supporting the American cause during the Revolution. The *American Museum* was to be a compilation of pieces previously printed in newspapers or as pamphlets and now hard to obtain, ranging from the Revolutionary period to the present. Each monthly issue would have ninety-six pages (twice as many as the *Columbian*), yet the subscription would be only eighteen shillings, of which only half need be paid up front. By the March 1787 issue of the *Columbian*, Carey's name had been dropped from the list of publishers, and he was devoting all his energy to the *American Museum*.

During the transition period Carey began a correspondence with Ebenezer Hazard, postmaster of the United States, collector and publisher of American historical documents, and one of the leading literary men of New York. His purpose was both to find a new editor for the *Columbian Magazine* and to attract talent for his own. Hazard proposed as editor his young friend the Reverend Jeremy Belknap of Boston, who had already published the first volume of his famous *History of New Hampshire* (1784-1792). Belknap ultimately decided not to leave Boston, and Francis Hopkinson, Philadelphia's own man of wit, got the job. All three men later became important contributors to the *American Museum*.

Belknap was skeptical about the prospects for either magazine's success. On 2 February 1787 he wrote Carey,

> Several attempts have been made within my memory both here & at the Southward to *establish* such a repository of Literature, but after a year or two they have uniformly failed [due to] the *too frequent* publication of them. We are fond of imitating our European Brethren . . . in their *monthly* productions–without considering the difference between our Circumstances & theirs. A Country full of learned men, full of business, literary, political, mercantile–having inexhaustible Resources of knowledge of every kind–may be able to keep up one or two monthly vehicles . . . but such a Country as this is not yet arrived at such a pass of Improvement.

Carey soon found that a shortage of material was the least of his problems. It was typical of Carey's optimistic and even impetuous approach to publishing that he should rush a second magazine into a market which, only a few months before, had none, in a country which had yet to support a single magazine for more than a couple of difficult years. Previous American magazines had been general, something for everyone, like the *Gentleman's Magazine*. But recently England had begun to support a variety of more specialized magazines, and Carey obviously believed America was ready to do the same.

Despite their similarity of appearance and (frequently) of subject matter, the two magazines were, as Carey advertised, different. The *Columbian Magazine* was more genteel and literary, lighter and more amusing. With its high proportion of original contributions, it was always in step with the latest fashion. The *American Museum,* with its reprints of speeches, old pamphlets, and documents, was more historical and political, high-minded, and serious. Its editorial desire to instruct, improve, and inspire was obvious. According to the preface to the first issue, its purpose was to rescue from oblivion fugitive pieces, mainly American but occasionally European, which "may have reference to the situation of this country, and be well calculated to promote the cause of liberty, religion, and virtue."

The first issue attracted great attention and was eagerly sought after; an edition of one thousand copies was quickly exhausted. It contained an article by Franklin, "Consolation for America"; an Address by Benjamin Rush on the defects of the Confederation, ending with a rousing "PATRIOTS of 1774, 1775, 1776–HEROES of 1778, 1779, 1780! come forward! your country demands your services! . . . THE REVOLUTION IS NOT OVER!"; "On the propriety of investing Congress with power to regulate the trade of the United States," by William Barton; a letter "On American manufactures," probably by Carey; Thomas Paine's *Common Sense;* a paper by Rush read before the American Philosophical Society on Dr. Martin's Cancer Powder; several shorter agricultural and medical articles; several "characters," a familiar moralizing genre; essays against drunkenness, prostitution, and slavery; "On the happy influence of female society" and several similar "women's" pieces, probably by Carey; and poems by Hopkinson, Philip Freneau, Provost Smith, and others, all fairly moralizing in the Augustan mode. It ended with a "Friendly Monition

for America" from the French revolutionary Comte de Mirabeau, which began, "Americans! Place constantly before the sight the deplorable scenes of your servitude, and the enchanting picture of your deliverance! . . . Begin with the infant in the cradle. Let the first word he lisps, be WASHINGTON." This was to set the tone of the *American Museum* for years to come.

Subsequent issues included a complete reprint of Trumbull's *M'Fingal* (1775-1782), Hopkinson's "Dialogue" on the filth in the streets of Philadelphia, and his "Plan for the Improvement of the art of paper war," showing how large and exotic type faces could be used to express a writer's emotions. Anthony Benezet's friendly protest against slavery was printed, as was the famous "Plan of an African Ship's lower Deck, with Negroes, in the proportion of not quite one to a Ton," in May 1789, one of the few engraved plates in the whole run. Various issues carried the first printed excerpts from the holograph of Benjamin Franklin's *Autobiography;* innumerable letters and historical documents of the Revolutionary era which Carey borrowed from Washington and many others involved in the war; and poems and essays, signed and unsigned, original and reprinted, by practically every literary person in the country. As a literary journal, the magazine's greatest strength was its section of original and reprinted poetry. No other magazine of the period published so much verse; the best anthology of American poetry for the half century before 1792 remains the *American Museum*.

The publication of papers excerpted from the second volume of *Transactions* of the American Philosophical Society (1786) and the first volume of *Memoirs* of the American Academy of Arts and Sciences (1785) caused some offense. In May and June 1788 Franklin in Philadelphia and Belknap in Boston objected on the grounds that these papers should not be treated as fugitive pieces, and that publication by Carey would cut into the sale of their journals. Indeed both societies had had a hard time finding enough material to fill their volumes, which had therefore appeared infrequently. Carey felt that in a free society knowledge should be freely available. He countered by repeating Belknap's own argument against imitation of English formats in periodicals (see above). The journals of American learned societies were published in the large quarto format used for the *Philosophical Transactions* of the Royal Society, whereas a smaller octavo format (like that used by the *Museum*) would permit more regular appearance at a lower price. He continued to advocate this change all his life. His advice was not taken.

The Federalists were quick to see that the *American Museum* had potential as a national propaganda organ, and Carey was eager to help. He had already established his lifelong pattern of using his political contacts to aid his publishing business while using the publishing to advance his political agenda. The issues published during and after the Constitutional Convention included articles by Washington, John Dickinson, Noah Webster, and Tench Coxe advocating a new Constitution. Dickinson's "Address" to the Annapolis Convention in September 1786 appeared in the April 1787 issue, and the first magazine printing of the Constitution appeared in September. During the ratification conventions in New York and New England, Coxe and the Hazard brothers began pointedly to urge Carey to publish Federalist essays to help the cause. In June 1788 Nathaniel Hazard wrote the Massachusetts Federalist Theodore Sedgwick, saying, "There is a valuable work published monthly in Philadelphia, called the American Museum. . . . It is calculated to dispel the Clouds of political Ignorance, and instruct and enlighten America. I must entreat your Exertions to procure Subscribers, and circulate this patriotic, and useful work. . . . Carey is a Federalist to enthusiasm." The July 1788 issue opened with two pages of warm endorsements from Washington, Dickinson, Rush, and others. Washington wrote, "A more useful literary plan has never been undertaken in America, or one more deserving of public encouragement. . . . I entertain an high idea of the utility of periodical publications; insomuch that I could heartily desire copies of the Museum . . . might be spread through every city, town, and village in America. I consider such easy vehicles of knowledge, more happily calculated than any other, to preserve the liberty, stimulate the industry, and meliorate the morals of an enlightened and free people." These endorsements were rewards; they gave the *American Museum* immense prestige and boosted its circulation.

In Washington's first administration, the Hamiltonian economic program dictated a foreign policy which favored England over France. While Carey was personally inclined toward France and against England, he supported parts of Hamilton's program, especially the idea of a national bank and the assumption of the states' Revo-

lutionary debts. His magazine thus continued to support the Federalists. But during the years 1790 and 1791 a group of dissatisfied men formed within the administration the nucleus of what was to become a party of opposition, and one of the ties that drew them together was opposition to Hamilton's pro-British policy and an inclination toward France. Some of Carey's closest friends were in this group, for example Tench Coxe, whose *Brief Examination of Lord Sheffield's Observations on the Commerce of the United States* he published in March through July 1791. Coxe argued that America's economy was capable of functioning without English support, and that our policy should be based on trade with France. This brought Carey the favor of Coxe's powerful friend John Beckley, Clerk of the House, who helped arrange credit with London booksellers for the wholesale book business Carey was just beginning. Coxe and Beckley soon emerged as strong allies of Thomas Jefferson, and Carey was drawn into the orbit. This affiliation was to have a profound effect on Carey's later career.

Though he never ceased to admire Washington, Carey lost the great man's confidence when in 1789 he indiscreetly sent a sensitive letter of Washington's unsealed through the public mail. Having frayed this strongest tie with the Federalists, when Carey published in September 1791 a "Declaration of the Belfast Volunteers" in favor of the French Revolution, he put himself even more firmly in Jefferson's camp. By the time the *American Museum* ceased publication in December 1792, it was a distinctly anti-British, anti-Hamiltonian, and pro-French Revolution magazine. The Federalists were not sorry to see it go.

As the orientation of the political articles in the *American Museum* changed, other parts either remained the same or became more like the *Columbian Magazine*. The January 1790 issue had been prefaced, "In conformity with the sentiments of a number of the friends of this work, who conceived that there was not a sufficient portion of it devoted to entertainment, the plan is considerably changed, so as to unite with the original design, that of magazines in general." Carey changed the title to the *American Museum, or, Universal Magazine*. From then on "Original Prose and Poetry" was segregated from "Selected Prose and Poetry" (extracts and reprints), while the "Public Papers" were relegated to an appendix. He even began to include a little fiction, such as a reprint of Hopkinson's *A Pretty Story*, which is considered the first American novel.

The *American Museum* continued to enjoy great prestige right up to the end, but it never actually made money. In fact, it was always on the brink of failure, and its demands kept Carey in a continual state of anxiety. In his autobiography, written in 1834, Carey said, "Never was more labour bestowed on a work, with less reward. During the whole six years, I was in a state of intense penury. I never at any one time, possessed 400 dollars,–and rarely three or two hundred. . . . I was, times without number, obliged to borrow money to go to market, and was often unable to pay my journeymen on Saturday." Financial troubles began immediately. He did not have enough type of his own and was forced to buy some of the old, battered type Franklin had used at Passy, which did not really suit his purposes. Having sold his extra copies of the first issue to nonsubscribers, he had to reprint it for later subscribers at great expense. Then, in hopes of building up his subscription list, he began to print too many copies. He soon found that in his zeal to undersell the *Columbian Magazine* he had set the price too low: eighteen shillings ($2.40) per year for over a thousand pages was extraordinarily cheap for that time.

Carey saw that the success of the magazine depended on national distribution, yet there was no mechanism in place in the American book trade to achieve this, and so he had to invent one. He recruited not only booksellers (and those in every part of the country) but also literary men, postmasters, and country-store owners to circulate advertisements, collect subscriptions, distribute copies, and forward payment. Ebenezer Hazard in New York and Jeremy Belknap in Boston were especially helpful in this regard. They also collected contributions and wrote little essays of their own. For all this help Carey paid them a small cash commission, though when money got tight he tried to pay them in copies of the magazine.

The wrapper of the December 1789 issue, for example, advertised that subscriptions were received by thirty-nine individual agents located in all the major coastal towns from Boston to Charleston, as well as in more remote outposts to the south and west of Philadelphia, such as Chambersburg, Pennsylvania, Hagerstown, Maryland, and Winchester, Virginia.

By July 1788 Carey already was able to print a list of about 540 subscribers, headed by Washington, Franklin, and Edmund Randolph. (Carey was proud of the many illustrious people on his subscription list, and he often highlighted the "Hon.'s" or the members of Congress.) Six months later the list had reached 850, including about 400 in Pennsylvania and 240 in New York, with every state represented, as well as Europe and the Caribbean Islands. By 1789 he had almost 1,500 names, with almost all the growth coming from New England and the South. From a high of about 1,600 in 1790, the print run declined to under 1,000 by 1792.

This far-flung network was held together by a steady stream of letters from Carey. Eloquent though they were, they could not overcome the lack of strong transportation and communication links between the regions of the country. Shipments of magazines were often delayed, lost, or damaged irreparably in transit. Carey was unprepared for the unbelievably wretched condition of American roads; his lifelong passion for internal improvements began with this experience. Weather posed a special problem: how could a magazine be sent out on time every month throughout a large territory when rivers were frozen and roads impassible from December to February? Communication by letter with agents whom Carey had not actually met caused problems almost as great as the poor transportation. The correspondence shows many misunderstandings and arguments; letters often crossed or were lost in the mail. Many agents were unable or unwilling to follow through with the business of maintaining the flow of copies to subscribers. Carey often misunderstood the number of copies needed for a particular area. Many subscribers became disgruntled with delays and irregularities; they withheld payment, necessitating collection proceedings which consumed as much as a third of his profit. Carey had simply set the subscription rates too low to allow for these costs of distribution to the back country, and he stubbornly refused to raise the rate or reduce the size of the magazine, because of the competition in the cities. In a sense, America was not ready for a truly national magazine. It was too hard to get the magazines out and even harder to get the money back.

The final blow came in 1792 when a new postal law was passed. It was unclear whether magazines were to be sent at the cheap newspaper rate, as before, or at the much higher letter rate. The Philadelphia postmaster interpreted the law the latter way and refused to accept either the *American Museum* or the *Columbian Magazine* at the old rate. Both periodicals folded immediately, because both relied on the post office to deliver to their many subscribers in the area around Philadelphia. (The magazine was sent to more distant towns in bundles by ship or wagon and distributed by local agents.) Postmasters in Boston and New York ruled the opposite way, and Carey probably would have been able to appeal, but in fact he seems to have welcomed the opportunity to bow out gracefully.

Carey issued just one further volume of the *American Museum* in 1799 as the *American Museum: or Annual Register of Fugitive Pieces Ancient and Modern. For the year 1798.* He continued to offer bound sets of the magazine in twelve volumes at least up to 1820. (It was issued in wrappers, but most subscribers had their sets bound, or traded unbound issues for bound volumes, so that today a copy in the original wrappers is quite rare.) The *American Museum* was seen as a treasure house of national historical documents, and, like the English magazines, it continued in demand long after its demise as a current periodical.

Before troubles began to beset the *American Museum*, Carey had projected yet another magazine. In August 1788 he wrote to William Livingston, governor of New York, of his wish to begin a "purely moral periodical publication," consisting of abridgments of important French and English writers, so that the "inhabitants of Carlisle, Pittsburgh—of Kty., would be rendered familiar with the writings of an Addison, a Steele, a Hawkesworth, a Johnson, in a way best calculated to make a lasting impression." He complained that "Of moral writing, the harvest in this Country has been hitherto very small. Politics—politics engross almost all the time that men of talent can spare for writing." Within a year he hoped to see the *American Museum* and this projected moral magazine "going hand in hand to serve the interests of Society." Nothing came of the project, but the *American Museum* certainly featured moral essays throughout its run. In later years Carey was to publish several books of that sort in cheap editions for sale in those same western towns. He even published his own schoolbook of moral essays called *The School of Wisdom: or, American Monitor* (1800).

On 24 February 1791 Carey married Bridget Flahavan, daughter of an Irish-American merchant who had been ruined by patriotically buying Continental currency during the Revolution. Ten years younger than her husband, she was prudent, frugal, and a good businesswoman who was quite capable of minding the store and at-

tending to the correspondence if Carey was away. She exercised a moderating influence on her husband's fiery temper. They eventually had nine children, two of whom died in infancy. Their son Henry Charles went into his father's business, while their daughter Frances Anne married Isaac Lea, who became a partner in the firm Carey and Lea in 1822.

Not long after the demise of the *American Museum*, the yellow fever epidemic of 1793 rudely interrupted Carey's career. As people fled the city or died by the thousands, Carey stayed behind and served on the citizens committee that ran the city and attempted to succor the victims. At the request of the mayor he wrote and printed *A Short Account of the Malignant Fever* and sent it to all parts of the country, in part as news, in part as a directory of the dead, and in part to explain why the city's businessmen could not be expected to meet their obligations. It went through at least five editions, with updates of the list of the dead. It is a compelling piece of writing with pretenses to literature in its echoes of Daniel Defoe's *Journal of the Plague Year* (1722). Being placed in the spotlight during such a tumultuous time caused Carey trouble. He was accused of profiting by his work (though he gave away at least one whole edition), of stealing the Committee's papers to write it, of deserting the city (he had once left with permission on a short business trip), and with refusing help to the poor. He became embroiled in a controversy with Rush over the origin of the fever and the best method of treatment; Rush's violent bleeding-and-purge treatment had caused large numbers of his patients to die. Finally, a word in Carey's account about the black people who heroically tended the sick led to a quarrel with the black clergymen Absalom Jones and Richard Allen about whether blacks had robbed their white patients.

Once free of the plague and the *American Museum*, Carey expanded his business rapidly in two directions: importing English books and publishing his own editions. About 1795 he sold his printing press; from then on he was primarily a wholesale bookseller and publisher. His printing was done by a host of independent printers. This was an early sign of a great shift in the American book trade, as printing and publishing slowly became separate businesses, with publishers emerging by the 1820s as the capitalists and the printers as mere mechanics.

By 1800 Carey had published about three hundred titles, and he estimated that the volume

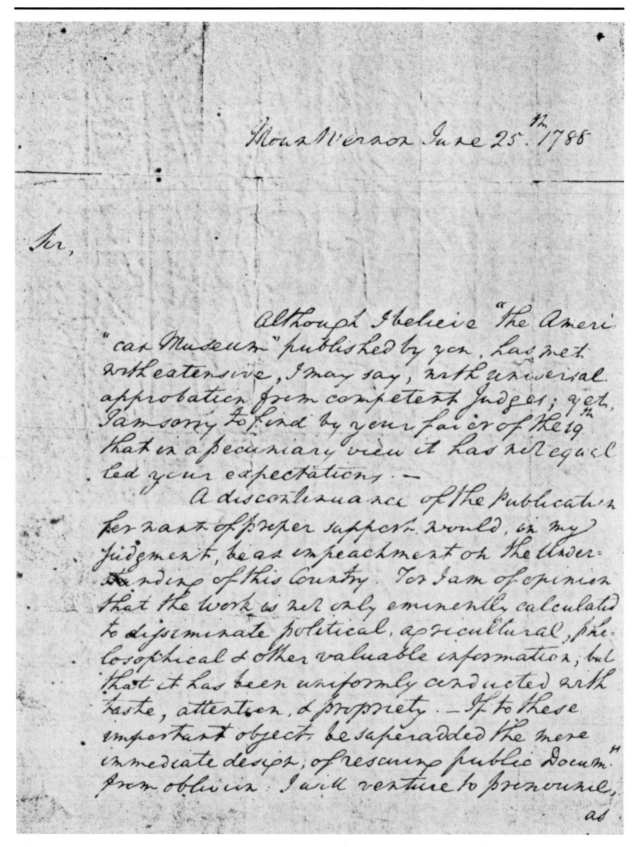

George Washington's letter to Carey commending him on the quality of American Museum *(Henry Charles Lea,* One Hundred and Fifty Years of Publishing, 1785-1935, *1935)*

as my sentiment, that a more useful literary plan has never been undertaken in America, or one more deserving public encouragement. — By continuing to prosecute that plan with similar assiduity and discernment the merit of your Museum must ultimately become as much known in some Countries of Europe as on this Continent, and can scarcely fail of procuring an ample compensation for your trouble & expence. —

For myself, I entertain an high idea of the utility of periodical Publications: insomuch that I could heartily desire, copies of the Museum and Magazines, as well as common Gazettes, might be spread through every city, town & village in America. — I consider such easy vehicles of knowledge more happily calculated than any other, to preserve the liberty, stimulate the industry and meliorate the morals of an enlightened and free People. — With sincere wishes for the success of your undertaking in particular, and for the prosperity of the Typographical art in general

I am — Sir

Y.r most Obed.t & most c.ble

Go. Washington

Mr Mathew Carey
Bookseller Phil.a

of his business in the decade had been three hundred thousand dollars. Among the more important were the first American literary anthology, *Select Poems, on various occasions chiefly American* (1787); the first American Catholic Bible (1790); the first American best-seller, *Charlotte Temple* (1794), by his friend Mrs. Rowson, who had just come from England to act and write for the New Chestnut Street Theatre; and the text of John Jay's secret treaty with England (1795) which rocked the nation and hastened the rise of Jefferson's party. During the same period Carey was also among the largest importers of English and Irish books in America.

During these years Carey built up the largest and densest book distribution network the country had ever seen. Its nucleus was the network of agents he had used for the *American Museum.* Around 1796 he hired the legendary itinerant book peddler Mason Locke Weems to sell his books in western Pennsylvania, Maryland, and Virginia, a territory which he had cultivated with special success in his magazine days. Weems sold tens of thousands of books for Carey; his feel for the taste of his customers was unsurpassed. The letters between them, edited by Emily E. F. Skeel in 1929, are an astonishing record of one of the most dynamic partnerships in the history of publishing.

In 1801 Carey published his first edition of the book which was to make his fortune, the quarto family Bible. In later years he purchased the type in which it was set and kept it standing; so spared the expense of composition and proofreading (especially costly when the Bible's reputation for accuracy was essential), he was able to print Bibles in almost unlimited quantities at a low price. His Bibles were offered in over two dozen varieties, differing in their binding, the size and quality of the paper, the inclusion of a concordance or the Apochrypha, and the number of maps and plates. Carey was shortly America's leading Bible publisher. In the next twenty years he published at least two hundred thousand copies. The Bible provided the first sure foundation his business ever had; as capital accumulated, he used it to expand his general publishing business. After the economic difficulties of the War of 1812, he emerged as the largest publisher in the country.

In 1801 Carey organized the first American book fair, at which he and booksellers from other cities met face to face, exchanged books, and planned joint publishing ventures by which books were published simultaneously in several cities. Though these fairs lasted only a few years, they transformed the American book trade by giving even small publishers access to a national market for the first time.

Carey returned to periodical publishing three times, but two of these ventures were short-lived, and the third was really the initiative of his son. Always a passionate theatergoer, he wrote and published a little magazine called the *Thespian Monitor, and Dramatick Miscellany. By Barnaby Bangbar, Esq.* It lasted only four weeks in late 1809. In 1820 he began to publish quarterly the *Philadelphia Journal of the Medical and Physical Sciences,* edited by Nathaniel Chapman, whom Carey had known since Chapman was a boy studying with a kinsman of Weems in Virginia. His successor firm of Carey and Lea continued to publish this prestigious journal until 1827, when it became the *American Journal of the Medical Sciences.* It is still going strong. Finally, in 1824 Carey began the *Political Economist,* edited by himself and published by his friend J. R. A. Skerrett. Thirteen weekly issues appeared (with some gaps) between 24 January and 1 May, by which time he declared that subscriptions were not meeting expenses, and publication ceased. The *Political Economist* is much like many of Carey's political and economic pamphlets which appeared in long series (for example his *Hamilton,* series 1 through series 12, 1822-1826), but since there was no frequency of publication stated, these pamphlet series were not true periodicals.

Carey's passionate interest in social and economic affairs kept him constantly involved in public life. Whenever a cause moved him, he would write a pamphlet, call a public meeting, or form an organization, with himself as secretary. While editing the *American Museum,* he had usually let others speak for him, but once he became established in business, he began to speak for himself. Curiously, he only once held elective office, a short term on city council. He felt he could be more useful if he remained free of party politics, and so his public career consisted of what today is called lobbying. He was a prototype of the species in America. The common thread that tied together the amazing variety of causes he embraced was his love of liberty, which in politics meant whatever made America united and strong, and in social issues meant compassion for the poor and enslaved.

This lobbying career really began with the controversy over the renewal of the charter of the Bank of the United States, which was due to expire in 1811. Carey had come to believe a strong national bank was essential to a strong economy and national unity. *Desultory Reflections upon the Ruinous Consequences of a Non-Renewal of the Charter of the Bank of the United States* (1810) was one of the few arguments in favor of the Bank. But when his prediction that nonrenewal would cause a severe depression came true, he began to be taken seriously as an economic advisor. In 1816 his considerably more sophisticated arguments were of great assistance to Nicholas Biddle and Henry Clay in their successful movement to charter a Second Bank of the United States.

During the War of 1812 the New England states' lack of support for "Mr. Madison's War" created a breach that threatened civil war or secession. In the midst of the crisis Carey wrote *The Olive Branch; or, Faults on both sides, Federal and Democratic* (1814), which attempted to show that the breach had been instigated by a few extremists, and that the vast majority of Americans of both parties wanted to preserve the Union. It became the most widely read political book since *Common Sense,* going through ten editions by 1819. Many contemporaries believed that it saved the Union.

During and after the panic of 1819, Carey emerged as a leading proponent of a protective tariff. He founded the Philadelphia Society for the Promotion of National Industry and wrote for the society a series of addresses on protection. By 1826 he had written at least forty separate pamphlets on the subject; his most famous convert was Henry Clay, who in 1824 dubbed his tariff program the "American System."

Carey believed that in order to extend the benefits of native manufactures to farmers and merchants, strong transportation links between cities and between cities and their hinterlands were essential. In 1824 he founded the Pennsylvania Society for the Promotion of Internal Improvements in the Commonwealth; from then on, pamphlets flowed from his pen advocating canals, turnpikes, and later, railroads.

After his retirement in 1822, hardly a day passed that Carey did not publish a pamphlet, write a piece for the newspapers, or call a meeting, large or small. He was not a powerful writer, but he was quick, often sending part of a piece to the typesetter before he had finished, and then revising in proof. He was especially eloquent in his writings on behalf of the poor and oppressed. In addition to his many public labors for the common good, Carey's many acts of private charity, es-

pecially to his fellow Irish-Americans, made him one of the best-loved men of Philadelphia. When he died in 1839 at age seventy-nine, after a carriage accident, his funeral procession was one of the largest the city had ever seen.

Carey's contribution to American literature consists largely of the influence of the *American Museum.* The magazine was a great stimulus to American writers because of the national exposure it gave to their writing. By lending the authority of its sophisticated format to American writers and by extending critical sympathy to their works, it helped to overcome a widespread cultural inferiority complex. Carey was an early and powerful proponent of the idea that American writings were worth attention because they were the product of a free political system, unstifled by the oppression of the Old World. To read and prefer American writers became, under his editorial influence, an expression of national pride and the love of liberty. No publisher did more to foster American literature in the early Federal period.

He made his contribution, however, as a publisher, not a patron. His chief worries were making money, pleasing his readers, and finding enough material. He was a scissors-and-paste editor; most of the *American Museum* consisted of reprints of pieces published elsewhere. Much of the prose was documentary, not literary. Authors of both prose and poetry whose names were already well known to the public received credit for their contributions, but works by unknowns were usually published unsigned or under a pseudonym. Nor was Carey a patron of letters in the sense of providing a source of income to writers. Since America did not have a copyright law until 1790, the payment for original works was minuscule, when it was offered at all. When in 1789 Jeremy Belknap began to ask for payment for his contributions to the *American Museum,* it was a mere two dollars per printed page. Carey tried to get him to take his payment in copies of the magazine. Many others offered their works at no charge, because the *American Museum* provided them with an unmatched national forum for their views. Carey never got accustomed to the idea of paying an author for a text. After the demise of the *American Museum* Carey published very few American literary works.

Ultimately a greater contribution to American literature was Carey's central role in the creation of a national book distribution network. Clearly the creation of a national market for books–even for reprints of English books–was a necessary preliminary to the creation of a national audience for American writing. Carey's son Henry Charles carried on where his father left off and became one of the leading publishers of American literature in the 1820s and 1830s. The father and the son each symbolize a stage in American literary development; Mathew Carey helped make Sir Walter Scott all the rage, and then Carey and Lea became the publishers of the American Scott, James Fenimore Cooper.

Carey was thus truly a pioneer, making smooth the way for those who followed him. His editorship of the *American Museum* manifested a principle which governed his entire life: America may have achieved its political independence and equality with England in 1783, but the Revolution was not over. The fight for cultural equality and economic independence still remained.

Letters:

Emily Ellsworth Ford Skeel, ed., *Mason Locke Weems: His Works and Ways*, volumes 1 and 2 (New York: Privately printed, 1929).

Bibliography:

William Clarkin, *Mathew Carey: A Bibliography of his Publications, 1785-1824* (New York: Garland, 1984).

Biographies:

Earl L. Bradsher, *Mathew Carey, Editor, Author and Publisher: A Study in American Literary Development* (New York: Columbia University Press, 1912);

Kenneth W. Rowe, *Mathew Carey: A Study in American Economic Development,* Johns Hopkins University Studies in Historical and Political Science, Series 51, no. 4 (Baltimore: Johns Hopkins University Press, 1933);

Edward C. Carter II, "The Political Activities of Mathew Carey, Nationalist, 1760-1814," Ph.D. dissertation, Bryn Mawr College, 1962;

James Gilreath, "Mason Weems, Mathew Carey and the Southern Booktrade, 1794-1810,"

Publishing History, 10 (1981): 27-49;

James N. Green, *Mathew Carey, Publisher and Patriot* (Philadelphia: Library Company, 1985);

Green, "From Printer to Publisher: Mathew Carey and the Origins of 19th Century Book Publishing," in *Getting the Books Out: Papers from the Chicago Conference on the Book in 19th Century America*, edited by Michael Hackenberg (Washington, D.C.: Center for the Book, 1987).

References:

William Charvat, *Literary Publishing in America, 1790-1850* (Philadelphia: University of Pennsylvania Press, 1959);

David Kaser, *Messrs. Carey & Lea of Philadelphia: A Study in the History of the Booktrade* (Philadelphia: University of Pennsylvania Press, 1957);

Rollo G. Silver, *The American Printer, 1787-1825* (Charlottesville: University Press of Virginia, 1967).

Papers:

The Lea and Febiger Collection and the Edward Carey Gardiner Collection at the Historical Society of Pennsylvania contain about fifty thousand letters to and from Carey from 1785 to 1824, as well as a few diaries and memoranda books. The Mathew Carey Papers at the American Antiquarian Society contain twenty-nine bound volumes with about twenty-seven thousand separate manuscript receipts and accounts. A diary for the years 1822-1826 is at Van Pelt Library, University of Pennsylvania. Much smaller groups of correspondence are to be found at the Library Company of Philadelphia; Clements Library, University of Michigan; the Massachusetts Historical Society; Houghton Library, Harvard University; the Franklin Papers, American Philosophical Society; and in the papers of other figures of the period at various repositories. The largest collection of books and pamphlets written and published by Carey is at the Library Company of Philadelphia.

Stephen Cullen Carpenter

(birth date unknown-1820?)

David E. Matchen
Auburn University

MAJOR POSITIONS HELD: Editor (1805-1807), publisher (1805-1806), *Monthly Register and Review of the United States*, renamed the *Monthly Register, Magazine, and Review of the United States*; editor, *New York Daily Advertiser*, renamed *People's Friend* (1806-1807); editor and publisher, *Mirror of Taste and Dramatic Censor* (1810-1811); editor, *Bureau; or Repository of Literature, Politics, and Intelligence* (1812).

WORKS: *Memoirs of the Hon. Thomas Jefferson*, 2 volumes, edited by Carpenter (New York: Printed for the purchasers, 1809);
Select American Speeches, Forensic and Parliamentary, with Prefatory Remarks; a Sequel to Dr. Chapman's Select Speeches, edited by Carpenter (Philadelphia: J. W. Campbell and E. Weems, 1815).

Stephen Cullen Carpenter, probably born in Ireland and eventually transplanted to Charleston, South Carolina, in the early part of the nineteenth century, was neither boldly innovative nor particularly perceptive either as a critic or arbiter of aesthetic standards in the magazines he edited and published. The chief importance of his periodicals in the history of American journalism is that they provide information about the tastes and interests of educated people in New York, Philadelphia, and the more isolated Charleston. His particular interests in the history of drama and the American stage also make his magazines valuable repositories for the student of theater.

Few biographical facts can be discovered about Carpenter, either from the periodicals he edited or from secondary sources. Magazine historians Frank Luther Mott and Sam G. Riley refer to Carpenter's reporting of the speeches at Warren Hastings's trial, and his arrival in Charleston, where, with Loring Andrews, in 1803 he founded the *Courier*, a paper with strong Federalist sympathies.

In January 1805 he founded the *Monthly Register and Review of the United States*. After publishing twelve issues over a period of eighteen months he moved to New York. There, with John Bristed as coeditor, he produced the second volume of the magazine. Retitled the *Monthly Register, Magazine, and Review of the United States*, the periodical underwent some alterations in format. After coediting six issues, Carpenter left the magazine to Bristed, who carried it on another six months until December 1807.

While in New York Carpenter also edited a newspaper, the *Daily Advertiser*, which he renamed and issued from 1 September 1806 to 3 August 1807 as the *People's Friend*. He may have continued to work on the newspaper after his departure from the *Monthly Register*. Nothing is known, however, of his activities until he appeared in Philadelphia in January 1810 with a new monthly, the *Mirror of Taste and Dramatic Censor*. Upon the sudden demise of this magazine, after four volumes of six issues each, Carpenter became editor of the *Bureau; or Repository of Literature, Politics, and Intelligence*, a short-lived Philadelphia magazine published from 28 March to 30 December 1812. Following this first magazine venture, he apparently held government positions in Washington, D.C., and is thought to have died in or around 1820.

Something of Carpenter's personality can be gleaned from studying the periodicals he edited. As writer and editor, he was expansive. His prose style suggests a man enamored with decoration for its own sake. He seems to have loved the extended metaphor and parallel structure, especially the repetition of an idea through a series of words or phrases meaning essentially the same thing. His essays, although clearly organized, rarely equal in substance the volume of words expended on the subject. As editor Carpenter seems to have been unable to focus the scope of his magazines. The *Monthly Register* seems to be unlimited in subject. It contains history, biography, current events, congressional proceedings, book reviews, poems, reports of technical develop-

PROSPECTUS

OF THE

MONTHLY REGISTER,

AND

REVIEW OF THE UNITED STATES.

It is allowed, that nothing of the literary kind is at this time so much wanted as a periodical publication, which would combine within itself the two-fold advantage of diffusing general knowledge, and standing as a permanent record of all the public transactions of the time; which would enlighten the minds, and improve the morals and the manners of the existing generation, and deliver down to posterity, for the use of the future historian, all the political facts and public transactions of the day, untinged with false colouring and unsullied by political prejudice.

Such a work has been long contemplated by the Subscriber, and he is encouraged to proceed in it by the promise of support from many respectable acquaintances, with whose influence and patronage he hopes to publish it soon, under the title of

THE MONTHLY REGISTER,

AND REVIEW OF THE UNITED STATES.

This work will be conducted, as nearly as possible, on the plan of the English Annual Register, whose reputation for utility and agreeableness has not been equalled by that of any other production of the same kind. Each number will be divided into two parts; the first historical and political, the second miscellaneous and literary.

The historical part will contain a regular and impartial history of the great political occurrences of the past month, the first place, and the largest room, being always allotted to those of the United States. The debates of Congress, and such debates of the several state legislatures, as may be of general importance to the union, and make a part of its history, shall be given in a concise form. In this part, all acts of Congress will be recorded; and thus not only the substance of our na-

First page of Carpenter's prospectus for the magazine he founded in Charleston, S.C., in 1805

ments and medical experiments, as well as excerpts from other periodicals.

He wanted to be both a truthful and objective historian, and he seems to have been unable to condense or summarize. In the *Monthly Register* he set out to give a detailed history of the politics in England and the colonies that led to the American Revolution; he then gave a history of the war. In the *Mirror of Taste* he intended to present a history of drama; in the two-year life of the magazine he completed only his discussion of Greece, Rome, and France.

As literary critic his criteria for judgment were Christian morality, sentiment, and utility. Any work that failed to teach Christian virtues, presented insensitive characters, or functioned only to entertain was likely to be deemed meritless or dangerous. Carpenter's reviews, which often contain lengthy quotations for the benefit of those unable to read the book or see the play, sometimes continue for several issues.

The *Monthly Register and Review of the United States* was originally published in two parts, a historical issue and a literary and miscellaneous issue, each appearing monthly and designed to be bound separately with their own title pages and indexes. The historical section had four divisions: "Retrospective History," the serial history of the American Revolution and the circumstances leading up to it; "History of the Passing Times," a report on the daily activities of the U.S. Congress (often more than six months in arrears); "Biography," serial biographical essays on a variety of people, from a stage prodigy named Betty to Admiral Nelson; and "Domestic Occurances [sic]," a collection of news items usually compiled from domestic newspapers in major cities.

The *Monthly Review and Literary Miscellany*, the second section, had ten divisions, although they never appeared at once in any issue. It usually began with "Literature and Criticism," a review, often carried on for several issues, of a recently published book. Carpenter apparently reviewed whatever came his way but sometimes reviewed books he had not read. "Review of French Literature," which followed, was written as a warning to young women who read French romances and to their mothers, who might be expected to keep such works out of their hands. He thought most of these novels particularly dangerous because they advocated free thinking and unfeminine behavior. Also included in the *Literary Miscellany* were reviews devoted to publications by American authors; an assortment of usually anonymous poems, often sent by subscribers and no better than they could be expected to be; "Useful Inventions," a collection of reports, usually taken from British periodicals, of scientific experiments and discoveries or of technical breakthroughs of particular interest to farmers; "Miscellanies" and "Variety," collections of news items and other information, jokes, anecdotes, and moral essays, taken from other publications; "Extracts," a collection of pieces taken from books and magazines; and "Notice of Books Printed in American Editions."

Carpenter's inclination toward multiple sections put demands upon him not easily met on a monthly basis, especially in Charleston. Almost from the beginning the *Monthly Register* fell behind schedule. In the issue for June 1805 Carpenter apologized for delays, explaining that he had to gather much of his material by "visiting the Seat of Government, and the chief Metropolitan cities of the union, which he proposes to do in the summer months when he hopes to make arrangements which will remove, in future, every obstruction on that account to the regular and satisfactory progress of the work." He also mentioned hiring a "co-adjutor" to help with the *Monthly Review and Literary Miscellany*. This advertisement of his intentions is dated 3 March 1806, suggesting that he was about a year behind schedule. After two more numbers, dated July and August 1805, the ninth issue is dated April 1806. Possibly the July and August issues appeared in March 1806 so that current dating could resume with the April 1806 issue. The last issue for volume 1 is dated June 1806.

Carpenter's purpose in publishing the magazine was lofty. In his role as historian he would avoid all bias, party politics, and portraits of public figures; and he usually kept to this policy, the one notable exception being his representation of Lord Bute as an ambitious monster who caused the American Revolution. His reports on Congress were politically neutral. As literary critic and editor he sought to "contribute to the happiness of . . . fellow citizens by a vigorous defense of the principles of truth and morality, and by rallying . . . round the sacred ALTARS OF CHRISTIANITY." Carpenter and his fictitious editorial staff would "endeavor to improve the manners, while they correct the heart; and to strengthen the understanding while they amuse the imagination and refine the taste." Such ideals resulted in his warning readers against Voltaire, Jean-Jacques Rousseau, and Thomas Paine while extolling the virtues of Madame de Genlis, that "QUINTILIAN of novel writers" whose *Le Marie Corrupteur: A Moral Tale* (1804) exposes the "misery to which a young woman may be led, even by her husband." The husband in the novel apparently distorts the heroine's thinking with "principles of fashionable philosophy."

After morality Carpenter valued sentiment. Thus, Thomas Cowper, whose "equally pure and heavenly spirit" illustrated "the more attractive and gentle influences of our divine religion," surpassed Milton in his estimation. Understandably, the poems printed in the "Poetry" section reflect the same taste. Typical examples are "Cottage Happiness," a poem about rustic joys; "Lines Sent to Young Lady with a Bunch of Jassamine," an overheated love poem; "To Mary," a poem to the speaker's dead wife; and "Lines Addressed to a Flute," verses exhorting the flute to "Thrill with despair, and breathe the sigh–/Despair that rends the trembling breast/The sigh, that wrings a heart opprest!"

In theory and practice Carpenter's prose style seems appropriate for the audience of "Lines Addressed to a Flute." Historical writing, he said,

must be made attractive, and, to that end, decorated with the finest, but most simple drapery which judgment can select from the stores of imagination, to embellish truth, without concealing her natural form, altering her complexion, or encumbering her superfluous ornament; a task of no small difficulty, since when the rein is once given to fancy, it is hard to restrain its career, and the best writers, in the warmth of composition, are often, imperceptibly, allured away from the strict line of truth, by the eager pursuit of meritorious finery; or a flowing period, a lofty climax, or a pointed, striking antithesis.

THE
HISTORY
OF
THE AMERICAN REVOLUTION,
INCLUDING

AN IMPARTIAL EXAMINATION OF THE CAUSES

WHICH PRODUCED THAT IMPORTANT EVENT;

AND

MONTHLY REGISTER
OF THE

UNITED STATES,

FROM THE DATE OF THEIR INDEPENDENCE TO THE
PRESENT TIME.

VOLUME THE FIRST.

[COPY-RIGHT SECURED ACCORDING TO LAW.]

CHARLESTON, S. C.

PRINTED FOR THE PROPRIETOR,

BY GABRIEL MANIGAULT BOUNETHEAU,

AT THE APOLLO PRESS, NO. 3, BROAD-STREET, NEAR THE EXCHANGE

1806.

THE
Monthly Register,
AND
REVIEW OF THE UNITED STATES.

HISTORY.

HISTORIA vero testis temporum, lux veritatis, vita memoriæ, magistra vitæ, nuntia vetustatis; qua voce alia, nisi Oratoris, immortalitati commendatur.   CICERO DE ORATORE.

CHAPTER I.

OF the many who read history, few are aware of the difficulties which beset the historian. To record truth is his business; to convey instruction, should be his object; and to the superficial observer, the detailing of a regular succession of facts, with precision, and sincerity, may appear easy; but, truths may be related without conveying instruction, and instruction can never be successfully administered if it be not recommended by those graces of composition, which relieve subjects of a dry nature from wearisome dulness, which attract attention, where interest flags, and give animation, and spirit, to the most cold and lifeless materials. Upon the reading of a dry, jejune narrative of events, utterly destitute of ornament, few will bestow time or trouble. To render history generally useful, therefore, it must be made attractive, and, to that end, decorated with the finest, but most simple drapery, which judgment can select from the stores of imagination, to embellish truth, without concealing her natural form, altering her complexion, or encumbering her with superfluous ornament; a task of no

VOL. I.   A

Title page for volume 1 and first page of the first issue of Carpenter's ambitious attempt to chronicle the American Revolution

The overly wordy and ornate style of this condemnation of superfluous decoration is commonplace in Carpenter's periodical writing.

Whatever his faults, Carpenter knew his audience in Charleston. They were planters and merchants and their families, people who were educated and enjoyed some leisure to read and pursue the arts but who were out of touch with artistic developments in England and on the Continent. Thus, discussion abounds of Cowper, Milton, Shakespeare, Daniel Defoe, Henry Fielding, James Thompson, Oliver Goldsmith, and Mozart, while William Wordsworth, Samuel Taylor Coleridge, and Beethoven are completely ignored.

Carpenter's move to New York and his association with Bristed brought changes to the magazine, including a new title–*Monthly Register, Magazine, and Review of the United States*–in January 1807. Under the new format each issue began with a moral essay by Bristed entitled "The Wanderer," followed by "Men and Women: A Moral Tale." The writing of this serial romance seems to have been shared by the two editors. Both also wrote reviews of American literature, but "Biography," "Poetry," "Retrospective History," and "History of the Passing Times" were handled by Carpenter as before. Material from British periodicals was replaced by "Anecdotes," a series of brief stories about well-known people, and "Communications," containing letters to the editors and, frequently, an essay by "the Archer," identified as a gentleman from South Carolina. The Archer, incidentally, contributed to the final issues of the *Monthly Review and Literary Miscellany*. Issues for January through May 1807, when Carpenter quit the magazine, ended with a list of recent publications and books in press.

Carpenter's second magazine venture, while much more limited in scope, retained much of the personality of the *Monthly Register*. The *Mirror of Taste and Dramatic Censor*, described by Mott as "the most important magazine devoted chiefly to the drama of this period, and the only one which outlasted a single theatrical season," was established in January 1810 in Philadelphia, where plays were regularly performed and where there was considerable interest in drama.

Each issue opens with a segment of a history of the drama, beginning with the origin of the Greek theater and continuing through French drama. The magazine folded before Carpenter could write a history of English drama or a history of the American stage. He had intended, however, through the history, to provide his readers with background for understanding the plays being produced in Philadelphia and subsequently reviewed by the magazine.

Following the history appear brief reviews of plays performed locally. Sometimes, through correspondents, there are reports of theatrical activities in New York, Boston, and Baltimore. Also included in the magazine are biographies of current and former stars of the stage, with emphasis given to those appearing in Philadelphia; lengthy analyses of the acting and staging of recent plays; excerpts from British theater periodicals; and, curiously but perhaps characteristically, a report on other forms of entertainment, primarily sporting activities in England, from foot races to fox hunts. Each issue of the first three volumes culminates with the publication of a new play, often one soon to be produced on the local stage. For so much material Carpenter charged eight dollars for a one-year subscription.

Carpenter's goals in this magazine were once again to record history; instruct through history, biography, and literary analysis; and entertain. He maintained his distaste for modern literature, which he saw as an unfortunate reflection of the degraded morality and taste of the public. He complained, for example, that the dramatic taste in London was so "corrupted by the spectacles and mummery of the Italian opera, by the rage for preternatural agency acquired from reading of ghost novels and romances, and by the introduction of German plays and translations, the people can relish nothing but melodrame [*sic*], show, extravagant incident, stage effect and situation–goblins, demons, fiddling, capering and pantomime. . . ." Stephen Cullen Carpenter, from the beginning of his curious Charleston magazine, was active in both recording and retelling history. It is remarkable that he attempted, as he indicated in his first magazine's prospectus, to provide for his readers "a permanent record of all the public transactions of the times."

References:

Frank Luther Mott, *A History of American Magazines*, 5 volumes (Cambridge, Mass.: Harvard University Press, 1938-1968), I: 260-261;

Sam G. Riley, *Magazines of the American South* (Westport, Conn.: Greenwood Press, 1986).

Lewis Gaylord Clark

(5 October 1808-3 November 1873)

Kathleen Kearney Keeshen
College of Notre Dame, Belmont, California

See also the Clark entries in *DLB 3: Antebellum Writers in New York and the South* and *DLB 64: American Literary Critics and Scholars, 1850-1880.*

MAJOR POSITION HELD: Editor (1834-1860) and publisher (1834-1841), *Knickerbocker Magazine, or New York Monthly.*

BOOK: *Knick-Knacks from an Editor's Table* (New York: Appleton, 1852).

OTHER: *The Literary Remains of the Late Willis Gaylord Clark. Including the Ollapodiana Papers, The Spirit of Life, and a Selection from his Various Prose and Poetical Writings,* edited by Clark (New York: Burgess, Stringer, 1844);

The Knickerbocker Sketch-Book: A Library of Select Literature, edited by Clark (New York: Burgess, Stringer, 1845);

The Lover's Gift; and Friendship's Token, edited by Clark (Auburn, N.Y.: Derby, 1848);

The Life and Eulogy of Daniel Webster, edited by Clark (Rochester: Hayward/New York: De-Witt & Davenport, 1853); enlarged and republished as *The Life, Eulogy, and Great Orations of Daniel Webster* (New York: McKee, 1855).

Lewis Gaylord Clark

Lewis Gaylord Clark's reputation rests largely upon his thirty years as pioneering editor of the *Knickerbocker Magazine, or New York Monthly,* the first popular literary magazine of the nineteenth century. Founded in 1833 by Samuel Langtree, who sold controlling interest in his then-failing periodical to Clark and his friend Clement M. Edson, the *Knickerbocker* attracted first-rate contributors. From 1834 to 1861 Clark screened some of the best contemporary literature of the day. He encouraged and promoted the careers of a host of writers, shaped public reception of their literature by writing and commissioning critical reviews, and expressed his own aesthetic standards through numerous essays published in the periodical's pages.

Captain Eleakim and Lucy Driggs Clark were the parents of Lewis Gaylord Clark and his twin, Willis Gaylord. The brothers were born on 5 October 1808 in the town of Otisco, in Onandaga County, New York. Exceptionally gifted, the boys seemed to have inherited their interest in writing and reading from a maternal relative who had been editor of the *Genessee Farmer and Albany Cultivator.* Although Lewis did not enjoy the popular recognition as a writer or editor his brother did, his contributions to the nineteenth-century American scene may be more significant historically.

Though little mention is made in biographical accounts of Clark being married or having children, *Harper's New Monthly Magazine* (March 1894) makes reference to his settling in "Wooster Street, near Broome," following his marriage in 1834 to Ellen Maria Curtis, and later moving to a second home on Henry Street near Rutgers University, both of which would be considered suburban by modern standards. The article describes Charles Dickens's wife, who was accompanying her husband on a visit to the Clark home. She asked to see the rollicking Clark children, whose boisterous play could be heard on the floor below where guests were assembled.

Clark began his journalistic career on the *Philadelphia Daily Inquirer,* the periodical Willis edited from 1834 to 1841, the year of his death from tuberculosis. Clark worked on the *Inquirer* briefly before taking over the editorial reins of the *Knickerbocker* from Charles Fenno Hoffman's successor, Timothy Flint.

Clark envisioned the *Knickerbocker* as the premier literary journal of its kind, and he energetically addressed the task of establishing it. To that end he courted contributors he thought would be able to provide works worthy of inclusion. From Philadelphia, Willis sent a potpourri of columns called "Ollapodiana." Dr. Ollapod, a character from the play *The Poor Gentleman,* was himself named for *olla podrida,* a spicy Spanish meat-and-vegetable stew that features a variety of ingredients. Willis's columns, too, were an olio of commentary on nature, literature, and life.

Other writers with whom he corresponded assiduously to keep them contributing to the magazine included Washington Irving (after whose pseudonym the magazine was named), William Cullen Bryant, James Fenimore Cooper, Charles Dickens, Letitia Elizabeth Landon, Fanny Kemble, William H. Seward, Francis Parkman, and William Wadsworth Longfellow. He formed a special bond with Irving, who ultimately became a regular contributor. A collection of Irving's sketches were later collected and published as *Wolfert's Roost* (1855). Irving's nephew, John T. Irving, wrote for the *Knickerbocker* under the pseudonym "Quod." Other contributors of the New England school were Nathaniel Hawthorne, John Greenleaf Whittier, and Oliver Wendell Holmes. Philadelphia contributors were Mathew Carey, Bayard Taylor, Joseph Neal, and William E. Burton; and from the Midwest and West were Albert Pike, Francis Parkman, and former *Knickerbocker* editor Timothy Flint. Fred Cozzens and Charles

G. Leland contributed humorous copy. In sum the magazine offered its readers a rich variety of content and authorship.

Always the champion of struggling artists and beginning writers, Lewis was one of the twelve organizers of New York City's Century Club (others included artist Asher B. Durand and William Cullen Bryant), established to foster advancement of the arts and literature and originally limited to one hundred members.

Clark's love of New York was manifested in a column that was a forerunner to "The Talk of the Town" in today's *New Yorker*. Called "The Editor's Table," the column appeared each month, in addition to the magazine's sketches, poetry, and other literary contributions. Over time its length increased, and other publications throughout the country ran it as a popular feature. Clark's friends might find that conversations they enjoyed with him in assumed privacy were detailed in the column, along with gossip about New York's literati. His memory was prodigious, and the column benefited from it.

Despite the *Knickerbocker*'s claim to be apolitical, the magazine reflected the conservative values of the upper class and most powerful New York circles. Nonetheless, in another sense, the *Knickerbocker* represented boosterism at its best, promoting the growing intellectual influence of New York, supporting its claim to a cultural status that rivaled its sister city of Boston.

While the *Knickerbocker*'s important contributions were those enhancing and extolling American literature, it also brought the works of Dickens before the public, and the admiration expressed in its pages for Sir Walter Scott and William Cullen Bryant was not insignificant.

Beginning in 1841 the *Knickerbocker* had passed through a rapid succession of publishers: John Bisco, John Allen, Samuel Hueston, John Gray, and J. R. Gilmore. By 1850 the quality of the magazine had lessened, partly due to disagreements between Clark and Clement M. Edson, his copublisher.

Nonetheless, the *Knickerbocker* continued to exercise a draw upon the reading public. Clark's *The Knickerbocker Sketch-Book* (1845) was made up of pieces from the magazine and represented somewhat of a counterpoint to the subsequent collection of chatty, gossipy excerpts from his collection of monthly columns, which appeared in 1852 as *Knick-Knacks from an Editor's Table.* His conservative bent extended into the realm of theology as well and found reflection in his 1853

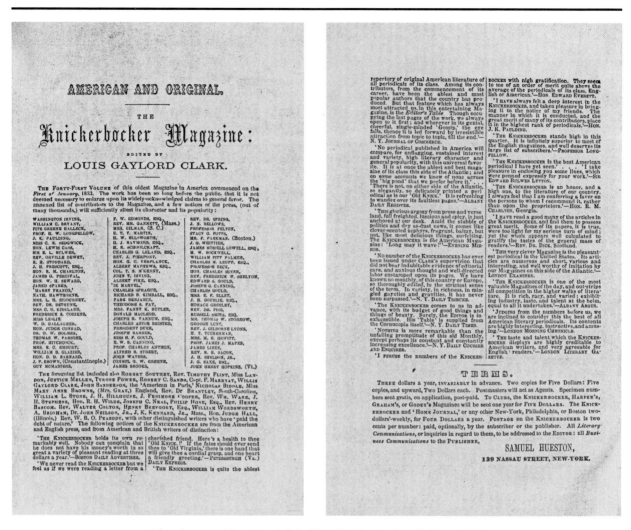

Advertisement with testimonials in The Knickerbocker Gallery, *1855*

publication of *The Life and Eulogy of Daniel Webster.*

With the approach of the Civil War, the financial fortunes of the publication ebbed. The magazine ceased publication in 1861, only to be revived in 1863 before its ultimate demise. In addition to its financial problems, the magazine had also suffered from Clark's failure to find new and younger writers to fill the places of the magazine's regular contributors as they aged and stopped writing.

Clark later wrote occasionally for then-popular magazines, such as the *Evening Post,* the *Home Journal, Harper's,* and *Lippincott's,* from his retirement cottage at Hudson in Piermont, New York. An exceptionally likable person to the end, he had been the recipient from his friends and the magazine's contributors of a special gift. The group banded together and in 1855 compiled an anthology specifically written and expressly de-

signed to be sold as a testimonial to him and to provide funds for his retirement home, an act perhaps unique in any editor's experience. The group realized the financial straits to which Clark's commitment to the magazine had led him, and its efforts reflected the esteem in which they held him personally and professionally. His "collaborators," as they called themselves, those surviving writers, all of whom had previously contributed to the *Knickerbocker,* agreed to contribute gratis original individual works for the resulting miscellany. Profits were sufficient to provide funds for "on the margin of the Hudson, a cottage, suitable for the home of a man of letters, who like Mr. Clark, is also a lover of nature and of rural life." *The Knickerbocker Gallery: A Testimonial to the Editor of the Knickerbocker Magazine from its Contributors* included works by Irving, Longfellow, Bryant, Oliver Wendell Holmes, Bayard Taylor, James Russell Lowell, William H. Seward, and Richard Henry Stoddard. Some forty-eight portrait engravings of the contributors and of Clark finished off the special tribute. Clark lived in the house on the Hudson until his death at sixty-five on 3 November 1873.

His *New York Times* obituary of 5 November 1873 pointed out that in "the twenty-seven years Clark presided over the fortunes of the *Magazine,* he was called upon to disappoint the expectations of thousands, yet he never made an enemy." The *Times,* in recapping Clark's achievements, found fault with the contributions of the literary period as a whole but noted that Clark "may be said to close the literature of the past, of which Washington Irving may be taken as its chief exponent. It was scholarly, it was humorous, it was pleasing, but it produced no strong man and was, indeed a reproduction of English classics, an echo from the Addisonian era." In balance Frank Luther Mott's assessment

should also be considered. Mott said in volume 1 of his *A History of American Magazines* (1938) that "No American magazine has ever been regarded with more affection by its readers than was 'Old Knick' under Lewis Gaylord Clark's editorship."

Letters:

The Letters of Willis Gaylord and Lewis Gaylord Clark, edited by Leslie W. Dunlap (New York: New York Public Library, 1940).

References:

The Knickerbocker Gallery: A Testimonial to the Editor of the Knickerbocker Magazine from Its Contributors (New York: Samuel Hueston, 1855);

"Lewis Gaylord Clark," *Harper's New Monthly Magazine,* 48 (March 1874): 587-592;

Frank Luther Mott, *A History of American Magazines,* 5 volumes (Cambridge, Mass.: Harvard University Press, 1938-1968), I: 606-614.

Joseph Dennie

(30 August 1768-7 January 1812)

James S. Featherston
Louisiana State University

See also the Dennie entries in *DLB 37: American Writers of the Early Republic; DLB 43: American Newspaper Journalists, 1690-1872;* and *DLB 59: American Literary Critics and Scholars, 1800-1850.*

MAJOR POSITIONS HELD: Editor, *Boston Tablet* (1795); *New Hampshire Journal: or the Farmer's Weekly Museum,* renamed *Farmer's Museum: or Lay Preacher's Gazette* in 1799 (1796-1799); *Gazette of the United States* (1800); *Port Folio* (1801-1812).

SELECTED BOOKS: *The Lay Preacher, or Short Sermons for Idle Readers* (Walpole, N.H.: Printed & sold by David Carlisle, Jr., 1796);
A Collection of Essays, on a Variety of Subjects, in Prose and Verse (Newark, N.J.: Printed by John Woods, 1797);
The Lay Preacher, edited by John E. Hall (Philadelphia: Printed by J. Maxwell & published by Harrison Hall, 1817).
Collection: *The Lay Preacher,* edited by Milton Ellis (New York: Scholars' Facsimiles & Reprints, 1943).

OTHER: *The Spirit of the Farmers' Museum, and Lay Preacher's Gazette. Being a Judicious Selection of the Fugitive and Valuable Productions, Which Have Occasionally Appeared in That Paper, since the Commencement of Its Establishment,* edited, with contributions, by Dennie (Walpole, N.H.: Printed for Thomas & Thomas by D. & T. Carlisle, 1801);
The Plays of William Shakespeare . . . with the Corrections and Illustrations of Various Commentators, volume 2, edited by Dennie (Philadelphia: C. & A. Conrad/Baltimore: Conrad, Lucas, 1805); volume 1, probably edited wholly or in part by Dennie (Philadelphia: C. & A. Conrad/Baltimore: Conrad, Lucas, 1809);
Thomas Moore, Esq., *Epistles, Odes and Other Poems,* second edition, edited, with notes, by Dennie (Philadelphia: John Watts, 1806);

Robert Hutchinson Rose, *Sketches in Verse,* edited by Dennie (Philadelphia: Printed for C. & A. Conrad by Smith & Maxwell, 1810).

PERIODICAL PUBLICATIONS: Review of *Joan of Arc* by Robert Southey, in "An Author's Evenings," *Port Folio,* 1 (29 August 1801): 274;
"Biography. The Life of the Right Hon. William Windham," *Port Folio,* 2 (15 May 1802): 149-151;
Review of *American Dictionary* by Noah Webster, in "An Author's Evenings," *Port Folio,* 2 (28 August 1802): 268;
"The Lay Preacher," *Port Folio,* 3 (9 July 1803): 217; (15 July 1803): 226;
"Polite Literature," *Port Folio,* third series 6 (22 October 1808): 264-266.

Joseph Dennie, an ardent Anglophile who detested democracy, was a leading literary figure during the latter half of the eighteenth century, which has been described as the "Dark Ages of American Journalism," and the ensuing first decade of the nineteenth century. He founded and edited the *Port Folio,* which was considered the finest magazine in America during his editorship. It was also the only early American magazine to survive for a considerable length of time. Politically Dennie was such a reactionary that one historian has described him as a monarchist. He strongly supported the Federalists and bitterly opposed Thomas Jefferson and his administration. Dennie was more accomplished as an essayist than as a political commentator, and he was sometimes compared with England's Joseph Addison. A frail, sickly individual who died relatively young, Dennie is best remembered for his literary criticism and his "Lay Preacher" essays.

Born 30 August 1768, Dennie was the only child of Mary Green and Joseph Dennie, Sr., both of whom were members of distinguished colonial families. His father, at the time a prosperous businessman importing and selling such West

THIRD EDITION.

PROSPECTUS

OF A NEW WEEKLY PAPER,

SUBMITTED TO MEN OF AFFLUENCE, MEN OF LIBERALITY, AND MEN OF LETTERS.

A YOUNG MAN, once known among village-readers, as the humble historian of the hour, the conductor of a *Farmer's Museum*, and a *Lay Preacher's Gazette*, again offers himself to the public as a volunteer-editor. Having, as he conceives, a right to vary, at pleasure, his *fictitious* name, he now, for higher reasons than any fickle humour might dictate, assumes the appellation of OLDSCHOOL. Fond of this title, indicative of his moral, political, and literary creed, he proposes issuing, every Saturday, on a super-royal quarter ...

A NEW WEEKLY PAPER,

TO BE CALLED

THE PORT FOLIO,

BY OLIVER OLDSCHOOL, ESQ.

Warned by the waywardness of the time, and the admonitions of every honest printer, the Editor begins his work on a Lilliputian page; and, like a saving grocer, gives of his goods only a small sample ...

First page of Dennie's prospectus for Port Folio

Indies staples as molasses, rum, hemp, and sugar, came from the "merchant aristocracy," and his mother's family had distinguished itself in the printing industry. His parents were loyal to the Crown, and there must have been much pro-Tory, antipatriot political talk in Dennie's home while he was a boy.

Dennie grew up in a Boston community that was rocked by the events that led to the American Revolution. Dennie was two years old at the time of the Boston Massacre, five when the Boston Tea Party took place. A year later the first armed clash occurred at Concord, and the small boy must have witnessed victims being returned to Boston. Joseph, Sr., moved the family to nearby Lexington, then a rustic, almost wholly agricultural hamlet with a population of between eight hundred and one thousand.

Dennie was a precocious child and began writing at an early age. He studied at a New England dame school, where ladies taught children in their homes. Dennie also may have attended the tiny, one-room grammar school in Lexington, but he probably learned more at home from his parents and from the literary classics in his father's library. When Dennie was fifteen, his father sent him to Boston to learn bookkeeping at a commercial school, and later Dennie was hired as a clerk at a counting house in Boston. One year at this position made it evident that Dennie's talents "were not of the mercantile variety." He was then placed under the supervision of the loyalist minister Samuel West of Needham, who would prepare him for entrance to Harvard College. Dennie joined the class of 1790, which consisted of forty-two members and later produced eleven ministers, three physicians, and twelve lawyers, five of whom would serve as members of Congress. His closest friend was Roger Vose, who would later serve in Congress and then become chief justice of the Circuit Court of New Hampshire. Another classmate was Josiah Quincy III, who was a member of Congress from 1804 to 1813, the first mayor of Boston from 1823 to 1828, and president of Harvard College from 1828 to 1845.

While at Harvard, Dennie wrote essays and poems, some of which were probably published in the *Massachusetts Magazine* under various pen names. During his senior year he was suspended for six months for insolence toward a faculty member, but during this "rustication" Dennie was permitted to pursue the same course of studies under the supervision of a minister in Groton.

He then was readmitted and permitted to graduate with his class. Dennie, however, felt he had been wrongly disgraced, and he never forgave Harvard. After graduation he prepared himself for a legal career by securing a clerkship in the law office of Samuel West's brother Benjamin, in Charlestown, New Hampshire.

Although he was initially enthusiastic about his legal apprenticeship, he began to regard the law as "a nauseous pill, not be poured down the throats of even the vulgar without gilding." In a letter to his father, he added: "I can appreciate my own talents. I never shall be profound. I never shall be a silent, unenterprising lawyer. My talents to you I can freely confess are superficial, but they are showy, and the deficiencies of Judgment in the thought are in vulgar opinion compensated by the boldness and glitter of Fancy in the expression."

Despite ill health, which would plague him for life, and the demands of his legal career, Dennie continued to write, and in 1792 the first of his "Farrago" (Latin for "mixed fodder") essays began to appear in the *Morning Ray: or the Impartial Oracle,* a newspaper published in Windsor, Vermont. In these essays Dennie satirized the foibles and faults of the times "in a pleasing manner." Only four essays were published in the Vermont paper; they were discontinued probably because of Dennie's illnesses. The amusing essays, which eventually numbered twenty-nine, were well received by readers and appeared in other New England newspapers. In a letter to his mother, Dennie wrote: "In moments of dreary vacancy I have amused myself, and enlarged my knowledge of English style, by writing, at different times and in various vehicles, the Farrago. . . . In the press of Obscurity I knew I should risk nothing either in censure or praise. The public, however, saw or fancied some merit; and as American essays have been heretofore unmarked, except for flimsy expression and jejeune ideas, they have allowed me praise for reviving, in some degree, the Goldsmith vivacity of thought, and the Addison sweetness in expression."

During the summer of 1793 Dennie was invited to read the liturgy and sermon during a Sunday service at a Claremont church. The congregation was favorably impressed, and Dennie was hired to serve as a lay reader for four months. The church experience proved valuable to Dennie for it provided the "suggestion and design" for his celebrated "Lay Preacher" essays.

Dennie completed his three-year legal clerkship and was admitted to the bar of New Hampshire in March 1794. He opened his law office in the home of a widow in Charlestown, determined "to assert my independence, to uphold and to defend causes with unspotted hands" and to be "ready for business whether clients enter or avoid my doors." Clients were scarce, unfortunately, and when he did appear in court his persuasive oratory was sometimes wasted on ill-educated rural judges. Trying cases before such judges was like attempting "to batter down a mud wall with roses," Dennie said. Although his law practice did not succeed, Dennie later said this was the happiest part of his life, a period when he slept soundly "unscared by the spectre of poverty."

Meanwhile, Dennie's "Farrago" essays began to appear in the *Eagle: Or Dartmouth Centinel*, published in Hanover, New Hampshire. The first "Farrago" essay in the *Eagle*, the eighth in the series, appeared in the 19 August 1793 issue, and the articles continued irregularly until 18 September 1794, numbering fifteen in all. Among others writing for the *Eagle* was Royall Tyler of Guilford, Vermont, with whom Dennie formed a lasting literary partnership. They called the partnership the "Shop of Colon and Spondee" and offered for sale literary works of "all sorts, verse or prose, grave or witty, moral or political, parody or elegy, etc., etc." The plan was for Dennie, as "Colon," to contribute prose and for Tyler, as "Spondee," to provide verse. In actuality both wrote prose and poetry, using the initials "C" or "S" to identify their work. They contributed satiric paragraphs, epigrams, anecdotes, poems, and other materials to the *Eagle*. Their work was widely reprinted in Federalist newspapers in New England.

Early in 1795 Dennie visited Boston seeking to capitalize further on his literary talents in order to earn money to supplement his meager law practice income. He first contacted such leading publishers as Benjamin Russell and Isaiah Thomas but received little encouragement. Dennie then decided to begin his own magazine, a small, weekly miscellany which would feature a "Farrago" essay as the principal article in each issue. William Spotswood, a publisher and bookseller, agreed to assume the entire financial risk and to share profits, if any, with Dennie. The first issue of the magazine, the *Boston Tablet*, appeared on 19 May 1795 with Spotswood as publisher and Dennie as the anonymous editor. The

magazine was patterned after the British essay papers, and Dennie wrote in the style of Joseph Addison and Richard Steele of *Spectator* and *Tatler* fame.

Dennie remained in Boston until the midsummer, returning to his neglected law practice in Charlestown with expectations of earning fame and fortune from the *Tablet*. Spotswood wrote, however, informing him that the *Tablet* was being discontinued because of a lack of public support. The thirteenth and last issue appeared on 11 August 1795.

During the autumn of 1795 Dennis moved his law office to Walpole, a village of about fifteen hundred inhabitants ten miles down the Connecticut River from Charlestown. The village already had three lawyers, including his friend Roger Vose, so the prospects of building a thriving practice were not promising for Dennie. What probably attracted him to Walpole was the *New Hampshire Journal: or the Farmer's Weekly Museum*, a newspaper published there by Isaiah Thomas and David Carlisle, a former apprentice Thomas had taken in as a partner. Thomas had other interests in Boston, Worcester, Newburyport, and Brookfield, so Carlisle managed the newspaper in Walpole. Some of Dennie's articles had previously been reprinted in the *Museum*, and on 12 October 1795 the first of a new series of essays, titled "The Lay Preacher," began to appear in the newspaper. The first article, "Wine and New Wine," was well received, and thereafter "Lay Preacher" essays began appearing weekly in the *Museum*.

Dennie was offered and accepted a "pecuniary" position and practically ran the literary and political departments of the newspaper. He wrote satires attacking New England democrats, and soon the newspaper, which previously had been politically impartial, was vigorously supporting the Federalists. When Thomas withdrew from the partnership and turned the *Museum* over to Carlisle, Dennie was made editor at a salary far more than the income from his law practice, which he had more or less abandoned. Under Dennie the *Museum* became the best and most popular rural publication in New England "as far as literature and politics were concerned." The *Museum* became less of a newspaper and more of an essay publication. Biographer Harold Milton Ellis notes: "He [Dennie] cared little for local items of news and the cataloguing of deaths, marriages, and prices, and left advertisements to the care of Carlisle. Colon and Spondee

THE PORT FOLIO.

BY OLIVER OLDSCHOOL, ESQ.

"VARIOUS, THAT THE MIND
OF DESULTORY MAN, STUDIOUS OF CHANGE,
AND PLEAS'D WITH NOVELTY, MAY BE INDULGED."
COWPER.

VOL. I.]　　　　　　　　　　　　　　　　　　　　　　　　**[No. 1.**

PHILADELPHIA, SATURDAY, JANUARY 3d, 1801.

TRAVELS.

FOR THE PORT FOLIO.

[The subsequent letter is the commencement of a series, which will be regularly published in this paper. It is unnecessary to dwell upon the general excellence of the following tour. It will be obvious to every intelligent reader that it has been made by no vulgar traveller, but by a man of genius and observation, who, in happy union, combines the power of selecting the most interesting and picturesque objects, and of describing them gracefully.]

JOURNAL OF A TOUR THROUGH SILESIA.

LETTER I.

Frankfort, on the Oder, 20th July, 1800.

As I have bespoken your company, upon our journey into Silesia, I begin this letter at our first resting station from Berlin. Hitherto, we have indeed seen little more than the usual Brandenburg sands, and perhaps you will find our tour as tiresome, as we have found it ourselves. I cannot promise you an amusing journey, though I hope it will prove so to us. My letters to you, on this tour, will be in the form, and serve as the substitute of a journal. They will, of course, be fragments, written at different times and places; nay, perhaps in different humours. Therefore, make up your account, to receive patiently all my tediousness.

On Thursday, the 17th inst. we left Berlin, just after three in the morning, and arrived here at about nine the same evening. The distance is ten German miles and a quarter; which you know is a very long day's journey in this country. In the course of a few years, it will be an easy journey of eight hours; for the present king, who has the very laudable ambition of improving the roads through his dominions, is now making a turnpike road, like that to Potsdam, the whole way hither; as yet, not more than one German mile of it is finished, and the rest of the way is like that, which on every side surrounds the *Todtner* of modern times. As we approach within a few miles of Frankfort the country becomes somewhat hilly, and of course more variegated and pleasant than round Berlin; but we could perceive little difference in the downy softness of the ground beneath us, or in the *air* of the pines within our view. Part of the country is cultivated, as much as it is susceptible of cultivation, and here and there we could see scattered spires of wheat, rye, barley, and oats shoot from the sands, like the hairs upon a head almost bald. We came through few villages, and those few had a miserable appearance. A meagre composition of mud and thatch composed the cottages, in which a ragged and pallid race of beggars reside; yet we must not be unjust, and confess, that we passed by one nobleman's seat, which had the appearance of a handsome and comfortable house.

We arrived here just in time to see the last dregs of an annual *fair*, such as you have often seen in the towns of Holland, and as you know are customary in those of Germany. But we hear great complaints against the minister Struensee, for having ruined the value of the *fair*, by prohibiting the sale of foreign woollen manufactures, which have heretofore been the most essential articles of sale at this fair. This prohibition is for the sake of encouraging the manufactures of this country, a principle, which the government pursue on all possible occasions. They are no converts to the opinions of Adam Smith and the French economists, concerning the balance of trade, and always catch with delight at any thing which can prevent money from *going out of the country.* Of this disposition we have seen a notable instance in the attempts lately made here or producing sugar from beets, of which I believe you heard something while you were here, and about which much has been said and done since then. At one time we were assured beyond all question, that one mile square of beets would furnish sugar for the whole Prussian dominions. The question was submitted to a committee of the Academy of Sciences, who, after long examination and deliberation, reported, that in truth, sugar, and even brandy, could be produced from beets, and in process of time might be raised in great quantities; but that, for the present, it would be expedient to continue the use of sugars and brandies, such as had been in use hitherto. Since this report, we have heard little or nothing of beet sugar.

This is an old town, pleasantly situated, and containing about twelve thousand inhabitants, of which a quarter part are Jews. It is therefore distinguished by those peculiarities, which mark all European towns where a large proportion of Israelites reside, and to express which, I suppose, resort must be had to the Hebrew language. The English at least is inadequate to it; for the word *filth* conveys an idea of spotless purity, in comparison to the Jewish nastiness. The garrison of the town consists of one regiment. There is here likewise an university; and by the introduction of a letter from Berlin, we have become acquainted with two of the professors. The number of students is less than two hundred; and of them, one hundred and fifty are students of law; ten or fifteen of divinity; and not more than two or three of medicine. The library, the museum, and the botanical garden, the professors tell me, are all so miserable, that they are ashamed to show them.

The banks of the Oder, on one side, are bordered with small hills, upon which at small distances, are little summer-houses with vineyards, at which, during summer, many inhabitants of the town reside. On the other side, the land is flat, and the river is restrained from overflowing only by a large dyke, which has been built since the year 1785. At that time the river broke down the smaller dyke, which had, until then, existed, and overflowed the country to a considerable extent. Prince Leopold of Brunswick, a brother of the present reigning duke, was then colonel of the regiment in garrison here, and lost his life in attempting to save some of the people, whom the inundation was carrying away. You have probably seen prints of this melancholy accident, and there is an account of it in the last edition of Moore's *Travels.* (I mean his first work.) There is a small monument erected in honour of the prince, upon the spot where his body was found. It was done by the free-masons of this place, of which society he was a member. But there is nothing remarkable in it. There is likewise in the burying ground a little monument, or rather tomb-stone, to *Kleist*, one of the most celebrated German poets, whom his countrymen call their Thomson. He was an officer in the service of Frederick the second, and was killed at the battle of Cunersdorf, a village distant only a couple miles from this place.

Just at the gate of the town, there is a spring of mineral water, at which a bathing house has been built, with accommodations for lodgers. This bath has been considerably frequented for some years past, and the physicians of the town say, that the waters are as good as those of Freyenwalde. I am willing to believe them as good as those of Toeplitz; for my faith in mineral waters in general, was not much edified by the success of our tour there last summer.

22d July. Still at Frankfort. We had left Berlin without being fully aware of the precise nature of the journey we had undertaken; and had not thought of taking with us furs, and winterclothing for a tour in the dog-days. But one of the professors, whose acquaintance we have made here, had formerly gone the same journey; and from his representations, we have been induced to send back to Berlin for thick clothing, and this circumstance has prolonged our stay here a couple of days more than we at first intended. Yesterday we took a ride of three or four miles, to the country seat of a Mr. Schoening, the *landrath of the circle.* The functions of his office are to collect the territorial taxes within a certain district called a *circle*, which is a subdivision of the province. You know the importance and extent of this title of *rath* or *councillor*, in the constitutions of the German states. It is a general name, designating every officer in all the subordinate parts of the administration; and sometimes a mere honorary title, which Frederic the second, by way of joke, once granted to a person, *upon condition that he should never presume to give any counsel.* For the principle upon which the name is founded is, that the person holding the title gives the king occasionally counsel, and the first part of it usually designates the particular department in which he gives it.

Mr. Schoening and his lady, received us with great kindness and hospitality. From the neighbourhood of their house, and on our return, we had the pleasure of agreeable prospects of the

Front page of the first issue of Dennie's most successful periodical

reopened their shop, supplying the paper with political satirical paragraphs and parodies. . . ." The "Lay Preacher" essays, however, were the most notable feature of the *Museum;* these articles ran weekly until 24 May 1796 and later appeared irregularly, once or twice a month, until April 1797. Writing in the style of a country parson, Dennie in these essays commented on a wide variety of subjects, usually in a playful manner.

The stay in Walpole apparently was a happy time for Dennie. His income was adequate, and his literary reputation was growing. He was enjoying his work, and he was spending his leisure time among congenial and admiring companions. Joseph Buckingham, later a successful printer and editor, served as an apprentice at the *Museum,* and he once recalled that Dennie was "pleasant and instructive" at the *Museum* office and must have been a "delightful and fascinating companion" in the company of his friends. Buckingham added: "Dennie wrote with great rapidity, and generally postponed the task until he was called upon for copy. It was frequently necessary to go to his office, and it was not uncommon to find him in bed at a late hour in the morning. His copy was often given out in small portions, a paragraph or two at a time; sometimes it was written in the printing office, while the compositor was waiting to put it into type. One of the best of his lay sermons was written at the village tavern, in a chamber where he and his friends were amusing themselves with cards."

Meanwhile, the *Museum* was growing in circulation. On 24 July 1797 Dennie announced the *Museum* had subscribers in all of the states except Georgia, Kentucky, and Tennessee. By December the *Museum* boasted a circulation of two thousand, the largest of any village newspaper in the nation. Among its readers were some of the most prominent people in the United States. Dennie and the other contributors to the *Museum,* including his friend Vose and Thomas Green Fessenden, had transformed the little village of Walpole into a literary center. A collection of Dennie's essays, *The Lay Preacher, or Short Sermons for Idle Readers* (1796), published in book form, added to his personal prestige.

All was not well, however. The *Museum,* despite its growing popularity, was in financial trouble, largely because of nonpaying subscribers and partly because of mismanagement. Carlisle went bankrupt, and Dennie lost money he had invested in the newspaper. Thomas took over the *Museum* again in February 1798, retaining Car-

lisle as the printer and Dennie as editor at a reduced salary. In June Thomas hired a relative, Alexander Thomas, as general manager, leaving Dennie as editor of the literary and political departments. To capitalize further on the popularity of Dennie's essays, Thomas changed the name of the newspaper in April 1799 to the *Farmer's Museum: or Lay Preacher's Gazette.* By then Dennie had become disenchanted and had turned his attentions elsewhere. He ran for Congress but lost to the incumbent.

Dennie, although tiring of his work at the *Museum,* turned down attractive offers to edit other influential newspapers in Boston, New York, Philadelphia, and Baltimore. James White, a Boston bookseller and a friend, offered Dennie twelve hundred dollars, three times his Walpole salary, to edit the nonpartisan *Independent Chronicle.* "If he had offered me 12 millions of dollars annually, I must have refused his offer. It would have belied my feelings, my habits, my principles, my conscience," he wrote his mother. Nonetheless, he realized he had remained too long in rustic New Hampshire.

In October 1799 he moved to Philadelphia, at the time the nation's capital, and, through political friends, he secured an appointment as a personal secretary to Secretary of State Thomas Pickering. He had literary opportunities as well. John Ward Fenno offered to pay Dennie eight hundred dollars, plus a percentage of all new subscriptions, to edit the Federalist *Gazette of the United States.* Dennie's income was enough for him to live elegantly and to pay debts left over in Walpole. He became good friends with Pickering, whose tastes and political views were much the same as his. Pickering's advocacy of Alexander Hamilton's extreme views soon led the more moderate John Adams to dismiss him from his cabinet on 12 May 1800. In a long letter to his parents Dennie noted his pessimism about the future of American democracy. He wrote: "Our government is so weak that it is powerless to hold out much longer against the assaults of Faction, and another war with Great Britain, and civil commotion, are now at hand." Although his views seem treasonable, such opinions were not unusual among some Federalists. There was deep distrust and hostility between the Federalists and the Anti-Federalists, and the newspapers were bitterly partisan during this era. In 1800 the nation had been in existence only eleven years under the Constitution, and the democratic government was still an experiment. The pro-English Federalists, the party of Washington, Hamilton, and Adams, favored by the "well born and rich," had been in power since the birth of the nation and were being challenged by the pro-French Anti-Federalists (later the Republicans), led by Thomas Jefferson, the party of the yeoman middle class.

Dennie, writing for the *Gazette of the United States,* gleefully entered the journalistic warfare. He attacked William Duane, editor of the Anti-Federalist *Aurora,* as a "gin drinking pauper" and described another rival editor as a "blockhead and an ass." He lambasted Jefferson, and, after his election, Dennie predicted that a "civil convulsion in the heart of our republic" would follow. During his brief time as editor of the *Gazette,* Dennie republished some of his "Lay Preacher" essays and occasionally wrote new ones. In one essay he blamed much of the world's trouble on the "frantic madness of liberty, equality, fraternity" that had inflamed France and was invading America. Dennie stepped down as editor when the *Gazette* changed ownership, but he continued as head of the literary and miscellaneous departments until December 1800.

In the 16 October 1800 issue of the *Gazette,* Dennie announced plans for a new magazine to be called the *Port Folio,* which would be backed financially by Asbury Dickins, a prominent Philadelphia bookseller and publisher. A prospectus for the new magazine appeared the following December, and it whimsically began: "A young man, once known among village readers, as the humble historian of the hour, the conductor of a *Farmer's Museum* and a *Lay Preacher's Gazette,* again offers himself to the public as a volunteer-editor. Having, as he conceives, a right to vary, at pleasure, his *fictitious* name, he now, for higher reasons, than any fickle humor dictate, assumes the appellation of *OLDSCHOOL.* Fond of this title, indicative of his moral political and literary creed, he proposes publishing every Saturday, on super-royal quarto sheets, a new weekly paper, to be called, *The Port Folio* by Oliver Oldschool Esq." Dennie promised he would not publish an impartial magazine, though he would not cast aspersions on the "government, church, or literature of England." The price would be five dollars a year.

The time and place were auspicious for the debut of a new, well-conducted magazine. Several Philadelphia magazines had gone out of business, leaving a void that Dennie's journal could fill. Despite Dennie's political extremism, his personal magnetism had attracted a number of talented contributors to the magazine. They included John Quincy Adams; Joseph Hopkinson, author of *Hail, America;* Gouverneur Morris, the diplomat; Alexander Wilson, the ornithologist; Richard Rush, later minister to England and France; John Blair Linn and Charles Jared Ingersoll, each a dramatist and poet; and Charles Brockden Brown, a noted literary figure of the time.

The first issue of the *Port Folio* appeared on 3 January 1801, and it was mostly the work of Dennie and Adams. The opening article, "Journey of a Tour Through Silesia," was one of a series of letters Adams had written to his brother, Thomas Boylston Adams, in Philadelphia. The letters continued to be published on the front page of the *Port Folio* until 7 November 1801. Adams also contributed a verse translation of the Thirteenth Satire of Juvenal that took up three of the eight pages of the first issue.

In the first issue, Dennie began a series called "An Author's Evenings" in which he reviewed the work of various writers. Although this series was credited to "The Shop of Colon and Spondee," it is believed Dennie wrote nearly all of it. A poem in the first issue called "The Misanthrope" is also believed to have been Dennie's work. He wrote a column of "Literary Intelligence," and there was a "Theatrical Review." The first issue also published, for the first time, letters written to Tobias Smollett, the British novelist, by James Boswell, David Hume, Samuel Richardson, John Armstrong, and William Pitt the Younger. The letters had been found in a trunk and given to Dennie by an anonymous but "learned friend, whose good taste selects, and whose care preserves, many a literary gem, and many a valuable fragment." The first issue contained no political article, an omission for which apologies were offered.

The *Port Folio* was a success from the start. Dennie had planned an initial printing of one thousand copies, but his partner insisted on fifteen hundred, and these soon sold out. The *Port Folio* exceeded Dennie's expectations, and the press run was increased to two thousand copies within a few months. Dennie basked in the praise for his creation that had "turned out to be a literary magazine eclipsing in its range and excellence anything on the continent before it." The magazine also established Dennie in literary circles as "the most influential American of the nineteenth century's first decade." The magazine's success, however, curtailed Dennie's own writing. After several years his desk work became so consuming that Dennie devoted all of his time to editing.

Politically the *Port Folio* was, of course, strongly Federalist and bitterly opposed to President Jefferson and his administration. The magazine verbally assailed Jefferson in nearly every issue and even scorned the Declaration of Independence as "that false, flatulent, and foolish paper." The magazine ran a protest of the reading of the document on the Fourth of July. Dennie railed against the return of Thomas Paine, the famed pamphleteer and friend of Jefferson, to America, calling Paine a "drunken atheist" and describing him as "loathsome." The *Port Folio* was unflagging in its attacks on Jefferson, and between 1802 and 1804 fourteen anonymous poems slanderously insinuated that Jefferson was cohabitating with his quadroon slave, Sally Hemings.

Dennie's distaste for democracy prompted him to write a paragraph in the 23 April 1803 edition that would result in an indictment against him. He wrote:

A democracy is scarcely tolerable in any period of national history. Its omens are always sinister, and its powers are unpropitious. With all the lights of experience blazing before our eyes, it is impossible not to discern the futility of this form of government. It was wicked and evil in Athens. It was bad in Sparta, and worse in Rome. It has been tried in France, and has terminated in despotism. It was tried in England, and rejected with the utmost loathing and abhorrence. It is on trial here, and the issue will be civil war, desolation, and anarchy. No wise man but discerns its imperfections, no good man but shudders at its miseries, no honest man but proclaims its fraud, and no brave man but draws his sword against its force. The institution of a scheme of polity so radically contemptible and vicious is a memorable example of what the villainy of some men can devise, the folly of others receive, and both establish, in despite of reason, reflection, and sensation.

The paragraph was reprinted in a number of Federalist newspapers whose editors agreed with Dennie; at the same time, Dennie was denounced as a traitor by the democratic press. On the Fourth of July the paragraph was presented before a grand jury that indicted Dennie for "inflammatory and seditious libel" on the same day. Action was postponed, however, and Dennie was not brought to trial until 28 February 1805. Ably defended by Joseph Hopkinson, Dennie was awarded a unanimous verdict of not guilty on Monday, 2 December 1805. The following Saturday the *Port Folio* exulted: "Thus far the editor has been triumphant in his warfare against Democracy, a fiend more terrible than any that the imagination of the classical poets ever conjured up from the 'vasty deep' of their Pagan Hill."

Although Dennie toned down his most virulent attacks after the trial, he continued to lambaste democracy and its adherents. He remained a resolute, class-conscious snob, greatly admiring the highly educated, cultured, and wealthy aristocracy while scorning the "ignorant and giddy multitude." He favored a classical education for the rich but thought the poor should receive only the rudiments of schooling. He did not believe in upward mobility and contended that "difference in rank and subordination are . . . of God's appointment, and consequently essential to the well being of society." He once described his favorite few as "men of genius, talents, principle, and property" and denounced the great majority as "democrats, fanatics, knaves, and fools . . . an impious, impudent, and savage gang, whom every man of genius and virtue is bound to meet with defiance on his brow and horse whip in hand."

Dennie even suggested that only the aristocracy could be entrusted with the proper use of language and insisted that advocates of democracy used "impure and incorrect" English. Dennie contended there was a close connection between false politics and spurious literature, and he blamed the party of Jefferson for exaggeration, boastfulness, weak logic, and improper innovation in words and pronunciations. He sneered at Noah Webster's *American Dictionary* and insisted on linguistic purity and elegance. "To resist and ridicule absurd innovations in literature, to cherish the classical and established forms of diction, and preserve the purity, and resort to the standards of English style is the constant aim of the editor," Dennie wrote.

In Philadelphia Dennie helped organize the Tuesday Club, a literary society similar to one he had supported earlier in Walpole. The Tuesday Club attracted a number of convivial young men who were imbued with a love of literature. Most of them were lawyers and Federalists, and they held meetings at various places that "overflowed with eloquent conversation and rollicking fun." Some of the Tuesday Club members became regular contributors to the *Port Folio*. Dennie also advocated the formation of an elite group to safeguard good American literature and the proper use of language. Members of the group, "not exceeding the number that of the French academy," would be "men of fortune, of the fairest character, the staunchest principles, and the greatest intrepidity." The group, Dennie wrote, would also "revive classical discipline, create a passion for pure undefiled English, guide the taste and fortify the judgement of youth, multiply the editions of sterling authors, and absolutely eradicate every bad book in the country."

The years 1802 to 1805 were good ones for the *Port Folio*. Its circulation was larger than that of any earlier magazine, and it was publishing the work of some of the best American and British writers. At the end of 1802 Dennie dissolved his partnership with Dickins and became the sole proprietor. Two years later the magazine's price was increased from five to six dollars a year. In 1806 the *Port Folio* changed from an eight-page newspaper format to a small magazine size containing sixteen pages. The magazine also began a new series of "Lay Preacher" essays.

Dennie was chronically ill after 1807, and the quality of the magazine declined. He lost some of his more talented contributors and was forced to rely more and more on reprints. Delinquent subscribers owed him ten thousand dollars, and they failed to respond to his anguished appeals for payment. Deeply in debt, Dennie was forced to relinquish ownership of the magazine. The firm of Innskeep and Bradford became the publishers and proprietors after January 1809. Dennie stayed on as editor even though he was bedridden for long periods of time; he was retained largely for his prestige.

The *Port Folio* in 1809 also became "A Monthly Miscellany, dedicated chiefly to original communications in the departments of science, combined with occasional criticism, classical disquisitions, miscellaneous essays, records of the progress of all the fine and useful arts, with all the extensive and variegated departments of literature, merriment, and wit." The magazine also became nonpartisan, a condition that Dennie would not have accepted in his healthier days. The pseudonym "Oliver Oldschool" disappeared in the first issue of 1810 and was replaced by the words, "Conducted by Joseph Dennie, Esq." The new prospectus announced that the magazine would seek to be solidly and entertainingly useful and would in the future exclude the "squabbles of the State, and polemical brawls in the Church."

Dennie became desperately ill during the autumn of 1811, and he died on 7 January 1812 at the age of forty-three. The February 1812 issue of *Port Folio* eulogized Dennie, saying, "The great purpose of all his exertions, the uniform pursuit of his life, was to disseminate among his countrymen a taste for elegant literature, to give to education and to letters their proper elevation in the public esteem, and reclaiming the youth of America from the low career of sordid interests, to fix steadily their ambitions on objects of a more exalted character." In the same issue Nicholas Biddle, the new editor, decided to revive the "Oliver Oldschool" pseudonym, and it again appeared on the front page. The *Port Folio* continued publication until 1827, a record unparalleled in America at that time, but it never regained the standards of excellence it had attained under Dennie's editorship.

Although some considered Dennie the finest American essayist of his era, his work did not stand the test of time, and his talents were forgotten as newer and more vigorous authors emerged. Dennie thought he was writing his "Lay Preacher" essays for posterity, but a later critic, Fred Lewis Pattee, has dismissed the "Lay Preacher" series as the "posings of a transplanted Puritan before what he considered the esthetes of old Philadelphia." Pattee preferred Dennie's "Colon and Spondee" columns. He wrote: "Here there is humor, here there is more naturalness. It is a relief to descend from the forced elegance of the 'Lay sermon' essays, the conscious posings and primpings for the literary few, to the spontaneous naturalness of this democratic column." Dennie's greatest achievements were the creation of the *Port Folio*, the most successful literary journal that had been published up to that time, and the influence the magazine had in enhancing the appreciation of literature in the young nation.

Letters:
The Letters of Joseph Dennie, 1768-1812, edited by Laura Green Pedder (Orono, Maine: Printed at the University Press, 1936).

Biographies:
William C. Clapp, Jr., *Joseph Dennie* (Cambridge, Mass.: John Wilson, 1880);
Harold Milton Ellis, *Joseph Dennie and His Circle* (Austin: University of Texas, 1915).

References:

Joseph Tinker Buckingham, *Specimens of Newspaper Literature*, 2 volumes (Boston: Little, Brown, 1850), II: 74-202;

Annie Russell Marble, *Heralds of American Literature* (Chicago: University of Chicago Press, 1907), pp. 193-231;

Frank Luther Mott, *A History of American Magazines*, 5 volumes (Cambridge, Mass.: Harvard University Press, 1938-1968), I: 223-246;

Fred Lewis Pattee, *The First Century of American Literature, 1770-1870* (New York: Appleton-Century, 1935), pp. 184-190, 210-212;

Randolph C. Randall, "Joseph Dennie's Literary Attitudes in the *Port Folio*, 1801-1812," in *Essays Mostly on Periodical Publishing in America*, edited by James Woodress (Durham, N.C.: Duke University Press, 1973), pp. 57-91.

Papers:

Most of Joseph Dennie's papers are held by Harvard University; other papers and correspondence can be found in the Adams Papers and Pickering Papers at the Massachusetts Historical Society, and in collections at the New Hampshire Historical Society and the Historical Society of Pennsylvania.

Ralph Waldo Emerson

(25 May 1803-27 April 1882)

Donald R. Avery
University of Southern Mississippi

See also the Emerson entries in *DLB 1: The American Renaissance in New England* and *DLB 59: American Literary Critics and Scholars, 1800-1850.*

MAJOR POSITION HELD: Editor, *Dial* (1842-1844).

SELECTED BOOKS: *Nature* (Boston: Munroe, 1836);

Essays [First Series] (Boston: Munroe, 1841; London: Fraser, 1841; expanded, Boston: Munroe, 1847);

Nature; An Essay, and Lectures on the Times (London: Clarke, 1844);

Orations, Lectures, and Addresses (London: Clarke, 1844);

Essays: Second Series (Boston: Munroe, 1844; London: Chapman, 1844);

Poems (London: Chapman, 1847; Boston: Munroe, 1847); revised and enlarged as *Selected Poems* (Boston: Osgood, 1876); revised and enlarged again as *Poems* (Boston & New York: Houghton, Mifflin, 1884 [volume 9, Riverside Edition]; London: Routledge, 1884; revised, Boston & New York:

Houghton, Mifflin, 1904 [volume 9, Centenary Edition]);

Nature; Addresses, and Lectures (Boston & Cambridge: Munroe, 1849); republished as *Miscellanies; Embracing Nature, Addresses, and Lectures* (Boston: Phillips, Sampson, 1856); republished as *Miscellanies* (London: Macmillan, 1884);

Representative Men: Seven Lectures (Boston: Phillips, Sampson, 1850; London: Chapman, 1850);

English Traits (Boston: Phillips, Sampson, 1856; London: Routledge, 1856);

The Conduct of Life (Boston: Ticknor & Fields, 1860; London: Smith, Elder, 1860);

May-Day and Other Pieces (Boston: Ticknor & Fields, 1867; London: Routledge, 1867);

Society and Solitude. Twelve Chapters (Boston: Fields, Osgood, 1870; London: Sampson, Low, Son & Marston, 1870);

Letters and Social Aims (Boston: Osgood, 1876; London: Chatto & Windus, 1876);

Miscellanies (Boston: Houghton, Mifflin, 1884 [volume 11, Riverside Edition]; London: Routledge, 1884);

Ralph Waldo Emerson (photograph by John S. Notman &
Co., courtesy of the Boston Athenaeum)

Lectures and Biographical Sketches (Boston & New
  York: Houghton, Mifflin, 1884; London:
  Routledge, 1884);

Natural History of Intellect and Other Papers (Boston
  & New York: Houghton, Mifflin, 1893 [vol-
  ume 12, Riverside Edition]; London:
  Routledge, 1894);

Two Unpublished Essays: The Character of Socrates;
  The Present State of Ethical Philosophy (Boston
  & New York: Lamson, Wolffe, 1896);

The Journals of Ralph Waldo Emerson, 10 volumes,
  edited by Edward Waldo Emerson and
  Waldo Emerson Forbes (Boston & New
  York: Houghton Mifflin, 1909-1914);

Uncollected Writings: Essays, Addresses, Poems, Re-
  views and Letters (New York: Lamb, 1912);

Young Emerson Speaks: Unpublished Discourses on
  Many Subjects, edited by Arthur Cushman
  McGiffert, Jr. (Boston: Houghton Mifflin,
  1938);

The Early Lectures of Ralph Waldo Emerson, volume
  1, edited by Stephen E. Whicher and Robert E. Spiller (Cambridge, Mass.: Harvard
  University Press, 1959); volume 2, edited by

Whicher, Spiller, and Wallace E. Williams
  (Cambridge, Mass.: Harvard University
  Press, 1964); volume 3, edited by Spiller
  and Williams (Cambridge, Mass.: Harvard
  University Press, 1972);

The Journals and Miscellaneous Notebooks of Ralph
  Waldo Emerson, 16 volumes, edited by William H. Gilman and others (Cambridge,
  Mass.: Harvard University Press, 1960-
  1983).

Collections: *Emerson's Complete Works,* 12 volumes
  (Boston & New York: Houghton, Mifflin,
  1883-1893 [Riverside Edition]; London:
  Routledge, 1883-1894);

Complete Works of Ralph Waldo Emerson, 12 volumes
  (Boston & New York: Houghton, Mifflin,
  1903-1904 [Centenary Edition]);

The Collected Works of Ralph Waldo Emerson, 3 volumes to date (Cambridge, Mass.: Harvard
  University Press, 1971-).

OTHER: Thomas Carlyle, *Sartor Resartus,* edited,
  with a preface, by Emerson (Boston: Munroe, 1836);

Memoirs of Margaret Fuller Ossoli, 2 volumes, written and edited by Emerson, William Henry
  Channing, and James Freeman Clarke (Boston: Phillips, Sampson, 1852); 3 volumes
  (London: Bentley, 1852);

Parnassus, edited by Emerson (Boston: Osgood,
  1875).

Ralph Waldo Emerson's contribution to magazine journalism consists of his work in connection with the *Dial,* the voice of early American
transcendentalism. A major force in the creation
of the journal, from 1840 to 1842 Emerson
served primarily as contributor under Margaret
Fuller's editorship. He then edited the journal
himself from 1842 to its demise in 1844.

Emerson, born 25 May 1803 in Boston, was
the second of five sons of William and Susan
Haskins Emerson. He began grammar school at
eight years of age and the Boston Latin School at
twelve. He was graduated from Harvard College
(A.B.) in 1821. Emerson attended the Harvard
Divinity School in 1825 and 1827 but did not
graduate. He showed few unusual abilities (mathematics seemed simply beyond him; philosophy
not much better) throughout his education. As
an undergraduate he was thirtieth out of a class
of fifty-nine and fared little better as a divinity student. His studies in divinity school were sporadic
and lacked distinction. In September 1829

Henry is quite unable to labor lately since his sickness, & so must resign the garden into other hands, but as private secretary to the President of the Dial, his works & fame may go on into all lands, and, as happens to great Premiers, quite extinguish the titular Master. My reading lately is to the subject of Poetry, which has at least this advantage over many others, that it pays the student well day by day, even if it should fail to reward his inquisition with one adequate perception after many days & nights. The custom of that enchanted hall I have often heard of, I have often experienced. The Muse receives you at the door with godlike hospitality gives bread & wine & blandishment, will turn the world for you into a ballad drives you mad with a ballad with a verse with a syllable, leaves you with that & Behold! afar off shines the Muse &

Emerson's letter of 10 April 1842 to Margaret Fuller, written as he prepared to take over the editorship of the Dial *(courtesy of Ralph Waldo Emerson Memorial Association Collection, Houghton Library, Harvard University)*

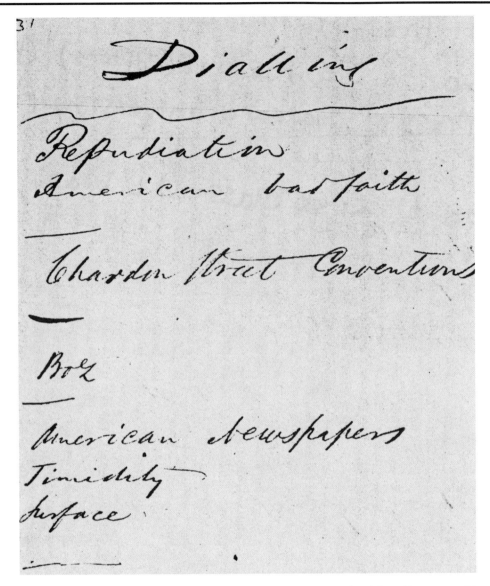

Page of notes Emerson made listing topics he wanted to include in the Dial *(courtesy of Ralph Waldo Emerson Memorial Association Collection, Houghton Library, Harvard University)*

Emerson married Ellen Louisa Tucker, who died without children in February 1832. In September 1835 Emerson married Lydia Jackson. They had four children.

Emerson taught school during his summers at Harvard and turned to the teaching profession as a career upon his graduation. It was during his five years as a Boston teacher that Emerson attended divinity school at Harvard. It was his connections and perhaps his ancestry rather than his academic prowess that led in 1826 to his being approved as a preacher by the Middlesex association of ministers. However, he was unable to take a post because poor health forced him to spend some months in South Carolina and Florida.

When he returned to New England in 1827, he turned to preaching and began actively to seek a church. During the next two years Emerson preached at various places in New England. It was not until January 1829 that he received an invitation to join the Second Church in Boston. The church's pastor was in ill health, and within eighteen months Emerson had taken his place.

Emerson appears to have been an effective and eloquent preacher, if somewhat stern in his bearing. He was involved in the city affairs of Boston and state government, serving on the Boston school committee and as chaplain of the state senate. He was involved in several philanthropic movements, either giving of his own funds or assisting in fund-raising. He early opened his church to antislavery champions although he himself did not speak publicly on the subject. Emerson seemed destined to remain in the calling for the remainder of his life. However, a year after his first wife's death he resigned his pastorate. Whether his withdrawal was the result of his wife's death or Emerson's spiritual and philosophical growth is unclear. However, it appears that after this period his life began to take on the shape it was to follow for his remaining years.

He went to Europe in 1832, visiting France, Italy, Sicily, London, and Edinburgh. Emerson preached extensively in the last two places and met William Wordsworth, Samuel Coleridge, and Thomas Carlyle. His friendship with Carlyle lasted for thirty-five years, and their correspondence was published in 1883 under the editorship of Charles Eliot Norton. Following his return from Europe Emerson began to preach and lecture, but it was not until the following year that his writings began to take on a distinctly literary flavor. Shortly before his second marriage he moved to his ancestral home in Concord and following the wedding to a plain frame house in Concord, where he spent the rest of his life as a writer, poet, and lecturer.

In 1836 he published his first book, *Nature*, anonymously in Boston. In this thin volume of less than one hundred pages may be found the seed from which grew all Emerson's subsequent work. Virtually everything he wrote after *Nature* merely expanded on the themes contained in that work. *Nature* talks of the universe consisting of nature and the soul. According to Emerson, everything in nature corresponds to some state of mind. Natural laws in the scheme of things always become moral laws and teach the worship of God, the idea of the absolute, that God cannot be described, and, indeed, that nature is but one form of God.

Nature was not universally well received and came in for considerable negative comment from the clerical community. Among other accusations, Emerson was labeled a deist and a pantheist. Ex-president John Quincy Adams, a family friend, said of him in 1840 that "after failing in the every-day vocations of a Unitarian preacher and school master, he starts a new doctrine of transcendentalism, declares all the old revelations superannuated and worn out, and announces the approach of new revelations." However, there were others, most notably those transcendentalists who gathered about him in Concord (called

"the Delphi of New England"), who believed the work ushered in a new era of American literature.

Emerson remained busy during the latter years of the 1830s writing, lecturing, and editing manuscripts. It was about this time that Emerson became active in the Transcendental Club, which began to meet at the home of George Ripley in 1836. Emerson was probably the group's leader from the beginning. Among the members of the loose federation were Bronson Alcott, Margaret Fuller, Frederic H. Hedge, James Freeman Clarke, Convers Francis, Theodore Parker, Rev. Cyrus A. Bartol, Orestes A. Brownson, and Elizabeth P. Peabody. It was the Transcendental Club which led directly to Emerson's only experience with running a magazine. He and other members of the Transcendental Club, primarily George Ripley and Margaret Fuller, founded the *Dial*, a publication designed to present the views of the transcendentalists. Primarily because Emerson refused to take on the job himself, Margaret Fuller became the first editor; however, she received considerable assistance from Emerson and George Ripley.

The *Dial* was an exercise of the young. Most of the magazine's contributors were in their early thirties or late twenties (only Alcott was over forty). Not surprisingly, much of the material that appeared in the publication was crude, undeveloped, and at times self-indulgent. Emerson wanted to offer a forum for his young and inexperienced friends, particularly those whom he considered writers of promise. He makes his position clear in a letter to Margaret Fuller: "Were I responsible, I would rather trust for its wit and its verses to the eight or nine persons in whose affections I have a sure place than to eighty or ninety celebrated contributors." The prospectus states well the magazine's purpose: "The pages of this journal will be filled by contributors who possess little in common but the love of intellectual freedom and the hope of social progress; who are united by sympathy of spirit, not by agreement in speculation; whose faith is in Divine Providence rather than in human prescription; whose hearts are more in the future than in the past, and who trust the living soul rather than the dead letter. It will endeavor to promote the constant evolution of truth, not the petrifaction of opinion"—and in a final sentence much that was Emerson can be found—"and in religion it will reverently seek to discern the presence of God in nature, in history, and in the soul of man."

MASSACHUSETTS QUARTERLY REVIEW.

NO. I.—DECEMBER, 1847.

TO THE PUBLIC.

THE American people are fast opening their own destiny. Their material basis is of such extent that no folly of man can quite subvert it; for the territory is a considerable fraction of the planet, and the population neither loath nor inexpert to use their advantages. Add, that this energetic race derive an unprecedented material power from the new arts, from the expansions effected by public schools, cheap postage, and a cheap press, from the telescope, the telegraph, the railroad, steamship, steamferry, steammill, from domestic architecture, chemical agriculture, from ventilation, from ice, ether, caoutchouc, and innumerable inventions and manufactures.

A scholar who has been reading of the fabulous magnificence of Assyria and Persia, of Rome and Constantinople, leaves his library, and takes his seat in a rail-car, where he is importuned by newsboys with journals still wet from Liverpool and Havre, with telegraphic despatches not yet fifty minutes old from Buffalo and Cincinnati. At the screams of the steam-whistle, the train quits city and suburbs, darts away into the interior,—drops every man at his estate as it whirls along, and shows our traveller what tens of thousands of powerful and weaponed men, science-armed and society-armed, sit at large in this ample region, obscure from their numbers and the extent of the domain. He reflects on the power

NO. I. 1

1847.] *Editors' Address.* 7

cause they know his religious constitution,—that he must rest on the moral and religious sentiments, as the motion of bodies rests on geometry. In the rapid decay of what was called religion, timid and unthinking people fancy a decay of the hope of man. But the moral and religious sentiments meet us everywhere, alike in markets as in churches. A God starts up behind cotton bales also. The conscience of man is regenerated as is the atmosphere, so that society cannot be debauched. That health which we call Virtue is an equipoise which easily redresses itself, and resembles those rocking-stones which a child's finger can move, and a weight of many hundred tons cannot overthrow.

With these convictions, a few friends of good letters have thought fit to associate themselves for the conduct of a new journal. We have obeyed the custom and convenience of the time in adopting this form of a Review, as a mould into which all metal most easily runs. But the form shall not be suffered to be an impediment. The name might convey the impression of a book of criticism, and that nothing is to be found here which was not written expressly for the Review; but good readers know that inspired pages are not written to fill a space, but for inevitable utterance; and to such our journal is freely and solicitously open, even though every thing else be excluded. We entreat the aid of every lover of truth and right, and let these principles entreat for us. We rely on the talents and industry of good men known to us, but much more on the magnetism of truth, which is multiplying and educating advocates for itself and friends for us. We rely on the truth for and against ourselves.

First and last pages of the editor's address Emerson wrote for Theodore Parker's magazine. Although listed on the masthead as a coeditor, Emerson's only contribution to the magazine was this preface.

Although Margaret Fuller was editor, it is clear that Emerson played an important part in the publication. In addition to writing the first issue's introductory article, "The Editors to the Reader," Emerson contributed some forty of his own poems and essays, plus a number of unsigned pieces. Among Emerson's better-known poems first published in the *Dial* are "Fate," "The Problem," "The Sphinx," and "Woodnotes." Many young writers (mostly of the Transcendental school) first appeared in print in the *Dial,* including Henry David Thoreau, who provided either a poem or a prose work for virtually every issue of the *Dial.*

After two years Margaret Fuller tired of the uphill battle to create a viable publication and begged out of the editorship. She cited two reasons for stepping down as editor: her own poor health and the magazine's poor financial condition. The *Dial* simply did not pay its own way, and Fuller could not afford to carry it. Rather than ask others to take on the task (and perhaps desiring greater control over the publication), Emerson was forced to take over the magazine or see it fail. As he makes clear in his diary, "The *Dial* is to be sustained or ended; and I must settle the question, it seems, of its life or death. I wish it to live, but I do not wish to be its life. Neither do I like to put it into the hands of the Humanity and Reform men, because they trample on letters and poetry; nor in the hands of the scholars, for they are dead and dry. . . ."

Despite the fact that Emerson had kept a strong hand in the early numbers of the publication, it began to change from the literary vehicle that had been originally intended and became something of a reform journal as soon as he became sole editor. Emerson wrote quite favorable essays on the socialists and Fourierism, and noted in his journal: "And now I think our Dial ought not to be a mere literary journal but that the times demand of us all a more earnest aim." As had been the case under Fuller, the subscriptions did not cover the printing costs, and Emerson was forced to pay them out of his own pocket. After two more years of devoting time and money that he could ill afford, Emerson let publication of the *Dial* cease.

The *Dial* did not succeed because there were not enough regular subscribers, contributors were mostly inexperienced writers, it had little support in the reading community of the day, and the founders of the publication never had consensus among themselves as to the magazine's

purpose–a ready formula for failure. It was a noble experiment, for despite the self-indulgence of many of its writers, the *Dial* was fresh in its writing and original in much of its thought. Certainly, critics were able to lambast its deficiencies, but it must be recognized as a vigorous attempt at originality and freedom of expression.

Emerson continued to write, lecture, and travel for the remaining thirty-eight years of his life, but he never attempted the management of a publication again. He contributed the "Editor's Address" to the first number of the *Massachusetts Quarterly Review,* which began publication in Boston in 1847. Its editor, Theodore Parker, listed Emerson as coeditor on the magazine's masthead, but Emerson had no interest in the position and asked that his name be removed. He was an early contributor to the *Atlantic Monthly,* founded in 1857, and some of his most important poems and prose appeared in that magazine, including "The Titmouse," "Brahma," "The Romany Girl," "Days," "Waldeinsamkeit," "Boston Hymn," and "Terminus." He also contributed material to a second *Dial,* established in Cincinnati in 1862.

When the *Dial* ceased publication in 1844, only three of Emerson's major works had been published. He had much left to do, and when one considers his frustrating experience with the magazine, it is not surprising that he was perfectly willing to let others carry on the business of providing a voice for transcendentalism. He continued writing and speaking out on certain important issues, such as slavery, woman suffrage, and politics, and his home in Concord became a meeting place for leading thinkers and writers of the Western world. Although his mental powers began to fail, and he lost the power to converse toward the end of his life, he kept busy revising his early work. In April 1882 Emerson contracted a severe cold that developed into pneumonia. He died on 27 April 1882.

Letters:

The Correspondence of Thomas Carlyle and Ralph Waldo Emerson 1834-1872, 2 volumes, edited by Charles Eliot Norton (Boston: Osgood, 1883; London: Chatto & Windus, 1883);

A Correspondence Between John Sterling and Ralph Waldo Emerson, edited by Edward Waldo Emerson (Boston & New York: Houghton, Mifflin, 1897);

Letters from Ralph Waldo Emerson to a Friend, 1838-1853 [Samuel Gray Ward], edited by

Norton (Boston & New York: Houghton, Mifflin, 1899; London: Watt, 1899);

Correspondence between Ralph Waldo Emerson and Herman Grimm, edited by Frederick William Holls (Boston & New York: Houghton, Mifflin, 1903);

Records of a Lifelong Friendship, 1807-1882: Ralph Waldo Emerson and William Henry Furness, edited by Horace Howard Furness (Boston & New York: Houghton Mifflin, 1910);

Emerson-Clough Letters, edited by Howard F. Lowry and Ralph Leslie Rusk (Cleveland: Rowfant Club, 1934);

The Letters of Ralph Waldo Emerson, 6 volumes, edited by Rusk (New York: Columbia University Press, 1939);

One First Love: The Letters of Ellen Louisa Tucker to Ralph Waldo Emerson, edited by Edith W. Gregg (Cambridge, Mass.: Harvard University Press, 1962);

The Correspondence of Emerson and Carlyle, edited by Joseph Slater (New York & London: Columbia University Press, 1964).

Bibliographies:

Walter Harding, *Emerson's Library* (Charlottesville: University Press of Virginia, 1967);

Joel Myerson, *Ralph Waldo Emerson: A Descriptive Bibliography* (Pittsburgh: University of Pittsburgh Press, 1982);

Robert E. Burkholder and Joel Myerson, *Emerson: An Annotated Secondary Bibliography* (Pittsburgh: University of Pittsburgh Press, 1985);

Manfred Putz, *Ralph Waldo Emerson: A Bibliography of Twentieth-Century Criticism* (New York: Peter Lang, 1986).

Concordances:

George S. Hubbell, *A Concordance to the Poems of Ralph Waldo Emerson* (New York: H. W. Wilson, 1932);

Eugene F. Irey, *A Concordance to Five Essays of Ralph Waldo Emerson* (New York: Garland, 1981);

Mary Alice Ihrig, *Emerson's Transcendental Vocabulary: A Concordance* (New York: Garland, 1982).

Biographies:

George Willis Cooke, *Ralph Waldo Emerson: His Life, Writings, and Philosophy* (Boston: Osgood, 1881);

Moncure Daniel Conway, *Emerson at Home and Abroad* (Boston: Osgood, 1882);

Alexander Ireland, *In Memoriam: Ralph Waldo Emerson* (London: Simkin, Marshall, 1882); revised as *Ralph Waldo Emerson: His Life, Genius, and Writings* (London: Simkin, Marshall, 1882);

James Eliot Cabot, *A Memoir of Ralph Waldo Emerson,* 2 volumes (Boston & New York: Houghton, Mifflin, 1889);

Denton J. Snider, *A Biography of Ralph Waldo Emerson* (St. Louis: William Harvey Miner, 1921);

Townsend Scudder, *The Lonely Wayfaring Man: Emerson and Some Englishmen* (New York: Oxford University Press, 1936);

Ralph L. Rusk, *The Life of Ralph Waldo Emerson* (New York: Scribners, 1949);

Henry F. Pommer, *Emerson's First Marriage* (Carbondale: Southern Illinois University Press, 1967);

Joel Porte, *Representative Man: Ralph Waldo Emerson in his Times* (New York: Oxford University Press, 1979);

Gay Wilson Allen, *Waldo Emerson* (New York: Viking, 1981);

John McAleer, *Ralph Waldo Emerson: Days of Encounter* (Boston: Little, Brown, 1984).

References:

Oliver Wendell Holmes, *Ralph Waldo Emerson* (Boston: Houghton, Mifflin, 1885);

Perry Miller, ed., *The Transcendentalists* (Cambridge, Mass.: Harvard University Press, 1950);

Edward Wagenknecht, *Ralph Waldo Emerson: Portrait of a Balanced Soul* (New York: Oxford University Press, 1974);

Stephen E. Whicher, *Freedom and Fate: An Inner Life of Ralph Waldo Emerson* (Philadelphia: University of Pennsylvania Press, 1953).

Papers:

The majority of Emerson's papers are deposited in the Ralph Waldo Emerson Memorial Association collection at the Houghton Library at Harvard University.

Timothy Flint

(11 July 1780-16 August 1840)

Elizabeth M. Fraas
Eastern Kentucky University

MAJOR POSITIONS HELD: Editor, *Western Magazine and Review*, renamed *Western Monthly Review* in 1827 (1827-1830); coeditor, *Knickerbocker: or New-York Monthly Magazine* (1833-1834).

BOOKS: *A Sermon, Preached May 11, 1808, at the Ordination of the Rev. Ebenezer Hubbard, Over the Second Church and Society in Newbury* (Newburyport, Mass.: From the press of E. W. Allen, 1808);

A Sermon, Delivered in Leominster, at the Commencement of the Year, Lord's Day, Jan. 1st, 1815 (Leicester, Mass.: Printed by Hori Brown, 1815);

An Oration, Delivered at Leominster, July 4, 1815, before the Washington Benevolent Society of Lancaster and Sterling and of Leominster and Fitchburg (Worcester, Mass.: Printed by William Manning, 1815);

Recollections of the Last Ten Years, Passed in Occasional Residences and Journeyings in the Valley of the Mississippi, From Pittsburg [sic] and the Missouri to the Gulf of Mexico, and from Florida to the Spanish Frontier: In A Series of Letters to the Rev. James Flint, of Salem, Massachusetts (Boston: Cummings, Hilliard, 1826);

Francis Berrian, or the Mexican Patriot, 2 volumes (Boston: Cummings, Hilliard, 1826);

A Condensed Geography and History of the Western States, or the Mississippi Valley, volume 1 (Cincinnati: Printed by Wm. & O. Farnsworth, published by E. H. Flint, 1828); volume 2 (Cincinnati: Printed by William M. Farnsworth, 1828); enlarged as *The History and Geography of the Mississippi Valley. To Which is Appended a Condensed Physical Geography of the Atlantic United States, and the Whole American Continent* (Cincinnati: E. H. Flint & L. R. Lincoln, 1832) and *The United States and the Other Divisions of the American Continent* (Cincinnati: E. H. Flint & L. R. Lincoln, 1832);

The Life and Adventures of Arthur Clenning, 2 volumes (Philadelphia: Towar & Hogan, 1828);

Flint's birthplace in North Reading, Massachusetts

George Mason, the Young Backwoodsman; or 'Don't Give Up the Ship.' A Story of the Mississippi (Boston: Hilliard, Gray, Little & Wilkins, 1829);

The Lost Child (Boston: Carter, Hendee, Putnam & Hunt, 1830);

The Shoshonee Valley: A Romance, 2 volumes (Cincinnati: E. H. Flint, 1830);

Lectures upon Natural History, Geology, Chemistry, the Application of Steam, and Interesting Discoveries in the Arts (Boston: Lilly, Wait, Colman & Holden/Cincinnati: E. H. Flint, 1833);

Indian Wars of the West; Containing Biographical Sketches of Those Pioneers Who Headed the Western Settlers in Repelling the Attacks of the Savages, Together with a View of the Character,

Manners, Monuments, and Antiquities of the Western Indians (Cincinnati: E. H. Flint, 1833);

Biographical Memoir of Daniel Boone, The First Settler in Kentucky, Interspersed with Incidents in the Early Annals of the Country (Cincinnati: N. & G. Guilford, 1833); republished as *The First White Man of the West or The Life and Exploits of Col. Dan'l Boone* (Cincinnati: George Conclin, 1847); republished as *The Life and Adventures of Daniel Boone . . . New Edition to which is Added an Account of Captain Estill's Defeat* (Cincinnati: Published by J. P. James, 1868);

The Bachelor Reclaimed, or Celibacy Vanquished. From the French (Philadelphia: Key & Biddle, 1834).

OTHER: "Preface" and "A Dissertation upon the True Taste in Church Music," in *The Columbian Harmonist: In Two Parts . . .* (Cincinnati: Printed by Looker, Palmer & Reynolds, published by Coleman & Phillips, 1816), pp. iii-v, vii-xiv;

"Oolemba in Cincinnati," in *The Western Souvenir, a Christmas and New Year's Gift for 1829*, edited by James Hall (Cincinnati: Published by N. & G. Guilford, 1828), pp. 68-101;

"The Indian Fighter," in *The Token; a Christmas and New Year's Present*, edited by S. G. Goodrich (Boston: Carter & Hendee, 1830);

The Personal Narrative of James O. Pattie, of Kentucky, During an Expedition from St. Louis, through the Vast Regions between That Place and the Pacific Ocean, edited by Flint (Cincinnati: Printed & published by John H. Wood, 1831);

The Art of Being Happy: From the French of Droz, 'Sur l'Art d'être Heureux;' in a Series of Letters from a Father to His Children: With Observations and Comments, translated by Flint (Boston: Carter & Hendee, 1832);

"Nimrod Buckskin, Esq.," in *The Token; a Christmas and New Year's Present*, edited by Goodrich (Boston: Gray & Bowen, 1832);

"The Blind Grandfather," in *The Token and Atlantic Souvenir. A Christmas and New Year's Present*, edited by Goodrich (Boston: Gray & Bowen, 1832).

Timothy Flint, a Harvard graduate and man of the cloth, was one of several early American writers to describe and interpret western lands, legends, and mores to readers in the East and across the Atlantic Ocean. He turned to writing relatively late in life, after a dissatisfactory stint in the ministry, but his first full-length book, *Recollections of the Last Ten Years* (1826), was followed by several romantic adventure novels, western histories, and a popular biography of Daniel Boone. During his most prolific writing period he also founded and edited the *Western Monthly*, a literary magazine in Cincinnati, from 1827 to 1830. He served as coeditor of the *Knickerbocker: or New-York Monthly Magazine* for several months in 1833-1834 until chronic ill health forced him to resign.

In ill health most of his life and a failure at his first career in the ministry, Flint's intellectual and imaginative talents were ignited by the flow of immigrants to the West and the new mix of nationalities, communities, and characters it inspired. To the extent that his works were read by others as a guide to the land across the Allegheny Mountains, he did achieve some measure of the goal he articulated in his preface to *The History and Geography of the Mississippi Valley* (1832). He wanted "something towards bringing about an acquaintance of good feelings between the elder sister, whose fair domain is the east country, the fresh breeze and the shores of the sea and her younger sister whose dotal portion is the western woods, and the fertile shores of the western streams."

At his worst, Flint was careless with facts: Daniel Boone's birthplace is given as Pennsylvania in one book, Maryland in another. His fiction is often morally simplistic and sentimental. At his best, Flint was an astute observer of the changes in American manners in the 1820s, not only in the West. On a visit back East, for example, he commented on how the growth of industry in the East had changed the social structure of the family: he feared that the rise of the working girl employed in factories would result in a loss of moral influence and maternal control in the American home.

Flint was born on 11 July 1780 in the North Reading, Massachusetts, homestead built by his great-grandfather around 1700. The fifth child of William and Martha Kimball Flint, he was educated at North Reading Grammar School and Phillips Academy in Andover before he entered Harvard College in 1796. Upon graduation in 1800 he studied theology and was invited to be pastor of the Congregational church in the parish of Lunenburg. He held this position, despite occasional disagreements with members of the congregation, until his resignation in June 1814.

Three of his sermons were published in pamphlet form the following year. His pastorate brought him little personal satisfaction, but missionary work and a quest for a better climate to nurse his chronic ill health led him eventually to his new career in the West.

Flint married Abigail Hubbard, a relative of wealthy Salem shipping merchant Joseph Peabody, on 12 July 1802. The couple had five children, most of whose birth dates are unknown. The eldest son, Micah, was baptized in 1803 and became a lawyer and a minor poet. His work appeared occasionally in both the *Western Monthly Review* and *Knickerbocker*. Ebenezer Hubbard, born 19 January 1808, and James, the youngest son, became well-to-do planters, and the Harvard-educated James was also a noted lawyer. Emeline, the elder daughter, helped her father with translations from French and Spanish and married a general whose last name was Thomas. The youngest of the five children, Martha Elizabeth, was born in 1828.

As a missionary for the Massachusetts Society for Promoting Christian Knowledge, Flint preached in newly settled areas of New Hampshire, western Massachusetts, and western New York. In 1815 he was commissioned by the Missionary Society of Connecticut to preach in Ohio and Kentucky and later Missouri. These assignments furnished him with the opportunity to gather the material that he later incorporated into his writing. He found clerical life in the West even less financially and spiritually rewarding than in the East and resigned from missionary work in 1818. After a desperate and unsuccessful effort to make a living on a farm near St. Charles, Missouri, and equally unsuccessful ventures in merchandising and real estate, he accepted a position teaching and supervising a college in Alexandria, Louisiana, from 1823 to 1825.

Alexandria offered Flint and his family some stability, but Flint's health continued to worsen. In 1825 he left his family and set off to his native New England believing he was to die. Instead he was nursed to health by his cousin the Reverend James Flint and encouraged to write his first book.

Recollections of the Last Ten Years is perhaps the most interesting of Flint's works to the modern reader because of its fresh description of emerging society in the western states and territories. An autobiographical account of his western experiences, the book is written ten years after Flint and his family emigrated down the Ohio River and is organized as a series of letters to his cousin in Salem, Massachusetts; the account of the difficulties they encounter and the places they visit is detailed and firsthand. With some regrets and homesickness for the order and neatness of his native New England, he gradually finds more to admire than condemn in the westerner, putting to rest the "horror inspired by the term backwoodsman" on the East Coast.

Much of Flint's experience during his travels in the Mississippi Valley from 1816 to 1826, chronicled in *Recollections of the Last Ten Years*, became the basis for the works to follow. A side trip into Spanish-territory Texas with his friend Judge Henry Bullard provides the background for *Francis Berrian, or the Mexican Patriot* (1826). The American hero of the two-volume novel goes to Mexico during the Mexican Revolution and encounters Comanches, while also experiencing resentment from the Spanish, romance, and eventually success on the battlefield. While the writing is stiff and melodramatic by today's standards, *Francis Berrian* is noted as the first English-language novel to be set in the American Southwest. Flint's first two books received appreciation from eastern writers, and Flint was highly praised by the English author Frances Trollope, who lauded the "vigor and freshness in his writing that is exactly in accordance with what one looks for in the literature of a new country."

With his literary career launched and inspired by his success, Flint threw his energies into a different type of missionary work–the encouragement and promotion of western writers and literature. By 1827 Flint had moved to Cincinnati and established the *Western Magazine and Review*, which was renamed the *Western Monthly Review* after two issues. With the help of his sons Micah, who contributed poetry, and Ebenezer, who published the magazine and several of his father's books, Flint spent the next three years writing prolifically. His daughter Emeline helped with French and Spanish translations.

The motto of the *Western Monthly Review* was "Benedicere Haud Maledicere"–"To bless rather than to curse"–an apparent rejection of "the curl of the lip and crook of the nose of the Atlantic reviewer" contemplating the idea of a work written west of the Allegheny Mountains. In the first issue Flint promised poetry and works of original and "domestic fabric." Many of the stories and articles, however, were excerpted from Flint's previously published work. Some of the stories which

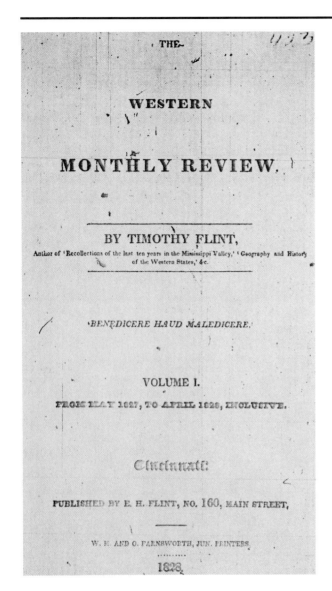

THE

WESTERN

MONTHLY REVIEW.

BY TIMOTHY FLINT,

Author of 'Recollections of the last ten years in the Mississippi Valley,' 'Geography and History of the Western States,' &c.

'BENEDICERE HAUD MALEDICERE.'

VOLUME I.

FROM MAY 1827, TO APRIL 1828, INCLUSIVE.

Cincinnati

PUBLISHED BY E. H. FLINT, NO. 160, MAIN STREET,

W. M. AND O. FARNSWORTH, JUN. PRINTERS.

1828.

ADVERTISEMENT

TO THE FIRST VOLUME OF THE

WESTERN MONTHLY REVIEW.

In making the collections of matter in these numbers, we find them insensibly to have swollen under our hands, to the size of a large volume. They are too painfully identified with our own wear and tear of brain, not to inspire the belief, that they will be bound and preserved. We can easily enjoy in anticipation, the eagerness, with which the future historian will repair to them, as a synopsis, of most of what has been said, and written, in the Western Country, touching its own natural, moral, and civil history. It would be useless for any one, to imagine the difficulties we have had to encounter, unless he were placed precisely in our situation. It seems to be a common opinion, that it is the easiest of all things to edit a Public Journal, and that a Hercules of this sort, may be made out of any kind of timber. Let those who so deem make the experiment. You wish the reputation of being learned and grave. Some twenty of your readers award you that honor; and the rest fall asleep over your writings. On the other hand, you wish to be facetious and free and familiar, and you insensibly slide into coarseness and vulgarity. On the one side, you wish to preserve the dignity of literary and philosophic discussion inviolate; and the million, who are used only to the foul feeding of politics, as soon as they come to a fair estimate of your writing, never cut your pages, nor subscribe for you, but once. To steer between Scylla and Charybdis, to clear the due medium between these extremes, is an enterprise, that has more perils, 'than war or women have,' and requires a tact and delicacy of judgment, and a calmness of temper, and a steadiness of self-possession, which fall to the lot of but a very few.

Every one knows the utter impossibility of pleasing all. Some pronounce your serious articles Jeremiads, and your gay ones buffoonry. The very subject, which moved the deepest fountains of feeling within yourself, perhaps, discourses grating jargon in the minds of a majority of your readers. Each one has his notions, and most frequently immoveable ones, touching education, politics, philosophy and religion, and all points of opinion and taste. Proteus himself could not have assumed shapes enough to satisfy all.

When this Journal was commenced, our course was mentally marked out, as well as our resolution, that nothing should swerve us from it, but the demonstration of experience, that it would not be well received by the discriminating and intelligent among the public. Self-respect has withheld us from blazoning notices and testimonials, as flattering, as we could desire, from people, in whose taste and judgment we had confidence, before they praised us; and whose discriminating praise was unbought, unsolicited; and bestowed, when it was known, that our views of propriety would prevent us from availing ourselves of the common editorial balance of paying back in praise again. We have, more than once, felt a disposition to use our privilege of eulogy, and have been withheld by having received such a notice, as would cause, what we intended to have said, to have the aspect of unworthy attempts to repay in kind. In the same spirit, we have, except in a single instance, forborne to notice strictures. Kind and well intentioned criticism, every man, who possesses a particle of the real spirit of a scholar and a gentleman, will always receive with courtesy and an answering spirit. Our critics, for the most part, have no higher object in view in their microscopic efforts at fault finding, than to create a reverend and proper estimate of their own learning, taste and acute-

Title page and advertisement for the first volume of Flint's morally instructive showcase of western literature

ADVERTISEMENT.

iv

ness. Whenever we notice strictures upon us, we intend it as clear evidence of our respect for those, who have passed them. We leave others to the course of their own judgment. For us, we have seen nothing to incline us to swerve from a measured silence.

The public has judged, and correctly, that most of the articles in this work, have been from one hand. A few contributors are now pledged for the coming year, who would do no discredit to the first journals in this, or in any country. We feel sure of our mark, so far as our judgment can reach, that mere ordinary and common place writing, shall find no admittance into our pages. To exclude whole masses of such writing has been one of our most painful duties, during the past year. Those, who have taken the trouble to read our pages, will discover, that our plan has been original. We have seen no model for such an arrangement and distribution, as we have made of our matter. Some have found fault with us for not naming the Journal, ' Miscellany,' and others, ' Magazine.' What a trifling ground of objection is a mere name! Our plan was obvious, and would be the same, call the work by what name we might.

The poetry, except two articles, has been altogether original, and of domestic fabric. That the public begins rightly to estimate the powers of the chief contributor in this department, we have the most grateful and consoling testimonials. Every one remarks, and most truly, that editors ought to have good steel wire, instead of nerves. But we do not see the cruel necessity, that an editor should not have a heart. The 'Camp Meeting,' we are told, has found its way into the most extensively circulated journal in the United States, a religious paper, edited with a great deal of talent, which we used formerly to read, and with which we should be pleased to exchange. We allude to the 'Methodist Magazine of New York.' Whatever be the general dearth of poetical feeling, and however capricious the standard of poetical excellence, it can not but be, that some kindred eye will rest upon the poetry in this volume, and that a congenial string will be harped in some heart. In the structure of poetry, the public seems to demand nothing more than pretty words, put into ingenious rhythm, with a due regard to euphony. In conformity to that taste, we have inserted some poetry, which we considered made up rather with reference to words, than pictures and thoughts. But we have flattered ourselves, that the greater amount has had something of the ancient simplicity and force, to recommend it to those, who had a taste for that, and has had an aim, to call the mind ' from sound to things, from fancy to the heart.' We have an humble hope, that, if the author of these verses survive the chances of the distant and deadly climate, in which his lot is cast, and is not, in the hackneying cares of life, deprived of the visitings of the muse, the time will come, when no man, that has any living and permanent name, as a writer and a poet, will be forward to proclaim, that he did not discover the powers of the writer; or after investigation, viewed them with disapprobation.

Most of the tales, moral essays, and articles of natural history, have been copied into the papers; and in many instances have been seen wandering over the country, without ' a local habitation and a name.' As regards the Reviews, our narrow limits restricted us to brief notices and abstracts. We have considered the latter the most useful, as it is certainly the most difficult and laborious part of our function. Let those, who doubt us, put themselves into the editorial chair, and abstract the contents of five hundred pages, and condense them into ten. We have in this way gone over forty volumes, most of which were to all, but some twenty readers, as completely sealed books, as though they had never been. Yet they are books that every western man, who lays any reasonable claims to be estimated a reading man, ought to consider it a discredit not to know. Our readers have been brought acquainted with the names and general scope of these works, and know where to repair, if they wish for further information. These books could not have been purchased, except at the expense of an hundred dollars. The reader can not but see, that in condensing the contents of these volumes, we have encountered not only wearing labor, but a very considerable degree of expense.

We hope, we shall be sustained, in supposing, that our researches, touching the natural, moral, civil and geographical history of the Mississippi valley, have been of public utility. If any person should dispute this point, the worst

ADVERTISEMENT.

infliction, which we wish him, for his heterodoxy and hard judgment of us, is, that he may be qualified the better to try us in the case, by being obliged to read the twentieth part of what has passed under our eye upon the subject. We could not wish our worst enemy, to purchase our personal observations at the expense of time, money, and disease, which it has cost us. We console ourselves with the confident persuasion, that it will one day be allowed us, that we have done something towards illustrating the country, over which we have so extensively travelled. The time is at hand, when the political and moral claims of this great region, will be as well understood, and as promptly admitted, as its physical extent and resources are at present.

The religious views, that we have incidentally taken, we are perfectly aware, will be too stern for some, and too liberal for others. This is a point upon which we felt, there was no ground for compromise, seeing that we had a tribunal of conscience, to which to be responsible as well as our readers. We exult in the best of all liberty, which our country possesses, *Religious Liberty*. We deprecate, above and beyond all other tyranny, that which attempts to establish its despotism over conscience. We have our own views of religion. They can never be changed, except upon conviction. But we have felt no call to commit them before the public. Temperate and well written discussions of this subject have been acceptable to us from the most opposite quarters of opinion. Upon no sentiment of religion have we expressed an opinion of praise, as coincident with our own, except that, which inculcated *peace on earth and good will to men*; and urged the strain with moderation, dignity, and in a tone of christian feeling. We are prepared to allow the reader to put his own construction upon this course. We have chosen it deliberately, and we mean to pursue it independently.

We are not apprehensive of the charge of arrogance, when we say, that the Western public needs a Journal of this kind—that the one portion of the citizens of this great valley, may not be ignorant what is written of its natural and civil and literary history in another. Our task is to buy, condense, and serve up this information, in a manner the most brief, unexpensive and attractive, that may be to our readers. From the past they must argue to the future; except, that, as we shall be more disengaged, we hope to produce another volume, more worthy of their patronage. We are sufficiently instructed, that many, who expected to find in this work the character only of a newspaper, will be disappointed; and that to many others, the kind of writing in this Journal has been, of all others, the most uninteresting. Those, who now continue their patronage, will act understandingly, and will know, what kind of fare they may expect.

In regard to the administration of praise and blame in this volume, we can only say, that there is a difference in books, which exists independent of us, and which we can not help. Every respectable man knows, that he has a higher purpose in life, than to administer to the vanity of another, or expect another to devote his powers to soothing his. Since we can not endow minds with the same powers, it is folly to speak of all mental efforts in the same terms of maudlin praise, as disgraceful to the receiver, as the giver. Let us learn not to distribute, nor expect flattering words; but to be ' just and fear not.'

THE

WESTERN

MAGAZINE AND REVIEW.

MAY, 1827.

EDITOR'S ADDRESS.

In presenting our readers with the first number of our proposed Journal, they will expect of us our inaugural speech, for in our country no one enters on the duties of a new office without one. We shall not follow the common example of reviewers by making our portico larger than our house, but shall come to our point at once;—Where is the use of a review at Cincinnati? At the census of 1830 the Mississippi valley will contain more than four millions of inhabitants. We are physically, and from our peculiar modes of existence, a scribbling and forth-putting people. Little, as they have dreamed of the fact in the Atlantic country, we have our thousand orators and poets. We have not a solitary journal expressly constituted to be the echo of public literary opinion. The teeming mind wastes its sweetness on the desert air. The exhausted author, after the pains of parturition, is obliged to drop the dear offspring of his brain into the immense abyss of a public, that has little charity for any bantlings, that do not bring money in their hands, and

'Where it is gone and how it fares,
Nobody knows and nobody cares.'

The ornament, the grace, the humanity and even the lesser morals of society, as has been said a thousand times, essentially depend upon the cultivation of literature. A community without it is like a rude family without politeness, amenity and gentleness. It may be a family of wealth and power, and courted, as such, by

Vol. I.—No. 1.   2

Statement of purpose for the first issue of Flint's magazine

appeared in the magazine, such as "The Lost Child" and "The Shoshonee Valley," were later expanded and separately published in book form. Flint's magazine generally favored and encouraged western writers as long as the literary piece was morally instructive. He defended the novel and short story against attacks by some orthodox religious critics of the day, saying that readers could be made virtuous "through the medium of imagination, love, tenderness, . . . and appeals to feelings." In the *Western Monthly Review* Flint took stands against slavery, dueling, and demagogic politicians and wrote in favor of temperance.

Flint's *A Condensed Geography and History of the Western States, or the Mississippi Valley* appeared in 1828 and was an exhaustive effort to collect in one work the many observations and facts about the western states which had been recorded in books, pamphlets, or journals. The author cited as references thirty or more works he scrutinized for the publication. Later expanded as *The His-*

tory and Geography of the Mississippi Valley (1832) and *The United States and the Other Divisions of the American Continent* (1832), the work became a popular reference for nineteenth-century readers seeking knowledge about the West. Its contents are an encyclopedic amalgam of historical tales, meteorological tables, population data, and descriptions of the flora and fauna of the western states from Ohio to the Oregon Territory.

Two adventure novels followed. *The Life and Adventures of Arthur Clenning* (1828) is a Robinson Crusoe-like story of a New York farmer's son who goes to sea, is stranded on a South Seas island, and eventually finds fame and fortune in Illinois. Another tale, *George Mason, the Young Backwoodsman; or 'Don't Give Up the Ship.' A Story of the Mississippi* (1829), parallels Flint's own experiences; the title character is a minister with five children who immigrates in 1816 to a settlement on the lower Mississippi River.

Throughout his three-year editorship of the *Western Monthly Review*, Flint was forced to remind readers to pay their subscription bills, threatening at one point to print the names of delinquent subscribers. Although the magazine had at its peak a circulation of a thousand copies, according to Flint's estimation, he was forced to discontinue publication because he could not afford the printing bill. Following the last issue in June 1830, Flint remained in Cincinnati completing several books.

In 1831 *The Personal Narrative of James O. Pattie, of Kentucky* appeared, with Flint as editor. An ostensibly true narrative of a young man's adventure in California and Mexico, the book was criticized for errors in its geographical descriptions and for failing to identify Pattie's companions on the adventure who could corroborate parts of the story. Flint's second attempt at pioneer biography was more favorably received, and it is the work for which he is best known today.

The *Biographical Memoir of Daniel Boone, The First Settler in Kentucky* (1833) was reprinted in several editions and reappeared throughout the 1800s under different titles. In his *Recollections of the Last Ten Years* Flint had noted that Daniel Boone, "this Achilles of the West, wants a Homer, worthily to celebrate his exploits." While living in St. Charles, Missouri, Flint was aware that Boone lived on the nearby farm of his son Nathan Boone, but apparently the author had no personal encounter with the famous pioneer. In the preface to the book Flint laments the lack of primary data from the pioneer days and notes that he relied on a balance between "doubtful authorities" and a "rigorous scrutiny of newspapers and pamphlets, whose yellow and dingy pages gave out a cloud of dust at every movement, and the equally rigid examination of clean modern books and periodicals." The result does not provide direct insight into Boone's character but instead chronicles in heroic prose Boone's role in the exploration and early settlement of Kentucky.

Flint concluded his Cincinnati years with the publication of the ambitious *Lectures upon Natural History, Geology, Chemistry, the Application of Steam, and Interesting Discoveries in the Arts* (1833), published both in Boston and Cincinnati. The topics range from steam engines to vaccinations, from definitions of "true wisdom" to the purification of the air by volcanoes. The book was poorly received by critics, and James Hall, who had included a Flint piece in his annual anthology, suggested that Flint keep "away from the natural sciences and other matters of which he is ignorant" (*Western Monthly*, August 1833).

Criticism of the *Lectures* rankled Flint throughout his short tenure as editor of the *Knickerbocker: or New-York Monthly Magazine*. This literary magazine, which grew tremendously under the editorship of Flint's successor, Lewis Gaylord Clark, was in its shaky fledgling year in 1833. After the first editor, Charles Fenno Hoffman, left in disagreement with the publishers Peabody and Company, Flint, who had contributed several articles to the magazine earlier in the year, was recruited by acting editor Samuel Daly Langtree to salvage the magazine's fortunes. In an early article he had decried the lack of support for American literature by the national government ("Literature, science, what are they at Washington, more than they would have been in the day of Attila?") and the nation's literary dependence upon Great Britain.

Assuming the editorship in the October 1833 issue, Flint stated his goals: to foster genuine American literature and to encourage latent talent and good taste. As later revealed in an April 1834 editor's column by Langtree, the October 1833 number was the only issue edited by Flint alone. His precarious health prevented his residing in New York for the remainder of the time he was listed as the editor of the *Knickerbocker*—until after the January 1834 issue. During these months he and Langtree acted as coeditors.

The early issues of the magazine showed considerable interest in the Old World. Numerous translations appeared, and most of the original

Monument to Flint at Harmony Grove Cemetery, Salem, Massachusetts

prose in the first six-month volume was run without bylines, though some of the poetry, including contributions from William Cullen Bryant and Lydia Sigourney, was signed.

Articles with bylines became more common in the second volume, which included Flint's own "Phrenology," in which he attacked an earlier piece on this topic in *North American Review* as dogmatic and bigoted. Other Flint contributions to this volume were a two-installment personal experience story with the names changed, "The First Steamboat on the LaPlata; or, 'The Monogamist'"; an essay on "The Influence of Education on the Formation of Character"; and of greatest interest, "Obstacles to American Literature." In the latter Flint wrote:

With more writers than any other people, in proportion to our numbers, with innumerable aspirants after the fame of literature, with nearly two thousand editors, with poets to fill the corners of our fifteen hundred periodicals, with American books to endanger the bookseller's shelves with their weight, why have we not a national literature?

His answers to this question included lack of government support, absence of a central literary metropolis, continuing literary dependence on Great Britain, overblown public interest in money-making and politics, and the puffery of overly generous reviewing. Flint's last article in the *Knickerbocker* during his period as coeditor was "A Chapter in the Life of a Bachelor, A South American Story," in January 1834. He had also used the literary review to respond caustically to his critics. In his introductory announcement to readers of the *Knickerbocker,* he had expressed regret that "the career editorial should be a life-militant," but he was not reluctant to return a cutting blow to those critics who had attacked his works. The magazine's Cambridge rival, the *American Monthly Review,* was labeled "a work as malingering as it is dull and lumbering." Flint also used his new position as editor to even the score with Cincinnati's Judge James Hall, who had run a satire on Flint's "Lectures Upon Natural History" in volume 1 of his *Western Monthly Magazine.*

Of greater interest was Flint's relationship at this time to Frances Trollope, who had spent a year and a half in Cincinnati prior to publishing her work *Domestic Manners of the Americans* (1832). Flint appears to have been one of the few Americans the ascerbic Trollope liked; she wrote of him:

The most agreeable acquaintance I made in Cincinnati, and indeed one of the most talented men I ever met, was Mr. Flint, the author of several extremely clever volumes, and the editor of the *Western Monthly Review.* His conversational powers are of the highest order: he is the only person I remember to have known with first-rate powers of satire, and even of sarcasm, whose kindness of nature and of manner remained perfectly uninjured. In some of his critical notices, there is a strength and keenness second to nothing of the kind I have ever read. He is a warm patriot, and so true-hearted an American that we could not always be of the same opinion on all the subjects we discussed; but whether it were the force and brilliance of his language, his genuine and manly sincerity of feeling, or his bland and gentleman-like manner that beguiled me, I know not, but certainly he is the only American I ever listened to, whose unqualified praise of his country did not appear to me somewhat over-strained and ridiculous.

In spite of these compliments, Flint devoted space in the *Knickerbocker* to far less generous criticism of her book and of her as a person. He was especially critical of her appearance, choice of society while in Cincinnati, and business acumen.

A combination of ill health and critical abuse led to Flint's resignation from the *Knickerbocker* in January 1834. He returned to Alexandria, Louisiana, to live near his son and daughter but made annual trips to the East. His last published work was a series of letters on the obstacles to American literature which appeared in the *London Athenaeum* (1835). Flint left the West for the final time in 1840 to visit relatives in New England. A steamboat accident on the Mississippi, which exposed him to the cold and wet, contributed to his death on 16 August 1840. He was buried in Salem, Massachusetts.

Biography:
John Ervin Kirkpatrick, *Timothy Flint: Pioneer, Missionary, Author, Editor* (Cleveland: Arthur H. Clark, 1911).

References:
James K. Folson, *Timothy Flint* (New York: Twayne, 1965);

W. H. Venable, *Beginnings of Literary Culture in the Ohio Valley* (Cincinnati: Robert Clarke, 1891), pp. 323-360.

Papers:
Limited collections of Flint papers are held by the American Antiquarian Society and Boston Public Library.

Benjamin Franklin

(17 January 1706-17 April 1790)

Alf Pratte
Brigham Young University

See also the Franklin entries in *DLB 24: American Colonial Writers, 1606-1734* and *DLB 43: American Newspaper Journalists, 1690-1872.*

MAJOR POSITIONS HELD: Typesetter, contributor, nominal editor, *New-England Courant* (1721-1723); publisher and editor, *Pennsylvania Gazette* (1729-1748); publisher, *Philadelphische Zeitung* (1729); publisher and editor, *General Magazine, and Historical Chronicle* (1741); copublisher, *Pennsylvania Gazette* (1748-1766).

SELECTED BOOKS: *A Dissertation on Liberty and Necessity, Pleasure and Pain* . . . (London, 1725);

A Modest Enquiry into the Nature and Necessity of Paper-Currency . . . (Printed & sold at the New Printing-Office, 1729);

Poor Richard, 1733. An Almanack . . . , as Richard Saunders, Philom (Philadelphia: Printed & sold by B. Franklin, 1732);

Poor Richard, 1734. An Almanack . . . , as Saunders (Philadelphia: Printed & sold by B. Franklin, 1733);

Poor Richard, 1735. An Almanack . . . , as Saunders (Philadelphia: Printed & sold by B. Franklin, 1734);

Some Observations on the Proceedings against The Rev. Mr. Hemphill; with a Vindication of His Sermons (Philadelphia: Printed & sold by B. Franklin, 1735);

A Letter to a Friend in the Country, Containing the Substance of a Sermon Preach'd at Philadelphia, in the Congregation of The Rev. Mr. Hemphill, Concerning the Terms of Christian and Ministerial Communion (Philadelphia: Printed & sold by B. Franklin, 1735);

A Defense Of the Rev. Mr. Hemphill's Observations: or, An Answer to the Vindication of the Reverend Commission . . . (Philadelphia: Printed & sold by B. Franklin, 1735);

Poor Richard, 1736. An Almanack . . . , as Saunders (Philadelphia: Printed & sold by B. Franklin, 1735);

Benjamin Franklin (portrait by Philippe-Amédée Vanloo; courtesy of the American Philosophical Society)

Poor Richard, 1737. An Almanack . . . , as Saunders (Philadelphia: Printed & sold by B. Franklin, 1736);

Poor Richard, 1738. An Almanack . . . , as Saunders (Philadelphia: Printed & sold by B. Franklin, 1737);

Poor Richard, 1739. An Almanack . . . , as Saunders (Philadelphia: Printed & sold by B. Franklin, 1738);

Poor Richard, 1740. An Almanack . . . , as Saunders (Philadelphia: Printed & sold by B. Franklin, 1739);

Elegy Franklin wrote for his sister, circa 1720
(American Art Association/Anderson Galleries Inc., Catalogue #4107, 2-3 May 1934)

Poor Richard, 1741. An Almanack . . ., as Saunders (Philadelphia: Printed & sold by B. Franklin, 1740);

Poor Richard, 1742. An Almanack . . ., as Saunders (Philadelphia: Printed & sold by B. Franklin, 1741);

Poor Richard, 1743. An Almanack . . ., as Saunders (Philadelphia: Printed & sold by B. Franklin, 1742);

Poor Richard, 1744. An Almanack . . ., as Saunders (Philadelphia: Printed & sold by B. Franklin & Jonas Greene, 1743);

An Account Of the New Invented Pennsylvanian Fireplaces . . . (Philadelphia: Printed & sold by B. Franklin, 1744);

Poor Richard, 1745. An Almanack . . ., as Saunders (Philadelphia: Printed & sold by B. Franklin, 1744);

Poor Richard, 1746. An Almanack . . ., as Saunders (Philadelphia: Printed & sold by B. Franklin, 1745);

Poor Richard, 1747. An Almanack . . ., as Saunders (Philadelphia: Printed & sold by B. Franklin, 1746);

Plain Truth: or, Serious Considerations On the Present State of the City of Philadelphia, and Province of Pennsylvania, as A Tradesman of Philadelphia (Philadelphia: Printed by B. Franklin, 1747);

Poor Richard improved: Being an Almanack and Ephemeris . . . for the Bissextile Year, 1748 . . ., as Saunders (Philadelphia: Printed & sold by B. Franklin, 1747);

Poor Richard improved: Being an Almanack and Ephemeris . . . For the Year of Our Lord 1749 . . ., as Saunders (Philadelphia: Printed & sold by B. Franklin & D. Hall, 1748);

Proposals Relating to the Education of Youth in Pensilvania (Philadelphia, 1749);

Poor Richard improved: Being an Almanack and Ephemeris . . . For the Year of Our Lord 1750 . . ., as Saunders (Philadelphia: Printed & sold by B. Franklin & D. Hall, 1749);

Poor Richard improved: Being an Almanack and Ephemeris . . . For the Year of Our Lord 1751 . . ., as Saunders (Philadelphia: Printed & sold by B. Franklin & D. Hall, 1750);

Experiments and Observations on Electricity, made at Philadelphia in America . . ., part 1 (London: Printed & sold by E. Cave, 1751);

Poor Richard improved: Being an Almanack & Ephemeris . . . For the Year of Our Lord 1752, as Saunders (Philadelphia: Printed & sold by B. Franklin & D. Hall, 1751);

Poor Richard improved: Being an Almanack and Ephemeris . . . For the Year of Our Lord 1753 . . ., as Saunders (Philadelphia: Printed & sold by B. Franklin & D. Hall, 1752);

Supplemental Experiments and Observations on Electricity, Part II. Made at Philadelphia in America . . . (London: Printed & sold by E. Cave, 1753);

Poor Richard improved: Being an Almanack and Ephemeris . . . For the Year of Our Lord 1754, as Saunders (Philadelphia: Printed & sold by B. Franklin & D. Hall, 1753);

Some Account of the Pennsylvania Hospital . . . (Philadelphia: Printed by B. Franklin & D. Hall, 1754);

New Experiments and Observations on Electricity. Made at Philadelphia in America . . ., part 3 (London: Printed & sold by D. Henry & R. Cave, 1754);

Poor Richard improved: Being an Almanack and Ephemeris . . . For the Year of Our Lord 1755 . . ., as Saunders (Philadelphia: Printed & sold by B. Franklin & D. Hall, 1754);

Poor Richard improved: Being an Almanack and Ephemeris . . . For the Year of Our Lord 1756 . . ., as Saunders (Philadelphia: Printed & sold by B. Franklin & D. Hall, 1755);

Poor Richard improved: Being an Almanack and Ephemeris . . . For the Year of Our Lord 1757 . . ., as Saunders (Philadelphia: Printed & sold by B. Franklin & D. Hall, 1756);

Poor Richard Improved: Being an Almanack and Ephemeris . . . For the Year of Our Lord 1758 . . ., as Saunders (Philadelphia: Printed & sold by B. Franklin & D. Hall, 1757);

Father Abraham's Speech To a great Number of People, at a Vendue of Merchant-Goods; Introduced to The Publick By Poor Richard (A famous Pennsylvanian Conjuror and Almanack-Maker) . . . (Boston: Printed & sold by Benjamin Mecom, 1758); republished as *The Way to Wealth, as clearly shewn in the Preface of An Old Pennsylvania Almanack, Intituled, Poor Richard Improved* (London: Printed & sold by H. Lewis, 1774; London: Printed & sold by R. Snagg, 1774);

The Interest of Great Britain Considered, With Regard to her Colonies, And the Acquisitions of Canada and Guadaloupe. To which are added, Observations concerning the Increase of Mankind, Peopling of Countries, &c. (London: Printed for T. Becket, 1760; Boston: Printed by B. Mecom, 1760);

A Narrative of the Late Massacres, in Lancaster County, of a Number of Indians, Friends of this Province, By Persons Unknown . . . (Philadelphia: Printed by Anthony Armbruster, 1764);

Cool Thoughts on the Present Situation of Our Public Affairs . . . (Philadelphia: Printed by W. Dunlap, 1764);

Remarks on a late Protest Against the Appointment of Mr. Franklin an Agent for this Province (Philadelphia: Printed by B. Franklin & D. Hall, 1764);

Oeuvres de M. Franklin, 2 volumes, edited by Jacques Barbeu-Duborg (Paris: Quillau, 1773);

Political, Miscellaneous, and Philosophical Pieces . . ., edited by Benjamin Vaughan (London: Printed for J. Johnson, 1779);

Watercolor of London's Little Britain section, circa 1725, where Franklin lived while working at the printing trade (courtesy of the British Museum)

Observations on the Causes and Cure of Smokey Chimneys (London: Printed for J. Debrett, 1787);

Philosophical and Miscellaneous Papers. Lately written by B. Franklin, LL.D., edited by Edward Bancroft (London: Printed for C. Dilly, 1787);

Rules for Reducing a Great Empire to a Small One (London: Printed for James Ridgway, 1793);

Autobiography of Benjamin Franklin, first complete edition, edited by John Bigelow (Philadelphia: Lippincott/London: Trübner, 1868);

Benjamin Franklin Experiments. A New Edition of Franklin's Experiments and Observations on Electricity, edited by I. Bernard Cohen (Cambridge, Mass.: Harvard University Press, 1941);

Benjamin Franklin's Autobiographical Writings, edited by Carl Van Doren (New York: Viking, 1945);

Benjamin Franklin's Memoirs. Parallel Text Edition, edited by Max Farrand (Berkeley: University of California Press, 1949);

Benjamin Franklin: His Contribution to the American Tradition, edited by Cohen (New York: Bobbs-Merrill, 1953);

Franklin's Wit and Folly: The Bagatelles, edited by Richard E. Amacher (New Brunswick: Rutgers University Press, 1953);

The Autobiography of Benjamin Franklin, edited by Leonard W. Labaree, Ralph L. Ketcham, and others (New Haven: Yale University Press, 1964);

First issue of Franklin's magazine

The Political Thought of Benjamin Franklin, edited by Ketcham (Indianapolis: Bobbs-Merrill, 1965);

The Bagatelles from Passy by Benjamin Franklin, Text and Facsimile (New York: Eakins Press, 1967);

The Autobiography of Benjamin Franklin, A Genetic Text, edited by J. A. Leo Lemay and P. M. Zall (Knoxville: University of Tennessee Press, 1981).

Collections: *The Works of Dr. Benjamin Franklin,* 6 volumes, edited by William Duane (Philadelphia: Duane, 1808-1818);

Memoirs of the Life and Writings of Benjamin Franklin, 3 volumes, edited by William Tem-

ple Franklin (London: Henry Colburn, 1817-1818);

The Works of Benjamin Franklin, 10 volumes, edited by Jared Sparks (Boston: Hilliard, Gray, 1836-1840);

The Writings of Benjamin Franklin, 10 volumes, edited by Albert Henry Smyth (New York: Macmillan, 1905-1907);

The Papers of Benjamin Franklin, edited by Leonard W. Labaree, Whitfield J. Bell, Jr., and others, 23 volumes to date (New Haven: Yale University Press, 1959-);

The Complete Poor Richard Almanacs published by Benjamin Franklin, edited by Bell (Barre, Mass.: Imprint Society, 1970).

Rarely remembered as a magazinist, Benjamin Franklin throughout his life paid tribute to the print shop which served first as his schoolroom and later as a pulpit for his ideas on government and the media. Although Franklin's direct contributions to the evolution of the magazine industry in America are not extensive, he exercised a stimulating influence upon the development of the field. In fact, it was Franklin's idea that generated the first American magazines in Philadelphia in February 1741. By 1749 he had moved on to the other interests–science, government, politics, and international affairs–for which he is better known today.

A remarkably versatile man, described by D. H. Lawrence as the first "down-right" American, Franklin was born to Josiah Franklin and his second wife, Abiah Folger, in Boston on 17 January 1706. A voracious reader, at the age of eight Franklin was put into grammar school but removed to a less expensive one a year later. During his two years of formal education he excelled in writing but failed arithmetic. At the age of ten he was taken home to work in his father's cottage business, boiling soap and making candles.

He was not successful in Josiah's shop. At the age of twelve he was coerced by his father to sign indenture papers to apprentice with his older brother James, who owned a print shop. During his time in James's shop he learned the basics of the print business that, in the next decade, he would use as a foundation for technical innovations for print media. He also absorbed much from James Franklin's unconventional journalistic experiment, the *New-England Courant,* the newspaper James had founded in August 1721. The formula Franklin later devised for spicing up his own Philadelphia weekly with hoaxes and moral essays owed much to his brother's iconoclasm in print, though Benjamin would never become as radical a journalist as his brother.

The *Courant* represented a marked departure from earlier colonial journalism. Its flag did not contain the words "published by authority," meaning that content had been approved by colonial officials. Modeled after the earlier English essay papers the *Spectator, Tatler,* and *Guardian,* the *Courant* was intended to be readable and witty. It dared criticize, even poke fun at authority, especially the politics of Puritan leaders Increase and Cotton Mather, whose supporters fired back at the *Courant* in other Boston papers and in a broadside called the *Anti-Courant.*

Ben Franklin's earliest newspaper copy was published in the *Courant.* Like James, Benjamin had read and studied the clever, urbane style of the English essayists Joseph Addison, Richard Steele, and others, an influence that showed clearly in the "Silence Dogood Papers," a series of fourteen satirical essays he wrote in the guise of Mrs. Silence Dogood, a minister's widow. Franklin's initial aim was to spoof Cotton Mather's "Essays To Do Good"; later the apprentice printer aimed his satire at Harvard College. These essays were left anonymously on the *Courant*'s doorstep; even James did not know the identity of their author. When James finally discovered their authorship, he began to envy his apprentice's talents, which led to strained relations between the two brothers, and at length to Benjamin's fleeing, at age eighteen, the remaining term of his apprenticeship and sailing to New York, and then later to Philadelphia, where he found work with printer Samuel Keimer.

While still in his teens, Franklin sailed to London, where he worked as a compositor for the leading London printer Samuel Palmer and learned type founding at the shop of Thomas James. After a year and a half in London Franklin took his new skills back to Philadelphia and in 1728 set up a printing business in partnership with his friend Hugh Meredith. Learning that Franklin had plans to found a newspaper to compete with Andrew Bradford's *Philadelphia Mercury,* Franklin's former employer Keimer sought to preempt him by starting his own paper, the *Universal Instructor in all Arts and Sciences: and Pennsylvania Gazette.* In a series of Addisonian essays in the *Mercury* that became known as the "Busy-Body Papers," Franklin made use of his flair for cosmopolitan satire to poke fun at Keimer, whose paper then lost circulation, and in 1729 Franklin

bought the paper from Keimer. He shortened its title to the *Pennsylvania Gazette,* bought out Meredith's interest, and earned for his new property the reputation of the most readable newspaper in the colonies. Rather than follow the outspoken, belligerently anti-establishment tradition of James's *Courant* and risk jail and bankruptcy, Franklin took a more reasoned middle road, criticizing those in power only moderately and within the bounds of what they would tolerate.

Franklin increased his sphere of influence by working with a succession of younger printers, the first of whom was Lewis Timothy. The two men founded America's first foreign-language newspaper, the *Philadelphische Zeitung,* in 1729. This venture failed after six weeks, but in 1731 Franklin sent Timothy to Charleston, South Carolina, to work with Thomas Whitemarsh on the *South Carolina Gazette,* a paper Franklin helped finance. Franklin provided similar help to several other promising young printers, establishing the first chain of newspapers in America.

Another publishing venture that brought Franklin wider fame and substantial fortune was *Poor Richard's Almanac,* first published in 1732 and continued until 1757. As with his newspaper and later his magazine, Franklin borrowed heavily from English periodicals and almanacs for *Poor Richard's* but also contributed to it his own witticisms, which secured for him the reputation of being America's first native humorist.

As with his *Philadelphische Zeitung,* Franklin's plan for publishing the first American magazine was less than successful. Having seen the success of English magazines, Franklin wanted to develop a similar vehicle to explore political, social, and scientific issues in greater depth than could be done in newspapers, but his plan to be first was anticipated by his major rival in Philadelphia publishing, Andrew Bradford.

Busy with his other publishing operations and with his appointments as clerk of the General Assembly and postmaster of Pennsylvania, Franklin in the autumn of 1740 engaged printer John Webbe to edit the planned magazine. Dissatisfied with his compensation, Webbe revealed Franklin's magazine plans to Bradford, who decided to preempt Franklin and engaged Webbe's editorial services at a higher rate of compensation. Minus his editor, Franklin pressed on with his magazine project but was beaten by three days by Bradford, who on 13 February 1741 launched his thirty-page *American Magazine, or A*

Benjamin Franklin in a 1766 portrait by David Martin (courtesy of the White House Historical Association)

Monthly View of the Political State of the British Colonies.

Franklin's *General Magazine, and Historical Chronicle, For all the British Plantations in America* was seventy to seventy-six pages per issue and somewhat more varied in content, though both magazines were dominated by official government pronouncements. The title page of the *General Magazine* featured a large woodcut of the coronet of the Prince of Wales and the motto "Ich Dein," meaning "That I May Serve." The contents Franklin selected for his first issue reflect the Old World orientation and colonial nature of his readership: brief historical notes on the monarchies of Great Britain and twenty other European principalities; a section providing historical information on several American colonies, plus Newfoundland, Nova Scotia, and several Caribbean islands; official proclamations on coinage in New York and use of bills of credit in lieu of silver and gold as a medium of exchange in Massachusetts; an act of Parliament for naturalizing foreigners in the British colonies. Following were accounts and extracts from colonial sermons, pam-

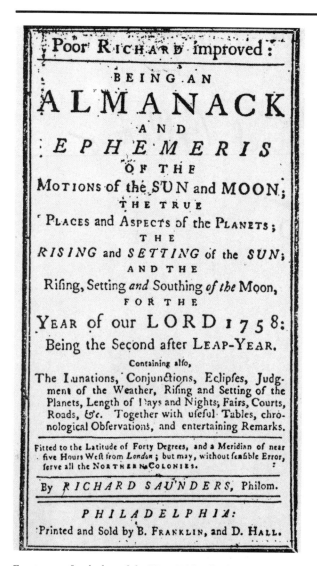

Front cover for the last of the "Poor Richard" almanacs (Parke-Bernet Galleries, Inc., Catalogue #627, 23-24 January 1945)

phlets, and books, then essays from various colonial newspapers, including advice to the lovesick from the *Virginia Gazette* and queries on the nature of God and other theological topics from the *Boston Weekly Post-Boy, Boston News-Letter,* and *Boston Evening Post.* Nine pages of mainly religious poetry were also included. The back pages of the magazine consisted of a three-page section of news notes, a selection of exchange rates in the British colonies, and a page summarizing Pennsylvania's exports for 1740. The *General Magazine* was not illustrated except for decorative borders and colophons.

The five issues that followed were similar in content, though the March 1741 number gave twenty-two pages to the colonial manual of arms, presenting complete details as to commands and

motions. The selection of poetry only rarely showed Franklin's whimsical touch, as in "The Gardener's Curse, For Such Visitors As Leave His Gate Open," which also appeared in the March issue. The final number, June 1741, contained no notice that the magazine was to be discontinued. Franklin's venture was only marginally more successful than Bradford's, which had lasted for but three issues.

Though neither magazine survived, Franklin's idea that the colonies needed magazines soon took hold, and before the end of the 1700s more than a hundred magazines had been published, though many of these, too, were short-lived. It is not accurate to suggest, as the Curtis Publishing Company did for so many years, that the *Saturday Evening Post,* founded in Philadelphia in 1820, can trace its roots to Franklin. The *Post* was established in the same physical plant and printed on the same press that Franklin used, and based on this slim genealogical root, the magazine's owners in the 1890s began an advertising campaign built around Franklin's presumed association. For the next fifty years the *Post* continued to run Franklin's picture in its masthead. This in part has contributed to Franklin's identification with the magazine industry. Franklin would have probably been surprised; in his *Autobiography* (1868) he did not mention even his actual contribution to magazine publishing in America.

In 1748, at the age of forty-two, Franklin sold his printing shop, almanacs, and newspaper to devote more time to public service and the sciences. His book *Father Abraham's Speech* (1758) and his pamphlet on fair play, *Morals of Chess,* broadened his reputation as a man of letters. In 1753 he was named joint deputy postmaster of the colonies; in 1757 he served as colonial agent from Pennsylvania in London. From 1770 to 1775 he represented Pennsylvania, Georgia, New Jersey, and Massachusetts in their dealings with the king and Parliament, then returned to America in 1775 and helped draft the Declaration of Independence and signed several other key public documents, including the United States Constitution.

As a self-taught scientist and scholar, Franklin made contributions in the fields of electricity, medicine, botany, hydraulics, physics, engineering, agronomy, chemistry, and ethnology. He continued, too, to contribute to the field that earned him his early fame and fortune, printing. He helped devise ways to make counterfeiting of

Five-pound note printed by Franklin for the Province of Pennsylvania. The leaf pattern was designed to discourage counterfeiters (courtesy of the American Philosophical Society).

printed currency more difficult and was instrumental in forming in Philadelphia in 1778 the earliest organization of American printers, which after his death was named the Franklin Society. He also bequeathed to Boston and Philadelphia the sum of five thousand dollars, to be loaned in limited amounts to journeyman printers who wished to start their own business.

Franklin can rightfully be said to have originated the idea of launching the first American magazine. Though this brief chapter in his incredible career is vastly overshadowed by his other accomplishments in printing and publishing, public life, and science, his fathering the *General Magazine* in 1741 earns him a place in any work devoted to American magazines and their creators.

Letters:

Les Amitiés américaines de Madame d'Houdetot, d'après sa correspondance inédite avec Benjamin Franklin et Thomas Jefferson, edited by Gilbert Chinard (Paris: E. Champion, 1924);

"My Dear Girl": The Correspondence of Benjamin Franklin, Polly Stevenson, Georgiana and Cather-

ine Shipley, edited by James M. Stifler (New York: Doran, 1927);

The Letters and Papers of Benjamin Franklin and Richard Jackson, 1753-1785, edited by Carl Van Doren (Philadelphia: American Philosophical Society, 1947);

Benjamin Franklin and Catherine Ray Greene: Their Correspondence, edited by William G. Roelker (Philadelphia: American Philosophical Society, 1949);

Benjamin Franklin's Letters to the Press, 1758-1775, edited by Verner W. Crane (Chapel Hill: University of North Carolina Press, 1950);

"Franklin's Letters on Indians and Germans" and "Franklin and Jackson on the French War," edited by A. O. Aldridge, in American Philosophical Society *Proceedings,* 94 (August 1950): 391-395, 396-397;

The Letters of Benjamin Franklin and Jane Mecom, edited by Van Doren (Princeton: Princeton University Press, 1950);

" 'All Clear Sunshine!' New Letters of Franklin and Mary Stevenson Hewson," edited by Whitfield J. Bell, Jr., in American Philosophical Society *Proceedings,* 100 (December 1956): 521-536;

Mr. Franklin: A Selection from His Personal Letters, edited by Leonard W. Labaree and Bell (New Haven: Yale University Press, 1956).

Bibliographies:

Paul Leicester Ford, *Franklin Bibliography: A List of Books Written by, or Relating to, Benjamin Franklin* (Brooklyn: Historical Printing Club, 1889);

I. Minis Mays, *Calendar of the Papers of Benjamin Franklin in the Library of the American Philosophical Society,* 6 volumes (Philadelphia: University of Pennsylvania Press, 1908);

C. William Miller, *Benjamin Franklin's Philadelphia Printing, 1728-1766. A Descriptive Bibliography* (Philadelphia: American Philosophical Society, 1974).

Biographies:

James Parton, *Life and Times of Benjamin Franklin,* 2 volumes (Boston: Mason Brothers, 1864);

Frank L. Mott and Chester E. Jorgenson, Introduction to *Benjamin Franklin: Representative Selections* (New York: American Book Company, 1936), pp. xiii-cxli;

Carl Van Doren, *Benjamin Franklin* (New York: Viking, 1938);

Franklin, circa 1780, in an idealized portrait by Rosalie Filleul
(courtesy of the American Philosophical Society)

Carl L. Becker, *Benjamin Franklin, A Biographical Sketch* (Ithaca: Cornell University Press, 1946);

William E. Lingelbach, "B. Franklin, Printer— New Source Material," American Philosophical Society *Proceedings,* 92 (May 1948): 79-100;

Clinton Rossiter, "Benjamin Franklin," in his *Seedtime of the Republic* (New York: Harcourt, Brace, 1953), pp. 281-312;

Charles L. Sanford, ed., *Benjamin Franklin and the American Character* (Boston: Heath, 1955);

A. Owen Aldridge, *Benjamin Franklin: Philosopher and Man* (Philadelphia: Lippincott, 1965);

Claude-Anne Lopez, *Mon Cher Papa: Franklin and the Ladies of Paris* (New Haven: Yale University Press, 1966);

Catherine Drinker Bowen, *The Most Dangerous Man in America: Scenes from the Life of Benjamin Franklin* (Boston: Little, Brown, 1974);

Lopez and Eugenia W. Herbert, *The Private Franklin: The Man and His Family* (New York: Norton, 1975);

David Freeman Hawke, *Franklin* (New York: Harper & Row, 1976);

Arthur B. Tourtellot, *Benjamin Franklin: The Shaping of Genius, The Boston Years* (Garden City, N.Y.: Doubleday, 1977);

Ronald W. Clark, *Benjamin Franklin: A Biography* (New York: Random House, 1983).

References:

Frederick A. Birmingham, "And Ben Begat The Post," *Saturday Evening Post* (April 1982): 54-55, 115;

Henry Lewis Bullen, "Benjamin Franklin, and What Printing did for Him," *Americana Collector* (1926);

Verner W. Crane, *Benjamin Franklin and a Rising People* (Boston, 1954);

Bernard Fay, *Franklin: The Apostle of Modern Times* (Boston: Little, Brown, 1929);

Sydney George Fisher, *The True Benjamin Franklin* (Philadelphia: Lippincott, 1898);

David Freeman Hawke, *Franklin* (New York: Harper & Row, 1976);

Robert V. Hudson, "The English Roots of Benjamin Franklin's Journalism," *Journalism History*, 3 (Autumn 1976): 76-79;

Wilbur R. Jacobs, *Benjamin Franklin: Statesman-Philosopher or Materialist?* (New York: Holt, Rinehart & Winston, 1972);

John Clyde Oswald, *Benjamin Franklin Printer* (New York: Doubleday, 1917);

Henry P. Rosemont, "Benjamin Franklin and the Philadelphia Typographical Strikers of 1786," *Labor History* (Summer 1981): 398-429;

Phillips Russell, *Benjamin Franklin: The First Civilized American* (New York: Brentanos, 1926);

James A. Sappenfield, *A Sweet Instruction: Franklin's Journalism as a Literary Apprenticeship* (Carbondale: Southern Illinois University Press, 1973);

William David Sloan, "America's First Editorial?," *Masthead* (Spring 1984): 34;

Albert H. Smyth, *Philadelphia Magazines and Their Contributors: 1741-1850* (New York: Books for Libraries Press, 1970), pp. 23-27;

Pete Steffens, "Franklin's Early Attack on Racism," *Journalism History*, 5 (Spring 1978);

Lawrence C. Wroth, *The Colonial Printer* (Charlottesville: University Press of Virginia, 1964);

Wroth, *The Pictorial Life of Benjamin Franklin: Printer, Published in Commemoration of the 200th anniversary of the arrival of Franklin in Philadelphia* (Philadelphia: Dill & Collins, 1923);

Wroth, *Printing in the Americas* (Port Washington, N.Y.: Kennicat Press, 1965).

Papers:

By far the greatest collection of Benjamin Franklin's manuscripts is held by the American Philosophical Society Library, Philadelphia. Other sizable holdings are in the Stevens Collection, Library of Congress; the University of Pennsylvania Library; the Library of the Historical Society of Pennsylvania; and Yale University.

Sarah Margaret Fuller, Marchesa D'Ossoli

(23 May 1810-19 July 1850)

Nora Baker
Southern Illinois University at Edwardsville

See also the Fuller entries in *DLB 1: The American Renaissance in New England* and *DLB 59: American Literary Critics and Scholars, 1800-1850.*

MAJOR POSITIONS HELD: Editor, *Dial* (1840-1842); literary critic, foreign correspondent, *New York Daily Tribune* (1844-1849).

BOOKS: *Summer on the Lakes, in 1843* (Boston: Little, Brown/New York: C. S. Francis, 1844); enlarged as *Summer on the Lakes. With Autobiography . . . and Memoir,* by Ralph Waldo Emerson, et al. (London: Ward & Lock, 1861);

Woman in the Nineteenth Century (New York: Greeley & McElrath/London: Clarke, 1845); enlarged as *Woman in the Nineteenth Century, and Kindred Papers Relating to the Sphere, Condition, and Duties of Woman,* edited by Arthur B. Fuller (Boston: Jewett/Cleveland: Jewett, Proctor & Worthington/New York: Sheldon, Lamport, 1855);

Papers on Literature and Art, 2 volumes (New York & London: Wiley & Putnam, 1846); enlarged as *Art, Literature, and the Drama,* edited by Arthur B. Fuller (Boston: Brown, Taggard & Chase/New York: Sheldon/Philadelphia: Lippincott/London: Sampson Low, 1860);

Memoirs of Margaret Fuller Ossoli, edited, with contributions, by Emerson, James Freeman Clarke, and William Henry Channing (2 volumes, Boston: Phillips, Sampson, 1852; 3 volumes, London: Bentley, 1852);

At Home and Abroad, or Things and Thoughts in America and Europe, edited by Arthur B. Fuller (Boston: Crosby, Nichols/London: Sampson Low, 1856);

Life Without and Life Within; or, Reviews, Narratives, Essays, and Poems, edited by Arthur B. Fuller (Boston: Brown, Taggard & Chase/New York: Sheldon/Philadelphia: Lippincott/London: Sampson Low, 1860);

Margaret Fuller (engraving of the portrait by Chappel)

Margaret and Her Friends, or Ten Conversations with Margaret Fuller upon the Mythology of the Greeks and its Expression in Art, reported by Caroline W. Healey (Boston: Roberts Brothers, 1895).

Collections: *The Writings of Margaret Fuller,* edited by Mason Wade (New York: Viking, 1941);

Margaret Fuller: American Romantic. A Selection from her Writings and Correspondence, edited by Perry Miller (Garden City, N.Y.: Anchor/Doubleday, 1963);

The Woman and the Myth: Margaret Fuller's Life and Writings, edited by Bell Gale Chevigny (Old Westbury, N.Y.: Feminist Press, 1976);

Margaret Fuller: Essays on American Life and Letters, edited by Joel Myerson (New Haven, Conn.: College & University Press, 1978).

OTHER: Johann Eckermann, *Conversations with Goethe in the Last Years of His Life,* translated by Fuller (Boston: Hilliard, Gray, 1839);

Günderode, translated by Fuller (Boston: E. P. Peabody, 1842).

PERIODICAL PUBLICATIONS: "A Short Essay on Critics," *Dial,* 1 (July 1840): 5-11;

"The Atheneum Exhibition of Painting and Sculpture," *Dial,* 1 (October 1840): 260-263;

"Menzel's View of Goethe," *Dial,* 1 (January 1841): 340-347;

"A Dialogue: Poet. Critic," *Dial,* 1 (April 1841): 494-496;

"Goethe," *Dial,* 2 (July 1841): 1-41;

"To Contributors," *Dial,* 2 (July 1841): 136;

"Lives of the Great Composers, Haydn, Mozart, Handel, Bach, Beethoven," *Dial,* 2 (October 1841): 148-203;

"Festus," *Dial,* 2 (October 1841): 231-261;

"Bettine [*sic*] Brentano and Her Friend Günderode," *Dial,* 2 (January 1842): 313-357;

"Entertainments of the Past Winter," *Dial,* 2 (July 1842): 46-72;

"Romaic and Rhine Ballads," *Dial,* 3 (October 1842): 137-180;

"The Great Lawsuit. Man *versus* Men. Woman *versus* Women," *Dial,* 4 (July 1843): 1-47;

"Dialogue," *Dial,* 4 (April 1844): 458-469;

"Emerson's Essays," *New-York Daily Tribune,* 7 December 1844, p. 1;

"Monument to Goethe," *New-York Daily Tribune,* 16 December 1844, p. 1;

"Miss Barrett's Poems," *New-York Daily Tribune,* 4 January 1845, p. 1;

Review of *The Waif: A Collection of Poems,* edited by Henry Wadsworth Longfellow, *New-York Daily Tribune,* 16 January 1845, p. 1;

Review of *Conversations on Some of the Old Poets,* by James Russell Lowell, *New-York Daily Tribune,* 21 January 1845, p. 1;

"Edgar A. Poe," *New-York Daily Tribune,* 24 January 1845, p. 1;

Review of *Scenes in My Native Land,* by L. H. Sigourney, *New-York Daily Tribune,* 28 January 1845, p. 1;

"French Novelists of the Day: Balzac . . . George Sand . . . Eugene Sue," *New-York Daily Tribune,* 1 February 1845, p. 1;

"English Writers Little Known Here: Milnes . . . Landor . . . Julius Hare," *New-York Daily Tribune,* 4 March 1845, p. 1; 28 March 1845, p. 1;

"Library of Choice Reading," *New-York Daily Tribune,* 4 April 1845, p. 1;

"Hazlitt's *Table-Talk,*" *New-York Daily Tribune,* 30 April 1845, p. 1;

"Mrs. Child's Letters," *New-York Daily Tribune,* 10 May 1845, p. 1;

Review of *Essays on Art,* by Goethe, translated by S. G. Ward, *New-York Daily Tribune,* 29 May 1845, p. 1;

Review of *Philothea,* by L. M. Child, *New-York Daily Tribune,* 5 June 1845, p. 1;

Review of *Margaret: A Tale of the Real and Ideal,* by Sylvester Judd, *New-York Daily Tribune,* 1 September 1845, p. 1;

Review of *The Wigwam and the Cabin,* by William Gilmore Simms, *New-York Daily Tribune,* 11 October 1845, p. 1;

Review of *The Raven and Other Poems,* by Edgar Allan Poe, *New-York Daily Tribune,* 26 November 1845, p. 1;

Review of *Poems,* by Longfellow, *New-York Daily Tribune,* 10 December 1845, p. 1;

"Farewell," *New-York Daily Tribune,* 1 August 1846, p. 2.

Margaret Fuller has been the target of more praise and more criticism for her work and her life than any other woman of the Transcendental period. She has been dismissed on one hand as a "bluestocking," and on the other as a coarse, conceited, immoral, and blasphemous woman. She has also been hailed as America's first female foreign correspondent, as the most brilliant woman of the age, and as the author of the first important feminist book in America. Her blessings were her formidable intellect and education; her curse was the fact that she was a woman. In the forty years of her life, perhaps her greatest contributions came from her intellectual influence on her peers and through the force of her personality upon the women with whom she had contact. That there were many Margaret Fullers indicates the rapid evolution of her life from prodigy to teacher to editor-writer-poet to critic to journalist and, finally, to revolutionary. She was not a "great" writer; her permanent status in journalistic and literary history stems more from what she

The Greene Street School, Providence, Rhode Island, where Fuller taught from 1837 to 1838 (courtesy of the Rhode Island Historical Society)

did and the handicaps under which she labored. She set an example for other women and encouraged them to follow.

Sarah Margaret Fuller, later Marchesa D'Ossoli, was the eldest of nine children born to Timothy and Margaret Crane Fuller. Her father, a lawyer, had expected and wanted a son; swallowing his disappointment, he gave his daughter a boy's education. She began learning Latin at the age of six. At fifteen she was on a schedule which included reading literature and philosophy in four languages from five in the morning until eleven at night, with a few breaks for exercise and music. This regimen, while providing Fuller with a unique and incomparable education, led to a breakdown of her physical and emotional health. Aside from a short period at a school run by the Prescott sisters in Groton, Massachusetts, when she was fourteen and fifteen, most of Fuller's education took place at home.

Shortly after her return home from Groton the family moved close to the Harvard campus. Fuller became friends with some members of the Harvard class of 1829, who would later distinguish themselves, and also with future Transcen-

dentalist Frederick Henry Hedge, home from a five-year sojourn in Germany. He introduced her to German literature and philosophy, and she began an intensive study of the subjects. Transcendentalism, the belief that the knowledge of reality is arrived at intuitively rather than by objective experience, had its roots in Germany. Because of her interests, Fuller soon met many other people who would later become involved with the Transcendentalist's Symposium Club and its quarterly journal, the *Dial*.

In 1833 the family moved to a farm at Groton. With her mother ill and her father writing his memoirs, it fell to Fuller to care for the family and to begin teaching her young siblings. At the same time, she managed to continue her own studies and to begin some writing projects. In 1835 Timothy Fuller died unexpectedly of Asiatic cholera, and Fuller embarked on a teaching career in order to support the family.

She began teaching in 1836 at Bronson Alcott's Temple School in Boston, a progressive institution, but the pay was not enough. In 1837 she moved to Providence, Rhode Island, to teach at the Greene Street School, where the salary was

Fuller's mother, Margaret Crane Fuller (standing at right), with four of her children: (seated, left to right) Arthur Buckminster, Ellen, Richard Frederick, and (standing) Eugene.

better and where she stayed for two years. In that same year she joined the Transcendentalist Symposium Club, becoming the first woman member. Elizabeth Peabody, the publisher, was the second.

In Rhode Island Fuller keenly felt her exile from Cambridge and the Transcendentalists. She kept up a voluminous correspondence with them and at the same time, in addition to her teaching duties, began to develop her literary skills. As early as 1835 she had been contributing occasional poems and literary reviews to the *Western Messenger,* a liberal Unitarian journal. She now began working on a biography of Goethe and provided two translations for John S. Dwight's edition of *Select Minor Poems, Translated from the German of Goethe and Schiller,* part of George Ripley's series *Specimens of Foreign Standard Literature.*

The Goethe biography proved to be a massive undertaking, and in December 1836 Fuller resigned her Providence post and moved to Boston, devoting her energies to the book while giving private language lessons to supplement her income. Unfortunately, the only tangible result of her labors on the biography was the translation of Johann Eckermann's *Conversations with Goethe in the Last Years of His Life,* published in 1839.

In Boston Fuller was restored to all that she held most dear: art, music, literature, lectures, the conversation of kindred spirits. With the publication of her first book Fuller was both proud and temporarily at loose ends for another project which would stimulate her mind and supplement her income. She conceived the plan of a series of meetings with educated women of the community in order that they might "ascertain what pursuits are best suited to us, in our time and state of society, and how we may make best use of our means for building up the life of thought upon the light of action...." This meeting was the first of Fuller's famous "Conversations With Women," which she held annually every winter for the next five years.

The opening session was held 6 November 1839 in Elizabeth Peabody's parlor; the topic was Greek mythology. Initially there were thirteen

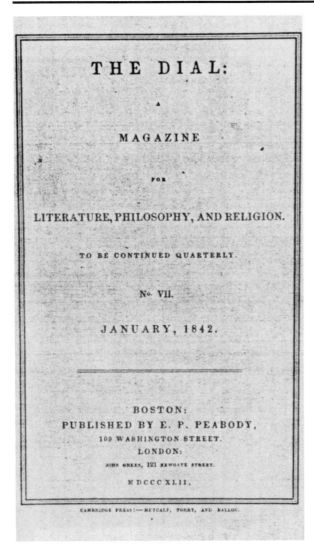

THE DIAL:

A

MAGAZINE

FOR

LITERATURE, PHILOSOPHY, AND RELIGION.

TO BE CONTINUED QUARTERLY.

No. VII.

JANUARY, 1842.

BOSTON:
PUBLISHED BY E. P. PEABODY,
109 WASHINGTON STREET.
LONDON:
JOHN GREEN, 121 NEWGATE STREET.
MDCCCXLII.

CAMBRIDGE PRESS:—METCALF, TORRY, AND BALLOU.

Front cover for the next-to-last issue of the Dial *edited by Fuller*

meetings, each two hours long. Fuller would introduce the topic, present some ideas, and suggest a direction for the discussion. Then she would ask the participants to express their thoughts. The series became so popular that she was asked to repeat it the following year, when the subject was fine arts. By 1841 evening sessions, which included both men and women, were being held. Although the topics varied, the common denominator adhered to by Fuller was a moral ethic. She believed that all people, regardless of race or gender, possessed moral freedom within themselves and a moral sense which would provide direction to the will, and insight and inspiration to the intellect. Many of the ideas expressed in the "Conversations" were later incorporated into Fuller's writing. The "Conversations" also marked

the beginning of her influence on women of culture and position.

During the first winter of the "Conversations," Fuller was planning a new career as editor of a Transcendentalist journal. The men of the Symposium Club had been debating the pros and cons of the wisdom of such a publication–when to begin, who to be editor–for quite some time, with no consensus on anything. The problem lay inherent in the tenets of Transcendentalism: a nebulous faith in individual inspiration, in the power of will, in everyone's birthright of universal good. In addition, no one member wished to be responsible for a publication which was certain to provoke controversy and which could possibly endanger livelihoods. Ralph Waldo Emerson, a member of the club, wrote, "Never will *I* be editor. We all wish it to be but do not wish ourselves to be responsible." However, Emerson was mainly responsible for persuading Fuller to take the position and promised her his "best assistance."

The months of hard work which Fuller put into the inauguration of the *Dial* were an indication of her reverence for Emerson and the esteem in which she held the other members of the club. She had no illusions about the success of the venture but hoped to initiate a "perfectly free" periodical which would encourage people to think noble thoughts through mental self-reliance. The problem was that the very people upon whom Fuller was to rely for the successful publication of the magazine were all, by the very nature of their belief in Transcendentalism, rugged individualists, not the best candidates for a team effort. She was promised the quarterly salary of fifty dollars, funds permitting. Emerson told her, "I rely on Ripley and Dwight and Parker and on young Thoreau and Ellery Channing and on Sam Ward, who will lend eagle wings whilst the car is yours. I should think we had the best group that ever made a Journal if all these were added unto You." George Ripley was persuaded to become business manager.

Fuller took up her new position officially in January 1840. The name of the publication had been suggested by Bronson Alcott: "I call my own Scriptures–that is, my own Diaries–the Dial. Why not call our journal by that name?"

There were problems from the start. Every periodical needs contributors, and those who wrote for the *Dial* were expected to do so for free. Also they were well aware that their Transcendentalist ideas were bound to land them in trouble. Fuller pleaded and begged: "What part do you propose to play in the grand symphony? Pray answer directly, as we proceed to tune the instruments." "We are planning by the yard—will you give philosophy or poetry and how much?" "Write, my friend, write!" "You can help and let it be nobly." "Let me hear from you!" "We count on *you*." Even Fuller's old friend Hedge, the club's expert on German philosophy, declined; he would not risk his ability to provide for his family by becoming involved in controversy. Fuller begged him: "Henry, in the name of all the Genii, Muses, Pegasus, Apollo, Pollio, Apollyon . . . to send me something good for this journal before the 1st May." Hedge's reply caused Emerson to term it a "sad letter for his biography."

And even Fuller's editorial colleagues disagreed. Emerson thought the preface to the first issue was too strong; Ripley thought it not strong enough. Fuller despaired of ever reaching publication. Emerson's preface described the journal "as a bold bible for Young America," calling on young writers to contribute. "Let *The Dial* measure none but sunny hours," he wrote, and he challenged New England convention and the mind-set resistant to new ideas. "Everything noble is directed upon life and this is. From the experience of spirits seeking in what is new somewhat to appease their inappeasable longing we hope to draw thoughts and feelings which, being alive, can impart life." This philosophy presented many problems for Fuller, as it forced her to accept work which her critical judgment would otherwise have rejected; as long as the authors qualified as sincere and thoughtful and anxious to impart their ideas to society, they met the criteria for publication.

The first issue of the *Dial* was dated July 1840 and contained 136 octavo pages, a pattern which would continue. It included Theodore Parker's "The Divine Presence in Nature and the Soul," John Sullivan Dwight's "The Religion of Beauty," Alcott's "Orphic Sayings," Fuller's "Short Essay on Critics," William Henry Channing's sketches of ecclesiastical Rome, Ripley's study of Orestes Brownson and his socialism, and reviews of books, art, and music. And there was poetry, including verse by Emerson and Thoreau. Fuller promised that the next issue would be better.

Subtitled *A Magazine for Literature, Philosophy, And Religion,* the quarterly was more a literary journal than a historical or theological one. The heavy use of prose, poetry, and criticism was, however, Fuller's way of coping with the problems of

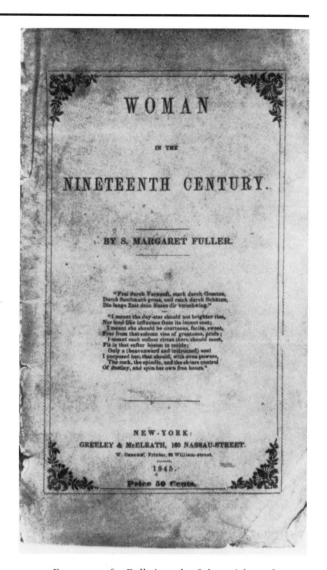

Front cover for Fuller's study of the sociology of male-female relations

putting out the *Dial.* Although Emerson was often critical of her efforts, Fuller was doing the work of an entire editorial staff. By the beginning of the second year of the *Dial,* the editor still had not been paid her salary for the first year. She was constantly cajoling and begging for contributors, a chore which was becoming increasingly difficult. Other magazines were paying as much as seven or eight dollars a page; the *Dial* paid nothing. Indeed, the magazine could not afford to. When Fuller informed Emerson that there were only thirty subscribers in Boston, he blithely remarked, "No matter, the thing will sell in a short while," and ordered an extra five hundred copies from the printer. The publishing fad of running pieces anonymously or by identifying authors only by an initial masked the fact that often much of an issue's content was hastily improvised by Fuller in order to fill the pages. For example, in the October 1841 edition, 85 of the 136 pages were written by the editor.

The reviewers were vicious in their attacks on the *Dial*. The *Boston Quarterly Review*, while allowing that the magazine was "full of rich thought," called Fuller and her friends "radicals in satin slippers." The *Philadelphia Gazette* called them "zanies and Bedlamites." The *Boston Times* referred to the magazine as "Transcendentally ridiculous." The *Knickerbocker Monthly* despaired of Emerson's "literary euphemisms" and Alcott's "inane twattle." Only the *Western Messenger* rallied to their defense. In its pages Fuller's old friend William Channing wrote, "The *Dial* is the windflower of a new literary spring. Subscribe as you love yourselves! Believe not the Geese that hiss!"

Yet even more calamity was to befall the troubled magazine. The publishers, Weeks & Jordan, declared bankruptcy and assigned their assets in trust for their creditors. Then it was discovered that the original contract had not been drawn with Weeks & Jordan but with Weeks and his brother. It was held by Jordan's brother, the assignee, who demanded payment for the subscription list and for the use of the magazine's name. When told that there was no money he suggested continuation of the publication at a rate of fifty cents for every copy sold so that he would be reimbursed. In addition, all paper and printing contracts would be in Emerson's name, and he would have total responsibility. Emerson had to hire a lawyer in order to settle the matter. Jordan backed away, and an agreement was reached with Weeks. The new publisher was to be Elizabeth Peabody, and Fuller, still unpaid, would continue as editor. Peabody immediately promised that Fuller's salary would be increased to seventy-five dollars per quarter. Peabody then began an audit of the account books. She quickly discovered the truth; the firm of Weeks & Jordan had looted the *Dial*, even absconding with the cash receipts. Two-year-old bills had not been paid. The supposed six hundred subscribers were actually closer to three hundred. Peabody advised that the magazine either halt publication at once or else cut the editions to a few hundred copies, the sale of which would pay for production costs. And, she added, Emerson or Parker must take over as editor. Fuller was in poor health due to expending her energies at the *Dial* while trying to earn her living with teaching, writing for other publications, and with the "Conversations."

Peabody, while sympathetic, was firm on this matter. "Margaret is unable any longer to give gratuitous labor; she has gone on in the hope of compensation that would enable her to give up teaching, but the two labors together are too much for her."

In March 1842 Fuller's career as editor of the *Dial* ended after more than two years of unpaid labor. She wrote to Emerson: "I grieve to disappoint you after all the trouble you have taken. I am also sorry myself, for if I could have received a maintenance from this '*Dial*,' I could have done my duties to it well, which I never have all this time, and my time might have been given to my pen; while now, for more than three months I have been able to write no line except letters. But it cannot be helped. It has been a sad business."

Emerson became the new editor, and Fuller was one of his most faithful contributors. On the bright side, in March 1842 Fuller saw the publication of her second book, the Günderode translation. Although Fuller felt she had failed in her editorship of the *Dial*, Emerson and others who knew how much she had really done later attested to the fact that without her hard work and many sacrifices, the magazine would never have survived. In addition to nurturing unknown talent, she had provided proponents of an unpopular cause with a platform from which to communicate their ideas. Fuller also learned from the experience, developing talents in writing reviews and in turning out great masses of copy when the need arose.

Now freed of her duties at the *Dial* Fuller took some time off to rest and recuperate. She visited relatives and friends, including Emerson at his home in Concord. She was, as she had been from its inception, a frequent visitor at Brook Farm, although she never joined Ripley's experiment in communal living. In November 1842 she began another series of the "Conversations" in Boston; these were so successful financially that she was able to go on tour in the Midwest by the following spring.

Under Emerson's editorship, the *Dial* survived–barely. Paid subscriptions were now down to 220. Peabody's efforts to increase sales were futile. Frantic, Emerson wrote to Fuller begging for copy. What she sent to him was the article which would make her famous on two continents–"The Great Lawsuit. Man *versus* Men. Woman *versus* Women." In July 1843 it appeared as the lead article in the only issue of the *Dial* ever to be completely sold out. It became the basis for a later book and was the first major published plea for woman's rights in America.

The full power of her reformer's zeal was channeled into "The Great Lawsuit." She wrote, "By Man I mean both man and woman; these are two halves of one thought. I lay no especial stress on the welfare of either. I believe that the development of one cannot be effected without that of the other." She wrote that women need "as a nature to grow, as an intellect to discern, as a soul to live unimpeded, to unfold such powers as were given her when we left our common home."

Fuller returned to Boston in September 1843. She embarked on another round of "Conversations," contributed some reviews to the *Dial*, and began work on a new book, *Summer on the Lakes, in 1843* (1844), an account of her travels. The "Conversations" ended in April 1844, and Fuller was able to devote all her energies to her book, raising quite a few eyebrows when she entered the all-male bastion of the Harvard University Library to do her research. The book was not well received, selling less than half of its nearly seven hundred copies.

The *Dial* had expired in January 1844. After the publication of *Summer on the Lakes* Fuller received an invitation from Horace Greeley to come to New York as literary critic of the *New-York Daily Tribune,* replacing Arthur Brisbane, who had resigned to take up socialism at Brook Farm. Greeley liked Fuller's book, as he liked all things western. Moreover, his wife had attended some of the "Conversations" and had praised the writer to her husband. Greeley had read Fuller's work in the *Dial* and was especially taken with "The Great Lawsuit." As an added inducement, if she wished to revise and expand the article into a book, he offered to publish it for her. Before leaving for her new job Fuller worked on the project, finishing in November. The book, *Woman in the Nineteenth Century,* was published in February 1845 and was her most important work. In its pages she attacked the hypocrisy of men and called for equality for women, especially in education. She deplored the stereotypical roles in which both men and women were cast. In spite of mixed critical reviews, all fifteen hundred copies were sold.

Fuller began her duties at the *Daily Tribune* on 1 December 1844; her first review appeared six days later. She had been hired to write two articles on literary topics and one on social questions every week for the daily edition. Several of these pieces were reprinted in weekly and semiweekly editions. She was also responsible for finding items in the foreign press for use in Greeley's editorial columns. Although Fuller felt most comfortable when writing about literature and art, she quickly became immersed in writing about the city's hospitals, prisons, and charitable institutions, which she visited in order to report on conditions to her readers. She was enjoying life in New York, with all its cultural attractions, and had moved in with the Greeleys in their home on the East River. Greeley gave her a free hand at the newspaper, although he deplored the length of time it took her to write a single article. Her reviews were well accepted, as was *Woman in the Nineteenth Century* when it was published. And she felt that she was continuing the work she had begun as editor of the *Dial*, that of interpreting European culture for Americans. The only dark cloud was Fuller's recurring migraines, the result of nearsightedness. The headaches were so severe that they totally incapacitated her for days.

The *Daily Tribune*'s circulation grew, in great part because of the popularity of articles by Fuller, all of which she signed with an asterisk. Her newspaper writing was, in general, better than any she had done for the *Dial*, sparer and not so florid, in adherence to the journalistic style demanded by her editor. Many of the new readers were women, a fact which did not surprise Greeley; he had hired Fuller to attract them.

Fuller's method for all the critical reviews she wrote for the *Daily Tribune* was to divide literature into three classes: the work of genius, the work of scholars who act as interpreters of genius, and the work of those with something to communicate. Although she believed in bringing the work of the latter two classes to public attention, she did not formally criticize them. She did assess and critique those writers she deemed geniuses. Even in her state of perpetual ill health, a condition aggravated by an unhappy love affair with James Nathan, Fuller wrote nearly 250 reviews and essays for the *Daily Tribune* during her tenure as literary critic.

In 1846, overcoming her lifelong dread of the sea, she sailed for Europe in the company of Marcus and Rebecca Spring, a wealthy New York couple who had befriended her. Ten years earlier an impending European trip had had to be canceled because of the death of her father. Fuller saved one thousand dollars and borrowed

Fuller in Rome (engraving by M. Haider from the painting by Thomas Hicks)

five hundred more from old friend Sam Ward, who had renounced art for banking. Greeley assured her she could continue to write for the *Daily Tribune* from abroad. Fuller's family and friends were delighted that her dream was to be realized at last; Emerson was so pleased that he gave her a letter of introduction to Thomas Carlyle. On 1 August 1846 Fuller and the Springs set sail aboard the *Cambria,* arriving in Liverpool ten days and sixteen hours later.

Almost from the moment she landed Fuller began entering her impressions and descriptions in a notebook, recording the people and places which she thought would be of interest to the *Daily Tribune*'s readers. She later expanded these entries into articles. After Fuller's death her brother Arthur collected them into the book *At Home and Abroad, or Things and Thoughts in Amer-*ica and Europe (1856), and together with the *Memoirs of Margaret Fuller Ossoli* (1852), edited by Emerson, Channing, and Clarke, they provide a fairly comprehensive picture of her three months in England and Scotland.

A month after arriving in England Fuller's newest book, *Papers on Literature and Art* (1846), a collection of some of her essays, was published. It was comprised of critical reviews of American and European literature and art. Well received, it went into a second printing in 1848. Partly as a result of this publication, but mostly as a result of the fact that her fame had preceded her, Fuller found herself lionized and entertained, especially by the *literati*. She was surprised to learn that the *Dial* had been very highly thought of by English readers. The British had discovered *Woman in the Nineteenth Century,* and Fuller received several invitations to contribute to various periodicals. She had to regretfully decline; she was far too busy. Among the literary giants she met were William Wordsworth, Thomas DeQuincey, and Carlyle. In London, through the Springs, she met Giuseppe Mazzini, the exiled Italian revolutionary whose dream was to free Italy and unite the country as a socialist republic. Fuller became the patriot's friend and confidant.

In November she sailed for Europe and finally situated herself in Paris, where she stayed until the following February. Her reputation had also preceded her to the continent. *La Revue Indèpendante* had already printed one of Fuller's essays and was planning to publish *Woman in the Nineteenth Century*. The editor invited her to become his American correspondent when she returned home, and she promised to think about it. Fuller did much sightseeing, went to the theater and the opera, worked on her French, and finally met her idol, George Sand.

On 25 February 1847 Fuller and the Springs traveled to Italy, visiting Livorno, Pisa, and Naples. In April she settled in Rome, living on the Corso. While there she faithfully visited the studios of American artists living abroad so she could inform her readers at home of the caliber of these expatriates' work. Because of her dispatches to the *Daily Tribune*, she played an important role in preparing a favorable reception for such artists as Luther Terry, Thomas Hicks, Christopher Cranch, and the sculptor Thomas Crawford.

Shortly after her arrival in Rome Fuller had a chance meeting with the Marchese Giovanni Angelo D'Ossoli, a member of an old and noble Italian family. Ossoli, some ten years Fuller's junior, was considered handsome but was intellectually Fuller's inferior. The seeds of revolution, already planted in Fuller by Mazzini, were nurtured by Ossoli, who was strongly allied with the republican cause. In the summer of that same year Fuller left Rome to tour northern Italy; she reported her impressions in letters to the *Daily Tribune*. She returned to Rome in October, and she and Ossoli became lovers. The couple were soon caught up in the Italian revolution. Then Fuller discovered that she was pregnant.

In July 1848 Fuller moved to Rieti, outside Rome, to await the birth of her child and to work on a book about Italy and the revolution. On 5 September 1848, her son, Angelo Eugene Philip, was born. Many biographers believe that Fuller and Ossoli later married, but no adequate docu-

mentation of such a marriage has ever been found. Fuller was a Protestant, a liberal, and a foreigner; finding a priest who would marry her to a member of the Italian nobility with ties to the Vatican would have been nearly impossible. However, if they were wed, it was probably in a civil ceremony in a small town or village outside Rome. Fuller kept the "marriage" secret for a year after Angelo's birth, but Ossoli's family learned of it, and he was disinherited.

Back in New York, Greeley, who had caught the revolutionary fever from Fuller's dispatches, had been busy on behalf of the cause–writing supportive editorials, making speeches, and raising money. When Mazzini's government took power in February 1849 Fuller left Angelo in the care of a nurse and returned to Rome. She joined Ossoli, a sergeant in the Civic Guard, and while the French besieged the city, Fuller supervised the government's military hospital. The city fell in July, and the French general ordered all foreigners who had helped the Republic to be out of Rome in twenty-four hours. Fuller and Ossoli left for Rieti, where they found Angelo seriously ill. After nursing him back to health, the family traveled to Florence in November. By this time Fuller was openly calling herself "Ossoli," and it is as "Margaret Fuller Ossoli" that libraries catalog her works.

There was no longer any reason to keep the "marriage" secret. The revolution had failed and with it, Ossoli's hopes of a government position and reconciliation with his family. The announcement of her liaison produced mixed reactions. Some, like Greeley, were morally affronted; others rallied to her defense. The English-speaking community in Florence considered the couple scandalous, although Elizabeth Barrett Browning eventually relented and invited Fuller into her literary circle.

The loss of Greeley as a friend and ally hurt Fuller in several ways. He had dropped her columns when he learned about Ossoli. Fuller had counted on that income to support her family and had also counted on him to publish her book on the Italian revolution, which she had nearly completed. In addition to losing her livelihood, Fuller and Ossoli were the target of relentless police surveillance. In April 1850 Fuller began to make plans to go home. She borrowed three hundred dollars on a note guaranteed by Marcus Spring and booked passage for her family on the merchant ship *Elizabeth*.

Memorial to Fuller in Cambridge, Massachusetts

On 17 May 1850 they set sail from Livorno. The voyage was calamitous. The captain died of smallpox and was buried at Gibraltar. Angelo came down with the same disease but finally recovered. They were almost home when a sudden storm blew the ship off course. It went aground off Fire Island, and the cargo of heavy Italian marble broke through the ship's bottom. During a lull in the wind and rain, some of the passengers and crew were able to swim to shore. The steward took Angelo, vowing to save him. Then the gale resumed and the ship went down. The bodies of Fuller and Ossoli were never recovered; the bodies of Angelo and the steward were washed ashore. Some of Fuller's diaries and letters were found, but the manuscript about the Italian revolution was lost.

For many years after her death Margaret Fuller was considered one of the minor writers of the period, overshadowed by such giants as Emerson, Thoreau, Nathaniel Hawthorne, and James Russell Lowell. More recent critical assessments, judging Fuller's work without the anti-female prejudice common to the nineteenth-century commentators, have found merit in it, especially in her criticism, her feminist writings, and her serious studies on European, especially German, culture. Her writing was uneven and often badly organized, but it was developing and getting better. Fuller felt that her manuscript on the Italian revolution was the best writing she had ever done; maybe it was. Certainly Fuller's idealistic efforts to civilize American culture and to promote American literature and art through her work in the *Dial* make her significant. Fuller deserves the credit for nurturing and sustaining the journal through its first two very troubled years, thus ensuring that the ideas and the writings it contained would find an audience.

Although Fuller was plagued by ill health from childhood, she worked at a killing pace all her life. In an age when women were expected to be either ornaments or drudges, the miracle is that she did anything at all. She had a powerful effect on the people with whom she came in contact: the women of the "Conversations" to whom she imparted her ideas; and influential men such as Greeley, Emerson, Thoreau, Carlyle, and Mazzini. Her causes–be they social reform, women's equality, or revolution in Italy–produced no immediate results, but her efforts were among the prophetic warnings of changes to come. She was born too soon, yet her ideas and ideals have relevance today.

Letters and Journals:
Love-Letters of Margaret Fuller 1845-1846, introduction by Julia Ward Howe (New York: Appleton, 1903; London: T. Fisher Unwin, 1903);

The Letters of Ralph Waldo Emerson, ed. Ralph L. Rusk, 6 volumes (New York: Columbia University Press, 1939);

Leona Rostenberg, "Margaret Fuller's Roman Diary," *Journal of Modern History,* 12 (June 1940): 209-220;

Joel Myerson, "Margaret Fuller's 1842 Journal: At Concord with the Emersons," *Harvard Literary Bulletin,* 21 (July 1973): 320-340;

Letters of Margaret Fuller, edited by Robert N. Hudspeth, 4 volumes to date (Ithaca: Cornell University Press, 1983-1987).

Bibliographies:
Joel Myerson, *Margaret Fuller: An Annotated Secondary Bibliography,* (New York: Burt Franklin, 1977);

Myerson, *Margaret Fuller, A Descriptive Bibliography* (Pittsburgh: University of Pittsburgh Press, 1978).

Biographies:
Julia Ward Howe, *Margaret Fuller (Marchesa Ossoli)* (Boston: Roberts Brothers, 1883);

Thomas Wentworth Higginson, *Margaret Fuller Ossoli,* American Men of Letters Series (Boston: Houghton, Mifflin, 1884);

Mason Wade, *Margaret Fuller: Whetstone of Genius* (New York: Viking, 1940);

Madeleine B. Stern, *The Life of Margaret Fuller* (New York: Dutton, 1942);

Faith Chipperfield, *In Quest of Love: The Life and Death of Margaret Fuller* (New York: Coward-McCann, 1957);

Joseph Jay Deiss, *The Roman Years of Margaret Fuller* (New York: Crowell, 1969);

Paula B. Blanchard, *Margaret Fuller: From Transcendentalism to Revolution* (New York: Delacorte Press/Seymour Lawrence, 1978).

References:
Barbara Belford, "Margaret Fuller," in her *Brilliant Bylines* (New York: Columbia University Press, 1986), pp. 7-19;

Arthur W. Brown, *Margaret Fuller* (New York: Twayne, 1964);

Lawrence Buell, *Literary Transcendentalism: Style and Vision in the American Renaissance* (Ithaca: Cornell University Press, 1973);

Russell E. Durning, *Margaret Fuller, Citizen of the World: An Intermediary Between European and American Literatures* (Heidelberg: Carl Winter, 1969);

Wilma R. Ebbitt, "Margaret Fuller's Ideas on Criticism," *Boston Public Library Quarterly,* 3 (July 1951): 171-187;

Francis Edward Kearns, "Margaret Fuller's Social Criticism," Ph.D. dissertation, University of North Carolina, 1960;

Helen Neill McMaster, "Margaret Fuller as a Literary Critic," *University of Buffalo Studies,* 7 (December 1928): 35-100;

Marie Mitchell Olesen Urbanski, "Margaret Fuller's *Woman in the Nineteenth Century,*" Ph.D. dissertation, University of Kentucky, 1973;

Stanley M. Vogel, *German Literary Influences on the American Transcendentalists* (New Haven: Yale University Press, 1955).

Papers:
The Fuller Family Papers are at Harvard University's Houghton Library. The Boston Public Library also has an extensive collection.

William Davis Gallagher

(21 August 1808-27 June 1894)

John Nerone
University of Illinois

MAJOR POSITIONS HELD: Editor, *Backwoodsman* (1830-1831); *Cincinnati Mirror* (title varies, 1831-1835); *Western Literary Journal and Monthly Review* (1836); *Ohio State Journal* (1837); *Hesperian, or Western Monthly Magazine* (1838-1839); *Cincinnati Gazette* (1839-1841, 1843-1850); *Cincinnati Daily Morning Message* (1841-1843).

BOOKS: *Erato, Number 1* (Cincinnati: Published by Josiah Drake, 1835);
Erato, Number II (Cincinnati: Published by Alexander Flash, 1835);
Erato, Number III (Cincinnati: Published by Alexander Flash, 1837); *Address and Poem Delivered before the Philalathean [sic] Society of Hanover College, Indiana, at the Annual Commencement, August 17, 1846,* by Gallagher and T. H. Shreve (Cincinnati: Printed by L'Hommedieu, 1846);
Facts and Conditions of Progress in the North-West; Being the Annual Discourse for 1850, before the Historical and Philosophical Society of Ohio; Delivered April 8, the Sixty-third Anniversary of the First Settlement of the State (Cincinnati: Published by H. W. Derby, 1850);
Miami Woods, A Golden Wedding, and Other Poems (Cincinnati: Robert Clarke, 1881).

OTHER: *Selections from the Poetical Literature of the West,* edited, with contributions, by Gallagher (Cincinnati: Published by U. P. James, 1841).

PERIODICAL PUBLICATIONS:
NONFICTION
"The Autumn Lay," *Western Messenger,* 1 (November 1835): 358-360;
"On the Western Press," *Hesperian,* 1 (May 1838): 90-94;
"Ohio in 1838," *Hesperian,* 1 (May 1838): 1-17; (June 1838): 95-103; (July 1838): 183-191;
"An Historical Sketch of the Early Settlements and Early Men of Kentucky," *Hesperian,* 2 (December 1838): 89-101;

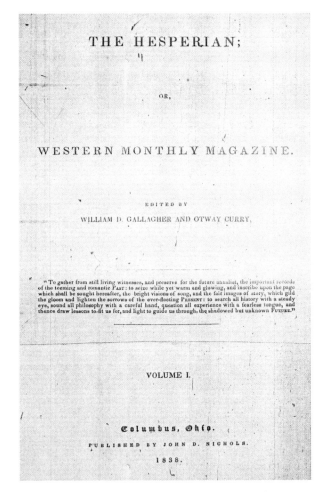

THE HESPERIAN;

OR,

WESTERN MONTHLY MAGAZINE.

EDITED BY
WILLIAM D. GALLAGHER AND OTWAY CURRY,

" To gather from still living witnesses, and preserve for the future annalist, the important records of the teeming and romantic PAST: to seize while yet warm and glowing, and inscribe upon the page which shall be sought hereafter, the bright visions of song, and the fair images of story, which gild the gloom and lighten the sorrows of the ever-fleeting PRESENT: to search all history with a steady eye, sound all philosophy with a careful hand, question all experience with a fearless tongue, and thence draw lessons to-fit us for, and light to guide us through, the shadowed but unknown FUTURE."

VOLUME I.

Columbus, Ohio.
PUBLISHED BY JOHN D. NICHOLS.
1838.

Title page for the first volume of Gallagher's ambitious attempt to promote the idea of a distinctive western literary culture

"A Periodical Literature for the West: What Has it Been? What Ought it to Be?," *Western Literary Journal and Monthly Review,* 1 (November 1844): 1-9;
"Educational Effort in Cincinnati: The Common Schools," *Western Literary Journal and Monthly Review,* 1 (December 1844): 85-88.

POETRY
"The West," *Hesperian,* 2 (December 1838): 160;

"Be Firm! Be True!," *Western Literary Journal and Monthly Review,* 1 (December 1844): 70.

William Davis Gallagher was one of the most important promoters of literary culture in the trans-Appalachian West in the first half of the nineteenth century. Himself a poet and essayist of considerable repute, he edited and published a series of literary magazines and journals in Cincinnati and Columbus, Ohio, especially in the 1830s. He combined his artistic concerns with a frank western boosterism and the promotion of common schools and internal improvements. Throughout his editorial career he maintained a profile of high principle. An early biographer records that "the boys in the printing office used to call him William 'Dignity' Gallagher."

Gallagher was born to Bernard Gallagher and Abigail Davis in Philadelphia in 1808. His father died in 1814, and shortly thereafter the Gallagher family moved to southwestern Ohio. As a boy William enjoyed roving the unspoiled woods of the Ohio River valley, and his youthful appreciation would remain characteristic of his more mature nature poetry. When an adolescent, Gallagher was put out to work by his mother on a couple of local farms. During the winter months he attended a log schoolhouse, where he received a rudimentary education. Later he attended the Lancasterian Seminary in Cincinnati, where he learned printing, working in the office of a locally published religious weekly, called the *Remembrancer.* He was apprenticed to a printer in 1821. Thus while his formal education was slight, he was an attentive student in the print shop and the forest.

In 1826 he went to work as general assistant to James Gazlay, a local Jacksonian lawyer and politician who edited an agricultural and political weekly called the *Western Tiller.* In the next few years he also worked on two general newspapers, the *Emporium* and the *Commercial Register,* the first daily newspaper in the Ohio country.

While learning printing, Gallagher was also writing energetically. He was a regular though anonymous contributor to John Foote's *Cincinnati Literary Gazette* (1824-1826) and edited with an older brother, Francis, a modest literary journal called the *Western Minerva* (1824-1825), of which, unfortunately, no copies survive. In 1827 Gallagher and another aspiring literatus, Otway Curry–also a notable poet–kept up a pseudonymous rivalry in two local papers. Gallagher wrote

as Roderick, Curry as Abdallah. The fanciful aliases are characteristic of an early western desire to imitate more refined, prestigious, and traditional eastern and English writers and publications.

Another common strain of western literary enterprises was apparent in Gallagher's teenage productions–a concentration on the country itself and its natural potential. In 1828 he traveled south through the Mississippi Valley and wrote a series of letters–again under a pseudonym–which were published in the Cincinnati *Saturday Evening Chronicle,* edited by Benjamin Drake, whose tales and sketches had received wide favorable notice. Gallagher's descriptions were popular, and when Drake let his identity be known, Gallagher found himself with a considerable regional reputation.

Politics as well as literature occupied Gallagher during these early years. In the late 1820s Gallagher became an active supporter of Henry Clay, and in 1830 he was offered the editorship of the *Backwoodsman,* a partisan organ in Xenia, Ohio. His tenure was short-lived, largely owing to matters of temperament. Apparently his political stands alienated too many readers. But he was also lured by the gentler muses. He married Miss Emma Adamson and moved back to Cincinnati to edit the *Mirror,* a literary paper issued first every two weeks, then weekly.

The next decade was Gallagher's most fruitful. He edited three literary journals: the *Mirror* (which merged with other journals and changed names several times) from 1831 to 1835; the *Western Literary Journal and Monthly Review* in 1836; and the *Hesperian, or Western Monthly Magazine* from 1838 to 1839. He also contributed to other regional literary magazines, wrote poetry and song lyrics, belonged to several local benevolent, fraternal, and educational organizations, and was an active participant in partisan politics, serving in 1837 as editor of the politically important *Ohio State Journal* and writing for other Whig newspapers. He also published three collections of his poetry.

Gallagher's obsession as an editor was the literary development of the West, and through the decade of the 1830s his ideas became more clearly defined until a formula for western periodical literature had been constructed. Other editors and writers contributed to this construction–Timothy Flint and James Hall are the most noteworthy–but Gallagher was as significant as anyone and certainly the most persistent and energetic of the bunch, if not the most talented.

The *Mirror* was Gallagher's first really significant instrument. It was an eight-page paper, issued first every two weeks and then weekly in Cincinnati, and was priced between two and three dollars for an annual subscription. Its name and format were borrowed from the popular New York *Mirror,* and in general it imitated eastern periodicals. It usually printed short poetry, fiction, essays, reviews, and occasional editorials, sometimes of a political nature, both original and selected. The topics covered included a full range of current interests: literature and the arts, science, geography, economic development and internal improvements, educational reform, and, to a lesser extent, religion and politics. Gallagher described the *Mirror* as having "at once an elevated rather than a popular tone, and a useful rather than an amusing character. . . ." Its motto was "A Voice in the Wilderness." And it was a fairly successful journal, enjoying the support of a good number of western writers and drawing a decent subscription list of eight hundred. Despite its avowed seriousness, it was an entertaining publication and remains interesting reading. But it was never economically successful due, according to Gallagher, to its subscribers' failure to pay up.

There are conflicting accounts of Gallagher's departure from the *Mirror.* One rendition has Gallagher being forced out for refusing to print a favorable review of Thomas Paine's *Age of Reason*; another, and equally likely, story has Gallagher fired because of financial incompetence. Both accounts point up significant characteristics. Gallagher often drew battle lines on editorial issues, and similar disagreements on principle appear to have been associated with his departures from the *Ohio State Journal* and later the *Cincinnati Gazette.* He was also plagued throughout his editorial career by money problems, and none of his literary journals was profitable. Usually he would, with some justification, blame this on tardy subscribers or uncooperative or incompetent publishers.

In 1836 Gallagher became editor of the *Western Literary Journal and Monthly Review.* The format of this periodical was different, though the topics included were much the same as in the *Mirror.* As a monthly, the *Literary Journal* featured longer and more elaborate articles and stories and in general had a more somber tone. It drew less support in terms of contributions and subscriptions: according to Buley, "The editor drew upon his own talents for approximately half of contents." After six months it merged with James

Hall's *Western Monthly Magazine,* and the two passed out of existence together in a couple of months. Gallagher himself noted that after the subscription lists of the *Journal* and the *Magazine* were combined, "it was discovered that both did not amount to one thousand names." The audience for such projects seems to have been rather narrow.

With the demise of the *Western Literary Journal* Gallagher moved to Columbus, where a younger brother helped Gallagher find employment as an editor at the *Ohio State Journal.* Gallagher's tenure was brief, but when he stepped down–or was let go–he had already made arrangements to establish another monthly magazine, the *Hesperian.* More substantial and ambitious than his previous efforts, Gallagher and later commentators called this his most important accomplishment as a literary promoter.

Gallagher sought to make the *Hesperian* "deserving of the respectful consideration of the friends of education, morality, general intelligence, and polite literature." His appeal was to all educated people interested in useful knowledge, and again he sought a tone of seriousness that occasionally became simply ponderous. Gallagher would contrast the gravity of his enterprise with frivolous eastern periodicals–"that flood of mammoth newspapers and bepictured magazines which rolls over the Allegheny Mountains and inundates the broad plains of the West"– which were more successful both east and west. Like earlier efforts the *Hesperian* featured a broad range of material: stories, poems, essays, reviews, and editorials, many from Gallagher's own pen. As with the *Mirror* and *Literary Journal,* much of the material was copied from other periodicals, but by far the largest proportion was original. And as with his other endeavors, the guiding idea was the West.

Gallagher's formula for western literature had by this time reached maturity. In part it still depended upon imitation of eastern ideals, by way of demonstrating that civilization had penetrated the trans-Appalachian forests. The result was a large amount of derivative verse and fiction that often became verbose or precious. But more important to Gallagher's project was a pursuit of western themes. Thus he described the purpose of a periodical literature for the West: to "reflect the intellectual light of this region, assist to elevate and echo its moral tone, portray with distinctiveness its physical features, and exhibit the successive developments of its great and varied

Prospectus for the Hesperian

natural resources. . . ." The West needed a distinctive voice because it had a distinctive morality, derived in part from its unique physical resources and in part from its colorful history. Gallagher and his colleagues—his thought on these matters was characteristic of a large group of contemporaries—believed in a western character, both in the sense of a unique personality and of high-minded adherence to principle. Western periodicals should both depict and build western character. Hence, periodicals should be rigorously moral in tone. The *Hesperian* especially lacked playfulness.

Western literature in Gallagher's formula was to be practical. In part, the media for western literature discouraged both the refinement and the lack of concern for usefulness that was available to eastern writers, who could publish through a number of outlets. "Not so in the West, however, where our choicest thoughts flow through the dingy channel of a newspaper column. . . ." Such a medium necessarily kept western literature from drifting too far afield.

Consequently, concrete concerns would permeate Gallagher's western literature. The development of the western country, the preservation of frontier history, and the cultivation of western reputation in the East grounded Gallagher's projects, and his columns and editorials concerned

themselves with substantial questions like public education and the building of roads and bridges.

Such a literature could not be confined to the printed page, and Gallagher's efforts naturally extended to a variety of forums. He was a founding member of lyceums, mechanics' institutes, and historical societies in Cincinnati, Columbus, and later Louisville, Kentucky. One of the more lucid and influential pronouncements of his goals was his 1850 presidential address to the Historical and Philosophical Society of Ohio, published in pamphlet form as *Facts and Conditions of Progress in the North-West* (1850). But the most likely forum was politics. Hence, it is not surprising that in the 1840s—after the failure of the *Hesperian,* which appears to have affected Gallagher deeply—his attention turned more and more to politics, and he settled in as editor of a Whig daily.

Gallagher was famous in his own day as a poet more than as an editor, and whatever reputation he still enjoys today is based upon his verse. His poems were frequently set to music—his ballad "The Spotted Fawn" was a tremendous popular hit—and were included in common school readers and reprinted in newspapers. The three volumes of *Erato* (1835-1837), collections of his poetry, were favorably received, especially in the West, and, according to Rusk, seem to have influenced Edgar Allan Poe in the East. In 1841 he published a collection entitled *Selections from the Poetical Literature of the West,* including his long poem "Miami Woods," which again attracted favorable notice. During the next few decades he continued to write verse, though less compulsively; his hortatory poems were circulated widely during the Civil War. In 1881 he published another collection of poems, *Miami Woods, A Golden Wedding, and Other Poems,* which was intended to be the first of a two-volume set of collected works. But due to a lack of popular interest, the second volume never saw print.

An 1849 article in the *Western Quarterly Review* on Gallagher's writing succinctly summed up his career: "There are three distinctly marked periods in his poetical life. The poems of the first period exhibit no very decided individuality of character. They were suggested by reading and casual occurrences, and show the influence which a study of Coleridge and Byron exerted over his mind. . . . The second period is marked by poems which indicate much familiarity with external nature. . . . The poems of the third period betoken much more sympathy with Humanity." In his poetry, then, he moved from youthful imitative romanticism to meditative nature poetry to allegory and didacticism. His best verse retains the vigor and grace that his contemporaries admired, though much of his poetry is guilty of the two faults which he consistently criticized in others: exaggeration and "rhyming mania."

The same themes that impelled his editorial career inspired his poetry. He proclaimed a conventional Christianity and frequently drew religious analogies in his nature poems, as in this comment on the evening dew after a hot summer day in "August":

> So, to the thirsting soul,
> Cometh the dew of the Almighty's love;
> And the seathed heart, made whole,
> Turneth in joy above,
> To where the spirit freely may expand,
> And rove, untrammel'd, in that 'better land.'

This religious creed included the ethical demand for hard work and self-denial as indicated in "The Laborer," in which Gallagher attributes the low status of the working man to:

> uncurb'd passions–low desires–
> Absence of noble self-respect–
> Death, in the breast's consuming fires,
> To that high nature which aspires
> Forever, till thus check'd:
> These are thine enemies–thy worst:
> They chain thee to thy lowly lot–
> Thy labor and thy life accurst.

Virtuous self-restraint promised equality, though:

> With this, and passions under ban,
> True faith, and holy trust in God,
> Thou art the peer of any man.

Gallagher's conservative morality thus did not prevent him from being a friend of democracy, and he was considered in his time to be sympathetic to Christian socialism. His attitudes toward political rectitude are similar to his more famous New England and eastern contemporaries, especially John Greenleaf Whittier and William Cullen Bryant. Both as poet and editor he sought to thunder on behalf of truth, justice, and reform, in accordance with his injunction in "Truth and Freedom": "He who seeks the Truth, and trembles/At the dangers he must brave,/Is not fit to be a Freeman:/He, at best, is but a slave." The union of these guiding ideas–God, virtue, freedom, democracy–produced a firm belief in progress, especially achieved through hard work.

Like his contemporaries, Gallagher believed that he could see the better day dawning in the rise of the western country. Chauvinistically, perhaps, he depicted the land itself as a unique setting for the development of a free and virtuous society. In the West a pure civilization, freed from the corruption that time had wrought in Europe and the eastern United States, could establish itself. Instrumental to this democratic civilization would be a viable western literature, expressing the new western character, celebrating western history, upholding morality and Christian virtue, and actively engaged in the work of material progress.

By 1839, however, when the *Hesperian* failed, Gallagher's enthusiasm had been tempered. For years he had been poorly rewarded for his literary activities; now, a man with a growing family, he needed steady work. While editing the *Hesperian* in Columbus he had reported on the state legislature for the *Cincinnati Gazette,* then edited by Charles Hammond, perhaps the most influential Whig editor of his day. Gallagher's letters, appearing over the pseudonym "Probus," were widely reprinted throughout Ohio and were credited, among other things, with crystallizing opposition to a harsh fugitive slave law. When Hammond offered Gallagher a position as literary editor of the *Gazette* in 1839, he accepted gratefully, and when Hammond died a couple of years later, Gallagher was his natural successor.

He continued to promote western literature through his newspaper columns, but his interests gradually turned more to politics. The slavery controversy especially attracted his efforts, and he left the *Gazette* for a brief period in the 1840s to edit the *Daily Message,* partly at least so he would have more freedom to editorialize on slavery. (Like all of Gallagher's independent journalistic enterprises, the *Message* failed quickly.)

In 1850 Gallagher left the *Gazette* to take a position as personal secretary to Thomas Corwin, who had recently been appointed Secretary of the Treasury. From Washington he moved to Louisville in 1853, where he had bought a half interest in the *Courier.* Gallagher's liberal views on slavery were controversial in Kentucky, a fact which made his continued association with the *Courier* problematical. With some encouragement, he sold his share of the newspaper and retired from political journalism to lead the life of a gentleman farmer. He continued to write, contributing to the *Columbian and Great West,* a magazine devoted to western literature in Cincinnati (more reminiscent of the mammoth, heavily illustrated papers of the East than Gallagher's austere monthlies), and to the *National Era,* an abolitionist weekly published in Washington, D.C., and edited by Gamaliel Bailey, a former resident of Cincinnati and longtime friend and collaborator. He also edited an agricultural journal called the *Western Farmer's Journal.*

As the Civil War approached, Gallagher was drawn to the Republican party. He was a delegate to the 1860 Chicago convention and was a member of the delegation that carried news of Lincoln's nomination to Springfield. During the war itself he held the important post of special customs agent for the Mississippi Valley. At the same time, he wrote patriotic verse that was widely reprinted.

In the three decades between the end of the Civil War and Gallagher's death in 1894, he turned his attention mostly to practical matters. He wrote several articles for the *Louisville and Ohio Valley Manufacturer and Merchant,* including a notable essay entitled "The Area of Subsistence, and its Natural Outlet to the Ocean and the World," about the geography and economy of the Southwest. (This was a companion to his 1850 address *Facts and Conditions of Progress in the North-West.*) In his final years renewed interest in the poetry of his younger days culminated in the publication of the collection *Miami Woods, A Golden Wedding, and Other Poems* (1881). He lived in or near Louisville until his death and was buried in Cincinnati.

As an editor Gallagher is more notable for energy than success. He was a tireless promoter of western literature, both in print and through organizations and associations. His contemporaries accorded him respect, and he was acknowledged to be among the most talented of western men of letters. But his conception of western literature failed to attract the wide support he sought.

The nineteenth century did see the maturation of a popular western literature, but it was not Gallagher's. The main characteristics of this popular literature–exaggeration, local color, dialect, adventure, lack of, or hostility toward, refinement–were in direct opposition to that he had envisioned. "Usefulness"–Gallagher's main concern–was not characteristic of this literature. Rather, the fruitful combination of practical and artistic concerns for which he had campaigned never came about. Art turned to entertainment,

and politics took over the pursuit of western developments. Gallagher's own literary contributions survived mainly in children's schoolbooks.

The reasons for Gallagher's failures were manifold. He blamed publishers, fellow editors, and delinquent subscribers but never acknowledged that the project itself might have been misconceived. He apparently never doubted that a literature that combined high moral seriousness with usefulness would be popular, or at least popular enough to support periodicals. Here he was wrong. Also he never doubted that there were enough talented writers in the West to fill the pages of such periodicals with worthy material. On this score, too, he was wrong, though to a certain extent this judgment remains a matter of taste.

References:

R. Carlyle Buley, *The Old Northwest: Pioneer Period, 1815-1840,* 2 volumes (Bloomington: Indiana University Press, 1950);

James Freeman Clarke, "Western Poetry," *Western Messenger,* 1 (July 1835): 60-68;

William T. Coggeshall, *The Poets and Poetry of the West, with Biographical and Critical Notices* (New York: Follett, Foster, 1864);

John T. Flanagan, Introduction to *Poetical Literature of the West,* edited by William D. Gallagher (Gainesville, Fla.: Scholars' Facsimiles and Reprints, 1968);

Ralph L. Rusk, *The Literature of the Middle Western Frontier,* 2 volumes (New York: Columbia University Press, 1925);

James A. Tague, "William D. Gallagher: Champion of Western Literary Periodicals," *Ohio Historical Quarterly,* 69 (July 1960): 257-271;

Emerson Venable, *Poets of Ohio* (Cincinnati: Robert Clarke, 1909);

William H. Venable, *Beginnings of Literary Culture in the Ohio Valley* (New York: Peter Smith, 1947);

William H. Venable, *A Selection from the Manuscripts of William Henry Venable* (Columbus: Ohio Historical Society, n.d.);

"William D. Gallagher," *Western Quarterly Review,* 1 (January 1849): 135-170.

Papers:

William Davis Gallagher's papers are held at the Ohio Historical Society, the Cincinnati Historical Society, and the Filson Club in Louisville, Kentucky.

William Gibbons

(birth and death dates unknown)

Ada Van Gastel
Auburn University

MAJOR POSITIONS HELD: Bookseller, printer, publisher (1792-1793), *Lady's Magazine; And Repository of Entertaining Knowledge.*

Very little is known about William Gibbons, the late-eighteenth-century printer and publisher who was largely responsible for producing the first American periodical intended for women readers. From his store on 144 North Third Street in Philadelphia he sold books, such as *Paradise Lost, Pilgrim's Progress, The Vicar of Wakefield*, Alexander Pope's *Essay on Man, Louisa, a Poetic Novel*, and Phillis Wheatley's *Poems*. In 1792 Gibbons was selected by a "Literary Society" to print a newly established periodical entitled the *Lady's Magazine; And Repository of Entertaining Knowledge*. From Gibbons's press also came an early edition of Mary Wollstonecraft's *A Vindication of the Rights of Woman*. The imprint of *A Vindication* carries the date 1792, which makes William Gibbons one of the first American printers of the book, which originally appeared in England in that same year. In 1793 Gibbons printed Edward Moore's *Fables for the Ladies. To which are added, Fables of flora* and Thomas Story's *The Means, Nature, Properties and Effects of True Faith Considered*. Gibbons printed Samuel Richardson's *Pamela* the subsequent year. Nothing else is known of his life.

It is not known who belonged to the "Literary Society" that established the *Lady's Magazine* and was responsible for its contents. In the "Original Plan" for the journal it called itself a "Society of Literary Characters," and in its "Address to the Ladies" its members called themselves the "editors" of the magazine. Anonymity among writers and editors was not unusual at the time; on the contrary, Frank Luther Mott records in volume 1 of *A History of American Magazines* (1938) that anonymity was the custom in eighteenth-century magazines.

The *Lady's Magazine* was, according to the "Original Plan," "the first attempt of the kind, made in the country." In England the women's magazine was established, and many were published during the century: the *Ladies' Mercury* (1693), the *Ladies' Diary; or, Women's Almanack* (1704), *Visiter* (1723), the *Ladies' Journal* (1727), *Parrot* (1728), the *Lady's Magazine; or, Universal Repository* (1733), the *Female Spectator* (1744), and others. Perhaps the business of settling into a new country slowed American recognition of women as potential readers. But as the eighteenth century progressed, attitudes were rapidly changing. It was the time when Charlotte Smith, Fanny Burney, and Mary Wollstonecraft rose to fame in England, and when Phillis Wheatley, Susanne Rowson, and Hannah Webster Forster acquired an audience in America.

The word "magazine" in the title of the *Lady's Magazine* was meant in its eighteenth-century sense: "a Monthly Collection, [intended] to treasure up, as in a Magazine, the most Remarkable Pieces" (*Gentleman's Magazine*, 1731). The *Lady's Magazine* announced that it would feature "a selection of miscellaneous pieces, taken from the works of the most entertaining and instructive writers that have appeared in the present century, whether in Europe or America." The new periodical was special in that it was "designed chiefly for the amusement as well as instruction of the FAIR SEX." "Essays, calculated to regulate the taste, form the judgment, and improve the mind" were to be the main feature of the journal. Along with "the most *lively prose*," it would further offer the most "*pathetic verse*." Occasionally "a general review of polite literature" would be included. The editors promised that "The DIVINE, the PHILOSOPHER and the NATURALIST, shall each have a treat, adapted to their different fancies and pursuits."

The *Lady's Magazine* set out with an attitude of respect for women and a high estimation of their abilities, although these abilities were judged to be of a different sort than men's. Thus, the frontispiece of the first issue consists of an emblematic engraving in which the Genius of the *Lady's Magazine*, accompanied by the Genius of Emulation bearing a laurel crown, approaches Liberty and presents the goddess with a copy of "The Rights of Woman." But in "Address to the Ladies" in the first issue, the editors also note that women are "to give ease to the weary traveller, in the rugged paths of science; and soften the rigour of intense study." They continue, "it is *theirs* to chace away the diffidence of bashful merit, and give real dignity to the boldest thought. In short, it is the province of *female excellence alone*, with the beame of intellectual light, which illuminates the paths of literature, to diffuse the glowing warmth of genial affection, and by a lively combination of sweet perfections, *add charms*—even to the native beauties of the most brilliant production." Intellectual light and charm were thus combined in the magazine's conception of the duty of woman and expressed in the motto "the Mind t'improve and yet delight." In addition to providing food for philosophical and spiritual thought, the "Literary Society" promised its readers "whatever tends to form the ACCOMPLISHED WOMAN, the COMPLETE ECONOMIST, and that greatest of all treasures—a GOOD WIFE."

The mode of execution of the *Lady's Magazine* was unique. To avoid the suspense and frustration of reading the phrase "to be continued" at the climax of every interesting piece, six monthly issues were offered at once: a volume of at least three hundred pages appeared semiannually, on 1 December and 1 June. A marbleized cover and a frontispiece adorned each work. Subscriptions ran for two dollars per annum (not much at the time: Philadelphia's *Columbian* and *American Museum* were $2.66 and $3.33, respectively). Subscriptions were taken in by the publisher and "principal Booksellers in this city," and by selected shops in Boston, Albany, New York, Baltimore, Richmond, Charleston, and Savannah.

The first issue of the *Lady's Magazine*, dated 1 December 1792, opens by invoking Aesop's fable of the man, the boy, and the ass. The editors, who had received contradictory advice from subscribers, felt like the man "who could not please the people, when he rode upon the ass, or when his boy rode upon the ass, or when both rode upon the ass, or when neither rode upon the ass, or when they agreed to carry the ass." Examples of the subscribers' advice were then printed. One correspondent expressed delight at the creation of a ladies' journal; another hoped there would be "articles that are calculated for the gentlemen." Some subscribers thought the magazine should offer a list of recently published novels; others cautioned against having women read "improper literature" such as "Eastern tales" or be exposed to "outrageous modes of dress." The editors finally promised to "endeavor to please all parties *at one time or other;* but they must see how impractical this will *be at all times.*"

The first issue contains pieces specifically aimed at the woman reader: a letter from a brother to a sister at a boarding school filled with precepts about proper feminine conduct; and an essay on love which talks of "your husband." The issue also contains pieces of general interest, such as a reprint of an account by a physician, C. P. Thunberg, to the president of the Royal Society in London, describing the government, manners, and customs of the inhabitants of Japan. There are sentimental tales such as "The NUN, an affecting story" in the mode of eighteenth-century novels; but there is also an essay arguing that authors are only good writers when they "record some moral sentiment." There is an essay advising ladies to take care of the appearance of their feet. The foot essay is counterbalanced by a poem inviting readers to envy Sophia because she possessed the only kind of charms which have lasting value: "those of the mind." There is a spicy tale set in Italy, but for the sake of "Philanglus," there is also an anecdote of a British lord and an essay larded with references to English writers such as Pope, Oliver Goldsmith, Richard Cumberland, and Edward Young. While most of the articles are extremely serious and authoritative in tone, there is also a satirical piece entitled "Matrimonial Creed," which presents the problem husband and wife face when they each expect to be obeyed by the other, "Yet they cannot both obey, but one must obey." The poem concludes, "This is the conjugal faith, which except a man believe faithfully, he had rather never be married."

To reach as wide an audience as possible each issue of the magazine also contained sections of "Interesting and Pleasing Reflections," anecdotes, marriages and deaths, and foreign and domestic news. Blank space was prohibited, and the pages were filled with riddles, rebuses, enigmas, or other testers of readers' wits in between the longer pieces. Many of the anecdotes were not humorous but, on the contrary, quite sorrowful. One tells, for instance, of a man weeping over his lost love in the woods, while another relates a legend of the insatiable curiosity of Frederick, King of Sicily, who pressed a famous diver to make a second exploration of a dangerous underwater area. The diver went down, "but was never since heard of." Marriages and deaths referred mostly to inhabitants of Philadelphia, though the names of some persons in New York, Brooklyn, Corlaer's Hook, Wilmington, and towns in Virginia and Georgia also were included.

Foreign news was usually European. Domestic news dealt with a variety of topics, from subscriptions to the Lancaster turnpike-road to the opening of a new coffeehouse in New York; from skirmishes with the Indians in Ohio to the threat of an earthquake in Montreal ("no material injury ha[s] ensued, a church, and two or three houses, having alone suffered some trivial damage").

The poetry in the *Lady's Magazine* is riddled with clichés, stilted diction, and forced word order for the sake of rhyme; most of it sounds like the following couplet:

To thee, this bleeding bosom must complain
Her woes on woes, a num'rous sable train.

"The Tear," "To Celia," "A Female Character," and "Thoughts after reading an Account of the Death of a YOUNG LADY" are typical titles. The last poem opens with words which do not sound like an admirer bewailing the death of a beautiful lady but more like a murderer congratulating himself for having committed the deed: " 'Tis done! she's gone!" Not all poetry is this poor; there are a few exceptions. One poem, which is neither hackneyed in content nor in expression or grammatical structure, is plagiarized. The title of the poem has been changed, and no name of the author is given, but "The Soul's Errand" is Sir Walter Raleigh's "The Lie."

The *Lady's Magazine* was very conscious of its position as the first American periodical primarily directed toward women. Not only was it soliciting from women, but it was also trying to build a female subscription base. On 1 June 1793, in a new "Address to the Ladies," the editors declared they had undertaken the magazine for motives other than "personal interest." They wanted to "rescue the *fair sex* from that obscurity in which the timidity of *female delicacy* would hide itself," they said, "as well as to *animate the breast* to seize the laurels to *their vivacity* and *their merits*." They rejected two submissions because of their portrayal of women: "*S.L.*'s piece we have received, but . . . he employs his pen . . . in degrading ideas of *female learning,* he will be viewed by us as an object of contempt"; and "If the *Old Bache-*

lor would *scour* himself, instead of '*endeavouring to scour the fair sex,*' he might perhaps be admissible– But, as '*charity begins at home,*' we think reformation ought also."

A few pieces published in the journal may be called genuinely feminist, such as an excerpt from Wollstonecraft's *A Vindication of the Rights of Woman.* Other pieces were reactionary. Instruction, for example, could take a form reminiscent of conduct books, albeit with a tone less condescending. The "Scheme for Increasing the Power of the Fair Sex" is a good example. Written by a man, the essay proceeds from the rhetorical query of Berkeley, late bishop of Coyne, "whether a *woman of fashion* ought not to be declared a *public enemy,*" to its counterposition, that "a woman of virtue and prudence is a public good–a public benefactor." The writer concludes, "that this power which the fair sex have over us, may be used to greater and better purposes than it has hitherto been generally employed to promote. I am persuaded, that nothing short of a general reformation of manners would take place, were the ladies to use their power in discouraging our licentious manners."

To help bring women into the limelight, the *Lady's Magazine* established the feature "SELECT LETTERS, or Specimens of FEMALE LITERATURE." This section appeared in seven of the twelve issues. A clever, entertaining letter by Lady Mary Wortley Montagu opens the series. Two letters of Anna Savigny follow about her courtship with, and marriage to, a man of a different creed and country and of limited finances. Another letter by Lady Mary describes life in Constantinople, and one from Queen Elizabeth to Henry IV of France warns: "It is, believe me, a dangerous experiment, *to do evil, that a good may come.*" There are also letters from Lady Jane Grey to her sister, written the evening before she was beheaded, and several epistles from unknown ladies with names like Clarinda, Maria Hervey, and Eliza Stanton.

The *Lady's Magazine* existed for one year. Why exactly it was dissolved is not known. Perhaps it had something to do with the semiannual form in which it was issued, or perhaps it had to do with the fact that there already were two thriving magazines in Philadelphia, the *Columbian* and the *American Museum.* In any case most magazines had only a very short life, according to Mott, who says eighteen months was the average life of an eighteenth-century American magazine. The *Lady's Magazine* deserves our brief attention for its pioneering effort to draw women into active participation in the medium.

References:

Joseph Blumenthal, *The Printed Book in America* (Boston: Godine, 1977);

Roger P. Bristol, *Supplement to Charles Evans' American Bibliography* (Charlottesville: University Press of Virginia, 1970);

Helmut Lehmann-Haupt, *The Book in America: A History of the Making and Selling of Books in the United States,* second edition (New York: Bowker, 1951);

Douglas C. McMurtrie, *A History of Printing in the United States* (New York: Franklin, 1969);

Frank Luther Mott, *A History of American Magazines,* 5 volumes (Cambridge, Mass.: Harvard University Press, 1938-1968);

Rollo G. Silver, *The American Printer, 1787-1825* (Charlottesville: University Press of Virginia, 1967);

John Tebbel, *A History of Book Publishing in the United States* (New York: Bowker, 1972);

Isaiah Thomas, *The History of Printing in America, with a Biography of Printers* (New York: Franklin, 1964).

Caroline H. Gilman

(8 October 1794-15 September 1888)

Maurine H. Beasley
University of Maryland

See also the Gilman entry in *DLB 3: Antebellum Writers in New York and the South.*

MAJOR POSITION HELD: Editor, *Rose-Bud, or Youth's Gazette,* renamed *Southern Rose-Bud* from 1833 to 1835, renamed *Southern Rose* from 1835 to 1839 (1832-1839).

BOOKS: *Recollections of a Housekeeper,* as Mrs. Clarissa Packard (New York: Harper, 1834);

The Poetry of Travelling in the United States (New York: S. Colman, 1838);

Recollections of a Southern Matron (New York: Harper, 1838); revised and enlarged as *Recollections of a New England Bride and of a Southern Matron* (New York: Putnam, 1852);

Tales and Ballads (Boston: W. Crosby, 1839);

Love's Progress (New York: Harper, 1840);

The Rose-Bud Wreath (Charleston, S.C.: S. Babcock, 1841);

Oracles from the Poets: A Fanciful Diversion for the Drawing-Room (New York & London: Wiley, Putnam, 1844);

Stories and Poems for Children (New York: C. S. Francis, 1845);

The Little Wreath of Stories and Poems for Children (New York: C. S. Francis/Boston: J. H. Francis, 1846);

The Sibyl, or New Oracles from the Poets (New York: Wiley & Putnam, 1848);

Verses of a Life Time (Boston & Cambridge: J. Munroe, 1849);

A Gift Book of Stories and Poems for Children (New York: C. S. Francis/Boston: J. H. Francis, 1850);

Oracles for Youth: A Home Pastime (New York: Putnam, 1852);

Vernon Grove; or Hearts As They Are (New York: Rudd & Carleton, 1859);

Stories and Poems by Mother and Daughter, by Gilman and Caroline Howard Jervey (Boston: Lee & Shepard, 1872);

The Poetic Fate Book; New Oracles from the Poets (Boston: Lee & Shepard/New York: Lee, Shepard & Dillingham, 1874);

Recollections of the Private Centennial Celebration of the Overthrow of the Tea, at Griffin's Wharf, in Boston Harbor, Dec. 16, 1773 (Cambridge, Mass.: Wilson, 1874);

Caroline Gilman

The Young Fortune Teller; Oracles for Youth, by Gilman and Caroline Howard (Boston: Lee & Shepard, 1874).

OTHER: *Letters of Eliza Wilkinson During the Invasion and Possession of Charlestown, S.C. by the British in the Revolutionary War,* compiled by Gilman (New York: S. Colman, 1839);

Record of Inscriptions in the Cemetery and Building of the Unitarian, Formerly Denominated the Independent Church, Archdale Street, Charlestown, S.C. from 1777 to 1860, compiled by Gilman (Charleston, S.C.: Walker, Evans, 1860).

PERIODICAL PUBLICATIONS: "Letters of a Confederate Mother," *Atlantic Monthly,* 137 (April 1926): 503-515;

"The Gamester," *Southern Rose,* 6 (1838): 214-216;

"The Lost Mail, A Tale of the Forest," *Southern Rose,* 6 (1838): 216-221.

Caroline Howard Gilman, a sentimental moralizer who chronicled middle-class domesticity, ed-

ited one of the earliest magazines for youth in the United States. Interesting today as a reflection of what Americans thought was suitable reading for the family hearth in the 1830s, her publication pictured women and children as the moral center of society.

As a popular literary figure of the pre-Civil War era, Gilman attempted to lessen the tensions between the North and the South through her varied writings, some of which appeared in her magazine before being published in book form. Her efforts to draw together the two sections of the country stemmed from her own divided loyalties.

Born in Boston, Massachusetts, Gilman was the third daughter and fifth of six children of Samuel and Anna Lillie Howard. Her father, a prosperous shipwright, died when she was two and her mother when she was ten. Her education was irregular as the family moved from one suburb of Boston to another, finally settling in Cambridge, where she lived until her marriage at the age of twenty-five to Samuel Gilman, a Harvard graduate and Unitarian minister. During her teenage years and early twenties she developed her writing skills and had several pieces published, including a story for the *North American Review.*

Immediately after their marriage the Gilmans moved to Charleston, South Carolina, so her husband could take an appointment at the Second Independent Church. They eventually had seven children. Their two sons and the youngest daughter died in infancy.

In 1832, while she was busy bringing up her children, Gilman began publication of the *Rose-Bud, or Youth's Gazette,* altering the name to *Southern Rose-Bud* the following year and changing the title to the *Southern Rose* in 1835 as the focus of the magazine changed from children to the entire family. The first issue, printed by J. S. Burges for Gilman, appeared on 11 August 1832; it presented an idealized picture of childhood. The journal had as its caption a line from Sir Walter Scott, "The Rose is Fairest When 'Tis Budding New," and a small woodcut of a rosebud decorated the first page. Gilman saluted her readers in a column beginning, "My dear Young Friends, I imagine at this moment that I see many an American boy and girl unfolding this tiny sheet, with sparkling eyes. 'What,' they exclaim, 'a real newspaper like father's!' "

A variety of motives apparently prompted her decision to start what she called "the first juvenile newspaper, if I mistake not, in the Union."

(Gilman was incorrect on this point. At least four earlier children's periodicals had been started in the United States: the *Children's Magazine* at Hartford, in 1789; the *Juvenile Magazine* and the *Juvenile Olio*, both at Philadelphia, in 1802; and the *Teachers' Offering*, also in Philadelphia in 1823.) Her publication, however, may well have been the first in the South. As an editor Gilman wanted to give "to the youthful mind a right direction." But she also used the magazine to expand her own literary endeavors.

In her column Gilman invited contributions from youthful readers but made plain her guiding principles: no mention of political or religious controversy. She explained she had selected the rosebud as an emblem for the magazine because it was a gift from God and a symbol for childish innocence. Children, she maintained, should be as pure and sweet as the rose. She beseeched them to be models of piety and industry with descriptions of such activities as a "Juvenile Industry Society," which met to sew clothing for the poor while listening to "judicious selections in reading."

Typical of the piety prescribed for children was an article titled "Saturday Reflections": "Have I deserved this holiday? Have I been respectful to my parents, obedient to my teachers, kind to my servants, and affectionate to my companions? Have I thought of God who gave me my parents, teachers, servants, friends?"

After one year of publication Gilman announced plans to issue the *Southern Rose-Bud* "adapted in many points to mature readers." Glowing tributes from men of high standing in Charleston appeared, along with a promise from the editor: "Nothing will ever be found in it to offend, on the most critical perusal." In 1834 the publication became an eight-page sheet published bimonthly (instead of weekly) on a better-quality paper. Although she continued to use material aimed at youthful readers, including journals purportedly written by children themselves, she expanded the contents by adding departments of miscellaneous news and wit, and reviews of other publications under florid headings: the "Leaf-and-Stem-Basket,–or Items of News"; "The Flower Vase"; "The Pruning Knife."

Still seeking a congenial format, Gilman announced in 1835 that the name of the magazine again would be changed and its contents greatly enlarged. This time it became the *Southern Rose* with a new caption, "Flowers of all hue, and without the Thorn the Rose." The subscription price increased from one to two dollars a year payable in advance, and it was to be sold by agents in various southern towns advertised in the magazine. Page length increased to twelve, giving it a more impressive appearance.

Lengthy articles appeared under the heading "Original Pieces," translations of popular European works ran in the "Exotic" section, religious subjects showed up in a column signed "Apollos" (written by Gilman's husband), and general news received attention in the "Leaf-and-Stem-Basket." For juveniles "The Bud" section included fiction and occasional obituary notices of youthful readers. Gilman commented on current events in the form of a Platonic dialogue between "Medora" and "Lisa" in a department called the "Editor's Boudoir." The last page contained verse, often by the editor herself, under the heading "Original Poetry."

In the pages of her publication Gilman established herself as an author as well as a poet. Her first book, titled *Recollections of a Housekeeper* (1834), was published under the pseudonym Mrs. Clarissa Packard. It chronicled the humorous tribulations of a middle-class lawyer's wife in New England as she attempted to train rustic young women to be her housemaids and cooks. A popular success, the book initially had been serialized in Gilman's magazine. Gilman referred to the *Recollections* as "the first attempt, in that particular mode, to enter into the recesses of American homes and hearts."

Subsequently she wrote a companion volume, *Recollections of a Southern Matron* (1838), depicting plantation life as close to perfection with happy slaves eagerly serving their masters. Convinced that slaves, whom she referred to as "servants," were better off than free laborers in the North, Gilman committed herself to the southern cause in spite of her affection for New England. She made frequent use of black dialect, contending it was necessary for the development of character.

As one who believed that she understood both North and South, Gilman strived to bridge the gap between the two regions. According to her, the bonds of family life and friendship transcended political differences, which she referred to as "mere state feelings." For example, in her 1838 book *The Poetry of Travelling in the United States* Gilman announced she sought "to increase a good sympathy between different portions of the country." She described the scene in Congress: "Amid the clanship, however, there is a gen-

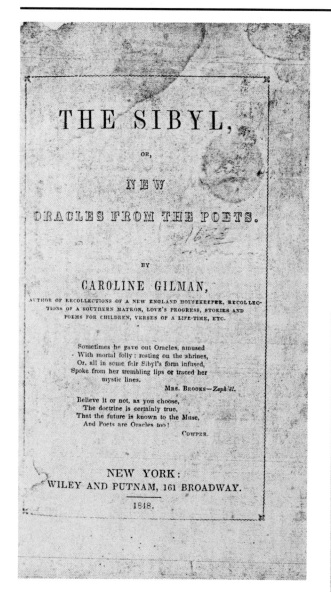

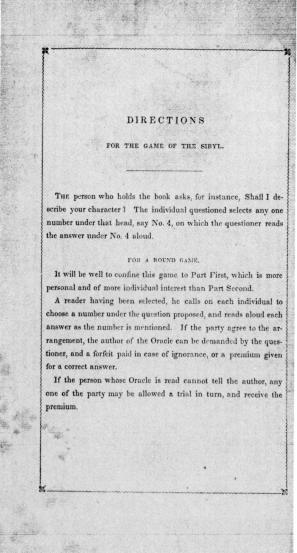

Front cover and game instructions from the second volume of Gilman's fortune-telling series

eral and beautiful courtesy, which in private leads to the happiest results; a pleasant jest is the very hardest weapon used, and that sparingly. The extreme Northern and Southern members are on terms of the most agreeable intercourse." She refused to recognize the storm clouds that would lead to war.

Gilman considered more important than politics the institution of the family, which she championed in the sentimental style that made her one of the most widely liked writers in the United States prior to the Civil War. Among works that ran in her magazine before being published as books were her novel *Love's Progress* (1840), numerous poems, and short stories for adults as well as children. Gilman was particularly proud of her works for juveniles, but today they are of interest mainly as examples of what Americans of the 1830s thought their children should read.

The *Southern Rose* and its predecessors were not the private preserve of Gilman. Each issue contained poems, translations, anecdotes, and articles attributed to some of the better-known literary figures of the nineteenth century. They included Harriet Martineau, Elizabeth F. Ellett, William Gilmore Simms, and Nathaniel Hawthorne, whose short story "The Lily's Quest" appeared in the *Southern Rose* on 24 November 1838. It was heralded as written "especially for *The Southern Rose*," apparently in gratitude for a complimentary review of his work. (It was published later as one of Hawthorne's *Twice-Told Tales*.) Two months earlier the editor had served notice to readers that many pieces had been rejected because they did not "afford sufficient novelty for the *Rose*." Weighty topics were not omitted. "The Pruning Knife" offered critical analyses of articles in important British journals: the *Westminster Review*, the *London Quarterly Review*, the *Edinburgh Review*, and the *Foreign Quarterly Review*.

Read today, the *Southern Rose* offers intriguing insights into the social history of the period, such as the report on the "street cry" of a learned slave, who in peddling spruce beer blended the Latin motto of South Carolina, "Animis, opibusque parati," with "E pluribus unum," added the phrase "anti-spasmodic," and ended with a jingle, "Spruce Beer - Made here - Manufactured by Shakespeare - And Sold by Voltere." Death notices of Charleston residents dotted its columns, classified into three groups: white, black, and colored. Under the heading "Interesting Item" appeared such glimpses of contem-

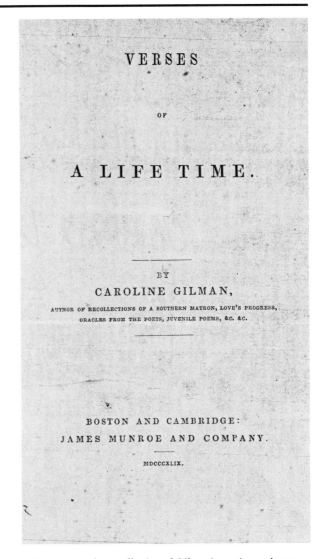

Front cover for a collection of Gilman's sentimental verse

porary life as these comments on whitewash: "Milk, eggs, sugar, and slacked lime, well mixed, are said to form an excellent paint for the outside of buildings."

In another example of the wide range of Gilman's interests, she published the titles of commencement orations given in 1834 at what is now the University of Georgia. Sample topics, which serve as illustrations of the subjects covered in Gilman's publication, are "Ought the United States to attach Canada and Texas?" "The price of Liberty is eternal vigilance" "The Study of the Ancient Languages", "The path of Science is strewed with flowers", "We have few great men! Why?", "American Literature vs. English Critics and Scotch Reviewers", "Political Associations", "The Influence of Mental Philosophy on National Character", "The foundation must be laid before the superstructure can be reared", "Benevolence", "The Influence of Literature upon Society", and "Can the mind cease to exist?"

Hints that financial problems confronted the *Southern Rose* appeared in the prospectus for volume 7, which turned out to be its final one in 1839. Gilman solicited from her readers "a continuation of their favors and from the public at large a more extended encouragement of the work." In addition, as Gilman's own literary career became well established, it appeared she lost interest in the magazine. The last year of publication saw increasing use of material copied from other sources. On 17 August 1839 the last issue of the *Southern Rose* appeared.

In a "Valedictory Address" Gilman gave her reasons for terminating the venture:

> With a thousand good wishes, and in perfectly happy humor towards her large circle of subscribers, the Editor bids them, in this number, an affectionate farewell. She ceases from her pleasant toils, not in consequence of any special discouragement, . . . but, as she approached her office seven years ago through an impulse perfectly voluntary, so she retires from it now with the same unimpaired feeling of liberty. Should she continue in the career of literature, towards which the public have in various ways extended such indulgent encouragement, she would prefer some mode of publication less exacting than the rigorous punctuality of a periodical work.

With the poetic flourish that marked her entire career, she ended her address: "Reader, have you ever left the door of a friend with her smile still impressed on your vision, and a freshly pluck'd blossom from her hand just fastened in your bosom? With such tokens of good will are you now dismissed by The Editor of *The Rose*."

As an editor Gilman had shown herself to be able and industrious. These qualities she brought to her writing after the *Southern Rose* vanished, publishing a total of ten more books, mainly poetry, before the Civil War broke out. According to a contemporary reviewer, her works were "valued for the spirit and fidelity with which she has painted rural and domestic life" as well as for her "skill in character writing" and "love of nature and good sense." Her popularity rose to enormous heights, only to be lost when the war came, shattering the rationale for the sentiments unifying the North and South that she had expressed.

After the death of her husband in 1858 Gilman continued to live in Charleston, becoming a strong southern partisan following the outbreak of the Civil War, although she had maintained her dual allegiance up to the time of the attack on Fort Sumter. When her home was shelled in March 1862, she moved to Greenville, South Carolina, where she helped with volunteer activities to aid Confederate soldiers. After the war was over she returned to Charleston to find that most of her possessions, including her papers, had been destroyed. Although she published four books in the 1870s (two written with her daughter Caroline Howard Jervey), she never regained her popularity.

Her last years were spent in the home of her daughter Eliza in Washington, D.C. She died there of paralysis when she was ninety-three. Gilman was buried beside her husband in the Unitarian cemetery in Charleston. For years she was referred to as South Carolina's "most eminent woman writer," praised particularly for her role as an unassuming and tender editor of one of the first family publications.

Biography:

Mary Scott Saint-Amand, *A Balcony in Charleston* (Richmond, Va.: Garrett & Massie, 1941).

References:

J. C. R. Dorr, "Caroline Howard Gilman," *Critic*, 13 (22 September 1888): 151;

John Seely Hart, *The Female Prose Writers of America* (Philadelphia: E. H. Butler, 1852);

William Stanley Hoole, "The Gilmans and the Southern Rose," *North Carolina Historical Review*, 11 (April 1934): 116-128;

Fronde Kennedy, "The Southern Rose-Bud and the Southern Rose," *South Atlantic Quarterly*, 23 (January 1924): 10-19;

Susan Sutton Smith, "Caroline Howard Gilman," *American Women Writers from Colonial Times to the Present*, volume 2, edited by Lina Mainiero (New York: Ungar, 1980), pp. 128-130.

Papers:

A collection of Gilman's letters, written between 1810 and 1880, is at the South Carolina Historical Society in Charleston.

Louis A. Godey

(6 June 1804-29 November 1878)

Edward H. Sewell, Jr.
Virginia Polytechnic Institute and State University

See also the Godey and McMichael entry in *DLB 49: American Literary Publishing Houses, 1638-1899*.

MAJOR POSITION HELD: Publisher and editor, *Godey's Lady's Book* (1830-1877).

"To the Ladies–" Louis A. Godey said in a toast. "It is my business and pleasure to please them, for to them–God bless the fairest portion of His creation–for to them I am indebted for my success." Inseparable from the popular culture of the nineteenth century, *Godey's Lady's Book* was published from 1830 to 1877. It was one of the most successful magazines of its era by most standards of achievement: it was the innovator in women's magazines, a financial success, one of the first periodicals to emphasize the value of American literature over English, the first to be edited largely by women, one of the first to offer relatively good payment for original stories, and a leader in the copyrighting of periodical literature. In sum it was the premier magazine of excellence for women.

The cultural impact of *Godey's Lady's Book* is best illustrated by the references made to it by contemporary writers and critics. Nathaniel Hawthorne, for example, in *The House of the Seven Gables*, has Phoebe Pyncheon ask Holgrave, the daguerreotypist, "Do you write for the magazines?" Holgrave assures her that his "name has figured . . . on the covers of Graham and Godey." Hawthorne later characterized his own writing, stating, "My poor story, it is but too evident, will never do for Godey or Graham!" In 1850 Philadelphian George W. Child recorded in his *Recollections* a "conversation in the office of the Harper's. . . . [We] were discussing the first number of Harper's *New Monthly Magazine*. It seemed so certain to us that the publication would be a failure. 'It can't,' said one Philadelphian, emphatically–'it *can't* last very long.' The only successful magazines then published in the United States were those issued in Philadelphia–

Louis A. Godey, 1850

Graham's, Godey's, Sartain's, and *Peterson's.*" Finally, in a letter to James Thomas Fields dated 24 November 1869, Henry Wadsworth Longfellow observed:

> I see by the morning paper [the *Boston Advertiser*] that "Georgia has a patent churn, which allows the *lady who operates it,* to nurse her baby, read Godey, and bring the butter in eight minutes."
>
> I wish any lady in this part of the country would bring me butter in eight minutes, or even in ten. I would allow her to read not only her Godey, but Ree's Cyclopedia and the bank [back] numbers of the North American Review.

Born of French immigrant parents, Louis and Margaret Godey, in New York City on 6 June 1804, Louis Antoine Godey had little formal education, but by the age of fifteen he was operating a combined newsstand and bookshop. In 1828 he moved to Philadelphia, where he spent most of his life, although he visited Europe three times. He was not involved in politics, and he remained detached from controversial issues. He married Maria Duke, daughter of a well-to-do Philadelphia family, on 31 August 1833, and they had five children. The employees of *Godey's Lady's Book* found him a generous and considerate employer, and some were to stay with the magazine for as many as forty years. Godey was genial, unostentatious, tolerant, and conservative. He was well liked as a businessman, and Edgar Allan Poe said of him, in spite of their occasional differences, "No man has warmer friends or fewer enemies."

In 1830–after working in Philadelphia for two years in the composing room and business department of a newspaper office–with a great deal of self-confidence and some financial support from Charles Alexander, his employer, he launched the *Lady's Book*. Godey saw the potential of a new and growing market in periodicals, and, even more important, he had the foresight to tap the female audience, a segment of the American public that had been growing in both numbers and sophistication.

Godey was involved in several other publication enterprises during his career, including the successful weekly newspaper *Saturday News and Literary Gazette*, which he established with Joseph C. Neal and Morton McMichael in 1836. Neal was a frequent contributor to the *Lady's Book*, and McMichael was editor of the *Saturday Evening Post* and *Philadelphia Saturday Courier*. In 1841 Godey and McMichael went into partnership to publish novels and magazines, including the *Young People's Book, or Magazine of Useful and Entertaining Knowledge*, established in 1841. They also published the works of T. S. Arthur, best known for his *Ten Nights in a Barroom*, who was a frequent contributor to the *Lady's Book*. In 1842 Godey published the *Lady's Musical Library*, a periodical containing fashionable parlor music.

The *Lady's Book*, however, was his most successful undertaking, the primary instrument in the transformation of the son of French immigrants into an American millionaire publisher. During its first seven years the *Lady's Book* was patterned after other American magazines of the

Front cover for an issue of the leading women's magazine of the nineteenth century

era, consisting almost entirely of pieces clipped from other sources, usually English publications. Godey's strength was his business acumen, and, observing the success and profitability of the ornate annual gift books that were in vogue as parlor table decorations in the 1820s, he fashioned his new publication in the format of a monthly version of the annuals. In addition to the typical poetry and fiction taken from anonymous sources the *Lady's Book* featured illustrated title pages, fine steel engravings, and colored fashion plates. Even his title suggested that this publication was more than another monthly magazine–it was a "lady's book" worthy of a place of honor in her parlor. After eighteen months of its publication Godey, a man known for his effusive self-promotional rhetoric, noted that his *Lady's Book* had "received in that time, the most unbounded patronage." He assured his readers he would continue "every exertion . . . to render it useful and entertaining." If readers had any doubts about the quality of the magazine, Godey put those doubts to rest by informing them that from the time of start-up "until the present time, the publishers have expended for Embellishments alone, upwards of SEVEN THOUSAND DOLLARS."

Godey, like his contemporary and friend P. T. Barnum, never shied away from promoting himself and his publications. Writing in the *Lady's Book* in December 1841, he boasted that, "From Maine to the Rocky Mountains there is scarcely a hamlet, however inconsiderable, where it is not received and read; and in the larger towns and cities it is universally distributed." Circulation statistics supported his claims that the *Lady's Book* was the most widely read magazine throughout much of the nineteenth century. In his monthly column, "Godey's Arm Chair," he claimed a circulation in 1849 of 40,000; growing to 70,000 by the end of 1850; 100,000 by 1856; and a high of 150,000 by 1860. After 1860, as a sectional conflict turned into the Civil War, his circulation declined. But even in 1865, after the loss of subscribers in the South, circulation was 110,000. The decline continued, however, and in 1873 circulation had fallen to 100,000.

Major changes were foreshadowed for the *Lady's Book* when in the December 1835 issue Godey noted, "We have received a copy of 'Traits of American Life,' from the pen of Mrs. S. J. Hale.... We read any thing from the pen of this lady with avidity, and can with confidence hand it on to our female friends, convinced that nothing but sound morality and wholesome piety will ever find its way to the public through her instrumentality." Sarah Josepha Hale, a widow with five children to support, had moved from rural New Hampshire to Boston at the request of an Episcopal clergyman, Rev. John L. Blake, who, impressed with her writing abilities, asked her to edit a new magazine, the *Ladies' Magazine*, which he planned to publish, and which he advertised as "the first magazine edited by a woman for women." Godey bought the Boston magazine in 1837 and incorporated it into the *Lady's Book*. He also hired Hale as his literary editor, and, until 1877 when both Godey and Hale retired from their positions, *Godey's Lady's Book* was the product of what Godey referred to as Hale's "literary" and Godey's "pecuniary" contributions. Godey described their working relationship over the forty-one years as that of friends who "have never had, in any one instance, a serious misunderstanding."

Godey attracted well-known writers, both men and women, by offering liberal payment for their works. For those without reputations, getting a story or poem published in *Godey's Lady's Book* was payment in its own right. Not even a personal recommendation from someone of the stature of Longfellow, however, could insure publication. In a letter of 26 March 1852 Longfellow took "the liberty of sending ... for your Magazine, a Sketch of a London Street, by Miss Wormeley ... now living in Boston." He described her as a "young lady of very decided talent," who "would like to become one of your contributors." Her story did not appear in *Godey's Lady's Book*. Perhaps she was at a disadvantage since her father was a rear admiral in the British navy, and *Godey's* preferred to publish American authors.

In its pages could be found the works of Longfellow, Ralph Waldo Emerson, John Greenleaf Whittier, William Gilmore Simms, T. S. Arthur, and Oliver Wendell Holmes, as well as those of leading women writers, including Harriet Beecher Stowe, Lydia H. Sigourney, Elizabeth Oakes Smith, Catherine M. Sedgwick, Lydia M. Child, and Sara Jane Lippincott writing under the pen name Grace Greenwood. Editorials by both Hale and Godey attested to the thoroughly American character of the *Lady's Book*. An editorial of March 1851 was addressed as "A Word to the American People": "We are sure our patrons are all patriots; therefore we solicit your aid in sustaining a true American work–even your own Lady's Book. We give you American literature ... we foster ... American genius.... That foreigners appreciate it is shown by their appropriations of its contents. The November number of one London magazine carried three stories selected from our Lady's Book.... How can we blame English publishers for their theft of American literature whilst American publishers are selecting wholesale from English publications? But we do not thus furnish forth our book. As we sustain the honor of our country, and pay liberally to foster American genius, art and industry we feel at liberty to ask from our own American people a large and liberal patronage."

In addition to publishing the works of American authors Godey was a leader in copyrighting the material appearing in his magazine. There had been a national copyright statute in effect since 1790, but, while books were often copyrighted, periodical publications had not taken advantage of the law. When Godey began copyrighting his material in 1845, followed very quick-

"The Daguerreotypist," an illustration from an 1849 issue of Godey's Lady's Book

ly by *Graham's Magazine*, protests were raised by the publishers of newspapers, other magazines, and the popular annual gift books which made extensive use of noncopyrighted materials from popular magazines such as *Godey's* and *Graham's*. The comment by the editor of the *Baltimore Visiter* [*sic*] was typical. He was pained that Godey had "resorted to the narrowly selfish course of taking out a *copyright* for his book." He predicted that Godey would "rue it bitterly" and continued, "Think of this insulting proposition, 'We have no objection to any paper copying any story from our magazine *if they will not do it until the succeeding number has been published*.' Wonderful liberality, Mr. Godey, towards that department of the press to which you are more or less indebted for a handsome fortune."

The comment about Godey's indebtedness to the newspapers derived from his habit of using quotations from small and large newspapers extolling the virtues of *Godey's Lady's Book*. In the October 1849 issue, for example, Godey printed a whole page of comments from newspapers around the nation praising the *Lady's Book* and castigating its imitators under the headline, "THE PRESS AWAKE UPON THE SUBJECT OF IMITATIONS." More typically his self-advertising strategy was to reprint short favorable descriptions from newspapers throughout his editorial comments in the "Arm Chair," such as the one in the October 1861 issue:

The *Clinton Messenger and Palladium* gets off a very good notice of the Book in the following:–

"Whoo! whoo! hallo, Postmaster–mail." In quick time it is ushered into the office, and the first thing that meets the eye when it is opened, is a package of Godey's Lady's Book. "Hurry up," says one, and they begin to flock in for their pretty magazine. And can any one wonder that there should be such a tremendous rush for this magazine, when the publishers take every pride in making it one of the most entertaining in the country? Take this, and if Uncle Sam is not at fault, you are sure of it every month at just such a date.

Another tactic Godey used in the marketing of his publication was a club offering group subscriptions to *Godey's Lady's Book,* either alone or in combination with other periodicals, such as *Arthur's Home Magazine.* Humor was often used in the "Arm Chair" as a means of advertising his magazine, as in an entry from July 1859 that plays on the theme of trying to get something for nothing: "We have been made a member of a society with an unpronounceable name. Why do not these literary societies choose some title that is plain and at once significant of their object? It is a remarkable fact that most of these societies very politely request us to send them the Lady's Book–for nothing, of course. Now, gentlemen, it is a very easy thing for one person to resolve himself into a committee of one, and call himself a society, sign three or four names to a paper, send it to publishers, and, if they are fools, get all his reading for nothing. Better try some other way; publishers are getting to know these tricks." It is interesting to note that the letter is addressed to "gentlemen" who are trying to pull the wool over his eyes and get a free subscription rather than to the ladies who made up the majority of his readership.

Many of the leading writers of the American literary renaissance were frequent contributors to the *Lady's Book.* Edgar Allan Poe, who edited the archrival *Graham's Magazine* for a brief time, was published often in *Godey's.* In a letter of 29 February 1848 written to George W. Eveleth, Poe described Godey as "a good little man" who "means as well as he knows how." A few years earlier, in 1846, when giving advice to Philip P. Cooke about the "usual pay of the Magazines" for manuscripts, Poe had said, "I furnish Godey regular papers (one each month) at $5 per page. The $5 Magazines do not pay quite so well and are by no means so prompt." While many magazines sold a year's subscription for $5, the *Lady's Book* sold for $3.00 or $3.50. Godey frequently referred to his ability to offer more to his readers at a more reasonable price because of his large circulation. In a December 1861 "Arm Chair" comment, he said, "Remember, that a work with

150,000 subscribers can give five times as much as a work with only half that number, and the embellishments can also be made of a very superior character." There were other authors who did not want to be associated with a magazine that James Russell Lowell is reported to have described as "thrice diluted trash in the shape of namby-pamby love tales and sketches." Lowell's evaluation, however, represents the exception rather than the norm.

Godey eschewed controversy and excluded from his magazine all discussion of political or religious themes that might cause public concern or division. It was even impossible to judge from the pages of *Godey's Lady's Book* that a major war was being fought in the 1860s, except for a few oblique references to declines in the number of subscribers in certain geographical regions of the nation or comments about the "current unpleasantness." Some regular contributors were, in 'fact, dropped when their views on topics such as abolition caused public controversy.

One conflict of a literary nature did disrupt the normal tranquillity. In his 1846 letter to Cooke, Poe made reference to a series he wrote for Godey that created quite a stir in the literary world of the day. "Never commit yourself as a pamphleteer," Poe advised; "I am now writing for Godey a series of articles called 'The N. Y. City Literati.' They will run through the year & include personal descriptions, as well as frank opinions of literary merit." In the first article of the series Poe wrote, "Hawthorne, the author of 'Twice-Told Tales,' is scarcely recognized by the press or by the public, and when noticed merely to be damned by faint praise. Now, my opinion of him is, that although his walk [work?] is limited and he is fairly to be charged with mannerism, treating all subjects on a similar tone of dreamy *innuendo,* yet in this walk [his work?] he evinces extraordinary genius, having no rival either in America or elsewhere. . . . Longfellow, who, although [a] little quacky *per se,* has, through his social and literary position as a man of property and a professor at Harvard, a whole legion of active quacks at his control. . . . "

He went on to say of Thomas Dunn English that his *"inexcusable"* sin was "imitation–if this be not too mild a term. . . . He has taken . . . most unwarrantable liberties, in the way of downright plagiarism, from a Philadelphian poet whose high merits have not been properly appreciated." Adding insult to injury, Poe placed "English on my list of New York literati, not on account of his poetry (which I presume he is not weak enough to estimate very highly) but on the score of his having edited for several months, 'with the aid of numerous collaborators,' a monthly magazine called the *Aristidean*." Poe then suggested that English would be well advised to study, since he had confused "lay" for "lie," and when the error was called to his attention, he blamed it on the printer. Poe's less-than-diplomatic retort was that "Nobody is so stupid as to suppose for a moment that there exists in New York a single proofreader–or even a printer's devil–who would have permitted such errors to escape. By the excuses offered, therefore, the errors were only the more obviously nailed to the counter as Mr. English's own."

English published a response in the *New York Mirror*, damning Poe's character and telling of several personal conflicts between the two men, including a thrashing he gave Poe. The implication, of course, was that this was the cause for Poe's caustic criticism. Poe then wrote a response to English, which he sent to Godey to publish, but, rather than publish it in his own magazine, Godey paid $10 to have it published in the *Spirit of the Times*, a small-circulation Philadelphia journal, and he sent the bill to Poe. It is no wonder that Godey, a man who disliked controversy, chose to exclude Poe's "Reply," which called English "the most unprincipled of Mr. Barnum's babboons [sic]." Poe was displeased with Godey's choice of the *Spirit of the Times*, and in a letter of 16 July 1846 he wrote: "I am rather ashamed that, knowing me to be as poor as I am, you should have thought it advisable to make the demand *on me* of the $10. I confess that I thought better of you–but let it go–it is the way of the world. . . . You should have done as I requested–published it in the 'Book.' It is of no use to conceive a plan if you have to depend upon another for its execution." The letter closed in a tone of harmony and friendship with the simple words, "In perfect good feeling Yours truly." A note was added to the letter about including a piece by Poe in the next number of the magazine. Poe also added some comments inquiring whether Godey had seen the flattering notices about the *Lady's Book* in several newspapers, the *St. Louis Daily Reveillé*, the *New Orleans Picayune*, and the *Charleston Daily Courier*.

Most of the material in *Godey's Lady's Book* did not cause controversy. Volume 40 (1850), for example, contained four pieces by T. S. Arthur, an article on "English Fairies" by Washington Irving, "Scripture Sketches" by Nathaniel Parker

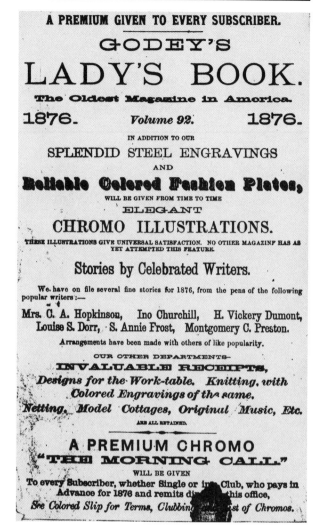

Advertisement on the back cover of an issue of Godey's magazine

Willis, the poem "Song for a Temperance Dinner" by Oliver Wendell Holmes, Longfellow's poem "The Evening Star," a sonnet by Elizabeth Oakes Smith, a story by Grace Greenwood, and three poems by Hale. As literary editor Hale selected pieces that would appeal to her readers, and her own sentimental poetry demonstrates the general tenor of much that was published in the magazine. These lines from "The Orphans" illustrate her style:

Brother, while the breath of even
Woos the starry eyes of heaven;
And the stealthy shadows, creeping,
Softly as an infant's sleeping,
Seem but as the brooding fancies,
Which the poet's soul entrances,
When the outward world is turning
Dark beneath his spirit's burning;

Then I stand amid the shrouding
Memories on my vision crowding;
Then I see our sainted mother–
Thou art with me, too, my brother.

While literature was an integral part of the success of the *Lady's Book,* it certainly was not the most popular aspect of the magazine. The *North American Review* correctly captured the character of *Godey's* in the 1860s and 1870s with the observation, "It condemns idle gossip in one story, social malice in another; commends improvement in dress, cookery and house decoration as worthy of woman's ambition; continues the drawing lessons, work department and recipes and furnishes a number of sprightly tales." A sample recipe from July 1835 is interesting both for its content and for the progressive concept of "artificial" foods:

> Artificial Anchovies–To a peck of sprats [small minnow-like fish] put two pounds of salt, three ounces of bay salt, one pound of salt-petre, two ounces of prunella [a French liqueur derived from prunes], and a few grains of cochineal [a red dye]; pound all in a mortar, put into a stone pan first a layer of sprats and then one of the compound, an [sic] so on alternately on the top. Press them down hard; cover them close for six months, and they will be fit for use, and will really produce a most excellent flavored sauce.

Each issue contained fine steel engravings on a variety of thoroughly Victorian subjects, a plan for a house or cottage, patterns for sewing and knitting, music, and features on health and beauty. There were some topics on which the *Lady's Book* took firm editorial positions, ranging from the almost comical to the major social issues of the day. Primarily under the pen of its literary editor *Godey's Lady's Book* was the foremost advocate of education for women, the right of women to attend medical school, and their right to serve as medical missionaries. Exercise for women was promoted through articles about the value of dancing–an activity of questionable social and religious standing–and equestrian skills, calisthenics, and the proper use of dumbbells. Exercise, according to Hale, was appropriate for women who were "by nature, far more inclined than man to movement, however slight its description."

While much of the editorial work in the realm of literature was done by Hale, Godey re-served to himself the embellishments that were his pride and joy, and about which he justifiably boasted in each issue of the magazine. Most outstanding were the fashion plates. The fine engravings in each copy of the magazine were hand-colored by women working in their homes. When asked by a reader why the colors varied from one copy of the magazine to another, Godey quickly pointed out that it was done so the readers could see how the dress would look when made from different cloth. In addition to the fashion plates each issue also contained columns about new conveniences for the wife and tips on how to solve common problems such as stains. Each issue featured a model home or cottage complete with a floor plan and description. Some of the model homes were quite impractical, featuring thatched roofs and spacious villalike designs, perhaps brought back by Godey's friends who had been traveling in Europe. Godey also used his magazine to market a wide range of goods, such as drawing pencils, household devices, and patterns.

In 1877 Godey sold the magazine and retired. In his final "Arm Chair" he observed that, for over three generations of readers, the *Lady's Book* had provided the readers with content that exemplified "the purity of the magazine and its eminent fitness for family reading."

References:

Ruth E. Finley, "The Prince of Publishers," in her *The Lady of Godey's: Sarah Josepha Hale* (Philadelphia: Lippincott, 1931), pp. 41-63;

Esther Forbes, "Around the Family Reading Lamp: Mr. Godey Passes Judgment on Life and Letters," *Independent,* 120 (31 March 1928): 294-296;

Sarah Josepha Hale, "Louis A. Godey," *Godey's Lady's Book,* 40 (February 1850): 87-88;

Lawrence Martin, "The Genesis of *Godey's Lady's Book,*" *New England Quarterly,* 1 (January 1928): 41-70;

Frank Luther Mott, *A History of American Magazines,* 5 volumes (Cambridge, Mass.: Harvard University Press, 1938-1968), I: 580-594;

F. L. Smith, Jr., "When the 'Lady's Book' Was Young," *Independent,* 119 (24 September 1927): 307-308, 320;

Richard Fay Warner, *"Godey's Lady's Book,"* *American Mercury,* 2 (August 1924): 399-405.

Samuel Griswold Goodrich
(Peter Parley)

(19 August 1793-9 May 1860)

Judith Serrin
Columbia University

See also the Goodrich entries in *DLB 1: The American Renaissance in New England,* and *DLB 42: American Writers for Children Before 1900.*

MAJOR POSITIONS HELD: Publisher, editor, *Token* annuals (1828-1842); editor, *Parley's Magazine* (1833-1834); editor, *Robert Merry's Museum* (1841-1854).

Bibliographical Note: Goodrich never clearly distinguished between the books he wrote, those he commissioned, and those he edited. His Peter Parley was so popular that many books have been falsely attributed to Goodrich. Because it is impossible to compile a comprehensive bibliography of his works, this list includes only works for which Goodrich's authorship can be established with some certainty. In England numerous pirated editions were published. According to Goodrich in *Recollections of a Lifetime* (1856), many of these were "counterfeits, every means being used to pass them off upon the public as by the original author of Parley's tales." British "counterfeits" cited by Goodrich are omitted from this list.

SELECTED BOOKS: *The Child's Arithmetic, Being an Easy and Cheap Introduction to Daboll's, Pike's, White's, and Other Arithmetics* (Hartford: S. G. Goodrich, 1818);
Blair's Outline of Chronology, Ancient and Modern, Embracing Its Antiquities (Boston: S. G. Goodrich, 1825);
The Tales of Peter Parley about America (Boston: S. G. Goodrich, 1827);
The Child's Botany (Boston: S. G. Goodrich, 1828);
Tales of Peter Parley about Europe (Boston: S. G. Goodrich, 1828; London: Tegg, 1834);
A Geographical View of the United States. Embracing Their Extent and Boundaries, Government, Courts and Laws (New York: W. Reed, 1829);

Samuel Griswold Goodrich (photograph by Mathew Brady; courtesy of the Library of Congress)

Peter Parley's Method of Telling about Geography to Children (Hartford: H. & F. J. Huntington, 1829);
Stories about Captain John Smith, of Virginia; for the Instruction and Amusement of Children (Hartford: H. & F. J. Huntington, 1829);
A System of School Geography, Chiefly Derived from Malte-Brun, and Arranged According to the In-

ductive Plan of Instruction (Boston: Carter & Hendee, 1830);

Atlas, Designed to Illustrate the Malte-Brun School Geography (Boston: Carter & Hendee, 1830);

Peter Parley's Tales about Asia (Boston: Gray & Bowen, 1830; London: Allman, 1839);

Peter Parley's Tales of Animals; Containing Descriptions of Three Hundred Quadrupeds, Birds, Fishes, Reptiles, and Insects (Boston: Carter & Hendee, 1830; London: Tegg, 1832);

Peter Parley's Winter Evening Tales (Boston: Carter & Hendee, 1830);

Tales of Peter Parley about Africa (Boston: Gray & Bowen, 1830);

The Child's Book of American Geography (Boston: Waitt & Dow, 1831);

The First Book of History. For Children and Youth (Boston: Richardson, Lord & Holbrook, 1831);

Peter Parley's Tales about the Islands in the Pacific Ocean (Boston: Gray & Bowen, 1831);

Peter Parley's Tales about the Sun, Moon, and Stars (Boston: Gray & Bowen and Carter & Hendee, 1831; London: Tegg, 1836);

Peter Parley's Tales of the Sea (Boston: Gray & Bowen, 1831);

Peter Parley's Tales about South America (Baltimore: Jewett, 1832);

Peter Parley's Method of Telling about the History of the World to Children (Hartford: F. J. Huntington, 1832);

Peter Parley's Tales about Ancient and Modern Greece (New York: Collins & Hannay, 1832);

A System of Universal Geography, Popular and Scientific, Comprising a Physical, Political, and Statistical Account of the World and Its Various Divisions (Boston: Carter & Hendee, 1832);

The Second Book of History, Including the Modern History of Europe, Africa, and Asia (Boston: Carter & Hendee, 1832);

Peter Parley's Tales about the State and City of New York (New York: Pendleton & Hill, 1832);

Peter Parley's Tales about Great Britain, including England, Wales, Scotland, and Ireland (Baltimore: Jewett, 1832);

Peter Parley's Method of Teaching Arithmetic to Children (Boston: Carter & Hendee, 1833);

Peter Parley's Tales about Ancient Rome, with Some Account of Modern Italy (Boston: Carter & Hendee, 1833);

The Every Day Book for Youth (Boston: Carter & Hendee, 1834);

Peter Parley's Short Stories for Long Nights (Boston: Allen & Ticknor, 1834);

The Third Book of History, Containing Ancient History in Connection with Ancient Geography (Boston: Carter & Hendee, 1834);

The Benefits of Industry. An Address Delivered Before the Inhabitants of Jamaica Plain, July 4, 1835 (Boston: Ticknor, 1835);

The Story of Captain Riley and His Adventures in Africa (New York: Peaslee, 1835);

The Story of La Peyrouse (New York: Peaslee, 1835);

Bible Gazetteer, Containing Descriptions of Places Mentioned in the Old and New Testament (Boston: Otis, Broaders, 1836);

The Outcast, and Other Poems (Boston: Russell, Shattuck & Williams, 1836);

Peter Parley's Bible Dictionary (Philadelphia: Tower, 1836);

Peter Parley's Dictionary of the Animal Kingdom (New York: Hunt, 1836);

Peter Parley's Dictionary of Astronomy (New York: Hunt, 1836);

A Present from Peter Parley to All His Little Friends (Philadelphia: Pomeroy, 1836);

Peter Parley's Arithmetic (Boston: Hendee, 1837);

Peter Parley's Method of Telling about the Geography of the Bible (Boston: American Stationers' Company, 1837);

Fireside Education (New York: Colman, 1838; London: Smith, 1839);

Five Letters to My Neighbor Smith, Touching the Fifteen Gallon Jug (Boston: Weeks, Jordan, 1838);

Peter Parley's Cyclopedia of Botany (Boston: Otis, Broaders, 1838);

The First Reader for Schools (Boston: Otis, Broaders, 1839);

The Second Reader for Schools (Louisville: Morton & Griswold, 1839);

The Third Reader for the Use of Schools (Boston: Otis, Broaders, 1839);

The Fourth Reader for the Use of Schools (Boston: Otis, Broaders, 1839);

Peter Parley's Farewell (New York: Colman, 1840);

Peter Parley's Wonders of the Earth, Sea, and Sky (New York: Colman, 1840);

A Pictorial Geography of the World, Comprising a System of Universal Geography, 10 parts (Boston: Otis, Broaders/New York: Tanner & Disturnell, 1840);

Sketches from a Student's Window (Boston: Ticknor, 1841);

The Story of Alexander Selkirk (Philadelphia: Anners, 1841);

A Pictorial Natural History; Embracing a View of the Mineral, Vegetable, and Animal Kingdoms (Boston: Munroe, 1842);

The Young American; or, Book of Government and Law (New York: W. Robinson, 1842);

Make the Best of It; or, Cheerful Cherry, and Other Tales (New York: Wiley & Putnam, 1843); republished as *Cheerful Cherry; or, Make the Best of It* (London: Darton & Clarke, 1843?);

A Tale of Adventure; or, The Siberian Sable-hunter (New York: Wiley & Putnam, 1843); republished as *Persevere and Prosper; or, The Siberian Sable-hunter* (London: Darton, 1843);

What to Do and How to Do It (New York: Wiley & Putnam, 1844);

Fairy Land, and Other Sketches for Youth (Boston: Munroe, 1844);

Peter Parley's Little Leaves for Little Readers (Boston: Munroe, 1844);

Wit Bought; or, The Life and Adventures of Robert Merry (New York: Wiley & Putnam, 1844; London: Cassell, Petter & Galpin, 1844);

Dick Boldhero; or, A Tale of Adventure in South America (Philadelphia: Sorin & Ball, 1845; London: Darton, 1846);

A Home in the Sea; or, The Adventures of Philip Brusque; Designed to Show the Nature and Necessity of Good (Philadelphia: Sorin & Ball, 1845);

A Tale of the Revolution, and Other Sketches (Philadelphia: Sorin & Ball, 1845);

The Truth-Finder; or, The Story of Inquisitive Jack (Philadelphia: Sorin & Ball, 1845);

A National Geography, for Schools (New York: Huntington & Savage, 1845);

Right Is Might, and Other Sketches (Philadelphia: Sorin & Ball, 1846);

Tales of Sea and Land (Philadelphia: Sorin & Ball, 1846);

A Primer of Geography (New York: Huntington & Savage, 1850);

Take Care of Number One; or, The Adventures of Jacob Karl (New York: Huntington & Savage, 1850);

A Comprehensive Geography and History, Ancient and Modern (New York: Huntington & Savage, 1850);

Poems (New York: Putnam, 1851);

Faggots for the Fireside; or, Fact and Fancy (New York: Appleton, 1855; London: Griffin, 1855);

The Wanderers by Sea and Land, with other Tales (New York: Appleton, 1855; London: Darton, 1858);

A Winter Wreath of Summer Flowers (New York: Appleton, 1855; London: Trübner, 1855);

The Balloon Travels of Robert Merry and His Young Friends over Various Countries in Europe (New York: J. C. Derby/Boston: Phillips, Sampson, 1855; London: Blackwood, 1857);

The Travels, Voyages, and Adventures of Gilbert Go-Ahead in Foreign Parts (New York: Derby, 1856);

Recollections of a Lifetime; or, Men and Things I Have Seen: In a Series of Familiar Letters to a Friend, Historical, Biographical, Anecdotal, and Descriptive, 2 volumes (New York & Auburn: Miller, Orton & Mulligan, 1856);

Illustrated Natural History of the Animal Kingdom, 2 volumes (New York: Derby & Jackson, 1859).

OTHER: *Parley's Cabinet Library*, 20 volumes, edited by Goodrich (Boston: Bradbury, Soden, 1843-1845).

"My name and all I have done will be forgotten," Samuel Griswold Goodrich wrote in his autobiography, *Recollections of a Lifetime*. To Americans in the mid 1800s, and especially to children, the prediction would have been astonishing. "I think you have done more to diffuse useful knowledge among the rising generation than any other modern writer, either English or American," President Millard Fillmore wrote to Goodrich in 1850, in reference to Goodrich's series of books for children written under the name Peter Parley. Goodrich, hardworking and productive, said in his memoirs that he had written or edited 116 Parley books and fifty-four others; about seven million volumes had been sold and about three hundred thousand were being sold annually. As late as 1912 five Parley books were still in print. Total sales have been estimated at twelve million.

A champion of American writers in a time when the country was considered by many to be barren of literature, Goodrich was a publisher of books and of a popular annual, the *Token*, that featured American engravers and the early work of such later famous American writers as Nathaniel Hawthorne. But his renown was based on the Peter Parley character he created for children's books and textbooks. This work, reflecting his determination to educate and uplift the children of America, led Goodrich to venture into publication of two of the earliest children's magazines, *Parley's Magazine* and *Robert Merry's Museum*.

THE

MAGAZINE'S ADDRESS.

TO THE PUBLIC.

If a stranger were to knock at your door, and ask some favor, you would first look him in the face, and then decide whether you would grant it or not. Now I, Parley's Magazine, am a stranger. I come before the reader, and like him who knocks at your door, I ask you to take me in. Like him also, I come with a face, or rather with a cover, which is much the same thing. Pray will you look at it; nay, will you be so kind as to study it? It is, I assure you, unlike some other faces, or covers, only meant to deceive. It is, I hope, an honest index to my real character.

It is said, that men as they grow old, grow deceitful, but youth are supposed to be without guile. Now if I were an old magazine, professing to teach the black arts and misty sciences, you might distrust me. But as I am young, and only hold companionship with the young, I beg you to consider me an ingenuous youth, who means what he says, and says what he means; and who, having nothing to conceal, lets his plans and purposes shine out frankly in his face; one, in short, who has not yet learned the artifices, or adopted the disguises of the world, and whose countenance may therefore be taken as a certificate of his character.

What then does my face or my cover seem to say? It consists of a number of little round pictures, each of which bears a certain meaning. One of them exhibits a church, by which I intend to tell you, that in my pages you will occasionally find

something about religion, and those duties and pleasures which spring from it. Not that I mean to preach sermons, for that is not my calling; nor will I weary your patience with long moral lessons, for that would make you dislike me. But I believe that all good people find many sweet thoughts and pleasant feelings in that love, truth and kindness, which religion teaches, and as I only seek the favor of good people, you may expect, sometimes to find these topics in my leaves.

Another feature of my face, exhibits a man gazing at the stars, through a long tube, called a telescope. Seen through this instrument, a star looks as large as a great wheel, and the moon appears like a vast world with mountains, rivers and seas upon it. By this picture I mean to say that I shall often tell you of Astronomy, which means an account of the sun, moon and stars, and the wonders which are displayed in the heavens.

The next picture exhibits a sort of ball in a frame, which is called a globe, and represents the figure of the earth, which, you know is round. The study of the earth, its mountains, rivers, lakes, seas, cities and inhabitants, is called Geography. It is one of the most pleasing and useful of all studies, and I mean often to discourse of it to my readers.

Beneath the picture of the globe, is a ship, with its sails spread. It is crossing the deep sea, and by this I mean to tell you that I shall frequently relate tales of mariners' and

Goodrich's address to the reader in the first issue of Parley's Magazine

Goodrich was born in Ridgefield, Connecticut, on 19 August 1793 to a minister of the First Congregational Church, the Reverend Samuel Goodrich, and Elizabeth Ely Goodrich. The family distinguished itself early and included prominent clergymen, lawyers, and, in Samuel's uncle, Chauncey, a United States senator. Goodrich received an elementary education at West Lane School House and at Master Stebbins's seminary and at fifteen went to work as a merchant clerk for his brother-in-law. He entered the army briefly during the War of 1812. Two years later, while a clerk in Hartford, he struck up a friendship with George Sheldon, a clerk for a book publisher. In 1816 the friends arranged to publish Scott's Family Bible in the United States. Sheldon died, but Goodrich continued publishing for several years, seeking out books he thought were needed in the United States, putting up the money for the printing, and arranging for book sales, with mixed results. He frequently sustained losses.

Goodrich married Adeline Gratia Bradley in 1818; she died in 1822. The following year he took a trip to Europe, where he met Hannah More, an English author who had written a successful series of moralistic tracts. He considered More's books "the first work [for children] that I read with real enthusiasm." After talking with her Goodrich determined to use a storytelling format to make the truth of history, geography, and biography simple enough for children and as interesting as fairy tales.

Back in America Goodrich married Mary Booth in 1826. They eventually had six children. He moved to Boston, where his publishing enterprises came to occupy the entire second floor above the Ticknor and Fields Old Corner Book Store. In 1827 he issued the first Parley book, *The Tales of Peter Parley about America*. The persona was named, according to Goodrich's daughter, Emily, for the French verb *parlez*, to talk. The book included a sketch of Parley as an old white-haired gentleman, leaning on a cane, wearing a dark coat and breeches. The series filled a need and was soon being sold to individuals and schools by the millions.

Goodrich's first venture into periodical editing was as editor of the *Token*, an annual printed from 1828 until 1842. A cross between magazines and books, such volumes developed in Europe and were regularly issued during this period by American booksellers. The annuals were intended as Christmas presents and were re-

garded as one of the few proper tokens of esteem single men and women could exchange. Goodrich was editor for most of the *Tokens*, and he was also a frequent contributor, writing more than fifty poems and sketches for them. He strove to focus on American authors and engravers and took pride in an 1836 boast that his was "the first annual, and the only highly embellished book, issued from the American press which could claim entire independence of foreign aid." Writers for the *Token* included Hawthorne, Lydia H. Sigourney, Henry Wadsworth Longfellow, and William Cullen Bryant. Goodrich later collected his own contributions and published them in books, *The Outcast, and Other Poems* (1836) and *Sketches from a Student's Window* (1841).

Goodrich was best, however, at writing for children, and his simple, didactic writing proved suitable for juvenile audiences. He expanded his Parley series with such books as *Tales of Peter Parley about Europe* (1828), and he eventually developed narrative accounts that blended adventure and morality, as he had first intended. Parley was sometimes the storyteller, sometimes the person to whom the story had been told, but always a strong presence. For *The Travels, Voyages, and Adventures of Gilbert Go-Ahead in Foreign Parts* (1856), Parley was the editor. "For my own part," Goodrich has Parley write in the introduction, "without pretending to vouch for everything that is here written, I may be permitted to say, that all which Mr. Go-Ahead relates is within the bounds of possibility. . . . I think the work may be safely commended to the lovers of amusement, mixed with instruction."

Goodrich's move into magazine publishing was a natural one for a book publisher. The magazines were often sold in booksellers' shops; they helped promote publishing companies and often introduced material that would later come out in books.

Goodrich founded *Parley's Magazine* in 1833 in Boston. His intent, he wrote in the first edition, was to offer children a magazine "that they will regard not as a thing which they *must* read as a task, but which they will love to consult as a companion and friend." The sixteen-page periodical, the editor promised, would contain geographical descriptions, travels, interesting historical notices, biographies, natural history, accounts of various trades, original tales, and cheerful and pleasing rhymes, all abundantly illustrated. *Parley's* was printed every other Saturday, and the cost was one dollar a year, payable in advance. Goodrich

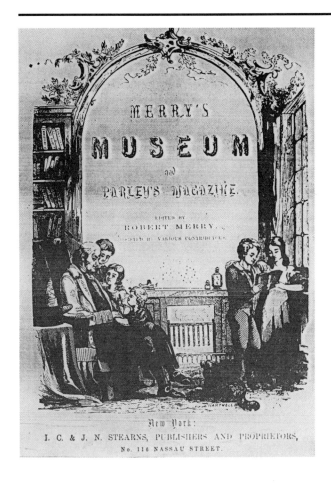

Front cover and address to the reader from the inaugural issue of the second magazine edited by Goodrich

published the magazine for a year and then sold it. It continued in publication until 1844, when it was merged into Goodrich's second magazine, *Robert Merry's Museum.*

The first issue of *Robert Merry's Museum* was published in February 1841. The popularity of the entire Goodrich troupe was indicated by a letter to the *Museum* from a child reader in Louisiana: "That good old gentleman, Peter Parley, has long since become a favorite among us," she wrote, and knowing Merry was a friend of Parley's was enough "to secure you the most ready reception."

Many Parley tales made their first appearance in the *Museum.* Both *Parley's Magazine* and *Robert Merry's Museum* were well illustrated and contained a variety of short informative articles, poems, puzzles, adventure tales, and paragraphs that made moral points. The *Museum* had the words and music for a song in each issue.

Like the Parley books, the magazines drew the devotion of young readers, who often sent their favorite author letters and gifts. A girl in Virginia had written to *Robert Merry's Museum* about Parley and received in reply a photograph of Goodrich, a younger, aristocratic-looking man with wire-rimmed glasses. "The reception of your likeness has disclosed the imposition," she wrote back. "You have come to us every month, in the form of a venerable old man ... we blush to think how familiar we have been." A Boston man likewise later recalled meeting the real Peter Parley as "a disillusion of childhood."

Goodrich published books and edited the *Museum* until 1850, when President Fillmore appointed him United States Consul to Paris. This venture was not Goodrich's first in the area of public affairs; he had served in the state legislature from 1837 to 1838 and had been involved in efforts at educational reform. Goodrich stayed involved with the magazine until 1854, when he sold it. The magazine continued until 1872.

After three years as consul Goodrich and his family remained in Europe for two more years, then returned to America, where he published his *Recollections of a Lifetime,* which remains valued for its look at early nineteenth century New England. Goodrich resumed publishing,

and in 1859 he published a natural history. On 9 May 1860, while visiting New York, he fell ill and, at age sixty-seven, died.

With the changes brought in the country by the Civil War, Goodrich's Parley slipped from popularity. In part, people looked for different things in both their children's literature and their textbooks. Goodrich himself had set the stage for his own obscurity; he had opened the market for juvenile literature, and more talented writers followed him. Reviewing his publications in his autobiography, he said, "I feel far more of humiliation than of triumph. . . . I have written too much, and have done nothing really well." Still, he said, he felt that "my example and my success have led others, of higher gifts than my own, to enter the ample and noble field" of publishing for juveniles. Indeed the popularity Goodrich achieved helped show the viability and national market for books and magazines for children.

Biography:

Daniel Roselle, *Samuel Griswold Goodrich, Creator of Peter Parley; A Study of His Life and Work* (Albany: State University of New York Press, 1968).

References:

L. W. Case, ed., *The Goodrich Family in America* (Chicago: Fergus Printing Company, 1899);

F. J. Harvey Darnton, "Peter Parley and the Battle of the Children's Books," *Cornhill Magazine,* 437 (November 1932): 542-558;

International Magazine of Literature, Art and Science (1 January 1851): 153-155;

Alice M. Jordan, "Peter Parley," *Horn Book Magazine,* 10 (January-February 1934): 96-101;

Rita Podell, "Samuel Griswold Goodrich or Peter Parley," Masters thesis, Columbia University, June 1939;

"Samuel G. Goodrich–his death," *Living Age,* 19 (9 June 1860): 619-620;

Emily Goodrich Smith, "Peter Parley–As Known to His Daughter," *Connecticut Quarterly,* 4 (July-September 1898): 304-315; 4 (October-December 1898): 399-407;

William Oliver Stevens, " 'Uncle' Peter Parley," *St. Nicholas Magazine,* 53 (November 1925): 78-81.

George Rex Graham

(18 January 1813-13 July 1894)

Alf Pratte
Brigham Young University

MAJOR POSITIONS HELD: Owner, *Casket* (1839); editor, *Saturday Evening Post and Philadelphia Saturday News* (1839); publisher (January 1840-July 1858), editor (1843-1847, 1850-1853), *Graham's Magazine*; partner, *Philadelphia North American* (1845-1846); partner, *North American and United States Gazette* (1847-1848); editor, *Saturday Evening Mail* (1853-1854); writer, *Newark Daily Journal* (1872-1882).

Although he is not as well known as Pennsylvanians Andrew Bradford, Benjamin Franklin, and Joseph Dennie, who helped pioneer magazine journalism, George R. Graham deserves special credit for his role in advancing the magazine form through *Graham's Magazine* (1840-1858). During his fourteen-year tenure as either editor or publisher of the Philadelphia-based publication Graham helped institute innovations still used by American magazines, including the promotional strategy of naming famous writers on the front cover, using pictures, and including subjects of interest to women readers. He also helped introduce a strong ethical component into magazine journalism during the medium's struggling early years. Along with *Godey's Lady's Book*, *Graham's Magazine* was one of the few periodicals that paid contributors, and thus, as pointed out by historian Frank Luther Mott, it played an important part in the economics of literature. According to critic J. Albert Robbins, *Graham's Magazine* was "the first of our periodicals to take a truly national view of our literature." Graham's policy was not to prate about the need of a national literature to rival England's; it was to use every means to gather work from all sections of the country and thus show the nation the scope and variety of its rapidly developing literature.

Graham eventually lost control of the magazine due to his poor financial investments in various newspaper endeavors and other speculations. Before he left, however, he had become recognized throughout the magazine business for his skill in hiring good editors and for his promo-

George Rex Graham

tion of American writers. Among his best-known editors were Edgar Allan Poe, Rufus Wilmot Griswold, and Bayard Taylor. Some of the contributors who helped *Graham's* become better known were William Cullen Bryant, Richard Henry Dana, Henry Wadsworth Longfellow, James Russell Lowell, and Poe. Although *Graham's* may not have started with lofty aims, it was, according to

James Playstead Wood, "addressed . . . to the entire literate public." *Graham's Magazine* in particular, he believes, "pointed the general direction that general popular magazines were to take."

Born in Philadelphia on 18 January 1813, the son of a shipping entrepreneur who later lost his fortune, George Rex Graham was educated in Pennsylvania schools and had hopes of becoming a lawyer. His plans were frustrated, however, with the death of his father when Graham was in his early teens. Graham moved to Montgomery County with his sister Mary and brother William to live with a maternal uncle, George Rex, after whom he had been named. During this time Graham first demonstrated his lifelong traits of curiosity and ambition through a self-improvement program that focused on reading. Not only did he cultivate an omnivorous appetite for books written by Henry Bolingbroke, Joseph Addison, Edmund Burke, and other classic authors, but he enjoyed reading aloud or having others read with him. His longtime friend and editor of *Peterson's Magazine* (1842-1898), Charles J. Peterson, later described Graham as one who inspired general affection. "The warmth of his heart and frankness of manners make for him friends wherever he goes. Generous to a fault, forgetful of injuries, conciliating in his deportment, he is one to be alike popular with the many and loved by the few. His faults, when he has them, are those of a noble nature. His sense of honor is keen."

After working for a short time as a storekeeper in rural Pennsylvania, Graham returned to Philadelphia in 1832 at the age of nineteen to work as a cabinetmaker's apprentice so he could make enough money to study law. He also read literature and later claimed that he devoted six hours daily to his literary pursuits after his work was completed. While carrying out both activities he also submitted articles to various publications in Philadelphia, including the *Saturday Evening Post,* founded in 1821 by Samuel Coate Atkinson as a publication to appeal to both men and women. Atkinson later purchased the *Philadelphia Saturday News* from L. A. Godey and with the issue of 12 January 1839 combined the two publications and named Graham as editor.

The year 1839 was important for Graham. Not only was he editor of the *Saturday Evening Post and Philadelphia Saturday News,* but on 23 April he married Elizabeth P. Fry. His childhood ambition of being admitted to the bar was also realized, but, because of his many journalistic enterprises and growing sense of himself as a

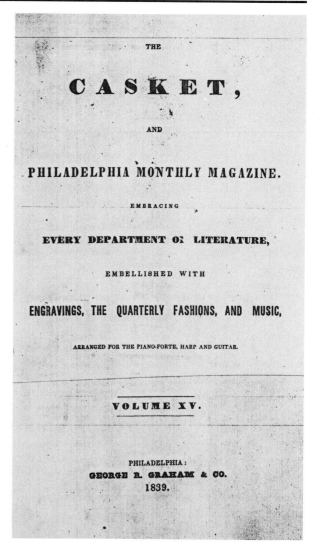

Title page for a volume of the Casket, *purchased by Graham in 1839 and combined with William E. Burton's* Gentleman's Magazine *to make* Graham's Magazine *in January 1840*

publisher, Graham never had an active practice. The same year Graham also bought the *Casket,* which had been started in 1826 by Atkinson and Charles Alexander out of the offices of the *Post.* Graham later combined the *Casket* with William E. Burton's *Gentleman's Magazine* (1837-1840) and issued the first *Graham's Magazine* in January 1840. As Mott notes, the publication became one of the most important American periodicals of the 1840s.

From the magazine's very first issue Graham stressed the importance of fine illustrations, short stories, criticism, material of interest to women, and essays. Before, the monthlies had been filled with secondhand stories from England or indifferently written original tales, while their poetry, except what was taken from well-known authors, was such as "both gods and men abhor." The prospectus for the magazine, printed on the cover of the December 1839 issue, promised that the "character of the articles . . . will be equally removed from sickly sentimentality, and from an affectation of morality, but while a true delineation of human nature in every variety of passion is aimed at, nothing shall be found in its pages to cause a blush upon the cheek of the most pure."

Graham was a leader in the use of new plate engravings expressly for each issue. Toward this end he hired one of the most outstanding engravers in the United States, John Sartain, who later went into the magazine business on his own. While at *Graham's* Sartain developed his art and helped increase the magazine's circulation. Sartain later wrote that, until the time of Graham's new publication, it had been unusual for the monthlies to have new plates engraved expressly for them; they were content, when they had pictorial embellishments at all, to use old worn-out plates picked up at a trifling cost. During the first year circulation of *Graham's* rose from five thousand to twenty-five thousand. By the end of the second year circulation had grown to about fifty thousand, in a nation with a population of seventeen million.

J. Albert Robbins attributes the instant success of *Graham's* to features which had proven popular in other periodicals of the day. Among the female contributors that Graham encouraged were Elizabeth Barrett Browning, Lydia H. Sigourney, Frances Sargent Osgood, Catherine M. Sedgwick, Emma C. Embury, and Elizabeth Oakes Smith. Inasmuch as the emphasis was on literary content, Graham avoided topical and controversial issues until his own financial troubles led him to become sensitive to such matters.

Graham's not only provided a fresh look but was an economic magnet for writers. Prompted in part by his days of near-poverty and the poor pay he had received as a struggling writer and lawyer, Graham made it a policy not to be niggardly with other writers. According to Nathaniel Parker Willis, the liberal payments offered by *Graham's* and *Godey's* in 1842 came "like a sunrise without a dawn." He called the two publishers the "most liberal of paymasters." Further, Graham could be relied on to run his magazine in an ethical manner. In contrast to Godey, he would not advertise as a "regular contributor" any writer who was not. Even after he was faced with fi-

nancial problems, Graham refused to pirate the writings of English authors and use them in his publication, a practice in which rival *Harper's Magazine,* founded in 1850, freely engaged.

Among those sharing in the liberal rates paid to writers for *Graham's* were Longfellow, James Russell Lowell, and James Fenimore Cooper, whom Graham later complained never brought him a new subscriber. In an aside Mott notes that Graham never had a right to complain about Cooper's articles, including a series on naval commanders, because, in addition to Cooper's writings, Graham was exploiting Cooper's name. In a letter encouraging Longfellow to sell "The Spanish Student," attorney George S. Hilliard also refers to Graham's "honorable character for liberal and prompt payment to his contributors."

Probably the most famous author identified with Graham during the golden days of his magazine was Poe, who for a time held the position of literary editor for *Graham's.* Despite his liking for Graham, Poe did not stay with the Philadelphia publication for long before leaving for New York and then Baltimore, where he eventually died. But, during his brief tenure working with Graham, Poe made an impact on American literature that is still felt today. Among the classic short stories that appeared in *Graham's* under Poe's byline were "The Murders in the Rue Morgue" (in the April 1841 issue), "A Descent into the Maelstrom" (May 1841), "To Helen" (September 1841), and "The Masque of the Red Death" (May 1842). Poe's well-known criticism of Nathaniel Hawthorne's *Twice-Told Tales* first appeared in *Graham's* in May 1842. Poe left *Graham's* in 1842 to work for the *Saturday Museum.* Hawthorne's "Earth's Holocaust" appeared in *Graham's* in May 1844, and Hawthorne later referred to the magazine in *The House of the Seven Gables* (1851) when the lodger Holgrave sarcastically states that his "name has figured . . . on the covers of Graham and Godey."

Graham's favorite author was not Poe, but Longfellow (1807-1882), of whom Graham spoke with special pride, claiming that the New England poet had brought more success to the magazine than any other contributor. *Graham's* helped Longfellow become famous throughout the New England states, and the magazine established a stronghold in New York as well as Philadelphia partly because of Longfellow's work. "The Spanish Student" appeared for the first time in *Graham's.* "Nuremburg" appeared in June 1844.

Other important contributions were "Childhood," "Belfry of Bruges," "The Arsenal at Springfield," and his translation of Dante's "Divina Comedia," published in June 1850. In addition to Poe, Graham employed other talented coeditors, including Rufus Griswold and his friend Peterson.

Prompted in part by the growing success of his magazine, Graham tried to expand into related publishing fields. In 1846 he purchased the *North American* and in 1847 merged it with the *United States Gazette*. With an estimated profit of fifty thousand dollars from his journalistic projects, Graham bought a mansion on Arch Street, kept a handsome carriage, and entertained lavishly. But his fine skills in writing, editing, and managing writers from around the country did not apply to his business investing or his appetite for speculation in copper mines. According to an obituary in the *New York Times*, Graham entered into an association with Morton McMichael, and it was not long before the literary man was inveigled into a bogus stock operation in which he lost nearly everything. In October 1848 Samuel D. Patterson and Company took over the management of Graham's holdings, and the following confession appeared in the October 1848 issue of *Graham's:*

> had I not, in an evil hour, forgotten all my true interests, and devoted that capital and industry to another business which should have been confined exclusively to the magazine, I should today have been under no necessity–not even of writing this note.

In a poignant reference to his struggling early years after being left as an orphan, Graham concluded:

> I can yet show the world that he who started life a poor boy, with but eight dollars in his pocket, and has run a career as mine, is hard to be put down by the calumnies or ingratitude of any. Feeling, therefore, that having lost one battle, "There is time enough to win another," I enter upon the work of the "redemption of Graham."

Despite such commitment, the efforts of new managers, and financial help from Graham's in-laws, *Graham's Magazine* was unable to regain its former popularity. Graham himself carried out routine editorial tasks and moved to a less fashionable home. But competition from other magazines that unashamedly borrowed many of his

techniques helped contribute to the decline of the journal. Of particular concern was *Harper's*, which Graham criticized in 1851 as "a good foreign magazine, but it is not *Graham's* by a long way." The major blow to the failing *Graham's* was a negative review of Harriet Beecher Stowe's *Uncle Tom's Cabin*. "It is a BAD BOOK," Graham bravely wrote, with a point of view out of kilter with northern sentiment.

In 1853 Graham became seriously ill with rheumatism, and he experienced failing eyesight. In 1855 he was appointed harbor master of the Port of Philadelphia, based on the recommendation of a friend whose political campaign had been supported by the newspaper Graham had worked for the previous year. Graham held the political position until November 1856. Two years later the magazine which had borne his name as well as the names of hundreds of other American literary greats ceased to exist. A "literary notice" on the last pages of the December 1858 issue noted that the *American Monthly*, the magazine into which *Graham's* was to be incorporated, "will retain all the old features which were so popular in *Graham's*, and will add to them many of the new ones of the most attractive nature." Despite the poignant plea to subscribers, however, the *Graham's* of the past did not survive. For a short period Graham lived in New York City, where the *Times* reports he continued his "financial misfortunes on Wall Street." A biographical note in *American Authors* states that after a stock swindle in 1870 Graham was "completely beggared."

Following the death of his wife in July 1871 Graham moved to Orange, New Jersey, to live with his wife's nephew, whom the Grahams had helped raise in their large Philadelphia home during the 1840s. During the 1870s Graham worked as a writer for the *Newark Daily Journal*. Such piecemeal work ended, however, in 1882 when cataracts formed on both Graham's eyes and slowly brought blindness.

The final years of Graham's life were spent in various boardinghouses and then at the Orange Memorial Hospital, where he was treated for heart and bladder problems. Before he died, on 13 July 1894, he was visited by former associates, including Philadelphia publisher George W. Childs, who contributed money for Graham's care. One editor wrote a letter noting the situation of the former magazine pioneer:

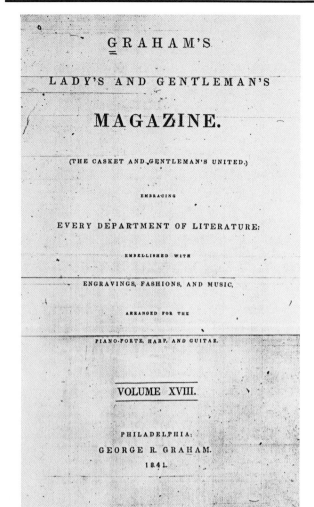

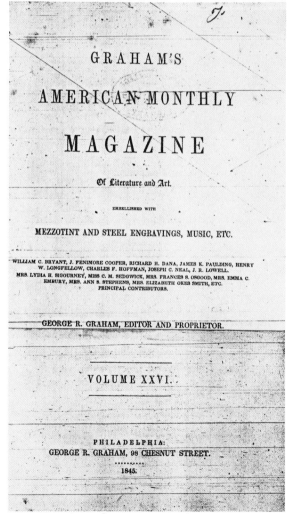

Variant titles for Graham's magazine

George R. Graham, the father of Graham's magazine and therefore the father of first class American periodical literature, has been for nearly two years now an invalid. . . . He is almost blind. . . . He is without a near relative or friend in the world, death having swept them all away.

When Graham's body was returned to Philadelphia there were no relatives to bury him, and few journalists remembered his contributions to the magazine world. He had no children. There is no biography of Graham. His death was not widely reported, and Pennsylvania newspapers generally carried only brief notices. One of the few publications to take note of Graham's accomplishments was the *Philadelphia Inquirer*, which noted the prominent position of the magazine that bore his name:

As a magazine of literature none of the popular magazines of the present day is producing anything like the results achieved by Graham in his "Philadelphia Magazine" a half century ago. . . . Until the "Atlantic Monthly" was founded, just before the war, "Graham's" had no successor and the success of the "Atlantic" was caused by many of the same contributors who in their earlier years had written for "Graham's. . . ." Without him, the most brilliant period of our literature might have been as dark as the years which preceded it and those that have followed it.

References:

Frank Luther Mott, *A History of American Magazines*, 5 volumes (Cambridge: Harvard University Press, 1938-1968), I: 343-344, 544-545;

Charles J. Peterson, "George R. Graham," *Graham's Magazine*, 37 (July 1850): 43-44;

J. Albert Robbins, "George R. Graham: Philadelphia Publisher," *North Carolina University Studies in Philology* (1928): 274-279;

Lawrance R. Thompson, "Longfellow Sells The Spanish Student," *American Literature*, 6 (May 1934): 141-150.

Sarah Josepha Hale

(24 October 1788-30 April 1879)

Edward H. Sewell, Jr.
Virginia Polytechnic Institute and State University

See also the Hale entries in *DLB 1: The American Renaissance in New England* and *DLB 42: American Writers for Children Before 1900.*

MAJOR POSITIONS HELD: Editor, *Ladies' Magazine,* renamed *American Ladies' Magazine* in 1834 (1827-1836); *Godey's Lady's Book* (1837-1877).

BOOKS: *The Genius of Oblivion; and Other Original Poems* (Concord, N.H.: Jacob A. Moore, 1823);
Northwood: A Tale of New England, 2 volumes (Boston: Bowles & Dearborn, 1827); republished as *Sidney Romelee: A Tale of New England* (London: Newman, 1827);
Sketches of American Character (Boston: Putnam & Hunt/Carter & Hendee, 1829);
Conversations on the Burman Mission (Boston: Printed by T. R. Martin for the Massachusetts Sabbath School, 1830);
Poems for Our Children (Boston: Marsh, Capen & Lyon, 1830);
Traits of American Life (Philadelphia: Carey & Hart, 1835);
The Good Housekeeper; or, The Way to Live Well and to Be Well While We Live (Boston: Weeks, Jordan, 1839);
Keeping House and House Keeping (New York: Harper, 1845);
Alice Ray: A Romance in Rhyme (Philadelphia: Printed by A. Scott, 1845);
"Boarding Out." A Tale of Domestic Life (New York: Harper, 1846);
Three Hours; or, The Vigil of Love: and Other Poems (Philadelphia: Carey & Hart, 1848);
Harry Guy, the Widow's Son. A Story of the Sea (Boston: Mussey, 1848);
Liberia; or, Mr. Peyton's Experiments (New York: Harper, 1853);
Manners; or, Happy Homes and Good Society All the Year Round (Boston: Tilton, 1868);
Love; or, Woman's Destiny. A Poem in Two Parts: With Other Poems (Philadelphia: Duffield Ashmead, 1870).

OTHER: *Flora's Interpreter: or, The American Book of Flowers and Sentiments,* edited, with contributions, by Hale (Boston: Marsh, Capen & Lyon, 1832); republished as *Flora's Interpreter, and Fortuna Flora* (Boston: Mussey, 1849; revised and enlarged, Boston: Sanborn, Carter & Bazin/Portland: Sanborn & Carter, 1856; revised again, Boston: Chase, Nichols & Hill, 1860);
John Mason Good, *Good's Book of Nature,* abridgment and adaptation attributed to Hale (Boston: Allen & Ticknor, 1834);

The School Song Book, edited by Hale and Lowell Mason (Boston: Allen & Ticknor, 1834); republished as *My Little Song Book* (Boston: Allen & Ticknor, 1841);

The Ladies' Wreath; a Selection from the Female Poetic Writers of England and America, edited, with contributions, by Hale (Boston: Marsh, Capen & Lyon, 1837; enlarged, Boston: Marsh, Capen, Lyon & Webb, 1839);

Jane Taylor, *The Pleasures of Taste, and Other Stories,* preface and "Sketch of Miss Jane Taylor" by Hale (Boston: Marsh, Capen, Lyon & Webb, 1840);

John Aikin, *The Juvenile Budget Opened,* introductory materials and "Biographical Sketch of John Aiken [*sic*]" by Hale (Boston: Marsh, Capen, Lyon & Webb, 1840);

Anna Letitia Barbauld, *Things by Their Right Names, and Other Stories, Fables, and Moral Pieces, in Prose and Verse,* preface and "Sketch of Mrs. Barbauld" by Hale (Boston: Marsh, Capen, Lyon & Webb, 1840);

The Countries of Europe, and the Manners and Customs of Its Various Nations. In Easy and Entertaining Verse for Children, edited by Hale (New York: Edward Dunigan, circa 1842);

Gift to Young Friends; or the Guide to Good, edited by Hale (New York: Edward Dunigan, circa 1842);

Good Little Boy's Book, edited by Hale (New York: Edward Dunigan, circa 1842);

Good Little Girl's Book, edited by Hale (New York: Edward Dunigan, circa 1842);

Happy Changes; or Pride and Its Consequences, edited by Hale (New York: Edward Dunigan, circa 1842);

Short Tales in Short Words, edited by Hale (New York: Edward Dunigan, circa 1842);

Spring Flowers, or the Poetical Bouquet, edited by Hale (New York: Edward Dunigan, circa 1842);

The Three Baskets; or How Henry, Richard, and Charles Were Occupied While Papa Was Away, edited by Hale (New York: Edward Dunigan, circa 1842);

Uncle Buncle's True and Instructive Stories, about Animals, Insects, and Plants, edited by Hale (New York: Edward Dunigan, circa 1842);

The Wise Boys, edited by Hale (New York: Edward Dunigan, circa 1842);

The Opal: A Pure Gift for the Holy Days. MDCCCXLV, edited, with contributions, by Hale (New York: Riker, 1845);

The Opal; A Pure Gift for the Holy Days. MDCCCXLVIII, edited, with contributions, by Hale (New York: Riker, 1848);

The Opal: A Pure Gift for All Seasons, edited, with contributions, by Hale (New York: Riker, 1849);

Mary Hughs, *Aunt Mary's New Stories for Young People,* edited by Hale (Boston: Munroe, 1849);

The Crocus: A Fresh Flower for the Holidays, edited by Hale (New York: Edward Dunigan, 1849);

The Poets' Offering: For 1850, edited by Hale (Philadelphia: Grigg, Elliot, 1850); republished as *A Complete Dictionary of Poetical Quotations* (Philadelphia: Lippincott, Grambo, 1850); republished again as *The Poets' Offering: For 1851* (Philadelphia: Lippincott, Grambo, 1851);

The Ladies' New Book of Cookery: A Practical System for Private Families in Town and Country, edited by Hale (New York: Long, 1852); republished as *Modern Household Cookery* (London: Nelson, 1863); enlarged as *Mrs. Hale's New Cookbook* (Philadelphia: Peterson, 1857);

The New Household Receipt-Book, edited by Hale (New York: Long, 1852); enlarged as *Mrs. Hale's Receipts for the Million* (Philadelphia: Peterson, 1857);

Woman's Record; or, Sketches of All Distinguished Women, From "The Beginning" Till A.D. 1850, edited by Hale (New York: Harper, 1853; London: Low, 1863; revised and enlarged, New York: Harper, 1855; revised and enlarged again, New York: Harper, 1870);

The White Veil: A Bridal Gift, edited, with contributions, by Hale (Philadelphia: Butler, 1854);

The Bible Reading-Book: Containing Such Portions of the History, Biography, Poetry, Prophecy, Precepts, and Parables, of the Old and New Testaments, As Form a Connected Narrative, in the Exact Words of the Scripture, edited by Hale (Philadelphia: Lippincott, Grambo, 1854);

The Letters of Madame de Sévigné, to Her Daughter and Friends, edited by Hale (New York: Mason Brothers, 1856; revised edition, Boston: Roberts Brothers, 1869);

The Letters of Lady Mary Wortley Montagu, edited by Hale (New York: Mason Brothers, 1856; revised edition, Boston: Roberts Brothers, 1869).

Mention of the nineteenth-century woman's movement immediately brings to mind the names of Elizabeth Cady Stanton, Susan B. Anthony,

Amelia Bloomer, and Lucretia Mott. There were other women, however, who made significant contributions, but, in Ida M. Tarbell's phrase, were women "who did not fight." "Fighting" is a matter of degree, and women like Margaret Fuller, Elizabeth Peabody, and Sarah Josepha Hale, included by Tarbell among those "who did not fight," were perhaps not highly militant in their public battles, but they were, nonetheless, effective. In her own way, Hale, as literary editor of *Godey's Lady's Book,* one of the most successful magazines of the nineteenth century, exerted tremendous influence on the attitudes and values of the American housewife of her era.

Sarah Josepha Buell was born on 24 October 1788 near Newport, New Hampshire, in what she described as "a pleasant village nestled among the green hills." She was the third child of Revolutionary captain Gordon Buell and Martha Whittlesey Buell. Her mother and brother Horatio, who attended Dartmouth College, were responsible for giving her an excellent, though informal, education. She considered her education the primary influence in her becoming "the Chronicler of my own sex." Though she never attended school, she acquired the equivalent of a college education, and for the years between ages eighteen and twenty-five she taught school in Newport.

In 1813 she married a lawyer, David Hale, with whom she continued her studying. After nine years of marriage, her husband died, leaving her, at age thirty-four, pregnant and with four children under seven. She briefly experimented with a millinery business before turning to writing. Before marrying she had published a few poems under the pen name "Cornelia," and later with the help of some of her husband's Masonic friends she had been able to publish a small volume of poetry, *The Genius of Oblivion; and Other Original Poems* (1823). In 1826 her poem, "Hymn to Charity," won a gold medal and a twenty-five-dollar prize in a Boston contest. Then in 1827 she published a novel, *Northwood: A Tale of New England,* describing the differences between life in the North and South. Her novel, the first by an American woman, was successful and was published in the same year in England under the title *Sidney Romelee: A Tale of New England.*

Episcopal clergyman John L. Blake, impressed with Hale's work, invited her to Boston to edit his new journal, *Ladies' Magazine,* which he advertised as "the first magazine edited by a woman for women." Her introduction to the first issue articulated what was to become one of her major crusades: "the granting to females the advantages of a systematic and thorough education." Hale pointed out that the privilege of favoring the intellect belonged, up until that time, "to the men of America." She drew the conclusion that the possibility of a woman's magazine meant that men "appear willing to risk the hazard of proving, experimentally, whether that degree of literature, which only can qualify woman to become a rational companion, an instructive as well as an agreeable friend, be compatible with the cheerful discharge of her domestic duties, and that delicacy of feeling, and love of retirement, which nature so obviously imposes on the sex. . . . " She noted, however, that the magazine, "although ostensibly designed for the ladies, is not intended to be exclusively devoted to female literature. The gentlemen are respectfully invited to examine its contents. If they find nothing which promises advantage to their own minds," she says, she hopes "they will not . . . withhold their support . . . . " Above all she hoped the magazine would be considered a national work that escapes the delimitations of gender.

These first editorial comments by Hale encapsulate much of the spirit of her career for the next fifty years. She was a crusader for the causes of women, but always within traditional roles and mores, and she was an advocate for the development of an "American" spirit in literature and in the home.

Most of what went into the first issues of the *Ladies' Magazine* was written by Hale. She even wrote her own letters to the editor in the first few issues and signed them "H***" as though that would disguise her true identity. She responded to her "Correspondents" in each issue caustically, although with humor. In the February 1829 issue, for example, she wrote:

We acknowledge the receipt of a prose article signed "Columbia." We concluded from the signature, it was written by a lady, but on looking it over, the spirit of the piece convinced us it was from one of the "lords of creation." The article will not appear, and should Columbia live two years, (if time makes him wiser) he will thank us for this hint.

Why is it that persons, who can doubtless converse with propriety on many subjects, when attempting to place their ideas on paper, fail so miserably? Because they will not write as they would speak. They imagine they must have a

The first fashion plate published in Ladies' Magazine, *November 1830*

lofty theme, and long words and pompous descriptions. We never read such, without feeling inclined to use Burchell's exclamation–fudge!

Most of the content of the *Ladies' Magazine* was like that of other periodicals of the era, consisting of correspondence, intellectual as well as romantic, anonymous stories, poetry, music, and fashion plates. The fashion plates, however, were not typical of those in similar magazines because Hale did not approve of American women wearing what she considered the ostentatious fashions of Europe, preferring simple fashions that were conducive to good physical education. In a January 1832 article titled "The Influence of Fashions," Hale remonstrated against extremism in matters of dress, saying "surely there is a difference between cultivating a taste for the graceful in costume, and making that costume the chief ob-

ject of our existence. Pope has very strikingly delineated the death scene of a woman, whose ruling passion had always been dress." She lost her battle to introduce simple American fashions, and rather than include what she considered the unacceptable European styles, Hale ceased the publication of the fashion plates in the *Ladies' Magazine*.

One benefit Hale derived from her editorship was the opportunity to have her magazine writing collected in books. *Sketches of American Character* (1829) and *Traits of American Life* (1835) are two successful examples. Perhaps a more important benefit she derived from her position was the social life of a literary editor in Boston. She lived in the same boarding house as Oliver Wendell Holmes, and she became friends with most of the New England literati. These friendships were invaluable for the remainder of her career as a magazine editor.

While the *Ladies' Magazine* (renamed the *American Ladies' Magazine* in 1834 when Hale discovered a London publication with the former title) was the first of its kind in America, it was not the most successful. In Philadelphia, Louis A. Godey had started the *Lady's Book* in 1830 and through his strong business acumen had turned it into a financial success. In 1836 he purchased the *American Ladies' Magazine* and persuaded Hale to become his literary editor. Since she had a son at Harvard, she agreed to the editorial position on condition that she would continue to reside in Boston until her son completed his college education. Godey agreed, and beginning with the January 1837 issue of *Godey's Lady's Book*, Hale began an association that would last for forty-one years. While Godey maintained control of the financial side of the business, the fashion plates, and the embellishments, Hale assumed responsibility for the literary department.

As literary editor Hale wielded power. Godey paid those authors with whom he contracted for a story in advance rather well, but he did not pay for much of what was published in the *Lady's Book*. Young authors were always trying to get a poem or story in the magazine, since being published in *Godey's* was payment in its own right. Hale printed notices in each issue of what had been accepted and rejected, and her comments could be caustic. In the May 1841 issue, for example, she notified one hopeful author, " 'My Mother's Grave'—the author, should he live ten years longer, will thank us for declining to publish this article." One "Notice to Correspondents" from 1849 read:

> We have been compelled to decline most of the articles sent to us lately. Where the request of return, in case of non-acceptance, was made, the MSS, have been sent back. But we hope the writers will retain copies of their communications, as we cannot answer for the safe-keeping of the multitude of articles that reach us every week. The following are accepted: "Woman's Rights," "The First Katydid," "L'Esprit!" "Loneliness," "A Gem from the French."
>
> "The Graveyard" will appear in the "Lady's Newspaper."
>
> The author of "Evaleen" had better try again. His letter evinces more talent than is displayed in his poem.

It would be a mistake to assume that everything rejected by Hale remained unpublished, even in the *Lady's Book,* for she, like other editors of the day, used snippets from rejected works in her monthly "Editor's Table" alongside selections from other magazines, often without attribution of the source.

In 1832, after the failure of several attempts to build a monument to honor the events of Bunker Hill, Hale took up the cause. She organized the women who read *Ladies' Magazine* into clubs which made financial contributions toward the completion of the monument. The final act was the organization of a large fair in Boston that raised more than enough money to complete the monument. Her editorials urged the women of America to contribute time and money to the project that the men of America had been unable to complete. She argued that America needed to preserve and remember its heritage through such monuments, an argument she later used in other patriotic crusades such as the restoration of Mount Vernon as a memorial to the memory of George Washington.

Because of her own experiences as a widow without the resources or skills needed to earn a livelihood for her family, she was active in women's benevolent societies. Elected president of the Seamen's Aid Society in 1833, she devoted significant energies toward the improvement of living and working conditions for the families of sailors who were at sea or who had died at sea. The result was more than a charity organization, however, and in addition to meeting the immediate needs of the families, the society established schools to train the women in trades and set up nursery schools for the children. It also fought to secure personal and property rights for the women.

Hale took up another patriotic cause: the establishment of a national holiday to celebrate Thanksgiving. She wrote editorials and letters urging Congress and five presidents, as well as governors and state legislators, to adopt a uniform date and declare a national Thanksgiving Day. As some state or person would take action to bring the establishment of the holiday closer to reality, she would publish names and events in *Godey's Lady's Book,* suggesting that those whose names were absent should rise to their patriotic duty and join the ranks of Americans in support of the holiday. Abraham Lincoln finally brought her campaign to its end when on 3 October 1863, in the middle of the Civil War, he declared the last Thursday in November a National Day of Thanksgiving.

Currier lithograph of David and Sarah Hale

While these campaigns were important, perhaps the most significant was Hale's work for the improvement of the position of women. Foremost among Hale's innovations was her almost exclusive publication of original American literature, especially the works of women authors such as Lydia H. Sigourney, Lydia M. Child, and Catherine M. Sedgwick. Another aspect of her battle for recognition of women as contributors to American culture focused on changing how people used gender terms in language. She objected to the use of the word "female" to refer to women because it was a term that was also used to refer to other species of animals. If the word "man" was used rather than "male" when talking about men, why should "female" be used rather than "woman?" She worked assiduously to establish educational opportunities for women, regularly printing information about speeches by women educators, such as Emma Willard, and events related to the advancement of what was then called "female education."

The extent of her influence is clearly seen in the case of the establishment of Vassar College. Quite supportive of the work of Matthew Vassar as he brought together the faculty and students for the first women's college in America, she devoted her "Editor's Table" of October 1861 to the proposed Vassar Female College, observing that, "While clouds and darkness overhang the land, we naturally welcome with double pleasure whatever promises permanent good for the future. The founding of an institution like Vassar Female College, in a year like the present, is a peculiarly cheering event." She praised Vassar but was also critical of him when she felt his actions were inadequate or misdirected. She exposed the more wrathful side of her personality in a letter of 30 March 1865 to Vassar:

> Female! What female do you mean? Not a female donkey? Must not your reply be, 'I mean a female woman'? Then . . . why degrade the feminine sex to the level of animals? . . . I write thus earnestly because I wish to have Vassar College take the lead in this great improvement in our language . . . . Pray do not, my good friend, disappoint me. It is not for myself that I expect any benefit. I plead for the good of Vassar College, for the honor of womanhood and the glory of God.

Over a year later, on 27 June 1866, Vassar wrote Hale "that the great agony is over—your long cherished wishes realized. Woman stands redeemed, at least so far as Vassar College is concerned, from the vulgarism in the associated name of 'female'.... Yesterday ... it was unanimously decided by vote to drop the middle letter [word?] to read thus–'Vassar College.' "

Hale used *Godey's Lady's Book* as a platform for advocating her views, but always within the guidelines set by Godey, guidelines that forbade publishing anything that might damage the sensibilities of the women who read the magazine, including all references to partisan politics and sectarian religious beliefs. Her causes were diverse but were always in keeping with the notion that the purpose of a quality magazine for women should "be conducive to the improvement, and advancement of women, by encouraging the cultivation of literary taste in union with domestic virtues and social accomplishments; and also to promote the interests of morality and piety, by examples of their excellence in both sexes."

In the 1830s she advocated the use of music in the schools, working with Lowell Mason as editor of *The School Song Book* (1834), which was republished in 1841 as *My Little Song Book*. In the 1840s she edited three volumes for the School Library Juvenile series for the Massachusetts Board of Education as well as a series of ten volumes of books for children. Her own works were included in the various editions of McGuffy's Readers, though usually without acknowledgment to the author.

She used the "Editor's Table" as a forum for advocating changes in the medical profession during the 1840s and 1850s. She supported Elizabeth Blackwell's struggle to obtain training as a physician when no medical college in the nation admitted women, and she defended Dr. William T. G. Morton as the inventor of anesthesia, a term suggested by her friend Oliver Wendell Holmes, when a strong religious controversy developed over the appropriateness of the use of anesthetics in medicine. Her most significant campaign in the medical arena, however, was for the rights of women to serve as medical missionaries. In 1851 she founded the Ladies' Medical Missionary Society of Philadelphia, and she fought for the right of single or married women to serve in medical roles. Missionary societies were willing to send a woman to a foreign land only if she accompanied her husband, and no consideration was given to the professional qualifications of the woman as an individual. In the end, women were

sent as medical missionaries to India, China, and Turkey.

Not all of Hale's campaigns were fought on a grand scale. In September 1852, for example, she introduced the use of the term "lingerie" to describe undergarments and to advocate their appropriate use in the everyday dress habits of American women.

Hale also made a significant contribution as editor of several gift books or annuals that were quite stylish from the 1820s to the 1850s. These books were collections of poetry, short fiction, and engravings, beautifully bound and sold as gift books, often around Christmas or some other holiday. Hale edited three volumes of the *Opal* (1845, 1848, and 1849) and one edition of the *Crocus* (1849). Her poetry also appeared regularly in numerous gift books and annuals.

In 1837 she edited *The Ladies' Wreath*, a collection of poetry by American and British writers. The book set out to prove that even though women poets wrote about different topics, there was no justification for believing that women exhibited a female style of writing that was inferior to a male style of writing. A second anthology of poetry, *The Poet's Offering* (1850), contained the works of American and British poets since Spenser, arranged on the basis of subjects. Both anthologies were significant for their comprehensiveness.

Hale's most popular edited work was *Flora's Interpreter*. First published in 1832, it came out in fourteen editions before 1848. It was retitled in 1849, revised and enlarged in 1856, and revised a third time in 1860. It was a variation on the gift book genre, a type of botanical encyclopedia that gave the common name and the scientific name for a flower followed by a poem. Most of the poets were British with a sprinkling of Americans, including John Greenleaf Whittier, William Cullen Bryant, and, of course, Hale.

By Hale's own estimations, the most important of her edited works was *Woman's Record* (1853). In her final "Editor's Table" of December 1877 she said that the book was "so closely bound up with thoughts and impressions which led me to attempt the guidance of my young countrywomen in the right way, that I must depart from this rule [of not mentioning books she edited].... My object was to prepare a comprehensive and accurate record of what women have accomplished, in spite of the disadvantages of their position, and to illustrate the great truth that woman's mission is to educate and amelio-

Hale in 1873 (courtesy of the Historical Society of Pennsylvania)

rate humanity. . . . " In her preface to *Woman's Record,* Hale advanced a theory arguing for the superiority of women based on an interpretation of the Bible, primarily the first chapters of Genesis and one chapter in St. Paul's Epistle to the Corinthians. She began her argument with the clear statement, "The want of the world is moral power," and after some explication of how men failed to provide the moral power so badly needed in the world, she continued: "I believe . . . that WOMAN is God's appointed agent of *morality,* the teacher and inspirer of those feelings and sentiments which are termed the virtues of humanity; and that the progress of these virtues, and the permanent improvement of our race, depend on the manner in which her mission is treated by man." After a lengthy discussion of the story of Creation and the Fall from Genesis, she concluded:

Who can read this, and not fail to perceive that there was a care and preparation in forming woman which was not bestowed on man?

Why was this recorded, if not to teach us that the wife was of finer mould, destined to the most spiritual offices,–the heart of humanity, as her husband was the head? She was the *last work* of creation. Every step, from matter to man, had been in the ascending scale. Woman was the crown of all,–the *last,* and must therefore have been the *best* in those qualities which raise human nature above animal life; the link which pressed nearest towards the angelic, and drew its chief beauty and strength from the invisible world.

Man, she argued, was deceived and should bear the blame for the Fall since "if man, who had the greatest strength of body, had also the greatest wisdom of mind, and knew, as he did, that the serpent was a deceiver, then surely man was the most criminal. He should have restrained or at least warned his wife."

Having built a solid case for the superiority of women, Hale presented the biographies of over six hundred women beginning with Eve and moving forward in history to 1854. She broke the history of women into four eras, beginning with the first era covering "the first four centuries from the creation to the Messiah's advent," followed by the second era from the birth of Christ to 1500, a time when women had "the aid of the blessed Gospel, which seems given purposely to develop her powers and sanction her influence." There followed a third era since 1500 during which the "Gospel had emancipated the soul of woman; the invention of printing gave freedom to her mind," and the fourth era devoted to the living.

Woman's Record was first published in 1853, the halfway mark of Hale's career as editor of the nineteenth century's most successful woman's magazine. Her ideas about the role of women were not excluded from the pages of the magazine that was known for its avoidance of controversy. In the July 1845 issue of *Godey's Lady's Book* Hale published a poem titled "The Empire of Woman" in which she argued for man's innate evil and woman's innate goodness: "The outward World, for rugged Toil design'd,/Where Evil from true Good the crown hath riven,/Has been to Man's dominion ever given;/But Woman's empire, holier, more refin'd,/Moulds, moves and sways the fall'n but God-Breath'd mind."

Hale continued the fight for the rights of women in her later publications. In an 1868 book, *Manners; or Happy Homes and Good Society All the Year Round,* Hale included a chapter on "Mistakes in Language" in which she cited the problem of using the term "female."

Hale's final words to her readers in the December 1877 issue of *Godey's Lady's Book* were a simple demonstration of her attitude about progress:

> And now, having reached my ninetieth year, I must bid farewell to my countrywomen, with the hope that this work of half a century may be blessed to the furtherance of their happiness and usefulness in their Divinely-appointed sphere. New avenues for higher culture and for good works are opening before them, which fifty years ago were unknown. That they may improve these opportunities, and be faithful to their higher vocation, is my heartfelt prayer.

Through what one author called a "subtle subversion," Hale used her position as editor to change the image of the American woman. Godey described their working relationship over the forty-one years as that of friends who "have never had, in any one instance, a serious misunderstanding." Hale retired from her editorship after the December 1877 issue and, after a short retirement, died on 30 April 1879.

References:

Isabelle Webb Entrikin, *Sarah Josepha Hale and Godey's Lady's Book* (Philadelphia: University of Pennsylvania, 1946);

Charles W. Ferguson, "Americans Not Everybody Knows: Sarah Josepha Hale," *PTA Magazine*, 60 (January 1966): 10-12;

Ruth E. Finley, *The Lady of Godey's: Sarah Josepha Hale* (Philadelphia: Lippincott, 1931);

Norma R. Fryatt, *Sarah Josepha Hale: The Life and Times of a Nineteenth Century Career Woman* (New York: Hawthorn Books, 1975);

Joseph Kastner, "The Tale Behind Mary's Little Lamb," *New York Times Magazine*, 13 April 1980, pp. 116-119;

Lawrence Martin, "The Genesis of *Godey's Lady's Book*," *New England Quarterly*, 1 (January 1928): 41-70;

Frank Luther Mott, *A History of American Magazines*, 5 volumes (Cambridge, Mass.: Harvard University Press, 1938-1968), I: 580-594;

Glenda Gates Riley, "The Subtle Subversion: Changes in the Traditionalist Image of the American Woman," *Historian*, 32 (February 1970): 210-227;

Emily Ross, "Madonna in Bustles," *Daughters of the American Revolution Magazine*, 105 (October 1971): 708-711;

Ida M. Tarbell, "The American Woman: Those Who Did Not Fight," *American Magazine*, 69 (March 1910): 656-669;

Richard Fay Warner, "*Godey's Lady's Book*," *American Mercury*, 2 (August 1924): 399-405.

James Hall

(29 July 1793-5 July 1868)

Elizabeth M. Fraas
Eastern Kentucky University

MAJOR POSITIONS HELD: Editor, *Illinois Gazette* (1820-1822); *Illinois Intelligencer* (1829-1832); *Illinois Monthly Magazine* (1830-1832); *Western Monthly Magazine* (1833-1836).

BOOKS: *An Oration Delivered in Commemoration of the Festival of St. John the Baptist, 24th. June 1818, Before Lodges Nos. 45, and 113, Ancient York Masons Held in the City of Pittsburgh* (Pittsburgh: Published by request, Ohio Lodge no. 113; printed by Butler & Lambdin, 1818);
Trial and Defence of First Lieutenant James Hall, of the Ordnance Department, United States' Army. Published by Himself (Pittsburgh: Printed by Eichbaum & Johnston, 1820);
Letters from the West; Containing Sketches of Scenery, Manners, and Customs (London: Henry Colburn, 1828);
The Western Souvenir, A Christmas and New Year's Gift for 1829. Edited by James Hall, for the most part written by Hall (Cincinnati: N. & G. Guilford, 1828);
An Address Delivered Before the Antiquarian and Historical Society of Illinois, at Its Second Annual Meeting, in December 1828 (Vandalia, Ill.: Printed by Robert Blackwell, 1829);
An Oration, Delivered at Vandalia, July 4, 1830 (Vandalia, Ill.: Printed by Blackwell & Hall, 1830);
Legends of the West (Philadelphia: Harrison Hall, 1832);
The Soldier's Bride and Other Tales (Philadelphia: Key & Biddle, 1833);
The Harpe's Head; A Legend of Kentucky (Philadelphia: Key & Biddle, 1833); republished as *Kentucky*, 2 volumes (London: Newman, 1834);
An Address Delivered Before the Erodelphian Society of Miami University, on the Twenty-Fourth of September, 1833, at Their Eighth Anniversary Celebration (Cincinnati: Corey & Fairbank, 1833);

Sketches of History, Life, and Manners in the West (1 volume, Cincinnati: Hubbard & Edmands, 1834; extended edition, 2 volumes, Philadelphia: Harrison Hall, 1835); republished in part as *The Romance of Western History: or Sketches of History, Life and Manners in the West* (Cincinnati: Applegate, 1857);
Tales of the Border (Philadelphia: Harrison Hall, 1835);
History of the Indian Tribes of North America, With Biographical Sketches and Anecdotes of the Principal Chiefs, by Hall and Thomas L. McKenney

(20 parts: parts 1-7, Philadelphia: E. C. Biddle, 1836-1837; parts 8-13, Philadelphia: F. W. Greenough, 1837-1838; part 14, Philadelphia: J. T. Bowen, 1841; parts 15-20, Philadelphia: Daniel Rice & James G. Clark, 1842-1844)–bound in three volumes;

A Memoir of the Public Services of William Henry Harrison, of Ohio (Philadelphia: Key & Biddle, 1836);

Statistics of the West, at the Close of the Year 1836 (Cincinnati: J. A. James, 1836); republished as *Notes on the Western States; Containing Descriptive Sketches of Their Soil, Climate, Resources and Scenery* (Philadelphia: Harrison Hall, 1838); republished as *The West: Its Soil Surface and Productions* (Cincinnati: Derby, Bradley, 1848);

The Catholic Question (Cincinnati: Catholic Telegraph Office, 1838);

The Wilderness and the War Path (New York: Wiley & Putnam, 1846);

Address before the Young Men's Mercantile Library Association, of Cincinnati, in Celebration of Its Eleventh Anniversary, April 18, 1846 (Cincinnati: Published by the Association, 1846).

OTHER: "The Soldier's Bride," in *Winter Evenings. A Series of American Tales* (Philadelphia: Ash, 1829); republished as *The Soldier's Bride and Other Tales* (Philadelphia: J. P. Ayres, 1829), pp. 1-47;

The Western Reader; a Series of Useful Lessons, selected and arranged by Hall (Cincinnati: Corey & Fairbank/Hubbard & Edmunds, 1833);

"Memoir of Thomas Posey," in *The Library of American Biography*, edited by Jared Sparks, second series, volume 9 (Boston: Little & Brown, 1846), pp. 359-403.

James Hall, an easterner of literary lineage, turned to the Ohio Valley of the 1830s for adventure, fortune, and subject matter. As editor of several publications in Illinois, he made his most lasting journalistic contribution through his promotion of western writing as editor of the *Western Monthly Magazine*, a successful literary periodical published in Cincinnati from January 1833 through June 1837.

The son of John and Sarah Ewing Hall, James Hall was born in Philadelphia in 1793. The family Bible and the records of the First Presbyterian Church in Philadelphia say he was born on 29 July, although the autobiography he sent

Evert A. Duyckinck for his *Cyclopedia of American Literature* and Hall's tombstone give his birth date as 19 August. His father was the son of a Maryland planter. His mother came from a family distinguished in both literature and education. Her father, James Ewing, a Princeton graduate, had become the first provost of the University of Pennsylvania. Her *Conversations on the Bible*, first published in 1818, was widely circulated in both America and England. Sarah Hall cultivated in several of her ten children an interest in writing. James's eldest brother, John Elihu Hall, edited the *Port Folio* in Philadelphia, a literary magazine published by another brother, Harrison Hall, and to which both James and his mother were frequent contributors.

Hall's early education came primarily through his mother. An unpleasant experience with the harsh discipline of a Philadelphia academy left him with "a deep-seated disgust for schools and schoolmasters," as he wrote in "The Academy" (*Western Monthly Review*, November 1827). Rejecting an apprenticeship in a counting-house, he studied law until the War of 1812 provided him the opportunity for romance and adventure.

Hall enlisted in a Philadelphia militia company at the age of nineteen, but he did not encounter significant action until he reenlisted in 1814 to join Gen. Jacob Brown's campaign on the Canadian frontier with the three-month battle of Fort Erie. When the campaign ended that winter with the Americans blowing up the fort, Hall, who had been made a lieutenant, was still eager for action. He volunteered for Commodore Stephen Decatur's campaign against Algeria, the response of the United States to repeated attacks on American shipping. Assigned as an artillery officer to accompany the naval expedition, Hall was forced to sail with a later fleet and missed most of the military action in the Mediterranean. But the experience provided him with an opportunity to see and write about Spain; a journal which he kept during his voyage was later published in serial form in the *Pittsburgh Gazette*.

In 1816 Hall was reassigned to the United States arsenal in Pittsburgh, a city which had become the commercial starting point for western migration. His military ambition, however, was dashed by an encounter with a contentious and demanding major, Abraham R. Woolley. The young lieutenant chafed under what he considered the older officer's pettiness and vindictiveness while Woolley seized every opportunity to

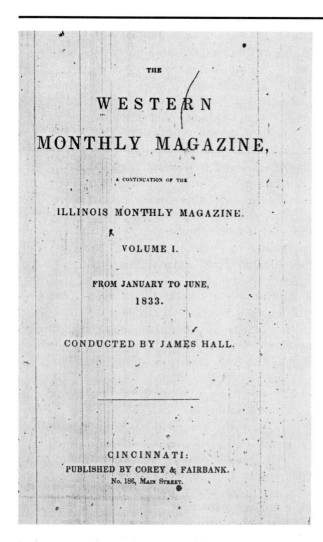

THE

WESTERN

MONTHLY MAGAZINE,

A CONTINUATION OF THE

ILLINOIS MONTHLY MAGAZINE.

VOLUME I.

FROM JANUARY TO JUNE,
1833.

CONDUCTED BY JAMES HALL.

CINCINNATI:
PUBLISHED BY COREY & FAIRBANK.
No. 186, MAIN STREET.

THE

WESTERN MONTHLY MAGAZINE.

JANUARY, 1833.

TO THE READER.

In presenting this Magazine to our readers, under a new name, and in an improved dress, the editor feels assured that the favorable reception which it has heretofore met with, will still be extended to it. Although devoted chiefly to elegant literature, it has always been our wish and endeavor, to render it useful, by making it the medium for disseminating valuable information and pure moral principles. The literature of the West is still in its infancy, and we trust that we are not unconscious of the responsibility which rests on those who attempt to direct it. Sensible that all literary effort, however refined or powerful, which does not promote the cause of virtue, and elevate public sentiment, is worse than useless, we have directed our humble energies towards the accomplishment of these important ends. How far we may have been successful, is not for us to decide.

Our future course will be directed by the same principles which have thus far governed our exertions. We shall endeavor to cull the flowers of literature, and to enliven our pages with the brilliant emanations of wit, so far as the contributions of wits and scholars may enable us to fulfil this pledge. We invoke the assistance of such gentlemen. We call on the man of genius, the classical student, the genuine lover of pure letters, to lend his aid to an enterprise, which is at least laudable and innocent, but which, if carried out to a successful accomplishment, will be honorable to our country, and beneficial to our fellow-citizens.

But we have other and higher views. We would promote the cause of science and useful knowledge. We invite the laborers in this wide and noble field, to enrich our pages with

VOL. I. NO. I.   i

Title page for volume 1 and prospectus in the first issue of Hall's Cincinnati-based magazine

scold his lieutenant. The friction between the two officers finally resulted in the mishandling of the capture of a deserter and the death of a soldier.

Woolley had Hall arrested and charged with insubordination. In the resulting court-martial, Hall was found guilty of unmilitary behavior and insubordination. Ordered to leave the service, Hall appealed his case to Washington and received a presidential pardon, restoring his rank. Nevertheless, the incident ended Hall's promising military career. He resigned from the service on 30 June 1818. Hall's account, a bitter attack on Woolley and a defense of his own behavior, was published in Pittsburgh a few months before he joined the westward migration.

At twenty-five Hall had emerged as an independent, witty, talented, and ambitious young man. During his five years in the military, he had periodically studied law with Pittsburgh lawyers and been admitted to the bar. Dozens of his poems were published in his brother's *Port Folio* and the *Pittsburgh Gazette*, edited by his friend Morgan Neville. His writings, usually published under the pseudonyms Orlando or "O," went beyond verse, however, to include several essays on the importance of the West and even to suggest the need for a western periodical. He had a sense of the vanishing West, expressing in *Letters from the West* (1828) a deep interest "in those young states which have sprung up in the wilderness and which, expanding with unexampled rapidity, are fast becoming the rivals of their elder sisters in the east." Promising to send back firsthand accounts of his experiences, Hall boarded a keelboat in April 1820 for his first trip west.

An account of his journey downriver, later published in the *Port Folio* and in London as *Letters from the West*, presents Hall as an enthusiastic, unsophisticated voyager. At times he is put ashore to "pop over the squirrels, talk with the men, take a peep at the women and kiss the children, while jogging on my way." His *Letters from the West* is a loosely organized collection of backwoods tales, chauvinistic attacks on English portrayals of America, and occasionally sharp sketches of the riverboatmen, farmers, and Indians he encountered in person or in folktale.

Hall had more than a sightseeing trip in mind when he joined the stream of settlers moving west. By 27 May 1820 he had purchased a half-interest in the *Illinois Gazette*, a weekly newspaper published in Shawneetown, situated just below the Wabash River's junction with the Ohio and noted for its salt deposits. By July he had also

opened a law office. His law partner, John McLean, and his newspaper partner, Henry Eddy, were both politically active, and Hall became involved in partisan politics. The following year Hall was named a prosecuting attorney for the southernmost counties of Illinois; he argued and won the first murder trial in the state.

Hall edited the *Gazette* for two years, writing stories, poetry, and editorials promoting western growth. Publication was sometimes suspended, however, for want of paper or during a session of the legislature. In November 1822 he sold his share of the paper to his partner.

Hall married Mary Harrison Posey, a Kentucky woman, on 2 February 1823, and they started a family. In 1825 he was appointed to a circuit judgeship in southern Illinois, a position he held until it was abolished by the legislature. His political career was revived in 1828, however, when the Illinois legislature made him state treasurer, necessitating a move to the capital, Vandalia, in central Illinois.

Hall did not desert journalism. Several of his articles appeared in Timothy Flint's Cincinnati magazine, *Western Monthly Review*. In 1828 Hall published *The Western Souvenir*, a 324-page gift book patterned after eastern publications. Though the publication's declared purpose was to provide a showplace for western talent, most of its contents are by Hall, who declared in a poetic introduction:

> We've seen your volumes o'erspreading the land,
> While the west country people strolled rifle in hand;
> And now we have come, with these hard palms of ours,
> To rival your poets in parlours and bowers.

Several of Hall's short stories, which presented western protagonists such as the Indian Hater and Peter Featherton, a whiskey-loving backwoodsman who matches wits with the devil, appeared in later collections of western writings and established Hall's reputation as an authority on the West and a storyteller of some talent. The *Souvenir* also introduced readers to Mike Fink, the famous riverboatman, in a story written by Hall's friend Morgan Neville, editor of the *Pittsburgh Gazette*.

In 1829 Hall purchased a half-interest in the *Illinois Intelligencer*, a weekly newspaper published by the state printer in Vandalia. The next year he established the *Illinois Monthly Magazine*, the first literary magazine in the state.

Portraits of Hall and his first wife, Mary Harrison Posey Hall (courtesy of Mrs. Elmer J. Rodenberg)

Active in both literary and political circles, Hall also helped found and was elected president of the Antiquarian and Historical Society of Illinois and encouraged the establishment of schools. But his involvement also made him vulnerable to attacks. The Illinois governor's race of 1830 was won by the opponent of the candidate his newspaper had endorsed, and Hall lost his position as state treasurer in 1831. Furthermore, his political enemies alleged that Hall left the office in debt to the state treasury. A lawsuit forced Hall to sell his newspaper and move his magazine to Cincinnati, where he could more easily find contributors and subscribers.

In January 1833 the *Illinois Monthly Magazine* became the *Western Monthly Magazine,* published in Cincinnati. It was characterized by shorter, more readable pieces than the earlier Cincinnati magazine edited by Timothy Flint. Hall wrote satirical and often pun-filled editorial notes and encouraged contributing writers. The magazine offered prizes of fifty dollars for short stories and essays on literary or scientific subjects.

By standards of the day the *Western Monthly* was successful. The magazine grew both in the size of the sheet, from octavo to duodecimo, and in the number of pages, to seventy-two; from five hundred subscribers in 1833 to three thousand in 1836. By the second volume Hall boasted contributions from thirty-seven different writers, including six women. Still, he was forced like other editors to face the reality that it cost more to collect from subscribers than to print. He reminded subscribers that "editors and publishers cannot live on air, and the inky face of the printer grows doubly black if he is not paid on a Saturday night" (*Western Monthly Magazine,* February 1835).

Most of Hall's published works appeared after his move to Cincinnati, although the writing and research had been going on for years. *Legends of the West,* published by his brother Harrison in Philadelphia in 1832, was followed by *The Soldier's Bride and Other Tales* (1833) and *The Harpe's Head* (1833), a novel based on a well-circulated legend of the cutthroat brothers who terrorized Kentucky's early settlers. *Tales of the Border* (1835) contains seven stories, including the "The New Moon," about an Omawhaw Indian princess who maintains dignity despite her humiliation by her white trader husband.

Hall's *Sketches of History, Life, and Manners in the West* (1834), "a collection of facts" about the development of the land west of the Appalachians, is based on Hall's observations and original source material, such as the papers of the Transylvania Company. In 1836 *Statistics of the West* offered a summary of facts and figures about the West as well as a description of the region's geography, wildlife, and trade.

Hall had also started to work with Col. Thomas L. McKenney, who had been in charge of the bureau of Indian affairs, on an ambitious history of the North American Indians. The project necessitated extensive correspondence and visits to St. Louis and Washington to collect information about the Indians who would be the subjects of the illustrated book. An expensive book, *History of the Indian Tribes of North America* was published in twenty parts in 1836-1844; later historians valued its collection and preservation of material that would otherwise have been lost.

Hall's other pursuits often necessitated his absence from the *Western Monthly Magazine*, but he continued to contribute articles and literary reviews. His criticism was sometimes satirical and biting, but never cruel; his essays on political issues of the day sought a middle ground, which brought him and his magazine into conflict with both the abolitionists and anti-Catholic movements gaining support in Cincinnati.

A spokesman for both movements was Lyman Beecher, the president of Cincinnati's Lane Seminary and the father of Harriet Beecher Stowe. In 1835 Hall reviewed Beecher's *A Plea for the West* (1835), which prophesied that European immigration would cause an end to American democracy. The review was followed by an article, "The Catholic Question" (published as a pamphlet in 1838), in which Hall, a Presbyterian, urged toleration, common sense, and an end to violence against Catholics. Hall's position was attacked fiercely by Cincinnati newspapers, and many of his readers canceled their subscriptions. A disagreement with his publisher over the printing of one of Hall's rebuttals forced Hall to take his work to other publishers who had "no feud with the Roman Catholics, or any other class of citizens."

In his magazine Hall printed letters which both attacked and supported his position and

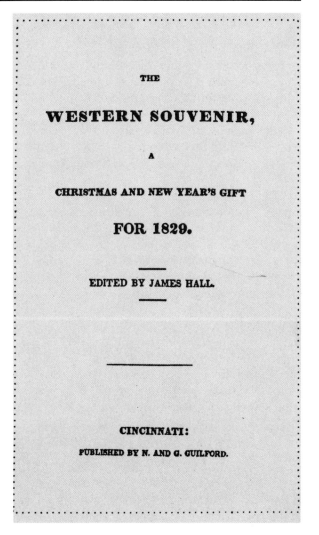

THE

WESTERN SOUVENIR,

A

CHRISTMAS AND NEW YEAR'S GIFT

FOR 1829.

EDITED BY JAMES HALL.

CINCINNATI:

PUBLISHED BY N. AND G. GUILFORD.

Title page for Hall's gift book, ostensibly a showcase for western literary talent, but mostly written by Hall

which disagreed with his position but defended his right to print his opinion. In subsequent issues of the magazine Hall kept readers informed of his difficulties and declared that his work would "continue to be, as it has been American, and not sectarian." The duty of an editor must at times provoke opposition, he said. "To shrink from the investigation of such topics would be to confess a weakness of intellect which would unfit him for his office or a timidity of spirit unbecoming a freeman or a scholar."

Hall had been spending less time with the magazine and more time researching his book, re-establishing his law practice, and directing the business affairs of the Commercial Bank of Cincinnati. By June 1836 a new editor had been hired for the *Western Monthly Magazine*, and by 1837 the journal had been sold to owners who merged it with a Louisville publication which lapsed in 1837.

It may be that Hall felt banking rather than journalism was a more direct way to influence the growth and development of the city. He continued to publish books but devoted most of his time to the reorganization of the bank. He was elected president of the bank in 1853 and held that office until his retirement in 1865. His last collection of short stories was *The Wilderness and the War Path* (1846).

Hall's literary contributions center around his efforts to cultivate and publish western literature, first in Illinois and later in Cincinnati. His writing style is for the most part free of the heavy sentimentalism characteristic of some writers of the period, and his sometimes overly enthusiastic promotion of the West was a balance to the critical and often inaccurate accounts of the West by English or eastern writers. His short stories preserve in printed form the sometimes haunting, sometimes humorous tales of life on the frontier, and both folklore and fact about the Indian race partially erased by the white man's migration. Hall's unabashed enthusiasm and optimism for what the West offered in literary and commercial terms led him eventually to financial success; in return he gave to the young state of Illinois and the growing city of Cincinnati an intelligent, sometimes argumentative, but always interesting voice.

Hall's first wife died in 1832, and he married Mary Louise Anderson Alexander, a widow, on 3 September 1839. They had four children. He died 5 July 1868 at his country home near Cincinnati and is buried in Spring Grove Cemetery.

References:

John T. Flanagan, *James Hall, Literary Pioneer of the Ohio Valley* (Minneapolis: University of Minnesota Press, 1941);

Randolph C. Randall, *James Hall, Spokesman of the New West* (Columbus: Ohio State University Press, 1964);

W. H. Venable, *Beginnings of Literary Culture in the Ohio Valley* (Cincinnati: Clarke, 1891), pp. 361 ff.

Papers:

Hall manuscripts are collected in several places, but there is a significant collection in the Cincinnati Historical Society, Cincinnati, Ohio.

Henry William Herbert
(Frank Forester)
(7 April 1807-17 May 1858)

Mary S. Mander
Pennsylvania State University

MAJOR POSITION HELD: Coeditor, editor, *American Monthly Magazine* (New York) (1833-1835).

BOOKS: *The Brothers. A Tale of the Fronde*, 2 volumes (New York: Harper, 1835);

Cromwell. An Historical Novel, 2 volumes (New York: Harper, 1838; London: Wiley, 1838);

Marmaduke Wyvil; Or, The Maid's Revenge. An Historical Romance (London: Henry Colburn, 1843; New York: J. Winchester, [1843]);

The Village Inn; Or the Adventures of Bellechassaigne. A Romance (New York: J. Winchester, New World Press, 1843);

Ringwood the Rover, A Tale of Florida (Philadelphia: William H. Graham, 1843);

Guarica, The Charib Bride. A Legend of Hispaniola (Philadelphia: A. J. Rockafellar, 1844; London: Ridgeway, 1844);

The Lord of the Manor; Or Rose Castleton's Temptation. An Old English Story (Philadelphia: A. J. Rockafellar, 1844);

Ruth Whalley; Or, the Fair Puritan. A Romance of Bay Province (Boston: Henry L. Williams, 1845);

The Warwick Woodlands, Or Things as They Were There, Ten Years Ago (Philadelphia: G. B. Zieber, 1845); revised as *The Warwick Woodlands; or, Things as They Were There Twenty Years Ago*, as Frank Forester (New York: Stringer & Townsend, 1851);

The Revolt of Boston. A Continuation of Ruth Whalley. Or, the Fair Puritan. A Romance of the Bay Province (Boston: Henry L. Williams, 1845);

My Shooting Box, as Frank Forester (Philadelphia: Carey & Hart, 1846);

The Roman Traitor; A True Tale of the Republic, 3 volumes (London: Henry Colburn, 1846); republished as *The Roman Traitor; A True Tale of the Republic. A Historical Romance[.]*, 2 vol-

Henry William Herbert

umes (New York & Baltimore: William Taylor, 1846);

The Miller of Martigne. A Romance (New York: Richards, [1847]);

Ingleborough Hall, and Lord of the Manor (New York: Burgess, Stringer, 1847);

Tales of the Spanish Seas (New York: Burgess, Stringer, 1847);

Isabel Graham, Or, Charity's Reward (New York: Williams, 1848);

Pierre the Partisan; A Tale of the Mexican Marches (New York: Williams, 1848);

Field Sports in the United States, And the British Provinces of America, 2 volumes, as Frank Forester (London: Bentley, 1848); republished as *Frank Forester's Field Sports of the United States and British Provinces of North America*, 2 volumes (New York: Stringer & Townsend, 1849);

Frank Forester and His Friends; Or Woodland Adventures in the Middle States of North America (London: Bentley, 1849);

The Deerstalkers; Or, Circumstantial Evidence: A Tale of the South-Western Counties, as Frank Forester (Philadelphia: Carey & Hart, 1849);

Dermot O'Brien: Or the Talking of Tredagh. A Tale of 1649 (New York: Stringer & Townsend, 1849);

Frank Forester's Fish and Fishing of the United States and British Provinces of North America (London: Bentley, 1849; New York: Stringer & Townsend, 1850);

Supplement to Frank Forester's Fish and Fishing of the United States and British Provinces of North America (New York: Stringer & Townsend, 1850);

The Captains of the Old World; As Compared with the Great Modern Strategists, Their Campaigns, Characters and Conduct, From the Persian to the Punic Wars (New York: Scribner, 1851);

The Cavaliers of England, Or the Times of the Revolutions of 1642 and 1688 (New York: Hall, 1852);

The Knights of England, France, and Scotland (New York: Hall, 1852);

The Quorndon Hounds: Or, A Virginian at Melton Mowbrey (Philadelphia: Getz, Buck, 1852);

The Chevaliers of France from the Crusaders to the Marechals of Louis XIV (New York, 1853);

American Game in Its Seasons (New York: Scribner, 1853);

The Captains of the Roman Republic, As Compared with the Great Modern Strategists, Their Campaigns, Character and Conduct from the Punic Wars to the Death of Caesar (New York: Scribner, 1854);

Persons and Pictures from the Histories of France and England. From the Norman Conquest to the Fall of the Stuarts (New York: Riker, Thorne, 1854);

Memoirs of Henry the Eighth of England: With the Fortunes, Fates and Characters of His Six Wives (New York & Auburn: Miller, Orton & Mulligan, 1855);

Wager of Battle: A Tale of Saxon Slavery in Sherwood Forest (New York: Mason, 1855);

Oliver Cromwell: Or, England's Great Protector (New York & Auburn: Miller, Orton & Mulligan, 1856);

The Complete Manual for Young Sportsmen: With Direction for Handling the Gun, the Rifle, and the Rod ..., as Frank Forester (New York: Stringer & Townsend, 1856);

Frank Forester's Horse and Horsemanship of the United States and British Provinces of North America (New York: Stringer & Townsend, 1857);

Fishing with a Hook and Line: A Manual for Amateur Anglers. Containing Also Descriptions of Popular Fishes, and Their Habits, Preparation of Baits ..., as Frank Forester (New York: Brother Jonathan Office, 1858);

The Tricks and Traps of Horsedealers, as Frank Forester (New York: Dinsmore, 1858);

Hints to Horsekeepers, A Complete Manual for Horsemen ... (New York: Moore, 1859);

Poems of "Frank Forester" (Henry William Herbert), edited by Morgan Herbert [Margaret Herbert Mather] (New York: John Wiley, 1888).

OTHER: *The Magnolia*, edited, with stories, by Herbert (New York: Monson Brancroft, 1836);

The Magnolia for 1837, edited, with stories, by Herbert (New York: Bancroft & Holley, 1837);

William Post Hawes, *Sporting Scenes and Sundry Sketches; Being the Miscellaneous Writings of J. Cypress, Jr.*, 2 volumes, edited by Frank Forester (New York: Gould, Banks, 1842);

Eugène Sue, *Matilda: Or the Memoirs of a Young Woman[.] A Novel*, translated by Herbert (New York: J. Winchester, New World Press, 1843);

Sue, *The Salamander. A Naval Romance*, translated by Herbert (New York: J. Winchester, New World Press, 1844);

Sue, *The Wandering Jew*, 8 parts, translated by Herbert (New York: J. Winchester, New World Press, 1844);

Sue, *Atar Gull, Or the Slave's Revenge*, translated by Herbert (New York: Williams, 1846);

Alexander Dumas, *Diana of Meridor; Or, the Lady of Monsoreau*, translated by Herbert (New York: Williams, 1846);

Sue, *The Fair Isabel; Or, the Fanatics of the Cevennes. A Tale of the Huguenot War*, translated by Herbert (New York: Richards, 1846);

Dumas, *Genevieve; Or, the Chevalier of Maison Rouge. An Episode of 1793*, translated by Herbert (New York: Williams, 1846);

Engraved title page and frontispiece for one of Herbert's sports manuals

M. A. Thiers, *The History of the Consulate and Empire under Napolean*, 12 parts, translated by D. Forbes Campbell, with notes by Herbert (Philadelphia: Carey & Hart, 1847-1852);

Dumas, *Acte of Corinth; Or, The Convert of Saint Paul. A Tale of Greece and Rome*, translated by Herbert (New York: Williams, 1847);

Frederick Soulié, *The Countess of Morion; Or, The Triumph of Woman*, translated by Herbert (New York: Williams, 1847);

The Prometheus and Agamemnon of Æschylus, translated by Herbert (Cambridge: John Bartlett, 1849);

Jonathan Peel, *The Sportsman's Vade Mecum; By "Dinks,"* edited by Frank Forester (New York: Stringer & Townsend, 1850); revised and republished with *And Dogs: Their Management* by Edward Mayhew (New York: Stringer & Townsend, 1856);

Major Walter Campbell, *The Old Forest Ranger; Or, Wild Sports of India on the Neilgherry Hills, In the Jungles, and on the Plains*, edited by Frank Forester (New York: Stringer & Townsend, 1853);

Charles Weiss, *History of the French Protestant Refugees, From the Revocation of the Edict of Nantes to our Own Days*, 2 volumes, translated by Herbert (New York: Stringer & Townsend, 1854);

Robert Smith Surtees, *Mr. Sponge's Sporting Tour*, edited by Frank Forester (New York: Stringer & Townsend, 1856).

PERIODICAL PUBLICATIONS:
POETRY
"M. De Lamartine's Reply to Sir Walter Scott's Farewell Address," translated by Herbert, *American Monthly Magazine* (March 1833): 20-33;

"Sonnet to a Butterfly," *American Monthly Magazine*, 1 (July 1833): 272;

"The Wreck," *American Monthly Magazine*, 1 (August 1833): 389-390;

"The Hostage's Release," *American Monthly Magazine*, 2 (October 1833): 92-95;

"The Hurricane," *American Monthly Magazine*, 3 (May 1834): 175-176;

"Cleopatra," *American Monthly Magazine*, 3 (June 1834): 223-224;

"The Etonian's Adieu," *American Monthly Magazine*, 3 (July 1834): 351-352;

"The Conscript," *Knickerbocker, or New-York Monthly Magazine*, 9 (January 1837): 38;

"To the Unsatisfied," *New World*, 1 (3 October 1840): 34;

"The Soldier's Song in Peace," *Knickerbocker, or New-York Monthly Magazine*, 21 (January 1843): 14;

"Twilight Musings," *Knickerbocker, or New-York Monthly Magazine*, 21 (February 1843): 133;

"A Riddle. Addressed to My Fair Cousin Elizabeth," *Knickerbocker, or New-York Monthly Magazine*, 21 (April 1843): 319-320;

"The Mother–A Sonnet," *Graham's American Monthly Magazine*, 23 (July 1843): 38;

"Song of the Poet," *New World*, 7 (2 December 1843): 531;

"The Hawking Party," *Graham's American Monthly Magazine*, 24 (January 1844): 42-43;

"Brownwood Female Seminary," *Graham's American Monthly Magazine*, 24 (June 1844): 42-43;

"The Woman Taken in Adultery," *Graham's American Monthly Magazine*, 25 (July 1844): 40;

"My Home," *Literary World*, 1 (10 April 1847);

"Sir Amelot de Vere. A Fragment," *American Review*, no. 79 (July 1851): 13-16;

"Hymn to the Sun. From the Greek of Dionysius," *Graham's American Monthly Magazine*, 41 (August 1852): 132;

"To Melancholy," *Graham's American Monthly Magazine*, 44 (March 1854): 334.

FICTION
"The Wanderer's Return," *American Monthly Magazine*, 1 (March 1833): 44-54;

"The Exile," *American Monthly Magazine*, 1 (April 1833): 72-80;

"Coleur de Rose," *American Monthly Magazine*, 1 (April 1833): 115-123;

"The Syrian Lady. A Sketch of the Crusades," *American Monthly Magazine*, 1 (June 1833): 251-258;

"The Fall of Murray, or The Bride of Bothwelhaugh," *American Monthly Magazine*, 2 (November 1833): 157-164;

"The Death of Pocahontas," *American Monthly Magazine*, 2 (December 1833): 272-277;

"The Veteran," *American Monthly Magazine*, 2 (January 1834): 310-312;

"The Golden Ganymede. A Scene on Mount Olympus," *American Monthly Magazine*, 2 (February 1834): 422-424;

"Passages from the Life of Mary Stuart Chastelar," *American Monthly Magazine*, 3 (March 1834): 9-18;

"Eustache de Saint Pierre. A Tale of the Surrender of Calay," *American Monthly Magazine*, 4 (September 1834): 63-67;

"The Queen's Remorse," *American Monthly Magazine*, 4 (November 1834): 128-135;

"The Death of Cleopatra," *American Monthly Magazine*, 4 (January 1835): 267-274;

"The Fortunes of the Maid of Arc. The Recognition," *American Monthly Magazine*, 5, new series 3 (May 1835): 233-238;

"The Poets of Chivalry," *American Monthly Magazine*, 5, new series 6 (August 1835): 434-441;

"The Death of a Pucelle," *American Monthly Magazine*, 1 (March 1836): 218-225;

"The Mother's Jewels," *American Monthly Magazine*, 3 (January 1837): 82-83;

"The Norman Arrow," *Lady's Companion. A Monthly Magazine*, 10 (January 1839): 64-68;

"The Fate of the Blanche Navire," *Lady's Companion. A Monthly Magazine*, 10 (March 1839): 135-138;

"The Norman's Vengeance," *Lady's Companion. A Monthly Magazine*, 10 (March 1839): 215-219;

"Adventure in the Life of Robert Leslie," *New-York Mirror*, 16 (2 March 1839): 286;

"The Outlaw's End," *Lady's Companion. A Monthly Magazine*, 11 (August 1839): 161-164;

"Hereward the Hunter," *American Miscellany*, 12 (7 December 1839): 177-183;

"The Crusader," *American Miscellany*, 14 (11 January 1840): 257-262;

"The Roman Duel," *Godey's Lady's Book and American Ladies' Magazine*, 20 (February 1840): [49]-51;

"The Charib Bride," *American Miscellany*, 26 (7 March 1840): 385-390;

"The Haunted Homestead. The Murder," *Lady's Companion. A Monthly Magazine*, 13 (August 1840): 185-187;

"The Death of Don Pedro," *United States Magazine and Democratic Review*, 8 (October 1840): 311-317;

"The Spanish Mother," *Godey's Lady's Book and American Ladies' Magazine*, 21 (November 1840): 214-216;

"Jugurtha. A Legend of the Commonwealth," *Graham's American Monthly Magazine*, 19 (July 1841): 3-5;

"The English Mariner. Three Days in the Life of Cavendish, the Rover," *Boston Notion* (1 August 1841);

"The Saxon's Bridal," *Graham's American Monthly Magazine*, 19 (September 1841): 115-119;

"The Woodsman's Daughter. A Tale of the Civil Wars," *Godey's Lady's Book and American Ladies' Magazine*, 23 (September 1841): 127-132;

"The False Ladye," *Graham's American Monthly Magazine*, 20 (January 1842): 27-30;

"The Doom of the Traitress," *Graham's American Monthly Magazine*, 20 (March 1842): 150-153;

"Bridal of Death," *Brother Jonathan*, 2 (30 May 1842): 130-131;

"The Sisters. A Tale of the Seventeenth Century. Part I," *Graham's American Monthly Magazine*, 21 (July 1842): 21-39;

"The Last Desmonds; or, The Graves of a Household," *United States Magazine and Democratic Review*, 12 (January 1843): 17-36;

"The Widow's Son. A Legend of the Scottish Persecution," *Lady's Companion. A Monthly Magazine*, 18 (January 1843): 122-125;

"The Narragansett's Vengeance," *Anglo-American: A Journal of Literature*, 1 (21 October 1843): 601-603;

"Honor O'Neil; or The Days of the Armada," *Columbian Lady's and Gentleman's Magazine*, 1 (March 1844): 97;

"The Pastor's Visit," *Godey's Lady's Book and American Ladies' Magazine*, 28 (April 1844): 153-157;

"Long Jakes, the Prairie Man," *New York Illustrated Magazine of Literature and Art*, 2 (January 1846): 169-174;

"The Rescue. A Tale of the 18th Century," *Anglo-American: A Journal of Literature*, 8 (30 January 1847): 342-343;

"The Death of the Red Deer. A Highland Rhapsody," *Godey's Lady's Book and American Ladies' Magazine*, 35 (August 1847): 61-63;

"The Wedding Day. An English Story," *Godey's Lady's Book and American Ladies' Magazine*, 38 (March 1849): 160-164;

"Anthony and Cleopatra," *Graham's American Monthly Magazine*, 41 (August 1852): 133-139;

"The Lady's Vow," *Gleason's Pictorial*, 4 (8 January 1853): 22-33;

"Love Laughs at Locksmiths. A Tale of the Storming of Rebadavia," *Mrs. Stephen's Illustrated New Monthly*, 4 (April 1858): 207-214.

NONFICTION

"Wild Sports in Many Lands," *American Monthly Magazine*, 4 (November 1834): 136-139;

"The Drama; Historically Considered in Reference to Its Moral and Intellectual Influence on Society," *Knickerbocker, or New-York Monthly Magazine,* 7 (January 1836): 7-12;

"Reminiscences of the Prairie," *Spirit of the Times,* 8 (19 January 1839): 388-389;

"A Week in the Woodlands; Or, Scenes on the Road, in the Field, and Round the Fire. Day the First," *American Turf Register and Sporting Magazine,* 10 (May-June 1839): 248-256;

"Canal Boat Travelling," *Spirit of the Times,* 9 (1 June 1839): 151-152;

"A Wolf-Hunt on the Warwick Hills," *American Turf Register and Sporting Magazine,* 11 (January 1840): 17-24;

"The Last Bear," *American Turf Register and Sporting Magazine,* 11 (March 1840): 107-116;

"Spring Snipe Shooting. Three Days at Pine Brook, New Jersey. Day the First," *American Turf Register and Sporting Magazine,* 11 (June 1840): 261-272;

"Ornithological Classifications of Quail," *American Turf Register and Sporting Magazine,* 12 (January 1841): 8-16;

"A Day in the Woods. Or English and American Game," *Graham's American Monthly Magazine,* 23 (December 1843): 289-295;

"The Ballad Poetry of England," *Godey's Lady's Book and American Ladies' Magazine,* 29 (December 1844): 262-265;

"Field Sports and Pastimes. No. 1. The Sportsman's Dray," *Graham's American Monthly Magazine,* 27 (September 1845): 133-135;

"Woodcock Shooting," *Spirit of the Times,* 15 (6 September 1845): 328-329;

"Bass and Bass Fishing," *Graham's American Monthly Magazine,* 36 (June 1850): 408-409;

"Indian Instinct vs. White Reason," *Gleason's Pictorial,* 5 (16 July 1853): 38;

"The Night-Buds of North America," *Putnam's Monthly,* 2 (December 1853): 616-626;

"Among the Mountains, or, Taking Times Along a Trout-Stream," *Graham's American Monthly Magazine,* 44 (February 1854): 144-147;

"English Sense Versus Websterian Nonsense," *Gleason's Pictorial,* 7 (9 December 1854): 358.

Henry William Herbert's literary reputation is derived primarily from the sports manuals he wrote under the pseudonym Frank Forester. He was, however, one of the first professional writers in the United States and an eccentric and engaging figure in the early history of American magazine publishing. He arrived in New York during a period when magazines, beginning to grow

to mass-market size, were the chief instrument for initiating a continuous literary tradition, one independent of the English. As an editor and writer of magazine literature, Herbert contributed an important, if not essential, impetus to the creation of flourishing industry.

Herbert's often troubled life began happily enough in early spring 1807 in London. His father, Rev. William Herbert, was a son of the first Earl of Carnarvon, Henry Herbert. Herbert's mother, the Honorable Letitia Emily Dorothea, daughter of Joshua, fifth Viscount Allen, was preoccupied with social obligations and had little part in her son's life, but his father set for him an important intellectual example and taught him sportsman's skills. William Herbert was a Doctor of Laws and a member of the British Parliament, where his reputation was tied to his authority on procedure and precedents. The elder Herbert also had a distinguished career in the Church of England, and in 1840 he was appointed Dean of Manchester. Probably the foremost influence on his son's life, he conducted botanical experiments and wrote variously. Byron noted William Herbert's poetry in his *English Bards and Scotch Reviewers* (1809), and Charles Darwin, in his *On the Origin of Species* (1859), praised his greenhouses as "unexcelled places of experiment." Linguist Henry Hallam visited the Herbert estate with his son Arthur, the man whose friendship with Alfred Lord Tennyson inspired Tennyson's hauntingly beautiful "In Memoriam." This was the kind of life and society that Henry would later bitterly miss and long for during his exile in the United States.

In 1819 Henry went to Rottingdam, where he began his formal education and cultivated the British sense of gentility, which American colleagues later misread as snobbery. The following year he entered Eton, where he spent about five years in good standing. He read widely and well and at the age of eighteen left Eton for Caius College in Cambridge, where his work was good but not outstanding. At the same time, he accumulated debts far beyond the generous allowance his father regularly sent him. Upon his graduation in 1830 he fled somewhat suddenly to France and, in 1831, to the United States, where he spent the remainder of his life.

The reason underlying Herbert's exile remains the most enigmatic circumstance of his life, a circumstance none of his three biographers explains satisfactorily. The official reason given at the time was that he lost funds through the dis-

Herbert's letter to publisher Abraham Hart inquiring about the status of his novel The Deerstalker *and other works (William Mitchell Van Winkle,* Henry William Herbert: A Bibliography of His Writings, *1936)*

honesty of a trustee. Herbert himself later intimated that bankruptcy proceedings were filed against him. According to the laws of the time, a debtor who flees makes himself subject to a writ of outlawry. This law remained in effect for almost the entire length of Herbert's life. However, evidence from his father's will indicates that all of Herbert's debts had been taken care of, thus canceling any writ of outlawry. Consequently, whatever offense Herbert committed was one his father could not settle—some infraction of the social or moral code so serious that, even after his death in 1858, Herbert's family refused to acknowledge his existence.

When Herbert took up residence in New York, he taught school for the Reverend R. Townsend Huddart and made friends with coworker A. D. Paterson, who for a short time coedited with Herbert the *American Monthly Magazine*. Before his magazine work began, Herbert had already coedited, at times with James Gordon Bennett, the *Courier and Inquirer*. He also made a number of contributions to its pages. During this period in American history the newspaper editor as well as the free-lance writer emerged and

gained definition. Thus, in the words of biographer William S. Hunt, Herbert "entered the mansion of literature through the tradesmen's doors." He also contributed several reviews, essays, and letters anonymously to a variety of periodicals of the day.

Herbert's attitude concerning "hack" work—that doing it was injurious to his reputation—is indicative of the degree to which the courtly order of letters lingered on well past the mechanization of the printing press, which created a new world of writing as a social practice. A print-based system of letters gave rise in England in the eighteenth century to a new kind of author who now was free of the patronage of the court but tied to the laws of the marketplace. However, for Herbert, who often intimated to friends that he expected someday to come into an earldom, the business of writing for the "common people" seemed beneath his dignity and social importance. For this reason he used the pseudonym Frank Forester for his manuals on sports and wildlife, though he retained his real name for a series of historical romances which he hoped would establish his "literary" reputation. It was always

Herbert's desire to make the *American Monthly Magazine* an organ of distinction. This determination made it virtually impossible for Paterson to initiate practical economical matters designed to keep the magazine afloat financially, and he resigned as coeditor in 1834. Herbert then edited the magazine by himself until early 1835.

In a 7 April 1833 letter to his cousin Algernon Herbert, Herbert characterized the first issue of the new magazine thus: "You will observe that it is all light stuff! So it is—but these Yankees are so superficial that the complaint is that there is not enough fun in it. The most we can venture upon inserting is one or at most two grave articles." His three years as editor of *American Monthly Magazine* marked his transition from an amateur to a professional writer. Much of the magazine's copy was written by Herbert himself, but he did succeed in procuring work from a few of the leading writers of the day, including James Kirke Paulding. The selections published in the magazine reveal that the critical tradition within which both American and English authors were working was one in which both writers and readers thought a close relationship existed between literature and human experience and that literature influenced public morals. Thus the first issue of *American Monthly Magazine* begins with an introduction on the utility of periodical literature.

William B. Cairns categorizes three kinds of magazine that appeared during this period: light reading for women, heavy reading for intellectuals, and a type for educating the masses. It was, of course, the last group to which the work of Herbert as editor belonged. This type of magazine was generally short-lived, and the *American Monthly Magazine* was no exception. Herbert resigned as coeditor in 1835 because he feared that Charles Fenno Hoffmann, who had replaced Paterson as coeditor (after a brief stint by Herbert as sole editor), would turn the magazine into a political organ, something he denigrated. Park Benjamin joined Hoffman as coeditor after Herbert's departure and was the magazine's sole editor for a year before turning the journal's subscription list over to Horace Greeley's *New-Yorker* in 1838.

By the time Herbert left the *American Monthly Magazine* he had developed a reputation as a truculent eccentric. He dressed foppishly and frequented many taverns and roadhouses, where he often became involved in brawls. At the same time, his prolific writings caught the atten-

tion of Edgar Allan Poe, who liked his poetry but who said that Herbert wrote "more trash than any man living, with the exception of [Theodore S.] Fay." Again, in his *Marginalia,* Poe wrote, "Nothing worse than his tone can be invented."

Herbert's private life continued to be marked by frustration and failure. In 1839 he married Sarah Barker, who died in 1844. Herbert's son by the marriage, William George, was subsequently sent to live in England. Herbert remarried in February 1858; however, his second wife, Adela R. Budlong, left him a few weeks later, and Herbert committed suicide in a New York hotel on 17 May.

Among his diverse contributions to early American magazines are several translations of French and Greek literature, and poetry and book reviews. His articles and translations appeared in leading periodicals of the day, including the *Democratic Review, Spirit of the Times, Peterson's Ladies' National Magazine,* and *Graham's Magazine,* edited by George R. Graham, who proved that a magazine could show a fair profit as well as pay reasonable prices for its selections.

In addition to his editorship of *American Monthly Magazine,* Herbert also attempted a Sunday magazine, the *Era,* the first family-oriented journal for general circulation. This venture failed because religious beliefs discouraged this kind of reading on Sundays and because several newspapers reproduced it, thus restricting the magazine's margin of profit. At the same time, republication in regional newspapers offered Herbert the benefit of extending his readership. Finally, Herbert attempted to launch a sports magazine and so can be identified as an important figure in the prehistory of general circulation sports magazines in the United States.

Given the relatively brief period of his life devoted to magazine editing, Herbert cannot be considered a major figure in magazine history. However, given the range and volume of his contributions to early American periodicals, he played an important part in the development of the magazine in the United States. His letters, which provide a firsthand account of the economics of periodical publishing in the first half of the nineteenth century, are especially informative. Herbert's role as a leading contributor to magazine literature and his editorship of the *American Monthly Magazine* render him a figure in early magazine history worthy of scholarly attention.

Letters:

The Letters of Henry William Herbert, "Frank Forester," 1815-1858, edited and annotated by Stephen Meats, Ph.D. dissertation, University of South Carolina, 1972.

Bibliographies:

William Mitchell Van Winkle, *Henry William Herbert [Frank Forester]: A Bibliography of His Writings, 1832-1858* (Portland, Maine: Southworth-Anthoensen Press, 1936);

Stephen Meats, "Addenda to Van Winkle: Henry William Herbert (Frank Forester)," *Papers of the Bibliographical Society of America,* 67 (First Quarter, 1973): 69-73.

Biographies:

Thomas Picton, "Henry William Herbert [Frank Forester], The Story of His Life," in *The Life and Writings of Frank Forester (Henry William Herbert),* volume 1, edited by David W. Judd (New York: Orange Judd, 1882), pp. 11-104;

William S. Hunt, *Frank Forester: A Tragedy in Exile* (Newark: Carteret Book Club, 1933);

Luke White, *Henry William Herbert & The American Publishing Scene, 1831-1858* (Newark: Carteret Book Club, 1943).

References:

Earl Bradsher, *Mathew Carey, Editor, Author and Publisher, a Study in American Literary Development* (New York: Columbia University Press, 1912);

William B. Cairns, *Development of American Literature, 1815-1833* (Madison: University of Wisconsin Press, 1898);

Alvin Kernan, *Printing Technology, Letters and Samuel Johnson* (Princeton: Princeton University Press, 1987);

Frederick Marryat, *A Diary in America: With Remarks on Its Institutions,* edited, with notes and an introduction, by Sydney Jackman (New York: Knopf, 1962);

Frank Luther Mott, *A History of American Magazines,* 5 volumes (Cambridge, Mass.: Harvard University Press, 1938-1968), I: 480-481, 618-619;

Vernon Louis Parrington, *Main Currents in American Thought,* 2 volumes (New York: Harcourt, Brace & World, 1958);

John Tebbel, *The American Magazine, A Compact History* (New York: Hawthorn Books, 1969);

Tebbel, "The Creation of an Industry, 1630-1865," in *A History of Book Publishing in the United States,* volume 1 (New York: R. R. Bowker, 1972).

Papers:

Henry William Herbert's letters and other materials are widely scattered. The British Museum holds a copy of one of his publisher's agreements. American institutions holding more than ten letters are the Yale University Library, the Boston Public Library, the New York Public Library, the New York Historical Society, and the Historical Society of Pennsylvania.

William Gibbes Hunt

(21 February 1791-13 August 1833)

William E. Huntzicker

MAJOR POSITIONS HELD: Editor, *Western Monitor,* renamed *Western Monitor and Lexington Advertiser* (1815-1824); *Western Review and Miscellaneous Magazine* (1819-1821); *Masonic Miscellany and Ladies' Literary Magazine* (1821-1823); *Nashville Banner,* renamed *Nashville Banner and Nashville Whig* and later renamed *National Banner and Nashville Daily Advertiser* (1824-1833).

William Gibbes Hunt gained his considerable reputation during the two years he edited one of the first and best literary magazines published west of the Allegheny Mountains. The *Western Review and Miscellaneous Magazine* contained poetry, political commentary, science, book reviews, natural history, and anecdotal history. It was an unusual publication in which a description of a battle with Indians followed an article lamenting the decline in the study of Greek. For most of his life Hunt was a newspaper editor who featured articles that were generally more literate than those of his contemporaries in frontier Kentucky and Tennessee.

Hunt was born in Boston, the son of Samuel Hunt and Elizabeth Gibbes Shepherd Hunt, the daughter of wealthy Charleston planter William Gibbes. Hunt studied under his father and Caleb Bingham, and, at the age of fifteen, he became the fourth in his family line to enter Harvard College, from which he graduated in 1810. Although he included law among his Harvard studies, it was not until 1824 that Hunt received an LL.B., which he earned at Transylvania University in Lexington, Kentucky. The same institution had awarded him an honorary A.M. degree two years earlier.

In 1815 he moved to the Ohio Valley and joined the staff of the *Western Monitor,* a Federalist paper in Lexington, Kentucky, owned by Thomas T. Skillman. In 1818 Hunt purchased the paper from Skillman, and the following year he became sole publisher and editor; the paper then became the *Western Monitor and Lexington Advertiser.*

Although Hunt and his *Western Review* are often mentioned in cultural histories of Kentucky and the nation, no biography of him exists. Consequently, little is generally known of his personal life, except that he married Fanny Wrigglesworth on 28 September 1820 in Lexington.

Hunt's two magazines, the *Western Review and Miscellaneous Magazine* (1819-1821) and *Masonic Miscellany and Ladies' Literary Magazine* (1821-1823), were published in the office of the *Western Monitor* in Lexington. (While editing his magazines, Hunt retained editorship of the weekly newspaper, took job-printing assignments, and operated a bookstore.) Lexington had been the site of the first frontier magazine in 1803 when Daniel Bradford published *The Medley, or Monthly Miscellany* for a year from the office of the *Kentucky Gazette.* But Bradford's short-lived publication was long forgotten when Hunt began Lexington's second literary magazine, which survived for two years (four volumes).

Drawing on Lexington's intellectual resources as the "Athens of the West," Hunt's magazine published original poetry and prose by local business and intellectual leaders, including faculty members of Transylvania University. "For two years," wrote F. Garvin Davenport, "this monthly was the medium through which Lexington's scientists, educators, and literati expressed themselves."

Hunt believed that using writers' names made journalism too personal. Consequently, very few bylines were carried in the *Western Review.* The major exception was Constantine S. Rafinesque, professor of botany and natural history at Transylvania University, whose byline became well known to the magazine's readers.

Rafinesque contributed articles on, among other things: botany in Kentucky; the salivation of horses; the oil of pumpkin seeds; Kentucky shrubs; an ancient monument near Lexington; de-

THE

WESTERN REVIEW

AND

MISCELLANEOUS MAGAZINE

A

MONTHLY PUBLICATION,

DEVOTED TO

LITERATURE AND SCIENCE.

VOLUME FIRST,

FROM AUGUST 1819 TO JANUARY 1820, INCLUSIVE.

LEXINGTON, KENTUCKY;

PUBLISHED BY WILLIAM GIBBES HUNT.

1820.

THE

WESTERN REVIEW

AND

MISCELLANEOUS MAGAZINE.

Vol. I.   AUGUST, 1819.   Num. I.

ART. 1. *The life of Andrew Jackson, Major General in the service of the United States: comprising a history of the War in the South, from the commencement of the Creek campaign, to the termination of hostilities before New-Orleans*—Commenced by JOHN REID, brevet major, United States Army—Completed by JOHN HENRY EATON. 8vo. pp. 425. *Philadelphia*, M. Carey and Son, 1817.

THERE is a splendor in military greatness, which renders it, to every one, an object of interest. The philosopher, the scholar, the philanthropist, and the statesman, may be approved and respected, but the achievements of the hero dazzle and enchant. The useful application of superior intellect to the purposes of civil and domestic life, will ultimately ensure veneration and gratitude: but what are these, compared with the enthusiastic glow of admiration, which the brilliant exploits of the warrior command! Vain are the efforts of reason to destroy this peculiar charm of military glory. Though associated with misery in its most distressing forms, and often with the display of the most ferocious passions, it still engages the understanding and captivates the heart. We may read unmoved of the discoveries of Newton, the philanthropy of Howard, the learning of Johnson, and even of the eloquence of Cicero or Demosthenes: but who can contemplate the exploits of Cæsar, or Alexander, or Bonaparte, without being animated, warmed, and interested. Nor would we wish to divest the hero of his dazzling qualities. Glory in any shape is a noble incentive, and though war is an evil of tremendous magnitude, opposed to the wishes of the philanthropist, as well as of the christian; yet, so long as it does and must exist, we cannot, as patriots, wish to destroy this greatest and most efficient stimulus to the exertions of the soldier.

Whatever doubts may have been entertained of the necessity or expediency of our late war with Great Britain, it had the

Title page and opening page from the first issue of Hunt's eclectic literary magazine

scriptions of two species of foxes; and an analysis of the types of lightning in the region. In a very different vein, he wrote poetry in English and Italian.

Most of the other essays, stories, travel articles, poems, and reviews were unsigned or signed by a single letter. At least ten different letters and four two-letter combinations were used. The editor often signed his comments with an *E*, but most authorship is a matter of speculation. Magazine historian Frank Luther Mott states that Transylvania University president Horace Holley wrote the poems and articles signed *T* and *U*. Hunt revealed John B. Clifford's authorship of the "Indian Antiquities" series and an article on western geology when the contributor died. Another frequent contributor was Holley's wife, Mary Austin Holley, who later became known for her writings about frontier Texas.

In literature the *Western Review* reflected the frontier's fascination with British authors, especially Lord Byron and Sir Walter Scott. Hunt particularly liked Scott and sought to be among the first to get copies of the author's books when they arrived in America.

The *Western Review* praised Byron's "The Prophecy of Dante" for its original and strong feelings but took offense at the poet's "constant attacks" on England. Like all its other reviews, this *Western Review* critique reprinted long excerpts from the work under review. And the reviewer rejected the idea that Byron had "exhausted his muse and lived down his genius." Byron provided ample proof that poetry remained a modern art form, and the critic expressed contempt for those who rejected modern poetry to find quality only in the classics.

Nevertheless, Hunt and the *Western Review* promoted classical learning. The *Western Review* even printed poems in Latin. It lamented the decline in the study of Greek and Latin and promoted higher education, encouraging interest in the area's two notable institutions, Transylvania University and the Lexington Female Academy. Throughout his career Hunt fought the notion that a liberal education was unnecessary in a frontier society. He also advocated education for women and slaves and called for improved professional and liberal education for ministers of the Gospel.

The first volume of the *Western Review* contained twelve book reviews and thirty-seven articles of "miscellany" ranging from anecdotes of Indian battles to Rafinesque's long-running natu-

ral history of fish in western waters. Titles of articles included "Education in the Western States," "Female Heroism," and "Geology of the Western Country." Thoughtful legal critiques were offered on the system of trial by jury and the idea of collecting bail for debtors.

The editor was already respected for his intellect by the time he founded the *Western Review*. He was elected to the American Antiquarian Society of Massachusetts—a sign of both his literary accomplishments and New England connections. In accepting the appointment, Hunt wrote on 19 November 1819 that his magazine would usually contain articles on Indian antiquity.

These articles began a running debate over the meaning of ancient mounds along the Ohio River and whether the ancient civilizations in the Ohio Valley practiced human sacrifice. One article stated that American Indians and slaves could communicate in a common language, leading the author to speculate that the African and American continents were once connected. Another series of articles discussed Indian manners and customs.

Decades before the first dime novel, the *Western Review* published hair-raising accounts of battles between whites and the region's original inhabitants. The magazine's adventure stories fulfilled a nationalistic need for an heroic American literature played out on the frontier, and they reinforced the white culture's morality in the conflict between civilization and savagery.

Kentucky's attractive climate, fertile soil, and natural beauty attracted pioneers, but the region was "infested with ferocious beasts" and wild, cruel, savage men, Hunt wrote. "There was not a tree, behind which a lurking Indian might not be apprehended; not a stump, from which a rifle ball might not, with deadly aim, be expected to be discharged by a concealed and cowardly foe. Defenceless women and children were exposed to the most cruel and barbarous outrages. Hosts of savages, well armed and confident of superior strength, would often rush with unexpected violence on a weak and unguarded settlement. Here was a theatre for valorous enterprise, and here was displayed feats of heroism unsurpassed perhaps in the annals of history."

These dramatic assumptions about the helpless whites versus vicious natives colored the adventure tales which appeared in the *Western Review*. Most anecdotes supported the assumption of the correctness of the "civilized" cause. But one story described a dramatic encounter be-

1821.　　　　　VALEDICTORY.　　　　　383

neighbourhood; while Brenda's fears were mingled with some share both of anger and of impatience. Norna paid no attention to either; but began her story in the following words. * * * * * *

VALEDICTORY.

THE present number, which completes the fourth volume of the *Western Review*, terminates also the existence of the work. It is with regret that we announce our determination to discontinue a publication, which we at one time fondly hoped would be a permanent repository of the numerous productions of the intelligence, and taste, and literary acquirements of the citizens of the west. The enthusiasm, indeed, with which we commenced this enterprise, has long since ceased to exist. Experience has taught us that our labours, valuable as they might appear to ourselves, were of little importance in the public estimation, and that the literary efforts, which, we are proud to say, have received the favourable notice of distinguished scholars in other parts of our country, were contemned and deemed unworthy of patronage at home. We have been well aware of the numerous defects of our little publication. It never aspired to an elevated rank among the literary productions of the country. It has been the result of the disconnected efforts of a few friends of learning, whose literary hours have been often broken in upon by the more essential and imperative duties of active life, and who have therefore been compelled frequently to disappoint the publisher at an hour when it was impossible to fill up the chasm in a manner satisfactory to himself. The work has for some time past been continued under circumstances peculiarly discouraging. Many who promised fairly, and who no doubt intended fairly, to rank among its liberal contributors, nev-

384　　　　　VALEDICTORY.　　　　　*July,*

er furnished a single article, and several others yielded only occasionally a reluctant essay to the often repeated solicitations of the editor or his friends. The melancholy loss of some of our most industrious and enthusiastic co-adjutors threw the entire labor and responsibility upon a few individuals, and the numerous other cares and duties by which those individuals have been surrounded, have prevented their devotion, so intently as they could have wished, to the interests of the work. We trust however that our efforts, humble as they have been, and far as they have fallen short of our own desires and intentions, have yet been productive of some good. If we have in any degree succeeded in creating or fostering a literary taste; if we have to any extent drawn out the resources of the scholars of the western country; if we have been instrumental in preserving, for the future historian and for the admiration of posterity, any of those interesting narratives, which contemporaries only could furnish, of the difficulties, and dangers, and almost incredible deeds of heroism, that distinguished and ought to immortalize the early settlers in the west; if, in fine, we have successfully repelled a single unjust aspersion cast upon the American character, our exertions have not been in vain, and we have no cause to regret the existence, feeble and short lived as it may have been, of the *Western Review.*

We have only in conclusion to express our hope, that the day may not be far distant, when the friends of literature and science in the western country may feel more generally disposed to encourage literary efforts in their own community, and when the public may, with more zeal than at present, afford to them that patronage, without which they cannot permanently succeed.

Hunt's farewell essay for the final issue of his short-lived Western Review and Miscellaneous Magazine

tween two white brothers and two Indians on a river bank and ended with a lament about an unnamed Indian's death. The writer stated that "this native was the most distinguished among five celebrated brothers belonging to the royal family of the tribe of Wyandots.... Notwithstanding he was engaged in this predatory expedition, he was acknowledged by all to be peculiarly magnanimous for an Indian, and had contributed, more than any other individual, to preserve and extend the practice, which was known to prevail in his tribe, that of not taking the lives of prisoners, and of not suffering them to be treated ill."

Hunt solicited adventure tales from his readers, promising to rewrite them if necessary. "To rescue from oblivion the interesting and numerous incidents of those days of peril, to preserve for the historian and for posterity the numerous anecdotes of cool, determined intrepidity, and of almost miraculous preservation from destruction, which live only in the memories of the spectators of the scenes, will be a prominent object in the publication of this work," he wrote in the *Western Review* of August 1819.

Despite his call for heroic exploits, the editor said the narratives should be "well-attested" and factual. "In making this request," the editor wrote, "we wish it to be understood that all we want is a *statement of facts,* properly attested. Gentlemen, who are not in the habit of writing for the public, and who are not even accustomed to composition of any sort, are still solicited to communicate, in the plainest manner, *the facts* within their knowledge. We shall consider it our business, in such cases, to reduce the narrative to a form adapted for publication in this work."

Hunt probably wrote the anecdote entitled "Female Heroism" (January 1820), which recounts the story of two women who held off an attacking band of Indians who had just killed their husbands. Having only one bullet for her gun, one of the women, Mrs. Cook, bit the bullet in half to make enough for two shots. She discouraged the attackers from burning her cabin by cutting open a chicken with an axe and throwing the moist entrails into the fire in the chimney. She then shot one of the departing Indians through a crack in the cabin, and Hunt goes on to verify the story by stating that the Indian's body was later found in the Elkhorn River.

The *Western Review* also sought to provide an intellectual rationale for white expansion and subjugation of the natives. The Indians simply did not use the land efficiently. "What they use

not, they cannot claim. Others may take it, and apply it to the purposes for which it was given." Productivity was another criterion to judge who should use the land. "No indulgence must be allowed to lazy and unproductive nations at the expense of the welfare and enlargement of the industrious, the productive, the intelligent, and the virtuous." The *Western Review* said the white civilization was superior in arts, letters, science, complex institutions, machinery, population growth, efficient investment of capital, and the ability to take and keep power.

Reacting to a book criticizing American expansion, the *Western Review* denied the charge that Americans had designs on the entire North American continent. But it added: "Even if we do cherish this idea, there is nothing improper in it, unless we adopt corrupt means to accomplish it. We ought, if any nation should command North America, to be the nation selected." Thus twenty years before the words "manifest destiny" appeared in print, the *Western Review* had outlined the basic idea. "The Creator did not intend that in any country a lazy, vagrant, ignorant, inefficient people should stand before an active, settled, intelligent, civilized, and energetic people."

The *Western Review and Miscellaneous Magazine* truly was a review. Much of the commentary on contemporary issues appeared in reviews of books, pamphlets, and speeches. The first issue opened with a twenty-two-page, two-part review of a book about Andrew Jackson written by a former aide to the general. The review, probably written by Hunt, took an analytical approach to both the general and the glowing biography of him. While acknowledging Jackson's courage and his contributions to the nation, the reviewer criticized his decisions to violate orders in both Florida Indian battles and the War of 1812. The reviewer warned of "being blinded by the glare of military and patriotic achievements, to real defects, perhaps dangerous traits, of character."

A twenty-three-page review of the second annual report of the Colonization Society solicited money for the cause of creating an African colony while promising that the group would not seek the emancipation of slaves. If the society created a successful colony, free blacks would voluntarily migrate, and masters would voluntarily free their slaves, resulting in the gradual removal of blacks from the United States, the reviewer wrote.

Slavery was evil, the *Western Review* admitted, but good slaveholders did a public service by owning slaves who might otherwise fall into the hands of cruel owners. Moreover, slaveholders were obligated to improve the slaves' living conditions and to provide them with an education. Given similar opportunities and education, the magazine said, blacks could achieve the same success as whites. But that success should be achieved in Africa. The *Western Review* attacked the slave trade and even suggested that U.S. ships intervene in Africa to stop it.

In much of his writing, Hunt promoted his region, especially its culture. "The advances," he said, "made by this infant section of our country in literature, science, morals, religion, and all the accomplishments of cultivated life, have excited the astonishment and admiration of distant observers. Within a few years past our progress has been unexampled."

In 1820 Hunt took Rafinesque's long-running articles on the natural history of fish in the Ohio River and its tributaries and published them as a book, *Ichthyologia Ohiensis or Natural History of the Fishes Inhabiting the River Ohio and Its Tributary Streams*. In the following year Hunt printed a number of the anecdotes about Indian attacks in *A Collection of Some of the Most Interesting Narratives of Indian Warfare in the West*, by Samuel L. Metcalf. This book also included a narrative by Daniel Boone and other material that did not appear in the *Western Review*.

Recalling his aspirations for the *Western Review* in an essay entitled "Valedictory" (July 1821), Hunt wrote that he had failed to meet them. Yet he mixed his departure with boasts of the critical acclaim his publication had received elsewhere. "The enthusiasm, indeed, with which we commenced this enterprise, has long since ceased to exist," he wrote. "Experience has taught us that our labours, valuable as they might appear to ourselves, were of little importance in the public estimation, and that the literary efforts, which, we are proud to say, have received the favourable notice of distinguished scholars in other parts of our country, were contemned and deemed unworthy of patronage at home." Volunteer staffers often failed to submit promised articles, and many others reluctantly contributed. Some who promised regular contributions never submitted a single article.

Hunt's "Valedictory" was not the only evidence that the *Western Review* had trouble maintaining a staff. Two articles announced the deaths of contributors: the Reverend Benjamin Birge, twenty-three, of Lexington's Episcopal Church; and Clifford, forty-two, a merchant and archaeologist. "One after another in rapid succession," Hunt wrote in the Clifford obituary, "our fellow labourers in the extensive field of literature and science are thus taken away, but we trust those of us who remain will be thereby excited to greater exertion."

Two of the major contributors had other problems. Despite his many contributions to the *Western Review*, President Holley faced constant pressure from a religious group who had opposed his appointment and who worked for his removal. In nine years Holley had built Transylvania into *the* major western university, but his opponents' rumors and vicious attacks were a constant plague until he resigned in 1827.

President Holley and Rafinesque had little use for each other, but there is no evidence to indicate how much their personality conflict caused problems for Hunt. Rafinesque was an irritable and eccentric man as well as a prolific writer. He became depressed upon the death of Clifford, his closest friend, and wrote an ode to him in Italian for the *Western Review*.

Rafinesque tried to begin his own rival publication, *Western Minerva*, in January 1821, but his printer destroyed the first and only issue before it was distributed because Rafinesque never paid his bill. Rafinesque, however, claimed his enemies prevented its release. Only about three copies survived. Not surprisingly, Rafinesque's byline no longer appeared in the *Western Review*.

Hunt took pains to see that material for the *Western Review* was original. In the February 1821 issue he apologized because a poem published the previous month had been published earlier. "As we intend our work to be a depository of *original articles*, we feel it to be a duty to notice this circumstance," he wrote.

No such ideals accompanied him on his next magazine, the *Masonic Miscellany and Ladies' Literary Magazine*, designed for lodge members in the West. Novelty could hardly be expected in interpreting the time-honored traditions of the lodge, he said, and the ladies' section would also borrow ideas and articles. "We shall cull flowers from the numerous, extensive, and variegated gardens of literature, occasionally transplanting valuable exotics, as well as rearing and cultivating products of our own soil. In doing this, we shall not always deem it necessary to notice the source from which our selected articles are taken," he wrote. After several issues, however, the editor began naming the sources of many borrowed articles.

The first *Masonic Miscellany* appeared the very month that the *Western Review* faded away. The editor promised that the new magazine would have a "light and popular character" with humble but valuable results. The major portion of the new magazine contained discussions of Masonic principles and reprinted orations delivered by Masons, primarily in Kentucky and New England. Hunt, who became grand high priest for the Kentucky Lodge while editing the magazine, often defended the lodge in both his magazines and his newspapers. At the same time, he called on Masons themselves to give their fraternity a better image by living up to the Christian ideals of the lodge.

The first part of each forty-page issue was devoted to news from other Masonic lodges. For example, the *Masonic Miscellany* printed a notice of Hunt's appointment as head of the Lexington Lodge and, within a month, Maj. Gen. Andrew Jackson's appointment to a similar position in Nashville.

The second part of the magazine contained the headline *Ladies' Literary Magazine*, but the quality of the material paled in comparison with the content of the *Western Review*. Romantic stories, jokes, and poetry filled much of this section. Many articles perpetuated sexist stereotypes; the very first article was a one-paragraph joke about an ugly woman in a freak show. Articles carried such headlines as "The Father, or Indian Magnanimity," "On Lips and Kissing," "Female Character," "On Taste in Female Dress," and "Matrimonial Happiness." Brief excerpts from James Fenimore Cooper's *The Pioneers* (1823) ran in several issues.

Despite its blatant sexism, the magazine printed anecdotes with positive female role models and advocated improved education for women. "If Adam had merely wished for a toy to amuse his vacant hours, the ape, the coney [rabbit], the squirrel or the bird of Paradise, might have answered his purpose," wrote a Massachusetts clergyman whose discourse Hunt printed. Women, he said, should be rational companions who could counsel and instruct their husbands.

The literary section's greatest contribution was the publication of promising poems by the teenaged girls in the Lexington Female Academy. Publishing the poetry, Hunt said, would reward writers of the best poems and provide an incentive for other students to write.

Like the *Western Review*, the *Masonic Miscellany* ran for two years (two volumes), and the editor again closed by expressing his disappointment at the lack of local support. But this publication ended with an upbeat message on the endurance of fraternal organizations. "Our principles," he concluded, "are the sober theory of human nature, which must bless the world." Hunt recommended two national Masonic publications to which his readers could subscribe.

The year after he permanently left the magazine business, Hunt also left Lexington, moving to Nashville, Tennessee, where he became editor in 1824 of the *Nashville Banner* newspaper, which became the *Nashville Banner and Nashville Whig* and then the *National Banner and Nashville Daily Advertiser*.

In Tennessee Hunt's newspaper promoted the American Colonization Society, and Hunt became a manager for the society in Nashville, helping free blacks relocate in Africa. He was a practicing attorney and remained an active Mason.

His newspaper usually showed more sympathy for Henry Clay of Kentucky and Andrew Jackson of Tennessee than for the politics of any political party. Hunt differed from other editors in his insistence that newspapers refrain from joining political parties. Like many other western editors, Hunt took much of his news from the exchanges. On at least one occasion he said the irregularity of the mail meant that there was "no late and interesting news to lay before our readers."

Instead of publishing magazines, Hunt encouraged the exchange of ideas in Nashville through the creation of the Nashville Lyceum, which he promoted through his newspaper by announcing forums, soliciting books for its library, and often reprinting speeches.

Hunt himself became well known as an orator, and in 1825 he delivered the welcoming oration in Nashville for General Lafayette when the former revolutionary soldier returned to the United States. Hunt often addressed the Lyceum and Masonic lodges, gaining a national reputation for his defense of Masonry.

The *Nashville Banner* published reviews of books, periodicals, and local theatrical productions. The newspaper printed items, such as the resignation of a professor of Greek literature at Harvard, that other frontier newspapers hardly noticed.

Hunt's erudite editorials apparently confused other editors. On 25 April 1831 Hunt debated the editor of the *Natchez Gazette* on the question of whether he ever "gave a *decided opinion*, even on an abstract question." Hunt retorted: "Those who have observed our editorial course, both in Kentucky and in this state, know full well that we have spoken most unequivocally, emphatically, and zealously, on all the important abstract questions, that have agitated the community. We have often observed indeed, that those who know the least, are the most *decided* and confident in the expression of their *opinions*." The Natchez editor, Hunt wrote, failed to understand the independent approach of the *Nashville Banner*, which was different from publications that required adherence to a party creed.

Hunt's newspaper, which he published with his brother, W. Hasell Hunt, often boasted about the strength of its patronage. Hunt took over the paper as a weekly, and by 1833 it appeared as a four-page daily with a tri-weekly edition for outlying areas. The paper appeared in very small type on "a sheet of the largest size used in the West," Hunt wrote.

Despite these boasts, the editor in early 1833 wrote: "And now permit us to add—for the first time, and we hope for the last—that feeling our share of the difficulties and embarrassments of the times, and being subjected to a constant and very heavy expense in the prosecution of a business of great public importance, we must insist, immediately, on the settlement of all our outstanding accounts and the payment of the large amount due us for subscriptions, advertisements, &c. We trust our friends and patrons will cheerfully render to us the sums respectively due—small to each of them, but in the aggregate of vast importance to us." With these words, Hunt admitted to a problem that often plagued frontier newspapers, especially those few which survived without political patronage.

The year 1833 proved to be difficult in other ways for both Nashville and the Hunt family. The *Nashville Banner* expressed even stronger fears of an impending civil war and the effect of the Tennessee bank's debts on the region's economy. Worse still, the region was hit by a cholera epidemic. On 15 June Hunt reported the death in Kentucky of his former partner and friend Thomas T. Skillman, "printer, a worthy, amiable, pious man."

Nearly two months later Hunt was struck suddenly by the disease. On 13 August he died.

"It cannot be expected of a distressed brother," W. Hasell Hunt wrote, "that he should prepare an elaborate obituary of the deceased—suffice it to say, that he has left a disconsolate widow and three infant children, an aged mother and a sister and brother" to mourn "a loss indeed irreparable." The obituary failed to mention that a daughter, Julia Gibbes Hunt, was born ten years earlier and preceded Hunt in death.

The paper's dependence upon its editor was shown by the fact that both the daily and tri-weekly editions missed a publication day because of his illness and death. And W. Hasell Hunt asked for his subscribers' indulgence, saying he could not match his brother's talent which was "surpassed by none and equalled by but few." Services were held 17 August at the Episcopal Church, and burial was at the old Nashville city cemetery.

In Hunt, the *Louisville Herald* said, "the Editorial corps has lost one of its most distinguished members; the cause of literature an able advocate; the society of the place in which he lived a valuable associate, and his family a kind and affectionate husband, father and friend." The *Herald* called him a vigorous political writer who maintained his good temper and discretion.

In his "Valedictory" in the final number of the *Western Review*, Hunt had summed up his accomplishment: "If we have in any degree succeeded in creating or fostering a literary taste; if we have to any extent drawn out the resources of the scholars of the western country; if we have been instrumental in preserving, for the future historian and for the admiration of posterity, any of those interesting narratives, which contemporaries only could furnish, of the difficulties, and dangers, and almost incredible deeds of heroism, that distinguished and ought to immortalize the early settlers in the west; if, in fine, we have successfully repelled a single unjust aspersion cast upon the American character, our exertions have not been in vain, and we have no cause to regret the existence, feeble and short lived as it may have been, of the *Western Review*."

References:

Milton L. Baughn, "An Early Experiment In Adult Education: The Nashville Lyceum, 1830-1832," *Tennessee Historical Quarterly*, 11 (March-December 1952): 238-242;

F. Garvin Davenport, *Ante-Bellum Kentucky: A Social History, 1800-1860* (Oxford, Ohio: Mississippi Valley Press, 1943), pp. 170-199;

T. J. Fitzpatrick, *Rafinesque: A Sketch of his Life with Bibliography* (Des Moines: Historical Department of Iowa, 1911);

Earl L. W. Heck, "William Gibbes Hunt, A Pioneer in Early Western Journalistic Literature," *Lexington Herald*, 17 April 1932, II: 10;

Samuel L. Metcalf, *A Collection of Some of the Most Interesting Narratives of Indian Warfare in the West* (Lexington, Ky.: William G. Hunt, 1821);

Frank Luther Mott, *A History of American Magazines*, 5 volumes (Cambridge, Mass.: Harvard University Press, 1938-1968), I: 311-312;

Ralph Leslie Rusk, *The Literature of the Middle Western Frontier*, 2 volumes (New York: Colum-

bia University Press, 1925), I: 164-203, 271; II: 1-38;

Charles Albert Snodgrass, *The History of Freemasonry in Tennessee 1789-1943* (Chattanooga: Masonic History Agency, 1944), p. 384;

Niels Henry Sonne, *Liberal Kentucky 1780-1828* (New York: Columbia University Press, 1939);

W. H. Venable, *Beginnings of Literary Culture in the Ohio Valley* (Cincinnati: Robert Clarke, 1891), pp. 58-71, 124;

Richard C. Wade, *The Urban Frontier: Pioneer Life in Early Pittsburgh, Cincinnati, Lexington, Louisville, and St. Louis* (Chicago: University of Chicago Press, 1959), pp. 240-262.

John Inman

(1805-30 March 1850)

Sam G. Riley
Virginia Polytechnic Institute and State University

MAJOR POSITIONS HELD: Editor, *New York Standard* (1828); coeditor, *New-York Mirror, and Ladies' Literary Gazette* (1828-1831, 1835-1836); assistant editor (1837-1844), editor (1844-1850), *New York Commercial Advertiser;* editor, coeditor, *Columbian Lady's and Gentleman's Magazine* (1844-1848).

PERIODICAL PUBLICATIONS:
FICTION
"Early Love and Constancy," *New-York Mirror, and Ladies' Literary Gazette*, 8 (2 April 1831): 305-306;

"Romeo and Juliet in Cheapside," *Columbian Lady's and Gentleman's Magazine*, 2 (July 1844): 14-17.

NONFICTION
"Magazine Literature," *Columbian Lady's and Gentleman's Magazine*, 1 (January 1844): 1-5;

"Holbein's Dance of Death," *Columbian Lady's and Gentleman's Magazine*, 2 (July 1844): 24-27;

"Le Compte De Gabalis," *Columbian Lady's and Gentleman's Magazine*, 2 (July 1844): 28-31;

"A True Story of Love and Death," *Columbian Lady's and Gentleman's Magazine*, 2 (July 1844): 32-34;

"The Process of Education," *Columbian Lady's and Gentleman's Magazine*, 2 (July 1844): 36-42;

"Death Under the Law," *Columbian Lady's and Gentleman's Magazine*, 7 (February 1847): 91-92;

"The Year That Has Gone," *Columbian Lady's and Gentleman's Magazine*, 7 (January 1848): 26-30.

POETRY
"The Joys of Absence," *Columbian Lady's and Gentleman's Magazine*, 2 (July 1844): 5;

"Grandeur," *Columbian Lady's and Gentleman's Magazine*, 2 (July 1844): 13;

"Town and Country–A Friendly Dialogue," *Columbian Lady's and Gentleman's Magazine*, 2 (July 1844): 17;

"Woman–A Scandalous Apostrophe," *Columbian Lady's and Gentleman's Magazine*, 2 (July 1844): 27;

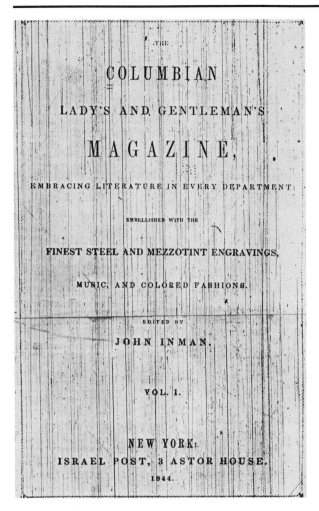

Title page for volume 1 of the magazine Israel Post founded to compete with Graham's Magazine

"The Glee Maiden," *Columbian Lady's and Gentleman's Magazine*, 7 (March 1847): 140.

John Inman, New York City magazine and newspaper journalist of the 1820s through the 1840s, has not often been remembered by media historians. Little has been written of his life and work, yet in his day he was a prominent member of New York's newspaper press, first as editor of the *Standard*, then of the *Commercial Advertiser*. His later magazine experience included six years as coeditor of the popular *New-York Mirror, and Ladies' Literary Gazette* and five years as editor of the *Columbian Lady's and Gentleman's Magazine*. Inman is an example of a journalist whose reputation rests more on his contributions as an editor than on what he contributed as a writer.

Inman was born in 1805 in Utica, New York, to English parents, William and Sarah Inman. In or around 1812 the family moved to

New York City, where the three Inman sons prospered, each in his own field of endeavor. The oldest, William (1797-1874), became a successful naval officer, rising to the rank of commodore before his retirement in 1867. The second son, Henry (1801-1846), gained considerable fame as a portrait painter and in 1824 was one of the founders of the National Academy of Design in New York. Prominent persons whose portraits he painted were William Wordsworth, John Marshall, DeWitt Clinton, John J. Audubon, Martin Van Buren, Nicholas Biddle, and William H. Seward.

Young John Inman appears to have had little formal schooling, but in 1823 he became a schoolteacher in North Carolina. After two years of teaching and saving most of his earnings, he spent a year traveling in Europe, then returned to New York and read for the law. Like so many other young men with legal training in this era, Inman found greater attraction in journalistic work. His first editorial experience was with the *New York Standard* in 1828.

Later in 1828 Inman became coeditor, with George Pope Morris and Theodore Sedgwick Fay, of a literary magazine, the *New-York Mirror, and Ladies' Literary Gazette*, which had been founded in 1823 with Morris as publisher and Samuel Woodworth as editor. This eight-page weekly, appearing on Saturdays, contained both original and selected tales, book reviews, biography, verse, essays, dramatic and art criticism, music, and miscellaneous notes on the mores of the time. Much of this material was run unsigned, making identification of Inman's own contributions difficult to assess. The *Mirror* was a quality journal of light literature that reached its greatest heights under a later editor, Nathaniel Parker Willis, and that employed Edgar Allan Poe during 1844 and 1845 as a contributor and critic prior to his employment with the *Broadway Journal*. Inman's involvement with the *Mirror* ran from 1828 to 1831, and later in 1835 and 1836. In 1833 Inman married a Miss Fisher, the sister of John Fisher, Clara Fisher, and Mrs. Vernon, English comedians who appeared at New York's Park Theater.

In 1837 Inman became an assistant editor of one of New York's better newspapers, the *Commercial Advertiser*, under head editor William L. Stone. Upon the death of Colonel Stone in 1844, Inman became editor and held this position until shortly before his own death in 1850. During these years he also wrote occasionally for the *New*

York Review, the *Spirit of the Times,* and other popular magazines.

Inman's greatest contribution to magazines, however, began in 1844 when he was picked by publisher Israel Post to edit the new *Columbian Lady's and Gentleman's Magazine,* which Post had founded to compete with the highly successful *Graham's.* The monthly *Columbian* was issued in two volumes yearly. Each volume was handsomely illustrated with eighteen to twenty steel and mezzotint engravings; six musical selections, usually written especially for the magazine; and in the early volumes, colored fashion plates.

Inman was a frequent contributor to his own magazine during its maiden year, though most of his contributions were quite brief. He adopted the unusual device of writing a page or less to accompany and amplify the magazine's engravings. These short selections in volume 1 bore such titles as "Columbus and the Egg," "Fortune Teller," and "The Victor in the Tournament." A larger Inman article occupied the first five pages of the first number of the *Columbian;* in it the editor gave his thoughts on the various journalistic forms of the day. "Decidedly this is the age of magazines," wrote Inman, adding that "newspapers, unable to emulate them in appearance, strive to do so in the variety and nature of their contents. In fact, the word *newspaper* has come to be almost a misnomer, for the purveying of news has ceased to be their characteristic vocation and object." Most newspapers, he continued, contained essays, short tales of fact and fiction, and long serialized stories taken from books or magazines. All dabbled in criticism and "good-naturedly afford space in their columns for the ambitious efforts of young gentlemen and ladies who labor under the mistake of believing that destiny calls on them to write poetry."

Not to be despised, wrote Inman, were the many weekly journals, even those published in the hinterlands, despite their coarseness, worn-out type, "ragged whitey-brown paper," and constant struggle for funds enough to continue publishing. Most of all Inman defended the quality of the era's monthlies, pointing out that Charles Lamb in England, Eugène Sue and Jules Janin in France, and such American writers as James Fenimore Cooper, Washington Irving, William Cullen Bryant, and Henry Wadsworth Longfellow first gained their fame by publishing their work in monthly magazines. The monthly, Inman said, hit the happy medium between

Self-portrait by Henry Inman, John Inman's brother (courtesy of the Pennsylvania Museum of Fine Arts)

ephemeral newspapers and the more ponderous book market.

The first number of volume 2 (July 1844) was entirely written by Inman himself, with the exceptions of the engravings, a fashion plate, and a song by Emma Embury and Mrs. C. L. Hall. A portrait of the editor, painted by brother Henry and engraved by W. L. Ornsby, appeared as a frontispiece to the July 1844 number, which also contained a portrait of Inman's young daughter, also by Henry Inman with engraving by Ornsby. The number's lead article is an Inman essay, "The Editor," reflecting on the different requirements for editors of newspapers, magazines, and books. In it Inman quotes Frederick Marryat: "He who enlists in the service of a monthly periodical makes himself a slave to a hard master."

In his essay "Talking of Birds" Inman concludes that the killing of these tiny creatures for mere sport "is a cowardly business." "The Key

Found" contains his reflections on a visit to a prison; "Romeo and Juliet in Cheapside" is his adaptation of this most famous of love stories, transposed to a modern urban setting in which the Montagues and Capulets are rival haberdashers.

"Newspaper Seedlings" is a collection of Inman's thoughts on the utility of newspaper copy as inspiration for imaginative writers who are always on the lookout for themes and story lines. Part of this article is devoted to duels, which then provided the substance for frequent stories in newspapers; another part, with the subheading "Judicial Murder," concerns the death penalty. Inman comes out against both. A third section of the article deals with "frigida mors," now called "cryonics"–the attempt to preserve human life for years, even centuries, by placing the person in intense cold.

"Le Compte De Gabalis" was inspired by a rare book Inman had bought at a Paris bookstall on the Quai Voltaire; "A True Story of Love and Death" is a tale in which love triumphs over poverty; and "The Process of Education" contains ex-teacher Inman's espousal of the Prussian and Scottish systems of teaching the young.

The July 1844 solo number also contained six of Inman's poetic efforts, the most quotable of which is "Grandeur":

> There's grandeur in the thunder's roar,
>   Loud pealing from on high;
> And in the vivid lightning's flash,
>   When storms sweep through the sky;
> There's grandeur in the swelling waves,
>   The mountains of the sea,
> That crush the pride and strength of man
>   When the winds blow wild and free.

Inman's other poems in this number were "The Joys of Absence," "Town and Country–A Friendly Dialogue," "The Farewell," "The Wail of the Jilted," and "Woman–A Scandalous Apostrophe." To the last of these he appended an apology, noting that he had written this poem some years earlier before taking a wife and discovering "how altogether charming, excellent, amiable and admirable women are, without variations or qualification."

Volume 3 was coedited by Inman and Robert A. West. Numerous items in this volume were signed "by one of the editors," making identification largely a matter of conjecture. In "Vague La Galerie," which opened the fifth volume of the *Columbian,* Inman tells his readers that due to the senior editor's poor health, West had done most of the editorial work for volume 4. In this address to his readers Inman claimed more than twenty thousand subscribers to the *Columbian.*

By January 1847 Inman's health had been sufficiently recovered for him to write again numerous one- or two-page pieces to accompany the magazine's engravings. In March 1847 "The Glee Maiden" appeared; it was a poem written to accompany an engraving. The early lines of this poem sound vaguely like Poe's "The Raven," though the similarity ends there:

> The prior he sat in his easy chair,
> Conning the page of an old tome rare;
> Before him a fire blazed warm and high,
> At his side was a goblet of Malvoisie.
>
> The prior was deep in his learned lore
> When tap, tap, tap came a sound at his door. . . .

Edgar Allan Poe, in fact, had been a fairly regular contributor to the *Columbian,* beginning with "Mesmeric Revelation," "The Angel of the Odd–An Extravaganza," and "Bryon and Mrs. Chaworth" in volume 2. Other frequent contributors of verse were Frances Osgood, Lydia Sigourney, William Cullen Bryant, coeditor West, and H. T. Tuckerman. Also making appearances, in prose and verse, were T. S. Arthur, Walter Whitman, Seba Smith, Park Benjamin, John Neal, Alfred Street, Charles Fenno Hoffman, Elizabeth Oakes Smith, and Catherine M. Sedgwick.

Ill health continued to plague Inman, and he resigned after the March 1848 issue. In the May number for that year appeared his farewell, in which he said that his original intention had been to edit the *Columbian* for only one year; instead, he had remained for more than four years. His poor health, he wrote, rendered him unable to summon the energy to serve two masters, the other being the *Commercial Advertiser,* which he continued to edit until 1850. The January 1848 issue of the *Columbian* also contained "The Year That Has Gone," a three-page essay in which a somber Inman addressed himself to the Indian wars of the previous decades, concluding that they "had no glory in them; they were vexatious and protracted, and cost monstrous sums of money, but somehow one could not help feeling ashamed of them; they had a kind of petty larceny aspect" and had been "wars to rejoice the hearts of contractors and all other people who had the fingering of Government money."

Inman went on to express hope of seeing an end to the Mexican War and wished that "never again, or at all events not soon, shall our rulers, our law-makers and our people be reduced, by any delusive glare of personal or national ambition . . . into a war that can by any means be avoided." He ended his unhappy piece by adding that "if the world, or any considerable part of it, is in the least better, as well as wiser, than it was a year ago, the evidence thereof is yet to be made available to the present editor."

Just prior to Inman's resignation the *Columbian* had been sold by Israel Post to John S. Taylor. Taking over from Inman and West as editor was Stephen M. Chester, who at the end of 1848 was replaced by the Reverend Darius Mead, founder of the *Christian Parlor Magazine*. The final number of the *Columbian* appeared in February 1849. Inman died in New York on 30 March 1850.

Though neither his accomplishments as a writer nor as an editor were sufficient to propel him into the front ranks of American magazinists, John Inman edited a magazine successfully and gave its readers a more than respectable diet of light literature. Surviving contemporaries remembered him as a genial, popular man. A member, with Bryant, Fitz-Greene Halleck, and Gulian C. Verplanck, of New York's Sketch Club, Inman was a prominent journalist of his day and a graceful, versatile writer who likely would have accomplished much more had his health been better and his life longer.

References:

Frank Luther Mott, *A History of American Magazines*, 5 volumes (Cambridge, Mass.: Harvard University Press, 1938-1968), I: 320-330, 743-744;

J. G. Wilson, *Bryant and His Friends* (New York: Fords, Howard & Hulbert, 1886), pp. 408-409.

Washington Irving

(3 April 1783-28 November 1859)

Jacqueline Steck
Temple University

See also the Irving entries in *DLB 3: Antebellum Writers in New York and the South; DLB 11: American Humorists, 1800-1950; DLB 30: American Historians, 1607-1865;* and *DLB 59: American Literary Critics and Scholars, 1800-1850.*

MAJOR POSITIONS HELD: Coeditor, *Salmagundi* (1807-1808); editor, *Analectic Magazine* (1813-1814).

SELECTED BOOKS: *Salmagundi; or, the Whim-Whams and Opinions of Launcelot Langstaff, Esq. & Others,* by Irving, William Irving, and James Kirke Paulding, 20 parts, published in 2 volumes (New York: Printed and published by D. Longworth, 1807-1808; London: Printed for J. M. Richardson, 1811; revised edition, New York: D. Longworth, 1814; revised by Irving, Paris: Galignani, 1824; Paris: Baudry, 1824);

A History of New York, from the Beginning of the World to the End of the Dutch Dynasty. Containing Among many Surprising and Curious Matters the Unutterable Pondering of Walter the Doubter, the Disastrous Projects of William the Testy, and the Chivalric Achievements of Peter the Headstrong, the three Dutch Governors of New Amsterdam; being the only Authentic History of the Times that ever hath been, or ever will be Published, as Diedrich Knickerbocker, 2 volumes (New York & Philadelphia: Inskeep & Bradford/Boston: M'Ilhenney/Baltimore: Coale & Thomas/Charleston: Morford, Willington, 1809; revised edition, New York & Philadelphia: Inskeep & Bradford, 1812; London: Murray, 1820); republished as volume 1 of *The Works of Washington Irving* (New York & London: Putnam, 1848; revised again, 2 volumes, New York: Printed for the Grolier Club, 1886);

The Sketch Book of Geoffrey Crayon, Gent., as Geoffrey Crayon, 7 parts (New York: Printed by C. S. Van Winkle, 1819-1820); revised edition, 2 volumes (volume 1, London: John

Washington Irving (painting by Henry F. Darby, courtesy of the Sleepy Hollow Press, Tarrytown, New York)

Miller, 1820; volume 2, London: Murray, 1820; revised edition, Paris: Baudry & Didot, 1823); republished as volume 2 of *The Works of Washington Irving* (New York & London: Putnam, 1848);

Bracebridge Hall, or the Humourists. A Medley, as Geoffrey Crayon, 2 volumes (New York: Printed by C. S. Van Winkle, 1822; London: Murray, 1822); republished as volume 6 of *The Works of Washington Irving* (New York & London: Putnam, 1849);

Letters of Jonathan Oldstyle, Gent., as The Author of *The Sketch Book* (New York: Clayton, 1824; London: Wilson, 1824);

Tales of a Traveller, as Geoffrey Crayon, 2 volumes (London: Murray, 1824; abridged edition, Philadelphia: Carey & Lea, 1824; unabridged edition, New York: Printed by C. S. Van Winkle, 1825); republished as volume 7 of *The Works of Washington Irving* (New York & London: Putnam, 1849);

The Miscellaneous Works of Oliver Goldsmith, with an Account of His Life and Writings, 4 volumes (Paris: Galignani/Didot, 1825); biography revised in *The Life of Oliver Goldsmith, with Selections from His Writings*, 2 volumes (New York: Harper, 1840); biography revised and enlarged as *Oliver Goldsmith: A Biography*, volume 11 of *The Works of Washington Irving* (New York: Putnam, 1849; London: Murray, 1849);

A History of the Life and Voyages of Christopher Columbus (4 volumes, London: Murray, 1828; 3 volumes, New York: G. & C. Carvill, 1828; revised, 2 volumes, 1831); republished in *The Life and Voyages of Christopher Columbus; to Which Are Added Those of His Companions*, volumes 3-5 of *The Works of Washington Irving* (New York & London: Putnam, 1848-1849);

A Chronicle of the Conquest of Granada, as Fray Antonio Agapida, 2 volumes (Philadelphia: Carey, Lea & Carey, 1829; London: Murray, 1829); republished as volume 14 of *The Works of Washington Irving* (New York: Putnam/London: Murray, 1850);

Voyages and Discoveries of the Companions of Columbus (London: Murray, 1831; Philadelphia: Carey & Lea, 1831); republished in *The Life and Voyages of Christopher Columbus; to Which Are Added Those of His Companions*, volumes 3-5 of *The Works of Washington Irving* (New York & London: Putnam, 1848-1849);

The Alhambra, as Geoffrey Crayon, 2 volumes (London: Colburn & Bentley, 1832); as The Author of *The Sketch Book*, 2 volumes (Philadelphia: Carey & Lea, 1832); revised as *The Alhambra: A Series of Sketches of the Moors and Spaniards by the Author of "The Sketch Book"* (Philadelphia: Carey, Lea & Blanchard, 1836); revised as volume 15 of *The Works of Washington Irving* (New York: Putnam, 1851);

A Tour on the Prairies, number 1 of *Miscellanies*, as The Author of *The Sketch Book* (London:

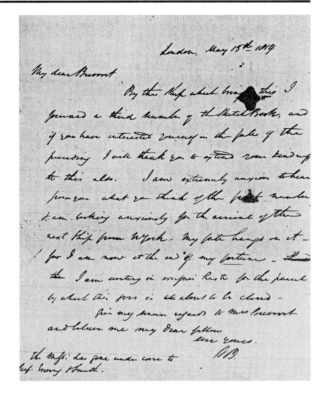

Letter Irving wrote to his friend Henry Brevoort (courtesy of the New York Public Library, Astor, Lenox and Tilden Foundations)

Murray, 1835); republished as number 1 of *The Crayon Miscellany* (Philadelphia: Carey, Lea & Blanchard, 1835); republished in *The Crayon Miscellany*, volume 9 of *The Works of Washington Irving* (New York & London: Putnam, 1849);

Abbotsford, and the Newstead Abbey, number 2 of *Miscellanies*, as The Author of *The Sketch Book* (London: Murray, 1835); republished as number 2 of *The Crayon Miscellany* (Philadelphia: Carey, Lea & Blanchard, 1835); republished in *The Crayon Miscellany*, volume 9 of *The Works of Washington Irving* (New York & London: Putnam, 1849);

Legends of the Conquest of Spain, number 3 of *Miscellanies*, as The Author of *The Sketch Book* (London: Murray, 1835); republished as number 3 of *The Crayon Miscellany* (Philadelphia: Carey, Lea & Blanchard, 1835); republished in *The Crayon Miscellany*, volume 9 of *The Works of Washington Irving* (New York & London: Putnam, 1849);

Astoria, or, Enterprise Beyond the Rocky Mountains, 3 volumes (London: Richard Bentley, 1836); published as *Astoria, or Anecdotes of an Enterprise Beyond the Rocky Mountains*, 2 volumes (Philadelphia: Carey, Lea & Blanchard,

1836); revised as volume 8 of *The Works of Washington Irving* (New York: Putnam, 1849);

Adventures of Captain Bonneville, or, Scenes beyond the Rocky Mountains of the Far West, 3 volumes (London: Bentley, 1837); republished as *The Rocky Mountains: Or, Scenes, Incidents, and Adventures in the Far West; Digested from the Journal of Captain B. L. E. Bonneville, of the Army of the United States, and Illustrated from Various Other Sources*, 2 volumes (Philadelphia: Carey, Lea & Blanchard, 1837); republished as *The Adventures of Captain Bonneville, U.S.A., in the Rocky Mountains and the Far West*, volume 10 of *The Works of Washington Irving* (New York & London: Putnam, 1849);

Biography and Poetical Remains of the Late Margaret Miller Davidson (Philadelphia: Lea & Blanchard, 1841; London: Tilt & Bogue, 1843);

Mahomet and His Successors, volumes 12 and 13 of *The Works of Washington Irving* (New York: Putnam, 1850); republished as *Lives of Mahomet and His Successors*, 2 volumes (London: Murray, 1850);

Chronicles of Wolfert's Roost and Other Papers (Edinburgh: Constable, Low/London: Hamilton, Adams/Dublin: M'Glashan, 1855); republished as *Wolfert's Roost and Other Papers*, volume 16 of *The Works of Washington Irving* (New York: Putnam, 1855);

Life of George Washington, 5 volumes (New York: Putnam, 1855-1859; London: Bohn, 1855-1859);

Spanish Papers and Other Miscellanies, Hitherto Unpublished or Uncollected, edited by Pierre M. Irving, 2 volumes (New York: Putnam/Hurd & Houghton, 1866; London: Low, 1866); republished as *Biographies and Miscellaneous Papers by Washington Irving* (London: Bell & Daldy, 1867);

The Complete Works of Washington Irving, edited by Richard Dilworth Rust and others, 29 volumes (Madison: University of Wisconsin Press/Boston: Twayne, 1969-).

The first American writer to be acclaimed as a literary figure of stature on both sides of the Atlantic, Washington Irving is today regarded as an important but obscure figure of American letters. Despite the decline in his popularity, our national memory is peopled with his creations–Ichabod Crane, Rip Van Winkle, and Father Knickerbocker. In his own day he was regarded by some as a dilettante; nevertheless, he wrote fiction and fact so gracefully that even his critics must concede that his work is rewarding to readers who come upon him more than two hundred years after his birth.

Washington Irving was a man of many parts. Often described as a "gentleman-author," he was also an editor, journalist, soldier, historiographer, translator, diplomat, lawyer, folklorist, explorer, satirist, playwright, and poet. Literary criticism of his writing is replete with words such as "sunny," "genial," "cheerful," "gentle," and "humane," with only occasional references to his style as "biting," "satiric," and "powerful." He was clearly influenced by English essayist Joseph Addison, whose work he greatly admired, and like Addison he took an amused view of people and events, realistic but understanding.

Washington was the youngest of the eleven children of Deacon William Irving and Sandra Sanders Irving. Born on 3 April 1783, shortly after the surrender of Cornwallis, he grew up in a New York home which happily combined British and American culture. Family life was secure, religious, and patriotic. Young Washington studied drawing, music, engraving, literature, and drama. He attended various "male seminaries" but did not study at Columbia College, as did his brothers. That institution, however, would one day bestow on him an honorary degree, as did Harvard and Oxford. Since there were no law schools in those days, he entered the law office of Josiah Hoffman to prepare for a career as a lawyer. He practiced law intermittently during his life, but it was never a passion for him, as writing was to become. He fell in love with his mentor's daughter, Matilda Hoffman. They eventually were engaged to marry, but Matilda died before their nuptials, and Irving remained a bachelor, though his name was linked romantically with other women in later years.

It was while he was studying law that he first experienced the excitement of writing for a newspaper and seeing his words in print. Newspapers of the day were a cantankerous lot of party organs, sometimes squabbling, sometimes libeling. The *Morning Chronicle*, edited by Washington's brother Peter, a nonpracticing physician, was no exception. A professed anti-Federalist publication, it embraced the faction of that group which supported Aaron Burr. It was here that a letter to the editor, signed "Jonathan Oldstyle," appeared on 15 November 1802. The letter, commenting not on politics but on the theater, was written by Washington Irving–young, opinion-

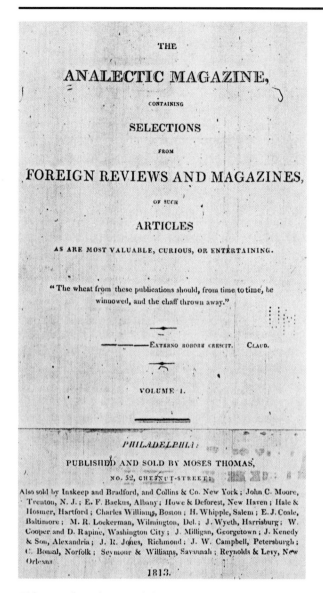

Title page for volume 1 of the magazine Irving began to edit in 1813. The demands of the business side of publishing and deadline pressures led Irving to resign in 1814.

ated, and passionate about drama, dramatists, and audiences. The persona Irving adopted here—that of a grumpy old man, outraged yet amused by modern dress, contemporary manners, silly music, bad drama—was the first of many he would use throughout his career.

There were nine letters in the Jonathan Oldstyle series. The last concluded with his wishes for all concerned:

> To the pit—patience, clean benches, and umbrellas.
> To the boxes—less affectation, less noise, less coxcombs.
> To the gallery—less grog, and better constables;

and
> To the whole house, inside and out, a total reformation.
> And so much for the Theatre.
> JONATHAN OLDSTYLE

The series of letters was published in 1824 as *Letters of Jonathan Oldstyle, Gent.* In later years Irving deplored these letters, viewing them as crude, amateurish, and immature; and in 1848, when he published a revised edition of his complete works, four of them were omitted from the collection.

He contributed political essays to another newspaper, the *Corrector*, also established by his brother Peter. These articles are not clearly identified, but they were said to have lampooned political targets with "the severest sarcasms."

His next excursion into journalism came with the publication on 24 January 1807 of the first issue of *Salmagundi*. The name provides a clue to the contents. Salmagundi was the name of a kind of hash, consisting of pickled herrings, oil, vinegar, pepper, and onions. In her study of Irving, Mary Weatherspoon Bowden summarizes the publication thus: "*Salmagundi* is, in truth, a veritable stew of humors, including puns, parodies, caricatures, burlesques, satires, invective, mock history, irony, and sarcasm. All the range of comedy is here. Not every word is a jewel, but every issue managed to irritate some New Yorker in his tenderest part—and the rest of New York laughed. *Salmagundi* is not genial; the objects of its humor are meant to feel the hurt, and undoubtedly did. But *Salmagundi* succeeded because its authors had the intelligence to hide its true faction-loving, discontented, probably irreligious, critical self underneath the costume of the gentle, genial, Spectator-like essay."

Actually, *Salmagundi* had a triumvirate of editors, Washington Irving, his brother William, and James Kirke Paulding, all of whom wrote under several freely shared pen names—among them Launcelot Langstaff, Anthony Evergreen, Pindar Cockloft, and Will Wizard. The latter is generally interpreted to be a caricature of inventor Robert Fulton. Launcelot Langstaff is a lampoon of New York Gov. Morgan Lewis. The authors saw most of the prominent people of the city as ridiculous eccentrics and portrayed them amusingly and often viciously, in a way that made them easily recognizable to their contemporaries. Thomas Jefferson, for example, is described as "a man of superlative ventosity, and comparable to nothing but a huge bladder of wind." One of the few persons who received sympathetic treatment was Aaron Burr, known in the essays as "The Little Man in Black." Irving had a great regard for Burr, even after his trial for treason. *Salmagundi* enjoyed great popularity but ceased after twenty issues.

After Matilda Hoffman's death in 1809 Irving began working intensively on a book he had been writing for many months. The two-volume *A History of New York, from the Beginning of the World to the End of the Dutch Dynasty* was published later the same year under the pseudonym Diedrich Knickerbocker. To promote this work, Irving circulated stories that the proprietor of a hotel had found the manuscript left behind by a vanished guest, Diedrich Knickerbocker. Whether or not the reading public was deceived or amused, the book was a success.

At the age of twenty-six Irving found himself a literary lion in New York City. *A History of New York* was dedicated to the city's historical society and looked authentic, but its pages were filled with caricatures of the Dutch stalwarts who had settled the town. A few dissenters objected to the frivolity with which the author treated their revered institutions, but most people were amused. Irving wrote: "It took with the public & gave me celebrity, as an original work was something remarkable & uncommon in America. I was noticed caressed & for a time elated by the popularity I gained."

Despite this success Irving seemed to feel that he had not yet found his niche in life. Another brief sojourn in journalism came in 1813 when he became editor of the *Analectic Magazine*, owned by Moses Thomas of Philadelphia. Induced by the publisher's offer of a salary of $125 a month, Irving commuted between New York and Philadelphia, writing reviews and essays, some of which he later incorporated in *The Sketch Book of Geoffrey Crayon, Gent.* (1819-1820). Eventually, however, the demands of the business side of the magazine and the pressure of deadlines combined with the dull basic routines left him disillusioned with magazine editing, and he left the journal in 1814. In the fall of that year he became aide-de-camp to New York Gov. Daniel Tompkins. He held the rank of lieutenant colonel when the War of 1812 drew to a close, but he never, in later life, used his military title.

Next Irving, in his capacity as lawyer, went to Liverpool to assist the family import-export firm, P.&E. Irving, which was experiencing legal

difficulty. There, he found that he had some devoted British readers. In Scotland he was warmly entertained by Sir Walter Scott, whom he greatly admired, and he was delighted to find the admiration was mutual. Scott had read Irving's *A History of New York* and called it a "most excellently jocose history" and said he had been entertained by it to "an uncommon degree." It is interesting to note that other famous literary figures in Britain, such as Charles Dickens and Samuel Taylor Coleridge, also expressed their delight with the work.

While in Britain, Irving finished his most significant work to date: *The Sketch Book of Geoffrey Crayon, Gent.* Its almost instant success confirmed him in the idea that writing was clearly his career. Irving's best-known short stories, "Rip Van Winkle," "The Legend of Sleepy Hollow," and "The Spectre Bridegroom," first appeared in *The Sketch Book*. Although some of the material in the book had been written before he left his native land, Irving also incorporated material using British sources and locales written while he was abroad.

An amalgam of stories, essays, and descriptive pieces, *The Sketch Book* had wide appeal. It combined pathos and humor, expert narration, and the graceful delicacy which critics have found the hallmark of Irving's work. The book enjoyed critical and popular success on both sides of the Atlantic. For Irving, it was also a financial success.

Further travels in France and Germany resulted in a short stint of play writing, in collaboration with John Howard Payne. He was pleased to find his works had been translated into French and sold well. He began *Bracebridge Hall, or the Humourists*, which was published in 1822. This series of sketches centered about a fictitious English manor house modeled on a great house near the home of Irving's sister and brother-in-law in Birmingham, where he spent much of his time in England. While critics generally consider *Bracebridge Hall* inferior to *The Sketch Book*, it was well received and solidified his literary reputation.

Irving was restless and experiencing some health problems, so he took refuge in further travels in Germany, occasionally writing pieces on the theater or doing translations for magazines. He was in demand as an editor but did not wish to be tied down to the routines that job required. In 1824, back in England, he published *Tales of a Traveller*, a hodgepodge of stories he had come across in Germany. It received poor reviews, and

Irving's letter to Edgar Allan Poe complimenting him on his story "William Wilson, A Tale," which appeared in the October 1839 issue of Burton's Gentleman's Magazine *(courtesy of the New York Public Library, Astor, Lenox and Tilden Foundations)*

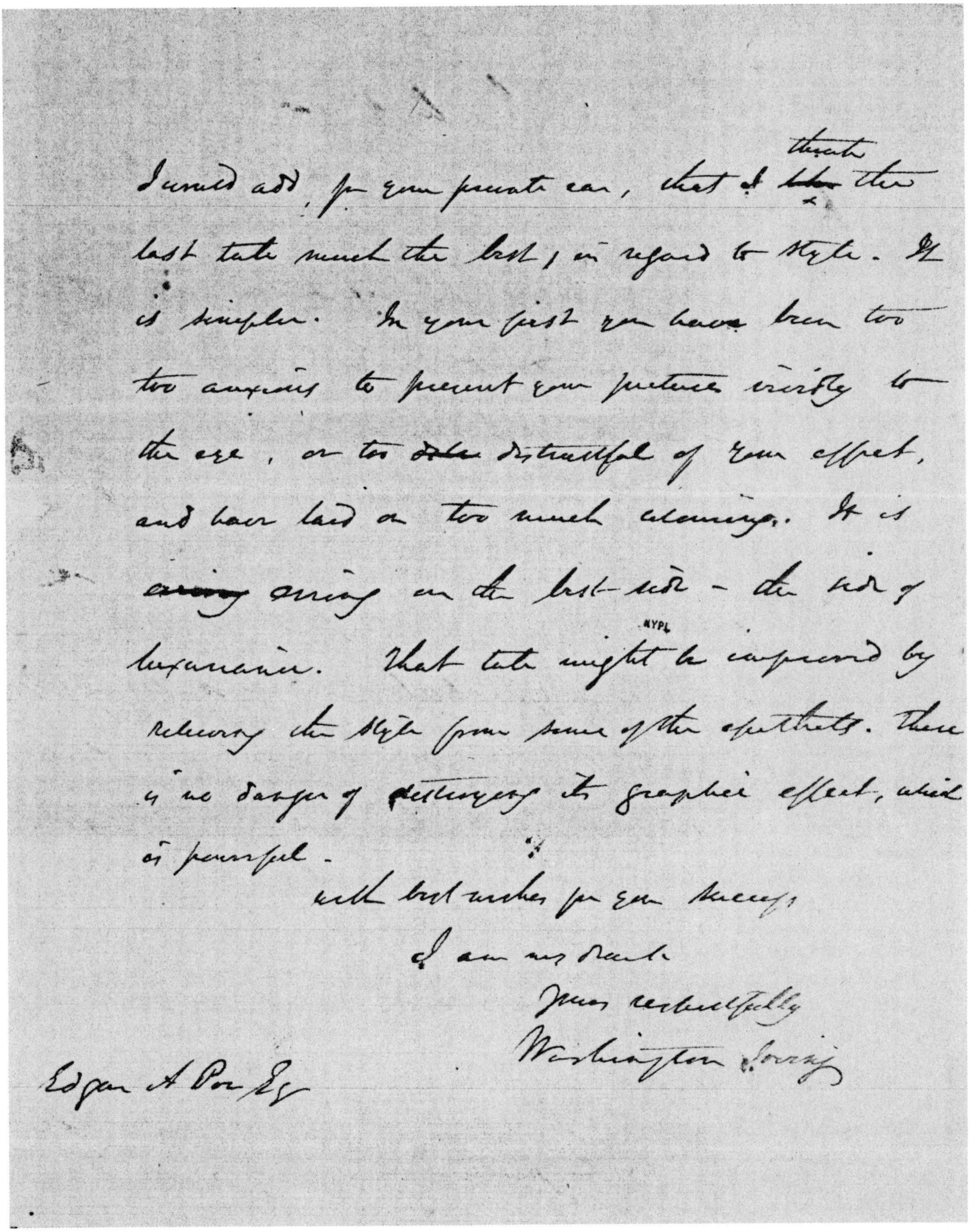

I would add, for your private ear, that I think the last tale much the best, in regard to style. It is simpler. In your first you have been too too anxious to present your picture vividly to the eye, or too distrustful of your effect, and have laid on too much colouring. It is erring on the best side — the side of luxuriance. That tale might be improved by relieving the style from some of the epithets. There is no danger of destroying its graphic effect, which is powerful.

With best wishes for your success

I am my dear

Yours respectfully

Washington Irving

Edgar A. Poe Esq

the author was greatly downcast. It is an interesting footnote to his literary history that John Murray, his publisher, paid him $2,400 for *The Sketch Book;* $5,250 for *Bracebridge Hall,* and $7,875 for *Tales of a Traveller.* Most critics would conclude that the money paid was in inverse proportion to the literary value of the works.

A welcome change occurred in Irving's life in 1826, when U.S. Minister to Spain Alexander H. Everett named him attaché to the American legation in Madrid. He had been studying Spanish and was most receptive to Everett's suggestion that he might undertake a translation of Martín Fernández de Navarrete's ongoing *Coleccion de los Viages y Descubrimientos que hicieron por mar los Españoles desde Fines del Siglo XV* (1825-1837). He found Navarrete's biography of Christopher Columbus exciting and provocative, plunging into the translation enthusiastically, only to conclude that he would be more satisfied with writing a popular life of the great explorer instead. This resulted in the publication of *A History of the Life and Voyages of Christopher Columbus* in 1828.

Irving had published the three works which appeared before the biography of Columbus under the pseudonym "Geoffrey Crayon, Gent.," but it was as Washington Irving that he published his popular history. It won him election to the Spanish Royal Academy of History. It remained the most significant biography of Columbus for many years, and while it falls short of today's more scientific approach to historiography, it is still a responsible, accurate, and appealing volume. It marks a change in the literary life of Irving, for after this he published more serious work, marked by scholarship as well as by the grace of his prose.

A Chronicle of the Conquest of Granada (1829) and *The Alhambra* (1832) followed, making Irving a preeminent interpreter of Spanish culture. Both were the result of scrupulous research and scholarly investigation, enhanced by long interviews with Spanish writers, peasants, and nobles. He infused his history with what we would today term "human interest," and the pleasing combination won him a devoted readership in Spain as well as at home.

He still functioned as a diplomat while his literary production increased. After his duties in Spain, he was named secretary to the U.S. Legation in London, where he served from 1829 to 1831.

On his return to New York in 1832 he was feted and acclaimed as a major celebrity. He basked happily in the limelight for only a short time, when his restless spirit sought more excitement by joining an expedition led by Henry L. Ellsworth to explore the land of the Osage and Pawnee Indian tribes. He had been stung by criticism about his preoccupation with foreign lands to the detriment of truly American themes, but his interest was more than professional. He had been fascinated by the frontier all of his life and welcomed the call to adventure.

The expedition was all he could have wished, with its rugged life-style, deprivations, and discoveries. He wrote about his experiences in *A Tour on the Prairies* (1835), the first volume of *The Crayon Miscellany.* Later came *Astoria, or, Enterprise Beyond the Rocky Mountains* (1836) and *Adventures of Captain Bonneville, or, Scenes beyond the Rocky Mountains of the Far West* (1837). Some commentators find the latter work generally inferior, but it did not detract from Irving's American popularity.

He also contributed many articles to the *Knickerbocker Magazine,* named in tribute to Irving's pseudonymous author of *A History of New York.* He was hired as a staff member at a salary of two thousand dollars per year, but most sources agree that he had difficulty collecting. He described his work to his readers in ingratiating fashion in March 1839: "I have thought, therefore, of securing for myself a snug corner in some periodical work, where I might, as it were, loll at my ease in an elbow chair, and chat sociably with the public, as with an old friend, on any chance subject that might pop into my brain." He contributed more than thirty articles during his tenure with the magazine, virtually all of which were included in later published volumes of his works.

Irving settled down in his Tarrytown home, Sunnyside, enjoying a tranquil life as country squire, surrounded by friends and relatives. In 1842 President John Tyler appointed him minister to Spain. It was a popular appointment nationally, and Irving set off once more to his beloved Spain. He was fifty-nine years old but was experiencing some difficulties with his health and with money. In a letter he wrote en route to his new post he said: "I shall endeavor to resign myself to the splendor of courts and the conversation of courtiers, comforting myself with the thought that the time will arrive when I shall once more return to sweet little Sunnyside, to be able to sit on a stone fence and talk about politics and rural affairs. . . ." In other letters written during his

Drawing of Irving by F. O. C. Darley, July 1848 (courtesy of Rare Books Division, New York Public Library, Astor, Lenox and Tilden Foundations)

four years in this post he deplored his lack of literary activity. He had expressed a conviction that he would accomplish much on his long-delayed life of George Washington while he was abroad, but little was written. He conscientiously fulfilled his duties, enjoyed Spanish life, then resigned from diplomatic service in 1846 and sailed home.

Back at Sunnyside, he worked intensively on a revised edition of his published works, requested by publisher George P. Putnam and completed in 1855. For the remainder of his life Irving labored on his five-volume *Life of George Washington* (1855-1859). It was a labor of love, for he admired his namesake and saw the work as a magnum opus. Careful research, sensitivity, a sophisticated historical perspective, and his literary gifts combined to make this a seminal work, indeed the definitive biography of Washington for many years. Writing in 1978, a literary commentator observed that part of the genius of the work was Irving's regard for "oral history," a tool not identified as such in those days. Irving tracked down persons who had known Washington or served under him. He interviewed dozens of individuals, seeking anecdotes about the first president. Allan Keller, writing in *American History*

Illustrated in April 1978, says: "He had no electronic tape recorder and no shorthand, but he had a wonderful ear. . . . Irving was able to get intimate anecdotes and word pictures that revealed his subject's character better than letters or state papers. . . . "

Volume 1 appeared in 1855, the second later the same year, volume 3 in 1856, volume 4 in 1857, and the fifth in 1859, less than a year before Irving's death. Now supplanted by biographies written with more precise tools of historiography, the *Life of George Washington*, nevertheless, was thorough, honest, vivid, appreciative, and wise. The last volumes show signs of Irving's declining health and increasing weariness.

He died at Sunnyside in Irvington on 28 November 1859. During his lifetime six hundred thousand volumes of his works had been sold in the United States. His passing was mourned by the nation. In a "Memorial of Washington Irving" by Louis Gaylord Clark in the *Knickerbocker Magazine*, he was praised: "We are giving expression to no extravagant eulogy; we are not overstating, in the slightest degree, the testimony which every one who had the happiness to know Washington Irving, while he was living, will bear as to his character, when we say, that aside from his preeminence as the most justly renowned American author of our time, he was one of the most genial, the most truthful, the most lovable authors in the world."

The encomiums that poured forth at his death were excessive in view of later assessments of his work. As early as 1882 an article in *Harper's Monthly Magazine*, noting that he was still probably the most famous son of New York, observed that numerous critics found his contribution to American letters "slender" and suggested that he would ultimately become obscure. But it quotes Washington Irving in a telling excerpt which may serve to induce a different evaluation: "If, however, I can by lucky chance, in these days of evil, rub out one wrinkle from the brow of care, or beguile the heavy heart of one moment of sadness, if I can, now and then, penetrate the gathering film of misanthropy, prompt a benevolent view of human nature, and make my reader more in good-humor with his fellow beings and himself—surely, surely, I shall not then have written entirely in vain."

Bibliographies:

William R. Langfeld and Philip C. Blackburn, *Bibliography of Washington Irving* (New York: New York Public Library, 1933);

Stanley T. Williams and Mary A. Edge, *A Bibliography of the Writings of Washington Irving* (New York: Oxford University Press, 1936).

Biographies:

Stanley T. Williams, *The Life of Washington Irving*, 2 volumes (New York & Oxford: Oxford University Press, 1935);

William L. Hedges, *Washington Irving: An American Study, 1802-1832* (Baltimore: Johns Hopkins University Press, 1965).

References:

Mary Weatherspoon Bowden, *Washington Irving* (Boston: G. K. Hall, 1981);

Edwin W. Bowen, "Washington Irving's Place in American Literature," *Sewanee Review* (April 1906): 171-183;

Louis Gaylord Clark, "Memorial of Washington Irving," *Knickerbocker*, 55 (January 1860): 113-128;

Clarence Cook, "The First Books of Some American Authors," *Bookman* (1898);

Curtis Dahl, "The Sunny Master of Sunnyside," *American Heritage* (December 1961): 37-52, 92-95;

"Editor's Easy Chair," *Harper's Monthly Magazine*, 66 (May 1882): 790-791;

Allan Keller, "Perspectives on the Past," *American History Illustrated* (April 1978): 35;

Philip McFarland, *Sojourners* (New York: Atheneum, 1979);

T. Edgar Pemberton, "Washington Irving in England," *Munsey's*, 30 (1903);

Albert H. Smythe, *The Philadelphia Magazines and Their Contributors, 1741-1850* (Detroit: Gale Research, 1970);

"Washington Irving," *Nation*, 36 (5 April 1883): 291-292.

Papers:

Washington Irving's papers are housed at the New York Public Library, Columbia University, and Harvard University.

Caroline M. Kirkland
(12 January 1801-6 April 1864)

Ada Van Gastel
Auburn University

See also the Kirkland entry in *DLB 3: Antebellum Writers in New York and the South.*

MAJOR POSITIONS HELD: Editor (1847-1849), coeditor (1849-1851), *Union Magazine of Literature and Art,* renamed *Sartain's Union Magazine of Literature and Art* in January 1849.

BOOKS: *A New Home–Who'll Follow? Or, Glimpses of Western Life,* as Mrs. Mary Clavers (New York: C. S. Francis, 1839); republished as *Montacute: Or, a New Home–Who'll Follow?* (London: Churton, 1840);
Forest Life, as Mrs. Mary Clavers, 2 volumes (New York: C. S. Francis/Boston: J. H. Francis, 1842; London: Longman, 1842);
Western Clearings, as Mrs. Mary Clavers (New York: Wiley & Putnam, 1845; London: Wiley & Putnam, 1846);
Holidays Abroad; or, Europe from the West, 2 volumes (New York: Baker & Scribner, 1849);
The Evening Book: Or, Fireside Talk on Morals and Manners, with Sketches of Western Life (New York: Scribner, 1852);
The Book of Home Beauty (New York: Putnam, 1852);
A Book for the Home Circle; or, Familiar Thoughts on Various Topics, Literary, Moral and Social (New York: Scribner, 1853);
The Helping Hand: Comprising an Account of the Home, for Discharged Female Convicts, and an Appeal in Behalf of That Institution (New York: Scribner, 1853);
Autumn Hours, and Fireside Reading (New York: Scribner, 1854);
Memoirs of Washington (New York: Appleton, 1857).

OTHER: *Spenser and the Faëry Queen,* edited by Kirkland (New York & London: Wiley & Putnam, 1847);
Garden Walks with the Poets, edited by Kirkland (New York: Putnam, 1852);

Caroline M. Kirkland (courtesy of the Burton Historical Collection, Detroit Public Library)

"Bryant," in *Homes of American Authors; Comprising Anecdotical, Personal, and Descriptive Sketches, by Various Writers* (New York: Putnam, 1853);
The School-Girl's Garland, A Selection of Poetry, edited by Kirkland (New York: Scribner, 1864).

PERIODICAL PUBLICATIONS: "An Apology for Authors," *Knickerbocker Magazine,* 19 (February 1842): 97-102;
"The Blighted Heart," *Graham's Magazine,* 23 (July 1843): 1-7;
"The Belles of Etherington," *Columbian Lady's and Gentleman's Magazine,* 1 (March 1844): 125-130;
"The Village School," *Union,* 1 (July 1847): 45-48;
"Harvest," *Union,* 1 (August 1847): 89-91;
"Goethe," *Union,* 1 (September 1847): 127-129;

"The Justice," *Union,* 1 (September 1847): 114-116;

"Goethe's Education," *Union,* 1 (October 1847): 168-169;

"The Country Funeral," *Union,* 1 (October 1847): 179-181;

"George Sand and the Journeyman Joiner," *Union,* 1 (November 1847): 221-223;

"Steps to Ruin," *Union,* 1 (November 1847): 229-231;

"The Singing School," *Union,* 1 (December 1847): 282-283;

"The Hard Winter," *Union,* 2 (January 1848): 43;

"A Love of a Singing Master," *Union,* 2 (March 1848): 137-138;

"Sunday in the Country," *Union,* 2 (April 1848): 166-167;

"Forest Literature," *Union,* 2 (May 1848): 201-212;

"The Log-House," *Union,* 2 (June 1848): 274-275;

"Sightseeing in Europe," 8 parts, *Union,* 3 (July 1848): 1-5; (August 1848): 49-54; (October 1848): 145-151; (November 1848): 193-199; (December 1848): 241-246; *Sartain's Union,* 4 (January 1849): 57-62; (February 1849): 127-132; (March 1849): 181-185; (April 1849): 232-235;

"English Characteristics," *Sartain's Union,* 4 (May 1849): 295-298;

"English and American Manners," *Sartain's Union,* 4 (June 1849): 401-404;

"Thoughts on Education," 2 parts, *Sartain's Union,* 5 (July 1849): 40-43; (October 1849): 236-239;

"Fastidiousness," *Sartain's Union,* 5 (August 1849): 102-106;

"Odds and Ends of Travel," *Sartain's Union,* 5 (September 1849): 139-142;

"Conversation," no. 1, *Sartain's Union,* 5 (November 1849): 292-296;

"Conversation," no. 2, *Sartain's Union,* 5 (December 1849): 369-371;

"Literary Women," *Sartain's Union,* 6 (February 1850): 150-154;

"Reading for Amusement," *Sartain's Union,* 6 (March 1850): 192-196;

"Mahomet," *Sartain's Union,* 6 (June 1850): 411-416;

"The Significance of Dress," 2 parts, *Sartain's Union,* 7 (August 1850): 99-102; (September 1850): 154-157.

Eight years after Caroline Kirkland had first received critical acclaim for her novel *A New Home–Who'll Follow? Or, Glimpses of Western Life* (1839), she was asked to serve as editor of the newly founded *Union Magazine of Literature and Art.* The publisher of the *Union,* Israel Post, wanted Kirkland's name to lend credit to his new enterprise; he also wanted her literary connections to facilitate soliciting contributions from famous authors such as William Cullen Bryant, William Gilmore Simms, Evert A. Duyckinck, Catharine Sedgwick, Lydia Maria Child, and Lydia H. Sigourney–all of whom were to publish in the *Union* during the one and a half years of Kirkland's editorship. Indeed, Kirkland strove hard to "elevate" the *Union* so as "to make the magazine more purely literary," as she phrased it. Nevertheless, the magazine had to remain marketable and therefore differed only slightly from the host of mid-nineteenth-century periodicals. Kirkland's own contributions to the magazine in the form of editorials, western sketches, and essays on various topics are marked by a combination of cool professionalism mixed with captivating charm, metropolitan sophistication delivered with rural straightforwardness, and serious didacticism tempered with humorous playfulness.

Kirkland was born Caroline Matilda Stansbury, the eldest of eleven children of Samuel and Eliza Alexander Stansbury. Samuel Stansbury worked for a New York insurance company, while Eliza Stansbury was a fervent reader of romances who composed two sentimental pieces which her daughter Caroline later published in the *Union.* After receiving her education in a Quaker school established by her aunt, Lydia Mott, Caroline became a student and later assistant in another school of her aunt's, one near Utica in upstate New York. There she met her future husband, William Kirkland, a scholarly, energetic man who had followed in the family tradition and had become an educator (an uncle had been president of Harvard University; a granduncle had taught Indians and founded Hamilton College in Clinton, New York). William left his teaching job at Hamilton College for two years of study in Germany after a college prank had severely impaired his hearing (a group of students fired a cannon). Upon his return in 1828 William and Caroline married and opened a seminary in Geneva, New York. The couple moved west in 1835 when William was appointed principal of Detroit Female Seminary. Caroline also

THE

UNION MAGAZINE.

JULY, 1847.

INTRODUCTORY.

ESTABLISHED forms are no doubt very excellent things in their way; but they are sometimes rather embarrassing and inconvenient. To be presented formally to a whole company, for instance; although it gives us the advantage of an accredited acquaintance, and may be productive of pleasant things in the end, is yet felt to be a most trying ceremony; and one would often be glad to slip in behind the chairs of the guests, and find a seat in some corner, trusting to chance and change for a piecemeal introduction, rather than face the whole line of eyes, and feel that we are making a very awkward reverence. Still more, in a case like the present, would a silent and unnoticed *entrée* be desirable to the unpractised editor, who might thus glide in with the crowd, without fear of special criticism. But imperious custom demands at least a few lines of self-introduction; insisting that without it a literary feast would be as imperfect as an elaborate dinner without a bill of fare. By the way, this same bill of fare affords some useful hints as to setting forth one's provisions of every kind. *Pommes de terre au naturel* are certainly much more attractive than plain boiled potatoes; and so would be the announcement of "An exquisitely simple poem after the manner of Wordsworth," than mere "Lines to a little girl on cutting her finger." We must remember this for future use. But at present we are rather disposed to say in plain and sincere earnest what we hope to accomplish by the establishment of the UNION MAGAZINE.

In offering our new venture to the public, we shall not adopt the apologetic strain fashionable of late; but rather take it for granted that the appearance of another candidate in the field is in fact a benefit to those who patronize the old, as securing that continuance of effort which alone can accomplish excellence. Nobody commences a new magazine without supposing that there is yet a literary or artistic want unsupplied; and we claim that an attempt to supply this want is praiseworthy, and we have little doubt the public will agree with us, at least after we have told our story.

There are more ways than one of exhibiting patriotism. To defend our country when she is attacked, is one which commands the loud applause of the world, and which is therefore the more popular. To elevate the intellectual and moral character of the people, is a work no less necessary and commendable, although far less showy; and this is the aim of the author and the artist. Magazines, though undervalued by the unwise, constitute, in a country like ours, a powerful element of civilization. Books are comparatively inert as to operation upon large classes of the community. They may be compared with heavy cannon, which require elaborate fixtures and much expense before they can be made available; while the magazine resembles rather the

VOL. I.—NO. 1.   1

---

flying artillery, which follows up the chase, and does execution under the most unfavorable circumstances. Instead of becoming less popular in consequence of abundance, periodical literature is growing every day upon public favor, as the best possible means of disseminating information, and diffusing the principles of a correct taste. A late writer in Chambers' Journal, proposes that instead of leaving books in the store to be sought for, they should be sent from house to house, in order to insure the greatest benefit from them; and this is just what the cheap monthly magazine can accomplish. It remains only to provide that its contents shall be all that can be desired for the purpose of this universal diffusion. As to our own plan for this purpose, we have a few words to say.

The literary merit of the monthly magazines already in circulation throughout the United States, is probably as great as the country can produce under similar circumstances. To promise to surpass this in ours, would be arrogant and deceptive. Our list of regular contributors will present nearly the same names with the other monthlies, and we can only hope our taste and judgment in selection will be such as to do justice to our desire to give general satisfaction to intelligent readers. Promise of assistance from those whose productions stand highest in public favor are not wanting; and should new stars rise, as we may hope, we shall not be slow in availing ourselves of their light.

But while we thus deprecate unmeaning boasting and arrogant promises, we feel that on the ground of artistic attraction we may safely claim for our novel and adventurous undertaking the suffrage of all who desire the elevation of American art, and the cultivation of taste among the large class who patronize the periodical literature of the day. The illustrations which have proved so attractive in the older magazines are deserving of high praise, especially when we compare those of to-day with those of only a few years since. The pictorial embellishments (so-called,) which then passed current, would now be received with contempt by the least-instructed magazine reader; and for this advance in the general power of appreciation we are largely indebted to the efforts and honorable competition of the periodicals. The Art-Union has been, confessedly, a potent instrument in this reform, and should as such be honored and supported. And why may we not consider our own present attempt a minor and auxiliary art-union? We are to have designs and engravings by American artists, each incited to his highest power by a generous ambition, and repaid by means of a noble list of subscribers, every one of whom is sure of not one picture, but many, in return for his contribution to the cause; while the vast body of entertaining, refining, and instructive literary matter which we shall be able to offer in the course of the year, will be a "prize" unsubjected to chance or contingency. We pray our friends to consider this matter; feeling confident that they will not withhold their support and encouragement to so original and arduous an enterprise.

It would be ungrateful in the editor to withhold the acknowledgment that she enters upon her task with the less reluctance, from her past experience of public indulgence. She ventures to hope that the favor shown to her works on the Western country will be extended to the present attempt in another and more laborious path of literary effort.

THE NEEDLE, PEN, AND SWORD.

BY MRS. L. H. SIGOURNEY.

WHAT hast thou seen, with thy shining eye,
   Thou Needle, so subtle and keen?—
"I have been in Paradise, stainless and fair,
And fitted the apron of fig-leaves there,
   To the form of its fallen queen.

The mantles and wimples, the hoods and veils,
   That the belles of Judah wore,
When their haughty mien, and their glance of fire
Enkindled the eloquent prophet's ire,
   I help'd to fashion of yore.

Kirkland's statement of intent for the magazine she edited from 1847 until 1851

taught in the seminary. A local newspaper described the newcomer Caroline as "charming in person and mind, and being possessed of executive ability and considerable force of character, a worthy helpmate" to her near-deaf husband. From 1837 to 1843 the Kirklands lived in Pinckney, a village they had planned and founded on the thirteen hundred acres of land they had purchased over the course of eighteen months. Located sixty miles west of Detroit, the village of Pinckney boasted (so a prospectus announced) all the essentials of a western town: a village store, a healthy climate, and "a good Temperance Tavern."

It was this personal experience of pioneer life that induced Caroline Kirkland to start writing. In a letter to her coeditor at the *Union*, John Hart, she said in retrospect: "I little thought of becoming an author before I lived in the wilderness— There, the strange things I saw and heard every day prompted me to description, for they always presented themselves to me under a humorous aspect." *A New Home–Who'll Follow?*, her first work, was published under the pseudonym Mrs. Mary Clavers (as were her next two books) and was well received by the critics. Edgar Allan Poe, in "The Literati of New York" (*Godey's Magazine*, August 1846), proclaimed that the book created "an undoubted sensation" because of its "*truth* and novelty": the novel is pervaded by "a fidelity and vigor that prove her pictures to be taken from the very life . . . 'scenes' that could have occurred only *as* and *where* she described them." Rufus Griswold, in *The Prose Writers of America* (1847), recommended the book as "a guide to those . . . labouring to create an American literature."

The success of *A New Home–Who'll Follow?* opened the doors of magazines for Kirkland. Feeling isolated and bereft of intellectual company, Kirkland also longed to write in order to communicate with kindred spirits. "People write because they cannot help it. The heart longs for sympathy, and when it cannot be found close at hand, will seek it the world over," she later declared. Kirkland began to publish regional sketches and essays in *Godey's Lady's Book*, *Knickerbocker Magazine*, *Boston Miscellany*, *Columbian Lady's and Gentleman's Magazine*, and the annual *Gift*. As the land enterprise turned out to cost more than it produced, money was another reason why Kirkland wrote. "I am busy penning some very dull stories for several publications. . . . I know not what we should do without this resource," she wrote her daughter Elizabeth at this time.

Fully aware of what sold well, Kirkland even submitted to *Graham's* "a very sentimental love story– or as near that as I can persuade myself to come." Furthermore, Kirkland composed during these years *Forest Life* (1842), a collection of sketches of frontier life in Michigan. The book differed from its predecessor in that it is more ethnographic in its intentions, more descriptive in its technique, and more mellow in its attitude toward immigrants. Meanwhile, William Kirkland had also started to contribute articles to such periodicals as *Godey's* and the *Democratic Review*. Disillusioned by frontier life and eager for cultural stimulation, the Kirklands decided in 1843 to return to New York City and to enter upon literary careers. Once in the metropolis William soon became editor of the *New York Evening Mirror* and coeditor of the weekly *Christian Inquirer*. According to Poe, all that William Kirkland wrote was "entitled to respect for its simplicity and evidence of scholarship and research." On 18 October 1846 William died tragically. His body was found in the Hudson River near Fishkill, New York, where he had gone to visit the Kirklands' son Joseph. It was believed that William, handicapped by his deafness as well as a strong nearsightedness, fell into the water while attempting to board the steamboat back to New York City.

A widow with four children to support, Caroline Kirkland opened up yet another school, taught in several others, and continued to write for magazines. The royalties from *A New Home* and *Forest Life* were especially welcome during these difficult years. Furthermore, Kirkland delved again into her reservoir of Michigan experiences to compose a few more frontier tales to be combined with reprints of essays from various periodicals into *Western Clearings* (1845). In a review of the book William Cullen Bryant remarked upon Kirkland's excellent "reputation . . . which gives all she writes a quick circulation over the whole country." It was this reputation combined with her literary connections which landed Kirkland the editorship of the *Union*.

In the preface to the first issue of the *Union* Kirkland declared the following about periodicals: "Instead of becoming less popular in consequence of abundance, periodical literature is growing every day upon public favor, as the best possible means of disseminating information, and diffusing the principles of good taste." Given the multitude of magazines, Kirkland announced that the *Union* was to stand out through its "artistic attraction": the magazine was to feature de-

First installment in Kirkland's series of sketches written especially for
the Union

signs and engravings by American artists, "each incited to his highest power by a generous ambition, and repaid by means of a noble list of subscribers." "Embellished with the Finest Steel, Mezzotint, and Wood Engravings, music and Colored Fashions," the title page boasted. Every issue contained two or three full-page engravings (in line or mezzotint), a colored steel plate depicting women sporting the latest fashion, and various woodcuts illustrating the featured tales and poetry. While the fashion plates were later abandoned, the magazine continued to provide colored pictures by way of lithographs of flowers. "In illustration the *Union* was especially brilliant," Frank Luther Mott declares in volume 1 of *A History of American Magazines* (1938).

However, to Kirkland it was the literature that mattered most. Noteworthy is that Kirkland continues the sentence about how the *Union* is to distinguish itself through its "artistic attraction" by mentioning literary quality: "the vast body of entertaining, refining, and instructive matter which we shall be able to offer in the course of the year, will be a 'prize' unsubjected to chance or contingency." Earlier, just after she had accepted the editorship, she had written to her friend Bryant: "I have sole editorial charge–The literary matter will be of course a good deal like that of the other *pictorials,* unless I can contrive to modify it a little in conformity with my own notions of what should be." Kirkland's own notions are most clearly stated in her essay "Periodical Reading": "Nine-tenths of the magazine stories, so popular among us, have nothing to do with life, and fiction which has no relation to what has been, or what is to be, must be both vapid and valueless." Furthermore, "Nobody has a right, morally speaking, to send forth in print that which has no good aim."

The prose and poetry of the first issue of the *Union* are representative of the later issues which appeared under Kirkland's editorship. There are pieces by well-known authors such as Sigourney, Hannah Gould, Child, and Sedgwick. Sigourney's poem, entitled "The Needle, Pen, and Sword," compares the relative merits and power of these three articles to conclude:

Then the terrible Sword to its sheath return'd,
While the Needle sped on in peace,
But the Pen traced out from a book sublime
The promise and pledge of that better time
When the warfare of earth shall cease.

Gould's poem is an apostrophe to the knowledge-able mastodon. Sedgwick's contribution is a sentimental tale about a store clerk unjustly accused of stealing and the love and fortitude of his devoted sister. And Child's contribution, based upon a real event, she assures us, tells of the purchase by a German immigrant of indentured servants who turn out to be his parents (they have followed him to New York three decades later).

The first issue of the *Union* displays a predilection for regional literature–clearly a sign of Kirkland's influence. Apart from the pieces by Child and Sedgwick, set in Germany/New York and New York, respectively, it contains a legend by C. Lanham of the Obivwa Indians on the shore of Lake Superior, a narrative by J. H. Mancur subtitled "A Legend of Tappan" (the tale is reminiscent of Washington Irving's "The Legend of Sleepy Hollow"), and an essay by W. A. Jones advocating the importance of "the literature of travel." Jones bewails that "at home, far too little has been done to illustrate our scenery, habits, and customs, by native travellers; Irving

for Dutchland and the far west; Miss Fuller for the lakes; and Bryant in his fine letters on the South–are the best." However, this was too little by far. To cap it off, the issue presents the first of a series of "Western Sketches," written by the editor. In the sketch, a delightful one in the manner of *A New Home,* Kirkland presents an array of mistresses and masters who quickly succeeded each other in the village school. The first one, Miss Cynthia Day, comes recommended as "a young woman of good parts and behaviour." Kirkland continues:

and so indeed we found her; but her parts were not the parts of speech.
        "Silas!" she would drawl out, "Si-ilas! let them 'are what's 'er names be, dew! You'll git it, if you don't!"

Miss Day is succeeded by Mr. Hardcastle, a young divinity student who stuns the functionaries because he can spell all the trap words in the spelling book and is able to define "orthography" and "ratiocination." Alas, he is "too delicate in mind and body for the place." The next teacher is "a disciplinarian": "Miss Pinkey had an ingenious instrument of torture, which consisted of a split quill that she placed on the ear of the offender. . . . If the offence was rank, the quill was exchanged for a small hickory twig, which being split and made to pinch the ear, produced such sounds as may be heard when a pig is caught unawares in a gate;–music which was seemingly pleasant in the ears of Miss Pinkey." Having established order in the school but "confusion and anger in the neighborhood," Miss Pinkey is replaced by Mr. Ball, a man who raises the villagers' suspicions by keeping a light in his room until midnight and by locking his chest of personal belongings. "This was not to be endured. Any attempt at privacy is considered *prima facie* evidence of guilt." The villagers thus decide to send two men to Mr. Ball to insist upon his opening the mysterious chest. Mr. Ball complies, but only on condition that he resign thereafter. The chest turns out to contain: "a very scanty amount of shirts and stockings, with a prodigious pile of James's novels, and a file or two of newspapers; a phrenological head, a few candles, and a bottle of blacking with brushes."

While the prose and verse of this initial issue are representative of the later *Union* issues under Kirkland's editorship, only one of the two full-page engravings is characteristic. Both engravings deal with war: one engraving depicts the dying moments of Col. Henry Clay, Jr., in the Battle of Buena Vista; the other engraving presents a lady who has fainted upon receiving news from the war. Only the latter engraving is representative. In fact, the two engravings reflect what seems to have been a diversity of opinion between Kirkland and T. H. Matteson, the person who designed the engravings. Subsequent issues carried moral, didactic, sentimental engravings such as "Innocence and Fidelity," "Steps to Ruin," "The Unwilling Bride," "The Wanderer's Return," and "Taking the Advantage" (a man stealing a kiss from a woman). Nearly all were accompanied by half a page of text written by the editor. However, when in January 1848 another war picture appeared, Kirkland deviated from her custom and did not provide the text for the illustration: Matteson had to write the text for "Gallant Exploit of Lieut. Schuyler Hamilton." Furthermore, Kirkland affixed a note from the editor to say that the military picture in the present issue frayed her feminine sentiment, and that, although she had of course "no rightful control over the illustrative department of the Magazine," she nevertheless had convinced Matteson to refrain from printing warlike pictures in the future.

Kirkland certainly had definite ideas about what was proper for the *Union*. Frequently she declared in her editorials that "nineteen-twentieths" of the verses submitted to the magazine fell below its standards. She devoted some three hundred words to the issue of "Indifferent Poetry" in the September 1847 editorial, boldly opening with "it is fearful to think of the deluge of this article [indifferent poetry] at present." According to Kirkland, most of the verse composed "lack[ed] vitality, and even common sense." Too little was it understood that good poetry, just as good prose, receives its value from its ideas, its "thoughts." Despite her remarks, submissions of poetasters kept pouring in. Kirkland complained in the November editorial: "Our sufferings still continue. We are under the spell of a poem which we are utterly unable to class." That is, Kirkland could not decide whether the poem was serious or a burlesque. The March 1848 editorial prints Bryant's poem "March" in order "to exemplify our notions of what is lacking in most of the verse sent to us. The poem illustrates that good poetry confines itself to what is essential; that adjectives should be sparingly used; that epithets should be 'significant'; and that ideas are crucial to all good literature."

When addressing any other subject than poetry submission, Kirkland strikes an amiable tone in her editorials. She pleasantly converses about the latest happenings in New York, the newest fashions, and the current museum exhibitions. She touches on a wide range of topics, from the funeral of John Quincy Adams to the proper pronunciation of the surname of Jane Eyre, from the question of prison discipline to the immense expansion of London (one hundred streets added to the city each year). The editorials occasionally display the light but sharp touch of humor which is the hallmark of Kirkland's best writing (one of the signs of progress is the refinements which gradually have been introduced on the Brooklyn-Manhattan ferryboats: "rich stained glass windows were installed, the seats were cushioned, . . . the floors *sometimes* attended to").

Kirkland further wrote essays on a variety of subjects. Two enthusiastic ones are on Goethe's then recently translated autobiography, *Dichtung und Wahrheit* (1811-1833). Kirkland immediately confesses that she too–like Goethe's contemporaries–is stunned and amazed by the man's genius, which casts a superior splendor over everything he touched. Even when, as a young boy, he threw out all his family's breakables in the street, he did so under loud applause from the neighbors, who found it diverting amusement. Kirkland especially emphasizes the excellent upbringing provided by Goethe's parents, who introduced the boy to many different subjects and allowed unrestrained browsing over the whole field of knowledge, yet never attempted to make a premature little old man of the brilliant boy: "If he chose to make nonsense-verses, he was not reminded of his deep study of Jewish Antiquities." Kirkland further remarks (with professional interest, it seems) upon the abundance of "characters" in Goethe's homeland (Kirkland always displayed a special interest in, and a special skill at, creating literary types in her writings).

As admiring as the Goethe essays are, as critical is Kirkland's essay on George Sand's *Le Compagnon du Tour de France* (1840; translated in 1847 as *The Journeyman Joiner; or, The Companion of the Tour of France*). Kirkland pronounces Sand's book "dull." Worse, the proposition of the book (a common carpenter is a worthy object of the devoted affection of an upper-class lady) is "the silliest in the world." The book is nothing but idealistic. According to Kirkland, "life is . . . very different, and as our phoenix of a carpenter would probably put his knife in the salt, or wipe

The Death of Washington.

From "Memoirs of Washington"

published in 1858.

— Can that solemn hour ever be forgotten? Can the feeling which thrilled over millions, under whatever skies, have passed away with the smoke of cannon, and the echo of funeral eulogies, that sought to give it utterance? Did all this luxuriance of grief spring from no deep root of love and reverence in the nation's heart?

Forbid it, Heaven! Forbid it truth, wisdom, honor, gratitude! The people who burst into spontaneous tears for the loss of Washington, had hearts to appreciate him; and to be able to appreciate him bespoke qualities in some degree akin to his own. He was no melo-dramatic hero, no meteor of war, no flimsy, popular idol for the worship of the vulgar. His character, his career, his personal qualities, mark the race from which they sprung; — grave, high-toned, generous, resolute, devoted; and such alone must ever be his true admirers. The sincerity of the

Fair copy page of an essay in Kirkland's volume of tributes to George Washington (from Autograph Leaves of Our Country's Authors, *compiled by Alexander Bliss and John P. Kennedy, 1864)*

his lips with the table-cloth, or object to much toilet labor, or smoke in the parlor, or keep his boots in the bed-room, we cannot but think he might become exceedingly disagreeable, with all his virtue."

Kirkland also reproves Sand for her ideas about divorce. Making divorce more readily attainable would lead, in the eyes of Kirkland, to the nullification of the institution of marriage. Sand's works thus were doing "mischief" to society. Sand was "the unsuspected flatterer of all who are discontented with their own lot, and who find gratification in shifting the responsibility from themselves to society and its institutions and abuses."

From July 1847 to June 1848 Kirkland contributed a western sketch to every *Union* issue but the February one. The sketches describe harvest, the "central point" of the year; justice and litigation, a practice westerners count "among their pleasures"; a hard winter; a log house; education; and religious services in the country. A country funeral is the topic of the October sketch: "There is perhaps no occasion on which the rougher sort of people appear to better advantage than in circumstances of illness and death in the neighborhood." While "delicacy, taste, disinterestedness, tenderness, may be lacking at other times among the uninstructed; when the hand of God touches 'the bone and the flesh' of any member of the community, all these come, by a beautiful instinct, just in proportion as they are needed." The November sketch, "Steps to Ruin," is actually more a moralistic warning against inconsistent behavior than a specific country sketch. The sketch on the singing master, started in December and completed in the March issue, is one of the most delightful. The first singing lesson conducted by the new master is described as follows: "Contortions dire and sad grimace, and sounds as when a flock of much maligned birds, disturbed from their resting place by the road-side, revenge themselves by screaming at the interloper–all were there. But not a muscle of the teacher's face showed that he was the conscious possessor of ears. With looks of unperturbed gravity, he gave the signal to begin–to stop–to stop–to stop again, and begin again. He himself led the panting host, his chin buried deep in his stock, and his eyebrows raised as if to be out of the way of the volume of sound that issued from the mouth that opened like an oyster below." While some of these tales seem to have been written merely for the sake of having a

sketch by the editor, others are among the best pieces Kirkland wrote about the West since in them she adds to her keen observations the insights of retrospect.

Book notices were also the responsibility of the editor. Between five and nine books were briefly discussed each month. Books included Henry Wadsworth Longfellow's *Evangeline* (1847), Charles Dickens's *Dombey and Son* (1846-1848), James Russell Lowell's *Poems* (1849), biographies of Oliver Cromwell and the Duke of Marlborough, and Emily Brontë's *Wuthering Heights* (1847). Kirkland seems to have spent very little time on these notices, something we can well understand when we consider that during this time she was also heading a school and teaching in addition to working for the *Union*. Moreover, she devoted much energy to soliciting contributions for the magazine. At times she almost had to plead for contributions. To Bryant she wrote, "My publisher is so truly orthodox that he declares we must be saved by a name. . . . Now under these circumstances can not . . . you come to rescue in the shape of *one single page* of prose?" "You must help me," she wrote to Duyckinck. Partly it was due to Kirkland's efforts that the *Union* was able to offer poems by Lowell, Poe, and Longfellow; essays by Henry David Thoreau, Bryant, and Duyckinck; and fiction by Sedgwick, Child, Simms, and Walt Whitman.

Always interested in local color and perhaps becoming a little tired of writing of the West (she had just completed the tenth installment of "Western Sketches" for the *Union*), Kirkland embarked for Europe in the spring of 1848. She had arranged with her publisher, Israel Post, that she would send back a series of impressions for the *Union*. The first of these appeared as the leading article in the July 1848 issue and treats the crossing of the Atlantic and sightseeing in Liverpool. Later installments render Kirkland's impressions of Oxford, London, Paris, Lyons, Genoa, Paris, and Florence. There are some nice observations ("Nobody above beggary wears a ragged shoe in Italy"), but on the whole these sightseeing essays are not as fresh and captivating as the western pieces.

Soon after her return from Europe in October 1848 Kirkland found that the *Union* had been sold to John Sartain, a famous copper engraver, and William Sloanaker, a former business manager of *Graham's Magazine*. The *Union* was renamed *Sartain's Union Magazine of Literature and Art,* and its headquarters was moved to Philadelphia. Moreover, John S. Hart, principal of a Philadelphia high school, was enlisted as coeditor. Hart assured the public in his first editorial that Kirkland would "continue, as heretofore, to contribute to [the *Union's*] pages." Kirkland indeed continued to contribute, writing essays on English and American manners, education, the significance of dress, conversation, Mahomet, and "fastidiousness." In "Reading for Amusement" she argues that "amusement is as wholesome for the mind as gymnastics are for the body." Reading is an "innocent pleasure." That some critical voices could be heard attacking novel reading was due, not to the activity in itself, which was harmless, but to the many bad novels that had lately been written. "Literary Women" seeks to dispel the misguided preconceptions about women writers. Literary women do not possess, Kirkland assures us, "inky fingers," "unkempt locks," "unrighteous stockings," or "disdain of dinner." Nor were there cobwebs in their parlours or neglected children in their nurseries. Kirkland also composed two more western sketches. From her correspondence we may gather that Kirkland continued to solicit contributions. However, she no longer had much input in editorial policies. At the end of 1850 she decided to sever her ties with the magazine altogether.

Energetic as ever, Kirkland selected and edited the anthology *Garden Walks with the Poets* (1852), wrote a long essay on Bryant for *Homes of American Authors* (1853), and compiled three collections of her own magazine articles, *The Evening Book* (1852), *A Book for the Home Circle* (1853), and *Autumn Hours* (1854). She also firmly advocated the cause and rehabilitation of women convicts in *The Helping Hand* (1853). In 1853 she became associated with *Putnam's Monthly*. All these years Kirkland continued to teach as well. Kirkland's *Memoirs of Washington* appeared in 1857. In the spring of 1864, having just published *The School-Girl's Garland* and busy with the preparations for a fair to benefit the Sanitary Commission (one of her many philanthropic activities), Caroline Kirkland suddenly died on 6 April from apoplexy.

"Of all [the *Union's*] brilliant array of contributors, there was not one whose articles gave such entire and uniform satisfaction as those of Mrs. Kirkland," John S. Hart wrote in *The Female Prose Writers of America* (1852). The high regard in which Kirkland's essays were held by her contemporaries likewise appears from a review of *The Evening Book* in Duyckinck's *Literary World*: "Mrs. Kirkland's Conversational Essays, . . . a mingling of description, home and travelled observations with touches of character, . . . form one of the most agreeable and withal profitable literary entertainments of the day." The critic added, "Her opinions on social topics are generally sound and always on the side of nature." Today, Kirkland is mainly remembered for her western writings and the impetus these gave to the emerging movement of realism, but in her own day it was Kirkland's work as an essayist which was thought to constitute "her strongest claim to distinction as a writer."

References:

John S. Hart, *The Female Prose Writers of America* (Philadelphia: Butler, 1852);

Douglas Hill, Foreword to Kirkland's *A New Home* (New York: Garrett Press, 1969);

Langley C. Keyes, "Caroline M. Kirkland: A Pioneer in Realism," Ph.D. dissertation, Harvard University, 1935;

Frank Luther Mott, *A History of American Magazines*, 5 volumes (Cambridge, Mass.: Harvard University Press, 1938-1968), I: 769-770;

William S. Osborne, *Caroline M. Kirkland* (New York: Twayne, 1972);

Daniel G. Riordan, "The Concept of Simplicity in the Works of Mrs. Caroline M. Kirkland," Ph.D. dissertation, University of North Carolina, 1973.

Papers:

Caroline Kirkland's papers are held at the Clifton Waller Barrett Library, the University of Virginia; Cornell University Library; the Michigan Historical Collections, University of Michigan; the Historical Society of Pennsylvania; and the Massachusetts Historical Society.

Hugh Swinton Legaré

(2 January 1797-20 June 1843)

Edward L. Tucker
Virginia Polytechnic Institute and State University

See also the Legaré entries in *DLB 3: Antebellum Writers in New York and the South* and *DLB 59: American Literary Critics and Scholars, 1800-1850.*

MAJOR POSITIONS HELD: Cofounder and editor, *Southern Review* (1828-1832).

BOOK: *Writings of Hugh Swinton Legaré, Late Attorney General and Acting Secretary of State of the United States . . . ,* 2 volumes, edited by Mary S. Legaré (Charleston, S.C.: Burges & James/ Philadelphia: Cowperthwait/New York: Appleton/Boston: Munroe, 1845-1846).

OTHER: "The Study of the Classics," in *The Charleston Book,* edited by William Gilmore Simms (Charleston, S.C.: Hart, 1845), pp. 14-19;
"Hugh Swinton Legaré: German Diaries," in *All Clever Men, Who Make Their Way: Critical Discourse in the Old South,* edited by Michael O'Brien (Fayetteville: University of Arkansas Press, 1982), pp. 89-124.

Hugh Swinton Legaré by Thomas Sully (courtesy of the Gibbes Art Gallery/Carolina Art Association)

Hugh Swinton Legaré held several important political posts in his native South Carolina, including that of attorney general of the state. On the national level he filled a diplomatic post in Brussels, was a member of the House of Representatives, and became attorney general and briefly secretary of state during the tenure of President John Tyler. But he is best remembered today by some as being a founder of the important periodical the *Southern Review,* published in Charleston. For several years he was its guiding force.

Legaré was born on Johns Island on the Ashley River near Charleston, South Carolina, of French Huguenot and Scottish Covenanter ancestry. The Legarés, who boasted in their background of goldsmiths, clockmakers, and members of the provincial assembly before the Revolution, became planters when the family purchased land on Johns Island. Hugh's father, Solomon, who had married Mary Splatt Swinton in 1791, was probably a planter. There were six children in all, although three died in infancy. Hugh was the fifth of the six children. His older sister, Eliza Catherine, married John Bryan, a state representative and later senator, in 1810 when she was sixteen, bore twenty-one children, buried eight of them, and was herself buried in 1842. Only his younger sister, Mary Swinton Legaré, survived him, and she played an important role in his life. Solomon died when Hugh was two years old, and the burden of running the plantation and taking care of the three surviving small children fell on the mother; however, she managed the estate with efficiency and reared her children well. James Mathewes Legaré (1823-1859), a southern poet, was a third cousin of Legaré.

217

When Legaré was four he was inoculated for smallpox because Charleston habitually suffered during epidemics. He almost died from the virus, which attacked his joints. He became an invalid, and his mother was forced to carry him about on a pillow. It took some time before he could walk again. Until he was about twelve or thirteen his growth was stunted; then, he grew robustly, but only in the upper portions of his body. The lower parts did not develop properly. Naturally his physical condition deprived him of some childhood activities, and, although he became sensitive and occasionally sulked, he handled the deformity well and seldom spoke to others about it. Perhaps because of his physical condition and his desire to excel, he developed a love of books and intellectual distinction.

His early education was handled first by his mother, then by an Englishman named Ward, followed by a Catholic priest, Simon F. Gallagher. Legaré then studied in a Charleston high school which later became the College of Charleston. When he was thirteen his mother sent him to the Willington Academy of the Reverend Moses Waddel, but Legaré rebelled against the spartan atmosphere there. In December 1811 he entered South Carolina College in Columbia (now the University of South Carolina) as a sophomore. He graduated at the head of his class in December 1814, and for the next three years he studied law in Charleston under the direction of attorney Mitchell King. In May 1818 he went abroad for further study, finally ending up at the University of Edinburgh. He returned to Charleston in 1820, managed his mother's plantation for a while, and then settled in the city as a lawyer.

As an orator he was unexcelled. Benjamin F. Perry stated that Legaré was "nearer to the finished Orator than any" other man he had ever heard; he was someone in "complete control" of his voice. Fellow students gave him the nickname of "Cicero."

In the political field Legaré, after serving in the state legislature from 1821 to 1822 and from 1824 to 1830, became attorney general of the state from 1830 to 1831. As a result of his argumentative skills in the United States Supreme Court, President Andrew Jackson offered Legaré the post of chargé d'affaires at Brussels, which the South Carolinian accepted. He served in Brussels for four years (1832-1836). Returning to Charleston in 1836, he was elected to the Twenty-Fifth Congress (1837-1839), and in the fall of 1841 he became attorney general in President John Tyler's cabinet. When Daniel Webster withdrew from the cabinet Legaré was made secretary of state ad interim on 8 May 1843. In June of that same year he went with Tyler to take part in the unveiling of the Bunker Hill Monument and there became critically ill with severe abdominal pains. He died on 20 June 1843 at the age of forty-six at the home of his friend George Ticknor. He was buried in Mount Auburn Cemetery in Cambridge, but fourteen years later his remains were removed and reinterred, on 8 October 1857, in Magnolia Cemetery in Charleston.

For the lover of literature Legaré is of most interest because of his association with the *Southern Review*, the first of the important magazines in the antebellum South. Before it emerged, he had written and published very little; however, the situation changed with this periodical. According to Michael O'Brien, the "opportunity for permanence had been wanting. That occasion the *Southern Review* was to provide"; with it he "entered a period of extraordinary productivity, the distillation of his years of reading and reflection."

The first issue was published in February 1828, the last in February 1832; each year had two volumes, and in all there were sixteen issues. The title pages gave little information; they simply stated that the journal was published in Charleston by A. E. Miller for the proprietors. The number of subscribers is unknown. Although the names of the authors were not given, they have been almost completely identified by O'Brien and others. For instance, copies exist with the authors' names written in by hand. For the most part the contributors were professional men in Charleston and professors at colleges in South Carolina. In addition, Legaré's sister Mary identified some of the works of her brother when she published his *Writings* (1845-1846).

A group of Charleston gentlemen–Legaré, Stephen Elliott, Sr., James Hamilton, Samuel Henry Dickson, Mitchell King, John Gadsden, James Louis Petigru, Robert Young Hayne, and William Drayton–felt the need for a journal that was distinctly southern and met in the fall of 1827 to make plans for such a magazine. A prospectus stated that the *Southern Review* wished to "vindicate the rights and privileges, the character of the Southern States; to arrest, if possible, the current which has been directed so steadily against our country generally, and the South in particular; and to offer to our fellow citizens one Journal which they may read without finding

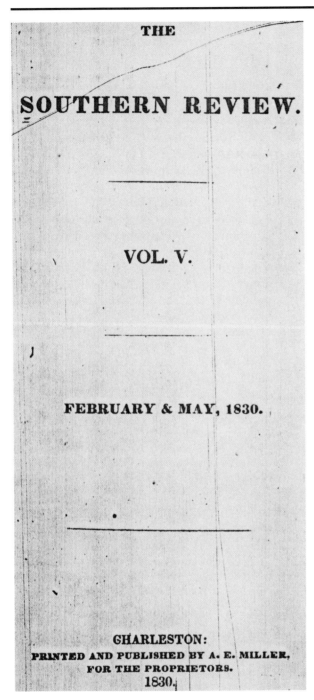

THE

SOUTHERN REVIEW.

VOL. V.

FEBRUARY & MAY, 1830.

CHARLESTON:
PRINTED AND PUBLISHED BY A. E. MILLER,
FOR THE PROPRIETORS.
1830.

Title page for volume 5 of one of the earliest important southern periodicals. Legaré began editing the journal with this volume.

glish, French, and German literature and contemporary American writing, the *Southern Review* published essays on such wide-ranging topics as the tariff, the mineralogy of North Carolina, the distribution of wealth, the Federal Constitution, mental development, and malaria.

Stephen Elliott, Sr., was probably the first editor; when he died in 1830 his son, Stephen Elliott, Jr., took over briefly; then Legaré edited the magazine for the last two years. According to John R. Welsh, the journal became "the child of one man," and it is appropriate to call it "Legaré's Review." A meticulous author and editor, Legaré wrote more than a thousand pages of its contents in the form of essays; he was the author of about twenty-five percent of all the review articles. Legaré spoke of his "immense *labor* for the *Southern Review*," which, in the last two years, he had been "saddled" with, "as if it had been an hereditary estate." In a typical Legaré essay there is generally a detailed historical background of the subject before a particular book is reviewed. Detailed comments and extended quotations, displaying impressive erudition, follow. Legaré's interests were the classical age; contemporary literary men and their writings; and the history, theory, and practical effects of law. He selected books to reflect these concerns. In the field of literature, though he might have spoken unkindly of his fellow Charlestonian William Crafts, he found much to admire in James Fenimore Cooper and William Cullen Bryant, as well as in the British romanticists Sir Walter Scott and Lord Byron.

The timing of the *Southern Review* is significant. The works of such southern writers as William Gilmore Simms, John Pendleton Kennedy, and the humorists were just beginning to appear. With a limited field for discussion and with financial problems, the magazine failed, just as almost all the other nineteenth-century southern journals failed. In November 1830 an editorial proclaimed that the "necessity of stopping the *Southern Review* arises, entirely," from "the want of money." Yet it struggled on until February 1832, the year Legaré left for Europe as the representative of the United States at the court of Brussels. Welsh states that, with his departure, Legaré "left behind the volumes of a true pioneer in Southern journals, one that died before the *Southern Literary Messenger* commenced publication in 1834." Linda Rhea believes that Legaré "wrote with the spirit of one who had a mission to perform, or a real duty to point out the best, and to

themselves the objects of perpetual sarcasm, or of affected commiseration." The editorial policy was to treat those works which detailed the "improvements of the age" and to give attention to books of literature, science, and agriculture, "as well as to our national and local concerns." In time nearly all of them became contributors. In its four-year history, in addition to articles on En-

lead readers away from the mediocre." O'Brien points out that Legaré "helped to found a model of critical discourse that was to be persistently emulated in the region."

During Legaré's lifetime no collection of his works was published. After his death his sister Mary corrected this deficiency with an edition of two volumes. Though she exalted her brother beyond his worth and though Paul Hamilton Hayne would later call her efforts "execrable" in arrangement and annotation, she nevertheless did make some of his works readily available. The first volume of the *Writings* contains a biographical notice by Edward Johnston, some diaries that Legaré kept while in Brussels and on his German travels, a section of letters, some orations, and three essays written for the *New York Review* between 1837 and 1841. Volume 2 consists entirely of sixteen essays selected from those that Legaré wrote for the *Southern Review*.

Even though Lord John Acton stated that Legaré was "the most accomplished scholar among American statesmen," O'Brien believes that he "can never be a popular writer" because he was "too confessedly learned." If readers wish to master Legaré, they must "know much recondite and difficult matter, across a span of time and cultures." Too much "bombastic eulogy," O'Brien continues, has been "heaped on the poor man's head"; he has become a "ponderous, formal, and very still corpse," and "plain" Hugh Legaré has been elevated to "Hugh Swinton Legaré." Yet, O'Brien concludes that the author "was a remarkable man, and no antebellum southern intellectual better deserves the attention of historians."

Biographies:

W.[illiam] C. Preston, *Eulogy on Hugh Swinton Legaré* . . . (Charleston, S.C., 1843);

E.[dward] W. J.[ohnston], "Biographical Notice," in *Writings of Hugh Swinton Legaré* . . . , volume 1 (Charleston, S.C.: Burges & James/ Philadelphia: Cowperthwait/New York: Appleton/Boston: Munroe, 1846), pp. vlxxii;

Paul Hamilton Hayne, *Lives of Robert Young Hayne and Hugh Swinton Legaré* (Charleston, S.C.: Walker, Evans & Cogswell, 1878);

Linda Rhea, *Hugh Swinton Legaré: A Charleston Intellectual* (Chapel Hill: University of North Carolina Press, 1934);

Michael O'Brien, *A Character of Hugh Legaré* (Knoxville: University of Tennessee Press, 1985).

References:

Merrill G. Christophersen, "A Rhetorical Study of Hugh Swinton Legaré: South Carolina Unionist," Ph.D. dissertation, University of Florida, 1954;

Jay B. Hubbell, "Hugh Swinton Legaré," in his *The South in American Literature: 1607-1900* (Durham: Duke University Press, 1954), pp. 263-274, 945-946;

Michael O'Brien, "Politics, Romanticism and Hugh Legaré: 'The Fondness of Disappointed Love,'" in *Intellectual Life in Antebellum Charleston*, edited by O'Brien and David Moltke-Hanson (Knoxville: University of Tennessee Press, 1986), pp. 123-151;

Edd Winfield Parks, "Hugh Swinton Legaré: Humanist," in his *Ante-Bellum Southern Literary Critics* (Athens: University of Georgia Press, 1962), pp. 23-50, 268-276;

Parks, "Legaré and Grayson: Types of Classical Influence on Criticism in the Old South," in his *Segments of Southern Thought* (Athens: University of Georgia Press, 1938), pp. 156-171;

Vernon Louis Parrington, "Hugh Swinton Legaré: Charleston Intellectual," in his *Main Currents in American Thought*, volume 2 (New York: Harcourt, Brace, 1927), pp. 114-124;

John R. Welsh, "Southern Literary Magazines, IV: An Early Pioneer: Legaré's *Southern Review*," *Southern Literary Journal*, 3 (Spring 1971): 79-97.

Papers:

Hugh Swinton Legaré's papers are held at the South Caroliniana Library, University of South Carolina; National Archives; Library of Congress; Southern Historical Collection, University of North Carolina; South Carolina State Archives, Columbia; and the Perkins Library, Duke University.

George Pope Morris

(10 October 1802-6 July 1864)

Jean Folkerts
Mount Vernon College

MAJOR POSITIONS HELD: Founder, editor, co-editor, *New-York Mirror, and Ladies' Literary Gazette,* renamed *New-York Mirror* (1824-1842); co-editor, *New Mirror* (1842-1844); editor, *Evening Mirror* (1844-1845); founder, editor, *National Press,* renamed *Home Journal* (1846-1864).

BOOKS: *The Deserted Bride; And Other Poems* (New York: Adlard & Saunders, 1838; enlarged edition, New York: Appleton, 1843); enlarged again as *The Deserted Bride, and Other Productions* (New York: Scribner, 1853);
The Little Frenchman and His Water Lots, with Other Sketches of the Times (Philadelphia: Lea & Blanchard, 1839);
Songs, Duetts and Chorusses in the New Opera of the Maid of Saxony, libretto by Morris, music by C. E. Horn (New York: J. C. House, 1842);
The Songs and Ballads of George P. Morris (New York: Morris, Willis, 1844).

PLAY PRODUCTION: *Brier Cliff; or, Scenes of the Revolution,* New York, Chatham Garden Theatre, 15 June 1826.

George Pope Morris, a sentimental poet and popular songwriter, grew up in Philadelphia and New York and secured his first job in a printing house, where he also began writing verses for the city's daily newspapers. Morris's professional life spanned the literary and journalistic worlds as he combined magazine editing with the writing of poetry and song. The invitations to society balls in the small collection of Morris's manuscripts at the Library of Congress (including one from Moses Beach to a party celebrating the twentieth anniversary of the *New York Sun*) attest to his popularity in New York society and his recognition as a leading member of the journalistic establishment.

During the first year of its existence, 1824, the *New-York Mirror, and Ladies' Literary Gazette* was the product of the twenty-one-year-old Morris and a distinguished editor, Samuel

George Pope Morris

Woodworth. Woodworth had written several plays and an operetta and was known in particular for the song "The Old Oaken Bucket." The partnership lasted for only a year, and Morris took over the magazine himself. The *Mirror,* one of the few literary journals of the period, opened channels for the Knickerbocker group of writers, who were specialists in writing the informal, half-humorous, half-satirical essay. As well as providing an outlet for an emerging group of American writers, including Nathaniel P. Willis, Fitz-Greene Halleck, and William Cullen Bryant, the *Mirror* also reprinted works of British poets.

221

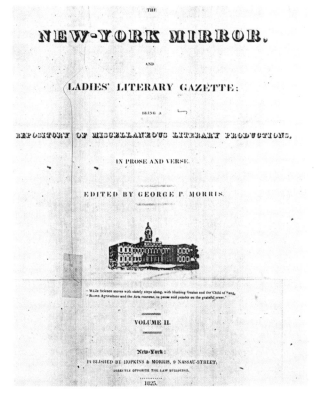

First page of the first issue of Morris's literary magazine, with his prospectus

Title page for volume two of the New-York Mirror. *Morris assumed editorial direction of the magazine in 1824, following the resignation of his friend Samuel Woodworth.*

Two years after the periodical's beginning Morris's revolutionary era drama, *Brier Cliff*, ran at the Chatham Garden Theatre and produced about thirty-five hundred dollars in income for the young author. In 1830 his poem "Woodman, Spare That Tree!" won popular acclaim and critical respect from Edgar Allan Poe, who labeled it and another Morris poem, "Near the Lake," as "compositions of which any poet, living or dead might justly be proud." The first stanza of "Woodman" remained a popular item in schoolbooks for many years:

Woodman, spare that tree!
   Touch not a single bough!
In youth it sheltered me,
   And I'll protect it now.

In October 1838 the *Southern Literary Messenger* congratulated Morris for being a pioneer in American literature and listed the characteristics of his poetry as "delicacy of perception, elegance of expression, liquid flow of syllables, and pervading smoothness of versification." The magazine noted that the "characteristic feature of the

poet's mind, seems to be gentleness, tenderness of feeling, playful humor, and a fancy, warm but chaste, that delights in picturing Love under his thousand varied and beautiful shapes." Nevertheless, while Morris's songs and poems were popular, some contemporary critics challenged them for being "soft as milk, and sage as Mother Goose."

Morris's only book of prose, *The Little Frenchman and His Water Lots* (1839), is a collection of sketches, with the title piece being the story of a shrewd New York realtor and a naive foreigner. "The Maid of Saxony," an operetta produced in 1842, was based on historical events in the life of Frederick II of Prussia. The opera ran for only two weeks. Morris's work appeared not only in the publications he edited but also in other journals, such as the *New York Ledger*.

In April 1842 Morris chose Nathaniel Parker Willis to help edit the *New Mirror*, an extension of the previous periodical, which, due to economic pressure, had ceased circulation four months earlier. Willis, an entertaining writer especially skilled in writing travel letters for publication, also joined Morris in his later venture, the weekly *Home Journal*. After difficulty with the postal laws in 1844, the *New Mirror* was abandoned and the short-lived *Evening Mirror* begun.

The *Home Journal* proved to be a popular periodical from its inception in 1846 through its transition to *Town and Country* in 1901. It was issued in a four-page newspaper format, with a scrolling masthead including Morris's name, as well as slogans such as "Repository of Letters," "Record of Art," and "Mirror of Passing Events." It sold for two dollars a year. The scrolling head was soon dropped and replaced with a simple masthead displaying the name "The Home Journal" in Roman type. In the first issue of the periodical, which had been initially entitled *Morris's National Press. A Journal for Home,* the editors addressed their intended readers in flowing nineteenth-century prose: "In choosing the kindliest day of all the year for the unfolding of our new hopes, we mean distinctly to refer the warm nest we are about to build among the widespreading branches of public favor. We are not, it is true, young at this kind of architecture, but we have not lost in enthusiasm what we have gained in experience. We have chosen a high place, liable to be rocked by storm, but all the more open to the genial sunshine. We mean to build firmly and well, choosing twigs from the tree of knowledge, leaves from the tree of liberty, straws from among those which show how the political winds blow, cement made of truth and good will, and the soft lining down which ladies love so well."

The editors thanked the "Gentlemen of the Press" for their congratulations on the prospectus of the *National Press* which had preceded the first issue. Morris did not ignore women readers either, noting that "No miscellaneous paper, whether daily, weekly, or monthly, can claim to be complete, or to possess its highest excellence, unless particular attention is paid to its female readers. We are past that period in the world, and that stage in society, when women, their improvement, their interests, their gratifications, or their very whims and caprices, can be overlooked by any editor who aspires to high and general usefulness."

The editors said women's place in the world was important, their influence great, their control over literature, society, and morals "too well ascertained." Perhaps ahead of their time, the editors announced that the paper would not carry a ladies' column as such, but that "our whole paper

Engraving of Morris by W. G. Jackson from a photograph by Mathew Brady

shall be one that our cultivated countrywomen can approve, and from which all our countrywomen can derive pleasure and instruction. Nothing shall appear in it to which the most fastidious in taste or morals can object."

In 1858 the editors boasted that the magazine was read "wherever run the gold threads of domestic happiness and true moral refinement, which are woven so thickly into the strong and coarser web of our country's industry and energetic prosperity." The magazine was clever, literary, and interested in art and amusement. It also devoted many columns to New York society gossip.

Richard Henry Stoddard, who often wrote for the magazine, said the *Home Journal* was so considerate to enterprising songwriters and poets that the writers referred to it as their "incubator." Stoddard described Morris as "a black-eyed, black-haired gentleman" and wrote, "there was something imposing and impressive in Morris's personal appearance. He had a broad, padded chest and a bulky waist, whose amplitude of girth was encircled by a military belt, which supported the long and dangerous weapon that dangled from it." He usually was referred to as "General Morris," out of respect for his connection with the New York State militia. Morris was married to Mary Worthington Hopkins and had several children. He lived for many years at his country estate in the Hudson River highlands. He was active in New York charities and was a trustee for the Samaritan House of Industry, a home for unemployed women. Morris died on 6 July 1864.

References:

"American Poetry," *People's and Howitt's Journal,* 10 (1850): 101;

Henry A. Beers, *Nathaniel Parker Willis* (Boston: Houghton, Mifflin, 1885);

James Cephas Derby, *Fifty Years Among Authors,* *Books and Publishers* (New York: Carelton, 1886), pp. 221-226;

Frank Luther Mott, *A History of American Magazines,* 5 volumes (Cambridge, Mass.: Harvard University Press, 1938-1968), I: 101-103; II: 57, 351-355, 361;

R. H. Stoddard, *Recollections* (New York: Barnes, 1893), pp. 25, 26, 44, 81, 83, 173;

James Grant Wilson, *Bryant and His Friends* (New York: Fords, Howard & Hulbert, 1886).

Papers:

The Library of Congress holds manuscripts of George Pope Morris's poetry, limited correspondence, and a partnership agreement between Willis and Pope. Other collections are located at the Harvard College Library, the Historical Society of Pennsylvania, the New York State Library, and the New York Public Library.

Thomas Paine

(29 January 1737-8 June 1809)

James Glen Stovall
University of Alabama

See also the Paine entries in *DLB 31: American Colonial Writers, 1735-1781* and *DLB 43: American Newspaper Journalists, 1690-1872.*

MAJOR POSITION HELD: Editor, *Pennsylvania Magazine* (1775-1776).

SELECTED BOOKS: *The Case of the Officers of Excise; with Remarks on the Qualifications of Officers; and on the Numerous Evils Arising to the Revenue, from the Insufficiency of the Present Salary. Humbly Addressed to the Hon. and Right Hon. the Members of Both Houses of Parliament* (London: Privately printed, 1772; London: Printed for J. S. Jordan, 1793);

Common Sense: Addressed to the Inhabitants of America . . . (Philadelphia: Printed & sold by R. Bell, 1776; revised and enlarged edition, Philadelphia: Printed by William Bradford, 1776; expurgated edition, London: Printed for J. Almon, 1776; unexpurgated edition, Edinburgh: Sold by Charles Eliot/Sterling: Sold by William Anderson, 1776);

The American Crisis, numbers 1-4 (Philadelphia: Printed & sold by Styner & Cist, 1776-1777); number 5 (Lancaster: Printed by John Dunlap, 1778); numbers 6-7 (Philadelphia: Printed by John Dunlap, 1778); numbers 8-9 (Philadelphia: Printed by John Dunlap?, 1780); *The Crisis Extraordinary* (Philadelphia: Sold by William Harris, 1780); *The American Crisis,* numbers 10-12 (Philadelphia: Printed by John Dunlap?, 1782); number 13 (Philadelphia, 1783); *A Supernumerary Crisis* (Philadelphia, 1783); *A numerary Crisis* [number 2] (New York, 1783); numbers 2-9, 11, and *The Crisis Extraordinary* republished in *The American Crisis, and a Letter to Sir Guy Carleton* . . . (London: Printed & sold by D. I. Eaton, 1796?);

Public Good, Being an Examination into the Claims of Virginia to the Vacant Western Territory and of the Right of the United States to the Same . . . (Philadelphia: Printed by John Dunlap,

Thomas Paine (Gale International Portrait Gallery)

1780; London: Printed by W. T. Sherwin, 1817);

Letter Addressed to the Abbé Raynal on the Affairs of North America . . . (Philadelphia: Printed by Melchior Steiner & sold by Robert Aitken, 1782; London: Printed for C. Dilly, 1782);

Dissertations on Government; The Affairs of the Bank; and Paper-Money (Philadelphia: Printed by Charles Cist & sold by Hall & Sellers, Robert Aitken, and William Pritchard, 1786; London: W. T. Sherman, 1817);

Rights of Man: Being an Answer to Mr. Burke's Attack on the French Revolution (London: Printed for J. Johnson, 1791; Baltimore: Printed & sold by David Graham, 1791);

Rights of Man: Part the Second (London: Printed by J. S. Jordan, 1792; New York: Printed by Hugh Gaine, 1792);

Letter Addressed to the Addressers on the Late Proclamation (London: 1792; New York: Printed by Thomas Greenleaf, 1793; Philadelphia: Printed by H. & P. Rice, 1793);

The Age of Reason: Being an Investigation of True and Fabulous Theology (Paris: Printed by Barrois, 1794; London: Sold by D. I. Eaton, 1794; New York: Printed by T. & J. Swords for J. Fellows, 1794);

Dissertation on First Principles of Government (London: Printed & sold by D. I. Eaton, 1795);

The Age of Reason: Part the Second. Being an Investigation of True and of Fabulous Theology (Paris: Printed for the author, 1795; London: Printed for H. D. Symonds, 1795; Philadelphia: Printed by Benjamin Franklin Bache for the author, 1795);

Letter to George Washington, President of the United States of America on Affairs Public and Private (Philadelphia: Printed by Benjamin Franklin Bache, 1796; London: Printed for H. D. Symonds, 1797);

The Decline and Fall of the English System of Finance (Paris: Printed by Hartley, Adlard & son/ London: Reprinted for D. I. Eaton, 1796; New York: Printed by Matt & Lyon for J. Fellows, 1796);

Thomas Payne à la législature et au directoire. Ou la justice agraire opposée à la loi agraire, et aux privilèges agraire (Paris: Ragouleau, 1797); republished as *Agrarian Justice, Opposed to Agrarian Law, and to Agrarian Monopoly . . .* (London: Printed for T. Williams, 1797; Philadelphia: Printed by R. Folwell for Benjamin Franklin Bache, 1797);

A Discourse Delivered by Thomas Paine, at the Society of the Theophilanthropists, at Paris, [1797] (London: Printed & sold by T. C. Rickman, 1798);

Compact Maritime, under the Following Heads: I. Dissertation on the Law of Nations. II. On the Jacobinism of the English at Sea. III. Compact Maritime for the Protection of Neutral Commerce, and Securing the Liberty of the Seas. IV. Observations on Some Passages in the Discourse of the Judge of the English Admiralty (Washington, D.C.: Printed by Samuel Harrison Smith, 1801);

Examination of the Passages in the New Testament, Quoted from the Old and Called Prophecies Concerning Jesus Christ. To Which Is Prefixed, An Essay on Dreams, Shewing by What Operations of the Mind a Dream Is Produced in Sleep, and Applying the Same to the Account of Dreams in the New Testament; with an Appendix Containing My Private Thoughts of a Future State, and Remarks on the Contradictory Doctrine in the Books of Matthew and Mark (New York: Printed for the author, 1807).

Collections: *The Writings of Thomas Paine*, edited by Moncure Daniel Conway, 4 volumes (New York: Putnam's, 1894-1896);

The Complete Writings of Thomas Paine, edited by Philip S. Foner, 2 volumes (New York: Citadel Press, 1945).

In 1776, when Thomas Paine wrote, "These are the times that try men's souls" (*The American Crisis*, number 1), he put into words the sentiments of all who believed in the cause of the American Revolution. Despite a resounding declaration of independence from Great Britain that summer, December found the army of the American colonies under George Washington cold, bitter, hungry, and deeply depressed. The army's numbers were dwindling, and the enemy seemed to grow in power.

Paine's clear, simple prose not only expressed what many Americans felt, but it also gave them reason for hope: "The summer soldier and the sunshine patriot will, in this crisis, shrink from the service of his country, but he that stands it NOW, deserves the love and thanks of man and woman. Tyranny, like hell, is not easily conquered, yet we have this consolation with us, that the harder the conflict, the more glorious the triumph. . . . "

It is difficult to accurately estimate the effect these words had on a weary cause. Washington was impressed with what Paine had written, and tradition says that he ordered the pamphlet read to all his men. Within a week Washington's army–following a shrewdly conceived and executed plan–crossed the Delaware River and routed the British forces to Trenton, New Jersey. Even James Cheetham, in writing a derogatory biography of Paine, acknowledged that Paine's words inspired the depressed army. "Hope succeeded to despair, cheerfulness to gloom, and firmness to irresolution," he wrote.

This was neither the first nor the last time that Paine's writing would capture the spirit of the times or would inspire Americans to action against the British. Paine was probably the most effective propagandist of the American cause. Time after time he spoke for Americans in voic-

Two anti-Paine cartoons published in the British press in 1791 (courtesy of the Library of Congress)

ing their grievances against the crown, in answering the difficult questions raised by the rebellion, and in giving voice to the feeling that Americans had about their trying times.

Yet, for all his skill and work, Paine is rarely numbered among the first order of American Revolutionary War patriots, and his life before, during, and after the Revolution has presented many problems for biographers. In fact, his reputation fell to such a point during the century after his death that Theodore Roosevelt termed him a "filthy little atheist," and many of Roosevelt's generation agreed. (In reality, Paine was a deist.) Paine was careless about his finances and appearance; his directness obscured the subtleties of many situations, and he was often irritatingly blunt; and his personal life left questions about his ability to maintain a marriage and resist the temptations of alcohol. During the twentieth century Paine's reputation has been rehabilitated to some extent, but many questions about his life, philosophy, and motivations still remain.

Paine was born in England on 29 January 1737 in the Norfolk village of Thetford. His father, Joseph Paine, was a Quaker and made stays for women's corsets, and his mother, Frances Cocke Paine, was an Anglican daughter of an attorney. He went to grammar school until he was thirteen and then was apprenticed to his father. Paine had learned enough to read and write, and, although he was accused in later life of being ignorant of the rules of proper grammar, he had the foundations of being able to use words with power. Six years after leaving school, Paine rejected his father's business and Quaker teaching to sign on with the privateer ship *King of Prussia*, engaged in England's latest war with France.

His seafaring career ended shortly thereafter, and Paine went to London to make his name and fortune. He did neither. He worked for a London staymaker for a time and attended scientific and philosophical lectures given by some of the leading thinkers of the day. The next year he was in Sandwich, a town west of

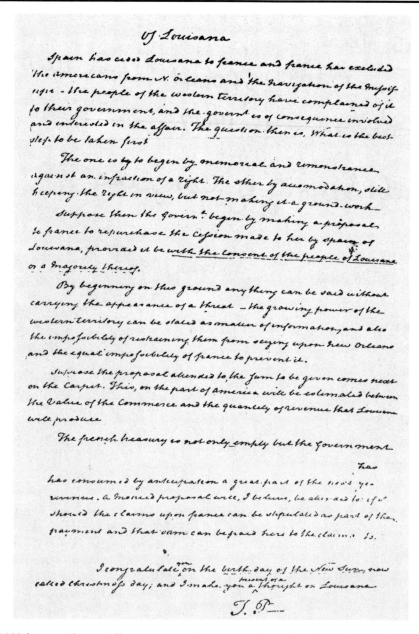

Paine's December 1802 letter to Thomas Jefferson recommending the purchase of Louisiana by the United States (courtesy of the Jefferson Papers, Library of Congress)

Dover, as a master staymaker, and in 1759 he married an orphan, Mary Lambert, who had been employed as a maid. Paine and his wife soon moved to Margate, a village on the North Sea side of Kent, but she died the next year.

Two years later Paine took up a new career, that of an exciseman. His duties were to patrol the coastline against smugglers. He was dismissed from that service in 1765 but applied for reinstatement in 1766. Although the application was accepted, there was no immediate opening, so Paine became a private schoolteacher. It was a

job of no higher position than staymaking and of no greater compensation. In 1768 he received another appointment as an exciseman, this time at Lewes.

In Lewes Paine became active in civic affairs, and he found a second wife. She was Elizabeth Ollive, the daughter of Samuel Ollive, a tobacconist with whom Paine had lodgings when he first arrived in the town. Samuel had since died, whereupon Paine had helped his widow continue the business. Once married (on 26 March 1771), he moved back into the Ollives' house. In 1774 the business failed, he lost his position as an exciseman, and he and Elizabeth separated. There is no evidence that the separation was rancorous, and, in view of what we know about Paine's personality from his later activities, the two may have simply come to the conclusion that they were unsuited for one another. Paine was never known to have any other romantic involvements.

Paine's first foray into political journalism came during this time, in 1772, when he wrote *The Case of the Officers of Excise*. Excisemen such as Paine were paid only fifty pounds a year, barely a livable wage, and Paine's pamphlet tried to set forth some reasoning why that wage should be increased. Paine paid for the printing and distribution himself, and he went to London to try to influence members of Parliament in his direction. For his trouble Paine was eventually dismissed from the service.

While in London Paine had the good fortune to meet Benjamin Franklin, and, when Paine lost his position, home, and family, his thoughts turned to the New World. In October 1774 he sailed for America, armed with a letter of introduction from Franklin to his son-in-law Richard Bache. Paine, Franklin said, was "an ingenious worthy young man" who could be put to work as a clerk, assistant tutor, or assistant surveyor.

Franklin's letter helped Paine obtain employment with a Philadelphia printer, Robert Aitken, and he soon became editor of the *Pennsylvania Magazine*, a publication begun by Aitken but which was finding little success. About six months later Paine wrote to Franklin that many gentlemen had asked him to tutor their sons and that the circulation of the magazine had grown from six hundred subscribers to more than fifteen hundred. "Your countenancing me has obtained for me many friends and much reputation," he told Franklin.

Paine began as the editor of the *Pennsylvania Magazine* in February 1775. (It was the only journalistic position he ever held, and there is some dispute among historians as to how long he held it. By the summer of 1776 Paine and Aitken had severed this relationship.) It was a momentous time in American history, and Paine was located squarely in the middle of it. His writings for this magazine and for other publications established him as a strong voice for the grievances of the colonists and the growing independence movement.

One of the issues Paine used to make a name for himself was slavery, which he saw as inconsistent with the liberty that Americans were seeking from Great Britain. His characterization of slavery as being on the level of "murder, robbery, lewdness, and barbarity" put him on record as being a major liberal thinker and writer. His was one of the first American calls to make slaves free citizens. Not long after his article appeared in March 1775, the American Antislavery Society was founded in Philadelphia. Paine took on other issues such as dueling, cruelty to animals, and international copyright laws, and he advocated the use of labor-saving devices and methods to increase the productivity of soil. He also began what was to be a lifelong campaign against privilege—particularly that of royalty and the aristocracy. "The lustre of the Star, and the title of My Lord, overawe the superstitious vulgar, and forbid them to enquire into the character of the possessor. Nay more, they are, as it were, bewitched to admire in the great the vices they would honestly condemn in themselves," he wrote. Paine also wrote sympathetically about the plight of women and their legal exploitation.

Less than a month after his article on slavery appeared, American militia were fired on by British forces in Concord and Lexington, Massachusetts. In June Washington was appointed commander-in-chief of the Continental Army, and the day after that the Battle of Bunker Hill occurred just outside of Boston. The tide of events was drawing Americans toward an open conflict with the British, and Paine was swept along with it. By his own account he was a somewhat reluctant convert. He wrote to Franklin of his feelings at the time, saying, "I thought it very hard to have the country set on fire about my ears almost the moment I got to it." Still, when he joined the fray he did so with enthusiasm and skill, bringing to the rebellion his considerable powers of logic and articulation.

The idea of American independence fired Paine's imagination with possibility, and in October he wrote an article for the *Pennsylvania Journal* that put forth reasons why it should happen. He cited the barbaric treatment of the natives of India and America by the British and concluded, "When I reflect on these, I hesitate not for a moment to believe that the Almighty will finally separate America from Britain." Despite all that had occurred to that point in the growing conflict between Britain and her American colonies, few had been willing to call for an independent nation. Most believed that the differences would find some other resolution. Paine, however, recognized that any solution less than independence was no longer feasible. Without meaning to, both America and Britain had gone too far along the road to open conflict.

Paine more clearly delineated these thoughts in January 1776 with the publication of *Common Sense,* a forty-seven-page pamphlet that Paine had printed at his own expense. It was an extraordinary document that from all accounts had a major effect on the thinking of the day. *Common Sense* represented one of the first major calls for American independence in the colonies, and, although there had been earlier such calls (most notably by John Adams), the timing of Paine's writing was such that many were waiting to be convinced. The language was plain and simple, and the arguments were easy to follow and absorb. Ultimately the continent of America could not remain tied to the island of Britain. As an independent nation America would have enormous markets opened to its trade that were now closed by British restrictions. Paine piled reason upon reason for an independent America until the case was overwhelming.

Common Sense not only was well reasoned, but it was also well read. One estimate put its circulation at five hundred thousand, and, although it may not have been that high, it spread through the colonies rapidly and was widely quoted and reprinted. A second edition appeared late in January, and later that spring it was exported to France, where historians have speculated that it had even more effect on the populace than in America. It had originally been published anonymously, but its authorship soon became known, and Paine's fame and position were quickly established. *Common Sense* did nothing for Paine financially, however. Paine donated all of the proceeds from sales of the pamphlet to the American cause, and he continued to do this when the work was published in subsequent editions.

The nation's British sympathizers, the Tories, fashioned answers to Paine's writing, but they were easily rebuffed by Paine himself. Paine's arguments were soon taken up by others, and his work is widely credited as pushing the members of the Continental Congress toward establishing a committee to draft a declaration of independence. (Despite some speculation, Paine apparently had nothing directly to do with the writing of that document.)

Portrait of Paine in 1806 by his friend John Wesley Jarvis (courtesy of the National Gallery of Art)

Paine spent much of 1776 with the army, first as part of a "flying camp" of mobile volunteers and militia from New Jersey, Pennsylvania, and Maryland and then as an aide to Gen. Nathanael Greene. (Greene called Paine "a man who has genius in his eyes.") Wherever he was, he kept writing, and his accounts of the army's actions were printed in the *Pennsylvania Journal.* Despite the issuance of the Declaration of Independence in July and Paine's extraordinary journalistic successes, the year was not a good one for the ragtag American army. The lack of Congressional backing and necessary supplies, expiring enlistments and discouragement among the men, and the presence of an overwhelming British force had forced retreat after retreat until Washington's troops found themselves spending a harsh winter at Valley Forge, Pennsylvania.

In December Paine began working on the first of what was to be sixteen publications entitled *The American Crisis,* designed to answer the needs of the Revolutionary Army and the rebellious public as they appeared. Published from 1776 to 1783, these pamphlets established and maintained Paine's influential role as a political journalist. In them he rallied the public during the dark and depressing hours of the Revolution; he effectively answered arguments against continuing the fight; and he set forth many of his ideas for establishing a just government once the Americans had won. For instance, the second number appeared in January in answer to British envoy Lord Howe, who had issued proclamations calling for reconciliation. Paine exposed the British efforts as shallow in light of their previous actions, and he launched an attack on Tory sympathizers in America.

Soon after these first issues appeared Paine was appointed secretary to Congress. He had made little money with any of his writings, but making money—or even making a living—was something he rarely thought about. He had managed to survive without concentrating on his means, and he would continue to give scant attention to his finances for the rest of his life. He continued to write and to find publishers for his writing. What money he did make he often donated to the revolutionary cause. In 1780, for instance, he gave five hundred dollars to begin a subscription drive for salaries for Washington's army. His donation was meant to encourage others with greater means to do the same, and it was reasonably effective.

Paine's position with Congress drew him into a complicated controversy that damaged his standing with many connected with the American government. The controversy concerned France's official position in aiding the revolution and the greed of merchants and businessmen who supplied the army. Before France had openly supported the American Revolution, it had sent supplies to the rebels through private sources. Whether these supplies were a gift or whether they deserved payment was the point in dispute. Silas Deane, the American agent who negotiated the trade and who stood to gain from it personally, said the Continental Congress should pay the claim. Arthur Lee, an American Commissioner to France, disputed this claim. Paine involved himself in the controversy by publishing a letter in the *Pennsylvania Packet* attacking Deane as a profiteer. Supporters of Deane struck back, and Paine was forced to defend his charges. He did so by revealing confidential papers to which his position as Congressional secretary had given him access. What he revealed made it appear that France had supplied the Americans while the French were still officially under a peace

treaty with Great Britain. The French were offended, and Paine was forced to resign his position.

Paine's motive in entering this fray was to fight against corruption and war profiteering. Inadvertently, however, he had involved himself in a power struggle between radicals and conservatives, particularly in the state of Pennsylvania. The fight continued long after Paine's resignation, but, once he had committed himself to the fight, he continued writing articles attacking Deane and those who supported him. He defended the Pennsylvania constitution against efforts to change it in favor of big businessmen and monopolistic practices. In doing so Paine made powerful enemies who were ultimately able to do some damage to his reputation.

The faction for which Paine fought won a majority in the state legislature in October 1779, and Paine was given the job of assembly clerk. It was an important and influential appointment, allowing Paine access to high-ranking officials. In this position he authored a bill that provided for the gradual emancipation of slaves in the state, the first such measure passed in any of the thirteen colonies.

Paine also continued the publication of his *American Crisis* series, and he continued to write on other subjects in other pamphlets. In late 1780 the states were faced with ratification of a set of Articles of Confederation passed by the Continental Congress. Maryland and Virginia balked because of claims on western lands, and Paine's pamphlet *Public Good* took the states (particularly Virginia) to task, saying public lands should not belong to the states but to a central government. In later writings Paine again called for the formation of a strong central government, and it became central to his beliefs about the future of his adopted country.

The fight against the British was continuing, however, and much of Paine's efforts were directed toward helping America achieve victory. In February 1781 Paine accompanied Col. John Laurens to France. Laurens was given the delicate task of asking the French for more aid for the fight. Laurens was only twenty-six at the time and insisted that Paine travel with him. Laurens was the only one commissioned to negotiate with France, but he realized the value of having someone like Paine with him. Ultimately the mission was a success, and Laurens and Paine returned in June with cash and two shiploads of supplies. The gift had come directly from Louis XVI, and

Paine never forgot this generosity. The money allowed Washington to pay and resupply his troops, and within six months they had won the decisive victory at Yorktown.

Paine was not so fortunate personally. He had gone to France at his own expense, and in doing so he had given up his lucrative job with the Pennsylvania legislature. The end of the war found him with no resources and no income. He appealed to Washington for some help, and Washington signed an agreement allowing him eight hundred dollars a year to write favorably on the legislatures. Paine was to become a propagandist for the government, and the deal was to remain secret. By 1783 Congress had also given him some back pay of three thousand dollars for his work during the war, and in June 1784 he was awarded a farm in New Rochelle, New York, by the state legislature. In granting the appropriation Congress passed the measure with the pronouncement, "The early, unsolicited and continued labors of Mr. Thomas Paine, in explaining and enforcing the principles of the late revolution by ingenious and timely publications upon the nature of liberty and civil government, have been well received by the citizens of these states and merit the approbation of Congress."

These grants enabled Paine to live in comfortable retirement, which for a time he was content to do. He enjoyed horseback riding, but he continued his writing and soon involved himself in the bank crisis that was facing the new nation. He joined a movement to prevent the revocation of the charter of the Bank of North America, and in doing so he aligned himself with many of the monied interests that he had opposed during the war. Yet, he believed that the bank was what the states needed for their economic development, and to that end he authored *Dissertations on Government; The Affairs of the Bank; and Paper-Money*, a pamphlet published in February 1786. Paine and the probank forces ultimately won the battle, but again Paine's reputation suffered because he appeared to have turned against those whom he had previously supported.

Despite this foray into politics, Paine remained relatively inactive on the political scene for several years. Instead, he revived an interest in science and technology that he had acquired during his first days in London. Paine came up with the idea of an iron, single-arch bridge—one whose piers would not be crushed by ice packs that formed during the winter. Many people expressed an interest in the idea, but Paine could not obtain financial backing for it. He decided to seek such backing in Europe, and in April 1787 he set sail for France.

There he met with the American minister Thomas Jefferson, who shared his interest in innovation, and he submitted his design to the French Academy of Sciences. The academy endorsed it as a "new extension of the application of iron," but that endorsement did little to further its construction. Paine went to his native England to promote the project. He found more support there for his idea, but the politics of revolution began to distract him again. Paine was in Yorkshire during the fall of the Bastille in 1789, and he traveled to Paris later that year to view the situation for himself. He was enthralled by the democratic uprising that was taking place and was convinced that what was happening in France needed also to happen in England. During the next two years he alternated between those countries, doing what he could to promote such a revolution. (Paine's bridge was eventually built, but characteristically he received neither money nor credit for it.)

Paine was shocked at the publication of Edmund Burke's *Reflections on the French Revolution*, which appeared in November 1790. Burke had been much admired by Paine for his stance favoring the American position against England in 1775. Burke's latest writing, however, bitterly denounced the French revolution, and Paine felt that it needed an answer. The answer from Paine developed into what many consider to be his best political work, *Rights of Man* (1791-1792).

Part 1 of *Rights of Man* is a treatise on Paine's philosophy of government and its place in the lives of the people. The purpose of government, Paine wrote, is to secure for the people rights they cannot secure for themselves. Paine called for a republican form of government, a constitution with a bill of rights, manhood suffrage, the outlawing of privilege by birthright, and many other reforms that were eventually to come to pass in most democratic societies. *Rights of Man* was aimed directly at the English, however, and Paine hoped that it would do the same for England that *Common Sense* had done for America.

The work gained a wide circulation in England—by one account it had sold two hundred thousand copies by 1793—but it caused much concern among powerful men in that country. Burke was forced to reply to it, and this reply spurred Paine to write a second part in which he set forth numerous proposals for social legislation (such as a progressive income tax, relief for the poor, popular education, old-age pensions, and help for the unemployed) and appealed directly to the English for the overthrow of their monarchy. *Rights of Man* was surpressed by the government, and Paine barely escaped England before his arrest. He was tried in absentia and convicted of sedition in 1792.

Paine found France much more receptive to his ideas than England. There he had been given French citizenship (along with other American heroes of the Revolution, such as Washington, Alexander Hamilton, and James Madison), and he quickly involved himself in the turbulent events of that nation. He was elected as a representative to the French Convention and aligned himself with the moderate Girondists. The Convention had been formed primarily to decide what to do about Louis XVI, who had been captured trying to flee the country. A proposal to execute him was a popular one, and few politicians felt they were in a position to oppose it. Paine did, however. He felt that the king's execution would be used by opponents of revolution in England to suppress any rebellion there, and he remembered the support that the king had given to the Americans during a time of desperate need.

Paine's point of view did not prevail, and it is probably the case that Paine did not fully understand what was happening in France at the time. (Paine did not speak French and had to have his speeches translated.) The fight over the fate of the king was part of a larger battle among the political factions in France. When the Girondists were overthrown Paine attended fewer and fewer meetings of the Convention, and when Robespierre and his associates came to power Paine was arrested. Ironically, his arrest was justified on the grounds that he was a citizen of England, a country that had just convicted him of sedition.

Paine's imprisonment at Luxembourg was not harsh, but his fate was uncertain. Many of those with whom he associated were being executed, and Paine himself wrote that once he escaped execution through the mistake of a guard at the prison. Others have disputed this story, and the amount of danger that Paine faced is not clear. In any event, Paine appealed to American officials in France to secure his release, but the American minister to France at the time was Gouverneur Morris, a man with whom Paine had clashed during the Silas Deane affair during the war. Morris took few steps to get Paine out of prison, and Paine later blamed his prolonged imprisonment on the lax attitude of President Washington.

Paine was released in November 1794, after ten months in prison, when James Monroe relieved Morris as the American minister to France. Monroe took Paine, then weakened by illness, into his home and kept him for many months as his illness refused to abate. Eventually he recovered and found a new political climate in the nation. He was given his old seat in the Convention in 1795, and he was offered a pension, which he refused.

Just before his imprisonment Paine delivered to his friend Joel Barlow a new manuscript entitled *The Age of Reason* (1794). It was published while he was still incarcerated, but Paine continued to work on revisions while in Luxembourg. *The Age of Reason* examines theology and the prevailing Christianity of his day and begins with the simple deist declaration, "I believe in one God, and no more; and I hope for happiness beyond this life." Paine took Christianity to task as a religion, however. "Of all systems of religions that ever were invented, there is none more *derogatory to the Almighty,* more unedifying to man, more repugnant to reason, and more contradictory to itself than this thing called Christianity." Paine's attacks on the prevailing religion of the day were not totally original, but they were direct and far-reaching. The manner of his writing seemed as much to offend as to persuade, and offense was taken in many quarters.

Paine sent a copy of *The Age of Reason* to Jefferson, then vice-president, and Jefferson sent it to an American printer with an accompanying note about its uses against the "political heresies" of the time–meaning those of the Federalists. They, of course, were greatly offended by both Paine and Jefferson, and they took every opportunity to link Paine to Jefferson.

While still living with Monroe in Paris Paine wrote his last great political pamphlet, published in England and the United States as *Agrarian Justice, Opposed to Agrarian Law, and to Agrarian Monopoly . . .* (1797). This pamphlet contributed to the debate then current in France over land reform. Paine saw the earth as the common property of all humans, but he realized that cultivation of the land by some was necessary for the benefit of all. He proposed a system of land sharing that he felt supported the principle of common ownership and the need for private cultivation.

France soon had a new leader, Napoleon, and the antipathy between France and England was growing. Despite France's problems Paine had great faith that the country would remain true to its democratic revolution, and he hoped France would go to war with England to spark the same kind of revolution there. To this end he submitted a plan to the government for the invasion of England–a plan that caught the eye of Napoleon and caused him to visit Paine to discuss it.

As the situation in France developed, however, Paine realized that his influence was diminishing. He wanted to return to America and finally did so in October 1802. His return sparked fires in the Federalist newspapers. Paine was denounced as a "loathsome reptile," "lily-livered rogue," "the scavenger of faction," and "an object of disgust, of abhorrence, of absolute loathing to every decent man except the President of the United States." The president, then, was Jefferson, and he received Paine openly in the White House and discussed with him political and scientific issues.

Despite the warm reception by Jefferson, Paine was avoided by many he formerly considered friends. Attacks on him in the newspapers increased, and he withdrew to his farm in New Rochelle and surrounded himself with a small circle of like-minded friends. In 1806 he was denied the right to vote in New Rochelle by Federalist officials on the grounds that he was not an American citizen. Paine was poverty-stricken, and his vilification–particularly as a drunkard–by the Federalist press continued until his death on 8 June 1809. In a bizarre post-mortem twist to the story of Thomas Paine, the radical journalist William Cobbett disinterred Paine's body ten years later and transported it to England with the idea of building a monument to Paine there. The monument was never built, and when Cobbett died in 1835 all of his property passed into a receiver's hands. The court refused to regard Paine's remains as an asset, and they were acquired by a furniture dealer and eventually lost entirely.

In Thomas Paine, revolutionary, America found one of its most potent journalistic voices. Paine's writings commanded vast audiences, and friends and enemies alike attested to his influence. With his pen Paine helped to begin and sustain a revolution. Paine's reputation after his death has suffered in part because he seemed to care so little for it during his life. He took little heed of his finances or his personal appearance; he was sometimes abrupt personally and always direct in his writing; he was a man without a family but with a temperament that was apparently unable to sustain close, personal relationships. All of these factors countered the monumental thinking and writing that he contributed to his era.

Paine's effectiveness as a journalist was the result of his ideas and his style. He was a master of the newspaper debates that were common in his era. He could pick apart the arguments of others and could organize his own thinking into rapid-fire ammunition when the occasion called for it. His writing style was possibly the best and most persuasive of his day. He spurned the florid prose that was common among many journalists and wrote in a simple, direct manner. His phrases were memorable then and are remembered today. Twelve years after Paine's death Jefferson wrote, "No writer has exceeded Paine in ease and familiarity of style, in perspicuity of expression, happiness of elucidation, and in simple and unassuming language." Jefferson, an effective user of the written word himself, knew the strength of Thomas Paine.

Biographies:

Moncure Conway, *The Life of Thomas Paine*, 2 volumes (New York: Putnam's, 1892);

W. E. Woodward, *Tom Paine: America's Godfather, 1737-1809* (New York: Dutton, 1945);

Alfred O. Aldridge, *Man of Reason: The Life of Thomas Paine* (Philadelphia: Lippincott, 1959);

Audrey Williamson, *Thomas Paine: His Life, Work and Times* (London: Allen & Unwin, 1973);

David Freeman Hawk, *Paine* (New York: Harper & Row, 1974);

Eric Foner, *Tom Paine and Revolutionary America* (New York: Oxford University Press, 1976);

David Powell, *Tom Paine: The Greatest Exile* (London: Helm, 1985).

References:

Alfred O. Aldridge, "Some Writings of Thomas Paine in Pennsylvania Newspapers," *American Historical Review*, 56 (1951): 832-838;

Howard Penniman, "Thomas Paine–Democrat," *American Political Science Review*, 37 (1943): 244-262.

Edgar Allan Poe

(19 January 1809-7 October 1849)

John A. Lent
Third World Media Associates

See also the Poe entries in *DLB 3: Antebellum Writers in New York and the South* and *DLB 59: American Literary Critics and Scholars, 1800-1850.*

MAJOR POSITIONS HELD: Editor, *Southern Literary Messenger* (1835-1836); assistant editor, *Burton's Gentleman's Magazine* (1839-1840); literary editor, *Graham's Magazine* (1841-1842); reviewer, *New York Weekly Mirror* (1844-1845); coeditor, editor, publisher, *Broadway Journal* (1845).

BOOKS: *Tamerlane and Other Poems. By a Bostonian* (Boston: Calvin F. S. Thomas, 1827);
Al Aaraaf, Tamerlane, and Minor Poems (Baltimore: Hatch & Dunning, 1829);
Poems. By Edgar A. Poe. Second Edition (New York: Elam Bliss, 1831);
The Narrative of Arthur Gordon Pym, of Nantucket . . . , anonymous (New York: Harper, 1838; London: Wiley & Putnam, 1838);
Tales of the Grotesque and Arabesque, 2 volumes (Philadelphia: Lea & Blanchard, 1840);
The Prose Romances of Edgar A. Poe (Philadelphia: William H. Graham, 1843);
Tales (New York: Wiley & Putnam, 1845; London: Wiley & Putnam, 1845);
The Raven and Other Poems (New York: Wiley & Putnam, 1845; London: Wiley & Putnam, 1846);
Eureka: A Prose Poem (New York: Putnam, 1848; London: Chapman, 1848).
Collections: *The Works of the Late Edgar Allan Poe: With Notices of his Life and Genius,* edited by Rufus Wilmot Griswold, 4 volumes (New York: J. S. Redfield, 1850-1856);
The Complete Works of Edgar Allan Poe, edited by James A. Harrison, 17 volumes (New York: Thomas Y. Crowell, 1902);
The Poems of Edgar Allan Poe, edited by Floyd Stovall (Charlottesville: University Press of Virginia, 1965);
Collected Works of Edgar Allan Poe, edited by Thomas Ollive Mabbott, 3 volumes (Cam-

bridge: Belknap Press of Harvard University Press, 1969-1978);
The Short Fiction of Edgar Allan Poe: An Annotated Edition, edited by Stuart Levine and Susan Levine (Indianapolis: Bobbs-Merrill, 1976);
Collected Writings of Edgar Allan Poe, volume 1, *The Imaginary Voyages: The Narrative of Arthur Gordon Pym, The Unparalleled Adventure of One Hans Pfaall, The Journal of Julius Rodman,* edited by Burton R. Pollin (Boston & New York: Twayne, 1981);

Essays and Reviews, edited by G. R. Thompson (New York: Library of America, 1984);

Poetry and Tales, edited by Patrick F. Quinn (New York: Library of America, 1984);

Collected Writings of Edgar Allan Poe, volume 2, *The Brevities: Pinakidia, Marginalia, Fifty Suggestions and Other Works,* edited by Pollin (New York: Gordian Press, 1985).

The story of Edgar Allan Poe's life remains one of the most disputed and slandered in the pages of American biography, despite conscious attempts to revise the story and rehabilitate the life. Decadence and immorality, in the form of alcoholism, opium addiction, and his relationships with women, and prolific production, as a journalist, editor, poet, reviewer, critic, and fiction writer, have been emphasized as characterizing his brief life.

Although very few authors have been written about as often as Poe, little is known of his whereabouts for months, or his activities and their motives. Some of the mystery was the doing of Poe himself. Hungering for literary fame, Poe, by acting at times as his own publicist, purposively misled and sensationalized. For example, invoking Byronic images, he passed himself off as an adventurer who traveled to South America or as a soldier of fortune who went to Russia to join rebel forces. He confused the record further by adopting assumed names: "Henri Le Rennent" as a teenager; "Edgar A. Perry" as a military enlistee; later, "Peter Prospero," "Sylvio Quarles," "E. S. T. Grey," "Thaddeus Perley," and "Lyttleton Barry."

Poe had much help in twisting the facts. Probably most damaging to how he has been remembered was a biographical sketch written by the Reverend Rufus Griswold, an editor appointed by Poe to be his literary executor. Poe had given Griswold a memorandum from which to write a biography. Upon Poe's death Griswold used the document to write an obituary in the *New York Tribune.* Shortly, he followed up with a fifty-page memoir, detailing Poe's life in very unjust terms. This sketch subsequently was used by many biographers, some already prejudiced adversely by tales of Poe's personal life, as well as by his unsavory literary subjects. Haldeen Braddy explains that Poe was maligned also because he was the "first great literary exponent in America of a way of life for the artist in opposition to Puritan tradition."

Poe's productivity belittles, if not belies, some of the claims of utter debauchery credited to him. Not many literary figures have left the written legacy of Poe. In twenty years he wrote at least 70 short stories, 62 poems, and over 250 critical and miscellaneous pieces–about 400 items in all. Braddy writes of Poe's prolific nature: "To have written and rewritten so much in uncomfortable surroundings, with insecure prospects for the morrow, and with never an abundance of food for his family is an incredible accomplishment."

Most of this body of literature was the fastidious work of a perfectionist. All of his work, but especially his poetry, is remarkable for its preciseness, although his prose shows the same dedication to brevity and experimentation. Poe liked to tinker, and he is considered by many to be the father of the American short story and mystery thriller.

In journalism his innovations were equally impressive. Poe helped make the magazine the main vehicle for literary fare during what became known as the "golden age" of magazine journalism. He is credited with coining the term "magazinist" to identify himself and other literary people who contributed to these periodicals. Almost everything Poe wrote was for the thirty magazines to which he contributed. He also was an editor of two magazines. Although his dream of establishing the "perfect" magazine never materialized, Poe's contributions to existing magazines changed the medium. Especially different was his literary criticism, noted for its severity and minute scrutiny.

Edgar Allan Poe was born to stage parents in Boston on 19 January 1809. Before he was three his father, David Poe, Jr., disappeared; then his mother, Elizabeth, died. The three Poe children were split up among Richmond relatives and friends, Edgar becoming the charge of a merchant, John Allan, and his wife, Frances. Despite bitter differences with his foster son later, Allan had dreams of Edgar becoming a cultured gentleman. He assured that the boy maintained a prosperous life-style and received a thorough education. Childless at that time, he groomed Poe to be his heir.

In 1815 Allan, hoping to expand his business, took his family to England where Poe began his formal education, first at the London school of the Dubourg sisters and, later, that of the Reverend John Bransby. He was considered an excellent student. When Allan's firm did not

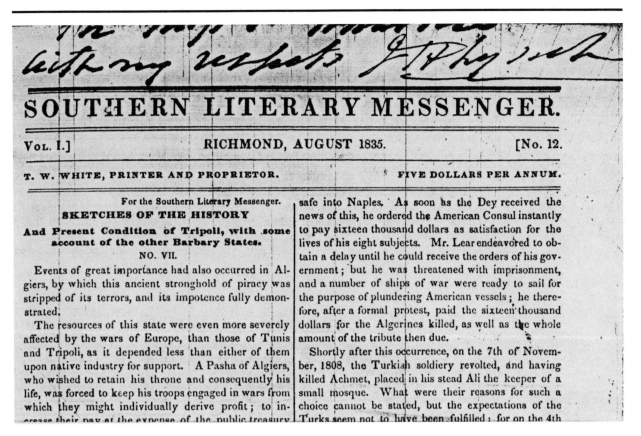

Head title of the leading southern journal of its time

achieve the success he had hoped for, the family returned to Richmond in 1820. Poe was enrolled in the school of Joseph H. Clarke for two years and then William Burke's academy, from which in 1825 he was removed to be tutored for admission to the University of Virginia. In February 1826 he started his studies in that university's schools of ancient and modern languages. He did well in classes, but, being only seventeen, he did not use mature judgment in other matters, running up debts at gambling tables and with local merchants. Allan bailed him out of some debts–those that he considered legitimate–but left others outstanding. By this time Poe and his foster father quarreled often, and Allan decided not to send him back to the university. Angry, Poe left the Allan home and gave his mailing address as a tavern in the name of "Henri Le Rennent."

Financially and domestically disgraced, as he was to be many times later, Poe left Richmond in April 1827, headed for Boston. Looking for a way out, he did the desperate act of generations of impetuous youth: he joined the army. His enlistment for a five-year stint was under a second new name, "Edgar A. Perry." That year, before

he was eighteen years old, he became a published author, having arranged the printing of *Tamerlane and Other Poems. By a Bostonian.*

Poe's intelligence even put him in good stead in the military, where, within eighteen months, he advanced to the highest non-commissioned rank. Encouraged by friends, he decided to become an officer by entering West Point. But first a reconciliation with his foster father was necessary in order to have this influential person's endorsement, not to mention his financial backing. While waiting for word from West Point Poe went to Baltimore in May 1829 to visit his brother Henry, his aunt Maria Clemm, and her daughter Virginia. While there he submitted a batch of new poems to Carey, Lea and Carey in Philadelphia, which agreed to publish them if Poe guaranteed payment for any financial losses. Again he approached Allan for money but was turned down. Poe withdrew the poems and submitted them to a Baltimore publisher, Hatch and Dunning, which published *Al Aaraaf, Tamerlane, and Minor Poems* in December 1829.

In the summer of 1830 he was informed that West Point had accepted him. In his first term Poe stood third in French and fifth in mathematics among his fellow cadets, but as usual he piled up debts. Again his foster father refused to come to his aid. Poe, who by then was drinking alone in his room, asked Allan's permission to resign from West Point, threatening that if permission were not given, he planned to disobey orders, necessitating a court-martial. In early 1831 he got his wish; he was court-martialed and dismissed. Poe proceeded to New York and, brazen as ever, wrote Allan for money. He also requested a letter of recommendation from the West Point commandant, so he could travel to Paris to enlist in the Polish Revolution. Meanwhile *Poems. By Edgar A. Poe. Second Edition* appeared under the imprint of Elam Bliss.

In May 1831 Poe returned to Baltimore and applied for his first editorial job, a post on the *Federal Gazette*, vacated by a cousin, Neilson Poe. Failing to obtain this position, and that of teacher at a local boys' school, he joined the Clemm household, consisting of his aunt, her children, and his grandmother. Poe's stay of four years in Baltimore–one of his longest habitats in his adult life–was marred by a hand-to-mouth existence. His only income came from odd jobs of copy editing and news reporting and an occasional sale of his fiction, which began to appear in periodicals in 1831. Five of Poe's tales, submitted for a contest which he did not win and carried in the *Philadelphia Saturday Courier* throughout 1832, marked his beginnings as a magazinist.

The record of his life in 1832 is more rumor than fact. One story said he enlisted in the army for a second time and was tossed out. Poe's version was that he went to St. Petersburg, Russia, intending to join the Greek revolt, but ran out of money and was sent home by U.S. diplomatic officials. What is fairly certain is that Poe was in miserable straits, reportedly starving and in ill health. Also it is a fact that he continued to write new and repackage old material. In 1833 he sought publication in the *New England Magazine* of what he called "Eleven Tales of the Arabesque," made up of the five tales published in the *Saturday Courier* and six others he submitted to a contest in the *Baltimore Saturday Visiter*. One of the tales, "MS Found in a Bottle," captured the first prize of fifty dollars and, along with a Poe poem, appeared in the October 1833 edition of the magazine.

Poe's entry in the *Saturday Visiter* contest was fortunate in another way, for he met one of the contest's judges, the novelist John Pendleton Kennedy, who encouraged him to submit one of the

Front cover for the issue in which publisher T. W. White announced that Poe would assist him in editorial matters

tales, "The Visionary" (later retitled "The Assignation"), to *Godey's Lady's Book*. Its appearance in that magazine in January 1834 was Poe's first publication in a widely circulated journal. Additionally Kennedy wrote a letter on Poe's behalf to T. W. White, publisher of the *Southern Literary Messenger*, soon after the magazine was established in Richmond; as a result Poe's "Berenice" was published in the March 1835 number. The magazine asked for more of Poe's work and offered him regular reviewing assignments.

The deaths of his foster father in 1834, who excluded him from his will, and his grandmother a year later, whose pension he could not depend upon any longer, forced Poe to look for more stable employment. He moved to Richmond where White offered him ten dollars a week salary, plus payment by the column for literary contributions to the *Southern Literary Messenger*.

While at the *Messenger* Poe was described as subject to despondency and states of "brutish drunkenness." In September 1835, after only a month, he left the *Messenger*, returned to Baltimore, and applied for a license to marry his thirteen-year-old cousin, Virginia Clemm. This impulsive act was brought on by a letter from his Aunt Maria, intimating that Virginia was to be adopted by another relative. He brought his aunt and future bride to Richmond, paid for their living in a boardinghouse at nine dollars a week, and sought back his *Messenger* position. White rehired him on the condition that the contract would be dissolved "the moment you get drunk." No doubt Poe hustled to keep his "family" together. Between the time of his first appearance in the *Messenger* in the spring of 1835 and the following spring Poe submitted revised versions of seven old stories, eight new poems, and seven new stories. In one year on the *Messenger* as an editor he wrote more than one hundred reviews and editorials, including a current literary events column and a series of partially satiric sketches of literary personalities, and he began his "Autography" series–176 contributions in all. He also kept busy doing the chores of editing, corresponding, and proofing necessary to bring out a magazine.

By December 1835 he was no longer just White's assistant, but a *Messenger* editor, with an increase in salary to $780 a year. His reviews built the magazine into the leading southern critical journal, and circulation increased from five hundred to thirty-five hundred. (Poe gave the increased figure as fifty-five hundred.) However, after the October and November 1836 issues were late and that of December failed to materialize, White announced in the January 1837 number that Poe's editorial duties with the *Messenger* were over. He said Poe would "continue to furnish its columns, from time to time, with the effusions of his vigorous and popular pen"; but eight years passed before Poe contributed another signed article to the *Messenger*.

Reasons given for the split-up varied. Poe provided at least three, saying it resulted from "being completely intoxicated" for days, or "the wretched taste of its proprietor which hampered and controlled me at all points," or "the drudgery [which] was excessive; the salary contemptible." Other reasons have been offered, including that his stringent reviews had made enemies for the *Messenger* and that Poe believed he could not cast the magazine's individuality because he had no proprietary interest in it. On the latter he was

wrong. The *Messenger* was changed drastically during Poe's short tenure, and the southern press was ecstatic in its praise of the journal, especially after Poe attacked the Knickerbocker clique of New York.

The timing of his departure was unfortunate; because of inflation some established magazines had stopped publishing. Nevertheless, Poe continued to seek his literary fortunes, this time in New York, where he was not very successful as a free-lance writer, completing a large critical article for the *New York Review*, two short stories, and a novel, *The Narrative of Arthur Gordon Pym* (1838), which began as a serialized work in the January and February 1836 *Messenger*. In 1838 *American Museum* in Baltimore published Poe's story "Ligeia" and "The Haunted Palace," one of his finest poems.

That same year he met William E. Burton, an actor who had recently founded *Burton's Gentleman's Magazine*. Poe was offered ten dollars a week for two hours daily on the journal beginning in May 1839. He was free to spend the rest of his time writing literary works. Apparently Burton was not enthusiastic about hiring Poe, but, because he had theatrical engagements that beckoned, he needed editorial assistance. In a letter to Poe on 30 May 1839 Burton expressed his reservations, saying "you must get rid of your avowed ill-feelings toward your brother authors." He said friends had warned him of Poe's "uncalled for severity in criticism." All of this was strange coming from Burton, who was a very harsh critic himself, admitting to such in his letter to Poe.

The one year he remained with Burton, Poe wrote 126 reviews and a few articles and revised or reprinted earlier work. His two most important literary works used by *Gentleman's Magazine* were "The Fall of the House of Usher" in September 1839 and the sonnet "Silence" in April 1840. He also contributed humorous pieces to the magazine, including "Peter Pendulum, The Business Man" and "The Philosophy of Furniture," in which he claimed Americans had no concept of interior decorating.

Rufus Griswold said Poe had allowed *Gentleman's Magazine* to fall behind schedule as he "prepared the prospectus of a new monthly, and obtained transcripts of his subscription and account books, to be used in a scheme for supplanting him [Burton]." In this instance Griswold is partially correct, for on 13 June 1840 Poe announced his plans for a new periodical, "Penn Magazine," to appear in January 1841.

Messenger. We are grieved, and mortified to hear that you cannot again contribute to its pages but your objection in respect to receiving a copy without equivalent is untenable — any one of your pieces already published in our Journal being more than an equivalent to a subscription *in perpetuo*. This we say as publishers, without any intention to flatter, and having reference merely to the sum usually paid, to writers of far less reputation for articles immeasurably inferior.

In respect to your question touching the Editor of the Messenger, I have to reply that, for the last six months, the Editorial duties have been undertaken by myself. Of course, therefore, I plead guilty to all the criticisms of the Journal during the period mentioned. In addition to what evidence of misconception on the part of your friends you will assuredly find in the January number, I have now only to say that sincere admiration of the book reviewed was the predominant feeling in my bosom while penning the review

It would afford me the highest gratific"n should I find that you acquit me of this "foul charge". I will look with great anxiety for your reply.

Very resp⁵ & truly

Yᵉ Ob. Sᵗ.

Edgar A. Poe

Final page of Poe's letter of 12 April 1836 to Lydia H. Sigourney, responding to her unfavorable criticism of a Poe critique that appeared in Southern Literary Messenger *(American Art Association/Anderson Galleries, Inc., Catalogue #4240, 11-12 March 1936)*

Poe and Burton, both vain and hot-tempered, were not destined to work together amicably. Burton thought Poe was intemperate; Poe considered Burton dishonest and resented the "absentee editor." By the spring of 1840 tension between the two was intense. Burton, claiming Poe owed him one hundred dollars, docked his wages. Poe, saying the loans amounted to sixty dollars, refused to pay a cent more. In a 30 May 1840 letter to Poe, Burton said he could "no longer afford to pay fifty dollars per month for two or three pages of M.S.," to which Poe responded it was more like eleven pages, plus numerous other editorial duties. They parted company in mid 1840, with Poe believing he had been slandered by accusations of excessive drinking. He did not bring suit because, as he wrote to a physician friend, "If I sue, he sues; you see how it is."

Burton sold his magazine in October 1840 to George R. Graham, who merged it with the *Casket* to form *Graham's Magazine*. Poe joined *Graham's* in February 1841 to ready the April issue. His post was literary editor in charge of book reviews; his literary works brought him extra remuneration. His eight hundred dollars per year salary was not as miserly as some biographers claimed. However, among literary contributors, even on the usually well-paying *Graham's*, Poe was low man, receiving four or five dollars per page. "The Gold Bug," perhaps the first American detective story, was accepted at four dollars per page. Before its publication, however, Poe withdrew the work and entered it in a contest where he won the one hundred dollar prize.

Graham sought to produce a first-rate periodical, hiring qualified editors and seeking the best literary talent, including Henry Wadsworth Longfellow, James Russell Lowell, William Cullen Bryant, James Fenimore Cooper, and Poe. The magazine featured writers' names on the cover, used illustrations, and, in an effort to appeal to women, had fashion plates, domestic scenes, and sentimental love stories. The fifteen months Poe was with *Graham's* were, and here Griswold is correct, "One of the most active and brilliant periods of his literary life." His contributions appeared in each of the numbers from April 1841 through June 1842 and included "Murders in the Rue Morgue," "A Descent into the Maelstrom," "To Helen," "The Masque of the Red Death," and others. Additionally Poe did some of his most trenchant criticism while with *Graham's* and contributed his "Autography" series

and papers on cryptology and cyphers. The "Autography" series attempted to illustrate character through analysis of handwriting. His cryptology series was developed on the assumption that humans could not develop secret writing that human ingenuity could not decipher.

Graham's circulation grew from five thousand to forty thousand and, in the words of press historian Frank Luther Mott, "became one of the three or four most important magazines in the United States." Mott says that during Poe's tenure the magazine "displayed a brilliance which has seldom been matched in American magazine history." It would seem the type of periodical that Poe wanted to be associated with, yet he left, again in disgust. He had differences with fellow editor Charles J. Peterson over what he termed the "namby-pamby character of the magazine." More specifically, Poe was disgruntled because he thought Graham had reneged on a promise to help Poe launch "Penn Magazine." He said: "Every exertion made by myself for the benefit of 'Graham,' rendered that mag. a greater source of profit, rendered the owner, at the same time, less willing to keep his word to me." George Woodberry said Poe's success on *Graham's* "put an end to the other scheme [he] had most at heart," meaning "Penn Magazine." To see the chance of publishing his own dream magazine slip away must have been very disheartening to a person such as Poe who craved independence. The summer he left *Graham's*, Poe wrote F. W. Thomas: "To coin one's brain into silver, at the nod of a master, is to my thinking the hardest task in the world."

But other reasons for Poe's departure might have been his own precarious mental and physical health, worry about his wife's poor health, and his drinking lapses. He may have needed more money as well. In 1841 Poe wrote a friend in Washington, D.C., that he was "disgusted" with *Graham's*, asking him to seek a clerkship there. Poe said he was poor and needed the job.

As he had no full-time position Poe's published work was slight in 1843. This was usual when he was not attached and could not command an immediate channel of publication. The places where he did publish did not provide much income. In 1843, for example, his contributions to magazines brought him three hundred dollars, ten dollars of which came from the *Whig Review* for publication rights to "The Raven." However, the poem appeared first in the *Evening*

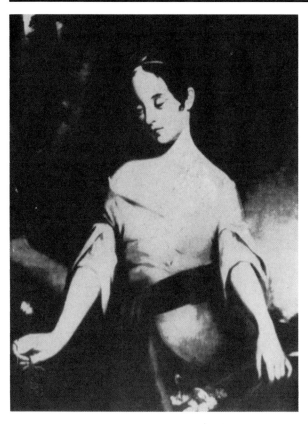

Portrait of Virginia Clemm Poe by Thomas Sully (courtesy of the Pierpont Morgan Library)

Mirror, which had merely clipped it from advance sheets the *Whig Review* had provided.

While still in Philadelphia Poe worked on a weekly, the *Saturday Museum*, which in an extra of 1 March 1843 listed him as a staff member and announced: "We have secured, at a high salary, the services of Edgar A. Poe, Esq., a gentleman whose high and versatile abilities have always spoken promptly for themselves, and who, after the first of May, will aid us in the editorial conduct of the Journal." The *Museum* planned a larger role for Poe–that of associate editor–which he had no intention of accepting. Some of his prose and verse appeared in the *Museum*, but, for the most part, Poe seemed to use the periodical to publicize his second proposed magazine, the "Stylus." In March 1843 he wrote James Russell Lowell, "I am *not* editing this paper, although an announcement was prematurely made to that effect; but have the privilege of inserting what I please editorially." Between 1843 and 1845 Poe also had editorial privileges with the *Citizen Soldier* of Philadelphia.

After Poe left *Graham's*, which was based in Philadelphia, he shifted his activities toward Bos-

ton, a city whose literary figures he had blasted often over the years. He sent tales to the *Boston Mammoth Notion, Boston Miscellany*, and the *Pioneer*, edited by Lowell, with whom he developed a cordial correspondence. In fact he requested a regular contributor slot on the *Pioneer*. The January 1843 debut issue of Lowell's magazine included Poe's "The Tell-Tale Heart." Lowell later introduced Poe to Charles Briggs, founder of the *Broadway Journal*.

Poe returned to New York in April 1844, where, still without salary, he depended on selling his work to newspapers and magazines. The month of his arrival one of his hoaxes appeared as an extra of the *New York Sun*. "The Balloon Hoax," which claimed eight people in a balloon crossed the Atlantic in three days, created a sensation that amused Poe. At this time he regularly wrote for the Pennsylvania-based *Columbia Spy* as its New York correspondent.

In 1845 Poe was affiliated in more than a contributory way with three periodicals–*Aristidean, Mirror*, and *Broadway Journal. Aristidean*, of which six numbers appeared, was published by Dr. Thomas Dunn English and several collaborators, one of whom was Poe. Perhaps Poe contributed a few reviews to the *Aristidean*, but he and English eventually had a bitter showdown. In the July 1846 *New York Evening Mirror*, English, after being embarrassed by Poe, accused him of being, among other things, a forger. Poe sued and was awarded $225 in libel damages.

Poe became associated with the *Mirror* in September 1844, when Nathaniel Parker Willis and George Pope Morris established the *Weekly Mirror* as a supplement to the daily *Evening Mirror*. After Poe's death Willis wrote of the connection: "Some four or five years since, when editing a daily paper in this city, Mr. Poe was employed by us, for several months, as critic and subeditor.... He ... was at his desk in the office, from nine in the morning till the evening paper went to press. With the highest admiration for his genius, and a willingness to let it atone for more than ordinary irregularity, we were led by common report to expect a very capricious attention to his duties, and occasionally a scene of violence and difficulty. Time went on, however, and he was invariably punctual and industrious.... With a prospect of taking the lead in another periodical, he, at last, voluntarily gave up his employment with us."

Poe stayed with the *Mirror* until February 1845, mainly as a critic. Willis, despite the kind

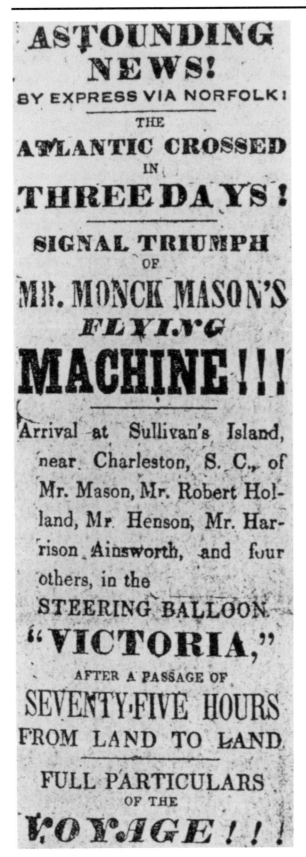

Head title for Poe's balloon hoax in the New York Sun,
13 April 1844

words of his eulogy, also referred to Poe as a "mechanical paragraphist." Poe got his licks in, too; soon after Poe moved to the *Broadway Journal*, the magazine featured an illustration of Willis and Morris preening themselves before a mirror. However, Poe had a high regard for Willis, considering him a real magazinist. It was not until Willis and Morris had withdrawn as publishers of the *Mirror* that Poe sued English and the *Mirror* for libel.

While still with the *Mirror* Poe began writing for the *Broadway Journal*, which began publication on 4 January 1845. Published by Charles F. Briggs, the *Broadway Journal*, a New York weekly of art, literature, and sciences, carried Poe's work in its first two numbers, after which Briggs made Poe a coeditor. Additionally Poe was given partial ownership of the journal with no investment required; he had a salary arrangement by which he received one-third of the editorial shares of profit. Poe called this "a third pecuniary interest." Briggs justified hiring Poe in a May letter to Lowell, saying he needed the editorial help while he handled the business end of the magazine. He recognized that Poe's name had "some authority," although he had "mounted a very ticklish hobby just now, Plagiarism, which he is bent on riding to death." This was a reference to the "Longfellow War," in which Poe accused the famous poet of plagiarism. Briggs added that Poe would be "only an assistant to me and will in no way interfere with my own way of doing things."

Poe contributed little of his work to the *Broadway Journal*, except for a considerable number of stories and poems previously published elsewhere. In the second half of the year the magazine carried a lot of Poe's reprints, some signed "Lyttleton Barry."

When no issue appeared during the first week of July, Briggs said Poe was on a "drunken spree, and conceived the idea that I had not treated him well." Briggs had written to Lowell on 29 June that he was getting a new publisher for the *Broadway Journal* and wanted to "haul down Poe's name" because he had gotten into "his old habits." However, when the magazine resumed on 12 July, it was Briggs's name that was hauled down; an editorial note reported: "The editorial conduct of the *Broadway Journal* is under the sole charge of Mr. E. A. Poe—Mr. H. C. Watson as heretofore controlling the Musical Department." By October John Bisco, a copublisher along with Poe and Watson, gave up on the journal and sold his interest to Poe for fifty dollars.

Of course Poe had no cash but gave Bisco a note which Horace Greeley had endorsed; the loan was never repaid to Greeley.

The *Broadway Journal* was described by George Woodberry as showing "vigorous management," and, while advertising increased, circulation dwindled. Poe found it increasingly difficult to keep it afloat, borrowing more money in November and inducing Thomas H. Lane to buy one-half interest. He steadily became disenchanted: his own reviews showed a deterioration in quality, and by mid December he had lost interest in the magazine altogether. Its "valedictory" appeared in the last December number thus: "Unexpected engagements demanding my whole attention, and the objects being fulfilled so far as regards myself personally, for which 'The Broadway Journal' was established, I now, as its editor, bid farewell–as cordially to foes as to friends. EDGAR A. POE." The last number was published on 3 January 1846.

Throughout the remainder of his life Poe was a contributor to, rather than editor of, periodicals, but through all the travails he faced the dream of his own magazine was not abandoned. The *Broadway Journal* was the closest Poe came to achieving that goal.

If the key literary personalities delighted in thinking that Poe without an editorship would spare them from his brutal attacks, they did not harbor that thought for long. In May 1846 *Godey's Lady's Book* published the first of six installments of his "The Literati of New York City," which, according to Mott, "pitilessly deflated" some of the greatest literary reputations in the country. The first installment had to be reprinted to meet the demand for copies, and so much commotion was caused by the series, *Godey's* printed a disavowal: "We have nothing to do but publish Mr. Poe's opinions–not our own." The quarrel with Dr. English, culminating in the libel suit, resulted partly because of Poe's reference to him in the series as "an ass." Poe's book reviews from 1845 until the end of his journalistic career showed the same scurrility and often vengeful resolve. Robert Jacobs wrote that these reviews "belong largely to the history of his controversies. Occasionally he did make an evaluation on the basis of his established principles, but often it was done in a captious manner that did not reflect his ideal standard of scientific objectivity in criticism."

Throughout the latter part of 1846 Poe lived with destitution and illness. Press reports mentioned his dire plight, and Willis, in the *Home Journal* for 26 December, called for a hospital for impoverished authors, mentioning Poe by name. Poe wrote to friends asking for handouts, telling them he and his wife were seriously ill and claiming he was the subject of much personal abuse in the journals. His wife died on 30 January 1847; he was dangerously ill afterwards. For a year Poe was seldom in the public notice.

As 1848 commenced Poe displayed renewed energy, working on his *Eureka: A Prose Poem*, published that year, issuing a prospectus for the "Stylus," and lecturing. *Union Magazine* published "An Enigma" in March and "To Helen" in November, and other works appeared in the *Columbian Lady's and Gentleman's Magazine, Graham's, Home Journal*, and *Southern Literary Messenger*. But during that fall Poe was at one of his lowest physical ebbs. Throughout the year he corresponded, and eventually forced a conditional engagement, with a poetess, Sarah Helen Whitman–the condition being he abstain from alcohol. Just before the marriage in late December he broke his promise and she, the engagement. On the rebound a few months later Poe announced his love for a happily married woman, Annie Richmond. In July he proposed marriage to an early love, Sarah Elmira Royster, by then the widowed, wealthy Mrs. Alexander B. Shelton.

In February 1849 Poe began contributing to the *Flag of Our Union*, a widely circulated Boston paper that paid well. In fact Poe wrote to Annie Richmond that the *Flag of Our Union* was "not a *very* respectable journal, perhaps, in a literary point of view, but one that pays as high prices as most of the Magazines."

A number of magazines published reprints or new works of Poe's in 1849. *Graham's* ran his "Fifty Suggestions"; the *Home Journal*, "For Annie"; *Sartain's Union Magazine*, "A Valentine"; and *Southern Literary Messenger*, "Marginalia." The *Messenger* had offered Poe an arrangement in 1845 by which he was to contribute a critical article monthly at three dollars per page. A series by him was announced in the April 1845 issue, but it never materialized. He did submit a satire, "The Editor of the Goosetherumfoodle," which the editor paid for but did not use. The *Messenger* published "The Literary Life of Thingum Bob" in December 1844 and reprinted "The Raven" in March 1845. Mott says Poe contributed nearly all of his important criticism to the *Messenger* during the last thirteen months of his life.

THE BROADWAY JOURNAL.

VOL. 1. NEW YORK, SATURDAY, JANUARY 4, 1845. N° 1.

Truth, whether in or out of fashion, is the measure of knowledge and the business of the understanding; whatsoever is beside that, however authorized by consent or recommended by variety, is nothing but ignorance, or something worse.

LOCKE.

INTRODUCTORY.

There is but one way of coming into the world, says Dean Swift, although there are a great many ways of going out of it, and we wish there were but one way of coming before the public in a newspaper for the first time; that we might be spared the possibility of a blunder in our first appearance, by following in the line of safe precedents. But since we are left to our own discretion, and have no kind friend to take us by the hand and present us to our dear friend, the Public, we will tell our own story as shortly as possible.

It is not improbable that somebody may object to our name, and exclaim with Milton's Stall-reader,

Bless us, what a word on
A title page is this!

but we have chosen it for the sake of individuality, and because it is indigenous, and furthermore is indicative of the spirit which we intend shall characterise our paper. Broadway is confessedly the finest street in the first city of the New World. It is the great artery through which flows the best blood of our system. All the elegance of our continent permeates through it. If there is a handsome equipage set up, its first appearance is made in Broadway. The most elegant shops in the City line its sides; the finest buildings are found there, and all fashions exhibit their first gloss upon its sidewalks. Although it has a character of its own, the traveller often forgets himself in walking through it, and imagines himself in London or Paris. Wall street pours its wealth into its broad channel, and all the dealers in intellectual works are here centered; every exhibition of art is found here, and the largest caravanseries in the world border upon it. Its pavement has been trod by every distinguished man that has visited our continent; those who travel through it are refreshed by the most magnificent fountains in the world. It has a sunny side too, where we have opened our office of delivery. It terminates at one end in the finest square in the city, doubtless in the Union, and at the other in the Battery, unrivalled for its entire beauty, by any marine parade in the world. So travellers say. For ourselves, we have seen many in the old world and the new, but none that equal it. As Paris is France, and London, England; so is Broadway, New York; and New York is fast becoming, if she be not already, America, in spite of South Carolina and Boston.

We have little hope of making our paper among other journals, what Broadway is among other streets, but we shall do what we can to render it in some degree worthy of the name that we have given it. We are fully aware that "we have a reasonable quantity of giants" to encounter in our undertaking, and that we have to rely more upon good intentions than good weapons to overcome them, but it must be an unreasonably tall giant that shall overcome our perseverance in the end.

In the conduct of our paper we shall follow the advice of Isocrates to his pupils, and "study the people," but rather with a view to profit them than ourselves. We have a prodigious respect for the people, tempered with no small amount of love, but we think with Falstaff, "that either well-bearing, or ignorant carriage, is caught, as men take diseases, one of another; therefore it is well to take heed of our company;" and we shall chose rather to talk to the people than with them. We do not arrogate to ourselves the character of a reformer; yet, we hope to reform some of the abuses which we sometimes hear spoken of as existing among us. The husbandman who never pulls up a weed in his garden can never hope to see them all removed from his enclosures.

We shall endeavor to make our paper entirely original,—and, instead of the effete vapors of English Magazines, which have heretofore been the chief filling of our weekly journals, give such homely thoughts as may be generated among us; and if our columns do not smack of home, it will be because "our spirits have been so married in conjunction with the participation of *foreign* society," that we cannot procure a divorce.

As we are entirely disconnected with any of the traders in literature, and have no personal friends among our literary producers,—saving an illustrious name or two, in Mr. Griswold's Pantheon—we have no inducements to indulge in the luxury of puffing; but we entertain so kindly a feeling towards the whole brood of unfortunates, called American authors, that we can never find it in our hearts to utter an ill word of them, or to treat them otherwise than with honest candor.

Although our daily and weekly press often contain admirable criticisms on literature and art, with the spirit of a quarterly review compressed into the limits of a half column, yet these are rather accidental than a general rule, and the public, in many cases, must submit to the actual cautery of buying and reading a new book before they can judge of its quality. There are too many good things to be had for time and money, to waste these precious commodities on uncertain productions. A sixpence worth of honest criticism will often save a dollar, or an hour, from being misspent.

We shall devote a good part of our columns to the interests of American Art; especially to Painting and Architecture,—and shall give specimens of American designs, in both departments, as often as they can be procured of sufficient merit to entitle them to notice.

The Lecture room, the Concert, and the Theatre, will all be dealt with; and though we hoist the signal of no political party, we shall dabble in politics when there is any thing in the wind worth heeding.

As the refinement of modern times has given birth to a ladies' literature, which, out of compliment to [illegible] made as unmeaning as possible, we shall so far conform to the complexion of the times as to have a LADIES' LEAF, wherein we shall do our best to be very lady-like and innocent. We can promise all, both ladies and gentlemen, that we shall raise no blushes on the cheek of modesty, because modest people are not easily put out of countenance; but the salacious and foul-minded are always changing colour. Our pen has two ends to it, and if we sometimes fail to

2 THE BROADWAY JOURNAL.

make an impression with the point, we shall occasionally reverse it and tickle with the feather.

We hope to receive the aid of true hearted and good people, in our undertaking, not only as subscribers but as contributors; to the first we will give the worth of their money, and to the others the worth of their articles.

As we infringe upon no man's quarter-section, but have squatted upon unoccupied ground, we hope to be allowed the privilege of sowing our dragon's teeth in peace; but if we are attacked, the enemy may expect an army of armed sentences falling upon his flank or rear, at all manner of unseasonable periods. *But as the eye can see every thing but itself,* so an Editor is very likely to see every body's mistakes but his own, and we shall certainly quarrel with no good-natured friend who reminds us of our slips.

REVIEWS.

"An author may be considered as a merciful substitute to the legislature. He acts, not by punishing crimes, but by preventing them. If the author be, therefore, still so necessary among us, let us treat him with proper consideration, as a child of the public; and indeed a child of the public he is in all aspects; for while so well able to direct others, how incapable is he frequently found of guiding himself."

MIND AMONG THE SPINDLES. [Republished from Charles Knight's weekly volumes.] Boston, Jordan, Swift, & Wiley, 1845.

OUR first review shall be of an American author, what one we will determine by lot, to save us from a partial feeling in the outset, when we have concluded our prefatory remarks. There should be no sectional feelings in literature or art. No political barriers or geographical distinctions can prevent our sympathies from embracing the whole world of mind; all the malice of ill-natured spirits that has been exerted the last half century, to make a gap between British and American minds, has been without the slightest effect. The authors of Great Britain are still our bosom friends, and such of our own authors as find their way to London, are kindly entreated, in spite of the Foreign Quarterly and Mrs. Trollope. We said a good many severe things, even malicious, about Dickens, as soon as he left us; but we seized on his Christmas Carol with as hearty a good will as old Scrooge poked his timid clerk in the ribs the morning after Christmas. It is the vainest of all efforts to fight against genius; no national prejudices are strong enough to contend with it; no laws can affect it; no earthly power control it. Mankind will gladly receive its productions, let them come whence they will. What matters it to us that Frederika Bremer is a Swede, inhabiting a country of which we hardly knew anything until we heard of it from her; she is our dear friend, and her name is often heard at our firesides, as though she were our cousin, or next door neighbour; and Mary Howitt's name is affectionately spoken by thousands in our country, who only know her by her pretty little stories; and her country people, too, are as fond of Mary Clavers, and Lydia Maria Child, as though they were the daughters of English soil. Many an Englishman, who thinks he does his country a service in speaking ill of America, entertains a feeling for Washington Irving, as for a kinsman. And we, who think it a proof of patriotism to abuse the land of our fathers, are ever on the alert to catch every ray of light that radiates from the minds of its people. We appear to feel no animosities against the better part of men, which is their mind, but only against their poor perishable bodies, which, if let alone, would soon enough come to naught of themselves.

It would ill become us, then, in the outset of our career as reviewers, to enter upon our duty with a narrow feeling of partiality for our own authors, to the unjust exclusion of foreigners, from our sympathies. But this liberal feeling wil compel us to give our first attention and widest space to the authors of our own country, because they have the greatest odds to contend with, having a forestalled opinion against them in the minds of their own countrymen, and the best paid and most fertile authors in the world for competitors, whose works are imported scot free to our markets.

An American author is one of those rare creatures, who think more seriously of the welfare of others, than of their own. He is *prima facie* a good fellow; and as a matter of course, an utterer of inspired thoughts; for having no inducements to exertion, he speaks because he must. He knows no law but the law of his own being, like the wind and the rain, the dew and the lightning. He is, because he is. There are no artificial stimulants to bring him out. No offers from booksellers; no demands from the public. His lightnings are produced by no machinery, but dart from the clouds of his imagination, because they will; they may not strike, nor dazzle always; but they flash of their own accord, without the aid of saltpetre or charcoal. They who sit in his light, think as little of his sufferings, from which they derive their enjoyments, as we do of the leviathan that was slaughtered in Coromandel, to afford us the luxury of spermaceti.

How different is the lot of the British author, who seizes his pen as Nelson did his sword, with thoughts of Westminster Abbey or a peerage. We have not even a "corner" for our poets; they are shoved aside entirely, unless one of their number, like Mr. Griswold, erects a Pantheon for the whole that he may have a niche for himself.

Numerous as English authors are, it is a marvel, considering the hot-bed in which they are forced, that their number should be so small. With such splendid rewards as are showered upon their poets and romancers, it is a wonder that the whole nation does not give itself up to literature.

Considering the rewards of authors with us, the appearance of even one, would be proof of national superiority. In England authors are sure of something. If not a peerage, a baronetage; if not that, knighthood, a pension, a consulship, employment in a public office, or a guinea a sheet at least. If none of these, they are sure to be lionized, and reviewed, and read, and illustrated, and at last put into Westminster Abbey. We must confess that some of these honors have not a very dazzling aspect seen from our point of observation, at the distance of three thousand miles, but they appear to have a strong influence upon British minds.

We have seen the British Parliament engaged day after day, debating the subject of copyright, and grave statesmen and great orators advocating the rights of an author to the control of his own productions; and we have seen our own national Legislature receive numerous petitions on the same subject, from different parts of the Union, and treat them with silent contempt. At the first session of the present Congress there were several petitions, signed by some of the best men in the nation, presented to both houses, praying for an international copyright, received in silence, referred to a committee, and never heard of again.

In France and in Germany, the most reliable instrument to carve a fortune with, or cut a road to preferment, is the pen; with us it is a magnet in the hands of those who use it, to draw upon them contempt and poverty.

The only author upon whom our Government, or the Nation, has bestowed an office, is Mr. Irving And among all of our foreign ambassadors, what one could be more safely trusted with the interests of the Republic? And among all of our literary men, what one could have so dishonored his

The first two pages of the last magazine with which Poe was affiliated

In late April 1849 publication of a magazine of his own finally seemed within his grasp when Poe received a mid-December 1848 letter from Edward H. N. Patterson, a printer from Oquawka, Illinois, who wanted to establish a national literary magazine with Poe as editor and half owner. Jubilant, Poe replied with an outline of the magazine idea, retaining the *Stylus* as its title, and said he would tour through the West and South, "visiting the small towns more particularly than the large ones–lecturing as I went, to pay expenses."

He left New York on 29 June to promote the proposed magazine in Richmond and other parts of the South. On a stop in Philadelphia he became very drunk, lost his valise with lectures he planned to give, and was jailed for a few hours. He asked "refuge and protection" from John Sartain, publisher of *Sartain's Union Magazine*, claiming "some men" were trying to kill him. Gratefully Poe sold Sartain his revised poem "The Bells," for fifteen dollars, and the new "Annabel Lee." He lectured in Richmond and Norfolk on the "Poetic Principle" in August and September, hit the bottle again, and joined the Richmond chapter of the Sons of Temperance, vowing to abstain from alcohol. On 22 September Sarah Shelton consented to marry Poe. Again he left for New York, intending to return in a few days with Mrs. Clemm. After stopping in Baltimore he drank heavily and was found in a comatose state on 3 October. He died of delirium tremens at Washington College Hospital on 7 October 1849.

On 8 October Greeley asked his friend Griswold to "prepare some account of the deceased" for the following day's *New York Tribune*. Griswold, according to his own diary, "hastily" wrote a long obituary under the pseudonym "Ludwig." In the piece Griswold said that "few will be grieved" by his death and that he "had few or no friends." In a longer version written later Griswold described Poe as a beggar and debauched individual, as well as a plagiarist: "He was not remarkably original in invention. Indeed some of his plagiarisms are scarcely paralleled for their audacity in all literary history." He also said Poe's realm was "on the shadowy confines of human experience, among the abodes of crime, gloom, and horror, and there he delighted to surround himself with images of beauty and terror, to raise his solemn palaces and towers and spires in a night upon which should rise no sun. His minuteness of detail, refinement of reasoning, and pro-

priety and power of language . . . gave him an astonishing mastery over his readers. . . ."

Poe deserved better. Among nineteenth-century literati Poe was one of the most staunch promoters of magazine journalism. In "Marginalia" Poe said: "The whole tendency of the age is magazineward. The magazine in the end will be the most influential of all departments of letters. . . . In a few years its importance will be found to have increased in geometrical ratio. We now demand the light artillery of the intellect; we need the curt, the condensed, the readily diffused–in place of the verbose, the diluted, the voluminous, the inaccessible. On the other hand, the lightness of the artillery should not degenerate into pop-gunnery–by which term we may designate the character of the greater portion of the newspaper press–their sole legitimate object being the discussion of ephemeral matters in an ephemeral way."

In a 22 June 1841 letter to Longfellow, Poe promoted magazines again, this time as the "signs of the times" because "the brief, the terse, the condensed, and the easily circulated will take place of the diffuse, the ponderous, and the inaccessible." As if to accentuate his point he said the finest minds of Europe were lending their spirit to magazines.

The type of periodical that impressed Poe had not yet been developed in the United States. Writing in 1845, Poe said American magazines had achieved very little and that the originality and variety of European journals alone permitted him to call the magazine field, "a *very* important branch of literature–a branch, which, moreover, is daily growing in importance."

From his youth Poe had been greatly interested in British magazines, particularly *Blackwood's Edinburgh Magazine* but also *London Magazine* and *New Monthly Magazine*. The pattern for *Blackwood's*, according to Michael Allen, was elitist, retaining an air of exclusiveness and authority, and incorporating "the curious and esoteric learning." These elements were fused into a "more relaxed, personal, and intimate ethos which permitted the inclusion of more blatant sensationalism, literary gossip, and fiction for the less erudite reader." However, for all its affected elitism, *Blackwood's* was careful to maintain relations with the popular audience.

Poe described a typical *Blackwood's* article as a Gothic tale of sensation and horror, whose appeal was sensational but "elaborated its central feeling with philosophical or psychological or popularly German mannerisms and ideas." He added that the article was "usually structured around a protagonist isolated in some strange, horrific, or morbid situation which is progressively exploited for effect." Poe thought of his own tales as either grotesque or arabesque, or "bizarreries and grotesques." The fiction in *Blackwood's*, according to Poe, was designed for an audience not exclusively mass or elitist–the horror tale appealed to the many, the sensation-minded; the burlesque to the few. Much as he claimed to want identity with the masses, Poe sometimes was out of step with them, giving the impression, according to Allen, that he was "infinitely superior to the mass-audience." Allen adds that Poe could "hardly have hoped to dazzle the mass-audience with his erudition."

Following the thinking of British magazines, Poe believed that the writer, rather than the proprietor, of magazines should be the arbiter of writing quality. In his "The Magazine Prison-House" of 1845 Poe described the relationship between the villainous "fat 'editor and proprietor' " and the poverty-stricken young author. His discontent with proprietors kept alive hopes for his own magazine, which he said was the "grand purpose of my life, from which I have never swerved for a moment."

By his criticisms of American magazines Poe gave an idea of the type of periodical he wished to create. Native magazines, he said, were faulty for substituting "articles or pieces for legitimate reviews," their "habit of anonymous reviewing, their verbosity, and their assumption of authority." He also chided American magazines for their excessive zeal in serving the causes of American artists. In a piece in the *Southern Literary Messenger* he wrote, "We get up a hue and cry about the necessity of encouraging native writers of merit–we blindly fancy we can accomplish this by indiscriminate puffing of good, bad and indifferent." On the other hand, he also wrote caustically about editors importing "British vogues." In 1845 he even threw off the influence of British periodicals, attacking *Blackwood's* and its editor. In sum, Poe wanted a magazine that appealed to the many and the few, with the backing of the high caste, upper-class audience.

All through his career Poe rewrote the prospectus of his ideal magazine, solicited manuscripts and money from friends, and announced different dates for its debut. In 1840, in a prospectus for the "Penn Magazine" and in letters to friends, Poe described the type of magazine he

planned. The prospectus mentioned Poe's work on, and reason for leaving, the *Southern Literary Messenger*, stating that in the early days of that magazine there was a "somewhat overdone causticity in its department of Critical Notices of new books." He assured that " 'The Penn Magazine' will retain this trait of severity insomuch only as the calmest yet sternest sense of justice will permit. Some years since elapsed may have mellowed down the petulance without interfering with the rigor of the critic." The magazine would be known for an "honest and a fearless opinion . . . an absolutely independent criticism;–and a criticism self-sustained; guiding itself only by the purest rules of Art."

Contributors' interests were to be looked after by "Penn," which planned to pay liberally. Poe, calling for an international copyright law, noted that authors were at the mercy of publishers: "Literature is at a sad discount. . . . Without an international copyright law, American authors may as well cut their throats."

In a letter to John P. Kennedy later in 1840 Poe reiterated his aims and begged Kennedy to write a piece for the first issue: "Any unused scrap lying by you will fully answer my purposes." In January 1841 he stated his goals to Joseph E. Snodgrass, saying he wanted a "good outward appearance–clean type, fine paper, etc.," and *"no articles but from* the best pens." In criticism he promised to be "bold and sternly, absolutely just, with friend & foe," resolving, "From this purpose nothing shall turn me."

His enthusiasm was dampened in early 1841 when a "disturbance in monetary affairs," his illness, and a national depression suspended the idea. But George R. Graham, in an article for the 20 February *Saturday Evening Post*, thought Poe had the "finest prospects of success" as the press and the South and West were warm to the cause. Poe then joined *Graham's* in 1841 with the belief that he and Graham were eventually to launch "Penn Magazine," a ninety-six-page monthly on "excellent quality" paper, "clear, and bold, with distinct face," and literary contributions from the "most distinguished pens (of America) exclusively." When he thought Graham was "less willing to keep his word," Poe wrote in 1841 that he needed a partner for the magazine. He changed the prospectus slightly and announced its publication for January 1842.

In late 1842 Poe had a new partner, after interesting Thomas C. Clarke, owner of the *Saturday Museum*, in his magazine now called the

"Stylus." The 4 March 1843 *Saturday Museum,* in fact, carried an editorial note and biographical sketch of Poe to introduce the "Stylus," which featured many of the attributes planned for "Penn." In February Poe wrote F. W. Thomas that the "Stylus" was "my old 'Penn' revived and remodelled under better auspices." He said the proposal was backed by ample capital and that he had complete editorial control. But Poe again snatched defeat from victory. Sent to Washington to solicit subscriptions and support from Pres. John Tyler and members of the cabinet, he shattered those hopes by becoming highly intoxicated. He was sent home by friends. Later, in letters, Poe admitted that he had made a fool of himself in Washington.

To others, however, he placed the blame for the magazine's delay on Clarke. Writing Lowell on 20 June 1843, Poe said, "my Magazine scheme has exploded–or, at least, I have been deprived, through the imbecility, or rather through the idiocy of my partner, of all means of prosecuting it for the present." Earlier, while soliciting a poem, he told Lowell the magazine was due out in July.

In a letter to Lowell on 30 March 1844 Poe tried a different tack. Repeating the need for an international copyright law and a "well-founded" monthly journal, he proposed setting in motion an idea where "each of elite of men of letters join secretly, subscribe $200 for the magazine." Articles were to be supplied by "members only" and an editor chosen from among them. He asked, "How could such a journal fail?" and warned that if such a publication did not appear, the literati would be "devoured, without mercy, by the Godeys, the Snowdens. . . ."

Poe's dream of an ideal magazine was still there in 1848 when he wrote Willis on 22 January that the "Stylus" was "to be *my* own, at all points," and that he planned to travel south and west, lecturing and gathering five hundred subscribers among old friends. The following year the dream came very close to being realized with the help of Patterson. But before an inaugural number could be launched, Poe had died.

Although the literary and journalistic worlds were not to know the type of magazine Poe had in mind, both benefited immensely from his contributions to journalism. His critical reviews made a lasting imprint upon that genre of journalism, and, if he had edited his essays the way he did his fiction, Braddy said Poe could have been the Defoe of his age. In addition to the "Literati of New York City," the "Autogra-

phy" series, and "The Philosophy of Furniture," Poe's other essays include: "Marginalia," a series of critical notations on Defoe, drama, *Antigone,* plagiarism, rhetoric, and men of genius, carried in the *Democratic Review* and *Southern Literary Messenger;* "Pinakidia," an early effort at assembling random notes, published in the *Messenger;* "Fifty Suggestions"; "A Chapter of Suggestions," a collection of epigrams in *Graham's* and *The Opal;* "Street Progress," in *Broadway Journal,* stating there had been no real progress in two thousand years of road making; and "Some Secrets of the Magazine Prison-House."

As a critical reviewer Poe was caustic, unpredictable, severe, meticulous, vituperative, unjust, sarcastic, and sometimes envious. His writings earned him names such as "tomahawk man" or "Bulldog the critick," and he was accused of being "magnificently snobbish and dirty" and stooping to "cutting and slashing" and "blackguard warfare."

The very prolific nature of his reviewing may have accounted for his unpredictability. Poe reviewed well over two hundred books on wide-ranging topics such as disease, drama, aesthetics, poetry, etiquette, games, literature, manners, politics, prejudice, printing, religion, science, and slavery. In most cases he scrutinized each book in detail and used outside materials to bolster his reviews. Overwhelmed as he was, it is possible he reversed himself often because he could not remember what he had said before. Also, the unpredictable trait was tied to his prejudices; he loved his friends and detested his enemies, and with Poe, a dear friend today often turned into a bitter enemy tomorrow.

Despite the apparent incongruities and contradictions, Poe had definite ideas about reviewing. He thought severity had to be part of the process and used frontal attacks in his impatience with mediocrity. He called one author a "ninety-ninth rate poet"; another, he said, had transplanted "the language of the chambermaid to the pages of a critical journal"; and still others' works were termed "drivel," "silly," "unworthy of a schoolboy," or "gibberish." He alleged Charles Dickens was insane; he attacked Longfellow as a plagiarist and regularly took on the New York and Boston literary cliques. After a break with his friend Lowell for failing to include southern writers in a survey, Poe wrote: "Mr. Lowell is one of the most rabid of the abolition fanatics," adding that if Lowell owned slaves, he would be atrocious in his ill-treatment of them. As for Ralph

His reviewing showed equal contempt for publishers' puffery about books and undeserved literary reputations. His notion of the ethics among reviewers was indeed pessimistic; he believed many did not even read the books. Further, he wrote: "The intercourse between critic and publisher, as it now almost universally stands, is comprised either in the paying and pocketing of blackmail, as the price of a simple forbearance, or in a direct system of petty and contemptible bribery." He disdained publishers who used tricks to get the public to purchase inferior works. Because readers could be fooled by sensationalistic tactics of promotion, Poe believed it was the critic's duty to avoid the common error of estimating a book's worth by its popularity.

Poe wrote both conventional reviews, dealing almost solely with the book in question, and longer critical ones, used as vehicles to present his doctrines, sometimes only remotely connected with the book under scrutiny. Edd Winfield Parks says that Poe was the "first important critic to develop and refine his critical theories through the media of book reviews and magazine articles."

In the longer reviews Poe sought to develop and set the critical theories and standards of literature. He believed the literary critic could help establish an intellectual climate in which great literary work could be produced. The critic's role was to point out demerits of works (the merits would be apparent, he said), to judge books fairly and without subservience to other critics, and to remain independent of the dictation of publishers and the influence of coteries. Critical theories espoused in Poe's reviews deal with brevity, unity, highlighting, and exaggeration, among others. Poe said literature needed lyric poems that could be read in thirty minutes or prose tales in two hours. He explained that to give the idea of an object, a writer had to tone down, or even neglect, certain parts, and to highlight those portions by which the idea of the object is afforded. A certain amount of exaggeration was needed to depict the truth, Poe said.

Others, such as Michael Allen, believe Poe used the longer reviews to show off his vast knowledge on a variety of subjects, such as languages, mathematics, cryptology, or autography. Allen writes: "At his best Poe brought his critical expertise directly to the literary work in self-assertive, superior, but shrewd textual analysis and comment. He rationalized this pragmatic critical tendency in his view that 'excessive *generalization*' is one of

Poe circa 1847 (portrait attributed to S. S. Osgood)

Waldo Emerson, Poe, after analyzing his signature in the "Autography" series, wrote: "Mr. Ralph Waldo Emerson belongs to a class of gentlemen with whom we have no patience whatever– The mystics for mysticism's sake. . . . His present role seems to be out-Carlyling Carlyle. . . . His MS is bad, sprawling, illegible, irregular– although sufficiently bold. The latter trait may be, and no doubt is, only a portion of his general affectation." Biographers have questioned whether Poe used such "distasteful" language out of envy or spite, a deep commitment to what he believed in, or as an attempt to appeal to a mass audience and bring publicity to himself.

Poe believed that as a reviewer he could exhibit impartiality by rooting generalizations in textual analysis. Poe devastated authors who committed grammatical errors, once justifying his attacks thus: "No spectacle can be more ludicrous than that of a man, without the commonest school education, busying himself in attempts to instruct mankind on topics of polite literature." In a review of Ellery Channing's poems Poe wrote, "They are not precisely English, nor will we insult a great nation by calling them Kickapoo; perhaps they are Channingese."

criticism's leading errors. . . . In his more flamboyant moods he wanted to play the expert on rather large lines and with grander gestures, which would draw attention to his performances in the realm of knowledge. Thus throughout his life he tried in various ways to use his specialized knowledge, however peculiar it might be, to bolster up his role of critical expert."

In attempting to prescribe a literary standard Poe attacked anonymity, literary monopolies, and plagiarism in his reviews. He termed anonymous writers "cowardly" and feared that because of anonymity, "someone else's 'twaddle'" would be credited to him. Personally, he liked to see his name on mastheads and signed his poems when it was not the style; obviously, some of this resulted from his wanting to build a reputation. Poe dealt with an author's craftsmanship only after asking if literary thievery was evident; he frequently charged authors with imitation or stealing, the most famous incident involving Longfellow. His attack on literary monopolies probably was tied to his self-perception as the southern champion of national literature. From his days on the *Messenger* he attacked the New York literati as one such monopoly, and later, the Boston clique, which he called "Frogpondium." His use of regional antagonism was reminiscent of *Blackwood's.*

The journalistic elements in Poe's work cannot be overstressed. He was an enterprising and efficient editor, with well-honed copyediting skills, and his journalistic sense kept him abreast of current public taste. At a time when the penny press played up a simpler style and sensationalistic and personal traits, Poe did likewise, promoting tight writing and authoring pieces on popular topics connected to the horrible and morbid. Throughout the 1840s he increasingly introduced gossip and personal descriptions of writers he profiled in his critical reviews.

Georges Zayad says that Poe's journalism was reflected in his connection to local traditions which he reported and wrote about, his taste for mystification through hoaxes ("The Balloon Hoax," "The Unparalleled Adventure of One Hans Pfaall," and "The Facts in the Case of Mr. Valdemar"), and his exploitation of current events for story ideas ("The Mystery of Marie Roget" and "The Oblong Box"). Further, Zayad says that in Poe one finds "an irreconcilable conflict between the practical journalist, mirror of his epoch, and the poet as dreamer and misfit, who criticizes that epoch and opposes all that it represents: democracy, industrialization, utilitarianism, perfectibility and the idea of progress."

Before 1839 the type of journalism Poe preferred was British–*Blackwood's,* more specifically–and elitist in nature. From the British he learned to engage in critical controversy, exploit the hoax, and imitate British modes of magazine fiction, particularly the burlesque and horror tale. But as he became attuned to the American mass audience Poe transformed some of these characteristics into formats and styles easily understood by the common person.

Biographies:

Rufus Wilmot Griswold, "Memoir of the Author," in *The Works of the Late Edgar Allan Poe,* 4 volumes (New York: J. S. Redfield, 1850-1856), III: vii-xxxix;

Oliver Leigh, *Edgar Allan Poe: The Man: The Master: The Martyr* (Chicago: Morris, 1906);

George Edward Woodberry, *The Life of Edgar Allan Poe, Personal and Literary,* 2 volumes (Boston: Houghton Mifflin, 1909);

Hervey Allen, *Israfel: The Life and Times of Edgar Allan Poe* (New York: Holt, Rinehart & Winston, 1934);

Arthur Hobson Quinn, *Edgar Allan Poe: A Critical Biography* (New York: Appleton-Century, 1941);

Marie Bonaparte, *The Life and Works of Edgar Allan Poe: A Psycho-analytic Interpretation,* translated by John Rodker (London: Imago, 1949);

Georges Zayad, *The Genius of Edgar Allan Poe* (Cambridge: Schenkman, 1985);

Dwight Thomas and David K. Jackson, *The Poe Log. A Documentary Life of Edgar Allan Poe 1809-1849* (Boston: G. K. Hall, 1987).

References:

Michael Allen, *Poe and the British Magazine Tradition* (New York: Oxford University Press, 1969);

Haldeen Braddy, *Glorious Incense: The Fulfillment of Edgar Allan Poe* (New York: Scarecrow, 1953);

Clarence S. Brigham, ed., *Edgar Allan Poe's Contributions to "Alexander's Weekly Messenger"* (Worcester, Mass.: American Antiquarian Society, 1943);

John C. French, "Poe and the *Baltimore Saturday Visiter,*" *Modern Language Notes* (May 1918): 257-267;

Alan Golden, "Edgar Allan Poe at the Broadway Journal," *Poe Messenger* (Summer 1982): 1-6;

A. Wigfall Green, "The Weekly Magazines and Poe," in *English Studies in Honor of James S. Wilson* (Richmond: William Bud Press, 1951);

David K. Jackson, "Four of Poe's Critiques in the Baltimore Newspapers," *Modern Language Notes* (April 1935): 251-256;

Jackson, *Poe and the Southern Literary Messenger* (Richmond: Press of the Dietz Printing Co., 1934);

Robert D. Jacobs, *Poe: Journalist and Critic* (Baton Rouge: Louisiana State University Press, 1969);

Benjamin B. Minor, *The Southern Literary Messenger, 1834-1864* (New York: Neale, 1905);

Frank Luther Mott, *A History of American Magazines*, 5 volumes (Cambridge: Harvard University Press, 1938-1968), I: 549-551, 674-675, 758-762;

Edd Winfield Parks, *Edgar Allan Poe as Literary Critic* (Athens: University of Georgia Press, 1964);

Claude Richard, ed., *Edgar Allan Poe, journaliste et critique* (Paris: Librairie Klincksieck, 1978);

John Tebbell, *The American Magazine: A Compact History* (New York: Hawthorne, 1969);

John Grier Varner, *Edgar Allan Poe and the Philadelphia "Saturday Courier"* (Charlottesville: University of Virginia Press, 1933);

Charles H. Warts II, "Poe, Irving, and the *Southern Literary Messenger*," *American Literature* (May 1955): 249-251;

William White, "Edgar Allan Poe: Magazine Journalist," *Journalism Quarterly* (Spring 1961): 196-202;

James Playsted Wood, *Magazines in the United States* (New York: Ronald Press, 1949).

William Carey Richards

(24 November 1818-19 May 1892)

Ernest C. Hynds
University of Georgia

MAJOR POSITIONS HELD: Editor, *Orion* (1842-1844); *Southern Literary Gazette: An Illustrated Weekly Journal of Belles-Lettres, Science, and the Arts*, renamed *Richard's Weekly Gazette* from 1848 to 1850 (1848-1852); *Schoolfellow* (1849-1857).

BOOKS: *A Day in the New York Crystal Palace, and How to Make the Most of It* (New York: Putnam, 1853);
Harry's Vacation; or, Philosophy at Home (New York: Evans & Dickerson, 1854; revised edition, New York: Appleton, 1863);
Electron; or, The Pranks of the Modern Puck: A Telegraphic Epic of the Times (New York: Appleton, 1858);
Great in Goodness: A Memoir of George N. Briggs, Governor of the Commonwealth of Massachusetts from 1844-1851 (Boston: Gould & Lincoln/ New York: Sheldon, 1866);
The Lord is my Shepherd (Boston: Lee & Shepard/ New York: Dillingham, 1883);
The Mountain Anthem; the Beatitudes in Rhythmic Echoes (Boston: Lee & Shepard/New York: Dillingham, 1885);
Science in Song; or, Nature in Numbers (Boston: Lee & Shepard/New York: Dillingham, 1885);
Our Father in Heaven; the Lord's Prayer in a Series of Sonnets (Boston: Lee & Shepard/New York: Dillingham, 1886);
The Apostle of Burma; a Missionary Epic in Commemoration of the Centennial of the Birth of Adoniram Judson (Boston: Lee & Shepard, 1889);
The Three Gems of the Bible, Comprising Our Father in Heaven, The Lord is my Shepard (and) The Mountain Anthem (Boston: Lee & Shepard/ New York: Dillingham, 1891).

OTHER: *Georgia Illustrated in a Series of Views*, edited by Richards (Penfield, Ga.: W. & W. C. Richards, 1842);
The Shakespeare Calendar; or, Wit and Wisdom for Every Day in the Year . . . , edited by Richards (New York: Putnam, 1850).

As a magazine editor, as an author of articles, essays, pamphlets, poems, books, and sermons, and as a minister of the gospel, William Carey Richards made significant contributions to the cultural development of the United States during the nineteenth century. More particularly, he helped develop the literary magazine movement in the South with the *Orion* and the *Southern Literary Gazette*, and he provided an early educational magazine for children, the *Schoolfellow*.

Richards was born in London on 24 November 1818, the son of William Richards, a Baptist minister, and Anne Gardener Richards. He was named in part after William Carey, one of the first Baptist missionaries from England to go to India. The family immigrated to the United States in 1831, and Richards's father became minister of a church in Hudson, New York. Within a few years the family relocated in Penfield, Georgia, where Richards's father served as a trustee of Mercer University. Young Richards remained in New York until 1840, when he graduated from Madison University and joined his family in Penfield. While he was in New York he met Cornelia Holroyd Bradley, and the two were married in 1841. Richards had a younger brother, Thomas Addison Richards, who became well known as an artist and engraver, and a younger sister, Kate Richards, who contributed a number of poems and stories to her brother's periodicals, often under the pseudonym of "Leila Cameron."

Aside from work he may have done while in college in New York, Richards's literary career began with contributions to the *Augusta Mirror*, a literary paper published between 1838 and 1841 by William Tappan Thompson, who became a friend as well as an editor. Subsequently, Richards's poems, stories, and other writings appeared in various periodicals, including *Southern Ladies' Book and Family Companion* in Macon, Georgia, *Southern Quarterly Review* in Charleston, South Carolina, the *Christian Review* in Boston, the *Knickerbocker* in New York, and in the three publications he started while living in Georgia in

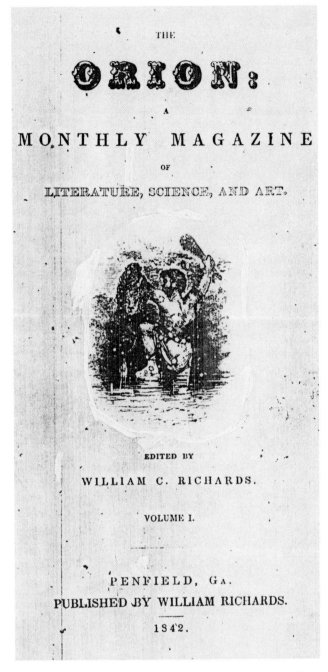

Title page for volume 1 of Richards's first magazine, named "for the most magnificent constellation in the southern hemisphere"

the 1840s. After he returned to the North and became active in the ministry in the 1850s, most of his writings were of a religious nature.

Richards's first magazine, the *Orion*, was started while he was living in Penfield, near where Georgia Baptists had founded Mercer University in 1833. It was not, however, a denominational, or even a religious, publication. Richards started the *Orion* to encourage the development of literature in the South. He emphasized that he was seeking a literature produced in the South, not Southern literature, "for we have a decided distaste for such local expressions, as if literature were of different characters in the South and in the North. It is the same every where except in degree and tone, and its advancement, its elevation in the South, is the proper object of our desires and efforts." At the suggestion of Thompson he named the magazine the *Orion* for "the most magnificent constellation in the southern hemisphere." The first issue, published in March 1842, somewhat resembled the *Knickerbocker*, but Richards denied any deliberate attempt to copy the form of that famed publication. It was octavo in size and contained a variety of literary forms in its sixty-four pages.

During slightly more than two years of publication the *Orion* published works by a number of leading writers in the South, including William Gilmore Simms, and a few well-known writers from the North as well. Richards himself was a leading contributor, and members of his family also provided some of the publication's best materials. His wife wrote various items which at times were signed "Mrs. Mannèrs," and at other times simply "C.H.B.R." His sister contributed a number of poems and tales, and his brother provided both articles and drawings. T. Addison Richards traveled throughout the South making drawings of interesting scenes and writing descriptive articles to accompany them. William Richards's desire to provide outstanding engravings as well as literature may have been a factor in his decision to have the *Orion* printed in New York City. Some criticized him for this, but it was not unknown among Southern publications at the time, and Richards distributed the publication from Penfield.

Some of the best materials in the *Orion* were written by Richards himself in his multiple roles as editor, literary critic, essayist, poet, and humorist. In the "Editor's Department" and "Monthly Chat" he exhibited a warm sense of humor as well as critical judgment. In the "Monthly Chat" he discussed why various submissions to the *Orion* were rejected and commended others which had been accepted for publication. Richards's literary standards were high, and he was not unwilling to criticize prominent writers if he believed some of their work was below expectations. He evidently believed that Simms was a better novelist than poet and, on one occasion, suggested that the publication of some of Simms's early poetry was "hardly adding to his reputation in publishing."

On another occasion in "Monthly Chat" Richards criticized a poem submitted to the *Orion* by Thomas Holley Chivers, a prolific Georgia poet, who some claim influenced the work of Edgar Allan Poe. Richards said the poem "To Allegra Florence in Heaven" was an uneven performance. "It contains some stanzas of *poetry*, and occasionally verses of much beauty, but as a whole we are compelled to decline it. We shall take the liberty, however, of presenting a few extracts from the poem by way of dealing poetical justice to the author."

Richards joined other Southern editors in attacking Rufus Griswold's anthology *The Poets and Poetry of America* (1842) because it devoted so little space to Southern poets. Of Griswold's effort Richards said in the *Orion*, "While he has given considerable space to the productions of second-rate bards in New England and other northern regions, he has not even named several of the south who have certainly written much that is superior to many of the specimens of the *favored* ones. . . . We regret this, inasmuch as a work professing to embody our *national* anthology should have done justice to *all* sections of the country."

Along with other Southern editors Richards also criticized Charles Dickens's *American Notes for General Circulation*, published in 1842 after a visit to the United States. Dickens was outspoken in his criticism of slavery even though he did not travel any farther south than Virginia. Richards rebutted Dickens's views on slavery and suggested that the Englishman was in a poor position to be critical. Richards wrote: "We . . . were gratified to find that Mr. Dickens had uttered no libels, none willfully at least, upon our country, our people, our manner, or our institutions, except that of slavery; in treating of which he displays his utter ignorance of the subject, and his natural and to-be-expected bitterness against the system and its upholders. We could wish that Mr. Dickens had visited the South and judged for himself, before he penned his stale and often-refuted calumnies upon our citizens, and his gross misrepresentations of a system which, at the worst, is infinitely superior, even by the confession of Mr. Lester, an abolitionist, to the system of white slavery so fearfully prevalent in some parts of the author's land." Richards conceded there were many beautiful passages in the work but suggested that, on the whole, it was not a happy literary performance.

One area in which Richards may have felt a special sense of responsibility was in writing reviews of novels. He was not kindly disposed to novels as a group but did on occasion cite individual works for his readers. He suggested that apart from the decidedly injurious tendency of many, perhaps most, their very numbers required that novels be selected carefully. As a prelude to favorable comments about a novel by G.R.P. James, he wrote of novels generally, "The mawkish taste, ridiculous philosophy, and threadbare sentiment, not to speak of the positive and openly vicious character, of the mass of novels, render them very unfit companions for the young and pure-minded reader."

In addition to essays and reviews Richards at times contributed poems and stories to the *Orion*, which were often sentimental but usually entertaining. At times they were attributed to "Orionis." He also wrote a number of humorous stories, such as "The Smithville Gas Frolic," "The Smithville Debating Society," and "Major Theophilus Bandbox Bubble, or the Nice Young Man."

The contents of the *Orion* included general articles, such as "The Origin of Slave Labor in Georgia" by William Bacon Stevens, "Autumn Reveries" by Henry Rootes Jackson, and "The Moral Character of Hamlet" by Simms; serial stories such as "The Trysting Rock: A Tale of Tallulah" by T. Addison Richards, "A Spanish Chronicle" by Mary E. Lee, and "The Hermytte of Drowsiehedde" by Simms; original poems such as "To a Mocking Bird" and "To Kate" by Richards, and "Orionis," and "Row Merrily, Fisherman, O'er The Sea" by John Love Lawrie; reviews of novels and other books; and drawings by T. Addison Richards and others. Richards said he had vigilant and able correspondents in cities such as New York, Philadelphia, Boston, and London to send him advance copies of new English and American publications so that he could mention them in the *Orion*.

In an effort to boost the circulation and influence of the *Orion* Richards moved the periodical to Charleston in early 1844. The move was taken, he said, "because we consider that city as the most important point in the South, and such a work as ours should, by all means, emanate from the headquarters of the region in which it is designed especially to circulate." But, for reasons not entirely clear, the magazine lasted only six months there and expired with the August issue.

Contemporaries were at times critical of the *Orion*, but, on the whole, they were complimentary of the magazine and its editor. Simms, who was editing the *Magnolia* in June 1842, wrote that in the *Orion* he had seen "nothing . . . indicative of very great intellectual superiority" but commented that Richards "writes with ease and good humor." The *Southern Miscellany* in Madison, Georgia, praised the *Orion*'s typography as equal to that found anywhere in the country but later called it "a precious humbug" for being printed in the North. The *Southern Literary Messenger* commended a lithographic representation in the September 1842 issue and suggested that some of the prose articles "are vigorous and spirited, and there is one exquisite poetic gem, 'He came too late,' contributed by Mrs. Welby of Kentucky." The *Knickerbocker* suggested the *Orion* was bidding to emulate the merit of and earn a popularity like that of the *Messenger*, which it praised. The *Knickerbocker* described the *Orion* as "a very neatly printed, well supplied, and admirably embellished monthly Magazine." B. H. Flanders, in his *Early Georgia Magazines: Literary Periodicals to 1865*, is complimentary of Richards's magazine and his work as a poet, humorist, and literary critic. He says Richards "was more cosmopolitan than William Gilmore Simms, perhaps the leading literary editor in the South, and much more ambitious to establish a popular periodical of the highest type in the South." He suggests that the "Editor's Department" and the "Monthly Chat" reflect a critical judgment above the average of antebellum Southern editors. In addition, Flanders suggests that Richards's work in literature deserves more attention than it has received. "His literary productions are not, of course, great pieces of literature, but they indicate a poetic talent above the average of Southern editors."

Although he was disappointed by the failure of the *Orion*, Richards did not despair of publishing a magazine that would encourage the development of literature in the South. He continued to write and plan, and in May 1848 he launched the *Southern Literary Gazette* in Athens, Georgia, where he had relocated in the early 1840s along with his wife and brother. Athens is the site of the University of Georgia, and in the 1840s the area ranked second only to Savannah in industrial development in Georgia. The state's first railroad had been started in part by entrepreneurs there, and the community had a substantial population of educated persons. Cornelia Richards was principal of a flourishing girls' school called the Athens High School, and Richards and his brother were described by a local historian as great additions to the growing town.

The *Southern Literary Gazette* was started, Richards said, "to develop and foster the intellectual capital of the South; to open a channel for literary communication between the scholars of our wide-spreading territory, to incite to diligence latent talent, and to awaken from its trance, slumbering genius in our midst, that 'the wilderness may blossom like the rose.'" He said, "We have engraved the title, 'Southern' upon our very name . . . to suggest, if no more, to our people, that Literature is as congenial and indigenous to the South, as to any other region. . . . Strictly neutral in partisanship, we shall present our readers with a bare synopsis of political intelligence, possessing general interest. Literature is the staple of our Journal."

In many respects the *Gazette* was similar to the *Orion*, although it was published on a quarto sheet with four columns to the page. It contained tales, essays, travel sketches, poetry, criticism, and a general miscellany of information in all departments of literature, art, and science. Richards and his family contributed to this publication as they had to the *Orion*. Although authors from throughout the country were published in the *Gazette*, there was a strong emphasis on Southern writers. Simms, Mary E. Lee, Robert M. Charlton, Henry Rootes Jackson, and many others were included among the magazine's authors. Through the "Editor's Department" and other writings Richards continued his efforts to stimulate literary thought and action in the South.

On one occasion Richards wrote of the challenges faced by an editor in providing instruction and pleasure for his readers. He suggested that the editor's articles were but a small part of his task. More of his efforts were devoted to providing for the various departments, determining the fitness of contributions, writing soothing letters to those rejected, ransacking old and new books for choice materials, and revising accepted manuscripts, particularly poetry, "supplying here a deficient foot; remedying there a disallowed rhyme—now furnishing a word to complete the author's meaning, and anon hunting up an idea to suit the author's rhymes." A message to "Charles" in the "Notices to Correspondents" column suggests some of the difficulties involved in selecting manuscripts: "We must respectfully decline your verses addressed 'To a young lady whom I saw washing her lily-white hands on the back piazza at sunrise in the morning.' The inscription reminds us forcibly of some stanzas once published in the Augusta Mirror, (if we mistake not), addressed 'To a child reposing in its nurse's arms under a rose-bush in Jasper county.'"

Some of the best material in the *Gazette* could be found in the "Editor's Department," where Richards discussed contemporary problems and sought to stimulate literary thought and writing in the South. The magazine included a variety of reviews, columns, and essays in addition to stories, poetry, and advertising.

Starting with the second volume in May 1848, the magazine adopted a new name, *Richard's Weekly Gazette*, and a new emphasis. It was to be "less exclusively devoted, than heretofore, to Literature, the Arts, and the Sciences," and more concerned with being a "Choice Family Newspaper." This approach apparently was followed for about a year. By the end of 1849 Richards had sold one-half interest in the publication to Joseph Walker of Charleston, and beginning with the first issue of 1850, the magazine was published in Charleston. The title *Southern Literary Gazette* was resumed in May 1850 and continued until the publication was merged with the *Weekly News*, edited by Paul Hamilton Hayne, in early 1853. Richards ceased his association with the publication in December 1852 when he moved himself and the *Schoolfellow*, the juvenile periodical he had founded in 1849, to New York City.

Contemporary editors in the North and West as well as the South praised the *Southern Literary Gazette*, and Flanders describes it as Richards's greatest success. The *Southern Literary Messenger* described it as "a promising coadjutor in the field of letters" and described its editor as a man "of taste and judgment" who will "walk worthily of the vocation wherewith he is called." The *Augusta Chronicle and Sentinel* said it "affords weekly a most agreeable and entertaining repast in the wide field of literary journalism—evincing tact, skill and ability on the part of the editor." The *Great West* (Cincinnati) said it "bids fair to maintain an elevated position among the weekly literary papers of the Union," and the *Yankee Blade* (Boston) said it was "brimful of choice matter, original and select, and the typography is worthy of the contents." Others had similar comments. Flanders says there was nothing pedantic about Richards's style, that he was "a master-editor in making the contents of his periodical interesting, yet of a high quality."

During the first year of the *Southern Literary Gazette*, while he was still in Athens, Richards had developed the idea for the *Schoolfellow*, the first magazine in the area aimed principally at children. It first appeared in January 1849, in a thirty-two-page twelvemo form with excellent woodcuts. Richards advised readers that the magazine would be both educational and entertaining. He said "the kind *Schoolfellow* is not less ready to help his associates to learn a hard lesson than he is to join them in any proper amusement, so he will be, at once, your teacher and your playmate–not less ready to inform you of curious facts in History, Philosophy, and other Sciences, than to share with you in those innocent pasttimes which constitute the charm of boyhood and girlhood." It was an immediate success, and by December 1849, when the editor moved his publishing office and both magazines to Charleston, it already had a circulation of ten thousand. Richards moved the *Schoolfellow* to New York City in 1852 and continued to publish it until 1857.

The editor was a principal contributor to the *Schoolfellow*, and his wife and sister also provided articles, as they had for his other publications. Charles L. Wheler, Mrs. Mary Howitt, Thomas Hood, Caroline Gilman, and many others also contributed.

The contents, as Richards promised, included stories, biographies, historical sketches, poetry, and articles on various subjects from table manners to animal life. The educational aspects of the magazine were emphasized, but there were many lighter pieces as well. Often the stories accomplished both goals.

The *Schoolfellow* received praise from various publications, including the *Floridian* (Tallahassee) in the South and the *Literary American* (New York) in the North, which praised Richards and both of his publications. The praise continued in subsequent years after the *Schoolfellow* moved to New York. *Godey's Lady's Book* described it as a "very neat and valuable little work. . . . It presents a great amount of information, conveyed in a familiar, but fascinating style, and embraces among the number of its contributors several of the most popular practical writers of the country."

In the 1850s Richards decided to enter the active ministry, and for several decades until his death in 1892 he served pastorates in Rhode Island, Massachusetts, and Illinois. He continued to write, especially on religious topics and on physical science, which he helped popularize through lectures in the United States and Canada. In a sense, Richards had two primary careers. During his young adulthood he was a magazine editor and writer in Georgia, South Carolina, and New York. Through his middle and later years he was a minister, writer, and public speaker in New England and the Middle West.

Although he spent fewer than fifteen years as a magazine editor, Richards made significant contributions to the field and to the development of literature, especially in the South. His first two magazines, the *Orion* and the *Southern Literary Gazette*, were especially concerned with encouraging Southern writers and developing literature in the area. These magazines not only provided a vehicle for good literature but also encouraged the development of other Southern publications. In his third publication, the *Schoolfellow*, Richards helped foster the development of children's magazines. Richards's efforts were generally well received throughout the country. He has been justly praised for his efforts to foster literature and to pioneer magazine development in the South.

References:

B. H. Flanders, *Early Georgia Magazines: Literary Periodicals to 1865* (Athens: University of Georgia Press, 1944);

Augustus Longstreet Hull, *Annals of Athens, Georgia with an Introductory Sketch by Dr. Henry Hull* (Athens: Banner Job Office, 1906);

David K. Jackson, "Letters of Georgia Editors and a Correspondent," *Georgia Historical Quarterly*, 23 (June 1939): 170-176.

George Ripley

(3 October 1802-4 July 1880)

Lloyd E. Chiasson
Loyola University in New Orleans

See also the Ripley entries in *DLB 1: The American Renaissance in New England* and *DLB 64: American Literary Critics and Scholars, 1850-1880.*

MAJOR POSITIONS HELD: Business editor, *Dial* (1840-1844); editor, coeditor, *Harbinger* (1845-1847); literary critic, *New York Tribune* (1849-1880).

BOOKS: *Discourse on the Philosophy of Religion. Addressed to Doubters Who Wish to Believe* (Boston: Munroe, 1836);
"The Latest Form of Infidelity" Examined. A Letter to Mr. Andrews Norton, Occasioned by His "Discourse Before the Association of the Cambridge Theological School" on the 19th of July, 1839 . . . (Boston: Munroe, 1839);
Defense of "The Latest Form of Infidelity" Examined; a Second Letter to Andrews Norton, Occasioned By His Defense of a Discourse on "The Latest Form of Infidelity" (Boston: Munroe, 1840);
Defense of "The Latest Form of Infidelity" Examined; a Third Letter to Andrews Norton . . . (Boston: Munroe, 1840).

OTHER: *Specimens of Foreign Standard Literature,* 15 volumes, edited by Ripley (volumes 1-11, Boston: Hilliard, Gray, 1838-1842; volumes 12-14, Boston: Munroe, 1842; volume 15, New York: Wiley, 1845);
Handbook of Literature and the Fine Arts, compiled by Ripley and Bayard Taylor (New York: Putnam, 1852); republished as *Cyclopedia of Literature and the Fine Arts* (New York: Barnes, 1854);
New American Cyclopædia, 16 volumes, edited by Ripley and Charles A. Dana (New York & London: Appleton, 1863); revised as *The American Cyclopædia* (New York: Appleton, 1873-1876).

PERIODICAL PUBLICATIONS: "De Gerando on Self-Education," *Christian Examiner,* 9 (September 1830): 70-107;

George Ripley

"Religion in France," *Christian Examiner,* 10 (July 1831);
"Pestalozzi," *Christian Examiner,* 11 (January 1832): 347-373;
"Herder's Theological Opinions," *Christian Examiner,* 14 (November 1835): 172-204;
"Schleiermacher as a Theologian," *Christian Examiner,* 20 (March 1836): 1-46;
"Martineau's Rationale," *Christian Examiner,* 21 (November 1836);
"Theological Aphorisms," *Christian Examiner,* 21 (January 1837): 385-398;
"Brownson's Writings," *Dial,* 1 (July 1840): 22-46;

"Letter to a Theological Student," *Dial*, 1 (October 1840): 183-187;

"Introductory Notice," *Harbinger*, 1 (14 June 1845): 8-10;

"Tendencies of Modern Civilization," *Harbinger*, 1 (28 June 1845): 33-35;

"Influence of Social Circumstances," *Harbinger*, 5 (26 June 1847): 46.

During his lifetime, George Ripley was many things: minister, philosopher, leader of a commune, writer and editor, literary critic. In some ways he represented the modern man, a product of the Enlightenment. Like many seventeenth- and eighteenth-century philosophers before him, Ripley believed in the rationality of man and was sure mankind would achieve an understanding of the universe through God-given intellect and revelation. Best known as one of the chief spokesmen of the transcendental movement during the nineteenth century, Ripley also became one of America's foremost literary critics. He also helped found and edit the *Dial*, the monthly organ of the transcendental movement, and the most noteworthy socialist newspaper of the period, the *Harbinger*. In addition, Ripley edited what was generally considered to be the best encyclopedia in the United States at that time.

Ripley was born on 3 October 1802, in Greenfield, Massachusetts, to Jerome and Sarah Franklin Ripley. In 1827 he married Sophia Willard Dana, who died in 1861. In 1865 he married Louisa Augusta Schlossberger. At the age of seventy-seven Ripley died on 4 July 1880.

Ripley's career is a particularly difficult one to analyze, primarily because he has to a great extent been overlooked by American historians. Although Ripley was at the heart of the transcendental movement in the 1830s, Ralph Waldo Emerson was its best-known spokesman. Also, Ripley was engaged in so many different enterprises during his life that no one endeavor seems to have received the attention it deserved. However, one common thread can be found running through Ripley's life: his desire to improve mankind by shaping the real into the ideal. Ripley always felt if men achieved their full development, a golden age would be attained.

Religion had a prominent role in Ripley's life as a child, and by the time he was a teenager he had been introduced to Calvinist, Shaker, and Unitarian teachings. When he graduated from Harvard University in 1823, and from Harvard Divinity School three years later, he was devoted to

Unitarian doctrine and immediately accepted a post as minister of the Purchase Street Church in Boston. For the next thirteen years Ripley remained in that position, although oftentimes his theological positions were considered extremely radical by mainstream Unitarians. Ripley, as did Emerson, championed the idea that man could not grasp God through reason alone and argued that the Scriptures were divinely inspired. This view differed from traditional American Unitarian belief based upon the doctrine that at birth man's mind was a clean slate upon which experience, through his senses, was recorded. In this way, man acquired knowledge over a period of time. To most Unitarians, this method of gaining knowledge meant that through the reasoning process, and only through the reasoning process, could insight into God be achieved. No supernatural help such as God-given revelation was required. Strongly affected by German philosophers of the period (Friedrich Schleiermacher, in particular), Ripley argued that intuition (revelation) provided men with the blocks upon which an understanding of God could be built. Essentially, Ripley tied reasoning and intuition together and in doing so touched the heart of the budding transcendental movement–a radical movement within the Unitarian Church–which recognized a spiritual/intuitive understanding of God beyond empirical evidence. This interweaving of reason with revelation can be seen in Ripley's "Essay Concerning Human Understanding" written in 1837 and included in the "Commonplace Book," located at the Houghton Library, Harvard University: "Reason is Natural Revelation, whereby the eternal Father of Right and Fountain of all knowledge communicates to mankind that portion of truth which was laid within the reach of their natural faculties; revelation is natural reason enlarged by a new set of discoveries communicated by God immediately, which reason vouches the truth of, by the testimony and proofs it gives that they may come from God."

It was a year before "Essay Concerning Human Understanding" was written, however, when Ripley became a widely known figure. In 1836 his review of Unitarian minister James Martineau's essay, "Rationale of Religious Enquiry," was printed in the official organ of the Unitarian Church, the *Christian Examiner*. In this highly controversial article Ripley first synthesized the spiritual (revelation) with the natural (reasoning abilities).

The house at Brook Farm, an experiment in communal living established by Ripley in April 1841

The first step in the proof of supernatural inspiration is the admission of natural inspiration. The foundation for this is laid in the primitive elements of our being. The power of the soul, by which it gains the intuitive perception of spiritual truth, is the original inspiration that forms the common endowment of human nature. This, we maintain, is established by the testimony of the absolute or intuitive reason of man. Our own consciousness assures us that a revelation of great spiritual truths is made to the soul. There are certain primitive and fundamental ideas which compose the substance of reason that exist, with more or less distinctness, in every intelligent mind. These ideas are the primitive perceptions on which all moral religious truth is founded, just as the whole science of mathematics is built upon a few simple definitions and axioms, which neither require, nor are susceptible of demonstration. These ideas, by the necessity of our nature, we refer to origin out of ourselves. They are not created by us, but they command us. They are not the products of our own will but should be its sovereigns. They are not limited to our own personality, but bear the signatures of universal and everlasting authority. Now, psychology and the history of man alike compel us to trace back their origin to God. We are conscious that they do not proceed from any act of volition of the personal causality which

acts within us, nor from the influence of nature, the material causality which acts without us; and we are, therefore, compelled by the authority of our reason to refer them to the Absolute Causality, –the Infinite Author of Truth and Good. They do not grow out of any deductions of our understandings, but are the fruits of a spontaneous and original inspiration, without which the understanding would have no materials to work upon.

Ripley's review, and the publication of his first book, *Discourse on the Philosophy of Religion* (1836), a collection of six essays delineating his beliefs, resulted in a public clash with Andrews Norton, his former Harvard Divinity School professor and one of the more prominent Unitarian leaders. In an open letter in the *Boston Daily Advertiser*, printed 9 November 1838, Norton condemned Ripley's philosophy. The next day Ripley replied in the *Advertiser*. The debate grew, and soon Ripley and Norton were responding to each other's charges with published book-length "letters." In 1838 the first volumes of Ripley's compilations, *Specimens of Foreign Standard Literature*, appeared. Eventually a fifteen-volume work published over a seven-year period, it provided translations of many of the more radical writings of European philosophers.

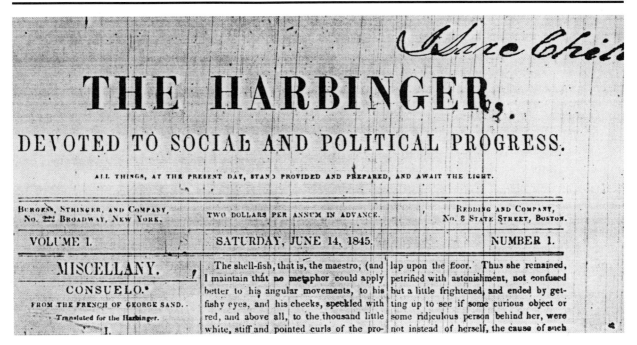

THE HARBINGER,

DEVOTED TO SOCIAL AND POLITICAL PROGRESS.

ALL THINGS, AT THE PRESENT DAY, STAND PROVIDED AND PREPARED, AND AWAIT THE LIGHT.

BURGESS, STRINGER, AND COMPANY, No. 222 Broadway, New York.	TWO DOLLARS PER ANNUM IN ADVANCE.	REDDING AND COMPANY, No. 8 State Street, Boston.
VOLUME I.	SATURDAY, JUNE 14, 1845.	NUMBER 1.

MISCELLANY.

CONSUELO.*

FROM THE FRENCH OF GEORGE SAND.

Translated for the Harbinger.

I.

The shell-fish, that is, the maestro, (and I maintain that no metaphor could apply better to his angular movements, to his fishy eyes, and his cheeks, speckled with red, and above all, to the thousand little white, stiff and pointed curls of the pro- lap upon the floor. Thus she remained, petrified with astonishment, not confused but a little frightened, and ended by get- ting up to see if some curious object or some ridiculous person behind her, were not instead of herself, the cause of such

Head title for the first issue of the Fourierist journal produced at Brook Farm

These activities undoubtedly increased Ripley's influence among members of the Transcendental Club, and along with Margaret Fuller, he began to call for the creation of a magazine of American transcendental philosophy. The *Dial* emerged in 1840 with Fuller as editor, and although it often contained brilliant essays and poems written by well-known figures like Emerson and Henry David Thoreau, it never had the journalistic impact Ripley and other club members hoped it would. Ripley served as business and office manager, contributed articles, and participated in almost every aspect of the journal's production. Although writers such as Thoreau and Emerson guaranteed superior contents, the *Dial* failed for a variety of reasons, primarily because it was an elitist journal aimed at a small, highly educated audience (circulation never exceeded three hundred), and it suffered from internal struggles concerning editorial content.

Even as Ripley espoused transcendental philosophy in the *Dial*, he was preparing to put into practice his reformist ideas. The result was Brook Farm, an experiment in communal living which Ripley hoped would serve as proof that the evils of capitalism and industrialization, and the corruption of values which he believed inherently came from both, could be avoided. Like others during the middle and late nineteenth century, Ripley became increasingly uneasy with the changes the United States was undergoing socially, reli- giously, and economically. Although he believed increased materialism was nothing more than a transition period to a golden age, Ripley was anxious to speed the process with the establishment of a Christian community separated from all authority but God's. Brook Farm would be an example of man's ability to conquer his dark, sinful side.

Although the change in life-style from minister in Boston to farmer in rural West Roxbury a few miles away may have appeared a complete role reversal for the scholarly Ripley, it was not. He knew Brook Farm would essentially be an educational institute emphasizing spiritual enrichment. For Ripley, Brook Farm was an idealistic haven from a capitalistic society.

Originally, about 20 scholars comprised the classless society of Brook Farm. The population did reach 150 persons, however, including novelist Nathaniel Hawthorne and Ripley's good friend Charles Anderson Dana. Frequent visitors included Horace Greeley, the editor of the *New York Tribune*, Margaret Fuller, the former editor of the *Dial* and a staff member on the *Tribune*, and noted transcendentalists Theodore Parker and Ralph Waldo Emerson.

Public curiosity surrounding Brook Farm was intense, and in one year about four thousand visitors came to see this strange transcendental community of scholar-farmers. By the end of 1844, however, the individual freedom embodied in the commune proved to be too anarchic, and in 1844 Brook Farm was restructured into a socialist community based upon the concepts of Charles Fourier, a French social theorist who advocated a cooperative organization of society into phalanxes of organized and closely united bodies of persons to allow for the social and economic needs of the group.

One-and-a-half years after Fourierism was adopted at Brook Farm, the *Harbinger* was established in June 1845. This weekly, produced at Brook Farm, became the foremost journal of Fourierism in the United States. It was published for four years, the first two at Brook Farm and the remaining two in New York City. While it was published at Brook Farm, Ripley served as editor in chief and produced one of the most unique periodicals of the nineteenth century. From the beginning the *Harbinger* was an improvement on the *Dial* from a production and editorial standpoint. Like the *Dial,* however, the *Harbinger* benefited from an impressive list of contributors such as Ripley, Dana, Greeley, Arthur Brisbane, and John Greenleaf Whittier. As was the case with the *Dial,* all contributors were afforded complete editorial freedom. In addition, Ripley and Dana wrote the editorials, many of which contained Fourier's socialistic ideas blended with Ripley's belief that the environment, not mankind, created the bulk of evils in society. As Ripley wrote in the 19 July 1845 edition of the *Harbinger:* "The whole tendency of modern society is to degrade man; once there were giants on the earth; now man is dwarfed, mutilated, monstrous; absorbed in a base, petty individualism; enervated in body and mind; greedy for gain, lustful for pleasure, contemptible in selfishness; his religious mechanism, his morality mummery, his God and idol. Not for these vile ends was human nature so magnificently endowed."

By 1847, however, Ripley was forced to close Brook Farm when his bold experiment could no longer financially sustain itself. Although the closing of Brook Farm marked the end of an important period of Ripley's life, it also meant the beginning of a financially successful career as a noted journalist and author. Ironically, from this point until his death, Ripley's ideas for reform were more available to the general public than ever before. In 1849 he began reviewing articles, essays, and books covering a wide range of subjects for the *New York Tribune.* Throughout the next thirty years he wrote thousands of social and literary commentaries for vari-

Beginning of Ripley's prospectus from the first issue of the Harbinger

ous publications while becoming one of the best-known literature critics in the country.

As a critic Ripley is most closely associated with Greeley's *Tribune,* but his reviews and essays also regularly appeared in numerous newspapers and magazines such as *Harper's New Monthly Magazine* (which he helped found) and *Putnam's Magazine.* His work was aggressively sought, in part because he was as much a teacher as a critic in his reviews and essays. Through his reviews (and in many of his letters to authors), Ripley always sought to evaluate in such a way that each work might be better than the last. He saw the role of critic as constructive, not debilitating. Essentially, he evaluated literary works according to their aesthetic qualities and to the degree of success the author achieved in accomplishing his particular goals.

It was also important to Ripley that his reviews were fair and balanced, a reflection, perhaps, of the democratic spirit embodied in transcendental philosophy. Ripley even gave positive reviews to works opposing Transcendentalism. In addition, he had the ability to write reviews which dealt solely with the work at hand, not the successes or failures of the past. For example, although in previous reviews he had criticized Herman Melville, Ripley praised *Moby-Dick* (1851) as a classic while many other reviewers were initially critical of the work. Instead, Ripley termed the novel a "pregnant allegory intended to illustrate the mystery of life. Certain it is that the rapid, pointed hints which are often throughout with the keenness and velocity of a harpoon penetrating deep into the heart of things, showing that the genius of the author for moral analysis is scarcely surpassed by his wizard power of description."

Although Ripley's journalistic career flourished, it was not until his major project, the *New American Cyclopædia,* was published in 1863 that he finally enjoyed financial security. The encyclopedia, which he edited with Charles Anderson Dana, was published in sixteen volumes and took five years to complete. Much less philosophical than his previous publications, it represented a deliberate attempt to write for a larger, less educated audience. Its success was no doubt bittersweet for the editor, however, since his wife and workmate of forty years, Sofia, had died the year before the work was published. Four years later, however, Ripley met a young German immigrant named Louisa Schlossberger, and they were married in 1865.

In his later years Ripley's work continued at a steady pace and covered topics as wide-ranging as philosophy, psychology, history, art, and science. His work also included evaluations of the work of such notables as Edgar Allan Poe, Voltaire, and Johann Wolfgang von Goethe. When not reviewing, he lent editorial support to the labor movement, abolitionism, socialism, and woman's rights. If he was no longer the active militant of Brook Farm days, he was in no way a passive bystander to the issues of the day.

Until his death in 1880 Ripley remained an active writer and reformer. For much of the previous fifty years he had been in the forefront of the transcendental movement and proved to be its chief activist. He also edited what many people considered the best encyclopedia of the period and was considered to be the major literary critic in the country. And always Ripley strived toward the same goal: to bring mankind closer to the perfection for which he believed it was destined.

Biographies:

Octavius Brooks Frothingham, *George Ripley* (Boston: Houghton, Mifflin, 1882);

Henry L. Golemba, *George Ripley* (Boston: Twayne, 1977).

References:

W. Arndt and others, *Popular Symbolics* (St. Louis: Concordia Publishing House, 1834);

Brian M. Barbour, ed., *American Transcendentalism* (Notre Dame: University of Notre Dame Press, 1973);

C. H. Faust, "The Background of the Unitarian Opposition to Transcendentalism," *Modern Philology,* 35 (1937-1938): 297-324;

Julia Franklin, ed., *Selections From The Works of Fourier* (London: Swan Sonnenschein, 1901);

Harold Clarke Goddard, *Studies in New England Transcendentalism* (New York: Hillary House, 1960);

Philip F. Gura and Joel Myerson, *Critical Essays on American Transcendentalism* (Boston: G. K. Hall, 1982);

Frank Luther Mott, *A History of American Magazines,* 5 volumes (Cambridge, Mass.: Harvard University Press, 1938-1968), I: 702-710, 763-765.

Papers:

The Boston Public Library holds 37 of George Ripley's letters in the Dwight collection; 35 in the Brook Farm collection; 18 in the Antislavery collection; and 17 in the Weston Papers; 1836-1847. The Fruitlands 'Museum, Harvard, Massachusetts, holds 10 letters written between 1841 and 1847. The Houghton Library at Harvard University has manuscripts, clippings, Brook Farm account books, and 15 letters collected in four Ripley folders. The Massachusetts Historical Society holds Ripley's memorandum book, sermons, manuscripts, and 34 letters in the Frothingham collection, 38 letters in the Bancroft collection, 18 in the Parker papers, and 17 in the Dana collection. The *New York Herald Tribune* files contain 106 letters, notes, and memoranda written from 1849 to 1880.

Lydia H. Sigourney

(1 September 1791-10 June 1865)

Dorothy A. Bowles
University of Tennessee

See also the Sigourney entries in *DLB 1: The American Renaissance in New England* and *DLB 42: American Writers for Children Before 1900.*

MAJOR POSITIONS HELD: Coeditor (titular), *Godey's Lady's Book* (1839-1842) and *Ladies' Companion* (1843-1844).

BOOKS: *Moral Pieces, in Prose and Verse* (Hartford, Conn.: Sheldon & Goodwin, 1815);

The Square Table, anonymous (Hartford, Conn.: Samuel G. Goodrich, 1819);

No. II. The Square Table, or the Meditations of Four Secluded Maidens Seated Around It, anonymous (Hartford, Conn., 1819);

Traits of the Aborigines of America, A Poem, anonymous (Cambridge, Mass.: Harvard University Press, printed by Hilliard & Metcalf, 1822);

Sketch of Connecticut, Forty Years Since, anonymous (Hartford, Conn.: Oliver D. Cooke & Sons, 1824);

Poems (Boston: Samuel G. Goodrich/Hartford, Conn.: H. & F. J. Huntington, 1827);

Female Biography, anonymous (Philadelphia: American Sunday-School Union, 1829);

Evening Readings in History, anonymous (Springfield, Mass.: G. & C. Merriam, 1833);

Letters to Young Ladies, anonymous (Hartford, Conn.: Printed by P. Canfield, 1833; revised edition, Hartford, Conn.: William Watson, 1835; revised again, New York: Harper, 1837; revised again, London: Jackson & Walford, 1841);

How to Be Happy, anonymous (Hartford, Conn.: D. F. Robinson, 1833);

Biography of Pious Persons, 2 volumes, anonymous (Springfield, Mass.: G. & C. Merriam, 1833);

The Farmer and the Soldier. A Tale, as L. H. S. (Hartford, Conn.: Printed by J. Hubbard Wells, 1833);

Memoir of Phebe P. Hammond, a Pupil in the American Asylum at Hartford (New York: Sleight & Van Norden, 1833);

The Intemperate, and The Reformed. Shewing the Awful Consequences of Intemperance and the Blessed Effects of the Temperance Reformation (Boston: Seth Bliss, 1833);

Sketches (Philadelphia: Key & Biddle, 1834);

264

Poetry for Children (Hartford, Conn.: Robinson & Pratt, 1834); enlarged as *Poems for Children* (Hartford, Conn.: Canfield & Robbins, 1836);

Poems (Philadelphia: Key & Biddle, 1834; enlarged, 1836);

Lays from the West, edited by Joseph Belcher (London: Thomas Ward, 1834);

Tales and Essays for Children (Hartford, Conn.: F. J. Huntington, 1835);

Memoir of Margaret and Henrietta Fowler, anonymous (Boston: Perkins, Marvin, 1835); republished as *The Lovely Sisters, Margaret and Henrietta* (Hartford, Conn.: H. S. Parsons, 1845); republished again as *Margaret and Henrietta* (New York: American Tract Society, 1852);

Zinzendorff, and Other Poems (New York: Leavitt, Lord/Boston: Crocker & Brewster, 1835);

History of Marcus Aurelius, Emperor of Rome (Hartford, Conn.: Belknap & Hamersley, 1836);

Olive Buds (Hartford, Conn.: William Watson, 1836);

Stories for Youth; Founded on Fact (Hartford, Conn.: William Watson, 1836);

The Girl's Reading-Book; in Prose and Poetry, for Schools (New York: J. Orville Taylor, 1838; revised, 1839); republished as *The Book for Girls* (New York: J. Orville Taylor, 1844);

Letters to Mothers (Hartford, Conn.: Printed by Hudson & Skinner, 1838; revised edition, New York: Harper, 1839);

Select Poems (Philadelphia: F. W. Greenough, 1838; enlarged edition, Philadelphia: E. C. Biddle, 1842; enlarged again, 1845);

The Boy's Reading-Book; in Prose and Poetry, for Schools (New York: J. Orville Taylor, 1839); expanded as *The Boy's Book* (New York: Turner, Hughes & Hayden/Raleigh, N.C.: Turner & Hughes, 1843);

Memoir of Mary Anne Hooker (Philadelphia: American Sunday-School Union, 1840);

Pocahontas, and Other Poems (London: Robert Tyas, 1841; New York: Harper, 1841);

Poems, Religious and Elegiac (London: Robert Tyas, 1841);

Pleasant Memories of Pleasant Lands (Boston: James Munroe, 1842; revised, 1844);

Poems (Philadelphia: Locken, 1842);

The Pictorial Reader, Consisting of Original Articles For the Instruction of Young Children (New York: Turner & Hayden, 1844); republished as *The Child's Book: Consisting of Original Arti-*

cles, in Prose and Poetry (New York: Turner & Hayden, 1844);

Scenes in My Native Land (Boston: James Munroe, 1845);

Poetry for Seamen (Boston: James Munroe, 1845); enlarged as *Poems for the Sea* (Hartford, Conn.: H. S. Parsons, 1850); republished as *The Sea and the Sailor* (Hartford, Conn.: F. A. Brown, 1857);

The Voice of Flowers (Hartford, Conn.: Henry S. Parsons, 1846);

Myrtis, With Other Etchings and Sketchings (New York: Harper, 1846);

The Weeping Willow (Hartford, Conn.: Henry S. Parsons, 1847);

Water-drops (New York & Pittsburgh: Robert Carter, 1848);

Illustrated Poems . . . With Designs by Felix O. C. Darley (Philadelphia: Carey & Hart, 1849);

Whisper to a Bride (Hartford, Conn.: H. S. Parsons, 1850);

The Poetical Works of Mrs. L. H. Sigourney, edited by F. W. N. Bayley (London: Routledge, 1850);

Examples of Life and Death (New York: Scribner, 1851);

Letters to My Pupils: With Narrative and Biographical Sketches (New York: Robert Carter, 1852);

Olive Leaves (New York: Robert Carter, 1852);

The Faded Hope (New York: Robert Carter, 1853);

Memoir of Mrs. Harriet Newell Cook (New York: Robert Carter, 1853);

The Western Home, and Other Poems (Philadelphia: Parry & McMillan, 1854);

Past Meridian (New York: Appleton/Boston: Jewett, 1854; London: Hall, 1855; enlarged edition, Hartford, Conn.: F. A. Brown, 1856; revised and enlarged again, Hartford, Conn.: Brown & Gross, 1864);

Sayings of the Little Ones, and Poems for Their Mothers (Buffalo: Phinney/New York: Ivision & Phinney, 1855);

Examples from the Eighteenth and Nineteenth Centuries (New York: Scribner, 1857);

Lucy Howard's Journal (New York: Harper, 1858);

The Daily Counsellor (Hartford, Conn.: Brown & Gross, 1859);

Gleanings (Hartford, Conn.: Brown & Gross/New York: Appleton, 1860);

The Man of Uz, and Other Poems (Hartford, Conn.: Williams, Wiley & Waterman, 1862);

The Transplanted Daisy: A Memoir of Frances Racillia Hackley (New York: Printed by Sanford, Harroun, 1865);

Letters of Life (New York: Appleton, 1866);
Great and Good Women; Biographies for Girls (Edinburgh: W. P. Nimmo, 1866).

OTHER: *The Writings of Nancy Maria Hyde, of Norwich, Conn. Connected with a Sketch of Her Life*, edited anonymously by Sigourney (Norwich, Conn.: Printed by Russell Hubburd, 1816);
The Religious Souvenir, for MDCCCXXXIX, edited by Sigourney (New York: Scofield & Voorhies, 1838);
The Religious Souvenir, edited by Sigourney (New York: Scofield & Voorhies, 1839); republished as *The Christian Keepsake. A Christmas & New Year's Gift* (New York: Leavitt & Allen, 1856);
"The Christian Going Home," in Joel Hawes, *Memoir of Normand Smith; or the Christian Serving God in His Business* (Springfield, Mass.: G. & C. Merriam, 1844);
"Eve," in *The Women of the Scriptures*, edited by Horatio Hastings Weld (Philadelphia: Lindsay & Blakiston, 1848);
"Memoir of Felicia Hemans," in *The Poetical Works of Felicia Hemans* (Boston: Phillips, Sampson, 1853);
Selections from Various Sources, edited by Sigourney (Worcester, Mass.: John H. Turnes, 1863).

PERIODICAL PUBLICATIONS: "Lines, Addressed to the Hon. Judge Mitchell, of Wethersfield Conn., on His 90th Birthday," *Hermethenean* (1833-1834): 146-147;
"Difference of Color," *Slave's Friend*, 2 (1837): 2;
"The Poet's Books," *Ladies' Companion*, 12 (April 1840): 287;
"Lines on the Plymouth Rock," *America*, 3 (1841);
"Grassmere, and Rydal Water," *United States Magazine and Democratic Review*, 9 (October 1841): 343-344;
"The Prince of Edom," *Democratic Review* (August 1842): 179-180.

Lydia Howard Huntley Sigourney's place in magazine history is deserved more for her prodigious production of prose and poetry than for her editorship of *Godey's Lady's Book* and the *Ladies' Companion*. Journalism historian Frank Luther Mott uses the adjectives "omnipresent" and "ubiquitous" in referring to Sigourney's presence in American magazines of the mid nineteenth century. No exact count exists of her published magazine pieces—many of them published anonymously—but the number is estimated at several thousand in nearly three hundred different publications. Most of those magazine articles and poems were compiled and republished in book form. By 1850 Sigourney, referred to as the "sweet singer of Hartford," was the most widely known woman writer in both America and Europe, a reputation that led several American magazine publishers to compete for her name on the title pages of their publications.

Sigourney was born in Norwich, Connecticut, the only child of Ezekial and Zerviah Wentworth Huntley. From all accounts she had a particularly strong attachment for her father, who had fought in the Revolution and then worked as a gardener for Dr. Daniel Lathrop. By the time Sigourney was born, Dr. Lathrop had died, but his widow had kept Huntley on as gardener. From her self-educated mother and Mrs. Lathrop, Sigourney received encouragement in reading and writing.

Mrs. Lathrop's family and social connections in both Norwich and Hartford and her attention to young Lydia turned out to be influential in shaping Sigourney's writings. When the eighty-eight-year-old woman died, Sigourney was at her side and later described the sentimental deathbed scene in her poems. In fact, at Mrs. Lathrop's funeral Sigourney was overcome with such emotion that a physician recommended that she be removed from familiar surroundings. So she was sent to stay awhile with the Wadsworths of Hartford, relatives of the deceased. Daniel Wadsworth became yet another influential benefactor to the young girl, introducing her to the volumes in his library, eventually setting her up as a teacher in her own school and helping get her first book published.

Sigourney began her long writing career with *Moral Pieces, in Prose and Verse* in 1815, a book drawn from the poems and prose that she composed for her students, and as early as 1816 her work began to appear in such periodicals as the *North American Review*. Her publishing career continued for half a century. Her writing style, in the fashion of the period, was excessively sentimental. Almost everything she wrote had a pious tone and conveyed a moral. Almost everything she experienced, thought, or heard about, extending to the trite routines of her daily homemaking, became subjects for her sentimental "effusions," as she called them. She drew upon her readings of historical and religious materials for much of her writing, as illustrated by the follow-

308　　　　　　EDITORS' TABLE.

EDITORS' TABLE.

Caption: Publisher William W. Snowden's announcement in the April 1843 issue of the Ladies' Companion *that Sigourney and Emma C. Embury would become coeditors of the magazine*

ing titles: "The Conflagration at Washington," "The Hartford Convention," "Paraphrase of Cleopatra's Advice to Mark Anthony When Angling," "Pocahontas," "The Distribution of Bibles at Malta," and "The Departure of Mrs. Nott with the Missionaries for India." She also wrote travel pieces about places that she had visited or had heard about. Temperance was another of her subjects.

Death—especially the death of a child—was her most frequent topic. Her poems often end with the spirit floating skyward. Indeed, a description of the same upward floating spirit concludes poems with vastly different themes, such as "The Gift of a Bible," "The Conflagration at New York," "The Ancient Family Clock," and "To the Cactus Speciosissimus." She composed thousands of elegiac poems, and one of her books, the three-

hundred-page *Zinzendorff, and Other Poems* (1835), is almost entirely a collection of funereal verse. In fact, she became so closely associated with poetry about death that she often received requests from total strangers who wanted elegies and epitaphs for recently deceased loved ones. She wrote in her autobiography, *Letters of Life* (1866), that some memoirs were composed to raise money for families of the deceased. She also said that one of the attractions of the Episcopal church, which she joined out of duty to her husband, was the pathos of its burial service. That she should seem preoccupied with death is not surprising, given the high infant mortality rate of the period and the fact that her first three children died at birth and a fourth died at age nineteen.

Moral Pieces, in Prose and Verse comprises genteel homilies from Sigourney's journals and material written as reading exercises for students. When she was twenty years old Sigourney turned to teaching, one of the only occupations open to women, to earn money to help support herself and her parents. She and a friend opened a school for young ladies in Norwich and charged tuition at the customary rate of three dollars a quarter. Two years later she moved to Hartford and opened a school after Daniel Wadsworth arranged for sixteen girls from the best families in town to enroll. Apparently, it was Wadsworth's idea to publish *Moral Pieces*. He financed it, read all the proof, did some editing, wrote the introduction, and arranged for all of his acquaintances to buy copies at one dollar each. Nearly a thousand copies were sold, producing more money than Sigourney—who had taught in Norwich for twelve dollars a year—had probably ever seen.

Gordon Sherman Haight, Sigourney's biographer, wrote that the volume was well named because "nothing she wrote could escape from her pen without a moral. The simple formulas she established in these poems remained practically unchanged throughout her life." Rufus W. Griswold, in *The Female Poets of America* (1849), wrote of *Moral Pieces*: "None of its contents are deserving of special commendation, but they are all respectable, and the volume procured her an accession of reputation which was probably of much indirect advantage." In 1816 Sigourney edited *The Writings of Nancy Maria Hyde* and wrote a biographical sketch of the woman who had died earlier that year and who had been like a sister since school days. Sigourney wrote in her autobiography that the work "was a solace to my feelings, and a source of profit to the bereaved mother."

When she was twenty-seven she married Charles Sigourney, a widower who owned a prosperous hardware business and was president of a local bank. He was respected by all who knew him and served as a warden of Christ Church and a trustee of Trinity College, then called Washington College. "Habitual industry did not forsake me, but was ready to enter untried departments," Sigourney later wrote of the early years of her marriage. Living in the house were her husband's two daughters and a son from his first wife, who had died a year before he met Lydia. In addition, the maiden sister of the first Mrs. Sigourney lived in the house, and two clerks from the hardware store, two gardeners, and three female servants were frequently about the house and grounds. Her remarks in her autobiography about this period in her life indicate that it was somewhat difficult for her to make a place for herself in the household and that she was intimidated by the legacy of the earlier Mrs. Sigourney. "In this new sphere I could scarcely hope to equal my predecessor–who was a model of elegance," Sigourney wrote almost fifty years later. After the deaths of her first three children–or in Sigourney's sentimental writing style, after they "fainted at the gate of life"–two children, Mary and Andrew, were born to the Sigourneys. Their mother would become the primary molder of their education, as she was for her three stepchildren. Several of her books were adapted from material that she originally composed to use for her children's lessons.

She continued her interest in writing, but she devoted the bulk of her attention to her new status as Charles Sigourney's wife. Her husband was insistent that literature should be a social accomplishment, an elegant pastime. He thought it beneath her–and perhaps a blemish on his reputation as the family provider–to publish, especially for money. She continued to have material published, and Charles Sigourney even helped her publish, so long as it was anonymous. For at least three years her poems, short stories, and essays were published anonymously in magazines, and *The Square Table* (1819), a reply to "Arthur's Round Table," was issued as a pamphlet in two parts. "I had great amusement in hearing its merits discussed and its authorship inquired after in circles where I visited," she later wrote.

In *Traits of the Aborigines of America* (1822), a 284-page poem in five cantos, Sigourney drew upon her acquaintance with the Mohegan tribe of Indians who lived a few miles from Norwich. In an impassioned appeal for the support of missionaries, the book urged Christian conversion of the Indians as a means to make the West safe for settlers. The poem included classical allusions and biblical similes, and the Indians all exhibited the virtues of friendship, gratitude, reverence for age, and piety. Griswold wrote that the poem "is too discursive to produce the deep impression which might have been made with such a display of abilities, learnings, and just opinions. Its tone is dignified and sustained, and it contains passages of considerable power and beauty." *Traits of the Aborigines of America,* which included elaborate notes so that the volume would be useful as a reference work on the Indians, was not popular when it appeared. As Sigourney's biographer pointed out, the Cherokee Nation had recently announced a firm resolution not to cede more land to the government, and John Adams, Thomas Jefferson, and John Marshall had rebuffed attempts at charity toward Indians as an interference with government policy, so as an appeal to charity the poem was ineffective.

During the 1820s Sigourney continued to publish anonymously in keeping with her husband's wishes. However, she did seek payment for her writings. By 1830 more than twenty periodicals were regularly accepting her poems. Sigourney needed money to help support her aging parents. Her father was approaching eighty and needed more than his soldier's pension could provide. Charles Sigourney was generous, but his finances were not as good as they had been earlier in the marriage. The dry goods and hardware businesses slacked off after an initial flurry of activity after the War of 1812; his salary from the bank never exceeded seven hundred dollars a year, and the mansion that the family had moved into soon after the marriage had cost more to build than estimated.

Sigourney drew subjects and inspiration for her writings from her travels and meetings with famous people. In 1824 Daniel Wadsworth arranged for her to meet the Marquis de Lafayette when he visited Hartford. She accompanied her husband to Virginia in 1825 and met Jefferson and Dolly and James Madison and dined with President John Quincy Adams. In 1827 she gathered her poems from the Virginia trip plus some others that had already appeared in periodicals and had them published by a Boston printer. The money from this anonymous effort went to her parents.

Throughout her life Sigourney recirculated poems, often sending the same work to more than one magazine. Then every few months she gathered the published poems together and sent them to a publisher to be issued as a book. She repeated stories that she wrote for children, first in the classroom or to her own children, then in magazines, and finally as chapters in books. Her *Biography of Pious Persons* (1833), for example, contained sketches that she composed originally to read to her students at the end of each week so that the students could keep the examples in mind until they returned to school on Monday. Within one ten-day period in 1833 she wrote a slim volume titled *How to Be Happy*, instructing children how to be good and obedient. The book sold well, and Sigourney received ten cents for each copy and twenty-five copies of each new printing.

In the same year, perhaps for financial reasons or perhaps because she no longer wished to yield to her husband's wishes, she broke out of her anonymity, allowing her initials to be used on *The Farmer and the Soldier. A Tale.* She would thereafter take credit for all but two of her publications, the exceptions being elegiac "memoirs." Evidence is strong that the Sigourney marriage was no longer happy by the mid 1820s. Ann Douglas Wood quotes an October 1827 letter from Charles Sigourney in which he accused his wife of evincing a "lust of praise" and having an "apparently unconquerable passion of displaying herself." He expressed resentment of the open flirtations she carried on with writers and editors, reminding her of her own precept that woman should be "like the sun behind a cloud, giving life & warmth & comfort to all around, itself unseen. . . . Who wants, or would value a wife who is to be the public property of the whole community." Further indication of the unhappy state of the marriage is the fact that of thousands of elegiac poems that Sigourney wrote, she apparently did not compose one for her husband. Her autobiography devotes only three sentences to his death and reveals little about their life together.

In 1834 and 1835 seven volumes by Sigourney were published, two of which were primarily funerary verse. *Zinzendorff, and Other Poems* was the subject of a review by Edgar Allan Poe in the January 1836 issue of the *Southern Literary Messenger.* Of the title poem Poe said that it was the longest, 580 lines, but not the best.

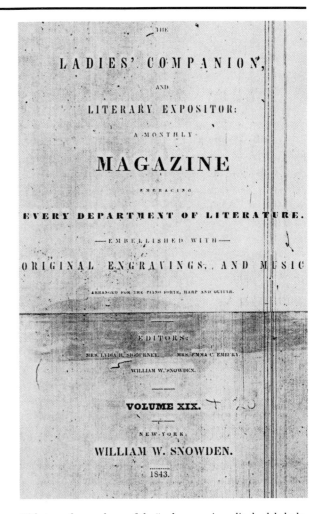

Title page for a volume of the "only magazine edited solely by ladies," according to publisher Snowden, who was in fact the magazine's only editor

"Many passages are very noble," Poe wrote, "and breathe the truest spirit of the Muse." However, he went on to fault Sigourney's imagery and what he viewed as her errors of accentuation. He criticized the conclusion of a poem titled "Female Education" as being "pathetic to a degree bordering upon the grotesque." Poe liked "Friends of Man," which he noted had first been published in the *Messenger.* The poem "Filial Grief " was "worthy of high praise," he said. In this same review Poe commented on Sigourney's growing comparison with the poet Felicia Hemans, a comparison that Sigourney herself promoted. Poe wrote that she had acquired the title of the "American Hemans" "solely by imitation. The very phrase 'American Hemans' speaks loudly in accusation: and we are grieved that what by the overzealous has been intended as complimentary should fall with so ill-omened a sound into the ear of the judicious." Poe then gave specifics to support his accusation: the character of Sigourney's subjects, the structure of her versification, the peculiar turns of her phraseology, use of quotations, use of an intitial motto–often a very long one–to inform readers of the subject matter. Poe wrote that the reader often must keep this motto in mind in order to understand the poem. Sigourney's biographer dismissed Poe's charge of imitation, arguing that it was more accurate to say that Sigourney modeled her verse on that of others, including Samuel Taylor Coleridge, William Wordsworth, Lord Byron, and Hemans.

Once she threw off the cloak of anonymity, Sigourney became the most widely known "authoress" in America. Helping to spread her fame were her contributions to several of the popular annual gift books. These were a source of income as well, as she received ten dollars for a piece of ordinary length and as much as one hundred dollars for three or four poems to fill twenty pages. Sigourney edited the *Religious Souvenir* in 1838 and 1839 but decided that the editorship involved too much time-consuming correspondence. She showed that she had a keen business sense in her dealings with the annuals and with magazines because after she became well known, she never allowed her material to be used unless she was paid for it. In addition, as part of her arrangement as editor of the *Religious Souvenir*, she gained rights to the stereotype plates, and for years afterward the books were occasionally reissued under various titles. Her attention to financial matters was important because, despite the embarrassment that her husband continued to feel by his wife's success, the family probably lived beyond its means and needed the extra income that she provided. By 1838 the Sigourney family could no longer afford the big house on the hill with its many servants. The move from their home of eighteen years to a more modest house was more a blow to pride than to comfort, and the sorrowful "dear retreat," as Sigourney began to refer to it, provided material for her poetry. By the 1840s the annuals were becoming less popular, but by that time Sigourney had shifted her attention to magazines, which were increasing in number and popularity, much to the dismay of those who thought that they were harmful, especially to young minds.

Once her popularity was established, magazine publishers began to bid against each other for the right to list Sigourney as editor of their periodicals. From 1839 to 1842 Louis Godey reportedly paid her five hundred dollars a year to have her name on the title page of *Godey's Lady's Book*. Sigourney shared billing for the first two years with Godey and Mrs. Sarah J. Hale, with Hale alone in 1841 and with Hale, Morton McMichael, and Godey in 1842. Godey wanted exclusive use of her name, but she continued to contribute poems to many publications, including competitors of the *Lady's Book*. Mott and other historians express doubt that Sigourney did much editorial work on any magazine, but there is no doubt that she was one of the most productive magazine contributors of the period.

Godey's Lady's Book and Sigourney's writings were particularly well matched. Godey never allowed anything to be published that was not suitable for ladies of the period. The magazine carried thousands of sentimental and moral stories and poems. While it was the most prominent of all the women's magazines of the period and published nearly all the best-known writers in America, it never became a first-rate literary magazine. The magazine almost never ran articles about current problems, politics, social concerns, or economic topics because Godey believed that women had no interest in such topics. However, Mrs. Hale frequently used the magazine to advocate education for women.

During the 1840s *Godey's Lady's Book*, *Ladies' Companion*, and *Graham's Magazine* all wanted exclusive use of Sigourney's name. In 1839 she signed with Godey, and correspondence between Godey and Sigourney indicates that it was supposed to be an exclusive contract. The Sigourney family's need for money probably compelled her to contribute poems to *Ladies' Companion* at the same time that the *Lady's Book* carried her name on its title page. *Ladies' Companion* paid better than most other magazines and paid promptly. With the May 1843 issue *Ladies' Companion* began to carry Sigourney's name on its title page. Her biographer speculated that perhaps the *Companion* wanted Sigourney's name to help secure respectability for the magazine, which tended to be more sensational than moral. It was owned by W. W. Snowden, who also owned a half interest in the Bowery Theater and puffed its shows in each issue of the magazine. Sigourney wrote a friend that she hoped to elevate the tone of the magazine, and she suggested that historic tales be published in place of some of the adventure stories that it was then running. Evidence that Sigourney's editorship was in name only is the fact that Snowden did not even answer her letter when she wrote suggesting that some "female supervision" was needed over each issue.

In the January 1844 issue of *Ladies' Companion* Snowden published an attack on Park Benjamin, editor of the rival *New World*. He had earlier called Benjamin "a literary hedge-hog." Now he printed an article referring to him as a "reptile," "scorpion," and "literary scarabaeus." In addition, Snowden heaped abuse upon Benjamin's physical appearance, writing that "whenever the poor creature is so unfortunate as to catch a glimpse of his disgusting form reflected in a mirror, he foams horribly at the mouth and pours forth savage imprecations upon all the human race." Ann Stephens, editor of *Peterson's Magazine*, wrote Sigourney in an attempt to entice her away from Snowden's employ and tried to convince her that a libel trial would likely ensue and damage Sigourney's good name. Sigourney did not join *Peterson's*, but she did write a humble letter to Benjamin, appealing to his chivalry and making sure that he knew that her duties with the magazine did not include receiving or revising articles. In the next issue of *New World* Benjamin published a long editorial about the situation, exonerating Sigourney from all blame but publicly rebuking her. He wrote that she was morally responsible for allowing herself to be named as editor, when she was not. He further asserted that she was also legally responsible for any slanderous defamation that may appear in its columns. Soon afterward Sigourney's name disappeared from the title page of the *Ladies' Companion*.

In addition to her name and influence Sigourney's literary efforts were also in demand. Poe may have thought her work imitative, but he recognized her popular appeal. In November 1841, as editor of *Graham's Magazine*, he wrote her and asked that she contribute to the magazine on a monthly basis, beginning with the January issue. The January issue included a Sigourney poem, "To a Land Bird at Sea." Also in that issue were contributions from Henry Wadsworth Longfellow and James Russell Lowell and Poe's favorable review of Sigourney's recently published *Pocahontas, and Other Poems*. Arrangements for the monthly contributions were never completed because in April 1842 Poe resigned, and Griswold took over as editor. Griswold's *Poets and Poetry of America* had recently been published, and Sigourney was irritated by the entry dealing with her. After a brief account of her life Griswold gave this opinion of her work: "Mrs. Sigourney has surpassed any of the poets of her sex in this country in the extent of her productions; and their religious and domestic character has made them popular with the large classes who regard more than artistic merit the spirit and tendency of what they read. Her subjects are varied, and her diction generally melodious and free; but her works are written too carelessly; they lack vigour and condensation; and possess but few of the elements of enduring verse...." She did not send any more work to *Graham's* in 1842, probably because Griswold had become editor. Among other magazines publishing or commenting on Sigourney's work were *Ladies' Repository, American Literary Magazine, Casket, Boston Miscellany, American Monthly, New-England Magazine, Knickerbocker Magazine, Literary World, Parley's Magazine, Ladies' Garland, Democratic Review, Hesperian, Christian Parlor Magazine, Columbian Lady's and Gentleman's Magazine,* and *Union Magazine.*

In addition to her frequent contributions to periodicals, Sigourney published fourteen volumes between 1840 and 1850, many of them containing works that had already been published either in magazines or other books. Material for much of her writing in the early 1840s came from her tour of Europe, which followed the usual itinerary of nineteenth-century travelers: from Liverpool to the Scottish lakes; Newcastle and York to London; two months in Paris; then back to London for three months. She was not much of a travel writer, but she took detailed notes filled with the dimensions, extravagant costs, and extreme antiquity of the monuments she visited. She wrote poems daily about almost everything she saw and everyone she met.

For Sigourney the primary purpose of the trip may have been a literary lion hunt. Her writings were already known in Great Britain, and she left Hartford armed with many letters of introduction. In all of her European travels she went to extraordinary lengths to try to meet authors such as Thomas Carlyle, Wordsworth, and Robert Southey, then the poet laureate. Later she would try to nurse even the briefest introduction into a literary friendship. Acquaintances were surprised, and some were regretful when *Pleasant Memories of Pleasant Lands* appeared in December 1842. Sigourney made it appear that she was close friends with people such as Mrs. Southey when she had in truth barely met them. Apparently, Sigourney used name-dropping as a type of advertising to boost the sales and the perceived importance of her writings. She took with her numerous volumes of her poems to give as gifts to important people she met or wanted to meet. For example, she sent the queen of France a beautifully bound volume of poems, along with a letter. Soon afterward the queen sent her a diamond bracelet. Sigourney's biographical notices immediately began to mention that the "Empress of the French" had bestowed it after reading her poems, which is unlikely since the queen could not understand English.

Three years later, in 1845, Sigourney's *Scenes in My Native Land* was published. The volume, which included prose and poetry, some of it recirculated magazine pieces about interesting places that she had visited in the United States, was more popular abroad than at home. Sigourney could not visit all the places, so she drew on descriptions from other writers. She did make a trip to Niagara in June 1844, accompanied by her son, Andrew, then fourteen, and she described the falls as they affected him. The book, however, was a failure. Apparently the American public, unlike readers in England, were not interested in reading secondhand impressions of familiar places. In England, however, *Scenes in My Native Land* sold better than *Pleasant Memories of Pleasant Lands*.

Continuing her pattern of gathering magazine poems and articles into books, Sigourney published *Poetry for Seamen* in 1845. This 152-page volume included all the poems she had written about ships and sailors plus many temperance hymns. In her autobiography Sigourney described the work as "a little book of poetry which might go with them (sailors) in their chests, a prompter of salutary thought when they should leave the charities of home. . . . Should I speak of it with that frankness of criticism by which we lady writers have too seldom an opportunity of profiting, I should say that some of its poems are not simple enough for sailors, and others too simple for those in command, so that it falls short of both classes." The first edition of one thousand copies was bought by a friend who distributed them to seamen through a chaplain.

In 1846 Sigourney brought together many of her poems and articles about flowers in *The Voice of Flowers*, followed the next year by *The Weeping Willow*, a collection of poems about the frailty of human life. *Myrtis, With Other Etchings and Sketchings*, published in 1846, contained thirteen tales in prose. One was set in ancient Athens, another in Poland during its struggle against Russian domination, and others in colonial America. This vol-

Sigourney in 1859 (photograph by Mathew Brady; courtesy of the Library of Congress)

ume depicted a young girl shutting herself off from the world in a convent or some similar retreat, a frequent theme for Sigourney and her peers. *Water-drops*, issued in 1848, promoted the cause of temperance and was another compilation of previously published work. Sigourney said that the volume was particularly addressed to females to help them influence their children against drink.

Illustrated Poems, which Griswold called the most complete and elegant edition of Sigourney's poems, was issued in 1849. Carey and Hart of Philadelphia asked her to compile her poems plus some new ones for an illustrated edition, the fourth in a series to include the work of William Cullen Bryant, Longfellow, and Nathaniel Parker Willis. The volume contained more than four hundred pages with fourteen fine engravings of illustrations designed by Felix O. C. Darley. In her autobiography Sigourney wrote that the book "was the first of mine that in all respects of paper, typography, and binding, was quite accordant with my taste." Illustrative, perhaps, of her opportunistic nature is the fact that she had planned to dedicate the book to Daniel Wadsworth, but he died in the summer of 1848. Three weeks later she wrote to the publishers and asked whether they thought a dedication to Samuel Rogers, the banker-poet of London, would be advantageous to the book. Carey and Hart assured her that such a dedication might be a nice touch, so the tribute to her deceased benefactor was replaced by a dedication to the eighty-five-year-old English poet, whom she had visited during her European trip.

Sigourney's most personal work of the 1850s was *The Faded Hope* (1853), a memoir of her only son, Andrew, who died of consumption in 1850 at the age of nineteen. Andrew had turned against his mother by the time of his death; like his father, he always seemed ashamed that his mother supported herself by writing. Andrew kept a diary and recorded the books that he read, all of a very moral character. By the time he was ten years old, in addition to the Bible, he had read such books as his mother's *Biography of Pious Persons, Doddridge's Rise and Progress of Religion,* and *Pilgrim's Progress.* Before he died he destroyed most of his personal writings because he did not want his mother to publish them as she had earlier published some of his school exercises without consulting him. Sigourney, however, had already set aside parts of his journals, and some material that he did not find to destroy was published in *The Faded Hope,* along with detailed descriptions of his last illness. Haight notes that modern readers would consider the book in deplorable taste, but her biographer maintains that Sigourney was simply following the fashion of the age.

During the 1850s and 1860s Sigourney's writings continued the pattern set in earlier decades, with most material being published first in magazines and then compiled into book form. In 1854 *Past Meridian,* a salute to old age, was published. According to her autobiography, the inspiration to write it came from Cicero's "De Senectute" and her belief that "if a heathen could discover so much beauty in age, Christian philosophy should be able more perfectly to illustrate how the latest drop of existence might exhale in a song of praise to the Giver." She quotes with pride a review of the work from the *North American Review,* which she characterized as "our highest umpire in the realm of intellect": "It is much more than 'De Senectute' Christianized. It is enriched and adorned by the association. . . . Above all, it blends with the serene sunset of a well-

spent life the young morning beams of a never-setting day. It will carry solace to many a fireside and rekindle hope and gladness in many a soul that scarcely dares to look into its earthly future."

The frequency of her books diminished in the last two decades of her life, and she completed her autobiography, *Letters of Life,* shortly before her death on 10 June 1865 at age seventy-three. She wrote: "My literary course has been a happy one. It commenced in impulse, and was continued from habit. Two principles it has ever kept in view—not to interfere with the discharge of womanly duty, and to aim at being an instrument of good." Of her journals she said: "These systematic records became a sort of necessity of my existence. They seemed an adjunct in religious progress, and to justify the adjuration with which one of them is consecrated: 'Give me Thine aid calmly to look upon the changes that are appointed me, and to love the little streams fed hourly from the fountain of Divine Mercy; and to hope that, when I fade, as I soon shall, like the grass, I may be renewed in the image of a glorious immortality.' "

Her writings have not brought immortality for Sigourney. The most popular female poet of nineteenth-century America is virtually unknown in the late twentieth century. In the preface to her biography Haight wrote that he had hoped to "find among her poems some few pieces that would establish her right to the reputation she enjoyed for half a century as America's leading poetess. But before reading many of the forty-odd volumes through which the search ultimately led me, I was forced to agree that posterity had judged fairly in denying her claim. I began then to wonder how she had achieved and maintained such popularity. Pursuit of this question revealed Mrs. Sigourney's wide acquaintance with famous people both at home and abroad during a lifetime that stretched from Washington's second term as President beyond the death of Lincoln."

As Ann Douglas Wood pointed out, Sigourney wrote tributes to feminine modesty and dependence, but she aggressively sought fame, as evidenced by her unsolicited correspondence with influential literary, social, and political figures, by the numerous volumes of her own work that she gave to important people, and by the maneuverings she used to meet the powerful, especially during her European tour. Wood asserted that this hypocrisy was encouraged in nineteenth-century culture because sentimental "effusions" were an acceptable way for women to succeed. Open competitive aggressiveness, either sexual or career-oriented, was absolutely unacceptable for women. Wood said that in adapting to and exploiting patterns laid out for women of her day, Sigourney "used poetry to gain social mobility, as an advertisement for piety and as a home substitute for church ritual; but equally important, she used it as a means for a kind of militant sublimation." Although Sigourney was unhappy in her marriage, she was held as an exemplar of feminine virtue.

Who were the readers that brought Sigourney widespread fame during her lifetime? Her biographer described them as ardent patriots, still conscious of the Revolution and anxious to have their literature independent from that of England. They wanted American subjects. They seemed to think that American literature could swallow up all others if only it could be produced in sufficient quantity. Haight noted, too, that the confusion of patriotism with literature worked to prevent criticism, as did acceptance of the principle that the religious or moral note automatically placed a poem above criticism, and, of course, Sigourney's major theme was morality. In an America that worshipped respectability and material success, Sigourney's image as a poor girl who had grown famous was appealing. Few critics, indeed, dared judge her work apart from her person. It would have been difficult to do otherwise because her work was filled with domestic notes. Her audience was composed primarily of women as romantic, pious, and patriotic as herself.

Sigourney wrote primarily for the heart rather than the intellect, a fact often mentioned in the more scholarly of the literary reviews of that time. But bad reviews probably had little effect on the sales of her books because her readers were neither scholarly nor critical. They were more concerned with sentiment than with scholarship. She became popular with the common folk because she was able to put their thoughts into words. She practiced the lessons that her poems taught: sobriety, thrift, patience, and virtue. Haight maintained that "when the inevitable decline of her reputation set in, it came, not from any deterioration in the quality of her verse, but from the changing taste of the public."

Biography:

Gordon Sherman Haight, *Mrs. Sigourney: The Sweet Singer of Hartford* (New Haven: Yale University Press, 1930).

References:

Rufus W. Griswold, *The Female Poets of America* (Philadelphia: Carey & Hart, 1849);

Griswold, *Poets and Poetry of America* (Philadelphia: Carey & Hart, 1842);

Frank Luther Mott, *A History of American Magazines*, 5 volumes (Cambridge, Mass.: Harvard University Press, 1938-1968), I: 584-585;

Ann Douglas Wood, "Mrs. Sigourney and the Sensibility of the Inner Space," *New England Quarterly*, 45 (June 1972): 163-181.

Papers:

Collections of Lydia Howard Huntley Sigourney papers are at the Connecticut Historical Library, the Connecticut State Library, Trinity College, the Huntington Library, the Schlesinger Library, the New York Historical Society, and the Boston Public Library.

William Gilmore Simms

(17 April 1806-11 June 1870)

James Everett Kibler, Jr.
University of Georgia

See also the Simms entries in *DLB 3: Antebellum Writers in New York and the South; DLB 30: American Literary Historians, 1607-1865;* and *DLB 59: American Literary Critics and Scholars, 1800-1850.*

MAJOR POSITIONS HELD: Staff editor, *Album* (1825-1826); coeditor, editor, *Southern Literary Gazette* (1828-1829); editor, *Charleston City Gazette* (1830-1832); editor or staff editor, *Cosmopolitan* (Charleston) (1833); editor, *Magnolia; or, Southern Apalachian* (1842-1843); editor, *Orion; Or, Southern Monthly* (Charleston) (1844); editor, *Southern and Western Monthly Magazine and Review* (1845); editor, *Southern Quarterly Review* (1849-1854); book review editor, *Charleston Mercury* (1854-1856, 1858-1860); editor, *Columbia Phoenix,* renamed the *Columbia Daily Pheonix* (1865); staff editor, *Charleston Daily South Carolinian* (1865-1866); staff editor, *Charleston Courier* (1870).

BOOKS: *Monody, on the Death of Gen. Charles Cotesworth Pinckney,* anonymous (Charleston, S.C.: Gray & Ellis, 1825);

Lyrical and Other Poems (Charleston, S.C.: Ellis & Neufville, 1827);

Early Lays (Charleston, S.C.: A. E. Miller, 1827);

The Vision of Cortes, Cain, and Other Poems (Charleston, S.C.: James S. Burges, 1829);

The Tri-Color; or The Three Days of Blood, in Paris. With Some Other Pieces, anonymous (London: Wigfall & Davis, 1830 [Charleston, S.C.: James S. Burges, 1831]);

Atalantis. A Story of the Sea: In Three Parts, anonymous (New York: J. & J. Harper, 1832; enlarged edition, Philadelphia: Carey & Hart, 1848 [i.e., 1849]);

Martin Faber; The Story of a Criminal (New York: J. & J. Harper, 1833; London: J. Clements, 1838 or 1839);

The Book of My Lady. A Melange, anonymous (Philadelphia: Key & Biddle, 1833; Boston: Allen & Ticknor, 1833);

William Gilmore Simms, circa 1859 (courtesy of the South Caroliniana Library, University of South Carolina)

Guy Rivers: A Tale of Georgia, 2 volumes (New York: Harper, 1834; London: J. Clements, 1841);

The Yemassee. A Romance of Carolina, 2 volumes (New York: Harper, 1835; London: N. Bruce, 1842);

The Partisan: A Tale of the Revolution, 2 volumes (New York: Harper, 1835);

Mellichampe. A Legend of the Santee, 2 volumes (New York: Harper, 1836);

Martin Faber, The Story of a Criminal; and Other Tales, 2 volumes (New York: Harper, 1837);

275

Slavery in America, Being a Brief Review of Miss Martineau on that Subject, anonymous (Richmond, Va.: Thomas W. White, 1838);

Richard Hurdis; Or, The Avenger of Blood. A Tale of Alabama, 2 volumes, anonymous (Philadelphia: Carey & Hart, 1838);

Pelayo: A Story of the Goth, 2 volumes (New York: Harper, 1838);

Carl Werner, An Imaginative Story; With Other Tales of Imagination, 2 volumes (New York: George Adlard, 1838); republished as *Young Ladies' Book of Romantic Tales* (Boston: E. Littlefield, 1839); *Carl Werner* republished as *Matilda: The Spectre of the Castle* (Boston: Gleason, 1846);

Southern Passages and Pictures (New York: George Adlard, 1839 [i.e., 1838]);

The Damsel of Darien, 2 volumes (Philadelphia: Lea & Blanchard, 1839; London: N. Bruce, 1843);

The History of South Carolina, from its First European Discovery to its Erection into a Republic: With a Supplementary Chronicle of Events to the Present Time (Charleston, S.C.: S. Babcock, 1840; revised, 1842); revised again (Charleston, S.C.: Russell & Jones/New York: Redfield, 1860);

Border Beagles; A Tale of Mississippi, 2 volumes (Philadelphia: Carey & Hart, 1840);

The Kinsmen: Or The Black Riders of Congaree, 2 volumes (Philadelphia: Lea & Blanchard, 1841; London: John Cunningham, 1841); revised as *The Scout Or The Black Riders of Congaree* (New York: Redfield, 1854);

Confession; Or, The Blind Heart. A Domestic Story, 2 volumes (Philadelphia: Lea & Blanchard, 1841; London: J. Cunningham, 1841);

Beauchampe: Or The Kentucky Tragedy. A Tale of Passion, 2 volumes (Philadelphia: Lea & Blanchard, 1842; London: N. Bruce, 1842); volume 1 revised as *Charlemont Or the Pride of the Village. A Tale of Kentucky* (New York: Redfield, 1856); volume 2 revised as *Beauchampe Or the Kentucky Tragedy. A Sequel to Charlemont* (New York: Redfield, 1856);

The Social Principle: The True Source of National Permanence. An Oration, Delivered Before the Erosophic Society of the University of Alabama, at its Twelfth Anniversary, December 13, 1842 (Tuscaloosa: The Society, 1843);

The Geography of South Carolina: Being a Companion to the History of that State (Charleston, S.C.: Babcock, 1843);

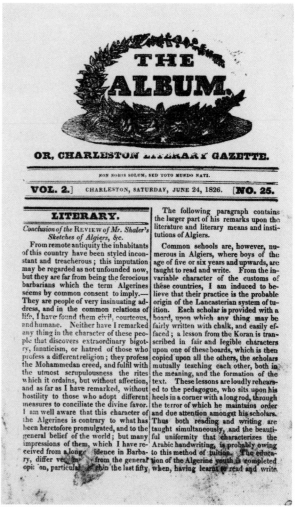

The only surviving copy of an issue from volume two of the first southern literary periodical (collection of James E. Kibler)

Donna Florida: A Tale (Charleston, S.C.: Burges & James, 1843);

The Prima Donna: A Passage from City Life (Philadelphia: Louis A. Godey, 1844);

The Sources of American Independence. An Oration, on the Sixty-ninth Anniversary of American Independence; Delivered at Aiken, South Carolina, Before the Town Council and Citizens Thereof (Aiken: Town Council, 1844);

The Life of Francis Marion (New York: Henry G. Langley, 1844);

Castle Dismal: Or, The Bachelor's Christmas. A Domestic Legend (New York: Burgess, Stringer, 1844);

Helen Halsey: Or, The Swamp State of Conelachita. A Tale of the Borders (New York: Burgess, Stringer, 1845);

Grouped Thoughts and Scattered Fancies. A Collection of Sonnets (Richmond, Va.: Wm. Macfarlane, 1845);

The Wigwam and the Cabin ... First Series (New York: Wiley & Putnam, 1845; London: Wiley & Putnam, 1846); enlarged as *Life in America* (Aberdeen, Scotland: George Clark, 1848);

The Wigwam and the Cabin ... Second Series (New York: Wiley & Putnam, 1845; London: Wiley & Putnam, 1845);

Count Julian; Or, the Last Days of the Goth. A Historical Romance (Baltimore & New York: William Taylor, 1845; London: Bruce & Wyld, 1846);

Views and Reviews in American Literature, History and Fiction ... First Series (New York: Wiley & Putnam, 1845; London: Wiley & Putnam, 1846);

Views and Reviews in American Literature, History and Fiction ... Second Series (New York: Wiley & Putnam, 1845; London: Wiley & Putnam, 1846);

Areytos: Or, Songs of the South (Charleston, S.C.: John Russell, 1846);

The Life of Captain John Smith. The Founder of Virginia (New York: Geo. F. Cooledge, 1846);

The Life of Chevalier Bayard: "The Good Knight," "sans peur et sans reproche" (New York: Harper, 1847);

Self-Development. An Oration Delivered Before the Literary Societies of Oglethorpe University, Georgia; November 10, 1847 (Milledgeville, Ga.: Thalian Society, 1847);

Lays of the Palmetto: A Tribute to the South Carolina Regiment, in the War with Mexico (Charleston, S.C.: John Russell, 1848);

Charleston, and Her Satirists; A Scribblement (Charleston, S.C.: James S. Burges, 1848);

Charleston, and Her Satirists; A Scribblement ... No. 2 (Conclusion) (Charleston, S.C.: James S. Burges, 1848);

The Cassique of Accabee. A Tale of Ashley River. With Other Pieces (Charleston, S.C.: John Russell, 1849; New York: Harper, 1849; New York: Putnam, 1849);

Father Abbot, Or, the Home Tourist; A Medley (Charleston, S.C.: Miller & Browne, 1849);

The Life of Nathanael Greene, Major-General in the Army of the Revolution (New York: George F. Cooledge, 1849);

Sabbath Lyrics; Or, Songs from Scripture (Charleston, S.C.: Walker & James, 1849);

The Lily and the Totem, Or, The Huguenots in Florida. A Series of Sketches, Picturesque and Historical, of the Colonies of Coligni, in North America (New York: Baker & Scribner, 1850);

Flirtation at the Moultrie House: In a Series of Letters, from Miss Georgiana Appleby, to her Friends in Georgia, Showing the Doings at the Moultrie House, and the Events Which Took Place at the Grand Costume Ball, on the 29th August, 1850; With Other Letters, anonymous (Charleston, S.C.: Edward C. Councell, 1850);

The City of the Silent: A Poem (Charleston, S.C.: Walker & James, 1850 [i.e., 1851]);

Katharine Walton: Or, The Rebel of Dorchester. An Historical Romance of the Revolution in Carolina (Philadelphia: A. Hart, 1851);

Norman Maurice; Or, The Man of the People. An American Drama (Richmond, Va.: Jno. R. Thompson, 1851; revised edition, Charleston, S.C.: Walker & Richards, 1852);

The Golden Christmas: A Chronicle of St. John's, Berkeley. Compiled from the Notes of a Briefless Barrister (Charleston, S.C.: Walker & Richards, 1852);

The Sword and the Distaff; Or, "Fair, Fat and Forty," a Story of the South, at the Close of the Revolution (Charleston, S.C.: Walker & Richards, 1852); republished as *Woodcraft or Hawks About the Dovecote* (New York: Redfield, 1854);

As Good as a Comedy: Or, The Tennessean's Story, anonymous (Philadelphia: A. Hart, 1852);

Michael Bonham: Or, The Fall of Bexar. A Tale of Texas, anonymous (Richmond, Va.: Jno. R. Thompson, 1852);

South-Carolina in the Revolutionary War: Being a Reply to Certain Misrepresentations and Mistakes of Recent Writers, in Relation to the Course and Conduct of this State (Charleston, S.C.: Walker & James, 1853; Charleston, S.C.: Courtenay, 1853);

Marie de Berniere: A Tale of the Crescent City, Etc. Etc. Etc. (Philadelphia: Lippincott, Grambo, 1853); republished as *The Maroon: A Legend of the Caribbees, and Other Tales* (Philadelphia: Lippincott, Grambo, 1855); "The Maroon" republished as *The Ghost of My Husband* (New York: Chapman, 1866);

Egeria: Or, Voices of Thought and Counsel, for the Woods and Wayside (Philadelphia: E. H. Butler, 1853);

Vasconcelos. A Romance of the New World, as Frank Cooper (New York: Redfield, 1853);

Poems Descriptive, Dramatic, Legendary and Contemplative, 2 volumes (New York: Redfield, 1853 [i.e., 1854]; Charleston, S.C.: John Russell, 1853 [i.e., 1854]);

Southward Ho! A Spell of Sunshine (New York: Redfield, 1854);

The Forayers or The Raid of the Dog-Days (New York: Redfield, 1855);

Eutaw A Sequel to the Forayers, or The Raid of the Dog-Days (New York: Redfield, 1856);

The Cassique of Kiawah A Colonial Romance (New York: Redfield, 1859);

Simms's Poems Areytos or Songs and Ballads of the South With Other Poems (Charleston, S.C.: Russell & Jones, 1860);

Sack and Destruction of the City of Columbia, S.C. to Which is Added a List of the Property Destroyed, anonymous (Columbia, S.C.: Power Press of Daily Phoenix, 1865);

The Sense of the Beautiful. An Address, Delivered by W. Gilmore Simms, Before the Charleston County Agricultural and Horticultural Association. . . , May 3, 1870 (Charleston, S.C.: The Society, 1870);

Voltmeier Or The Mountain Men, volume 1 of *The Writings of William Gilmore Simms Centennial Edition*, edited by James B. Meriwether (Columbia: University of South Carolina Press, 1969);

As Good as a Comedy: Or the Tennessean's Story. And Paddy McGann; Or The Demon of the Stump, volume 3 of *The Writings of William Gilmore Simms Centennial Edition*, edited by Meriwether (Columbia: University of South Carolina Press, 1972);

Stories and Tales, volume 5 of *The Writings of William Gilmore Simms Centennial Edition*, edited by John Caldwell Guilds (Columbia: University of South Carolina Press, 1974);

Joscelyn A Tale of the Revolution, volume 16 of *The Writings of William Gilmore Simms Centennial Edition*, edited by Keen Butterworth (Columbia: University of South Carolina Press, 1975).

OTHER: *The Remains of Maynard Davis Richardson, With a Memoir of His Life*, edited anonymously by Simms (Charleston, S.C.: O. A. Roorbach, 1833);

The Charleston Book. A Miscellany in Prose and Verse, edited anonymously by Simms (Charleston, S.C.: Samuel Hart, 1845);

A Supplement to the Plays of William Shakspeare, edited by Simms (New York: George F. Cooledge, 1848);

War Poetry of the South, edited by Simms (New York: Richardson, 1866);

Selections from the Letters and Speeches of the Hon. James H. Hammond, of South Carolina, edited by Simms (New York: John F. Trow, 1866);

The Army Correspondence of Colonel John Laurens in the Years 1777-8. Now First Printed from Original Letters. . . , edited by Simms (New York: Bradford Club, 1867); republished as *A Succinct Memoir of the Life and Public Services of Colonel John Laurens* (Albany, N.Y.: Williamstadt, 1867).

In his rich and varied career as writer, William Gilmore Simms expended no less energy on his magazine editing than on his poetry, novels, short stories, and essays. He brought to his magazine work the same vitality that distinguishes his literary work at its best. It is indisputable that he left his mark on the American literary scene in a way that few of his contemporaries did. From the age of nineteen until his death at sixty-four, he edited or helped edit a total of seven literary magazines and five newspapers to which he gave a literary cast. In the bulk of these his primary intention was to advance and encourage literature in his homeland. To "stimulate native productions," he wanted to give American authors a place to publish their works, provide a critical forum for discussion thereof, and, in general, help develop literary awareness, particularly as to the great part literature must play in the advancement or progress of American civilization. It is understandable that, as a pioneering advocate of American literature using native scenes, tone, subjects, character, and themes, he would become a member of the "Young America" movement of the 1840s. He used his magazines as the vehicle for this philosophy throughout this decade. The periodicals he edited from 1825 to 1840 show the sure development of this ideology. Within a career that never failed to demonstrate the primary importance of art and its practical value to the human being, he fought hard and long for the creation of a distinctive national literature free from the slavish imitation of foreign models. His magazines provided him a forum to voice this aim, to publish works that exemplified it, and to encourage their widespread production of such works by adventurous new native authors. It was a grand vision, a totally unselfish one, and one

First page of the first issue of the monthly magazine Simms coedited with James Wright Simmons

that, in the final analysis, triumphed. Simms, of course, did not win the victory single-handedly, but neither was his part insignificant.

Simms was born in Charleston, South Carolina, to William Gilmore Simms, Sr., a Scotch-Irish immigrant who came to this country soon after the American Revolution, and Harriet Singleton Simms. After the failure of his business in 1808 and the death of his wife around the same time, the elder Simms went to Mississippi territory and served as a volunteer in Andrew Jackson's army. His son remained with his maternal grandmother in Charleston, where he later studied law and was admitted to the bar in 1827.

Simms's career as a magazine editor began in 1825, when he was nineteen. There had been many periodicals in Charleston, some distinguished, but none devoted exclusively to literature. Throughout the South the magazine had always been a melange of literature, political es-

says, news, scientific writing, and religious, historical, and social essays. In 1825 Simms and a "Society of Young Gentlemen" of the city were to challenge this tradition with the publication of the *Album*, a magazine whose only interest was literature. This move perhaps took some courage in a politically minded region, but the city was ripe for such an undertaking. Simms himself recalled that there were in Charleston during the time of the publication of the *Album* "fully twenty or thirty . . . juvenile societies, counting each from twenty to forty members. . . . a period of great literary activity among all classes." These societies pooled their books and encouraged the performance of drama and the writing and discussion of essays, poetry, and fiction. The *Album* encouraged local contributors of original material and stated that it would not serve up European reprints and translations, as so often happened in other American magazines. Neither would they borrow heavily from the files of other periodicals for copy. The three great emphases of the *Album* throughout its history were on demanding high literary quality, publishing original productions, and "cultivating *Native Talent*." For the last-named purpose, the editors offered premiums for the best original essay and story.

The *Album* continued weekly publication for at least one year. The first issue appeared on 2 July 1825, and the last extant octavo is dated 24 June 1826. Styled as a "Weekly Literary Miscellany," the eight pages of a typical issue usually contained an installment of a long story or short novel, several sketches, notes, brief essays on literary matters, anecdotes, book reviews, five or six poems, and occasionally a complete short story. The *Album* lived up to its promise; the great majority of these contributions were original, and in some issues all were. Because the contributions were unsigned, it has been difficult to identify many of the authors. Simms, however, has been proved to be the most frequent contributor, with more than seventy items. These include sixty-one poems, eight works of fiction, reviews, and an important series of letters–his first known letters–that detail an 1826 journey to the West.

For its modest size, the *Album* made a spectacular mark on American literary history. Still, nothing is known of its contemporary reception. Just how many subscribers it had and who they were cannot be surmised. The fact that the contributions were original and competent points toward its connection with an intelligent circle of readers. As for its influence on Simms, John C.

PROSPECTUS.

THE Subscriber having assumed the entire management of " *The Southern Literary Gazette*," it may be well to devote a few remarks to its future conduct and publication. With regard to the nature of the material of which the work will be composed, little need be said. The favorable reception which the preceding numbers have met with from the public, will, perhaps, render idle the hope of much improvement upon our plan : some, however, is thought necessary, in order that all readers should be equally satisfied. The plan of publishing a regular series of Essays, in which abstract points are discussed, and opinions given, which are seldom read or understood by the many, will induce the Editor, so to vary the character of the contents of this Journal in future, as to put something within the reach of every patron, calculated, as well for amusement, as instruction. While he proposes to do this, however, he will endeavour to maintain the same stand in public opinion, which the work has heretofore taken. He has been enabled to add to the list of contributors, who have already done so much honor to its pages, the names of many able writers for whose voluntary pledges he is grateful, with whose aid, combined with that of his fellow-citizens, (from whom he begs leave to solicit all such papers as may come within the design of this Journal,) he can have no fear as to the result of his adventure.

Having entered into an arrangement with Mr A F CUNNINGHAM, Printer, for the *regular* publication of the Gazette at certain periods, he feels much satisfaction in assuring his patrons, that the delay heretofore experienced in several of the past Numbers, will be avoided.

The *Gazette* will, in future, be issued semi-monthly, on the 1st and 15th days of each month, and delivered to subscribers in the city on the days of publication.

The Work will be divided into three distinct departments—viz. 1. Critical Notices of New Publications, principally American, or, such of foreign original, as may bear upon our Institutions, or Literature. 2. Original Poetry. 3. A General Miscellany. It is contemplated to make this last department particularly comprehensive, and to include in its formula, Essays, Tales, Sketches, Anecdotes, &c. To these may be added a fourth department, appropriated to local occurrences entirely. The whole formed upon the plan of *The Critic* of New York.

The Arts and general Literature, have hitherto been rather tolerated in our community, than admired. A cold indifference has heretofore encountered and repelled the progress of these strangers, until "they have fallen it to a strange sickliness, and died without remark." It is high time that we should hope for better things. The season is rich in promise, and the sunshine of encouragement will bring the fruit to perfection. That we can do much more for the South, is evident, as we feel how much has already been done. It only requires an effort—and the application of individual energies, will go far to remove the contempt and apathy, into which our mental reputation has fallen.

The department appropriated to *Critical Notices* of new Works, will contain, not only a synopsis of the work reviewed, but a liberal portion of the most interesting parts, extracted, with a view to the full illustration of the text, and for the amusement or instruction of the reader. To this department we would beg leave to direct the attention of our correspondents. They will perceive from the outline of our plan, traced in the present number, the length of an article of the kind, generally. While we would not wish to curtail a valuable paper, or arrest the course and full expression of a writer's thoughts, it is necessary, in order to preserve the miscellaneous character of the Work, to remind them that we have certain defined limits, over which we cannot pass, unless under very necessary or particular circumstances. This department will afford to the general reader a perfect idea of the new publications, as they appear the model chosen for our work in this respect being the *London Literary Gazette.*

WILLIAM G. SIMMS, JUN.

CONDITIONS.

THE SOUTHERN LITERARY GAZETTE will be put to subscribers at *Four Dollars* per annum; and Collections made, as heretofore, semi-annually in advance, and upon the delivery of the first Number It is contemplated, should a liberal patronage warrant the measure, to publish, accompanying every other number, a fine engraving of some public building, either in the City or State. To these may be added, Fancy Sketches, illustrated by original papers.

Subscriptions received at the office of the Southern Literary Gazette, No. 36 Queen-street, where all papers intended for the Work, and addressed to the Editor, will be received.

This Number may be considered a specimen of the pervading features of the Work.

A. F. CUNNINGHAM.

Simms's prospectus for the new, semimonthly series of the Southern Literary Gazette, *which he took over from Simmons in May 1829. The magazine failed in October 1829.*

Guilds, Jr., summarizes that his contributions show "the spade work for some of his best poems and for at least one of his major novels [*The Partisan*, 1835]." In addition, his experience there gave him an opportunity to formulate editorial policy in that, already, "he had learned to strike out boldly and fearlessly as a critic" and had voiced what was to be the keynote of his career as magazinist: the advancement of a native literature. In the *Album* one is able to trace the beginnings of a significant career in American literature and to see the first serious stirrings of that movement to cultivate native genius in a distinctively native southern (hence American) literature, which he championed. Simms restated this

call in almost identical language a few years later in his next editorial endeavor, the *Southern Literary Gazette* of 1828-1829. With more intensive study of the *Album* and its southern milieu, and with the possible discovery of more of its missing issues, should that occur, future scholars should be better able to document the impact and significance of this first southern literary magazine.

With the issue of 7 January 1826 the *Album* added the subtitle *Or, Charleston Literary Gazette*, thus suggesting that the periodical may have been the parent of the *Southern Literary Gazette*, which continued essentially the same editorial policy as that of the *Album*. Advertised as early as June 1828 as the *Tablet*, an eight-page "Weekly Literary Gazette," and sounding in yet other ways much like the *Album*, this periodical, with the new title the *Southern Literary Gazette*, finally appeared in September 1828 as a monthly. Simms, who was now twenty-two, was practicing law at his Charleston office. He was also now a family man, having married Anna Malcolm Giles in October 1826 and having fathered a daughter in November 1827. The year 1827 had likewise seen the publication of two collections of his poetry, *Lyrical and Other Poems* and *Early Lays*. These were busy years for Simms, but he began his new endeavor with customary energy and eagerness. He had as his coeditor James Wright Simmons, a Charleston author in his late thirties, who provided a calming influence on his young and sometimes impetuous partner. Their collaboration continued for six months, until March 1829, when Simms became sole editor and changed the magazine to a semimonthly. The periodical ceased publication with the issue of 1 November 1829. It apparently had never been on a solid financial footing; and Simms, now having given up the practice of law, was about to embark on a new venture as newspaper editor.

Throughout the thirteen-month history of the *Southern Literary Gazette* as a monthly and semimonthly, the editorial policy was to do everything possible to encourage the progress of an indigenous literature. Perhaps the most eloquent expression of this philosophy came in Simms's review of the Virginia novel *Edgehill*:

> Let the good work go on, and we shall not tremble for the result. Let us only think that future days will receive as an inheritance from the present, a set of *American classics*, in which the North, East, West, all will have their representation but the South; and the niche which she should occupy, may be, (if we determine not otherwise)

Announcement of Simms's appointment to the editorship of the Magnolia

like the monument of the decapitated Doge, all black, blank and barren.

The editor thus challenged his local readers to join him in filling that empty southern niche, thereby furthering the cause of American letters as a whole. Here, put another way, was Simms's famous dictum that to be American in literature one must first be regional. If each new American author would remain true to his regional traits (in dialect, character, setting, tone, and themes), then the work of American illustration would be accomplished in a great body of distinctively American classics. As far as the *Gazette* was concerned, the worst sin a critic, poet, or fiction

writer could commit was slavish imitation of English novels, fashion, and taste. To a lesser degree it was also wrong for one region in America to ape the literature of another. The *Gazette* thus set out to publish and encourage the writing of works with local settings and topics. Such titles as "The Cypress Swamp," "Chronicles of Ashley River," "Indian Sketch," "The Wilderness," and "Great Is the Yemassee" should suffice to show that it at least partly succeeded. All of these works were by Simms and Simmons. Getting other writers to contribute good original pieces of this type was another matter, however. In his study of the *Gazette*, Guilds has estimated that first the two editors, and later Simms alone, wrote approximately eighty percent of the magazine's copy. In the absence of contributor support of the kind they desired, they thus bore the overwhelming responsibility for keeping its pages filled. Simms's own proven contributions for the entire periodical total at least 107 pieces, excluding book reviews and notices. Of these, there are 66 poems, 25 essays, 10 stories, and the six-part "Chronicles of Ashley River" series. Faced with overwork, for which he knew he would receive little or no financial recompense, Simms understandably felt impelled to move on. As he would frequently state throughout his career as magazine editor, "I hoped only to make my contribution to American literature"; he did not expect fortune or fame. His editorial duties took time away from his own writing, as he knew only too well; but he felt it his duty to his "calling" not to go too long without taking on yet another editorial job.

The works that Simms left posterity in the *Southern Literary Gazette* are not insignificant. "Indian Sketch" is one of the early realistic treatments of the Indian in our literature. "The Streamlet," "Cottage Life," "Ashley River," and "Song (I have no joy)" are among his best poems and compare well to other verse of the day. "Confessions of a Murderer" is the model for his first novel, *Martin Faber* (1833). But Guilds feels that "it is Simms the critic who is best revealed" in the *Gazette* and that, "despite his youth and inexperience, he emerges as a surprisingly sound and mature judge of literature." The critic should judge a work on its own artistic merits, not the personality of the author, Simms was quick to say. He must "wholly divest himself of every kind of prejudice" and "must not regard the person writing, but the thing written." Good critics "advance the literature of our country" as "guardians of the portals of Fame's temple." Some of his most significant remarks appear in the essay "Modern Criticism," where true criticism is defined as "a liberal and humane art, the offspring of good sense and refined taste; an art aiming to acquire a just discernment of the real merits of authors, which preserves us from that blind and implicit veneration which would confound their blemishes and beauties in our esteem. In short it teaches us to admire and to blame with judgment, and not to follow the crowd blindly." The critic must be no slavish follower of English fashion and English taste. As an independent thinker Simms would not wait for the nod of an English journal before accepting an American work. He regarded this vassalage to a foreign master's opinion as a true impediment to the progress of American art.

As the year 1829 closed, Simms used the remainder of his inheritance from his mother to purchase a daily newspaper of long standing, the *Charleston City Gazette*. He formed a partnership with the printer E. S. Duryea and set himself up as the paper's editor. The first issue under his editorship was published the first of January 1830. A comparison of Simms's paper with that which preceded it shows many changes. The local news is more fully reported under Simms's editorship, and more attention is paid to current literature. Its columns contain a scattering of his own newly written poems as well as revisions of older ones. Literature was a central concern of the paper alongside the political events of the day: there are essays on American and English authors, an important source yet to be sufficiently explored in Simms studies. In the political arena Simms chose what was to be the unpopular side. In 1830 nullification and secession had become table talk in Charleston; but Simms did not believe in disunion. At first he had planned to stay neutral, making the paper an objective review with emphasis on a free and open press, but as the controversy wore on, he threw his support behind the Unionist cause and wrote strong editorials favoring it. Further, he allowed pointed personal attacks to be printed in his columns. The editor of the rival *Charleston Mercury* attacked Simms's character as vulgar and ignorant and questioned his loyalty to the state. Simms and his paper helped the Union man carry the mayoral election, a stinging blow to the Nullifiers, and especially to the editor of the *Mercury*, who was, in fact, the defeated candidate for mayor. The tide turned, however. In September 1831 Nullifiers celebrating victories in the legislative elections with a torchlight parade found the editor of the *Gazette* in his office on Broad Street, where he was standing in the front door watching the procession. Some of the Nullifiers jeered at him and made a rush at the office. Simms stood his ground and defied them by calling them cowards. Prudent members of the crowd restrained the rash ones, and a violent clash was averted. Simms's courage and audacity were duly noted, and his editorials did not soften. This was the first of two times during his career as newspaperman that he was to place his life in jeopardy by writing what he felt he must.

EDITORIAL BUREAU.

OUR NEW MONTHLY.

FREQUENT applications to the present publishers, for the restoration of the Magnolia Magazine, and a conviction on their part that a work so well sustained by public favor should not have been allowed to perish, persuades them to make amends for whatever of the reproach may properly belong to them, by the establishment of a new journal as nearly on the plan of the old as possible. They have accordingly persuaded the Editor of that work to return to his *fauteuil*, and he in turn has succeeded in persuading to a resumption of their tasks, the greater number of his old contributors. To these, new names are to be added from various parts of the country, from whose co-operation the happiest variety may be expected in the pages of the new Magazine. This, though differing in name from the former, will maintain a not dissimilar character. The endeavour will be made to impart to it a more decided political complexion than was borne by the Magnolia, and, if possible, to impress upon it more of those sectional aspects, South and West, which need development quite as much as advocacy. It is frankly avowed that the characteristics of the work are to be sectional, since, it is believed, that whether this were the case or not, no periodical of the country, not published at one or other of the great cities of the North, could possibly hope for the countenance of the public in their vicinity. Our experience has been conclusive on this head. The Northern press claims to supply us in the South and West with all our Literature, and will take none of ours in return. While millions are sent away annually to recipients north of the Potomac, it will be within the mark to affirm, that what is brought to us, by similar means, from that quarter, may be expressed by hundreds. And this sweeping absorption of the literary employment and means of our region, includes all branches of business,—our works of taste and of authority, of science and of education. It seems not an unreasonable desire, that a literature which seeks no more than to seize upon passing events and suggestions,—to give form and pressure to the occasional moods and fancies,—which addresses itself at short intervals to our leisure, and much of the material for which must be of local provision,—should be made at home. It is but moderately tasking the patience of our neighbours of contiguous sections, and still more moderately the pockets of our own, that we should endeavor to build up a monthly journal, which shall address itself particularly to the people of the South and West. By this special purpose, however, it is not meant that we should exclude the reader from any section of our country. Much that our periodical contains, will be, we trust, of that general character, which must prove equally acceptable in every region; and its tone and temper will, we are persuaded, afford no cause of annoyance to any. Some of our most valued [pledged] contributors are citizens of the North,—men of that catholic sense which readily recognizes the necessity of many such journals as that which we contemplate, for the proper representation, in the world of literature, of every section of our common

---

68   EDITORIAL BUREAU.

country. Our work simply proposes that justice should be done to the mind which fills our region, to the development of which, as far as such purpose comes within the design of such a work, our Magazine will be honestly directed.—We may add, that our present issue is scarcely a fair specimen of what we propose hereafter. The work was too suddenly conceived, late in the year, when other labors were pressing upon the Editor, to suffer him to do justice either to the reader or himself. Some little time must be allowed before "the hang" of a new labor can be properly acquired, and for the due preparation of contributors, some of whom are amateurs, for the new tasks to which they are to be set. We claim from the reader's liberality the requisite forbearance and indulgence.

LIFE AND CORRESPONDENCE OF RALPH IZARD. New-York: CHARLES S. FRANCIS & CO

THE IZARD family is one of the oldest and most respectable in the State of South-Carolina. They came to America, according to the memoir before us, in the reign of Queen ANNE. RALPH, the subject of this memoir, was educated in England, as, at that period, were most of the young gentlemen of fortune in Carolina. He married Miss DE LANCEY of New-York, in 1767, and in 1771 took up his abode in London, leaving his large estates in Carolina to the care of an agent. RALPH IZARD was a gentleman of taste and letters, who collected a fine library, and was an enthusiastic admirer of painting and music. He was a thorough republican, refusing to be presented at court, for no other reason than that he would not "crook the pregnant hinges of the knee," to any mortal sovereign. He was a patriot, and strove, while in England, in conjunction with the other Americans there, to avert the great and protracted issue which finally separated the two countries. In 1777 he retired first to France, and next, as Minister of Congress, to the court of Tuscany. From this post, one, at that day, of honor rather than utility, he was removed by a resolution of Congress, owing, as is alleged in the memoir, to certain misrepresentations of SILAS DEANE. The memoir more than hints at the improper and dishonest action of Dr. FRANKLIN in this matter, and threatens revelations, should the publication of the correspondence go on, which may very much disturb the sanctity and repose of that reputation which has been so long enjoyed by the New-England philosopher. In this connection, we are reminded of certain similar revelations made by ARTHUR LEE, his associate in France, to which we shall take early occasion to refer. The truth is—though we shall not care to unsettle the hold of individuals upon the affectionate memories of the country—our revolutionary history has very much to be re-written. The Southern States, in particular, have good reasons to insist upon this. Our historians have but too frequently set aside the claims and slurred over the achievements and sacrifices of a region, which, agricultural in its character, sparsely settled, with no large cities, is naturally slow to assert itself, and exact that full justice from public opinion, which a more active condition of society always insures to itself. There is no doubt that FRANKLIN was a very remarkable man, but it is equally certain that he had some very striking foibles. His vanity appears to have been immense, and seems to have been at the bottom of his frequent neglect of business, while at Paris. It was more pleasant to the great man to play the lion in the saloons of Paris, than to attend at the sittings of the Commission with which he was connected. This is pretty much the accusation of ARTHUR LEE, though it goes, if we remember rightly, something farther. What the proofs

---

Simms's introductory essay for the first issue of his Southern and Western Monthly Magazine and Review

But personal danger was the least of the editor's troubles. Simms complained publicly of having lost subscribers due to his free expression of Unionist principles. Subscriptions were running short, and debts were running high. Then Duryea died on 25 March 1832; and by 9 April 1832 Simms was both sole editor and proprietor. He struggled on in heavy debt until 7 June 1832, when he announced that the paper had been sold. Creditors were politely informed that they could seek the former editor at Charles Carroll's law office (where Simms had studied law). They no doubt found him there, as Simms said of himself, "over head and ears in debt," with every desire to meet his obligations, but with little prospect of doing so in the near future.

Simms's stormy two and a half years as editor of the *City Gazette* may have been the hardest years of his life because of the deaths of loved ones during this span. His father died on 28 March 1830, his grandmother (who raised him) shortly thereafter, and his wife on 19 February 1832. Charleston had indeed become, as he phrased it, "a place of tombs." Leaving his daughter with in-laws, Simms traveled north, contemplating a move there; but after a brief period of exile and homesickness for his beloved city by the sea, he returned home to stay. His trip north did result in lasting valuable friendships with William Cullen Bryant and James Lawson (soon to become his literary agent). In a letter to Lawson of 28 October 1832 Simms wrote that he was at his fireside, watching the triumphs of Nullifiers all about him. His Charleston friends were in raptures over his newly published poem *Atalantis* (1832) and were welcoming him back with parties every night. He would settle down to work next week; but in the meantime, he would go dove hunting.

His country pleasures did not last long. By May 1833 he was editing, with the aid of Charles and Edward Carroll, an occasional, the *Cosmopolitan*, again devoted exclusively to literature. In his piece "Le Debut," Simms makes clear that the greatest threat to the progress of a native literature is political embroilment. After the Nullification struggle he could indeed speak from experience. "Should the talents of our country," he asks, "only find an outlet and direction in the turbulent and temporary notoriety of a partisan harangue...? Should it not be given a higher employ...? That our people are rich in all those qualities of mind and ambition, which constitute individual as well as national greatness, it will be

no extravagance to assert." Simms wished to channel some of that native energy and genius into high art and sought in the *Cosmopolitan* to provide an example "for other and more experienced adventurers." While not strictly a magazine (its pages were not open to contributors), this occasional was a literary collection by Simms and the two Carrolls in the form of a periodical. Still, it could provide, as pioneering example, a stimulus to native creativity. Although Simms's approach was somewhat different here, he struggled in the *Cosmopolitan* toward the same goal as he had in the *Album* and *Southern Literary Gazette*: the advancement of art in his region, and, by extension, the nation. The *Cosmopolitan* did indeed scrupulously avoid politics in this most highly charged political time.

The occasional was issued in two numbers, May and July 1833, for a total of 264 pages. It includes ten short stories, some 20 pages of literary "chitchat," and essays by the three authors. As Guilds summarizes the occasional's importance, the *Cosmopolitan* was a stepping-stone in Simms's development as a novelist and short-story writer; "perhaps its only significant bearing on his editorial career is that in it he gave voice once more to the demand for an American and a Southern literature." From this work he jumped into a flurry of literary efforts that produced four major works of fiction within the next two years: *Martin Faber* (1833), *Guy Rivers* (1834), *The Yemassee* (1835), and *The Partisan* (1835). By 1835 Simms's career as writer had come into full flower, and his life's direction as author was certain. He had received a deserved recognition North and South as one of the chief American authors of the time.

It would be nearly a decade before Simms would again take up his pen as magazine editor. This interim period was to see the publication of other major works in the canon: *Mellichampe* (1836), *Richard Hurdis* (1838), *Carl Werner* (1838), *Southern Passages and Pictures* (1838), *Border Beagles* (1840), *The Kinsmen* (1841), and *Confession* (1841). It also saw his marriage in 1836 to Chevillette Eliza Roach with the resulting division of his time between his wife's Woodlands Plantation in Barnwell County, South Carolina, and his town house in Charleston, along with regular business and social visits to New York. It was altogether a busy, fruitful, and happy time for the author. He gloried in his large family, and his reputation as writer continued its rise. Although he found it difficult, he was making his living by writing, the only southerner to do so at that time while still living in the region. Yet his old desire to promote a national literature had again been fired by the "Young America" controversy as well as the growing need to free his region from intellectual dependence upon the North. Thus he ventured forth again into magazine editing to do what he could for the cause he had the right to call, after twenty years of endeavor, *his* grand old cause.

The Charleston *Southern Literary Journal*, under the editorship of David Whitaker and B. R. Carroll, filled the need for a local literary magazine from September 1835 to December 1838. Perhaps this is one reason Simms had felt it unnecessary to task himself with the job. But the demise of the *Journal* left a gap, and Simms increasingly grew to feel that the literary magazine was the best medium through which to further the cause of sectional and national literature, at least in the South. He reasoned that the sparseness of the southern population did not make intellectual discussion as easy as in the large cities; the countryman lacked the stimulus to read because there was no one nearby to provoke his mind in discussion of his reading; the countryman found it difficult to purchase books, and they were apt to be expensive. The southern magazine would thus perform a great service because it was, in Simms's words,

> the cheapest, the most eligible, and, perhaps, the most useful form, in which Literature may yield them its advantages. The mail brings it to the door of the farmer, to the cottage of the peasant, to the stately mansion, embosomed in deep forests, of the lordly and secluded planter. It is, along with the newspaper, the chief mode by which he communicates with the distant world without.

Thus, in 1842, when the editor of the *Magnolia* called on Simms to salvage the periodical from imminent demise by assuming the position of editor, Simms consented. He did so, as he wrote R. H. Wilde, even though he did not "expect to *make* but to *lose* money by the process." He continued, "But I feel every day, more & more, the humiliating relation in which the South stands to the North.... To change this in some degree is my object, and for which I make some sacrifices." This letter shows an important shift in emphasis from America's need to become independent of Britain in literary matters to the South's need for intellectual independence from the North. Again, he wished to remain absolutely

true to its own character, thus furthering the work of American letters.

With the *Album* and the *Southern Literary Gazette*, Simms's aim had been to stimulate local southern genius, but his primary concern was still the goal of elevating the status of American letters. America could never establish its own literature until it stopped imitating British models. He criticized the English for condemning everything American and complained that his own countrymen ignored even the best American works until they were praised by the English journals. He called for American literary independence. Thus, from 1825 to 1829 Simms strongly and consistently voiced a view that was heard only after 1837 in the *Democratic Review* and other "Young America" journals in New York. He had unequivocally stated the principles of the movement which a decade later would be regarded as "radical" heresy by the *Knickerbocker, North American Review, New England Magazine, New York Review,* and *American Quarterly*. This advocacy of a national literature free from bondage to England was the primary doctrine underlying his editorial principles, developed over a decade before "Young America" did so. Although Simms is not often enough given due credit for it, he was a precursor of this important movement and well ahead of the times. It is no wonder that he would join this New York-based group and help further the cause against the vituperative criticism of the conservative journals, because, after all, their cause had first been his for over a decade and a half. With his assumption of the editorial position of the *Magnolia; or, Southern Apalachian* in 1842, he was able to lend support to "Young America." As a result, he was damned in the *Knickerbocker* of August 1842 for his nationalism, which it called a "device to secure an extrinsic and undue consideration for flimsy novels." There was, in fact, a heated running battle between the two monthlies.

Simms moved the *Magnolia* from Savannah to Charleston and, as biographer William P. Trent writes, "labored heroically," securing contributions from the best southern writers. Being a seasoned veteran, he was at the outset well aware of the problems he would encounter as a southern editor. He would find, Simms wrote, that

> his contributors, . . . devoted to other professions—only write at moments of leisure. [He] is compelled to wait upon them for their articles, which, good, bad, or indifferent, he is compelled to publish. The constant drain upon himself, enfeebles his imagination and exhausts his intel-

lect. . . . [His station becomes one of] mental drudgery. . . . The collections are to be made over an extensive tract of interior country . . . and are realized too slowly for the current expenses of his journal. The printer . . . clamors for his monthly dues, and the subscriber recedes from the subscription list, the moment he is called upon for his. Under the pressure of pecuniary difficulties, the publication of the work becomes irregular . . . [and] soon leads to the early abandonment of an attempt in which nothing has been realized but discredit, annoyance, and expense.

Despite his certainty that any attempt at editing was sure to fail in short time, Simms was also sure that the endeavor was worth his "mental drudgery, discredit, annoyance, and expense" in the cause of national letters, and now, with the *Magnolia,* the cause of southern letters in particular.

The *Magnolia* marks an important shift in emphasis to the sectional. Throughout the last decade Simms had become increasingly alarmed by the South's dependence on the North. Political developments had also helped widen the gap. As Guilds puts it, "Whereas in the 1820s he had editorialized largely against American imitation of British literary style and taste, in the 1840's–as editor of the *Magnolia* and the *Southern and Western Monthly Magazine and Review*–he was more concerned with freeing the South from its literary bondage to the North. This generalization holds true despite the fact that in the 1820's Simms was already speaking against Northern domination of American literature and that in the 1840s he still battled vigorously for American freedom from intellectual servility to England." Simms felt the southern writer to be in a doubly difficult situation. His country was still intellectually dependent on England, and his region was becoming ever more dependent on the North. What disturbed him most was the northern assumption that northern literature was *the* American literature, and that southern writing was regional rather than national. The unfairness of this assumption became even clearer when New England journals branded literature in the South "sectional" while not realizing that they were just as provincial. Simms felt, as Guilds says, that a "truly national magazine must assert the character of its people–must paradoxically, then, be sectional–because a magazine of one section could not fully represent the needs and wants of the people of another section. Therefore, a maga-

zine editor failed to be national only when he ceased to represent faithfully his own section."

Simms would tailor the *Magnolia* expressly to meet the needs and wants of the southern region by making it "a work in which the tone shall be manly and the character and sentiment essentially only Southern." What became the *Magnolia* had begun in 1840 as the *Southern Ladies' Book.* By Simms's plan the magazine would be rid of the excessive sentimentality usual in American journals for women and would address both sexes. The "manly" tone of this journal repudiated that "disparaging estimate" of the female "intellectual character" which supposed that women are capable of enjoying nothing but "nauseating and injurious sweets." Simms promised his female readers a "rude" but "wholesome" fare. Under Simms's editorship, the *Magnolia* does seem to have emphasized literature that provoked thought over that which merely entertained. In doing so, he was appealing to the southern reader who felt knowledge, rather than pleasure, to be the primary object in reading. Though he stressed belles lettres, he also published historical and cultural writings, which he felt to be equally important in the development of a southern literary culture. The journal's quality during Simms's tenure as editor has been judged equal, if not superior, to the *Southern Literary Messenger.* At the close of 1842 it was generally recognized as a magazine of high quality and promise. Still, it was in precarious financial condition. The subscribers had not paid their debts, which were "more than sufficient money [being] due," as the proprietor wrote, "if paid in, to cancel my liabilities." The debts were "in sums of five, ten and fifteen dollars, scattered over a district of more than a thousand miles" and therefore impossible to collect.

With the June 1843 issue Simms withdrew as editor, despite the rising reputation the *Magnolia* had as one of the South's leading periodicals. It was in debt; Simms had not been paid for his work; the proprietors were squabbling; and the situation was worsening. Simms decided to resign before the magazine perished under his hands. In his brief year as editor he had contributed over sixty works to the periodical, had engaged the help of many other noteworthy contributors, had encouraged the young writers of the South (he was forced to use a smaller type in order to print as many contributions as possible), and had brought the journal from comparative obscurity

Simms in a portrait by an unknown artist (courtesy of William Gilmore Simms, Washington, D.C.)

to a respected position among the better magazines of the nation.

Simms remained out of editorial harness for less than a year, however. In February 1843 William Carey Richards moved his *Orion; Or, Southern Monthly* from Georgia to Charleston in an effort to save it. Simms became a regular contributor and, a little over a year later, assumed the editorship for its last issues–May, July, and August 1844–in an effort to aid once more the cause of letters in his region. Recent scholarship indicates that, rather than simply joining other journals in the Charleston "graveyard of periodicals," the *Orion* had a different fate. The publishers of the *Magnolia* purchased it and offered to give Simms half the profits of a new periodical to merge with the older one, to be gotten up in a "new style and spirit" and to be called *Simms's Monthly Magazine*. Simms agreed to this plan and began editing the *Southern and Western Monthly Magazine and Review* (popularly called *Simms's Magazine*) in January 1845. It was to run for a total of twelve monthly issues, ending in December 1845.

Simms introduced his new magazine as a "restoration" of the *Magnolia*, made as nearly on the old plan as possible. He would, however, impart to it "a more decided political complexion . . . and, if possible, to impress upon it more of those sectional aspects, South and West." Despite Simms's statement, Guilds finds the magazine decidedly less devoted to politics than the *Magnolia* had been. To make the journal seem to have a wide southern and western base, Simms manufactured pseudonyms to affix to his own works and gave them fictional place-names: for example, Bernard Hilton, Greendale, Alabama, and others from Millefleurs, Virginia; Florence, Alabama; and Vidalia, North Carolina. Thus, his periodical would seem to have regional support and not appear to be, as it was, written largely by himself. (This was a ploy he had also used in the *Magnolia*.) He would stress literature "made at home" but would likewise publish northern authors who appreciated the regional approach to the creation of an American literature. His lead essay was "Americanism in Literature," a championing of the old familiar cause, now being popularized by "Young America." He explored the material for American writers in seven installments of "The Epochs and Events of American History, as Suited to the Purpose of Art in Fiction." In his editorials he criticized American readers, writers, critics, and publishers for a "colonial thraldom" to Britain and praised Bryant, Nathaniel Hawthorne, and others as the "equal in real genius to almost any import."

The southern emphasis was even more pronounced than literary nationalism, however. "Our Agricultural Condition" warned of the threat of northern economic and industrial domination. Other such essays touched on problems peculiar to the region. But, as always for Simms, sectionalism was a necessary condition of nationalism in literature. And this nationalism in the *Southern and Western* allied him ever more closely with "Young America." Simms, in fact, proposed to the acknowledged leader of the group, Evert Duyckinck of New York, that his new undertaking would be a voice for the movement: "it will, in some measure afford us the organ we desire. Until you can get your press in N. Y. you must be content with a wing of it in Charleston." Simms predicted that New York would eventually replace Boston as the nation's intellectual and publishing center and felt it expedient to ally himself and the South with New York writers, publishers, and institutions. Because New England periodicals snubbed both New York and the South, the two locations had much in common. In particular, he attacked Boston's *North American Review* in

"A Passage with 'The Veteran Quarterly'" as being blindly provincial and selfishly partial, treating "the one region to the wholesale neglect of all others," this coming in partial response to some northern criticism of southern periodicals as "narrow." Such periodicals, he felt, denounced sectionalism in the South while exclusively promoting their own sections. There is a certain arrogance, he complained, "in the assumption that our [a New England] magazine is the national magazine, and yours the sectional one."

The *Southern and Western* was well received by both northern and southern journalists who shared Simms's literary nationalism. The editors of *Godey's, Southern Quarterly Review,* and *Southern Literary Messenger,* for example, praised Simms's magazine and its important work in behalf of American letters. Edgar Allan Poe wrote in the *Broadway Journal* that it was "as ably edited as any journal in America–if not more ably edited than any." On the other hand, the opposition movement discussed Simms as one of those "small authors and smaller critics" and ridiculed his "Americanism in Literature" essay. This literary warfare swirled around the magazine; but throughout it all, Simms remained remarkably levelheaded and judicious. He even avoided renewal of the old conflict with the *Knickerbocker,* archenemy of "Young America."

Although Simms did everything in his power to encourage contributors to submit their works, once again he was forced to write the majority of the copy. As Guilds says, "It is doubtful if any editor of importance wrote so voluminously for his magazine as did Simms." Whereas Poe and James Russell Lowell would use three or four choice selections of their own in an issue, Simms would average ten or fifteen. The difference was that Poe and Lowell, with money to back them, could offer pay to contributors; Simms could only extend encouragement. *The Southern and Western* contains very good Simms short stories (including "Oakatibbe" and "The Snake of the Cabin") and most of the essays collected in his *Views and Reviews in American Literature* (1845). As David Tomlinson writes, the magazine displays Simms's "considerable capabilities . . . at their height."

In 1845 Simms was thirty-nine years old. The drudgery of editing the journal began to weigh on him, and he began to repent the "sentiment of patriotism." After the December 1845 issue he left the *Southern and Western* without receiving monetary recompense, for the journal had never had enough subscribers to turn a profit in which he could share. Although Simms claimed two thousand subscribers for the *Southern and Western* at its highest point, it never reached the three thousand necessary to break even. Simms, who made his living from literature, knew it would be bad business to take time away from the writing for which he got paid in order to expend further energy in a struggle already doomed to failure. The *Southern and Western* had served its ideological purpose well in providing a platform for "Young America" and had encouraged literary pursuits in the region. In its pages Simms had taken editorial positions that were strongly stated but voiced without prejudice. He offered fair literary judgment and sound and sensitive criticism in a way that encouraged the free development of art that "Young America" advocated. In the opinion of Tomlinson, "What gave the work its distinctive place among Southern magazines was its flexible design, the editor's expertise in using that format, and the sensitive intelligence displayed in the magazine's content." The journal ended with Simms's plea for southerners to wake up intellectually and support the arts, and declared that its editor would be withdrawing from editorial duties "in all probability, forever." Simms was obviously tired and somewhat despondent; but within four years he would again become an editor, this time of the *Southern Quarterly Review.*

His eighth venture was unlike those that went before. The *Album, Southern Literary Gazette, Magnolia, Orion,* and *Southern and Western* had all combined to good effect the features of the review and the magazine. In the *Southern Quarterly Review,* however, Simms was restricted by the format. This periodical could have no fiction or poetry; and, according to some, it was never as "exciting" as the *Southern and Western.* It was a departure for Simms and something of a challenge; but here he could fully exercise one of his strengths: that of the sound, impartial critic.

The *Southern Quarterly Review* was founded in 1842, but Simms did not assume the position of editor until April 1849. Even though he was promised an annual salary of a thousand dollars, he never really expected to receive it. As always, his devotion to the cause prompted him to accept the task. As the publisher had hoped, Simms rescued the foundering periodical; he did so by adding fifty new contributors, promising them a dollar per page of copy. The articles improved and so did the number of subscribers. Among the contributors were Beverley Tucker, A. B. Meek, M. C. M. Hammond, Joel Poinsett, Francis Lieber, J. D. B. DeBow, William Trescot, R. W. Gibbes, Benjamin Perry, Junius Nott, D. F. Jamison, Mitchell King, James Henry Hammond, Brantz Mayer, Henry Tuckerman, George Holmes, and W. A. Jones. Remaining true to form, Simms was his own most prolific contributor. In the period from April 1849 to October 1854 he wrote all the "Critical Notices," a highly interesting monthly review of current books, largely literary, comprising a total of 670 large pages in small print. In addition, he published several dozen literary essays, where one finds him skillfully practicing his expertise. Simms's ability to read hundreds of works and to comment intelligently and incisively on their merits and faults is here shown clearly. Even when limited to a few paragraphs, Simms had the uncanny ability to get at the heart of a work. He comments on such figures as Lord Byron, Samuel Taylor Coleridge, Robert Browning, Alfred Tennyson, James Fenimore Cooper, Ralph Waldo Emerson, Herman Melville, Henry Wadsworth Longfellow, Henry David Thoreau, Hawthorne, Margaret Fuller, Poe, John Pendleton Kennedy, and a host of lesser southern authors. Simms's essay on William Wordsworth is particularly good; and his evaluations of Robert and Elizabeth Barrett Browning, Charlotte and Emily Brontë, Coleridge, Charles Dickens, and Tennyson sound quite current and certainly not the standard ones during his day. He estimated Hawthorne to be destined for greatness; considered Thoreau's *Walden* a curious volume of Yankee philosophy, well written and noteworthy; and pronounced Whittier's poetry mediocre. Simms praised Melville's *Mardi*, found *Redburn* faulty in characterization, and liked *White-Jacket* as a social treatise but not as a story. He was far off the mark with *Moby-Dick*, which he called "sad stuff, dull and dreary"; he found Ahab a "monstrous bore." *Pierre* convinced him that both character and author should be locked away. While Simms made mistakes as a critic, he was on the whole remarkably perceptive and judicious.

After Simms's resignation in October 1854 the *Southern Quarterly Review* lasted less than three years. Like the *Southern and Western* before it, it was beset with the failure to collect subscribers' debts; when Simms took over the periodical, they owed thirteen thousand dollars. And Simms seldom agreed with its owners. The improvements he made were often only after a struggle.

In spite of all the difficulties, he took the review from a position of collapse and made it a very respectable publication, comparing favorably with such a work as the *North American Review*. From paying nothing to contributors he went to the recompense of a dollar a page. According to Trent, he got part of his own salary, which was in itself no mean achievement. After so long literature was becoming a paying profession in both the North and South. Simms at least was continuing to make a meagre living by his pen, and the veteran author felt he was making it somewhat easier to choose the profession for the young writers who followed him. He was no doubt correct.

The *Southern Quarterly Review* was Simms's last magazine, though he acted as the unnamed book reviewer of the *Charleston Mercury* from December 1854 until May 1856. In this capacity, under the pseudonym "Lorris," he wrote nearly a hundred review articles on literature, very much in the manner of his "Critical Notices" in the *Southern Quarterly*. He appears simply to have picked up where he left off two months earlier with his resignation from the *Quarterly*. It is a remarkable feat considering his incisive criticism of so many works from a wide range of authors. From 1858 to 1860 he also wrote literary review columns for the *Mercury*. Except for the "Lorris" material, the extent of his involvement with the *Mercury* is still largely uncharted.

But Simms was to be sole editor of another newspaper and the book review editor of two other newspapers before his career ended with his death in 1870. Caught in Columbia, South Carolina, during the last months of the Civil War, he needed employment as badly as the burned town needed a newspaper. It was a hard time for him. His wife had died, and Sherman's troops had burned Woodlands Plantation. He was living in various garrets in Columbia with his children and was finding it difficult to provide them with food and the barest necessities. Julian Selby, owner of the burned-out *South Carolinian*, acquired his services as the editor of the *Columbia Phoenix*, a new paper whose first issue came out on 21 March 1865, a month after the city's destruction. Although he was cognizant of its importance, Simms did not relish his new job, but he nonetheless set himself to the task with his old zeal. Searching through the ruins of the *Carolinian* office, he found a composing stick and suggested that the first lines of the new paper be set up in it for the sake of continuity and tradition. After three weeks as a triweekly, the paper became the *Daily*

Phoenix and prospered. The first issues were a large single sheet which was sold door-to-door. With its broken type, uneven margins, and coarse paper, its physical appearance was strikingly like that of the colonial gazettes. Though it was certainly unintentional, the resemblance provided fitting visual reinforcement to Simms's editorial stating that "we are really in the condition of a people just beginning to colonize in a strange land, whose resources we do not know."

As usual Simms wrote most of the original matter for the periodical himself. His constant emphasis on courage and endurance in a time of trial was a familiar theme from his earlier works now carried over into his editorials. Articles on this topic provided the largest group. In the six months that he edited the paper it was filled with original material, a situation which changed when he left 1 October 1865, when there was a fifty percent decline in editorials and essays, this space being taken over by ads and news service clippings.

One of the paper's main purposes was to help in the rebuilding of Columbia:

> We trust that the advent of *The Columbia Phoenix* will prove . . . favorable to the resuscitation of our brave old city from her ashes. . . . We must not sit and wring our hands idly, but go at once to our duties. . . . Like the Phoenix, our city shall spring from her ashes.

Simms provided guidance for the rebuilding, dealing practically with the homeliest of problems and insisting at the same time that the gardens and trees that had been the hallmark of the old city be replaced in the new. His policy was not the limited, utilitarian New South view. He emphasized the necessity for the area to remain absolutely true to its own traditional character.

During the six months Simms edited the *Phoenix*, he veritably bustled about his work. Editorials such as "Labor–Its Value" and "How We Should Work!" show his state of mind at the time. The subjects of his essays, an average of two or three per issue, range from his candid views of the Confederate cabinet to the poetry of Wordsworth. One essay is particularly noteworthy from a journalistic standpoint. In it Simms states that public opinion, which governs in a democracy, can be manipulated for good or ill by the press. He was aware of the propagandistic distortion of the South in the northern press and vowed that the reverse would not occur in the *Phoenix*. The opinions would be as "diversified" as pos-

sible and would include copious selections from northern papers. This was done most frequently without commentary, leaving the reader to make up his own mind. This was the expressed ideal of good modern journalism, perhaps an outgrowth of Simms's wonted fairness and objectivity in writing criticism, a trait seen so clearly in the magazines he edited throughout his career.

On political questions, he did not mince words. He wrote stinging criticism of the Northern occupation forces. In his memoirs, Selby described Simms's arrest for one such article. A squad of soldiers took Simms to the occupation general, whom an editorial had offended. He was placed before the officer, and the trial began. After a short time the charges were dismissed, and Simms was invited to a luncheon, which he attended. The general expressed to his colonel the following day that Simms "out-talked me, out-drank me, and very clearly and politely showed me that I lacked proper respect for the aged." The officers, wrote Selby, were great admirers of Simms, and two or three would drop by daily to chat. In a letter to a relative, Simms dismissed the event with a few words: "On Saturday, I was on the eve of being arrested for an article in the paper. The article of arrest was made out; but, cited to appear before the General in Command, I satisfied him that his arrest would be an error." Simms was far from frightened and intimidated, for his criticism of the military government continued to be printed at the steady pace of former times, one such article being entitled "Thieving as One of the Fine Arts." These forceful editorials are reminiscent of those from Simms's days with the *City Gazette*. His resolution to speak his mind in 1865 placed his life in jeopardy as it had with the Nullifiers in 1832. Both times he exhibited the same calm bravery in the face of more powerful opposition. Selby was not as cool about the matter as his editor. He reported that Simms "was disposed to call a spade by its proper name. I would sometimes suggest a little toning down of his articles. . . ."

In the issues of 17 and 21 June 1865 Simms wrote on his favorite periodical topic: the necessity of the writer to use native material. Other essays on literature were frequently included. Although literature was not the paper's primary interest, Simms managed to include nearly a dozen stories during his six months as editor, and forty-one of his own poems, some of which treat his recent personal experiences and are very good. His "Capture, Sack and Destruction of the City of Columbia" was serialized over a period of three weeks. As descriptive writing, it is among Simms's best works. Its stark and powerful prose style is memorable. He revised, shortened, and toned down this work as a separate publication, published by the Daily Phoenix Press in 1865.

With Simms's return to Charleston, Trent reports that he became an editor of the *Charleston Daily South Carolinian* in 1865-1866. He was affiliated with the *Charleston Courier* in some capacity in 1870. Virtually nothing is known of these last undertakings except the brief statement in Trent's biography.

Simms's editorial work rivaled, if not surpassed, in color, energy, competency, and accomplishment the editorial careers of other figures such as William Cullen Bryant, Philip Freneau, Poe, Lowell, and Walt Whitman. As a critic, he was unsurpassed. He was a strong formulator of pioneering ideas in American literature and an effective and practical editor. As a fiction writer, he has been called a realistic romancer; as an editor, he might be called a practical dreamer. It would be impossible to question the sincerity of his devotion to literature; no writer has ever put any more of himself into furthering its cause. His principles were high and unselfish.

Simms was always fully aware of the problems besetting a southern editor in trying to establish a permanent literary journal. That he was never able to do so never vanquished his courage and determination. Without resorting to the puffery he detested, he encouraged southern letters along a distinctively southern path. He defended southern letters from northern charges and through it all knew he was laboring for the progress of an American literature. In his personal life he became the embodiment of the South, and before his death he was recognized as its symbol by his countrymen. *DeBow's Review* states this fact clearly:

> He reflects . . . the spirit and temper of Southern civilization; announces its opinions, illustrates its ideas, embodies its passions. . . , and betrays those delicate shades of thought, feeling, and conduct, that go to form the character, and stamp the individuality of a people.

His works, as a reflection of the man, are portrayals of this unique southernness.

John Guilds wisely sums up Simms's editorial career:

> Although in the early 1830s some southerners frowned upon Simms for his national views and in the 1840s northerners generally upbraided him for his sectional views, he at all times considered himself a proponent of both nationalism and sectionalism because to his eyes the two forces were not opposed but conversely, were too closely allied to be separated. Fundamentally his outlook remained surprisingly steadfast. His early emphasis on American literature and his later emphasis on Southern literature represent changes in degree, not in position.

The record of Simms's life and career speaks for itself. His literary contributions are among the most unfairly overlooked achievements in the literary annals of America.

Letters:
The Letters of William Gilmore Simms, 6 volumes, volume 1-5 edited by Mary C. Simms Oliphant, Alfred Taylor Odell, and T. C. Duncan Eaves, volume 6 edited by Oliphant and Eaves (Columbia: University of South Carolina Press, 1952-1982);
James Everett Kibler, Jr., "The First Simms Letters: 'Letters from the West,' " *Southern Literary Journal*, 19 (Spring 1987): 81-91.

Bibliographies:
Alexander S. Salley, Jr., *Catalogue of the Salley Collection of the Works of Wm. Gilmore Simms* (Columbia, S.C.: State Company, 1943);
James E. Kibler, Jr., *Pseudonymous Publications of William Gilmore Simms* (Athens: University of Georgia Press, 1976);
Betty Jo Strickland, "The Short Fiction of William Gilmore Simms: A Checklist," *Mississippi Quarterly*, 29 (Fall 1976): 591-608;
Keen Butterworth, "William Gilmore Simms," in *First Printings of American Authors* (Detroit: Gale Research, 1977), I: 325-334;
Kibler, *The Poetry of William Gilmore Simms: An Introduction and Bibliography* (Spartanburg, S.C.: Reprint Company, 1979);
Butterworth and Kibler, *William Gilmore Simms: A Reference Guide* (Boston: G. K. Hall, 1980).

Biography:
William Peterfield Trent, *William Gilmore Simms* (Boston: Houghton, Mifflin, 1892).

References:

Maurice R. Cullen, Jr., "William Gilmore Simms, Southern Journalist," *Journalism Quarterly*, 38 (Summer 1961): 298-302, 412;

Janice L. Edens, "*Southern Quarterly Review*," in *American Literary Magazines*, edited by Edward E. Chielens (New York: Greenwood Press, 1986), pp. 399-404;

John C. Guilds, Jr., "Simms as a Magazine Editor, 1825-1845," Ph.D. dissertation, Duke University, 1954;

Guilds, "Simms and the *Southern and Western*," in *South Carolina Journals and Journalists*, edited by James B. Meriwether (Columbia, S.C.: Southern Studies Program, 1975), pp. 45-59;

Guilds, "Simms's First Magazine: *The Album*," *Studies in Bibliography*, 8 (1976): 169-183;

Guilds, "Simms's Views on National and Sectional Literature, 1825-1845," *North Carolina Historical Review*, 34 (July 1957): 393-405;

Guilds, "The Literary Criticism of William Gilmore Simms," *South Carolina Review*, 2 (November 1969): 49-56;

Guilds, "The 'Lost' Number of the *Southern Literary Gazette*," *Studies in Bibliography*, 22 (1969): 266-273;

Guilds, "William Gilmore Simms and the *Cosmopolitan*," *Georgia Historical Quarterly*, 41 (March 1957): 31-41;

Guilds, "William Gilmore Simms and the *Southern Literary Gazette*," *Studies in Bibliography*, 21 (1968): 59-92;

Guilds, "Simms as Editor and Prophet: The Flowering and Early Death of the Southern *Magnolia*," *Southern Literary Journal*, 4 (Spring 1972): 69-92;

Edward Thomas Herbert, "William Gilmore Simms as Editor and Literary Critic," Ph.D. dissertation, University of Wisconsin, 1958;

Hugh Holman, Introduction to *Views and Reviews in American History and Fiction, First Series* (Cambridge, Mass.: Harvard University Press, 1962), pp. vii-xliii;

James Everett Kibler, Jr., "Simms' Editorship of the Columbia *Phoenix* of 1865," in *South Carolina Journals and Journalists*, edited by Meriwether (Columbia, S.C.: Southern Studies Program, 1975), pp. 61-75;

Kibler, "*The Album*," in *American Literary Magazines*, edited by Chielens (New York: Greenwood Press, 1986), pp. 8-11;

Kibler, "*The Album* (1826): The Significance of the Recently Discovered Second Volume," *Studies in Bibliography*, 39 (1986): 62-78;

William M. Moss, "*The Magnolia*," and "*The Southern and Western*," in *American Literary Magazines*, edited by Chielens (New York: Greenwood Press, 1986), pp. 239-244, 370-375;

Edd Winfield Parks, *William Gilmore Simms as Literary Critic* (Athens: University of Georgia Press, 1961);

J. V. Ridgely, *William Gilmore Simms* (New York: Twayne, 1962);

Kate Esary Russell, "William Carey Richards and the Orion," Ph.D. dissertation, University of Georgia, 1987;

Julian A. Selby, *Memorabilia and Anecdotal Reminiscences* (Columbia, S.C.: R. L. Bryan, 1905);

David Tomlinson, "Simms's Monthly Magazine: the *Southern and Western*," *Southern Literary Journal*, 8 (Fall 1976): 95-125;

Jon L. Wakelyn, *The Politics of a Literary Man: William Gilmore Simms* (Westport, Conn.: Greenwood Press, 1973).

Papers:

The most important collection of Simms manuscripts, which includes unpublished letters, writings, notebooks, and scrapbooks, is in the South Caroliniana Library, University of South Carolina, particularly in the Charles Carroll Simms Collection.

John Stuart Skinner

(22 February 1788-21 March 1851)

Jack W. Berryman
University of Washington

MAJOR POSITIONS HELD: Editor and publisher, *American Farmer* (1819-1830); editor and publisher, *American Turf Register and Sporting Magazine* (1829-1835); editor, *Journal of the American Silk Society* (1839); editor, *American Farmer* (1839-1841); editor, *Monthly Journal of Agriculture* (1845-1848); editor and publisher, *The Plough, the Loom, and the Anvil* (1848-1851).

BOOKS: *A Christmas Gift to the Young Agriculturists of the United States* (Washington City, 1841); *The Dog and the Sportsman* (Philadelphia: Lea & Blanchard, 1845).

OTHER: "An Essay on the Ass and Mule," in William Youatt, *The Horse* (Philadelphia: Lea & Blanchard, 1843);
Francis Clater, *Every Man His Own Farrier*, notes and additions by Skinner (Philadelphia: Lea & Blanchard, 1845);
Francois Guénon, *A Treatise on Milch Cows*, introduction by Skinner (New York: Greeley & McElrath, 1846);
Henry Stephens, *The Book of the Farm*, notes by Skinner (New York: Greeley & McElrath, 1847);
Richard Mason, *Mason's Farrier and Stud-Book*, supplement by Skinner (Philadelphia: Grigg, Elliot, 1848);
John Badcock, *Farriery Taught on a New and Easy Plan*, supplement by Skinner (Philadelphia: Grigg, Elliot, 1849).

John S. Skinner, known for his involvement in military matters during the War of 1812, his agricultural publishing, and his political contributions as a government official, was also an avid sportsman and sports journalist. Beginning in 1819, when he initiated the *American Farmer*, Skinner published material concerning exercise, recreation, amusements, and sporting pursuits. In 1825 he added a regular sports section, the "Sporting Olio," to the weekly *American Farmer*.

John Stuart Skinner (courtesy of the National Sporting Library, Middleburg, Virginia)

Skinner carried his interest in sports a step further in September 1829, when he began publication of the *American Turf Register and Sporting Magazine*, America's first specialized sports magazine. In 1830 he sold the *American Farmer* in order to devote all of his literary efforts to sports journalism. The *American Turf Register and Sporting Magazine* served as a forum to unite, stimulate, and solidify the rapidly growing American interest in sports of all kinds.

The *American Farmer* was a pioneer, originator, popularizer, and stimulator for many American sports, especially those involving horses and hounds; and the *American Turf Register and Sporting Magazine* represented the first broad-scale attempt at the crystallization of American sports reporting. Together the two magazines provided a firm foundation upon which to build American sports journalism. Sporting magazines preceded newspapers and most other forms of literature in detailed sports coverage and showed that sport was a viable topic for other journalistic endeavors. Accordingly, on the basis of his accomplishments and contributions, John S. Skinner deserves the title of "Father of American Sport Journalism."

John Stuart Skinner, born in Calvert County, Maryland, was the fifth of eleven children of plantation owner Frederick Skinner and Bettie (Stuart) Skinner. He graduated in 1806 from Charlotte Hall Academy, St. Mary's County, and was admitted to the Maryland Bar in 1809. He married Elizabeth Glenn Davies on 10 March 1812, and they resided in Annapolis, Maryland, and later in Baltimore, New York, and Philadelphia. The Skinners had three sons.

Skinner was made inspector of European mail by President Madison after the outbreak of the War of 1812 and in 1814 was commissioned a purser in the navy. In this role he was with Francis Scott Key when Key wrote "The Star Spangled Banner." From 1816 to 1839 he served as postmaster for the city of Baltimore. In 1841 President Harrison appointed Skinner third assistant postmaster general, a post he held until his removal in 1845 by President Polk for political reasons.

While Skinner was well-known in political circles, his international reputation centered upon his role as an agricultural writer, sporting magazine editor, and avid proponent of the breeding and racing of thoroughbred horses. Concerned with the poor state of agricultural affairs in his home state and throughout the South, Skinner began on 2 April 1819 to publish the *American Farmer*, a four-page weekly with an annual subscription cost of four dollars. Although it was devoted to the improvement of all aspects of farming, the *American Farmer* also contained material pertaining to the rural life-style, usually including horse racing, fox hunting, angling, and other forms of hunting. During this time he also remained active in local agricultural and sporting matters by serving as corresponding secretary of the Maryland Agricultural Society, manager of the Maryland Association for the Improvement of the Breed of Horses, and secretary of the Maryland Society for Internal Improvement. From these roles and from correspondents in similar positions Skinner acquired much of the information

that he printed in the *American Farmer*. With the establishment of the "Sporting Olio" in the 21 January 1825 issue Skinner began America's first regular magazine section devoted to sports.

The contents of the "Sporting Olio" mirrored many contemporary sporting interests, introduced new sports, explained the rules and etiquette for certain sports, and served as an important inducement for increased participation in sports. Skinner urged women and children to take part in sporting activities and often included testimonials on the value of exercise for the health and well-being of young boys and girls. When he could not secure American sports news or wanted to include information concerning a sport not yet popular in the United States, he often reprinted material from major English publications. Much of the rationale for sport and exercise, the methodology and techniques of the sportsman, and the varieties of sports introduced by Skinner was borrowed from Great Britain.

As a result of the reporting in the "Sporting Olio," horse racing became more acceptable and was introduced to new locales, the collection and recording of horse pedigrees acquired new life, new fox hunting clubs were established, and more people were made aware of the values of an active participation in outdoor sports. The success of the "Sporting Olio" illustrated the viability of sports journalism as a profitable publishing endeavor. Whereas other editors had ignored sporting news or just touched upon it, Skinner emphasized it and brought sports reporting to the American magazine industry.

Skinner had a propensity for animals of all kinds and pioneered in the publication of articles dealing with the natural history of native American animals. He also printed stories detesting the cruel treatment of animals, and, since he valued animals so greatly, he published a regular veterinary section in the *American Farmer*. Skinner's interest in improving the breed of thoroughbred horses led him to solicit and publish pedigrees in the *American Farmer* toward the aim of establishing a permanent record and American stud book. This plan, coupled with the success of the "Sporting Olio," led Skinner to begin publication in September 1829 of the monthly *American Turf Register and Sporting Magazine*. In 1830 he sold the *American Farmer* to concentrate on the new magazine.

Like the *American Farmer*, the *American Turf Register* was utilized by Skinner to encourage the systematic breeding of thoroughbred horses.

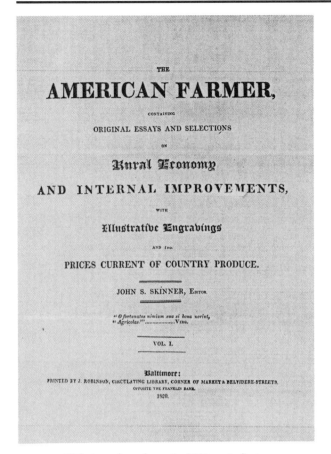

*Title page for volume 1 of Skinner's first
agricultural magazine*

*First installment (21 January 1825) of the first sporting col-
umn published in an American magazine (courtesy of the National Sporting Library, Middleburg, Virginia)*

Engraved title page for volume 1 of the first American sporting magazine (courtesy of the National Sporting Library, Middleburg, Virginia)

Engraved title page for volume 1 of Skinner's final agricultural magazine. He derived the title from his favorite maxim: "The plough profits by the successes of the anvil and the loom."

With the collection and verification of pedigrees as a major objective, Skinner published a regular "Stallion List," printed all available pedigrees of horses, and encouraged the formation of associations for the improvement of the breeding of horses. Since he believed the horse race or "trial of speed and endurance" was the only true test of breed, Skinner continued to encourage that sport. After he was appointed corresponding secretary of the Maryland Jockey Club in 1830, he used that position along with his editorship of the *American Turf Register* to help standardize and systematize horse racing. He introduced the use of the split-second timer for more accurate race results and imposed consistency in track lengths, weight allowances for riders, and general racing rules. Consequently, the Maryland Jockey Club and their Central Course became the mecca for all horse racing affairs in the early 1830s.

As editor and publisher of America's first magazine devoted exclusively to sports, Skinner was in the vanguard of a movement introducing the English athletic revolution to the American people. The *American Turf Register and Sporting Magazine* became a popularizer and stimulator for sports and a recorder of events, racing performances, and pedigrees of horses. Skinner also included in the magazine engravings of horses and dogs, and information on natural history. His emphasis on natural history influenced the formation of the Philadelphia magazine *Cabinet of Natural History and American Rural Sports* by the Doughty brothers in 1830.

When Skinner sold the *American Turf Register and Sporting Magazine* in 1835, it was apparent that he had recognized early the interest of Americans in reading about the amusements of others. Skinner's success did not go unnoticed. Aspiring sportsmen-editors and publishers already in the magazine business rapidly realized that Skinner had established a precedent for sports journalism as a profitable publishing endeavor. Accordingly, six new sports magazines began between 1826 and 1835, most of which had some direct relationship with Skinner and his two magazines. They shared news items, copied Skinner's format and style, and even utilized Skinner's correspondents, sometimes without formal credit. Skinner, however, never complained about rival publications. In fact, William T. Porter, founder and editor of the *Spirit of the Times* in 1831, and Cadwallader R. Colden, founder and editor of the *New York Sporting Magazine* (1833) and the *United States Sporting Magazine* (1835), were both close friends of

Skinner in his later years

Skinner. Colden gave direct credit to Skinner for encouraging his entrance into sports journalism. Other editors reprinted articles from the *American Farmer* and the *American Turf Register*; engravings first acquired by Skinner were used later by rival publishers; and other magazines looked upon the *American Turf Register* as the "official" record for horse racing and even referred to it as the "American Sporting Magazine." Despite the fact that only one of the new sports magazines, Porter's *Spirit of the Times*, survived longer than three years, their establishment was indicative of America's growing interest in sports and sports journalism.

At a time when sport for sport's sake was under suspicion the *American Turf Register* provided an extensive array of reasons for its practice. Skinner succeeded in demonstrating the possible functions of sport in American society by publishing articles that illustrated the viability of sport for measuring physical skills; promoting and maintaining health; stimulating socialization; attracting national attention to business enterprises; and molding the spirit, sentiments, and patriotic feelings of a distinct American character.

The work of the *American Turf Register* was a prelude to developments in still other sports during the 1840s and 1850s. By the beginning of the Civil War American sport magazines were in abundance. At a time when Americans were learning what to play and how to play, Skinner performed vital roles in the transformation of a general lifestyle.

In December 1838 Skinner was elected a member of the executive committee of the newly formed American Silk Society in Baltimore, and he became editor of their monthly *Journal of the American Silk Society,* which published its first issue in January 1839. However, Skinner's editorship was short-lived. His removal from his postmaster's duties for the city of Baltimore early that same year left him without steady employment. Consequently, he took up the editorship of *Farmer and Gardener,* which had been the old *American Farmer.* Skinner restored the magazine's original name and remained with it until August 1841.

After serving as assistant postmaster general from 1841 to 1845, Skinner was invited by the publishers of the *New York Tribune,* Horace Greeley and Thomas McElrath, to New York to plan and edit a new periodical called the *Monthly Journal of Agriculture.* It began in July 1845 and contained costly engravings and reprints of articles from some of the most noted foreign works. Skinner was given a three-year contract, and he became an agricultural editor once again. He kept active in sports writing as well, publishing a book called *The Dog and the Sportsman* (1845) his first year in New York.

When Skinner's contract with Greeley and McElrath expired in 1848 he remembered an earlier suggestion by Henry C. Carey of Philadelphia that he establish his own magazine once again. Keeping in mind his visits to large industrial centers and his knowledge of agriculture, Skinner made his favorite maxim–"The plough profits by the successes of the anvil and the loom"–a reality. He moved to Philadelphia, where he and his son Frederick began publishing and editing a new monthly, *The Plough, the Loom, and the Anvil.* He continued in this role until his death on 21 March 1851 from an injury to his head, sustained in a fall while he and his wife were visiting friends in Baltimore.

References:
Jack W. Berryman, "John Stuart Skinner and Early American Sport Journalism, 1819-1835," Ph.D. dissertation, University of Maryland, 1976;

Berryman, "John Stuart Skinner and the *American Farmer,* 1819-1829: An Early Proponent of Rural Sports," *Associates NAL Today,* 1 (October 1976): 11-32;

Berryman, "John S. Skinner's *American Farmer:* Breeding and Racing the Maryland 'Blood Horse,' 1819-1829," *Maryland Historical Magazine,* 76 (Summer 1981): 159-173;

Harold A. Bierck, Jr., "Spoils, Soils, and Skinner," *Maryland Historical Magazine,* 49 (March 1954): 21-40; (June 1954): 143-155;

Lucretia Ramsey Bishko, "The Agricultural Society of Albemarle and John S. Skinner: An Enduring Friendship," *Magazine of Albemarle County History,* 31 (1973): 76-113;

Harold T. Pinkett, "*The American Farmer,* A Pioneer Agricultural Journal, 1819-1834," *Agricultural History,* 24 (July 1950): 146-151;

Pinkett, "A Forgotten Patriot," *Social Studies,* 40 (December 1949): 354-355;

Ben Perley Poore, "Biographical Sketch of John Stuart Skinner," *The Plough, the Loom, and the Anvil,* 7 (July 1854): 1-20;

Harry Worcester Smith, *A Sporting Family of the Old South: With Which is Included Reminiscences of An Old Sportsman by Frederick Gustavus Skinner* (Albany, N.Y.: J. B. Lyon, 1936).

Papers:
Skinner's papers are at the Maryland Historical Society, Baltimore; the University of Virginia, Charlottesville; Cornell University, Ithaca, New York; and the National Sporting Library, Middleburg, Virginia.

Ann Sophia Stephens

(30 March 1810-20 August 1886)

Sam G. Riley
Virginia Polytechnic Institute and State University

See also the Stephens entry in *DLB 3: Antebellum Writers in New York and the South.*

MAJOR POSITIONS HELD: Cofounder and editor, *Portland Magazine* (1834-1836); associate editor, *Ladies' Companion; and Literary Expositor, a Monthly Magazine Embracing Every Department of Literature* (1837-1841); associate editor, *Graham's Lady's and Gentleman's Magazine* (1841-1842); coeditor, *Lady's World*, renamed *Peterson's Magazine* in 1849 (1842-1853); editor, *Frank Leslie's Lady's Gazette of Fashion and Fancy Needlework* (1854-1856); founder and editor, *Mrs. Stephens New Monthly* (1856-1858).

SELECTED BOOKS: *The Queen of a Week* (New York: W. W. Snowden, 1839);

High Life in New York, as Jonathan Slick, Esq. (New York: E. Stephens, 1843; London: J. How, 1844);

Alice Copley. A Tale of Queen Mary's Time (Philadelphia, 184?; Boston: "Yankee" Office, 1844);

David Hunt, and Malina Gray (Philadelphia: G. R. Graham, 1845; New York: F. M. Lupton, 1892);

The Diamond Necklace: and Other Tales (Boston: Gleason's Publishing Hall, 1846);

The Tradesman's Boast (Boston: Gleason's Publishing Hall, 1846);

Henry Longford, or, the Forged Will. A Tale of New York City (Boston: Gleason's Publishing Hall, 1847);

The Red Coats; or, The Sack of Unquowa (New York: Williams, 1848);

Fashion and Famine (New York: Bunce & Brother, 1854; London: Richard Bently, 1854);

Zana; or, The Heiress of Clair Hall (London: Ward & Lock, 1854); republished as *The Heiress of Greenhurst: An Autobiography* (New York: Edward Stephens, 1857);

Julie Warren, oder Glanz und Elend (Leipzig: C. E. Kollmann, 1855);

The Old Homestead (New York: Bunce & Brother, 1855; Philadelphia: T. B. Peterson, 1889);

translated as *Das Alte Familienhaus* (Leipzig: C. E. Kollmann, 1856);

Myra, the Child of Adoption. A Romance of Real Life (New York: Beadle & Adams, 1856; London: Beadle, 1861); translated as *Myra, oder Die Pflegetochter* (Leipzig: C. E. Kollmann, 1871);

Mary Derwent (Philadelphia: T. B. Peterson, 1858); republished as *Mary Derwent: A Tale of the Wyoming Valley* (New York: A. L. Burt, 1858); republished as *Mary Derwent: A Tale of the American Settlers* (London & New York: Beadle, 1861?); republished as *Mary Der-*

went; A Tale of the Wyoming and Mohawk Valleys in 1778 (Wilkes-Barre, Pa.: Fowler, Dick & Walker, 1908);

Malaeska; the Indian Wife of the White Hunter (London & New York: Beadle, 1860); republished as *Mahaska, the Indian Princess: a Tale of the Six Nations* (London: Beadle, 1863);

Ahmo's Plot; or, The Governor's Indian Child (New York: Beadle, 1860; London: G. Routledge, 1866);

Sybil Chase; or, The Valley Ranche. A Tale of California Life (New York: Beadle, 1861; London: E. F. Beadle, 1862);

Esther: A Story of the Oregon Trail (New York: Beadle, 1862; London: E. F. Beadle, 1863, 1864);

Pictorial History of the War for the Union, 2 volumes (New York: J. G. Wells, 1862);

The Rejected Wife (London, n.d.; Philadelphia: T. B. Peterson, 1863); republished as *The Rejected Wife; or, The Ruling Passion* (Philadelphia: T. B. Peterson, 1876);

The Indian Princess (New York: Beadle & Adams, 1863);

The Indian Queen (New York: Beadle & Adams, 1864; London: Beadle & Co., 187?);

The Wife's Secret (Philadelphia: T. B. Peterson, 1864); republished as *The Wife's Secret; or, Gillian* (Philadelphia: T. B. Peterson, 1876);

Silent Struggles (Philadelphia: T. B. Peterson, 1865);

The Gold Brick (New York: Lupton, 1866; Philadelphia: T. B. Peterson, 1866);

The Soldier's Orphans (Philadelphia: T. B. Peterson, 1866);

Doubly False (Philadelphia: T. B. Peterson, 1868);

Mable's Mistake (Philadelphia: T. B. Peterson, 1868);

Ruby Gray's Strategy (New York: F. M. Lupton, 1869);

Wives and Widows; or, The Broken Life (Philadelphia: T. B. Peterson, 1869);

The Curse of Gold (Philadelphia: T. B. Peterson, 1869);

Married in Haste (Philadelphia: T. B. Peterson, 1870);

A Noble Woman (Philadelphia: T. B. Peterson, 1871);

Palaces and Prisons (Philadelphia: T. B. Peterson, 1871);

The Reigning Belle (Philadelphia: T. B. Peterson, 1872); republished as *The Reigning Belle. A Society Novel* (Philadelphia: T. B. Peterson, 1885);

Bellehood and Bondage (Philadelphia: T. B. Peterson, 1873);

Lord Hope's Choice (Philadelphia: T. B. Peterson, 1873);

The Old Countess; or, The Two Proposals (Philadelphia: T. B. Peterson, 1873, 1888);

The Outlaw's Wife; or, the Valley Ranche (New York: Beadle & Adams, 1874);

Phemie Frost's Experiences (New York: G. W. Carleton, 1874);

Bertha's Engagement (Philadelphia: T. B. Peterson, 1875);

Norton's Rest (Philadelphia: T. B. Peterson, 1877);

Lily. In Memoriam (New York: J. J. Little, 1884);

The Lady Mary. A Novel (New York: F. M. Lupton, 188?, 1892);

Rock Run; or, The Daughter of the Island (New York: F. M. Lupton, 1893).

Collection: *The Works of Mrs. Ann S. Stephens*, 23 volumes (Philadelphia: T. B. Peterson, 1886).

OTHER: *The Portland Sketch Book*, edited by Stephens (Portland: Colman & Chisholm, 1836);

The Ladies' Complete Guide to Crochet, Fancy Knitting and Needlework, edited by Stephens (New York: Garrett, 1854);

Frank Leslie's Portfolio of Fancy Needlework, edited by Stephens (New York: Stringer & Townsend, 1855).

The prolific Ann Stephens found considerable fame in the mid 1800s as a writer of sentimental novels, short stories, and poems, and as an editor of magazines that specialized in light literature for women readers. She is best remembered today, when she is remembered at all, as the author of the first Beadle Dime Novel.

She was born Ann Sophia Winterbotham, the third of ten children of John and Ann Wrigley Winterbotham, on 30 March 1810 in Humphreysville, Connecticut. Her father had emigrated from Manchester, England, in 1806 to become part-owner and superintendent of woolen mills founded by the Connecticut poet-patriot Col. David Humphreys. Her mother died when Ann was a child, and her upbringing fell to her stepmother, Rachael. She was educated at a dame school in Humphreysville and later in South Britain, Connecticut. She was heavily influenced by the literary interests of Colonel Humphreys, who had been an aide to Gen.

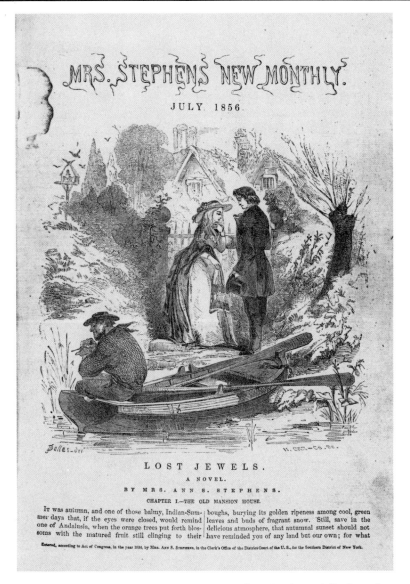

Engraved first page of Stephens's magazine, featuring her serialized novel

George Washington and later U.S. minister to Spain.

Stephens's first poem was written when she was seven; her first published work was a composition about a Yale student that appeared in the *New Haven Post*. Her early efforts, all published under pen names, appeared in a variety of newspapers.

In 1831 Ann Winterbotham was married to printer Edward Stephens of Plymouth, Massachusetts. The couple moved to Portland, Maine, where they founded the *Portland Magazine* (1834-1836), a women's journal containing both "selected" material and original romantic tales, poetry, essays, biographical articles, nature and travel articles, literary notices, and pieces on phrenology. Edward Stephens served as publisher, Ann Stephens as editor. Realizing the difficulty of her new venture, she wrote in an address that prefaced the first issue:

> Noah, when sending out the dove upon the waste of waters, could not have felt more anxiety for its safe return with the green leaf of promise in its bill, than is experienced for the success of the specimen number of the Portland Magazine, which we now offer to the Ladies of Maine. The editor is fully aware of all that can be said in opposition to the present undertaking.

The thirty-two-page monthly's early issues consisted largely of material from the editor's own pen. Her poems "The Polish Boy" and "My Natal

Bowers" were run in the first issue, as were her first published tales, "The Tradesman's Daughter" and "Romance and Reality." Other important contributors in later issues were local writers John Neal and Seba Smith, Henry Wadsworth Longfellow, and Nathaniel Parker Willis.

In the ninth number of her second volume Stephens announced her departure as editor due to a combination of ill health and a desire to devote more of her time to writing. In 1836 the *Portland Magazine* was merged with *Eastern Magazine* to form the *Maine Monthly Magazine*, and soon the Stephenses moved again, this time to New York City, where Edward had secured a position at the customs house.

In 1837 Ann Stephens became associate editor of William W. Snowden's *Ladies' Companion, and Literary Expositor, a Monthly Magazine Embracing Every Department of Literature* (1834-1844). The New York magazine was published in the mold of its older Philadelphia rivals *Godey's Lady's Book* and *Graham's Magazine*. Poe and Longfellow were contributors, and like most women's magazines of its era, the *Ladies' Companion* was heavy on fiction and ran sentimental poetry and romantic tales, as many fashion engravings as its publisher could afford, and articles on fashion, music, and theater.

During the years 1837 to 1841, the period in which she helped edit the *Ladies' Companion*, Stephens contributed to that magazine a number of articles that would eventually help establish her literary reputation. The first was "Mary Derwent, A Tale of the Early Settlers," which won her a two-hundred-dollar prize in a writing competition. Next came the three-part serialization of "Malaeska" (published in 1860 as *Malaeska; the Indian Wife of the White Hunter*), a sentimental tale of an Indian maiden—one of nature's noblewomen—who was married to a white hunter. After the hunter dies mother and child go to live with his parents in New York. The bigoted grandparents keep the child but demote Malaeska to the status of nursemaid. Malaeska returns to the forest, and her child is taught to hate Indians. Later, when Malaeska reveals her identity to him, the boy commits suicide out of shame, and in turn the heartbroken Malaeska dies a picture-perfect death on her husband's grave. Such a plot sounds unduly saccharine today but was conventional in the early and mid 1800s.

During the early years of her career Stephens also contributed to numerous periodicals, among them the *Lady's Wreath, Olive Branch, Phila-* *delphia Saturday Gazette, Columbian Lady's and Gentleman's Magazine, Flag of Our Union*, and *Brother Jonathan*, a short-lived New York story paper (1842-1843) edited for a time by her husband, Edward.

In 1841 Ann Stephens became an associate editor of *Graham's Lady's and Gentleman's Magazine* (1826-1858), which had earlier been published under the titles *Casket* (1826-1830) and *Atkinson's Casket* (1831-1839). The magazine was taken over in 1839 by George R. Graham, who aimed his new periodical at women readers, giving them the usual amalgam of politely sensationalized love tales, sentimental poetry, travel fare, and literary notices. Writing for *Graham's*, Stephens found herself in good company: James Fenimore Cooper, William Cullen Bryant, Richard Henry Dana, Longfellow, Poe, E. F. Ellet, Frances Osgood, Seba Smith, and Emma Embury. Such a talented stable of contributors eventually gave *Graham's* the largest circulation of any American monthly.

Stephens was lured away from *Graham's* in 1842 by Charles J. Peterson, publisher of a rival women's magazine then titled the *Lady's World of Fashion*. Peterson took his magazine in quick succession through several name changes—*Lady's World, Artist and Lady's World*, and *Ladies' National Magazine*—before finally settling on *Peterson's Magazine*, the title used from 1849 until 1892. Though Ann Stephens was listed as editor through 1847, then as coeditor until 1853, her actual position appears to have been more nearly that of an associate editor, as Charles Peterson maintained direct editorial control during this entire period.

During her years as a *Peterson's* editor, Stephens was a frequent contributor, her sentimental tales appearing alongside the work of Emily H. May, Elizabeth Oakes Smith, Frances Osgood, Lydia Sigourney, Lydia Pierson, and other of the period's best-known women writers. Among the magazine's male contributors, T. S. Arthur and John T. Trowbridge stand out.

Stephens's editorial position with *Peterson's* lasted from 1842 until 1853, though from 1850 to 1852 she left Edward and their two children, Ann (born in 1841) and Edward (born in 1845), at home in New York while she made the grand tour of Europe with her friend Col. George W. Pratt and his sister, Julia. While abroad she made the acquaintance of numerous literary greats, including Charles Dickens, William Makepeace Thackeray, and the Humboldts.

Engraving from the October 1856 issue of Mrs. Stephens New Monthly

Her connection with *Peterson's* was a most profitable one. Not only did her serialized tales in the magazine add to her literary fame, but some years later these stories would be sent to T. B. Peterson, Charles's brother, to be published as books. Stephens continued writing for *Peterson's* for most of the remainder of her life, and much of this output reappeared in book form under the T. B. Peterson imprint. T. B. Peterson became her most frequent publisher beginning in 1863, but prior to that time she had already had quite a number of books published by other firms.

Stephens's husband, Edward, who tried a few publishing ventures of his own, published in 1843 Ann's sole contribution to the humor of the period, *High Life in New York*, with Ann writing under the pseudonym Jonathan Slick, Esq., a take-off on T. C. Haliburton's "Sam Slick." This little book, a collection of articles that had originally appeared serially in the *New York Daily Express*, sati-

rized New York society in the style of the cracker-barrel humorists. The book was reprinted several times by a variety of publishers, including two abroad in London and Stuttgart. Six succeeding books, three of which were published in Boston by Gleason's Publishing Hall, do not appear to have made much of an impression on the reading public, but upon her return from Europe she brought out her first long novel, *Fashion and Famine*, published in 1854 by four different publishers in New York, London, and Philadelphia. Later it appeared in translation in Lisbon, Portugal. Her next novel to become popular was *The Old Homestead* (1855), introduced, as had been *Fashion and Famine*, by Bunce and Brother of New York, then translated into German and published in Leipzig.

In January of 1854, following her return from Europe, Stephens became editor of engraver-publisher Frank Leslie's first magazine, entitled *Frank Leslie's Lady's Gazette of Fashion and*

Fancy Needlework, a sixteen-page monthly featuring short stories, articles on the arts, music, folded dress and embroidery patterns, book reviews, and a feature on chess. Her connection with this magazine was brief, ending in 1856 when she founded her own magazine, *Mrs. Stephens New Monthly* (1856-1858). Much of the writing in this quarto was her own, but her friends John Neal, Frank Benedict, Alice Carey, Lydia Sigourney, and E. F. Ellet also contributed. Other prose writers for the *New Monthly* were Douglas Jerrold and George L. Aiken; contributors of verse were William W. Fosdick, John Cruger Mills, David Paul Brown, and James G. Clark.

The first issue of the *New Monthly* opened with Stephens's serialized novel "Lost Jewels." Later issues contained her serial tale "The Royal Sisters." Many items, prose and poetry, were illustrated with the fine engravings of J. A. Dallas. Only twenty-four numbers were published owing to the business failure of her publisher, playwright Oliver Bell Bunce. The last issue of the *New Monthly* was in June 1858, after which the little magazine was absorbed by *Peterson's*.

In 1856 the New York firm Beadle and Adams brought out another Stephens novel, *Myra, the Child of Adoption*, which was based on an actual lawsuit that had been brought by Myra Clark Gaines, who had been disinherited by her wealthy father. This novel, too, was republished in London and in Leipzig, in translation. Her novel *Zana; or, The Heiress of Clair Hall*, originally published in London in 1854, was retitled *The Heiress of Greenhurst: an Autobiography* and republished in 1857 by her husband, Edward, in New York.

Mary Derwent, which had first appeared in serial form in the *Ladies' Companion*, was brought out as a novel by T. B. Peterson in Philadelphia and was subsequently republished under slightly altered titles in 1858, 1861(?), and 1908. By the late 1850s her combination of magazine writing and editing, plus her books, had made Ann Stephens one of America's most popular writers.

Her fame and popularity reached a new height in 1860 when her historical Indian romance *Malaeska* burst onto the popular literature scene as the first Beadle Dime Novel. At least three hundred thousand copies of this 128-page book were sold, putting it in the category of a major mid-nineteenth-century best-seller. Due to the great success of *Malaeska*, the third in the prodigious series of Beadle novels was a resurrected *Myra, the Child of Adoption* (186?). Five more Ste-

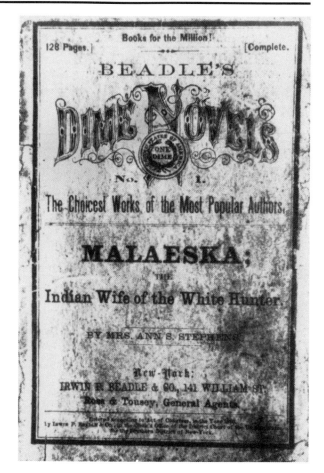

Front cover for Stephens's 1860 Indian romance

phens tales appeared as Beadle Dime Novels thereafter. Like most of the Beadle novels, Stephens's works were adventure stories, mostly historical fiction based on pioneer life. Most were nationalistic and moralistic in tone. Her attention to domestic detail created a sense of realism about frontier life.

Stephens's work has attracted new interest in recent years on the part of writers concerned with how women were portrayed in nineteenth-century American literature. One such commentator, Juliann E. Fleenor, finds Stephens's tales short on action but long on detailed descriptions of women's clothing, and points out that Stephens was more given to external descriptions of women's physical appearance than to examination of their thoughts. The women in Stephens's stories were put there to be acted upon by men, writes Fleenor. She also points out that Stephens sentimentalized poverty with her poor-but-sweet, innocent heroines, who were found to be appealing characters by the predominantly middle-class women who comprised most of the readership of both her books and magazine stories.

Writer Ann Douglas points out that Ann Stephens was one of a good many women writers of her time who were more successful than their husbands. Douglas also discusses these writers' literary careers and how some–Stephens, Sarah Hale, and Lydia Sigourney–entered into editorial positions with magazines partly as a means of gaining some control over the literary marketplace in order to further their own interests as writers.

Feminists would hold Stephens in somewhat lower esteem, however, if they read the comments of Herbert Ross Brown in his examination of sentimental American novels. Brown quotes a selection from *The Old Homestead* in which Stephens writes of the inherent "leaning" or "clinging" role of women, saying, "Women were born to look inward with their hearts and cling to others for their support. Men were made to give this support. You cannot change places and be happy!" One wonders how autobiographical these comments were inasmuch as she herself was already her family's primary breadwinner. That she truly held this conservative, prefeminist attitude is ratified by comments she had made in 1834 in the opening address to readers of her *Portland Magazine*, in which she said that business and politics were the man's proper domain, "but poetry, fiction, and the lighter branches of the sciences are woman's appropriate sphere, as much as the flower garden, the drawing room, and the nursery."

During the Civil War Stephens was vice president of the Ladies National Covenant, a Washington, D.C., organization that attempted to hold down extravagance on the home front. She also wrote and compiled a two-volume *Pictorial History of the War for the Union*, published in New York by J. G. Wells in 1862. In this same year her husband, Edward, died, leaving the tall, stout Ann as the sole, but perfectly capable support of herself and her children. For her remaining years she never returned to magazine editing but continued to contribute serials, most of them year-long stories, to *Peterson's Magazine*. Many of these were subsequently published as books by T. B. Peterson. After 1862 twenty-seven more of her books appeared; most were novels set in America, though a few were set in England.

Stephens was interested in a number of social causes and used her sentimental novels to raise readers' consciousness regarding such issues as prison reform, hospital conditions, orphan care, and better pay for working women. She was also an active writer for the "story papers" that were so popular during and after the Civil War. In 1860 she wrote for *Marie Louise Hankins' Family Newspaper*, for the *New York Weekly* from 1861 to 1869, and for *Saturday Night* for several years, beginning in 1869. In 1876 she wrote for *Frank Leslie's Chimney Corner*. Her work was frequently pirated by the London *Family Herald*, a weekly periodical of light literature that enjoyed a large circulation in England.

The writings of Ann Sophia Stephens are far too sentimental and moralistic for today's tastes, which accounts for her lack of lasting fame, yet in the mid to late 1800s she was one of the best known of our nation's writers. The romantic, sentimental appeal for her historically placed characters and her talent for vivid description gave two, perhaps three generations of women readers what they wanted. Ann Stephens died at age seventy-six in 1886 of nephritis at the home of longtime friend Charles J. Peterson in Newport, Rhode Island. She was buried in Greenwood Cemetery in Brooklyn, New York.

References:

Herbert Ross Brown, *The Sentimental Novel in America, 1789-1860* (New York: Pageant Books, 1959);

Ann Douglas, *The Feminization of American Culture* (New York: Knopf, 1977);

James Alfred Eastman, "Ann Sophia Stephens," M.A. thesis, Columbia University, 1952;

Juliann E. Fleenor, "Ann Sophia Winterbotham Stephens," in *American Women Writers*, edited by Lina Mainiero (New York: Ungar, 1982), pp. 163-164;

Frank Luther Mott, *A History of American Magazines*, 5 volumes (Cambridge, Mass.: Harvard University Press, 1938-1968), II: 306-309, 437-438;

Helen Waite Papashvily, *All the Happy Endings* (New York: Harper, 1956), pp. 142-144;

Madeleine B. Stern, *Books and Book People in 19th Century America* (New York & London: Bowker, 1978), pp. 162-164;

Stern, *Publishers for Mass Entertainment in Nineteenth Century America* (Boston: G. K. Hall, 1980), pp. 35-50, 229-234;

Stern, *We the Women: Career Firsts of 19th Century America* (New York: Schulte, 1963), pp. 29-54, 312-320.

Papers:

Letters by Ann Sophia Stephens are held by the Boston Public Library, Brown University Library, the New York Historical Society, the Connecticut Historical Society, and the Historical Society of Pennsylvania. Her manuscript scrapbook is held by the New York Public Library.

Thomas Swords
(1763-1843)

and

James Swords
(birthdate unknown-1844)

June N. Adamson
University of Tennessee

MAJOR POSITIONS HELD: Editors, publishers, *New-York Magazine; or, Literary Repository* (1790-1797); editors, publishers, *United States Christian Magazine* (1796); publishers, *Medical Repository of Original Essays and Intelligence* (1797-1824); publishers, *Monthly Magazine, and American Review* (1799-1800); publishers, *New York Missionary Magazine, and Repository of Religious Intelligence* (1800-1803); publishers, *American Review, and Literary Journal* (1801-1802); editors, publishers, *Christian Journal, and Literary Register* (1817-1830).

Important on the New York City publishing scene in the late 1700s and early 1800s were the Swords brothers, Thomas and James–printers, booksellers, book publishers, and publishers of seven periodicals. The most noteworthy of their magazines was the *New-York Magazine; or, Literary Repository* (1790-1797), one of the longest-lasting American magazines of the eighteenth century.

Thomas and James Swords were the two youngest of three sons of Thomas Swords and Mary Morell Swords of Albany, New York. There were also two daughters. Thomas Swords came from a town near Dublin, Ireland, and was the first of his family to come to this country. Unlike later Irish immigrants who came to America to escape poverty, the senior Swords came from a family of moderate means. He was granted a commission as ensign in the Fifty-fifth Regiment of Foot, British Army. Soon after his joining, the regiment was ordered to America. Ensign Swords was severely wounded in a disastrous British attack on Fort Ticonderoga. For his effort he was promoted to lieutenant and given several important commands. Four years later, however, he resigned his commission and took up residence in a house built on a huge tract of land near the banks of the Hudson River granted him by the British government as payment for his services. There he lived the life of a country gentleman until local patriots forced him to leave out of fear that he might try to communicate with the British in Canada. In the summer of 1777 he was permitted to return to his home in order to move his family to Albany, New York.

The Revolutionary War background seems important, since it must have created mixed feelings in his sons, especially because the senior Thomas's ambivalence was known. He loved the countryside where he lived and was repeatedly asked by important American patriots to accept the command of a regiment in the patriot army; but his devotion to duty, plus his fear of losing his land, kept him from accepting. In addition, part of his livelihood depended on the half-pay he received from the British government after he resigned his commission.

His sons also experienced some of the trauma of war. An infamous murder of a young loyalist woman took place a few miles north of Swordses' original homestead, and it was his youngest son, James, who carried her body to the British garrison at Fort Edward.

After the capture of the British Gen. John Burgoyne at Saratoga in 1777, the elder Swords

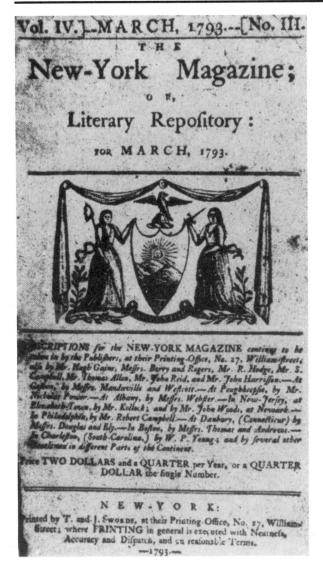

Front cover for an issue of one of the leading general magazines of the post-Revolutionary era

and other loyalists were not permitted to move to Canada, as they wished, but were granted a "flag" to proceed to the city of New York with their families. Their petition for this favor is on file in the library of the New York Historical Society. The senior Thomas Swords died in New York in 1780.

The outcome of the Revolutionary War directly affected Thomas and James. The family was deprived of its property, and the two sons were apprenticed to a printer and by 1784 were working in Nova Scotia for the *Port-Roseway Gazetteer* and the *Sherburne Advertiser*. After the peace of 1783 their mother went to England with her daughters, hoping for remuneration for what she had lost because of her husband's loyalty. She par-

tially succeeded, and, shortly after her return in 1786, her two sons established themselves on New York's Pearl Street as booksellers and printers, under the firm name of T. & J. Swords. Early on, the firm became identified with the Episcopal Church, and the brothers were recognized as publishers for that denomination. Their bookstore was a favorite visiting spot for all Episcopal clergy, whether New Yorkers or visitors from out of town. Thomas was for nearly thirty years a leader in the vestry of wealthy Trinity Parish.

While their firm operated successfully for almost a half-century, producing a variety of publications, it was dissolved when the junior partner, James, retired upon his election to the presidency of the Washington Fire Insurance Company, a position he held until his death and for which he received many honors.

With the dissolution of the firm, Thomas associated himself with his oldest son, Edward J. Swords, and Thomas N. Stanford, son of an Episcopal minister. The firm's name was changed to Swords, Stanford & Co. and remained so until Thomas's death.

Thomas Swords was married in 1799 to Mary White, by whom he had nine children. Following his death in 1843 the publishing firm was dissolved, Edward J. Swords devoting himself to a printing department, while Thomas N. Stanford continued the book business in connection with Thomas Swords's younger son, James R. Swords, undoubtedly his uncle's namesake. This new company was named Stanford & Swords and continued for sixty-nine years.

New-York Magazine; or, Literary Repository, the Swordses' most important periodical, was one of the longest-running continuing magazines of the eighteenth century. Frank Luther Mott, in volume 1 of *A History of American Magazines* (1938), says that the Swords brothers were probably editors as well as publishers. In any case, the greater part of the magazine was taken from books and other periodicals, and the original portions were so disguised that the Swordses' helpers are hard to identify. Mott states that they were probably members of the Friendly Club, citing Marcia Edgerton Bailey's *A Lesser Hartford Wit, Dr. Elihu Hubbard Smith* (1928) as his source. John W. Francis, in the February 1852 *International Magazine*, says that Charles Brockden Brown, William Dunlap, Anthony Bleecker, Josiah Ogden Hoffman, and James Kent were contributors to "The Drone," the magazine's chief essay series. Dunlap is known to be the author of "The Theatrical Register," carried by the magazine from 1794 to 1796. Mott credits the magazine with showing the most interest in theater of any eighteenth-century magazine and, consequently, being the most valuable to students of theater history.

Other contributors included Friendly Club members Dr. Elihu Hubbard Smith, Dr. Edward Miller, Dr. Samuel Latham Mitchill, the Reverend Sam Miller, William Johnson, Charles Adams, and John Wells, as well as Noah Webster. The only woman listed was Eliza Bleecker, who contributed elegiac and domestic poems.

The *New-York Magazine* also carried articles, many quite lengthy, on travel, agriculture, medicine, and legal problems. The first subscription list was headed by the names George Washington and John Adams, and the magazine at least once, on 5 November 1792, carried a speech by Washington to "Fellow Citizens of the Senate and the House of Representatives."

The *New-York Magazine; or, Literary Repository* was a direct outgrowth of the *American Magazine* published in New York by Noah Webster. Lyon N. Richardson, in *A History of Early American Magazines* (1931), writes that after the latter magazine was discontinued late in 1788, the city was without a magazine until the Swordses began their effort, with Webster among their many contributors. Richardson explains that Webster, upon realizing his magazine would have to be modified or discontinued, probably for financial reasons, "was planning an extensive federal magazine." He hoped to unite his New York publication with Isaiah Thomas's *Massachusetts Magazine* and also with one of the publications in Philadelphia. But it turned out that Thomas was wealthy enough to support his publication, which ranks, along with the *New-York Magazine,* as one of the four longest-running magazines of the period, the other two being the *Columbian Magazine* and the *American Museum,* both of Philadelphia.

The Swords brothers' second magazine venture was the short-lived *United States Christian Magazine* (1796), which carried a combination of Biblical interpretation, doctrinal essays, biographical articles on religious leaders, letters, reviews, and religious notes. The following year, during an epidemic of yellow fever, the Swordses began publishing a quarterly medical journal, the *Medical Repository of Original Essays and Intelligence, Relative to Physic, Surgery, Chemistry and Natural History,* which continued until 1824. The journal was edited by Samuel Latham Mitchill, assisted by fellow New York physicians Elihu Hubbard Smith

Announcement by Thomas and James Swords that they would assume editorial duties, in addition to their role as publishers, of the long-running Episcopal journal

and Edward Miller. The *Medical Repository* gained a solid reputation and devoted special attention to the study of epidemics.

In 1799 and 1800 the Swordses published the *Monthly Magazine, and American Review,* which for a little more than a year and a half presented its readers with a combination of verse, fiction, articles on science and literature, reviews, and some news items. In 1800 the brothers began their second religious periodical, the *New York Missionary Magazine, and Repository of Religious Intelligence,* edited by a C. Davis for the interdenominational New York Missionary Society. Probably the first American periodical devoted to missionary work, the magazine was published through December 1803.

In 1801 the firm of T. & J. Swords became publishers of editor Charles Brockden Brown's *American Review, And Literary Journal* (1801-1802). One section of the magazine dealt with literature; a second section was given over to information on new inventions, patents, and discoveries in science and mechanics. The last of the firm's magazines was also concerned with religion. The *Christian Journal, And Literary Register* was an Episcopal magazine initially edited by Bishop John Henry Hobard and the Reverend Benjamin T. Onderdonk, after which the Swordses themselves assumed editorship. Though never profitable, this magazine was carried by the Swordses until 1830.

Unfortunately, little is known about the Swords brothers' personal lives. Obviously, they were hardworking and successful. No record can be found of whether James married or had a family. One thing that is known is that they must have been hard taskmasters to their apprentices, perhaps treating them as they had been treated. Madeleine B. Stern, in *Books and Book People in 19th Century America* (1978), writes that James Bogert of Geneva, New York, "served his apprenticeship with the firm of Thomas and James Swords of New York, where, for forty dollars a year and board that included rancid butter, mouldy bread, and spoiled meat, he had learned the art of printing. When young James was forced to shake the snow from his bed on arising and retiring, it soon became apparent that many hogs were better fed and his articles were cancelled. . . ." This information is confirmed by Milton W. Hamilton in *The Country Printer* (1936) as he describes the Swordses' treatment of apprentices. "James Bogert was taken away from Thomas and James Swords of New York because the board 'was not up to standard.'" Presumably, being "taken away" means the same thing as "his articles were cancelled," so there must have been some supervision of apprentices and means of complaint.

Despite this case, and it may have been the only one, the Swords brothers were generally respected as printers. Indeed, they were well enough thought of that Isaiah Thomas, in preparing his history of printing, addressed a query to them which begins: "I have been long engaged in writing a History of Printing in America, and have nearly completed the very laborious work; one volume of which is printed. I have not been so fortunate in collecting materials respecting printing in New York. . . ." The letter continues with mention that this was not the first time he had queried the Swordses, and asks again "[if] you can inform me, I shall esteem it a great favor." Whether the brothers responded is unknown.

Largely forgotten today, the Swords brothers were active publishers and reasonably successful by the standards of their day. Their periodical contributions included one of the two longest-lived popular American magazines of the 1700s, a noteworthy early medical journal, and three religious magazines.

References:

Milton W. Hamilton, *The Country Printer: New York State 1785-1830* (New York: Columbia University Press, 1936), pp. 14, 85;

Frank Luther Mott, *A History of American Magazines*, 5 volumes (Cambridge, Mass.: Harvard University Press, 1938-1968), I: 114-116;

Lyon N. Richardson, *A History of Early American Magazines, 1741-1789* (New York: Thomas Nelson & Sons, 1931), pp. 282-283; 334-335;

Madeleine B. Stern, *Books and Book People in 19th Century America* (London & New York: Bowker, 1978), p. 14.

Papers:

A Swords family manuscript is held by the New York Historical Society.

Isaiah Thomas

(30 January 1750-4 April 1831)

Terry Hynes
California State University, Fullerton

See also the Thomas entry in *DLB 43: American Newspaper Journalists, 1690-1872* and the entry on his publishing house in *DLB 49: American Literary Publishing Houses, 1638-1899.*

MAJOR POSITIONS HELD: Printer, *Halifax Gazette* (1765-1766); publisher, *Massachusetts Spy* (1770-1786, 1788-1801); printer, *Massachusetts Spy* (1770-1776, 1778-1786, 1788-1801); copublisher, *Essex Journal* (1773-1774); publisher, *Royal American Magazine, or Universal Repository of Instruction and Amusement* (1774), *Massachusetts Herald* (1783), *Worcester Magazine* (1786-1788); copublisher, *Hampshire Chronicle* (1788); publisher, *Massachusetts Magazine: or, Monthly Museum of Knowledge and Rational Entertainment* (1789-1793); copublisher, *New Hampshire Journal: Or, The Farmer's Weekly Museum* (1793-1796, 1798-1801, 1803-1807, 1808-1809), *Worcester Intelligencer; Or, Brookfield Advertiser* (1794-1795), *Albany Centinel* (1797-1798).

BOOKS: *An Oration: Delivered in Free Masons-Hall, Lancaster, Commonwealth of Massachusetts, on Thursday, the Twenty-fourth of June, 1779 (A. L. 5779) to the Right Worshipful Master, Worshipful Wardens and Members, &c. of Trinity Lodge* (Worcester, Mass., 1781);
A Specimen of Isaiah Thomas's Printing Types. Being as Large and Complete an Assortment as Is to Be Met with in Any One Printing-Office in America. Chiefly Manufactured by That Great Artist, William Caslon, Esq, of London (Worcester, Mass.: Printed by Isaiah Thomas, 1785);
New American Spelling Book; or, The Child's Easy Introduction to Spelling and Reading the English Tongue. To Which Is Added, an Entire New, Plain and Comprehensive English Grammar. Also, The Shorter Catechism, by the Assembly of Divines, The Whole Adapted to the Capacities of Young Children; Rendering the Use of a Primer Unnecessary (Worcester, Mass.: Printed & sold by Isaiah Thomas, 1785);

Isaiah Thomas

Catalogue of Books to Be Sold by Isaiah Thomas, at His Bookstore in Worcester, Massachusetts. Consisting of Many Celebrated Authors in History, Voyages, Travels, Antiquities, Philosophy, Novels, Miscellanies, Divinity, Physick, Surgery, Anatomy, Arts, Sciences, Husbandry, Architecture, Navigation, Mathematics, Law, Periodical Publications, Poetry, Plays, Musick, &c. &c. (Worcester, Mass.: Printed by Isaiah Thomas, 1787);
Literary Proposal. Proposal of Isaiah Thomas and Company, for Publishing by Subscription, a New Periodical Work, to Be Entitled, The Massachusetts Magazine: or, Monthly Museum of Knowledge

and Rational Entertainment (Boston: Printed by Isaiah Thomas, 1788);

The Only Sure Guide to the English Tongue; or, New Pronouncing Spelling Book. Upon the Same Plan as Perry's Royal Standard English Dictionary (Worcester, Mass.: Printed by Isaiah Thomas, 1789);

Catalogue of Books to Be Sold by Isaiah Thomas, at His Bookstore in Worcester, Massachusetts. Consisting of History, Voyages, Travels, Geography, Antiquities, Philosophy, Novels, Miscellanies, Divinity, Physick, Surgery, Anatomy, Arts, Sciences, Husbandry, Architecture, Navigation, Mathematics, Law, Periodical Publications, Poetry, Plays, Musick, &c. &c. (Worcester, Mass.: Printed by Isaiah Thomas & Leonard Worcester, 1792);

Thomas and Andrews's Catalogue of Books, for Sale, Wholesale and Retail, at Their Book and Stationary [sic] Store, Faust's Statue, No. 45 Newbury Street. Boston. Consisting of a Very Extensive Collection of the Latest and Most Approved Authors, in Divinity, Law, Physick, Surgery, Chemistry, History, Biography, Voyages, Travels, Miscellanies, Novels, Poetry, Musick, Arts and Sciences, Philosophy, Navigation, Astronomy, Geography, Architecture, Trade and Commerce, Mathematicks, Bookkeeping, &c. &c. To All Which Large Additions Are Constantly Making (Boston: Thomas & Andrews, 1793);

The Massachusetts Compiler of Theoretical and Practical Elements of Sacred Vocal Music (Boston: Isaiah Thomas & Ebenezer T. Andrews, 1795);

Catalogue of Books to Be Sold by Thomas, Son & Thomas, at Their Bookstore, in Worcester, Massachusetts: Consisting of History, Voyages, Travels, Geography, Antiquities, Philosophy, Novels, Miscellanies, Divinity, Physic, Surgery, Anatomy, Arts, Sciences, Husbandry, Architecture, Navigation, Mathematicks, Law, Periodical Publications, Poetry, Plays, Music, &c. &c. &c. (Worcester, Mass.: Thomas, Son & Thomas, 1796);

Isaiah Thomas's Catalogue of English, Scotch, Irish and American Books for Sale, at the Worcester Bookstore. Consisting of History, Voyages, Travels, Geography, Antiquities, Philosophy, Novels, Miscellanies, Divinity, Physic, Surgery, Anatomy, Arts, Sciences, Husbandry, Architecture, Navigation, Mathematics, Law, Periodical Publications, Poetry, Plays, Music, &c. &c. (Worcester, Mass.: Printed by Isaiah Thomas, 1801);

Almanack, With an Ephemeris, for the Year of Our Lord 1803 (Worcester, Mass.: Printed by Isaiah Thomas, Jun., 1802);

Eccentric Biography; or, Memoirs of Remarkable Female Characters, Ancient and Modern (Worcester, Mass.: Printed by I. Thomas, Jun., 1804);

The History of Printing in America. With a Biography of Printers, and an Account of Newspapers. To Which Is Prefixed a Concise View of the Discovery and Progress of the Art in Other Parts of the World, 2 volumes (Worcester, Mass.: From the press of Isaiah Thomas, Jun. Isaac Sturtevant, printer, 1810);

An Address to the Most Worshipful Grand Lodge of Massachusetts, at the Close of the Constitutional Term of His Presiding as Grand Master (Boston: J. Eliot, Jun., 1811);

Communication from the President of the American Antiquarian Society to the Members, October 24th, 1814 (Worcester, Mass.: Printed by W. Manning, 1815);

A Catalogue of Publications in What Is Now the United States prior to the Revolution of 1775-6 (Albany, N.Y.: J. Munsell, 1874);

The Diary of Isaiah Thomas, 1805-1828, edited by Benjamin Thomas Hill, 2 volumes (Worcester, Mass.: American Antiquarian Society, 1909);

Extracts from the Diaries and Accounts of Isaiah Thomas from the Year 1782 to 1804 and His Diary for 1808, edited by Charles L. Nichols (Worcester, Mass.: American Antiquarian Society, 1916);

Three Autobiographical Fragments (Worcester, Mass.: American Antiquarian Society, 1962).

OTHER: *Laus Deo! The Worcester Collection of Sacred Harmony,* edited by Thomas (Worcester, Mass.: Printed by Isaiah Thomas, 1786);

The Perpetual Laws of the Commonwealth of Massachusetts from the Establishment of Its Constitution to the First Session of the General Court, A.D. *1788,* edited by Thomas (Worcester, Mass.: Printed by Isaiah Thomas, 1788);

The Perpetual Laws of the Commonwealth of Massachusetts, from the Establishment of Its Constitution to the Second Session of the General Court, in 1798, edited by Thomas (Worcester, Mass.: Printed by Isaiah Thomas, 1799);

The Perpetual Laws of the Commonwealth of Massachusetts, from the Establishment of Its Constitution, in the Year 1780, edited by Thomas (Boston:

Printed & sold by I. Thomas & E. T. Andrews, 1807).

One of the most important printer-publishers of his generation and generally known for publication of the newspaper, the *Massachusetts Spy,* and numerous children's books, Isaiah Thomas also is notable for publishing three magazines during his lifetime. His first magazine, the *Royal American Magazine, or Universal Repository of Instruction and Amusement,* was a general content, short-lived publication, which Thomas began in January 1774. His *Worcester Magazine,* published from 1786 until 1788, was a substitute for the *Spy,* whose publication Thomas suspended in protest of a tax on newspapers passed by the Massachusetts legislature. His last magazine venture, the *Massachusetts Magazine: or, Monthly Museum of Knowledge and Rational Entertainment,* published under various owners from 1789 through 1796, was one of the most important eighteenth-century American magazines.

Thomas's heritage also includes *The History of Printing in America,* the first history of its kind, which he published in 1810, and the founding of the American Antiquarian Society in 1812, to which he donated the major portion of his personal collection of early American imprints and which he intended as an organization for the preservation of materials related to the development of the United States.

Isaiah Thomas, son of Moses and Fidelity Grant Thomas, was born in Boston, 30 January 1750. He was the youngest of five children and a member of the fifth generation of his family in America. According to family tradition, his great-great-grandfather, Evan Thomas, arrived in Boston in 1632, settled in the Massachusetts Bay Colony in 1639 or 1640, and was established as a merchant by 1640. Isaiah's grandfather, Peter Thomas, was born in Boston in 1682. He married Elizabeth Burroughs, whose father, a minister, had been hanged at Salem for witchcraft. Their fourth son and Isaiah's father, Moses, was regarded as a shiftless adventurer by his family. He was a soldier in an expedition against Cuba in 1740, a sailor, and, in Hampstead, Long Island, where he met his future wife, Fidelity Grant, successively a schoolteacher, farmer, trader, and storekeeper. Peter Thomas finally disinherited his son when numerous efforts to help him become established in business did not succeed. Not long after Isaiah was born, Moses left Boston, ostensibly looking for work and a means

of providing for his family but probably also out of general restlessness. He died in North Carolina in 1752.

Although Peter Thomas was still alive after his son's death, he did not change his will to provide for Moses's family. Thus, Fidelity Grant Thomas was left with the responsibility of supporting herself and her three youngest children. (Moses and Fidelity had left their two oldest children in Hampstead, Long Island, in the care of Fidelity's relatives when they moved to Boston in the late 1740s). With the help of friends, Fidelity opened a small shop in Boston and sent her children into the country to board.

In 1755 Fidelity brought her youngest son, Isaiah, back to Boston and placed him with Zechariah Fowle, a printer of ballads and small books, who had no children of his own. Several months later, on 4 June 1756, Isaiah was formally apprenticed to Fowle, an arrangement which, according to the indenture papers, was to last fourteen years. In an agreement typical of the time, the Fowles promised to provide Isaiah's board, room, and clothing; teach him reading, writing, arithmetic; and—most relevant in terms of the apprenticeship—instruct him in the art and craft of printing. Thomas's duties were also typical of such apprenticeship agreements: "The said apprentice, his said master and mistress, well and faithfully shall serve; their secrets he shall keep close; their commandments lawful and honest everywhere he shall gladly obey; he shall do no damage to his said master, etc., or suffer it to be done by others without letting or giving seasonable notice thereof to his said master, etc.; he shall not waste the goods of his said master, etc., nor lend them unlawfully to any; at cards, dice, or any other unlawful game or games he shall not play; fornication he shall not commit; matrimony during the said term he shall not contract; taverns, alehouses or places of gaming he shall not haunt or frequent; from the service of his said master, etc., by day or night he shall not absent himself."

Years later Thomas charged that Fowle disregarded the terms of the agreement and that Fowle compelled him to perform a good deal of menial work, in violation of the indenture papers. In *The History of Printing* and in his autobiographical fragments, Thomas called Fowle ignorant and indolent. If true, this may help to explain Fowle's small, ill-equipped (even for his day) print shop. Thomas balanced his negative assessment of Fowle, however, by noting that he was "honest in his dealings, and punctual to his engagements."

By his own recollection, one of Thomas's earliest jobs for Fowle was helping to set the type for a reprint of a bawdy ballad. Such ballads, together with chapbooks, were Fowle's most staple product. The young Thomas was still so small that he had to stand on a bench eighteen inches high in order to reach the type, and, since he could not yet read, Thomas selected type for the fifty-six lines of "The Lawyer's Pedigree" by comparing pieces of type with the printed copy in front of him. It took him two days to finish the work. About a year after Thomas had been formally apprenticed, Fowle undertook one of the most ambitious jobs of his career: printing ten thousand copies of *The New-England Primer*.

The success of the primer caused Fowle to expand his business and print an edition of the Psalter, for which he needed additional help. He hired two journeymen printers, one of whom was Samuel Draper, who became Fowle's partner for five years beginning in 1758. It was Draper, more than Fowle, who taught Thomas the craft of printing, and, according to Thomas, the partnership between the two men was mutually advantageous: "Fowle had been in business seven years; but had made no progress in the advancement of his fortune. Draper was more enterprising, but had no capital to establish himself as a printer. He was a young man of correct habits and handsome abilities. He was industrious, and, for those times, a good workman." Together the partners printed several good-sized works in relatively large editions. Although not all sources agree, these appear to have included twenty thousand copies of *The Youth's Instructor in the English Tongue*, a speller widely used at the time and the one from which Thomas himself learned to spell. Draper left Fowle, probably in 1763, to become a partner with his cousin, Richard Draper.

During the next few years Thomas assumed more responsibility in the shop to counteract Fowle's neglect of the business. In the early 1760s Thomas produced the first volume under his own imprint: *The New Book of Knowledge, Shewing the Effects of the Planets and other Astronomical Constellations; with the Strange Events that Befall Men, Women and Children Born under Them.* Unable to rely on Fowle for professional help, Thomas sought advice of a former printer, Gamaliel Rogers, then in his fifties and operator of a kind of general store opposite the Old South Church. Rogers had been a partner with Daniel Fowle,

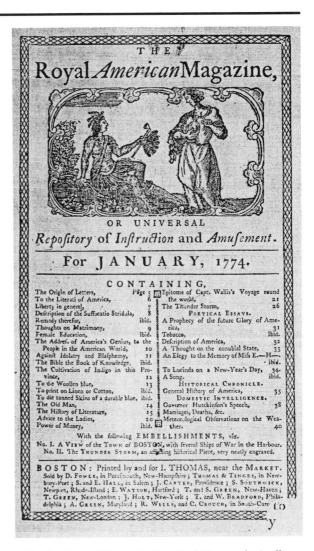

The first issue of Thomas's short-lived illustrated miscellany

Zechariah's brother, from 1742 to 1750. The partners were, according to Thomas, "correct printers. They used good types, paper, and excellent ink of their own manufacture. They were the only printers, I believe, who at that time could make good ink." Rogers and Fowle also had published a magazine, the *American Magazine,* for three years beginning in 1743. Although it is impossible now to know with certainty, it may be that Thomas's later efforts in magazine publishing began from conversations with Rogers. Rogers loaned Thomas some of his books on printing, and Thomas remembered the older man's kindnesses with fondness in *The History of Printing in America:* "He [Rogers] admonished me diligently to attend to my business, that I might become a reputable printer. I held him in high veneration, and often recollected his instructions, which, on many occasions, proved beneficial to me."

During his apprenticeship Thomas also demonstrated early stages of the business savvy that would mark his later career. The market for printed ballads, for example, was a highly competitive one, so Thomas taught himself engraving and matched his own type-metal cuts against other printers' woodcut illustrations. His recognition of the marketing importance of visual content for the ballads was a prelude to his use of engravings in his magazines. For a conscientious printer of that era, eager to learn the state of the art of his craft, however, London was the equivalent of Mecca. Thomas's desire to go there, combined with the increasing difficulty of working for a man whose professional abilities he did not respect, probably led to the "serious fracas" with Fowle which caused Thomas to break his indenture agreement in 1765. In late September of that year he sailed for Halifax, hoping to get inexpensive passage from there to London.

The London trip never materialized. In order to earn money for his passage Thomas sought work and was hired by the only printer in Halifax, Anthony Henry, who also printed the province's only newspaper, a weekly, the *Halifax Gazette*. Neither Henry, whom Thomas later described as indolent and "a very unskilful printer," nor the newspaper's editor, Richard Bulkeley, was very interested in the newspaper, so by default Thomas infused it with his own ideas. He used larger and cleaner type for greater legibility; he chose more interesting news items and included pointed editorial notes for increased readability. His arrival in Halifax nearly coincided with the effective date of the Stamp Act, and he inserted in the *Gazette* much news of the opposition to the act in other colonies as well as woodcuts that satirized the legislation. Local government officials warned Henry against publishing such offensive material and threatened to withdraw his government printing contract if it continued. Thomas attempted to evade the government warning by reprinting a replica (rather than publishing an original work which could be traced to his authorship) of William Bradford's *Pennsylvania Journal* of 30 October 1765, which depicted its front page as a tombstone, complete with skull and crossbones and black rules, the printer's symbol of mourning. The paper also contained a statement saying it was dying of a disorder known as the Stamp Act. Shortly after the *Gazette* reprinted this page, the Halifax stampmaster was hanged in effigy on the town gallows, and a local sheriff almost arrested Thomas for the affair. Not long after this incident, Thomas may even have been responsible for cutting the stamps off about a year's supply of paper which had arrived at the print shop from England. Perhaps to protect his position as government printer, Henry finally fired Thomas, probably in March 1766, but Henry lost his position anyway when local officials decided to import another printer whom they could trust to keep his apprentices under control.

For about two months after departing Halifax Thomas worked for printers in Portsmouth, New Hampshire, about two weeks with Daniel and Robert Fowle—Zechariah's brother and nephew, respectively—who printed the *New Hampshire Gazette*, and then with Ezekiel Russell and Thomas Furber, printers of the *Portsmouth Mercury and Weekly Advertiser*. Thomas later claimed that Zechariah initiated a truce in their quarrel because he recognized the quality of Isaiah's work on the *Mercury*. Thus, after an absence of about seven-to-eight months, Thomas returned to Boston to work for his old master. The reconciliation was short-lived, however, and Thomas set out for London via print shops in the Carolinas. After aborted attempts to establish a newspaper at Wilmington, North Carolina, and travel to England by working on board a ship, Thomas obtained a job with Robert Wells, the best printer in Charleston, South Carolina, and remained there for about two years. On 25 December 1769 Thomas married Mary Dill, who, he learned later, had borne an illegitimate son some years before and "had been prostituted to the purposes of more than one," a factor in their divorce almost eight years later.

In the spring of 1770 Thomas returned to Boston with his wife and entered a short-lived partnership of convenience with his old master, Zechariah Fowle. The partnership gave Thomas access to equipment and supplies for publishing a new triweekly newspaper, the *Massachusetts Spy*, which Thomas would make into a major vehicle for the patriot cause in the revolution against England. Sample copies of the new paper, about half the size of the four other newspapers published in Boston, were distributed free in mid July; its first regular issue was 7 August 1770. The partnership between Thomas and Fowle was dissolved after about three months, and Thomas acquired his former master's shop and equipment by assuming Fowle's debts. Thomas subsequently abandoned the triweekly tabloid form and, for about three months, printed the newspaper as a semiweekly half-sheet. By March 1771 he adopted the weekly, royal-sized, four-page folio format that became the standard for the *Spy*, making it the largest newspaper published in Boston to that time.

Although Thomas initially promised that the pages of the *Spy* would be open to loyalist as well as radical points of view—its motto was "Open to all Parties, but influenced by None"— within a few weeks after beginning regular publication, Thomas moved decisively toward the patriot side. He later said neutrality was simply an impossibility at that time, so he was forced to choose sides even though it was distasteful to him to do so. Clifford Shipton, however, one of Thomas's chief biographers, offers a more pragmatic explanation for Thomas's support of the patriots. Shipton notes that, when Thomas purchased Fowle's business, John Hancock assumed financial responsibility for the press, and the radicals Joseph Greenleaf and Thomas Young became regular contributors to the paper. Shipton suggests that Thomas provided unqualified support of the radicals' political cause in order to preserve his financial alliance and insure the paper's continued existence. In time, the *Spy* became an outspoken advocate of independence, but much of the radical rhetoric which originated in it was more bombastic, illogical, and less well reasoned than arguments crafted by Thomas Paine or by writers for the *Boston Gazette*. Thomas appears to have recognized the conflict of interest represented by his financial alliance and, in March 1772, sought to separate himself from the radicals by exploring the idea of moving his business to Bermuda. Nothing came of this, but some time between then and the outbreak of the Revolution he did sever his financial ties with the radicals, although he remained personally committed to that cause and continued to publish essays in the *Spy* supporting the patriots. Because his papers from this period have been lost, the details of the break remain unclear.

In 1771 Thomas published the first of his annual almanacs, *The Massachusetts Calendar* (entitled *Thomas's New-England Almanack* beginning in 1775), which helped make his name well known throughout the country in later years. Thomas's almanacs included important documents of enduring value, such as the Articles of Peace and the Declaration of Rights, as well as the typical astronomical information and other material published in eighteenth-century almanacs. In 1781

he published three thousand copies of his almanac; by 1797 the annual edition was twenty-nine thousand copies.

Thomas formed in 1773 the first of the many partnerships that became characteristic of his business style and fundamental to his financial success. Invited to establish a newspaper in Newburyport, Massachusetts, Thomas set up a former apprentice, Henry W. Tinges, to do business as his partner and publish the *Essex Journal*. Like some of the later arrangements Thomas made, however, this one failed due to his partner's mismanagement, and, with the newspaper deeply in debt, Thomas sold his interest within a year.

Thomas began publishing the first of his three magazines, the *Royal American Magazine, or Universal Repository of Instruction and Amusement*, in late January 1774. In *The History of Printing in America* Thomas noted that a prospectus for this magazine had appeared "many months" before the magazine itself, but publication had been delayed because of "the disordered state of public affairs, and the difficulties which individuals experienced from them." The prospectus had indeed appeared on the front page of the *Spy* on 24 June 1773 and contained Thomas's complaint that newspapers were not "fit to convey to posterity the labours of the learned." By 1774 no magazine of any kind had been printed in the colonies for almost two years, and no general magazine had appeared in more than four years.

The *Royal American* was an illustrated miscellany of forty octavo pages, designed to appeal to the general public. Thomas mixed original material with selections from English magazines, books, and other printed matter. Like other "miscellanies" of the eighteenth century, Thomas's magazine contained articles on a broad range of subjects: politics, medicine, agriculture, education, literature, and religion. In addition, it included advice to women, fiction, "poetical essays," and current news about such things as marriages, deaths, and the weather. Like Thomas's *Massachusetts Spy*, the politics of the *Royal American* were patriot, almost stridently so in the first six months of the magazine's publication. According to magazine historian Frank Luther Mott, among the early articles most likely to arouse the ire of British officials were "Liberty in General" and "The Address of America's Genius, to the People in the American World," in the January 1774 issue; "The Character of an American Patriot" in the February number; John Hancock's oration commemorating the Boston Massacre in

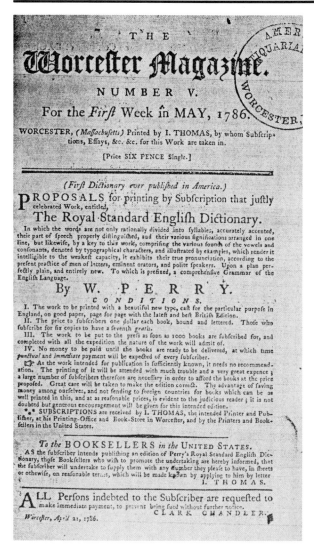

An issue of the magazine Thomas created to circumvent a tax on newspaper advertising levied by the Massachusetts legislature. The weekly replaced Thomas's newspaper the Massachusetts Spy

the March issue; and "Extracts from the Rev. John Lathrop's Artillery Election Sermon" in the June number.

The conclusion of Lathrop's sermon illustrates Mott's point about the inflammatory nature of some of the magazine's content: "Whoever makes an alteration in the established constitution, whether he be a *subject* or a *ruler*, is guilty of treason: Treason of the worst kind: Treason against the state. For such treason many rulers as well as subjects have lost their heads. . . . That we may and ought, to resist, and even make war against those rulers who leap the bounds prescribed them by the constitution, and attempt to oppress and enslave the subjects, is a principle on which alone the great revolutions which have

taken place in our nation can be justified." When Thomas reported the passage of the Boston Port Bill in the May issue, his account also reflected his patriot leanings: "Nothing can equal the distress the inhabitants of Boston and the adjacent towns are thrown into by the shutting up of the port; all the colonies think themselves interested in this alarming event, and all seem determined to aid and assist their brethren in Boston. How matters will end, God only knows, but it is thought that, by the blessing of heaven, if the colonies unite and stand firm, that they will preserve their liberties and cast off the iron yoke of bondage." Not all of the magazine's content was political, however. Serialized fiction and medical articles by Dr. Thomas Young appeared in several issues. Thomas also printed short stories beginning with "The Thunder Storm" in the first issue and "Justice and Generosity" in the February and March issues. An early version of today's personal-advice column, "The Directory of Love," offered solace to the lovelorn. A serialization of Governor Thomas Hutchinson's *History of Massachusetts Bay* was published as a supplement to the magazine.

After publication of the June 1774 issue Thomas suspended his operation of the magazine, explaining to his readers that the halt was necessitated by "the Distresses of the Town of Boston, by the shutting up of our Port, and throwing all Ranks of Men into Confusion." Publication was resumed in September under the direction of Joseph Greenleaf, a contributor to the *Massachusetts Spy* and a justice of the peace until he lost his commission because of his association with Thomas. Although he lacked formal training as a printer, Greenleaf had opened his own print shop in 1773. The actual printing apparently was done by his son, Thomas, who had learned the trade from Isaiah Thomas. Greenleaf published six additional numbers to complete the first volume of the magazine, but, due to the lack of adequate type, ink, and paper (with the port closed and a boycott of British goods in effect, these materials could not be imported as they usually were), these issues are of inferior printing quality to those published under Thomas's direction. Although muted, the patriot propaganda continued under Greenleaf and included political illustrations by Paul Revere. Revere's work and that of Paul Callender were among the twenty-two copperplates that appeared during the life of the magazine and which, Mott notes, are a landmark in American magazine publishing to that point, making it the first American magazine to be adequately illustrated. Revere's "The Able Doctor, or America Swallowing the Bitter Draught" appeared in the June 1774 issue and portrayed America half dressed, with her hands held down by a judge attired for court in wig and robe and her feet held by another man who also indecorously lifts her dress, while Parliament, personified as a gentleman of robust elegance, holds the spout of a teapot in her mouth and forces her to drink. The magazine's cover itself, according to Thomas's description, was a type-metal cut, depicting an Indian who represented America and was seated on the ground with a quiver of arrows at her feet and near her a bow on which her right hand rested. In her left hand she held a long-stemmed peace pipe "which she appeared to offer to the Genius of Knowledge standing before her dispensing instruction."

Greenleaf also published monthly issues of the magazine for January through March of 1775, but no additional issues appeared after the battles of Lexington and Concord in April. Thus, the *Royal American*, which had been the first magazine published in the colonies in almost two years, was also the last periodical established in Boston before the Revolutionary War began. Although little evidence exists of its circulation or readership, Thomas claimed it had "a considerable list of subscribers."

Late in 1774 Thomas was approached with a request to establish a newspaper in Worcester, a small town about forty miles west of Boston. By February 1775 he had prepared proposals for a newspaper to be called the "Worcester Gazette; or American Oracle of Liberty." When the war broke out in April, however, rather than establish a separate newspaper, Thomas moved himself and the *Spy* to Worcester, the town which would become his home for the rest of his life. After sending his equipment ahead to his new home on 16 April and leaving his family across the Charles River from Boston in Watertown, Thomas apparently joined the militia at Lexington early on 19 April, an experience which generated this hyperbolic report in the next issue of the *Spy*, dated 3 May: "AMERICANS! forever bear in mind the BATTLE of LEXINGTON!—where British Troops, unmolested and unprovoked, wantonly, and in a most inhuman manner fired upon and killed a number of our countrymen, then robbed them of their provisions, ransacked, plundered and burnt their houses! nor could the tears of defenceless women, some of whom were

in the pains of childbirth, the cries of helpless babes, nor the prayers of old age, confined to beds of sickness, appease their thirst for blood!– or divert them from their DESIGN of MURDER and ROBBERY!"

According to tradition, Thomas's other prewar activities included printing handbills for the Sons of Liberty at night, after his employees had gone home, and permitting the patriots to meet in his shop, which became known as the "sedition foundry." By the time of his move to Worcester, the circulation of the *Spy* was reported to be approximately thirty-five hundred, a high number for this period. Thomas had augmented the usual circulation by joining with William Goddard of Baltimore, John Holt of New York, and Thaddeus Burr of Fairfield, Connecticut, to establish a system of post riders for intercolonial delivery of the paper. Subscriptions outside Massachusetts appear to have been a fairly high proportion of the total. This transportation network may also have provided a useful communications network for the radicals' committees of correspondence. In addition, the arrangement is another relatively early example of Thomas's business savvy, in this case demonstrating his awareness of the important linkages between publishing and distribution.

Thomas's professional life in the prewar years thrived; his personal life was more mixed. His and Mary Dill's first child was stillborn in 1770. His daughter Mary Ann was born on 27 March 1772; his son Isaiah Jr., on 5 September 1773. Thomas and his wife grew further apart, however, and, when she traveled to Newburyport with a British officer early in 1775, Thomas stopped living with her. He obtained a divorce from her on 27 May 1777.

Sustaining his business during the war years was no easy task for Thomas. Basic materials like type, ink, and paper–often imported from England–were in short supply. Thomas was able to resume publication of the newspaper because he received a paper allotment through the help of Hancock and patriots on the Committee of Safety. He also received paper subsidies from the Provincial Congress in Watertown for which he did some printing for a short time after moving to Worcester. But the scarcity of paper continued to be a problem and caused Thomas to plead frequently for subscribers to donate rags, which he exchanged for paper at the mill. When the paper supply was inadequate, Thomas reduced the size of the newspaper accordingly.

Lack of money was an even more serious problem for Thomas. Due to his sudden departure from Boston he was unable to collect three thousand dollars he was owed for copies of the paper already printed and delivered during the subscription year which was nearing its end. In addition, with British-occupied Boston no longer a possible market, the *Spy*'s circulation plummeted to fifteen hundred, further reducing revenues. One of Thomas's two apprentices from this period, Benjamin Russell, later publisher of the *Massachusetts Centinel,* reported that circumstances were so straitened at times that Thomas and his apprentices had only bread and milk to eat. In March 1776 Thomas had to discontinue the paper for about a month, and, when he increased the price resuming publication in April, his creditors attached the paper. Thomas had been appointed postmaster at Worcester by the Provincial Congress in May 1775 and was formally appointed by Benjamin Franklin as U.S. postmaster for Worcester in November 1775. (This was the only public office Thomas ever held, and he was reappointed in succeeding years until he retired in 1802.) How much–if anything during the war years–Thomas was paid in this position, however, is unclear.

To satisfy his creditors and attain some financial stability, Thomas traveled around the countryside, collecting money owed to him. During that period, from 21 June 1776 to 2 July 1778, he leased the paper to other printers–although he returned to Worcester periodically to check on his operation, almost established another print shop in Salem, bought and sold a farm in New Hampshire, and, as noted above, was divorced from his wife.

Thomas's return to Worcester marked a turning point in his professional and personal fortunes. In 1778 he brought out the first Worcester edition of his almanac. Within a year after his return, on 26 May 1779, he married his twenty-nine-year-old half-cousin, Mary Thomas Fowle, widow of Isaac Fowle (no relation to Thomas's former master). The next year he became a partner in a drugstore, purchased new type for the *Spy,* and was able to obtain more adequate stocks of good paper. The *Spy* experienced a sharp decline in circulation in 1780, from 1,200 to 271, but the drop apparently occurred as a result of Thomas's efforts to remove delinquent subscribers. For about a month in 1783 Thomas also published a shorter edition of the *Spy,* called the *Massachusetts Herald.* By the time the war ended, Thomas's inter-

ests had shifted away from radical causes toward sustaining and enlarging his business. The Worcester *Spy* was much more temperate than its Boston counterpart, and Thomas's feistiness generally surfaced on issues which involved some threat to his growing business empire.

One such threat, from Thomas's perspective, was the tax levied in Massachusetts in 1785 on almanacs and newspapers. Thomas's second magazine venture was fundamentally a ruse to avoid paying this tax. In March 1785 the legislature passed an act requiring that newspapers and almanacs be stamped to indicate payment of taxes of two-thirds of a penny and one penny, respectively. The similarities between this and the British Stamp Act of 1765 made the legislation especially onerous, and the General Court was compelled to repeal it before it could be applied. To circumvent a comparison with the earlier tax and in an attempt to raise revenue sorely needed to pay the war debt, in July 1785 the General Court imposed a measure that, in effect, taxed all advertisements included in newspapers printed in Massachusetts. Years later, in *The History of Printing in America,* writing of himself in the third person, Thomas reported his reaction: "This act was thought by the publisher of the Spy, and by many others, to lay an improper restraint on the press. He therefore discontinued the Spy during the period that this act was in force, which was two years. But he published as a substitute a periodical work . . . in octavo."

Thomas prepared readers of the *Spy* for his new publication by inserting, in the last issue of the newspaper, 30 March 1786, and printing in separate broadside form, a notice of complaint of the near-mortal "wound" "inflicted" by the legislature. Thomas further complained in his notice that the tax violated the state's bill of rights, which guaranteed liberty of the press, and noted that, while the tax itself was not high, it set a precedent for even higher taxes. His concern for his own financial survival was also evident in the notice: "The tax on News-paper Advertisements has a direct tendency not only to restrain, but to destroy those necessary vehicles of publick Information, by taking away their only support; for Advertisements are the only support of News-papers in this country, where News-papers are at so low a price. . . ." Thomas promised the *Spy* would resume when the tax disappeared. Meanwhile, he offered his substitute so that "those who have encouraged the Press in this Country . . . may not be deprived of their weekly entertainment." And, he noted, since magazines were not subject to the tax, his new publication would contain ads. He promised also to send it to all customers of the *Spy*, unless they informed him that they did not want it.

Thomas's twofold complaint against the legislation, namely that it violated freedom of the press and would adversely affect the profitability of his business, was typical of printers' complaints regarding the act. In addition to criticizing the act's restraint of free expression, some printers argued that the tax would make Massachusetts newspapers so expensive that publishers from other states would thus be encouraged to market their newspapers in the commonwealth more cheaply than those originated locally and thus force native Massachusetts newspapers out of business. Massachusetts printers underscored their own complaints by reprinting in their newspapers concerns expressed in publications in other states. The depth of the printers' reaction may be seen in a quotation from an essay which appeared in August 1785: "May Providence avert the dire malady from sister states! May their crimes never entail this dreadful chastisement on them! But should any wretch pollute the air with such a proposal in the Pennsylvania senate, may the plagues of Pharaoh await him! May he wander a vagabond about the earth like the murderous Cain! And may he be accurst, sitting, standing, lying, and in every action of his detested life." Some printers even fought the measure in a not-so-subtle manner by inserting in local news columns items like the following, which appeared in the *Salem Gazette*, 2 August 1785: "Were it not for the tax upon advertising good Books, the Printer hereof would inform the publick, that he has just published 'Extracts from Dr. Priestly's Catechism,' which he sells at five coppers single, and two shillings the dozen." One of the printers' concerns seems to be borne out by evidence regarding the amount of space devoted to advertising in newspapers of the period: one historian has estimated that although all New England states experienced a drop in the total space devoted to advertising between 1784 and 1788, the drop in Massachusetts was most pronounced. In 1784 more than one-third of the space in the commonwealth's newspapers was allotted to advertising. In 1785 the amount was slightly more than twenty percent, and by 1786 this figure was slightly more than twelve percent. While the overall drop was due to many factors, including hard times and economic pressures, it is probable that the tax on advertisements exacerbated the drop in Massachusetts.

Thomas's substitute for the *Spy* was the *Worcester Magazine*, differing from the newspaper chiefly in its smaller paper size and larger type. Like the newspaper and unlike Thomas's other two magazines, which were monthlies, it was published weekly (although the word "weekly," in contrast to Thomas's claim in *The History of Printing*, did not appear in the magazine's title). Its content was almost identical to that of the *Spy*. For example, its first issue, for the first week of April 1786, continued a series which had been appearing in the *Spy* from the *British Annual Register* of 1776 on "the late War in America." The magazine also repeated advertisements that had appeared in the newspaper, including, for example, a personal ad, typical for that era, from one Hezekiah Gibbs announcing he would not be responsible for debts incurred by his wife Meriam who "has left my bed." Both the *Spy* and the *Worcester Magazine* contained letters to the printer-editor, which, like other media content during that era, were either unsigned or signed with pseudonyms. A letter published in the fourth issue of the magazine expressed one reader's pleasure with the new publication and his belief that newspapers and magazines would give readers "something more than the mere news of the day. It is a place for every man to speak his mind in. . . ." This issue also contains a summary of the trial of a Concord couple, William and Eunice Scott, for the murder of William's daughter, Mary. The narrative notes that Eunice abused the child. The verdict–the couple was found guilty of manslaughter–was reported in the story's last paragraph, as would have been typical of such chronological accounts. Personified, the magazine itself claimed a broader heritage than simply a tie with the newspaper: it described itself as an offspring of Thomas's first magazine, the *Royal American*, from 1774.

During the two years of its existence the *Worcester Magazine* contained substantial material about the significant political activities of the time, including Shays's Rebellion (Thomas supported the government, not the farmers), conditions under the Articles of Confederation, troubles in Rhode Island, the constitutional convention and the campaign for the adoption of the Constitution, as well as the proceedings of Congress and the Massachusetts General Court. In addition, agricultural articles, medical notes, the magazine's major literary content (an essay series called "The Worcester Speculator"), and a poetry department, which was included occasionally, to add to the "miscellany" quality which Thomas had claimed for his publication. The last issue of the *Worcester Magazine*, for the fourth week of March 1788, contained a small notice on page one above the title saying the legislature had restored constitutional liberty of the press, and the *Spy* would soon publish again.

Thomas delivered on the promise of this notice, for the *Spy* resumed publication one week later, on 3 April 1788. With nice irony, its first story continued the history of the war in America which had been appearing in the *Worcester Magazine* and which had begun in the newspaper before its publication had been suspended two years earlier. Thomas celebrated the renewed publication with a paean to freedom of the press: "Heaven grant that the FREEDOM of the PRESS, on which depends the FREEDOM of the PEOPLE, may, in the United States, be ever guarded with a watchful eye, and defended from shackles, of every form and shape, until the trump of the celestial Messenger shall announce the final dissolution of all things."

For most of 1788 Thomas was copublisher, with Ezra Weld, of a weekly newspaper, the *Hampshire Chronicle*, printed at Springfield, Massachusetts. In September of that year he formed his first major postwar partnership, I. Thomas & Co., with a combination printing office and bookstore in Boston. Within a year, one of the three partners dropped out, and Thomas and the remaining partner, Ebenezer T. Andrews (who was also one of Thomas's former apprentices), reorganized the firm solely in their names. This was the most successful and one of the longest-lived (it lasted until 1820) of Thomas's many partnerships and, at its peak, was the largest printing company in the United States. Although at first the Worcester parent company's seven presses exceeded the capacity of the five presses in Boston, by the mid 1790s the relative strength of the two offices seems to have been reversed. Due to the confusion of the business relations between the two offices (for example, type and composing sticks were sent from one shop to the other with no accounting of the exchange), it is difficult to sort out the situation completely.

Thomas and Andrews's publications included spellers and hymnbooks as well as the most ambitious of Thomas's magazine undertakings, the *Massachusetts Magazine: or, Monthly Museum of Knowledge and Rational Entertainment*,

which lasted for eight years beginning in January 1789 (although Thomas and his partner remained publishers for only four years). Thomas printed eight hundred copies of each sixty-four-page issue. He said the magazine's purpose was to "gratify and excite the natural inquisitiveness of the human mind . . . rouse and strengthen the latent powers of the soul . . . give birth to literary emulation and effort . . . enforce and reward studious application . . . improve the taste, the language and the manners of the age . . . increase an acquaintance with natural and civil history, with arts, manufactures and commerce, with law, physick and divinity. . . ." The periodical lived up to Thomas's promise to make it informative and entertaining. It was, as the above quotation suggests, and like the *Royal American*, a miscellany, including everything from announcements of marriages to philosophical treatises. Essayists included John Dennie, whose pseudonym was "Socialis"; William Bigelow, writing as "Charles Chatterbox"; and Judith Murray, wife of the Universalist minister John Murray, writing as "Gleaner." Thomas published fiction as well known as nonfiction, and (ironically, since Boston was not permitted a theater) the first volume included a full-length play, Dunlap's *The Father*, published over two issues, October and November 1789. For some years a page or two of music, much of it original American compositions, was printed with each issue. Some of these were signed by Hans Gram, organist at the Brattle Street church. Most of the selections were sentimental songs, although marches, anthems, and other pieces also were included. Just as he had done with the *Royal American*, Thomas usually issued a copper engraving with each number of the *Massachusetts Magazine*. Most of these were done by Samuel Hill, who was also one of the publishers in 1794.

In the same month that he began the *Massachusetts Magazine*, Thomas also printed in his Boston shop a novel, *The Power of Sympathy*, by William Hill Brown. This book is now generally regarded as the first American novel because it was written in America by an American-born author, was set in America and was concerned with issues endemic to this country and not simply transferred from England, and, finally, because it was first published in America. Brown's name did not appear on the title page, and during the nineteenth century some confusion emerged over the book's authorship. Because a portion of it so closely paralleled a well-known scandal of the

1780s and since this part of the book was emphasized in the copperplate frontispiece that appeared with the original edition, some literary critics assumed it was written by a woman intimately involved in the events which the novel recounted.

Thomas's printing of the novel is just one of the many examples of how he tried to promote an emerging American culture as he became more financially successful and secure. Thomas's shrewdness as a publisher is also reflected in the fact that, probably as part of his effort to generate interest in the novel, he published eleven excerpts from it, purportedly written by "Calista," in the first issue of the *Massachusetts Magazine*. Some of the titles under which the excerpts were published, for example, "Seduction" and "Suicide," seem to have been marketing ploys designed to emphasize the novel's sensational appeal and engender greater interest among readers. If so, they did not succeed, at least in any evidence visible to twentieth-century students of the period. The novel's publication seems to have elicited very little public discussion, and it is difficult to determine its sales. In the nineteenth century Joseph Buckingham was among those who publicized the idea that the two families involved in the real-life drama reflected in the novel bought most of the copies of the book to keep it out of circulation. This legend and others concerning the supposed suppression of the novel were basically discredited by the twentieth-century William Hill Brown scholar, Milton Ellis, whose examination of inventories showed that the novel was still available from both the publishers, Thomas and Andrews, and other Boston booksellers in the 1790s and that Thomas's Worcester shop still had the title as late as 1801.

News in the *Massachusetts Magazine* appeared under the heading, "The Gazette." Usually placed near the end of each issue, this section included proceedings of the Massachusetts legislature and of Congress and reports of fires, marriages, deaths, accidents, and a record of the weather. In the magazine's last issue this section consisted solely of Washington's farewell address. By the end of the periodical's third year it was apparently becoming harder to find original material to fill its pages, as suggested in the preface published with the December 1791 issue. As the editors wrote, "Three years of experience, the best school of man, has painfully taught them, [the editors] that expectations of *Originality*, were in some measure, delusively founded. A copious selection, both Foreign and Domestick, has therefore supplied those vacant pages, that long waited for the effusions of American Genius—and languished, but in vain—for the genial embrace of Columbian Science."

Andrews was not so skilled a craftsman as Thomas, and publication costs at the Boston office were thus higher than at Worcester. This may help to explain why the magazine accumulated annual deficits of up to one hundred pounds. At the end of 1793 Thomas and his partner sold the magazine to the printers Ezra Weld and William Greenough and the engraver Hill. In the preface to the fifth volume, issued with the December 1793 number, Thomas and Andrews apologized for the neglect in the periodical's printing, paper, and editing and explained that the magazine's failure to pay for itself required them to sell it. Regular issues of the magazine appeared throughout 1794, but apparently its financial stability did not improve and publication was suspended during the first three months of 1795. It reappeared from April through September 1795 under Greenough's sole editorship and then was published under three successive owners before it died after the December 1796 number was issued. Notwithstanding the magazine's lack of financial success, Mott rated it third in interest among eighteenth-century magazines, just below Mathew Carey's the *American Museum* and the *Columbian*.

No complete list of Thomas's partnerships is currently available, but a study of his business organizations and practices might well offer some important insights about the connections between publishers, printers, and booksellers as well as about distribution of printed materials in the late eighteenth century. According to the available evidence, Thomas formed at least twenty partnerships, including the brief one with Tinges at Newburyport in 1773-1774. Seven of the twenty included Andrews, although Thomas's bitterness over the dissolution of their Boston partnership in 1820 (Thomas felt he should have received seventy thousand dollars; the settlement was for twenty-two thousand dollars) suggests their relationship was not without acrimony. This is, of course, difficult to assess, especially since most of Thomas's partnerships appear to have been terminated with mutual dissatisfaction. As postmaster, Thomas had direct access to an important distribution system, and he may have franked the costs of some of his business correspondence. In addition, however, due to the relative infrequency of mail service and the high cost of parcel post, he maintained his own messenger service between the partnerships and employed his older brother, Joshua, as one of his post riders.

Thomas published more titles and numbers of copies than any other publisher of the colonial and early national period. With his partners he published more than nine hundred books; in contrast, Benjamin Franklin and his partners published approximately eight hundred. The staples of his business were his reprints of standard British and European medical and legal texts and schoolbooks, especially William Perry's speller, *The Only Sure Guide to the English Tongue*. Between 1785 and 1802 Thomas published fourteen editions of Perry's book for a total of about three hundred thousand copies. In addition, he published four editions of Perry's *Royal Standard English Dictionary* for a total of about fifty-four thousand copies. Thomas and Andrews had an exclusive, fourteen-year contract to print Noah Webster's speller, grammar, and selections in Massachusetts, New Hampshire, and Rhode Island. Before the contract expired in 1804 the firm had published thirty editions of the speller for a total of about three hundred thousand copies, six editions of the grammar, and fourteen editions of the selections. Another profitable schoolbook was Nicholas Pike's *New and Complete System of Arithmetic*, first printed by Thomas in Worcester in 1795 and subsequently printed in revised versions. Among the medical texts which Thomas published were William Smellie's *Set of Anatomical Tables* and Charles White's *Treatise on the Management of Pregnant and Lying in Women*, two of the most important books in their fields. Thomas brought out editions of these in 1793, thus enhancing his reputation as the most important publisher of standard medical works in New England.

Thomas published several editions of the Bible, beginning in 1786 and 1788, with two editions designed for children. He brought out his first major Bible in December 1791. His duodecimo version first appeared in 1797 and represents an aspect of Thomas's pioneering efforts in the mass production of books. He kept it set in type—in itself a sign of his financial success, because most printers could not afford to keep type idle for long periods—and thus was able to supply a relatively low-cost Bible to a broad audience. Most of the Bibles he published sold well. Thomas also specialized in music publishing. His first major work in this category was *Laus Deo!*, a

collection of hymns which he published in 1786 and which he revised for subsequent editions. He also brought out rival hymnals, mostly through the Boston shop with Andrews.

Thomas did not restrict his printing and publishing solely to established works for which he might anticipate a ready market, however. As noted above, one of the publishing risks he took was with the first American novel in 1789. Subsequently, he published from the Worcester shop an abridged version of Richardson's *Pamela* (1794), Goldsmith's *The Vicar of Wakefield* (1795), and Rousseau's *Letters of an Italian Nun* (1796). From the Boston partnership with Andrews he published Jeremy Belknap's *American Biography* (1794), one of the earliest American biographical dictionaries; Belknap's *The Foresters* (1792); and collections of poems by Sarah Apthorp Morton (one of the women intimately involved in the real-life scandal depicted in *The Power of Sympathy*) and by Mercy Warren, James Otis's sister. Even in schoolbooks he was somewhat innovative in publishing Caleb Alexander's Latin and Greek grammars, which were considered revolutionary at the time.

In 1779 Thomas entered the realm of children's books when he began selling imported copies of John Newbery chapbooks and the best of the British juveniles, including such standbys as *The History of Little Goody Two-Shoes, Robinson Crusoe*, and novels based on Shakespeare's plays. In addition, Thomas was probably the most important printer of children's books in his generation, although he had so little regard for this aspect of his work that he did not deposit any examples of this genre in the library of the American Antiquarian Society when he donated other materials in 1813—an irony considering the importance which has been attached to these editions by later historians and librarians. Beginning in 1785 he printed numerous editions of children's books, including the first American edition of *Mother Goose's Melody* in 1786. In 1787, the peak of this phase of Thomas's business, he published 19 titles in the children's category. In all, he listed 66 titles in 119 editions of children's books.

Although he took many risks, Thomas seems to have experienced relatively few major business failures in the post-Revolutionary era. A speller which he created himself and published in the late 1780s did not sell well, so he discontinued it. Sometimes he clashed with American writers over copyright interpretations. Some of his partnerships failed, and, in the early 1790s, he made several abortive efforts to expand his operations into additional towns, including a seven-month venture in 1794-1795 as copublisher with Elisha Waldo of a weekly newspaper, the *Worcester Intelligencer; Or, Brookfield Advertiser*.

In the overall pattern, however, it is Thomas's successes that dominate. His willingness to take risks and his savvy business sense caused him to expand beyond the immediate realm of printing and publishing whenever such opportunities might work to his advantage. In 1793, for example, he built his own paper mill at Quinsigamond, near Worcester, which produced about fourteen hundred pounds of paper each week until Thomas sold it in 1798. The printing operations, however, were always the most important part of his business. At the height of his success in the mid 1790s he employed 150 people at the Worcester shop. In 1796 the inventory of the Worcester printing plant and bookstore was valued at $39,679.02. He developed an avenue for reducing the number of slow-selling items while effectively increasing his own inventory inexpensively by exchanging stock with booksellers in other states, another aspect of distribution during this period which deserves further study. His other partnerships in the 1790s included one with David Carlisle, one of his former apprentices. Thomas sent Carlisle home to Walpole, New Hampshire, in 1793 and set him up as copublisher of the *New Hampshire Journal: Or, The Farmer's Weekly Museum*, which became a well-known newspaper chiefly because of the contributions of Joseph Dennie and Royall Tyler. Thomas remained involved sporadically as copublisher until he sold out his interest in 1809.

After the turn of the century Thomas retired from active involvement in the printing business. He yielded management of the Worcester print shop and *Spy* to his son Isaiah in 1802, although he retained ownership at least of the print shop and, on occasion, had to rescue the business from his son's mismanagement. Thomas even had to edit the *Spy* himself for six weeks in 1811. The last two books to bear his imprint were the 1802 editions of his 1793 Octavo Bible and *The New-England Primer*, one of the first books he had worked on as an apprentice to Zechariah Fowle. As his diaries and other evidence indicate, however, Thomas continued to be involved in bookselling, and he set up several partnerships between 1807 and 1813. During these years he also helped establish and for eleven years was a director of the first bank in Worcester, which for

An issue of Thomas's most ambitious magazine, published in an effort, according to the prospectus, to "gratify and excite the natural inquisitiveness of the human mind."

some time was the only banking institution between Boston and Pittsfield. He was a partner in a Worcester tannery (1809-1815), owned a paper mill in New Hampshire (1813-1818), helped organize the construction of the Boston-Worcester turnpike of which he also became a director, and was an active member of the Boston Athenaeum, which he helped found. Although during his retirement he had to deal with the financial troubles of some of the partnerships, he was at the time he retired one of the wealthiest Americans, with holdings valued at more than $150,000. In later years he donated separate lots of land to the city of Worcester for a charity house and for a courthouse.

Thomas's increased political conservatism after the Revolutionary War may help to explain why he was replaced as postmaster at Worcester in 1802 by one of President Thomas Jefferson's political appointees. In the War of 1812 he supported the punishment of mobs, a view directly contrary to his opinion in the Revolutionary War. A combination of his Federalism and his humanitarianism also was evident in the War of 1812: when British prisoners of war were held at Worcester, he intervened on their behalf in order to be sure they were fed, and he visited them in jail.

For many years Thomas was a prominent member of the Order of Masons. He appears to have joined the Massachusetts Lodge in Boston before fleeing the city in April 1775. During his early years in Worcester he was active in the Lancaster Lodge near his hometown until, with his help, the first lodge was established in Worcester in 1793. Thomas was made the first grand master of the Morning Star Lodge of Worcester in February 1793 and was selected for the same position in at least three subsequent years. For many years he traveled throughout New England on Masonic business, including the dedication of new lodges. New lodges were named for him beginning in 1796, and during the first decade of the nineteenth century he served as grand master of the Massachusetts Lodge for four years. Thomas also was an active member of a number of other organizations, including the fire societies of Boston and Worcester, the Worcester Associate Circulating Library, the Massachusetts Humane Society, and the Auxiliary Bible Society of Worcester County.

Substantial evidence indicates Thomas's love for the craft of printing and his concern for those who practiced it. Even his youthful escape from Fowle was tied to his desire to go to London and learn the state of the art in the field. In 1803 he organized the Society of Printers and Booksellers in Boston, later renamed the Faustus Association. This organization served as an early labor union and trade association as well as a benevolent society and social club. In 1816 Thomas was elected to this group's Philadelphia counterpart, the Typographical Society. He also made bequests in Boston and Worcester to fund the training of printers and the education of the children of poor printers, booksellers, and bookbinders.

By the turn of the century Thomas had become increasingly concerned about the potential loss of America's early history. After he retired he began to focus his attention on ways of preserving that heritage for posterity. His two most impor-

tant efforts in this regard are his collection of information about American printing, which he published in two volumes in 1810 as *The History of Printing in America,* and the formation of the American Antiquarian Society in 1812. Thomas had begun to collect copies of original newspapers in the early 1790s, and he used these, as well as his contacts with printers, as basic sources for the history of printing which he spent two years writing. He did not see his book as a definitive history but rather as a collection of notes which could be revised and expanded by future historians of printing. For decades, however, his book remained the sole source of American printing history, and, even after another major history of newspapers appeared in the 1870s, his book–though flawed–remained a major source of information about printing and newspapers in the colonial and early national periods. In 1874 the American Antiquarian Society published a second edition of his book with a biographical introduction by his grandson, Benjamin Franklin Thomas.

A modest, one-sentence entry in Thomas's diary for 13 January 1812 signaled the beginning of another of Thomas's major contributions to American culture: "Proposed to the Rev. Dr. [Aaron] Bancroft and Dr. Oliver Fiske the establishment of a Society by the name of the Antiquarian Society." Nine months later to the day he sent a petition to the General Court asking for incorporation of the American Antiquarian Society. The petition, signed by six men, including Thomas and Bancroft, stated that the society's purposes would be "to contribute to the advancement of the Arts and Sciences, . . . to aid . . . in collecting, and preserving such materials, as may be useful in making their progress, not only in the United States, but in other parts of the Globe; and . . . to assist the researches of the future historians of our Country. . . ." As Thomas noted in the petition, these objectives went beyond the basic purpose of other learned societies of his time, which generally existed to provide forums for the presentation of scholarly papers. Before the month ended, the General Court had approved the petition, and the society was incorporated. Not long after, Congress made the society a depository for all government documents, in keeping with the society's purpose to provide "a fixed, and permanent place of deposit" for all portable "relics of American antiquity."

Thomas was elected president of the American Antiquarian Society at its first meeting, in Boston, on 19 November 1812. He held that office until his death nineteen years later. In 1813, as promised in the original petition, he donated his personal library of about three thousand volumes to provide the society with a solid base of research materials. Thomas estimated his collection's worth to be about five thousand dollars, and it was housed in his home for the next eight years. He also bought the remains of the Mather Library and also gave it to the society. In addition, he donated the land and paid most of the costs for the society's first building in Worcester, which was completed in 1820, and he encouraged the society to begin its publications with a volume on American archaeology, which it published in the same year.

Thomas's contributions were recognized in several ways beyond those already noted. In 1811 he was elected to membership in the Massachusetts Historical Society, in 1813 to the New York Historical Society, and in 1816 to the American Philosophical Society of Philadelphia. Dartmouth College awarded him an honorary M.A. in 1814 and Allegheny College, Pennsylvania, presented him with an honorary LL.D. in 1818. In 1829 he was elected an honorary member of the Academy of Arts and Sciences.

Thomas's second wife–"My truly dear and beloved consort," as he noted in his diary–died on 16 November 1818. His son died at the age of forty-five on 25 June 1819 as a result of injuries received in a fall. Thomas's third marriage was to his second wife's sixty-two-year-old cousin and housekeeper, Rebecca Armstrong, on 10 August 1819. After being married and divorced three times, Thomas's daughter Mary Ann returned with her son and three daughters to live with her father in Worcester. Of this period Thomas wrote in his diary, "The year, that is from November 1818 to November 1819, has been attended with as many important events to me, as any one year of my life–during this period I have buried my best friend and wife, with whom I had lived 40 years–I have also buried my only son; and I have married another wife. I have with the proprietorship of the Massachusetts Spy, which I established in 1770, sold my printing materials.–Had a visit from my only daughter whom I had not seen for 10 years–My late son's family removed to Worcester.–Many other events of consequence, but the above are the most important." Thomas's third wife did not share his interests, and, after having lived apart for about six months, the couple separated for good in May 1822. Rebecca

died in October 1828. During the last decade of his life Thomas disposed of most of his businesses and real estate holdings and engaged in fewer activities (he was blind in one eye, probably by 1820), although his home continued to be a gathering place for family and friends. He died at Worcester on 4 April 1831.

Although in the specific field of magazine publishing Mathew Carey is generally regarded as superior to Thomas, in the broader aspects of printing and publishing as well as in the historical contributions of *The History of Printing in America* and the American Antiquarian Society, Thomas is without equal in his generation.

Biographies:
Benjamin Franklin Thomas, "Memoir of Isaiah Thomas," in *Transactions and Collections of the American Antiquarian Society*, 5 (Albany: Joel Munsell, 1874): xvii-lxxxvii;

Charles Nichols, *Isaiah Thomas: Printer, Writer and Collector* (Boston: Club of Odd Volumes, 1912; New York: Burt Franklin, 1971);

Annie Russell Marble, *From 'Prentice to Patron: The Life Story of Isaiah Thomas* (New York: Appleton-Century, 1935);

Clifford K. Shipton, *Isaiah Thomas: Printer, Patriot and Philanthropist* (Rochester, N.Y.: Leo Hart, 1948).

References:
Frank Roe Batchelder, "Isaiah Thomas, the Patriot Printer," *New England Magazine*, new series, 25 (November 1901): 284-305;

Joseph T. Buckingham, *Specimens of Newspaper Literature: With Personal Memoirs, Anecdotes, and Reminiscences*, 2 volumes (Boston: Little & Brown, 1850);

Cathy Davidson, *Revolution and the Word: The Rise of the Novel in America* (New York: Oxford University Press, 1986);

Worthington C. Ford, "The Isaiah Thomas Collection of Ballads," *Proceedings of the American Antiquarian Society*, 33 (April 1923): 34-112;

James Gilreath, "American Book Distribution," *Needs and Opportunities in the History of the Book: America, 1639-1876*, edited by David Hall and John Hench (Worcester, Mass.: American Antiquarian Society, 1987), pp. 103-185;

Carol Sue Humphrey, " 'That Bulwark of Our Liberties': Massachusetts Printers and the Issue of a Free Press, 1783-1788," *Journalism History*, 14 (Spring 1987): 34-38;

Luther Livingston, "An American Publisher of a Hundred Years Ago," *Bookman,* 11 (August 1900): 530-534;

Bruce M. Metzger, "Three Learned Printers and Their Unsung Contributions to Biblical Scholarship," *Journal of Religion,* 32 (October 1952): 254-262;

Frank Luther Mott, *A History of American Magazines,* 5 volumes (Cambridge, Mass.: Harvard University Press, 1938-1968), I: 83-86; 92-93; 108-111;

Charles Nichols, "The Portraits of Isaiah Thomas with Some Notes Upon His Descendants," *Proceedings of the American Antiquarian Society,* new series, 30 (October 1920): 251-277;

John R. Osterholm, "The Literary Career of Isaiah Thomas, 1749-1831," Ph.D. dissertation, University of Massachusetts, 1978;

Lyon N. Richardson, *A History of Early American Magazines, 1741-1789* (New York: 1931);

Clifford K. Shipton, "America's First Research Library," *Library Journal,* 74 (15 January 1949): 89-90;

Rollo Silver, *The American Printer, 1787-1825* (Charlottesville: University Press of Virginia, 1967);

Madeleine Stern, "Saint-Pierre in America: Joseph Nancrede and Isaiah Thomas," *Bibliographical Society of America,* 68 (July 1974): 312-325;

Richard Walser, "Boston's Reception of The First American Novel," *Early American Literature,* 17 (Spring 1982): 65-74;

John T. Winterich, "Early American Books and Printing," *Publisher's Weekly,* 124 (15 July 1933): 174-176;

Lawrence C. Wroth, *The Colonial Printer* (Portland, Maine: 1938);

Hollis R. Yarrington, "Isaiah Thomas, Printer," Ph.D. dissertation, University of Maryland, 1970.

Papers:

Isaiah Thomas's diaries, correspondence, business papers, imprints, newspapers, and other materials are collected in the Isaiah Thomas Papers, twenty-eight volumes and seven boxes, American Antiquarian Society, Worcester, Massachusetts.

John Reuben Thompson

(23 October 1823-30 April 1873)

George Green Shackelford
Virginia Polytechnic Institute and State University

MAJOR POSITIONS HELD: Editor, *Southern Literary Messenger* (1847-1860); editor, *Southern Field and Fireside* (1860); editor, *Southern Illustrated News* (1863); editor, *Record* (1863); contributor, *Index* (1864-1865); literary editor, *New York Evening Post* (1867-1873).

BOOKS: *Poems,* edited by John S. Patton (New York: Scribners, 1920);
The Genius and Character of Edgar Allan Poe, edited by J. H. Whitty and J. H. Rindfleisch (Privately printed, 1929).

John Reuben Thompson, Jr., was born in Richmond, Virginia, on 23 October 1823, where his Vermonter father moved after marrying Sarah Dyckman of New York. Prospering as the owner of a hat, cap, and fur store, Thompson's father in 1836 sent the boy to East Haven, Connecticut, for schooling before enrolling him in the Richmond Academy for three years. Between 1840 and 1842 Thompson was an indifferent student at the University of Virginia, but he graduated with a bachelor of arts in chemistry. After serving two years in Richmond as a law clerk for James A. Seddon, he returned to take his bachelor of laws degree in 1845. He returned to Richmond and practiced law until 1850.

Thompson was a lifelong bachelor with many women friends but without any known romances. He dressed so fashionably that some thought him a dandy, albeit sometimes a rather Bohemian one in a cape, plaid trousers, and a Tyrolean hat. Some contemporaries thought he affected languor. Besides being a witty raconteur, he excelled at playing whist with the ladies in their parlors and at billiards with the gentlemen. His friend John Esten Cooke said that, after William Makepeace Thackeray, Thompson was "the most delightful reader I ever listened to."

At the age of twenty-four Thompson became the owner-editor of the *Southern Literary Messenger* when his father bought it for twenty-five hundred dollars and gave it to him. As its fourth

John Reuben Thompson (courtesy of the John Reuben Thompson Collection, University of Virginia Library)

editor he brought to the journal during the next thirteen years its greatest success. As Rayburn S. Moore has said, the *Southern Literary Messenger* lived off Poe's fame and survived on Thompson's hard work. At the outset Thompson set three editorial goals: to be national in content and appeal, to champion southern literature and new authors, and to be nonpolitical. His chief obstacle was the journal's constantly shaky financial condition. While northern literary journals paid their contributors between three and five dollars a page, Thompson could pay only three. Seeking to cultivate contributions, endorsements, subscriptions, and books for review, Thompson traveled to New York and Charleston. He engaged some foreign correspondents. Among northern writers he enlisted Thomas Bailey Aldrich, Henry Wadsworth Longfellow, "Ik Marvel" (Donald G. Mitchell), Frances S. Osgood, Lydia H. Sigourney, Frank P. Stockton, and Richard H. Stoddard (who became his literary executor). Southern contributors included George W. Bagby, Joseph G. Baldwin, John Esten, Philip Pendleton Cooke, Paul H. Hayne, George F. Holmes, James Barron Hope, James L. Legaré, Matthew F. Maury, Edgar Allan Poe, Margaret Junkin Preston, William Gilmore Simms, and Henry Timrod.

In his literary criticism Thompson was in some respects a follower of the genteel tradition of his New York friends, but he differed from them in admiring Poe, Simms, Timrod, and Mark Twain. He so strongly disliked Walt Whitman's *Leaves of Grass* that he declined to review its first two editions, finally declaring in the 9 June 1861 number of the *Southern Field and Fireside* that the book was either a "hoax" or the work of a "lunatic." He praised Nathaniel Hawthorne and Longfellow, even while parodying *Evangeline.* He delighted in Alfred Tennyson's *Idylls of the King,* but his sense of moral and poetic propriety was offended by "Maude." That mere morality was not, however, enough for him was shown in his dislike of Edward Bulwer-Lytton's *Alfred.* In 1857 he helped arrange Thackeray's lectures in Richmond, and he praised *Vanity Fair.* Only with Ralph Waldo Emerson and the Transcendentalists was Thompson "intolerant and impatient."

Thompson recognized that as a poet he was inferior to his American contemporaries Poe, Timrod, and William Cullen Bryant. Almost all his poetry was topical, yet, before and during the Civil War years he was a kind of poet laureate of Virginia. Among his more serious efforts before the war were commemorative odes celebrating the 250th anniversary of the Settlement of Jamestown and the dedication of Thomas Crawford's equestrian statue of George Washington at Richmond. During the 1860s he published funeral odes commemorating William Latiné, John Ashby, J. E. B. Stuart, and George W. Randolph. Historian Allan Nevins's statement that "every Southern schoolboy" knew Thompson's poems on Ashby, Latiné, and Robert E. Lee was a great exaggeration in 1922 and is laughable today. If Thompson is remembered for his poetry itself,

Thompson in 1847, when he assumed the editorship of the Southern Literary Messenger. *He held the position until May 1860.*

rather than his patriotic subjects, it is for light verse, such as "The Window-Panes of Brandon" and "Music In The Camp."

From a literary point of view Thompson was important for his association with the *Southern Literary Messenger* and with Poe. He made the *Messenger* the acknowledged literary representative of the South. His association with Poe at Richmond during August and September of 1848 and July through September of 1849 gave him a vantage point from which to survey that great poet. During the first of these visits he offered Poe office space, a bedroom, and publication. During the second Poe delivered a public address on "The Poetic Principle," borrowed money from Thompson, and gave him the poem "Annabel Lee," which did not, however, achieve its first publication in the *Southern Literary Messenger* as planned.

When Poe died in 1849 Thompson gave a halfhearted, enigmatic approval of the derogation of Poe as a drunkard, expressed by Poe's literary executor, Rufus W. Griswold, by James

Russell Lowell, and in the *Southern Literary Messenger* by John M. Daniel. In the 1850s Thompson came to realize Poe's greatness, however, which he proclaimed in his 1859 lecture "The Genius and Character of Edgar Allan Poe." Because this lecture was not published until 1929, Thompson's considered opinion was misrepresented as condemnatory of Poe as late as 1941, when Arthur H. Quinn dismissed Thompson as a hostile and "unreliable witness." In fact, however, Thompson in his 1859 lecture urged posterity to look upon the flaws of Poe's character with "a larger and more liberal charity than is ordinarily extended to the infirmities of genius" in a man whom "a wayward impulse made . . . neglectful of the inexorable duties of life." Thompson did not respect Poe's "tomahawk" style of criticism, but he praised his poetry and declared that "as a writer of stories Poe was undeniably the most original and marvellous narrator." In Thompson's poem entitled *Virginia,* which he declaimed before the Alpha Chapter of Phi Beta Kappa at the College of William and Mary on 3 July 1856, he wrote:

> Unhappy POE, what destiny averse
> Still hung about thee both to bless and curse!
> The Fairies' gifts, who on thy birth attended,
> Seemed all with bitter maledictions blended;
> The golden crown that on thy brow was seen
> Like that Medea sent to Jason's queen,
> In cruel splendor shone but to consume
> And decked its victim proudly for the tomb.

Thompson was not a man of strong political views. In 1848 he was enough of a Whig to give his vote to Zachary Taylor for president. Standing aloof from the Whigs' subsequent factional divisions, Thompson was thereafter not interested in political organizations or candidates, although he continued to favor such Whiggish goals as improved educational facilities and internal improvements. He opposed both slavery and abolition. Even when in the late 1850s he encouraged southerners to write about slavery so that people outside the South could learn that it was benign, not evil, he was a strong advocate of the Union. He remained so until after Virginia had seceded. In his last editorial for the *Southern Literary Messenger* he declared, "We have endeavored to cultivate kindly feelings between the two divisions of the country."

As editor he used book reviews as a means of bringing to his subscribers extended discussion of pre-Marxian socialist writings, such as those by

Thompson in later life

George F. Holmes, professor at the University of Virginia, on Du Var Robert's *Histoire de la classe ouvrière* (1850) and George Fitzhugh's *Sociology for the South, or the Failure of Free Society* (1854) and *Cannibals All! or Slaves Without Masters* (1857). Because Thompson also led a small discussion group, one of whose members was the future Confederate Secretary of War George Wythe Randolph, it is possible to attribute to his intellectual leadership an influence in the adoption of advanced social and economic ideas by the Southern Republic of the 1860s. In the 1850s both Thompson's and Holmes's reviews of Harriet Beecher Stowe's *Uncle Tom's Cabin* were unfavorable but not so argumentative as to be unusual among Southern reviewers. They criticized her lack of factual information to sustain her literary invention. Yet, Thompson's epigram in the *Southern Literary Messenger* for January 1853 achieved dubious fame:

> When Latin I studied, my Ainsworth in hand,
> I answered my teacher that *sto* meant to stand.
> But if asked, I should now give another reply,
> For Stowe means, beyond any cavil, to *lie.*

In 1853 Thompson sold the *Southern Literary Messenger* to its printers-publishers but remained as editor for a small salary until 1860 when he accepted the editorship of the new Augusta, Georgia, *Southern Field and Fireside* at the enormous salary of two thousand dollars a year. The burning of Richmond's business district in 1865 destroyed records that might have proved the degree of the financial success of the *Southern Literary Messenger,* which was outstanding if judged on a comparative instead of an absolute basis. Throughout the 1850s Thompson suffered from tuberculosis, for the relief of which he went twice to Europe, meeting English literary lions such as Robert Browning, Bulwer-Lytton, Thomas Carlyle, Tennyson, and Thackeray. The heat of Georgia's summer caused him to resign from the *Southern Field and Fireside* after less than six months. After a brief journalistic stint in Baltimore he returned to Richmond, where he was given the positions of Assistant Secretary of the Commonwealth and State Librarian.

In 1864 Thompson's ill health caused him to run the Federal blockade in order to go to London, where he was a principal contributor to the Confederate journal *Index.* In England, from 1864 to 1867, he became more intimate with Carlyle and Tennyson, and he edited with much elaboration the memoirs of Heros von Borcke, the Prussian soldier-of-fortune who had served with J. E. B. Stuart's cavalry. Homesick, Thompson in 1866 returned to Richmond, but he found that he could not support himself there. In 1867 he moved to New York City, where Bryant made him literary editor of his *New York Evening Post* in 1867. Although Thompson always had urged others to join him in considering Bryant's poetry, which he admired, separately from his political views, which he did not admire, the association

of the two men was remarkable. The Virginian may have moderated the New Yorker's anti-Southernism, but the combination of the former's declining health and the character of New York journalism prevented any development of the *Evening Post* along more literary lines.

References:

Gerald M. Garmon, *John Reuben Thompson* (Boston: Twayne, 1979);

Jay B. Hubbell, *The South in American Literature* (Durham: Duke University Press, 1954), pp. 521-528;

Benjamin B. Minor, *The Southern Literary Messenger* (New York & Washington, D.C.: Neale, 1905);

Montrose J. Moore, ed., *Literature of the South* (New York: Crowell, 1910), p. 354;

Rayburn S. Moore, "Antebellum Poetry" and "Literary Magazines of the Old South," in *History of Southern Literature,* edited by Louis R. Rubin, Jr. (Baton Rouge: Louisiana State University Press, 1985), pp. 158-161, 184;

Allen Nevins, *The New York Evening Post: A Century of Journalism* (New York: Russell & Russell, 1922);

Arthur H. Quinn, *Edgar Allan Poe: A Critical Biography* (New York: Appleton-Century-Crofts, 1941), pp. 636-658;

J. V. Ridgeley, ed., *Nineteenth Century Southern Literature* (Lexington: University of Kentucky Press, 1980), pp. 26-27;

Edward L. Tucker, "A Rash And Perilous Enterprise: *The Southern Literary Messenger* And The Men Who Made It," *Virginia Cavalcade,* 21 (Summer 1971): 14-20.

Papers:

John Reuben Thompson's papers are held at the University of Virginia.

Tobias Watkins

(12 December 1780-1 November 1855)

June N. Adamson
University of Tennessee

MAJOR POSITIONS HELD: Editor, *Baltimore Medical and Physical Recorder* (1808-1809); coeditor, editor, *Portico: A Repository of Science and Literature* (1816-1818).

BOOKS: *A History of the American Revolution; Comprehending All the Principal Events Both in the Field and in the Cabinet,* projected by Paul Allen, written by Watkins and John Neal (Baltimore: Printed by Thomas Murphy, 1819);
Tales of the Tripod; or, A Delphian Evening, as Pertinax Particular (Baltimore: F. Lucas, Jr., 1821).

OTHER: Xavier Bichat, *Physiological Researches Upon Life and Death,* translated by Watkins (Philadelphia: Smith & Maxwell, 1809);
Luis de Onís, *Memoir Upon the Negotiations Between Spain and the United States of America, which Led to the Treaty of 1819,* translated by Watkins (Baltimore: F. Lucas, Jr., 1821).

Tobias Watkins, in addition to editing the *Portico: A Repository of Science and Literature,* practiced medicine as a private physician, published medical and scientific articles, edited the short-lived *Baltimore Medical and Physical Recorder,* translated articles from the French, and was a medical officer for the military. He was known as "an elegant scholar and accomplished gentleman," according to Eugene Fauntleroy Cordell. Yet he gave up both publishing and medicine to take a post with the U.S. government.

Tobias Watkins was born in Anne Arundel County, Maryland, on 12 December 1780. He graduated from St. John's College, Annapolis, in 1798 and earned the doctor of medicine degree in 1802. He served as assistant surgeon in the U.S. Navy from 20 July 1799 to 1 January 1801. After earning the M.D., he was licensed in midwifery and began practice at Baltimore in 1803 or 1804. Watkins became physician to the Marine Hospital and later, on 20 May 1813, was appointed major and surgeon, Thirty-eighth Infan-

try, U.S. Army. On 30 March 1814 he was appointed Maryland Hospital surgeon and provisionally retained on 15 June 1815. On 18 April 1818, after two years, he gave up the editorship of the *Portico* when he was appointed assistant surgeon general of the United States, a position that was eliminated on 1 June 1821. He was deputy grand master of Masons, 1809-1813; grand master, 1813-1814 and 1816-1818. In 1812 he was named high priest, Encampment of the Knights Templar, No. 1. From 1824 to 1829 Watkins served as fourth auditor of the United States Treasury in Washington, D.C. While in this office he was found guilty of appropriating public monies and was imprisoned from 1829 to 1833.

Whether the *Portico* grew out of Watkins's membership in the Delphian Club or the club grew, in part, from the magazine, is not clear, but certainly the two influenced each other. According to Frank Luther Mott, Watkins met John Neal, a "fiery man of letters," in the club. Mott states that "Neal appears to have been second only to Stephen Simpson, in the number of his contributions to *The Portico....* " Simpson was coeditor of the *Portico* from January 1816 to June 1817; Watkins was sole editor from July 1817 to June 1818, though Neal served as substitute editor for the magazine's final issue.

The Delphian Club, named for the oracle at Delphi, was a small organization but central to the literary activity of Baltimore, a city whose citizens wanted to keep up with the reputation of Philadelphia, which, in the first part of the nineteenth century, was known as "the Athens of America." Watkins was one of the club's seven founders, and as its president, it was he who wrote the club's constitution, which outlined two primary purposes: to foster members' interest in literary and scientific pursuits; and to amuse their leisure hours. It is probable that the club was officially organized after the founding of the *Portico,* the first issue of which appeared in January 1816. However, the record shows that it was at the thirty-second weekly meeting of the club

THE PORTICO.

CONDUCTED BY TWO MEN OF PADUA

Hic patet ingeniis campus: certusque merenti
Stat favor.   CLAUDIAN.

"Different minds
Incline to different objects; one pursues
The vast alone, the wonderful, the wild;
Another sighs for harmony and grace
And gentlest beauty.
Such and so various are the tastes of men."—AKENSIDE.

VOL. I.   JANUARY, 1816.   NO. I.

PROSPECTUS.

At a time when the numerous failures of similar attempts have inspired authors with diffidence and distrust, and produced in the publick mind weariness and satiety, the Editors, in offering to the publick attention the plan of a new periodical work, pause with hesitation, though determined to go forward, and confess their doubts, though bold in their hopes of success. When every variety of literary enterprize has long ceased to be a novelty to American readers; when every thing has been attempted, and almost every thing has miscarried; it will naturally be inquired, whether the authors of a new Literary project come better prepared to command success; whether they possess more exhaustless materials, and are less dependant on casual supplies and external accidents, for the permanence of their design, and the success of their undertaking, than their predecessors?

If a thorough knowledge of the causes that have swept away former works of this kind, could rescue the present from miscarriage: if the maturity of their plan, the independence of their principles, the fervour of their zeal, and the copiousness of their

1

PROSPECTUS.

2

materials, could ensure to them an auspicious career; the Editors would have nothing to fear, and little to hope for. In soliciting a general patronage, they do it with a conviction of the general utility of the proposed work. In pledging themselves for the greater extent of its duration, they do it with the express avowal, that they repose exclusively on their own resources, for its spirit and its substance. Bold in the consciousness of their aims, and familiar with the extent of their powers, they challenge a scrutiny of its defects without fear; and will labour it into excellence, if excellence be attainable. United in the scope of their design, and combined in the vigour of their efforts; they are still distinct in the direction of their attainments, and the complexion of their sentiments; possessing in this regard the double advantage of concord and variety.

To depend on adventitious aid for success, is to invite miscarriage; to reject it when it may be obtained, is to refuse the gift of perfection because it emanates from another. The Editors purpose to pursue a middle track, that will lead to splendid acquisitions. While they solicit, and firmly hope to receive, much substantial support from extraneous channels; they do not mean to waste the hours in expectations that may be disappointed, nor indulge in languid supinity on the promises of others.

To make vows and professions, however, is always easy: but it is still easier to violate them. Will it be any security against corruption and degeneracy, to be fearful of their occurrence, and aware of their insidious approaches?

The Editors propose to give to this work, as general and wide a scope as may be compatible with excellence in its uniform execution. To attempt every subject, might hazard failure in all; yet, under some restrictions it will combine the properties of many different periodical productions; and concentrate the rays of various departments of literature. Its matter will be arranged under the following general heads, viz. *Miscellany, Review, Chronicle* and *Repository.*

1st. *The Miscellany.* To this department shall be allotted *original letters* on various subjects; and essays of an interesting nature, connected with Life, Literature and Manners.

This division of the work will likewise embrace *Biography;* a branch of literature agreeable to every taste and fitted to every

Prospectus for the magazine founded by Watkins and his brother-in-law, Stephen Simpson, the "Two Men of Padua"
referred to above

capacity. To the lover of human nature, who delights to trace the mazes of passion and the vicissitudes of woe, through variety of character; and to treasure in his mind the solemn and impressive lessons of experience, Biography is always welcome, always captivating.

2d. *The Review* will comprise original and selected criticism. There are few persons of cultivated intellect, who cannot justly appreciate the advantages of a correct taste in subjects of literature, as well as estimate its influence on the happiness of life. It is chiefly in *taste*, and not in *genius*, that our country seems yet deficient. Learning may flourish by industry; wealth may attend toil; and ingenuity may discover improvement in every climate: but the efforts of genius, undirected by the hand of taste, shoot into rank luxuriance, or disgusting deformity. Criticism, as an auxiliary to taste, is a branch of letters eminently estimable. But, when it prevents the success of imposture, or exposes the errours of dulness; when it stimulates genius to exertion, and awakens curiosity to deeper researches it assumes a still nobler attitude, and extorts our veneration and applause for its salutary influence on the perfection of science and the felicity of life.

3d. *The Chronicle.* This department will comprehend a general record of interesting *national* facts, without regard to *political* principles. Whatever publick events, or private incidents may possess claims to attention, will be carefully embodied and preserved; and, among these, Philosophical and Literary notices will find a distinguished place. The Editors solemnly and explicitly renounce all intention of making *Politicks* a source of discord and contention to their readers. Learning can only flourish where passion and prejudice gain no entrance.

4th. *The Repository* shall embrace such *Poetick* effusions, as by their sterling merit, shall challenge the taste and judgment of the scholar. This department, however, will not be confined to original composition. Selections, from the copious stores of exotick genius, must often supply the scarcity of native productions—a scarcity, not so much the effect of a barren soil, as the consequence of a want of *patronage*, which is the *food* of genius, indispensable to its life, and essential to its perfection.

To this display of their plan, the Editors can only add, that whatever can extend the bounds of knowledge, or augment the

harmless pleasures of life; give dignity to science, or add embellishment to what is useful, shall be imparted with promptitude and appropriated with fidelity. The entertaining narrative, and the profound dissertation, will be equally regarded; and *variety*, as forming the chief excellence of a periodical work, will be studiously sought after.

REVIEW.

On the Nature, Origin, Progress and Influence of Consular Establishments, by D. B. Warden, Consul General of the United States of America at Paris; &c. &c. Paris Printed by Smith, 1815. Sold by M Carey, Philadelphia, 8vo. p. p. 351.

To a commercial community, eager to gain, and desirous to regulate the preservation of their wealth, nothing can command higher interest, than a knowledge of the laws, and customs, that influence and control the publick functions of American Consuls. Acting as the superior agents of a nation's commerce, in a foreign port, their office is important, and their power great. The property of the merchant is, or ought to be secured, by their jurisdiction; the rights of the seamen are protected; the fortune of the intestate wanderer, summoned by death, in a foreign land, is rescued from the gripe of avaricious strangers, and restored to his legal heirs, or dearest connexions; his grave is bedewed with the tear, at least, of one fellow citizen, alive to the same national sympathies, and tender emotions; and whether in Turkey, Africa, or Algiers, the corpse of the Christian is rescued from contempt, or brutality, and the person of the traveller, is protected from injury and abuse. Humanity rejoices at an institution, that secures her most sacred privileges, and fosters her noblest sentiments: and interest and industry applaud a regulation, that removes the embarrassment of the navigator, when landed on a strange scene, and among a foreign people, of whose language he is ignorant, and with whose customs and laws, he is totally unacquainted.

In the "nature, progress, and influence of Consular Establishments," both the merchant and the man, are therefore, eminent-

that the following bylaw was adopted: "A sheet of paper shall be furnished by the member providing refreshments for the Club, on which each Delphian shall be bound in honor to write such of his own thoughts as he may consider fit to appear in the scientific, witty, historical, poetical, erudite, widely circulating, and no doubt still-more-widely-to-be-circulated *Portico* of the learned President, and that such thoughts shall be entitled: 'Wise Sayings of a Knot of Queer Fellows.' "

The Delphians made substantial contributions to journalism, fiction, poetry, history, and science; there were twelve newspapers or magazines whose editors were members of the club, which certainly succeeded in its purpose of inspiring its own members with a love of literature. John Neal began his literary career in the club, and in 1869, in *Wandering Recollections of a Somewhat Busy Life,* he described the club in detail, concluding: "The Delphians were a great help to one another; and all to me, in a thousand ways . . . as writers, they were more or less distinguished, even the nervous and excitable [William H.] Winder having managed to bring forth and publish, in Paul Allen's 'Journal of the Times,' for which I also wrote profusely, in capital outline, 'History of Maryland.' "

Literary criticism of an astringent type was characteristic of the *Portico*. Simpson, Neal, and others discussed Lord Byron, Sir Walter Scott, Robert Southey, Thomas Moore, Henry Fielding, William Cowper, and others at length. American books were sometimes noticed, and articles on Russian, Greek, and French literature were included as well. Travel and biography took up much space, with some of the travel articles being original. Some of the last issues contained pages of mathematical problems, and music was occasionally published.

According to Mott, it was Simpson, Watkins's brother-in-law, who wrote most of the more serious pieces, including "The Life of Cowper" and a pessimistic serial entitled "View of the Present State of Polite Learning." However, there is no question, as Mott wrote, that "Watkins was the head and front of the magazine–genial and expansive, known to be generous to a fault, and talented."

The first issue of the *Portico* contained a long review, "On the Nature, Origin, Progress and Influence of Consular Establishment, by D. B. Wardry, consul general of the United States of America at Paris," as well as reviews in

French, Italian, and Latin. It included a section on arts and sciences; under the heading "Miscellany" there was one long letter "on the state of political learning" and the first installment of Simpson's biography "The Life of William Cowper, derived from authentic sources." Although illustrations were few, some engravings were included, including one illustrating Ali Bey's travels.

Later issues contained such articles as "Dialogues on Female Education," probably written by Watkins, and a narrative about the difficulties of Napoleon's campaign in Russia, translated from books by the captain of the Royal Geographical Engineers.

After Watkins left the magazine in 1818, Neal was left in charge as substitute editor. By his own account he "sunk the 'Portico' at her moorings" with an essay entitled "Man not a Free Agent," a nullification of the concept of free will. Whatever effect Neal's essay had on subscribers to the *Portico*, it is clear that Watkins was through with the magazine. He devoted the next eleven years to his various governmental positions and to a translation of Luis de Onís's *Memoir Upon the Negotiations Between Spain and the United States of America, which Led to the Treaty of 1819* (1821). Then, in 1829, he was imprisoned for misappropriating nearly three thousand dollars from the U. S. Treasury.

Watkins habitually suffered from financial pressures, in part, Neal states, because he was both extravagant and generous, "a man who would sooner empty his pockets into the lap of a stranger than pay his butcher or grocer. . . ." However, after Watkins's release from prison in 1833, Neal thought that "he became a changed man, heart and soul. . . . The last time I saw him, he was keeping a common school, in an old tumbledown brick building, one of a large block, in Alexandria; and though evidently impoverished, and well stricken in years, and more serious than I had ever seen him, he appeared to be both submissive and resigned, uttering no word of complaint or reproach, and looking as if, though ready to go, if called for, he was not weary of life, nor in any hurry for the translation." Despite the embarrassment and poverty of his last years, Watkins, and the *Portico*, made a significant contribution to the establishment of the magazine as a vehicle for ideas in the early years of the nineteenth century.

References:

"Baltimore's First Magazine," *Baltimore Evening Sun,* 6 October 1935;

Eugene Fauntleroy Cordell, *The Medical Annals of Maryland, 1799-1899* (Baltimore, 1903);

Charles Lanman, *Biographical Annals of the Civil Government of the U.S. During its First Century* (Washington, D.C.: James Anglim, 1870);

Maryland Historical Magazine, 20 (December 1925): 305-346;

Frank Luther Mott, *A History of American Magazines,* 5 volumes (Cambridge, Mass.: Har-

vard University Press, 1938-1968), I: 126, 293-296;

John Neal, *Wandering Recollections of a Somewhat Busy Life* (Boston: Roberts, 1869), pp. 100-224;

John R. Quinan, *Medical Annals of Baltimore from 1608-1880* (Baltimore: Press of L. Friedenwald, 1884), p. 175;

Edward T. Schultz, *History of Freemasonry in Maryland* (Baltimore: Medairy, 1885), pp. 326, 327.

Noah Webster

(16 October 1758-28 May 1843)

Lloyd E. Chiasson
Loyola University in New Orleans

See also the Webster entries in *DLB 1: The American Renaissance in New England; DLB 37: American Writers of the Early Republic; DLB 42: American Writers for Children Before 1900;* and *DLB 43: American Newspaper Journalists, 1690-1872.*

MAJOR POSITIONS HELD: Editor, *American Magazine* (1787-1788); editor, publisher, *American Minerva,* renamed *Commercial Advertiser* (1793-1803); *Herald,* renamed *Spectator* (1794-1803).

SELECTED BOOKS: *A Grammatical Institute, of the English Language, Comprising, an Easy, Concise, and Systematic Method of Education, Designed for the Use of English Schools in America. In Three Parts. Part I. Containing, a New and Accurate Standard of Pronunciation* (Hartford: Printed by Hudson & Goodwin for the author, 1783);

A Grammatical Institute of the English Language, Comprising, an Easy, Concise, and Systematic Method of Education, Designed for the Use of English Schools in America. In Three Parts. Part II. Containing a Plain and Comprehensive Grammar ... (Hartford: Printed by Hudson & Goodwin for the author, 1784);

A Grammatical Institute of the English Language; Comprising an Easy, Concise and Systematic Method of Education; Designed for the Use of Schools in

Noah Webster (courtesy of the Metropolitan Museum of Art, bequest of Charles Allen Munn)

America. In Three Parts. Part III: Containing the Necessary Rules of Reading and Speaking, and a Variety of Essays ... (Hartford: Printed by Barlow & Babcock for the author, 1785);

Sketches of American Policy. Under the Following Heads: I. Theory of Government. II. Governments on the Eastern Continent. III. American States; or the Principles of the American Constitutions Contrasted with Those of European States. IV. Plan of Policy for Improving the Advantages and Perpetuating the Union of the American States (Hartford: Printed by Hudson & Goodwin, 1785);

The American Spelling Book . . . (Philadelphia: Young & M'Culloch, 1787; revised edition, Philadelphia: Published by Jacob Johnson & Co., 1804);

An American Selection of Lessons in Reading and Speaking. Calculated to Improve the Minds and Refine the Tastes of Youth. . . . Being the Third Part of A Grammatical Institute of the English Language . . . , Greatly Enlarged (Philadelphia: Printed & sold by Young & M'Culloch, 1787; revised edition, New Haven: From Sidney's Press for I. Beers & Co. and I. Cooke & Co., 1804);

An Examination into the Leading Principles of the Federal Constitution Proposed by the Late Convention Held at Philadelphia. With Answers to the Principle Objections That Have Been Raised Against the System (Philadelphia: Printed & sold by Prichard & Hall, 1787);

An Introduction to English Grammar; Being an Abridgement of the Second Part of the Grammatical Institute (Philadelphia: Printed by W. Young, 1788);

Dissertations on the English Language; With Notes, Historical and Critical. To Which Is Added, By Way of Appendix, An Essay on a Reformed Mode of Spelling, with Dr. Franklin's Arguments on that Subject (Boston: Printed by Isaiah Thomas & Co. for the author, 1789);

Attention! or, New Thoughts on a Serious Subject; Being an Enquiry into the Excise Laws of Connecticut . . . (Hartford: Printed & sold by Hudson & Goodwin, 1789);

The Little Reader's Assistant . . . (Hartford: Printed by Elisha Babcock, 1790);

A Collection of Essays and Fugitiv Writings. On Moral, Historical, Political and Literary Subjects (Boston: Printed by I. Thomas & E. T. Andrews for the author, 1790);

The Prompter; or A Commentary on Common Sayings and Subjects, Which Are Full of Common Sense, the Best Sense in the World . . . (Hartford: Printed by Hudson & Goodwin, 1791);

Effects of Slavery, on Morals and Industry (Hartford: Printed by Hudson & Goodwin, 1793);

The Revolution in France, Considered in Respect to Its Progress and Effects (New York: Printed & published by George Bunce & Co., 1794);

A Letter to the Governors, Instructors and Trustees of the Universities, and Other Seminaries of Learning, in the United States, on the Errors of English Grammars (New York: Printed by George F. Hopkins for the author, 1798);

An Oration Pronounced before the Citizens of New-Haven on the Anniversary of the Independence of the United States, July 4th 1798 . . . (New Haven: Printed by T. & S. Green, 1798);

A Brief History of Epidemic and Pestilential Diseases; With the Principal Phenomena of the Physical World, Which Precede and Accompany Them, and Observations Deduced from the Facts Stated, 2 volumes (Hartford: Printed by Hudson & Goodwin, 1799; London: Printed for G. G. & J. Robinson, 1800);

Ten Letters to Dr. Joseph Priestly, in Answer to His Letters to the Inhabitants of Northumberland (New Haven: Printed by Read & Morse, 1800);

A Rod for the Fool's Back (New Haven?, 1800);

A Letter to General Hamilton, Occasioned by His Letter to President Adams (New York?, 1800);

Miscellaneous Papers on Political and Commercial Subjects . . . (New York: Printed by E. Belden & Co., 1802);

Elements of Useful Knowledge. Volume 1. Containing a Historical and Geographical Account of the United States: For the Use of Schools (Hartford: Printed & sold by Hudson & Goodwin, 1802);

An Oration Pronounced before the Citizens of New Haven, on the Anniversary of the Declaration of Independence; July, 1802 . . . (New Haven: Printed by William W. Morse, 1802);

An Address to the Citizens of Connecticut (New Haven: Printed by J. Walter, 1803);

Elements of Useful Knowledge. Volume II. Containing a Historical and Geographical Account of the United States: For the Use of Schools (New Haven: From Sidney's Press, for the author, 1804);

Elements of Useful Knowledge. Vol. III. Containing a Historical and Geographical Account of the Empires and States in Europe, Asia and Africa, with Their Colonies. To Which Is Added, a Brief Description of New Holland, and the Principal Islands in the Pacific and Indian Oceans. For the Use of Schools (New Haven: Printed by O. Steele & Co. and published by Bronson, Walter & Co., 1806);

A Compendious Dictionary of the English Language (New Haven: From Sidney's Press, 1806);

A Dictionary of the English Language; Compiled for the Use of Common Schools in the United States (New Haven: From Sidney's Press for John & David West in Boston, Brisban & Brannan in New York, Lincoln & Gleason and Oliver D. Cooke in Hartford, and I. Cooke & Co. in New Haven, 1807);

A Philosophical and Practical Grammar of the English Language (New Haven: Printed by Oliver & Steele for Brisban & Brannan, 1807);

A Letter to Dr. David Ramsay, of Charleston, (S.C.) Respecting the Errors in Johnson's Dictionary, and Other Lexicons (New Haven: Printed by Oliver Steele & Co., 1807);

The Peculiar Doctrines of the Gospel, Explained and Defended (New York: J. Seymour, 1809);

History of Animals; Being the Fourth Volume of Elements of Useful Knowledge. For the Use of Schools, and Young Persons of Both Sexes (New Haven: Printed by Walter & Steele and published & sold by Howe & Deforest and Walter & Steele, 1812);

An Oration Pronounced before the Knox and Warren Branches of the Washington Benevolent Society, at Amherst, on the Celebration of the Anniversary of the Declaration of Independence, July 4, 1814 (Northampton: Printed by William Butler, 1814);

A Letter to the Honorable John Pickering, on the Subject of his Vocabulary; or, Collection of Words and Phrases, Supposed to Be Peculiar to the United States of America (Boston: Printed by T. W. White and published by West & Richardson, 1817);

An Address, Delivered before the Hampshire, Franklin and Hampden Agricultural Society, at Their Annual Meeting in Northampton, Oct. 14, 1818 (Northampton: Printed by Thomas W. Shepard & Co., 1818);

A Plea for a Miserable World. I. An Address Delivered at the Laying of the Corner Stone of the Building Erecting for the Charity Institution in Amherst, Massachusetts, August 9, 1820, by Noah Webster, Esq. II. A Sermon Delivered on the Same Occasion, by Rev. Daniel A. Clark, Pastor of the First Church and Society in Amherst. III. A Brief Account of the Origin of the Institution (Boston: Printed by Ezra Lincoln, 1820);

Letters to a Young Gentleman Commencing His Education: To Which is Subjoined a Brief History of the United States (New Haven: Printed by S.

Converse and sold by Howe & Spalding, 1823);

An American Dictionary of the English Language . . ., 2 volumes (New Haven: Printed by Hezekiah Howe/New York: Published by S. Converse, 1828); republished as *A Dictionary of the English Language*, 12 parts (London: Printed for Black, Young & Young, 1830-1832);

The Elementary Spelling Book; Being an Improvement on the American Spelling Book (New York: Printed by A. Chandler & published by J. P. Haven & R. Lockwood, 1829);

A Dictionary of the English Language; Abridged from the American Dictionary . . . (New York: White, Gallaher & White, 1830);

Biography for the Use of Schools (New Haven: Printed by Hezekiah Howe, 1830);

An Improved Grammar of the English Language (New Haven: Published & sold by Hezekiah Howe, 1831);

History of the United States; to Which Is Prefixed a Brief Historical Account of Our English Ancestors, from the Dispersion of Babel, to Their Migration to America; and of the Conquest of South America, by the Spaniards (New Haven: Printed by Baldwin & Treadway and published by Durrie & Peck, 1832; revised edition, Cincinnati: Published by Corey, Fairbank & Webster, 1835);

Value of the Bible, and Excellence of the Christian Religion: For the Use of Families and Schools (New Haven: Published by Durrie & Peck, 1834);

A Brief View 1. Of Errors and Obscurities in the Common Version of the Scriptures; Addressed to Bible Societies, Clergymen and Other Friends of Religion. 2. Of Errors and Defects in Class-Books Used in Seminaries of Learning; Including Dictionaries and Grammars of the English, French, Greek and Latin Languages; Addressed to Instructors of Youth, and Students, with a Few Hints to Statesmen, Members of Congress, and Heads of Departments. To Which Is Added, 3. A Few Plagiarisms, Showing the Way in Which Books May Be Made, by Those Who Use Borrowed Capital (New Haven, 1834?);

Instructive and Entertaining Lessons for Youth . . . (New Haven: Published by S. Babcock and Durrie & Peck, 1835);

The Teacher; A Supplement to the Elementary Spelling Book (New Haven: Published by S. Babcock, 1836);

A Letter to the Hon. Daniel Webster, on the Political Affairs of the United States, as Marcellus (Philadelphia: Printed by J. Crissy, 1837);

Mistakes and Corrections. 1. Improprieties in the Common Version of the Scriptures; With Specimens of Amended Language in Webster's Edition of the Bible. 2. Explanations of Prepositions, in English, and Other Languages. These Constitute a Very Difficult Part of Philology. 3. Errors in English Grammars. 4. Mistakes in the Hebrew Lexicon of Gesenius, and In Some Derivations of Dr. Horwitz. 5. Errors in Butter's Scholar's Companion and in Town's Analysis. 6. Errors in Richardson's Dictionary (New Haven: Printed by B. L. Hamlen, 1837);

Appeal to Americans . . ., as Sidney (New York?, 1838?);

Observations on Language, and on the Errors of Class-Books; Addressed to the Members of the New York Lyceum. Also, Observations on Commerce, Addressed to the Members of the Mercantile Library Association, in New York (New Haven: Printed by S. Babcock, 1839);

A Manual of Useful Studies: For the Instruction of Young Persons of Both Sexes, in Families and Schools (New Haven: Printed & published by S. Babcock, 1839);

A Collection of Papers on Political, Literary and Moral Subjects (Boston: Tappan & Dennett/Philadelphia: Smith & Peck, 1843).

OTHER: *The New England Primer, "Amended and Improved . . . ,"* edited by Webster (New York: Printed by J. Patterson, 1789);

John Winthrop, *A Journal of the Transactions and Occurrences in the Settlement of Massachusetts and the Other New-England Colonies, from the Year 1630 to 1644*, edited by Webster (Hartford: Printed by Elisha Babcock, 1790);

A Collection of Papers on the Subject of Bilious Fevers, Prevalent in the United States for a Few Years Past, edited by Webster (New York: Printed by Hopkins, Webb & Co., 1796);

The Holy Bible, Containing the Old and New Testaments, in the Common Version. With Amendments of the Language by Noah Webster, LL.D. (New Haven: Published by Durrie & Peck, 1833).

Throughout his long and varied life Noah Webster worked for progress but often resented its course. An authoritarian both in politics and religion, he became in his later years a self-imposed castaway in a progressive America. While as a youth Webster supported the changes

the American Revolution offered (he felt it would bring enlightened ideas and the proper line of authority to the colonies), as an American elder he increasingly became disturbed by the growth of libertarianism and the changing values associated with it. In the end Webster was a Puritanical man desperately trying to hold onto a world which no longer existed while simultaneously making important contributions to the one which did.

Although he was critical of the course America had taken as it entered the nineteenth century, his contributions are nonetheless prodigious. He was the great educator of the period, working as schoolteacher, lawyer, newspaper editor, author, and most important, pioneer in the field of education. He produced essays in politics and religion, moralistic tracts and scientific treatises, schoolbooks, and dictionaries. It is no overstatement to classify his life's work as phenomenal. Taken alone, his spelling book had a tremendous impact on American education. Known as the "Blue-Back Speller," that book marked the beginning of a fascinating, although not lucrative, writing career. Between 1787 and 1789 Webster turned journalist, first publishing a magazine, then a book of collected newspaper essays, then a Federalist newspaper, then an innovative country weekly. Next came a remarkable two-volume study of epidemic diseases. This was followed by a small dictionary and later his unabridged "life's work." Webster still was not finished, however, for in 1832 his history of the United States was published, and two years later his version of the King James Bible appeared.

The above are but highlights of the career of one of the most intriguing colonial/post-colonial figures in American history. Born on 16 October 1758 in West Hartford, Connecticut, Webster was the son of Noah and Mercy Steele Webster. Webster's father, who owned a ninety-acre farm, apparently instilled in him an appreciation of hard work which became obvious in his years of writing. Although his family was not wealthy, it is evident from his writing that he viewed himself as a member of the elite, somewhat of an American aristocrat.

From 1774 to 1778 Webster attended Yale University, and after graduation he studied law, gaining admission to the bar in 1781. In 1789 he married Rebecca Greenleaf, and they had eight children: Emily, born in 1790; Frances Juliana, in 1793; Harriet, in 1797; William Greenleaf, in 1801; Eliza, in 1803; Henry Bradford, in 1806;

and Louisa, in 1808. On 28 May 1843 Webster died in New Haven, Connecticut, at the age of eighty-four.

Upon graduation from Yale, Webster tried teaching and practicing law before he returned to education by opening a school in Sharon, Connecticut. In 1781 Webster left Sharon for personal reasons and soon began teaching in Goshen, New York. Penniless and alone, Webster appears to have been at one of the low points in his life. However, it was at this point that he turned his energies to the support of the Revolution, which he hoped would ultimately bring some sort of utopian state to America. To this end Webster optimistically began writing schoolbooks as he undertook the great task of educating the colonists in the hope they would be prepared for the new way of life to follow.

Perhaps Webster's most important work, and certainly his most widely read, appeared soon afterward in 1783 with the publication of part 1 of *A Grammatical Institute, of the English Language*. This was the highly successful spelling book, to be followed by the grammar and reading selections in 1784 and 1785, respectively.

The speller did not bring the kind of financial success to Webster it should have, primarily because of inadequate copyright laws, but it did make him a national figure. Webster's prominence put him in the position to critique society, debate the key issues of the period, and serve as counsel to those who governed. To this means he entered the field of journalism, first as a contributor, and later as an editor.

Webster was a frequent newspaper contributor, taking advantage of the rapidly expanding audience in order to spread his ideas. In 1786 in the *Connecticut Courant* he wrote: "people in general are too ignorant to manage affairs that require great reading and an extensive knowledge of foreign nations. . . . For my own part, I confess, I was once as strong a republican as any man in America. Now, a republican is among the last kinds of government I should choose. I would infinitely prefer a limited monarchy, for I would sooner be the subject of the caprice of one man, than to the ignorance and passions of the multitude." This quote serves as a classic illustration of Webster's contradictory nature. His comments in the *Courant* appeared just one year before he published the first issue of *American Magazine*, which, without official approval, he could not have printed in most of the monarchies of the world. Perhaps more interesting, Web-

ster's distrust of the masses' ability to make rational decisions is somewhat paradoxical since his speller and other schoolbooks probably made him the greatest contributor to mass education in America during the postcolonial period.

Webster began his magazine career when he moved to New York City in 1787. There he established the monthly *American Magazine*. Unfortunately, the magazine suffered the same fate as others during the period and folded in less than a year. However, the journal did offer Webster the opportunity to write on various subjects, and his breadth of knowledge, as well as interests, was vast. He wrote essays about history, architecture, botany, and law, as well as romance stories and theological tracts.

Webster's narrative persona, "Giles Hickory," emerged as a prominent character in the pages of the magazine. Hickory often discussed authoritarian principles as they might be applied to the Constitution and American life. In most cases Webster simply used Hickory to restate his belief that control of the state rested at the top with elected officials, not with the people.

American Magazine had importance beyond being a strong Federalist organ, however. It was an attempt by Webster to create a national magazine with appeal for all types of readers. Unfortunately, lack of a solid financial base prevented Webster from turning the magazine into a successful venture.

Shortly after the failure of the *American Magazine*, Webster had a series of sixteen essays (later nine more were added) printed as a book. *The Prompter; or A Commentary on Common Sayings and Subjects . . .* (1791) may represent Webster's finest writing and has been compared to Benjamin Franklin's "Poor Richard" essays. In *The Prompter* Webster altered his usual humorless, dry writing style. Instead he wrote in a simple, straightforward manner with generous portions of humor, satire, and short stories intended to teach basic moral lessons. The book was an immediate success, probably because Webster's lighter touch was more acceptable to the general public. *The Prompter* may have more importance than historians have generally given it since Webster may have accomplished with this book what he intended for all his writing: to educate America in politics, in morals, and in life.

Following his success with *The Prompter*, Webster returned to journalism in 1793 when he established in New York the *American Minerva, patroness of peace, commerce and the liberal arts*, a Federalist newspaper known simply as the *American Minerva*. Four months later he began printing the *Herald*, a country weekly with rewritten *American Minerva* copy and with different advertising than the city journal. Both newspapers are important journalistically for different reasons. The *American Minerva* represented the new breed of journals edited by men of education rather than printers and, along with others, helped speed the changeover from newspaper printer to newspaper editor. The weekly's importance lies in the fact that it was an economically sound attempt to reach a scattered country audience, in part because Webster "recycled" *Minerva* copy in a different format. Both journals were financial successes, and in 1797 Webster changed the names of the newspapers to the *Commercial Advertiser* and the *Spectator*, respectively.

Although Webster's reputation as a journalist grew, his years as an editor became increasingly difficult, primarily because he was operating in the midst of the most partisan, and stormy, journalistic period in American history. And Webster did not emerge unscathed, having fought editorial battles over the construction and interpretation of the Constitution as well as the controversial treaty with England. However, as political power began to slip from the Federalists to the Jeffersonians at the turn of the century, Webster seems to have lost interest in the journals. By 1803 he sold his newspaper holdings, although he had already ceased active participation as editor five years before.

Although Webster drastically reduced his editorial duties by 1798, he continued to write, and in 1799 *A Brief History of Epidemic and Pestilential Diseases* was published. In it Webster attempted to solve the cause of the devastating yellow fever epidemics so common during the period. Although his theory proved incorrect, this two-volume work, like his other writings, demonstrated his unceasing willingness to work tirelessly toward the betterment of the nation and of mankind in general.

Even before his history of diseases was published, Webster had returned to his roots in New Haven. There he turned his energies to both language and religion. At this point Webster's life took an unusual twist. As a young man he showed no indication of developing strong religious commitments, once writing that he doubted "salvation by free grace, the atonement and the divinity of Christ. . . ." After 1800, however, Webster's attitudes changed, and he became in-

Webster in an 1833 portrait by James Herring

creasingly interested in, then devoted to, Calvinist doctrine. In so doing, Webster's educational and political beliefs changed drastically in that he no longer believed secular education (or Federalist polity by itself) was the road to a stable, well-structured nation. Webster felt that only through obedience to God could society achieve beneficial changes. For the remainder of his life his work was dominated by this belief. Amidst some ridicule because of his previous political and educational stances, in 1800 Webster announced plans to write a dictionary. In 1806 *A Compendious Dictionary of the English Language* was published. Though it was small compared to his unabridged dictionary still years in the future, Webster apparently learned the difficulties in producing a book about language. He then began a ten-year study of ancient languages in order to conduct research on the larger, more complete dictionary. In 1822 he traveled to Europe to continue his work, and in 1825 in Cambridge, England, he completed the massive *An American Dictionary of the English Language* (1828). Concerning the completion of the dictionary, Webster later wrote: "When I came to the last work I was seized with a trembling, which made it somewhat difficult to hold my pen steady for writing. The cause seems to have been the thought that I might not live to finish the work, or the thought that I was so near the end of my labors. But I summoned strength to finish the last work, and then walking about the room a few minutes, I recovered."

Even today Webster's monumental work is difficult to appreciate fully considering he compiled the dictionary alone whereas present-day dictionaries are usually revisions conducted by several scholars. Although Webster's work was a tremendous contribution to a growing America, it was flawed. Too often his definitions revealed his perceptions of life from a New England, as well as a Calvinistic, standpoint. Besides being somewhat provincial in nature, Webster also ignored etymological scholarship from Europe, perhaps in part because he felt that for America to progress it should divest itself of all European trappings. In addition, Webster's belief in a literal interpretation of the Bible led him to the conclusion that languages developed at the Tower of Babel. This was not the rock upon which most etymological study in Europe was based. For example, in the introduction of the dictionary, Webster's religious leanings can be found: "We may infer that language was bestowed on Adam, in the same manner as all his other faculties and knowledge, by supernatural power; or in other words, was of divine origin. . . ."

During the next six years the book went through several revisions, and by 1864 Webster's etymologies were replaced, at which point the book took on the appearance of a modern-day dictionary. By then Webster's philosophies had been removed, but his place in American history was secure.

Following the publication of the dictionary, Webster's devotion to hard work continued. In 1832 his *History of the United States* was published, and in 1834 he published his amended version of the King James Bible. This work, more than any other, held the deepest meaning for the septuagenarian. Even after its completion, however, Webster remained a prolific writer his final ten years, most often as a political and philosophical contributor to newspapers.

In some ways Webster's career is difficult to analyze. As he aged he lost faith in the people's ability to govern themselves in judicious fashion. Always he yearned for a system which placed political power in the hands of the educated elite. Not unlike many of his Federalist contemporaries, he

viewed the Constitution as an instrument of control. At some point, however, it seems clear that Webster was disabused of the idea that America could fulfill its utopian promise. When this happened, he became more fervent in the belief that a commitment to Christian doctrine was the only hope for political, educational, and moral growth in America.

Regardless of Webster's views, his importance to early America should not be underestimated. One of the most prolific writers in American history, he made important contributions in education, science, politics, and language. Like so many writers before and after him, his goal was to influence and to educate. What separates Webster, however, was his belief that in grasping the meanings of words, a better understanding of language would be achieved and result in some measure of control over the people where it mattered most: in politics and religion.

Biographies:
Ervin C. Shoemaker, *Noah Webster: Pioneer of Learning* (New York: Columbia University Press, 1936);
Richard Rollins, *The Long Journey of Noah Webster* (Philadelphia: University of Pennsylvania Press, 1980);
Richard J. Moss, *Noah Webster* (Boston: Twayne, 1984).

References:
Robert Keith Leavitt, *Noah's Ark, New England Yankees and The Endless Quest* (Springfield, Mass.: G. & C. Merriam, 1947);
E. Jennifer Monaghan, *A Common Heritage: Noah Webster's Blue-Black Speller* (Guilford, Conn.: Archon Books, 1983);
Arthur Schlesinger, *Prelude to Independence* (Boston: Northeastern University Press, 1980);
Fred Siebert, Theodore Peterson, and Wilbur Schramm, *Four Theories of the Press* (Chicago: University of Illinois Press, 1978);
Siebert, Peterson, and Schramm, *Picturesque Word Origins From Webster's New International Dictionary* (Springfield, Mass.: G. & C. Merriam, 1933).

Papers:
Noah Webster's papers are held, in part, at the Sterling Memorial Library at Yale University, the New York Public Library, and the Library of Congress.

Daniel K. Whitaker

(13 April 1801-24 March 1881)

Patt Foster Roberson
Southern University

MAJOR POSITIONS HELD: Editor and publisher, *Southern Literary Journal and Monthly Magazine* (1835-1837); *Southern Quarterly Review* (1842-1847); *Whitaker's Magazine: The Rights of the South* (1850); *Whitaker's Southern Magazine*, merged with *Southern Eclectic* in 1853 (1851-1854); *New Orleans Monthly Review* (1874-1876); *Southern Quarterly Review* (1879-1880).

BOOKS: *Questions, Adapted to the Arithmetic of S. F. Lacroix* (New Bedford, Mass.: B. Lindsey, 1821);

An Oration Pronounced at New Bedford, Mass., February 22, 1823. On the Anniversary of the Birth of Washington (Boston: Printed by R. M. Peck, 1823);

The Unity and Supremacy of God the Father, a Sermon Delivered in the Second Independent Church, Charleston, 22 April 1826, Published at the Request of the Charleston Unitarian Book Society (Charleston, S.C.: Printed by W. Riley, 1826);

Christian Perseverance; a Sermon Delivered in the Second Independent Church in Charleston, S.C., December 23, 1827 (Charleston, S.C.: Charleston Unitarian Book Society, 1828);

The Claims of Agriculture to be Regarded as a Distinct Science; an Address Delivered in Charleston, Before the Agricultural Society of South Carolina, August 20th, 1833 (Charleston, S.C.: Printed by A. F. Miller, 1833);

Sidney's Letters to William E. Channing, D.D., Occasioned by His Letter to Hon. Henry Clay, on the Annexation of Texas to the United States (Charleston, S.C.: Printed by E. C. Councell, 1837);

An Eulogy on the Late Washington Irving: Delivered by Appointment, Before the Washington Raven Club, December 22, 1859; Repeated, By Request, Before the Washington Art Association, the 20th February, 1860 (Washington, D.C., 1860).

Edgar Allan Poe once wrote that Daniel K. Whitaker was one of the best essayists in North America and in the foremost rank of elegant writ-

ers. Upon Whitaker's death, the *New Orleans Daily Picayune* ran a page-one story on 26 March 1881 which said in part, "He was a thorough classical scholar, a student throughout a long life, devoted to diligent inquiry, and fond of analyzing political and historical problems. He was a writer of rare merit."

Daniel Kimball Whitaker was born in Sharon, Massachusetts, to the Reverend Jonathan and Mary Kimball Whitaker. He was the second of ten children. His father was a Harvard graduate and Congregationalist minister. Whitaker's studies began at home under his father's tutelage. He subsequently attended Bradford Academy on the Merrimac River, then Derby Academy, Hingham, Massachusetts. His namesake uncle, the Reverend Daniel Kimball, also a Harvard graduate and, for a time, a Latin tutor at Harvard, served as Whitaker's teacher, after which Whitaker spent three years at Andrew Phillips' Academy, Andover, Massachusetts. At the academy's anniversary exhibition he was invited to deliver the Latin Salutatory Oration, the first pupil ever to be so honored.

He earned a bachelor of arts degree with honors from Harvard University in 1820 and a master's degree in 1823. His favorite subjects were the belles lettres, Greek, Latin, logic, moral and intellectual philosophy, politics, and rhetoric. In 1819 he won a Boylston gold medal for a dissertation, "The Literary Character of Dr. Samuel Johnson." John Quincy Adams and Daniel Webster were among the judges when Whitaker won a Bowdoin gold medal for oratory in 1820. He then studied theology under the Reverend Dr. Richmond in Dorchester, Massachusetts. Upon completion of the course, the Bridgewater (Massachusetts) Association of Divines awarded him a license to preach the gospel. In New Bedford, Massachusetts, he edited the *Christian Philanthropist,* a periodical devoted to literature and religion, from May 1822 to May 1823.

Having suffered continued frail health since childhood, he was advised by the family physi-

SOUTHERN LITERARY JOURNAL.

VOL. I.]   SEPTEMBER, 1835.   [No. 1.

CONDITION AND PROSPECTS OF AMERICAN LITERATURE.

THE influence of a popular national literature upon the social and political condition of those among whom it exists, is correctly regarded as of the highest importance. In a country like our own, where the sovereign power, in practice no less than in theory, resides in the people, it is necessary that the people should be intelligent. On this foundation only can the fabric of our institutions firmly rest. On this account, our country requires for its highest prosperity, a popular literature of a peculiar kind; a literature deserving the name of American, alike in its range of subjects, and its tone of feeling.

The intellectual history of the United States is singular, and almost unprecedented. Other nations have emerged, step by step, from barbarism, and, in the course of centuries, obtained successive heights of mental advancement. But we, from our earliest period of colonial existence, have possessed a share in the intelligence of older communities. With English frames and English courage, our forefathers bore across the Atlantic, English manners, civilization and literature. True, the lighter graces of poetry and fiction were not held in high regard either by the stern puritans of the North, or the first hardy adventurers of the South. Yet there was an intellectual spirit among our early settlers—an intellectual spirit like the men in whom it existed, of a vigorous growth, able to encounter successfully the dangers of migration to a foreign shore. The language too, of English literature was theirs; and as their first arduous toil gave place to a period of greater quiet, and the village rose where the forest had stood, the treasures of gifted minds beyond the Atlantic were received and appreciated.

But in that colonial state, few productions of original genius could be expected to appear. Forming a portion of the British Empire, the colonies had no separate character to maintain. All that they could contribute to the rich stores of English literature would be too unimportant to attract notice, when placed beside the works of their more favoured brethren. The colonies were too poor to encourage genius in its higher departments; and thus their situation excluded the influence of those motives, which have been found most powerful in exciting to mental activity—the hope of personal wealth and fame, and the ambition of adding to the glory of their country.

But our separation from England was at length effected, and the United States commenced their independent existence; between three and four millions of people, with half a continent to divide among them. The spirit of

1

First page of Whitaker's assessment of the state of American literature in the inaugural issue of his first magazine

cian in late 1823 to move to a less harsh climate. His father accompanied him, and on the journey south young Whitaker lectured and preached meaningful, impressive discourses and sermons. Large audiences gathered to hear him in New York City; Philadelphia; Washington, D.C.; Baltimore; Richmond and Petersburg, Virginia; Raleigh and Fayetteville, North Carolina; Cheraw, Camden, and Charleston, South Carolina; Savannah, Milledgeville, and Augusta, Georgia. In Charleston he served as the summer replacement for the Reverend Dr. Gilman, and the congregation subsequently honored him by publishing two of his sermons. He was instrumental in establishing a congregation and building a church in Augusta, where he preached for a year before illness forced him to leave the ministry permanently. He returned to his family, who by then had moved to South Carolina.

In 1828, after regaining his health, Whitaker married Mary H. Firth, the widow of a planter-physician and for ten years raised cotton and rice, working two large plantations with sixty-two slaves in St. Paul's Parish, south of Charleston. His health seemed to improve with outdoor work. Through other planters he was invited to join the State Agricultural Society of South Carolina, the oldest such society in the United States, having been founded in 1785. Whitaker presented an address to the society in August 1833 entitled "The Claims of Agriculture to be Regarded as a Distinct Science," proposing that the undervalued science of agriculture should be a separate area of education and that "some opulent individual" should endow a college with a professorship of agriculture. The society published this discourse, and it was republished in the *Southern Agriculturist,* one of the oldest of the regional farm magazines, in three segments (October, November, and December 1833) under the editorship of John D. Legaré. Georgia and South Carolina were soon thereafter to make agriculture a separate part of the college curriculum.

Life as a gentleman planter gradually became tiresome, and Whitaker's interests turned to the study of law. He trained under the guidance of a prominent South Carolina attorney, James L. Petigru, passed the bar examination, and became a partner with John Lyde Wilson, former governor of South Carolina. In 1832, as chairman of a committee of citizen-planters in St. Paul's Parish, he wrote several nullification resolutions that were adopted by the committee and published in the *Charleston Mercury.* Over the years he made frequent contributions to newspapers, including the *Charleston Courier, Charleston News, National Intelligencer* (Washington, D.C.), and *New Orleans Times.*

Whitaker became a member of the Literary and Philosophical Society of South Carolina when Joel R. Poinsett served as president. The society's members were renowned scholars from various professions in Charleston. In 1835, under the patronage of this society, he proposed the publication of a magazine, the *Southern Literary Journal and Monthly Magazine* which he subsequently founded, wrote for, and edited. Another magazine, the *Southern Review,* edited by the two Stephen Elliots (father and son) and Hugh Swinton Legaré, had just folded. Whitaker proposed the new magazine as an avenue for the expression of opinion by the same group of southern literary figures who had published in the *Southern Review.*

On the first page of the first number of the *Southern Literary Journal* Whitaker wrote, "The influence of a popular national literature upon the social and political condition of those among whom it exists, is correctly regarded as of the highest importance. In a country like our own, where the sovereign power, in practice no less than in theory, resides in the people, it is necessary that the people should be intelligent. On this foundation only can the fabric of our institutions firmly rest. On this account, our country requires for its highest prosperity, a popular literature of a peculiar kind; a literature deserving the name of American, alike in its range of subjects, and its tone of feeling."

Whitaker editorialized in a column entitled "From Our Arm-Chair." In the first number he compared the *Southern Literary Journal* to a chair: "It is not a rocking-chair, but is planted firmly on the floor upon its four legs, as if to indicate that the position of an editor should be a steady one—that he should not be always bobbing up and down like a man rocking himself to sleep after a hearty dinner. Neither is it a trundle-chair, which may be made to change places at the pleasure of every whimsical and capricious person who may wish to see it put in motion. Neither is it a high-backed, well-stuffed, old-fashioned easy-chair, fit only for an invalid who has a headache.... Neither is it a professor's chair from which he reads lectures, nor a chairman's chair in which he presides at literary, political, commercial, or agricultural meetings; but simply an editor's chair constructed after the most approved fashion."

Whitaker invited contributions dealing with "the customs, opinions, peculiarities, and general tone of thinking" in the South. This publication, "projected at the South, and chiefly supported by the citizens of the South, will, at all times, breathe a Southern spirit, and sustain a strictly Southern character." The *Southern Literary Journal* was printed by James S. Burges in Charleston and ran from September 1835 until December 1838, at first with sixty-four pages, later eighty. The last number under Whitaker's editorship appeared in August 1837, after which Whitaker relinquished control to Bartholomew Rivers Carroll, who served as editor until December 1838. The demise of the *Southern Literary Journal* has been attributed to the rise of the *Southern Literary Messenger,* which was founded in 1834 and estab-

FROM OUR ARM-CHAIR.

EDITOR'S INTRODUCTORY.—Well! we are, at length, fairly seated, and, in the first place, owe an apology to our good friends and patrons for not having appeared before. We regret that we have no other than a very stale one to offer, and one which has been nearly 'used up' at barbecues and political dinners, viz. 'that circumstances entirely beyond our control' have hitherto deprived us of the eagerly anticipated pleasure of paying our personal respects to you. We now make our bow to the public, and would more particularly express our warmest thanks to you, sir—and to you, madam—and to you, miss—and to you—and to you—and to you—for the very kind efforts which you have, up to this day, exerted in our humble behalf. To one and all of you we would say, that if you remember us, and are glad to see us, the recognition and the pleasure are reciprocal. We greet you with most heartfelt gratitude and the kindest wishes. We hope, in a short time, to be better acquainted with you all, than we even now are. By frequent interviews seasoned with good humor, and evincing a desire to please, we trust that this object may be fully accomplished, and that, at last, a mutual friendship and esteem, and a thoroughly good understanding may be established between us.

And now to proceed, without further remark, to the business before us. Our first task, in regular order, is a description of our *sella curulis*—the chair itself that we occupy. This, like most articles of the kind constructed either 'for ornament or use,' is made of wood, and does not differ very materially either in form, dimensions, or general appearance, from the large arm-chairs that are to be seen in the libraries and studies of most of the literary loungers of the present century. To those, however, who have never ventured to penetrate the *sanctum sanctorum* of one of our modern literati, we very cheerfully furnish a more particular description of it. We will, in this description, pursue the ingenious course of some divines, who first tell us what happiness is not, and then what it is. In like manner, we will begin by informing inquirers what our arm-chair is not, and afterwards what it is. Well, then, it is not a rocking-chair, but is planted firmly on the floor upon its four legs, as if to indicate that the position of an editor should be a steady one—that he should not be always bobbing up and down like a man rocking himself to sleep after a hearty dinner. Neither is it a trundle-chair, which may be made to change places at the pleasure of every whimsical and capricious person who may wish to see it put in motion. Neither is it a high-backed, well-stuffed, old-fashioned easy-chair, fit only for an invalid who has a headache. Neither is it a riding-chair to go abroad in, it being, on the contrary, always housed in the most retired apartment of our domicil. Neither is it a professor's chair from which he reads lectures, nor a governor's chair of state in which he appears on great occasions—nor a chairman's chair in which he presides at literary, political, commercial, or agricultural meetings; but simply an editor's arm-chair, constructed after the most approved fashion. To its nether part is affixed a drawer divided into two apartments, in one of which is deposited pure white paper, and in the

First page of Whitaker's "arm-chair" editorial in the first issue of the Southern Literary Journal

lished its reputation under the editorship of Edgar Allan Poe from 1835 to 1837.

Times were harsh, and a more solemn publication seemed appropriate to deal with literary and political issues. Again the Literary and Philosophical Society of South Carolina supported him, and in January 1842, with a subscription list worth sixteen thousand dollars, Whitaker founded, edited, and commenced publication of the *Southern Quarterly Review* in New Orleans. It had been decided to publish the journal in New Orleans, instead of Charleston, in order to capture a larger circulation in the growing South and Southwest. Benjamin Jenkins was its first printer. After the first number, however, the place of publication moved to Charleston, where it remained until 1855. It moved again in 1856 to Columbia, South Carolina, where it was published until 1857.

Whitaker's lead article in the first number concerned itself with the newspaper and periodical press. He called the newspaper "the greatest agent in promoting civilization known to modern times" and said, "How dull and stupid a city or a village must be, where there is no newspaper!" He discussed abuses of the press in publishing anything untrue, whether false statements, erroneous opinions, or "the withholding of the truth, by partial representations of acknowledged facts, and the addition to the truth of false and extraneous matter, not true, and the employment of the truth for purposes calculated to disturb the public peace." He thought the interests of literature and science could not be represented fully and thoroughly in a newspaper already crowded with advertisements, shipping news, and legislative proceedings, and furthermore, because ideas and arguments are lost in serialization.

Where the newspaper is lacking, the periodical press saves the day, whereupon Whitaker gives "a passing glance at the character and fortunes of the leading periodicals," including the *Knickerbocker, Southern Literary Messenger, New England Magazine, United States Magazine and Democratic Review, Hunt's Merchant's Magazine and Commercial Review, Graham's Magazine, Lady's Book, Magnolia, Augusta Mirror, Western Monthly Magazine, North American Review, American Quarterly Review, New York Review, Southern Review, Boston Review, Boston Christian Examiner,* and the *Biblical Repertory.* He concludes the article with an explanation of the commencement of the *Southern Quarterly Review,* "to protect the rights of our Southern soil from invasion, and to promote the cause of learning, arts and literature among us."

The *Southern Quarterly Review* appeared in January, April, July, and October, in two volumes and four numbers a year. The first number ended with a quarterly list of new publications of interest to subscribers in the fields of biography, drama, education, history, law, medicine, natural science, poetry, theology, and travel. In 1846 Whitaker claimed a circulation of two thousand, but subscribers were so slow in paying that he was ten thousand dollars in debt. Whitaker served as editor until 1847, followed by J. Milton Clapp from 1847 to 1849; William Gilmore Simms, 1849 to 1855; and James H. Thornwell, 1856 to 1857. In February 1847 Whitaker sold the publication to Simms for six or seven thousand dollars, according to the July

1850 *DeBow's Review,* partly because of sagging subscriptions and partly because of the readers' dissatisfaction with Whitaker's criticism of John C. Calhoun in the October 1846 number. The new editors carried on until the outbreak of the Civil War, when the *Southern Quarterly Review* ceased publication.

Following the death of his first wife, with whom he had two sons, Whitaker married Mary Scrimzeour Furman Miller, daughter of the Reverend Samuel Furman, of the High Hills of Santoe, South Carolina, in 1848. She was a celebrated writer of fiction and poetry, and the widow of John Miller, advocate of Edinburgh, Scotland, and the queen's attorney general for the British West Indies. They had six children. With her he founded and edited *Whitaker's Magazine: The Rights of the South* for seven numbers in 1850 in Charleston. From 1851 to 1853 he published *Whitaker's Southern Magazine* in Columbia. This publication was merged in August 1853 with the *Southern Eclectic,* which Whitaker edited in Augusta during 1853 and 1854, at first assisted by J. H. Fitten and later on his own.

Under President James Buchanan's administration Whitaker worked as a government employee in Washington, D.C., until South Carolina seceded. He then moved to Richmond and worked in the Confederate government post office and in the War Office. He left Richmond on the day it was evacuated by Confederate troops and journeyed to New Orleans in January 1866. For about eighteen months he worked on the *New Orleans Times* as associate editor. He was corresponding secretary of the New Orleans Academy of Sciences and edited the *New Orleans Monthly Review* at irregular intervals from 1874 to 1876.

The first article in the first issue of the *New Orleans Monthly Review,* appearing in April 1874, was Whitaker's "Editor's Salutatory," which contained his editorial philosophy. He wrote, "In the sphere of literature no sensation is ever produced by plodders, and every number of a magazine that expects to lead opinion, and every article in it, must possess something original, something brilliant, something captivating. Its learning must be rich and varied, its suggestions timely, its criticisms trenchant and just, and its style terse. There must not be too much philosophy, too much poetry, nor too much fiction, but a judicious and spirited intermingling of each in its pages. The imagination is sometimes to be approached, oftener the judgment, the passions never, except when indignation has ceased to be a fault and becomes a duty."

He thought his aversion to procrastination explained his determination to start a magazine at this time: "The difficulties which the literary adventurer encounters, in starting a Monthly Review in New Orleans, in these disastrous times, is readily admitted, but life is full of difficulties, before which the courageous mind will not give way, but only summon up superior skill, and put forth greater strength than usual, for their removal.... The conductors of the Daily, Weekly, Monthly and Quarterly press have duties imposed upon them in this crisis, of a more serious character than ever before devolved on them. It is no time for excuses or faint-heartedness.... It is only necessary that rights should be maintained, and wrong rectified, and, these ends attained, that we should employ every effort, ply every oar, stretch every nerve, and spread every sail, that can waft us to the future."

The July 1875 issue began with Whitaker's article "What Do We Read?" to which he answered, newspapers. He then criticized newspaper reporters: "Reporters should be compelled to write according to the rules of grammar, to keep their private opinions private, to submit their work to the inspection of judicious, critical authority before it goes to press."

Whitaker, with L.L.D. after his name, was shown as editor and proprietor of the *New Orleans Monthly Review*. W. A. Weed, of New Orleans, was the printer. Advertising rates were $20 for an inside full page, $12 for a half, and $7 for a quarter page. The inside cover cost $25 for a full page; $15, half; and $8, quarter. An outside full page cost $30; outside half, $20; outside quarter, $12. Business card size was $5. The cost of a subscription was "$5 per annum, payable invariably in advance." Clubs could get bulk subscriptions at five copies for $20.

A prospectus appeared on the inside back cover of the first number of volume 2 in which Whitaker states, "The objects to which this 'Monthly Review' is devoted, are Literature, Science, Industry, Government, and the Fine Arts. To the best thinkers and ablest writers of the South, irrespective of parties, it supplies an opportunity for the expression of their 'well considered views' on these subjects. To the commercial community, it affords a favorable advertising medium, on reasonable terms." The magazine ceased publication in 1876. Whitaker tried to bring it back as the *New Orleans Quarterly Review*

with a few numbers in 1878. Another attempt was made when he republished the latter as a new series of the old *Southern Quarterly Review* during 1879-1880.

A prospectus was printed in the first issue of the new *Southern Quarterly Review* that appeared in January 1879. In it Whitaker wrote:

> The establishment of a work representing the literature and intelligence of the Southern and Western Portion of the Union, in the able and thorough discussion of all great questions connected with literature, commerce, government, art and science, was never more important than at the present period, when the country, emerging from the results of the late fearful and herculean contest, is preparing to make new and extraordinary efforts.
>
> With a view to these objects, the subscriber projected the *New Orleans Monthly Review;* subsequently the *New Orleans Quarterly*. The occurrence of yellow fever in that metropolis having prevented its continuance there during the past summer, the undersigned has decided to recommence this Quarterly under the style and title of the work formerly established and edited by him, viz: "The Southern Quarterly Review," to be issued in the city of Louisville, Kentucky.

A notice to subscribers followed which explained the delay in the appearance of the January number as due to the severe illness of the editor. Subscribers to the *New Orleans Quarterly* would receive the new *Southern Quarterly Review* as publication of the *New Orleans Quarterly* was suspended during the epidemic. It was printed at the Masonic Widows and Orphans' Home in Louisville. Subscriptions were four dollars a year, payable in advance.

In this first number of the new series of the *Southern Quarterly Review* Whitaker wrote the lead article, titled "The Scotch Element in English Literature," which recognized Scottish authors and philosophers for their contributions to nineteenth-century literature. "Most of these have passed from a world which, so long as they lived, was illuminated by their discoveries, surprised by their varied attainments, encouraged by their lofty examples, electrified by their wit, and enriched by their elegant productions; and, on dying, they bequeathed to their contemporaries, and to their successors in all ages who speak the English tongue, the rich intellectual treasures they had accumulated."

The article closed with an anonymous tribute to the "distinguished excellence" of poet

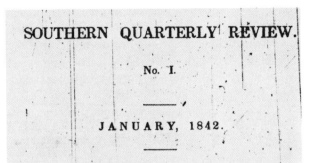

SOUTHERN QUARTERLY REVIEW.

No. I.

JANUARY, 1842.

ART. I—1. *The North American Review, No. CXIII.*
October 1841. Boston: Published by James Munroe &
Co.

2. *The New-York Review, No. XVIII. October* 1841.
New-York: Published for the Proprietor by Alexander
V. Blake.

3. *The United States' Magazine and Democratic Review, No. XLII. December* 1841. New-York: J. &
H. G. Langley.

4. *The Charleston Courier, No.* 11,954. *December* 1841.
Charleston, S. C.

5. *The Richmond Enquirer, No.* 62. *December,* 1841.
Richmond, Va.

WE have placed at the head of this article, the titles of
certain Reviews and Newspapers, as a text upon which to
offer some remarks upon the Newspaper and Periodical
Press of the United States.

The discovery of the Art of Printing about four hundred
years ago, gave rise to the publication of books, among
which the Bible, next the classical works of antiquity, next
the ponderous tomes of divines and schoolmen, and then
works of science and literature, were among the earlier
triumphs of the Art. No mode of publishing and giving
durability and almost immortality to the works of genius,

VOL. I.—NO 1.   1

66   *Currency and Exchanges.*   [Jan.

to this great, growing, interesting and prosperous emporium
of our country, where the voice of truth can be heard far and
wide, through the vallies and mountains of the whole
South, in order to promote and accomplish objects of great
weight and interest to the durability of our institutions, the
salvation of this dear region, the glory of the whole Union,
and the fame of American literature,—objects in which all
denominations of Christians, and all orders of men, may
cordially co-operate, and heartily aid us in promoting, with
all their ability.

And now, commending this work to the protection of that
Providence, without whose smiles all our efforts, however
ambitious, are vain, we proceed, after many toils and labors
expended in its establishment, to dedicate it to the citizens
of the Southern States in particular, and, more generally,
to the citizens of the United States, and, offering our grateful
acknowledgments to our patrons, we lay before them, and
commend to their generous clemency, the first number of
THE SOUTHERN QUARTERLY REVIEW.

ART. II.—1. *Message of the President of the United*
States, returning to the Senate with his objections the
bill entitled "An Act to Incorporate the Subscribers to
the Fiscal Bank of the United States," August 16,
1841.

2. *Message of the President, returning to the House of*
Representatives with his objections, the bill entitled
"An Act to provide for the better collection, safe keeping
and disbursement of the Public Revenue, by means of
a Corporation to be styled the Fiscal Corporation of the
United States," September 9, 1841.

The documents, of which the titles are given above, have
every where produced a degree of interest which seems to
require some notice of the subject, beyond those contained
in the ephemeral publications of the passing hour. Every
individual in the community is dependant on commercial
interchange, in some of its various forms, for most of the
comforts, if not the actual necessaries of life. Custom,
founded on universal convenience, has established currency

First and last pages of Whitaker's introduction to his second magazine

Thomas Campbell, apparently written by Whitaker's wife Mary Scrimzeour Whitaker. A footnote by Whitaker followed the poetry, indicating that Campbell gave the writer, upon "hearing some of her verses recited, the compliment of being his 'spiritual daughter.' She is a South Carolinian by nativity, and favorably known as a poetess, novelist, and critic on both sides [of] the Atlantic." Mrs. Whitaker had been educated in Edinburgh and published her first poetry in Scotland under Campbell's guidance and support. A collection of her poems was published in Philadelphia in 1850. Mrs. Whitaker wrote often in her husband's publications, using the bylines M.S.W., Mrs. M.S.W., Mrs. M. S. Whitaker, and Author of "Albert Hastings," the latter being the title of a novel she wrote in 1867. This first number of the *Southern Quarterly Review* ended with an essay-review by Whitaker on two books about Shakespeare, one questioning the authorship of his plays and the other analyzing the system of his dramas.

Whitaker maintained a home and office in New Orleans. His daughter Lily C. Whitaker was educated in New Orleans and contributed poetry to the *Southern Quarterly* under Whitaker's direction.

As a young man Whitaker had been prejudiced against Catholicism; however, in 1878 he became a Roman Catholic and affiliated with St. Patrick's Church. He died on a visit to Houston on 24 March 1881, and his body was returned for burial in Washington Cemetery in New Orleans. Four of the ten pallbearers were gentlemen representing the Society of Leonites.

According to Frank Luther Mott, Whitaker was not well-thought-of by some of his colleagues: "Whether it was because his northern birth was resented in the editor of a magazine for Southerners, whether his northern 'hustle' was repellent to the more leisurely aristocracy with which he had to deal, or whether the trouble was simply an unpleasant personality, certain it is that Whitaker lacked that necessary quality of the successful editor which may be called personal magnetism."

Editor Edwin L. Jewell in his *Crescent City Illustrated* (1874) said of Whitaker, "As a writer, he is distinguished by a style critically correct, and in argumentative powers is rarely surpassed. A total absence of affectation assists in establishing the cogency of his reasoning and the logical accuracy of his deductions. Few care to measure swords with him in a fairly conducted argument. His blows fall with persevering force, and, even when diffuse, as he sometimes is, he seldom fails in establishing any point for which he contends."

When the *Daily Picayune* published the news of Whitaker's death on 26 March 1881, it stated in part, "The value of his editorial work was, perhaps, best shown in his conduct of the Southern Quarterly Review, printed in Charleston, half a century ago.... Prof. Whitaker was a friend of Calhoun, Toombs, Buchanan, Stephens, Marcy and Douglas. During more than 50 years he was well known and thoroughly respected throughout the South. His life was a noble one."

References:

Robert Bain, Joseph M. Flora, and Louis D. Rubin, Jr., *Southern Writers: A Biographical Dictionary* (Baton Rouge: Louisiana State University Press, 1979), pp. 481-482;

Richard J. Calhoun, "Literary Criticism in Southern Periodicals: 1828-1860," Ph.D. dissertation, University of North Carolina, Chapel Hill, 1959;

Eugene Current-Garcia, "Criticism and the Problem of Literary Expression in a Democratic Society," Ph.D. dissertation, Harvard University, 1947;

Edwin L. Jewell, ed., *Jewell's Crescent City Illustrated: The Commercial, Social, Political and General History of New Orleans, Including Biographical Sketches of Its Distinguished Citizens* (New Orleans, 1874), pp. 159-160;

Frank Luther Mott, *A History of American Magazines,* 5 volumes (Cambridge, Mass.: Harvard University Press, 1938-1968), I: 383, 664-665, 721-725;

Albert L. Rabinovitz, "The Criticism of French Novels in American Magazines, 1830-1860," Ph.D. dissertation, Harvard University, 1941;

Edward R. Rogers, "Southern Periodicals prior to 1860," Ph.D. dissertation, University of Virginia, 1902;

Frank W. Ryan, "The Southern Quarterly Review, 1842-57: A Study in Thought and Opinion in the Old South," Ph.D. dissertation, University of North Carolina, Chapel Hill, 1956.

Nathaniel Parker Willis

(20 January 1806-20 January 1867)

John J. Pauly
University of Tulsa

See also the Willis entries in *DLB 3: Antebellum Writers in New York and the South* and *DLB 59: American Literary Critics and Scholars, 1800-1850.*

MAJOR POSITIONS HELD: Editor, *American Monthly Magazine* (1829-1831); coeditor, *New York Mirror* (1831-1839); coeditor, *Corsair* (1839-1840); coeditor, *Home Journal*, originally called *National Press* (1846-1864).

SELECTED BOOKS: *Sketches* (Boston: S. G. Goodrich, 1827);

Fugitive Poetry (Boston: Pierce & Williams, 1829);

Poem, Delivered Before the Society of United Brothers, at Brown University on the day Preceding Commencement, September 6, 1831 (New York: Harper, 1831);

Melanie and Other Poems (London: Saunders & Otley, 1835; New York: Saunders & Otley, 1837);

Pencillings by the Way, 3 volumes (London: J. Macrone, 1835; Philadelphia: Carey, Lea & Blanchard, 1836);

Inklings of Adventure, 3 volumes (New York: Saunders & Otley, 1836; London: Saunders & Otley, 1836);

A l'abri, or The Tent Pitch'd (New York: Colman, 1839); reprinted as *Letters from under a Bridge* (London: G. Virtue, 1840; New York: Morris & Willis, 1844);

Tortesa the Usurer (New York: Colman, 1839);

Bianca Visconti; or The Heart Overtasked (New York: Colman, 1839);

Romance of Travel, Comprising Tales of Five Lands (New York: Colman, 1840);

American Scenery, 2 volumes (London: J. S. Virtue, 1840);

Loiterings of Travel (London: Longman, Orme, Brown, Green & Longmans, 1840);

Poems of Passion (New York: Mirror Library, 1843);

The Sacred Poems of N. P. Willis (New York: Mirror Library, 1844);

The Lady Jane and Other Humorous Poems (New York: Morris & Willis, 1844);

The Poems, Sacred, Passionate, and Humorous, of Nathaniel Parker Willis (New York: Clark & Austin, 1844; revised and enlarged, 1849);

Lectures on Fashion (New York: Mirror Library, 1844);

Dashes at Life with a Free Pencil (New York: Burgess, Stringer, 1845; London: Longman, Brown, Green & Longmans, 1845);

Poems of Early and After Years (Philadelphia: Carey & Hart, 1848);

349

Rural Letters and Other Records of Thought at Leisure (New York: Baker & Scribner, 1849);

People I Have Met; or, Pictures of Society and People of Mark, Drawn Under a Thin Veil of Fiction (Auburn: Alden & Beardsley/Rochester: Wanzer & Beardsley, 1849; London: H. G. Bohn, 1850);

Life Here and There; or, Sketches of Society and Adventure at Far-Apart Times and Places (New York: Baker & Scribner, 1850);

Hurry-graphs; or, Sketches of Scenery, Celebrities & Society, Taken from Life (Auburn & Rochester: Alden & Beardsley, 1851; London: H. G. Bohn, 1851);

Memoranda of the Life of Jenny Lind (Philadelphia: Peterson, 1851);

Summer Cruise in the Mediterranean (Auburn: Alden & Beardsley, 1853; London: T. Nelson, 1853);

Fun-Jottings; or, Laughs I Have Taken a Pen To (New York: Scribner, 1853);

Health Trip to the Tropics (New York: Scribner, 1853; London: Sampson, Low, 1854);

Famous Persons and Places (New York: Scribner, 1854; London: Ward & Lock, 1854);

Out-doors at Idlewild; or, The Shaping of a Home on the Banks of the Hudson (New York: Scribner, 1855);

The Rag Bag, a Collection of Ephemera (New York: Scribner, 1855);

Paul Fane; or, Parts of a Life Else Untold. A Novel (New York: Scribner/Boston: A. Williams, 1857; London: C. Clarke, 1857);

The Convalescent (New York: Scribner, 1859).

Collections: *The Complete Works of N. P. Willis* (New York: J. S. Redfield, 1846);

The Prose Works of N. P. Willis (Philadelphia: Carey & Hart, 1849);

Poems of Nathaniel Parker Willis, edited, with a memoir, by H. L. Williams (New York: Hurst, 1882);

The Poetical Works of N. P. Willis (London: Routledge, 1888).

PLAY PRODUCTIONS: *Bianca Visconti; or, The Heart Overtasked*, New York, Park Theatre, 25 August 1837;

Tortesa the Usurer, New York, National Theatre, 8 April 1839.

OTHER: *The Legendary, Consisting of Original Pieces, Principally Illustrative of American History, Scenery, and Manners*, 2 volumes, edited by Willis (Boston: S. G. Goodrich, 1828);

The Token: A Christmas and New Year's Present, edited by Willis (Boston: S. G. Goodrich, 1829);

The Opal: A Pure Gift for the Holy Days, edited by Willis (New York: J. C. Riker, 1844);

The Prose and Poetry of Europe and America, compiled by Willis and George Pope Morris (New York: Leavitt & Allen, 1845);

The Gem of the Season, for 1850, edited by Willis (New York: Leavitt, Trow, 1850);

Trenton Falls, Picturesque and Descriptive, edited by Willis (New York: Putnam, 1851).

During his own lifetime Nathaniel Parker Willis was widely recognized in Europe as well as the United States as one of the preeminent magazine writers and editors of his age. Today his literary achievements dim next to those of his contemporaries, such as Herman Melville, Nathaniel Hawthorne, and Edgar Allan Poe, whose work he often praised and encouraged. Yet, as journalist, travel writer, critic, raconteur, and celebrity, Willis appears time and again as one of his age's most notable writers.

Willis's grandfather, Nathaniel, founded the *Independent Chronicle* in Boston and a series of frontier newspapers in western Virginia. His father, Nathaniel Willis, was a noted clergyman who founded a series of publications, including the religious newspaper the *Boston Recorder* and the long-lived juvenile magazine *Youth's Companion*. Not surprisingly, then, the younger Willis received a strong, religiously oriented education. He attended the Boston Latin School in Andover, and then Yale, where he graduated in 1827.

Willis's literary career began at Yale, where he was eventually named class valedictorian poet. While still in school he regularly published his verse in the *Boston Recorder*. According to Henry Augustin Beers, Willis's first biographer, by graduation the boy had already achieved some note because "the suffrages of a few hundred readers in New York, Boston, New Haven, and Philadelphia, and the praises of a few dozen journals were enough to bestow fame." After graduation Willis toured Canada and New York State, producing his first set of travel sketches, which were published in 1828 as "Leaves from a Colleger's Album" in Samuel P. Goodrich's magazine *Legendary*. The following year Willis became editor of Goodrich's *Token*, an annual. Off and on throughout his career Willis would contribute to such annuals, which were often lavish volumes combining literature with expensive illustrations.

Willis in a portrait by Chester Harding

In April 1829, only a year and a half out of college, with little money or practical experience as an editor, Willis introduced the *American Monthly Magazine*. The two-page prospectus proclaimed his intention to focus on literary matters. He vowed to make his review interesting but not to descend to "ungentlemanly seasoning of personal abuse, or allusions to private differences." Willis warned his readers not to expect his new magazine to perform at the level of its English counterparts. (Magazine historian Frank Luther Mott wrote that the *American Monthly* was modeled on Englishman Thomas Campbell's *New Monthly Magazine*.) Perhaps wishing to temper the financial demands of his contributors as well, Willis also warned that his magazine could not afford to pay handsomely, as English periodicals could, because only one or two thousand Americans might subscribe, "and the profit arising from such a subscription is necessarily inadequate to an expensive establishment."

Willis distinguished his editorial stance from that of many partisan journals of the Jacksonian era. He promised not to take sides in politics. "Our pages," he said, "will be open to fair and

manly discussion on every political topic, and by men of every party." Willis said he aimed to avoid a "licentious tone" and to discuss political questions "in their higher and more general bearings."

The early issues of *American Monthly Magazine* showed Willis's heavy emphasis on literature. The seventy-six-page first issue carried six book reviews, five poems, and essays on "The Republic of Letters," "Aborigines of America," and "Unwritten Music" (a meditation on the sounds of nature), as well as two pages of news and notices of recent publications. The format of the *American Monthly* changed slightly in the first few months, but mostly in ways that made it even more consistent with Willis's literary interests. Starting with the fourth issue, Willis introduced a new feature, "The Editor's Table," in which he exuberantly and unapologetically displayed his wide-ranging tastes and bon vivant sensibility. A typical Willis column contained several short, appreciative reviews, often with long quotations from the works under discussion. Such a style, which gradually replaced most of the individual, formal reviews, better suited Willis's role as an aficionado of literature who wished to share his enthusiasms with his fellow readers. Out of seventy-two pages per issue, "The Editor's Table" might occupy as many as thirty pages, suggesting how much of the *American Monthly* Willis produced himself. Beers claimed that Willis often wrote as many as forty pages of each issue, contributing everything from poems to tales to essays, book reviews, and travel sketches.

Although short news items disappeared altogether from the magazine after the first seven months, Willis continued to run long analyses of contemporary politics. *American Monthly* published profiles of well-known politicians, such as Henry Clay and Daniel Webster, and of the preacher Lyman Beecher. (The rather routine character of these particular three sketches suggests that Willis chose his subjects with an eye on the marketplace, for they were all popular figures with his New England readers.) Even though it avoided harping partisan criticism, the magazine occasionally took strong stands on important reform questions of the day. For example, a January 1830 article disagreed with President Jackson's policy of removing Indian tribes, such as the Cherokees, from lands given them under treaties and also took issue with the feeble attempts of the *North American Review* to justify that policy. A December 1830 article com-

First and last pages of the magazine Willis cofounded with T. O. Porter in response to what he perceived to be the inequities of British copyright laws

plained about the brutal treatment of animals in America, particularly horses. Sometimes Willis lent his journal to exchanges of opinion on controversial issues. A writer in the September 1829 issue, for example, complained about the "gratuitous administration of justice," vigorously attacking lawyers for defending only the rich and for making laws too complex. The writer proposed public financing of licensed lawyers, who would be paid a standard fee. The next issue featured a four-page response defending current practices. Willis even allowed opinions with which he disagreed. When a contributor criticized a report absolving a Boston theater of charges of immorality, Willis printed the critique despite his ardent love for theater, and he invited readers to respond to the article if they wished.

Willis occasionally used the columns of the *American Monthly* to defend himself against attacks by literary rivals and critics. That criticism was often the result of Willis's self-conscious attempts to devise a social and literary persona for himself. Reared in a strict Calvinist household, he nonetheless cultivated a taste for things urbane, amusing, and frivolous. According to Beers, Willis's love of the theater and absence from church (and apparent lack of penitence about either) led his Park Street congregation to excommunicate him in 1829.

Willis's dandyism and self-conscious posturing, though it offered him a distinctive and widely appealing literary voice, drew vehement attacks from Boston newspapers. For a time he bandied opinions with Joseph T. Buckingham, editor of the *Boston Courier*, one of the most influential Whig papers of its age. Willis's wit often defended him well. In the October 1830 issue, for example, Willis wondered whether the "mild and genial criticisms" of Buckingham were not, in reality, "bitter and envious." He asked "if even the open and upright look with which the kind old Scissors meets you, were to look plaguily like one's idea of a certain gentleman whom it is not polite to mention."

Throughout his career Willis would tangle with other editors and writers as well, including the editor of the *New-England Galaxy*, William Joseph Snelling, whom Willis dubbed "Smelling Joseph"; Capt. Frederick Marryat, whose criticisms nearly led Willis into a duel; and the writer Lydia Maria Child. Years later Willis would renege on promises to pay William Thackeray for letters to his magazine the *Corsair* and incur the undying wrath of that English author.

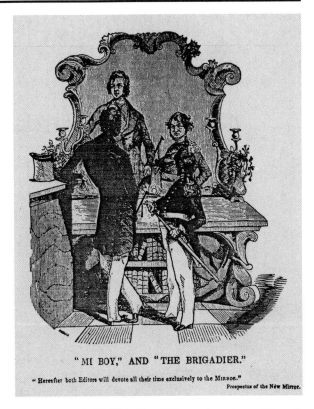

"MI BOY," AND "THE BRIGADIER."

"Hereafter both Editors will devote all their time exclusively to the Mirror."

Prospectus of the New Mirror.

An 1845 spoof of Willis's "dandy" image in an issue of Broadway Journal. *Willis's companion in the cartoon is George Pope Morris, "the Brigadier."*

In general the magazine displayed the light touch that Willis valued in his own work. He advised would-be contributors to be "brief and crisp" and to avoid being "too grave." He urged a gentlemanly stance that would "avoid the familiar impudence and slang into which smartness so easily degenerates." Though he paid little, Willis nonetheless attracted contributions from such talented young writers as Richard Hildreth, J. L. Motley, Rufus Dawes, Albert Pike, Park Benjamin, and Lydia Sigourney.

Willis proved less able at the business aspects of magazine publishing, however. When *American Monthly* folded in summer 1831, it was three thousand dollars in debt. Willis signed over the subscription list to the *New York Mirror*, becoming an associate editor of that publication and beginning a collaboration with George P. Morris that would span five different publications over thirty years. The *Mirror* sent Willis to Europe, where he began to write the descriptive travel sketches that would eventually be collected in volumes such as *Pencillings by the Way* (1835) and *Inklings of Adventure* (1836). While at the *Mirror* Willis also reworked material from his *American Monthly* articles for his new, cosmopolitan, largely female New York City audience. Though Willis did not think highly enough of his *American Monthly* pieces to include them in collections of his work, many of the characters and ideas of later books and articles first appeared in those early tales, sketches, and editorials.

From time to time during his tenure at the *Mirror* Willis's jaunty style offended one or another group. Catholics complained of his irreverent travel notes on the Vatican, Britains of his gossipy whisperings about amorous aristocrats, and his fellow American editors of his apparent lack of good taste and breeding. Throughout such controversies Morris generally supported Willis. But in 1839, after Morris had apologized in print for a Willis article impugning Letitia E. Landon, a British contributor to the *Mirror*, Willis resigned.

In March 1839 he began publishing the *Corsair* with T. O. Porter, brother of William T. Porter, who had founded the popular sporting weekly *Spirit of the Times*. In the original prospectus the Willis-Porter journal was named the *Pirate* because it planned to reprint, without permission or payment, the most popular works from England and the Continent. The *Corsair* was in part Willis's response to an 1838 act by the English Parliament that refused copyright protection to American authors until the United States began protecting English authors. That law then affected few American writers, but Willis was one. Throughout the 1830s his work had appeared in such English magazines as *Metropolitan Monthly*, *Court Magazine*, and *New Monthly*, and his travel writing had won him a following overseas. Thus Willis proposed to retaliate by making the *Corsair* a symbol of the battle for copyright protection in the United States. In part, however, the *Corsair* seized upon publishing possibilities offered by recent improvements in transportation technology. Beers notes that Willis's magazine was only one of a series of weeklies, such as *Brother Jonathan* and *New World*, made feasible by the regular transatlantic steamship travel that began in 1838: "It was now possible to get the freshest supply from the London literary market within a fortnight, and the news of Europe before it was cold." The free and ready availability of quality foreign writing thus placed the *Corsair* in an odd position. Willis's magazine vociferously defended the need for copyright as a means to encourage indigenous American literature, but it apologetically excluded American writers from its own pages on the grounds that, relying as it did on free foreign

material, it saw no particular need to pay for any stories.

The *Corsair* described itself as "A Gazette of Literature, Art, Dramatic Criticism, Fashion and Novelty." In practice it emphasized news of the theater much more than *American Monthly* ever had. The first issue featured a passage from Willis's own new play, *Tortesa the Usurer* (1839). The magazine's home in New York City and the weekly deadlines also encouraged a more newsy, gossipy tone. Like later magazines that Willis would edit, the *Corsair* saw itself as the voice of the beau monde. It regularly reprinted local news items under the heading "Items from the Daily News of the Gayest Capital of the World" and, in a similar spirit, reprinted short snippets of foreign news under the heading "Plunderings by the Way."

From the beginning the financial base of the *Corsair* seemed shaky. The magazine's management said it had no plans to establish permanent agencies for soliciting subscriptions, though it did offer a twenty percent commission to canvassers "who transmit, with the name and residence of the subscriber, the amount of one year's subscription, deducting the commission." The *Corsair* refused to take part in exchanges with other American periodicals: "as all our 'plunderings' are from abroad, and as we have no time to open even a score of papers every morning, our friends will see that it [exchanging papers] amounts to an *entire gratuity* on our part, of five or six hundred numbers of the *Corsair* weekly." The marginal status of the operation even prompted ironic self-reflection in the magazine's own columns. The 23 March 1839 issue reprinted the following "Bill of Mortality among Periodicals for 1836-7-8" in its letters column:

Died, of uncollectable debts 2
---- of faint praise 4
---- of the editors' own contributions 1
---- of dishonesty in publishers 0
---- of virulent "original" poetry 3
---- of "fragments of unpublished novels" 2
---- of compliments to their "Americanism" .. 5
---- of imaginary lists of contributors 3
---- of reciprocating puffs 2
---- of a succession of new editors
        (epidemic) 6
---- of "to be continued" 5
---- of excessive "Lines to ----" 2
---- of unhappy marriages 7
---- of intemperance in the use of "Boz" 1

Willis's 12 November 1847 letter to Edgar Allan Poe (Richard Henry Stoddard, editor, The Works of Edgar Allan Poe, *volume 1, 1896)*

Willis commented, "If we are to swell the next [list] we trust we shall have invented a new disease to die by," and added, in a footnote, that in the list of magazine diseases "there is no case of plethora, either of the head or purse."

In May 1839 Willis left Porter in charge and sailed for England again; by March 1840 the *Corsair* had collapsed. But Willis's reputation was secure. He was perhaps the best-known magazine writer of his age, and during the 1840s his work continued to appear in well-known publications such as *Godey's*, *Graham's*, *Brother Jonathan*, and *Ladies' Companion*. In 1843 he reunited with Morris to found the *New Mirror*, and after that publication folded in 1846 he and Morris began the *Home Journal* (originally called the *National Press*), which he edited with Morris until 1864. In those last twenty-five years before his death in 1867 Willis continued to edit literary magazines and annuals, write stories and novels, and publish collections of his travel sketches and poetry.

Most modern commentaries on Willis's career attempt to fix his place in the canon of nineteenth-century American literature, assessing the influences on his work, his place as a minor Knickerbocker writer, and his influence as a literary critic. But in some ways his career, as much as that of any nineteenth-century American writer, illustrates the economics and editorial practices of antebellum publishing. Willis's career advanced alongside every major trend in the magazine business of his day. He was an outspoken participant in the movement for copyright protection. He was one of the first writers to devise a genteel, personal style to help lure a middle-class, female audience to magazines. He created

around himself an aura of celebrity that blurred the boundaries of his public and private identities. He may have been the very first writer in American history to live off the profits of his own writing and editing alone, and his work illustrates the literary strategies and compromises such a career has forever dictated. Though modern readers might find his writings mannered, giddy, or superficial, for better or worse Nathaniel Parker Willis was one of the progenitors of the modern professional writer.

Biography:

Henry Augustin Beers, *Nathaniel Parker Willis* (Boston: Houghton, Mifflin, 1885).

References:

Cortland P. Auser, *Nathaniel Parker Willis* (New York: Twayne, 1969);

Van Wyck Brooks, *The World of Washington Irving* (New York: Dutton, 1944);

William Charvat, *The Origins of American Critical Thought 1810-1835* (Philadelphia: University of Pennsylvania Press/London: Oxford University Press, 1936);

Frank Luther Mott, *A History of American Magazines*, 5 volumes (Cambridge: Oxford University Press, 1938-1968), I: 320-330, 356-358, 366, 384, 577-579, 808;

Edgar Allan Poe, "N. P. Willis," in *The Works of Edgar Allan Poe*, volume 7 (New York: Putnam & Armstrong, 1884);

John W. Rathbun, *American Literary Criticism, 1800-1860* (Boston: G. K. Hall, 1979);

Kendall Bernard Taft, *Minor Knickerbockers* (New York: American Book Co., 1947).

Frances Wright

(6 September 1795-13 December 1852)

Earl L. Conn
Ball State University

MAJOR POSITIONS HELD: Co-owner and editor in chief, *New Harmony Gazette* (1828), renamed *New Harmony and Nashoba Gazette, or Free Enquirer* and *Free Enquirer* (1829-1832).

BOOKS: *Views of Society and Manners in America—in a series of Letters from that Country to a Friend in England, During the Years 1818, 1819, 1820* (London: Longman, Hurt, Ress, Orme & Brown, 1821; New York: Bliss & White, 1821);

A Few Days in Athens—Being the Translation of a Greek Manuscript Discovered in Herculaneum (London: Longman, Hurt, Ress, Orme & Brown, 1822; New York: Bliss & White, 1825); expanded edition, with four additional chapters from *New Harmony Gazette* (New York: Matsell, 1835);

England the Civilizer: Her History Developed in Its Principles (London, 1848);

Biography, Notes, and Political Letters of Frances Wright D'Arusmont (Boston: Mendun, 1849).

PLAY PRODUCTION: *Altorf, a Tragedy*, New York, Park Theatre, 19 February 1819.

Frances Wright

Frances (Fanny) Wright was one of America's pioneers of what today would be called the woman's movement, as well as a social reformer and an advocate of free thinking. She conveyed her message from the lecture platform and through the publication of her writings, principally as a writer and editor of early American periodicals, and in books and collections of writings published both in the United States and in England.

Frances Wright was born on 6 September 1795 in Dundee, Scotland. Her father, James Wright, was a wealthy merchant but a person much in sympathy with the political liberalism of his day. Frances was orphaned by the age of two, and with her sister, Camilla, and a brother, Richard, she was cared for by maternal relatives. The brother was separated from his sisters and died

at fifteen in a military engagement against the French.

The sisters, meanwhile, had been taken to England under the care of their grandfather Gen. Duncan Campbell and a young aunt. Brought up amidst considerable wealth, Wright wrote in her autobiography that she constantly asked searching questions about the social conditions of her day and found that men seemed afraid of the truth. Her search for truth and its implications consumed the remainder of her life.

In her late teens she developed a strong interest in the United States as a country where her developing sense of social justice seemed not only possible but put into practice. She was only twenty-three when she and her younger sister sailed alone to the United States.

She was accepted into the society of New York City, and shortly after her arrival a play she had written earlier and brought with her was per-

357

formed at the Park Theatre. Titled *Altorf, a Trag-edy* (produced in 1819), the play centers on the Swiss war of independence during the fourteenth century. Its hero dies a tragic death at the end of the play, whose authorship was kept secret from the audience. According to the *New York Evening Post*, the play was exceptionally well received. "There was a greater share of applause than we have ever before witnessed. At every fall of the curtain between the acts, peals of approbation resounded through the House. . . ."

That success proved short-lived, however. The very next day New York City turned its attention to welcoming the hero of the hour, Gen. Andrew Jackson. After his departure Wright's play received two more presentations, but the audience was disappointing and her financial rewards were limited.

Soon her authorship of the play became common knowledge, but, because the play had offended a number of persons with its politics and morals, Wright became the subject of uncomplimentary discussion. After all, she was a young, unmarried woman who already had shocked public opinion through her apparent disregard for some of the social customs of the day, including being seen as the frequent companion of a young Irish soldier of fortune, Wolfe Tone.

Wright and her sister shortly thereafter left New York City on their trip to see the United States, which became the subject of her first book, *Views of Society and Manners in America—in a series of Letters from that Country to a Friend in England, During the Years 1818, 1819, 1820*, published in London in 1821. They traveled up the Hudson, then into the valley of the Mohawk River, and across to Lewiston on the Niagara River. They traveled into New England before going south to Philadelphia, New Jersey, and Washington, D.C. She returned to England in 1820, having compiled a great number of impressions and much information about the United States.

The book brought her immediate attention and a certain amount of fame. It quickly was translated into French and Dutch and even today is considered one of the important first books of travel about the United States. Her writing contains full descriptions of both the country and the people she encountered during her travels. She was especially struck and impressed with what she considered to be the kindly manners of the American people: "I verily believe that you might travel from the Canada frontier to the gulf of Mexico,

Painting of Wright as a resident of New Harmony, Indiana

or from the Atlantic to the Missouri, and never receive from a native born citizen a rude word, it being understood always that you never gave one." One account of finding an address in New York contains three incidents of persons not only providing directions but insisting on leaving their work upon perceiving her to be a stranger so they might walk with her toward her destination, making certain she did not make a wrong turn.

Perhaps it was these references coupled with her uncomplimentary statements about British actions in the War of 1812 which excited unfavorable comment among conservatives in England. However, the book was well received in the United States. For one thing it contained none of the critical tone which seemed to characterize the writing of other British contemporary travelers in the United States. She found herself enchanted with the land of political liberty, and her picture of the country is one long, glowing tribute to an idealized democratic society.

She also found herself encouraged by what she saw to be an enlightened view of women,

Drawing of the Nashoba community by resident Auguste Hervieu

whom she found held in high esteem and appreciated, enjoying a form of liberty which first startled but greatly pleased her. What she did not find for women, however, was any program of formal education. The advance of the nation could be "doubly accelerated when the education of women shall be equally a national concern with that of the other sex," Wright wrote. It was to this matter that she was to devote a considerable part of her attention for the remainder of her life.

But it was the political institutions of the country that particularly excited her interest. She found Americans to be politically well versed and able to talk with her in great detail about what was occurring in the administration of James Monroe. Equally important, they saw themselves as integrally involved in the affairs of the country. "I have observed, that it is usual for an American, in speaking of political matters to say *our* president does so and so; *we* passed, or shall bring forward, such a bill in Congress; *we* took such and such a measure with a view, &. To speak in short . . . I should say that it were impossible for a people to be more completely identified with their government, than are the Americans," she wrote.

The critique of her book which appeared in the *North American Review* was generally favorable but did note her conclusions were too sweeping and unwarranted and that the book's "principles are borrowed from the *London Quarterly*, the organ of government by influence and corruption, coercive and restrictive laws, every abomination practiced by the old governments of Europe." Perhaps what the book's publication chiefly accomplished for Wright, however, was the attention of prominent liberals in England and on the Continent. Among the latter was the Marquis de Lafayette, who wrote her expressing great interest in her work. Within a short time, Wright was in France preparing to meet the Revolutionary War hero, who had become a widower, at the family estate, LaGrange. There she spent much of the next three years in a developing friendship while she attempted to write a life of the general.

When the general was invited to visit the United States in 1824, and with his family distressed about her desire to become his adopted daughter, Wright's French visit came to an end. When the general left for the United States, Wright and her sister followed, apparently with the blessing of the Lafayette family after some form of reconciliation had been reached.

The general visited former presidents Thomas Jefferson and James Madison in Virginia, and Wright joined them, seeing the practice of slavery firsthand in the nation she idealized. She set out to eliminate slavery by establishing an experiment in the South in which slaves would gain their freedom through a program of cooperative labor, while their children were educated to better handle their own ensuing freedom. Her plans may have taken form after she had contact with Robert Owen in Washington. He was on his way to take charge of his utopian community at New Harmony, Indiana. In 1825 Wright purchased a large tract of land in Tennessee, which she called Nashoba, and there established her "colony" of slaves working for their freedom.

Her next step in her efforts to bring universal education and freedom of thought and action was to become co-owner and editor in chief of the *New Harmony Gazette* at the Owen experiment in Indiana. Under its new editor, the renamed weekly periodical (*New Harmony and Nashoba Gazette, or Free Enquirer*) promised to devote itself "without fear, without reserve, without pledge to men, parties, sects or systems, to free, unbiased, and universal inquiry." It would "aid in the diffusion of truth, in the spread of liberal principles, and in the dissipation of those prejudices which observation and experience may designate as obstacles to the progressive march of the world from error and suffering toward wisdom and enjoyment."

Wright combined her editorship with a series of lectures in Cincinnati in 1828 and later in principal cities throughout the East, published copies of which were also widely circulated in the late 1820s and early 1830s. Wherever she spoke, she tended to create a sensation. Her friend Frances Milton Trollope wrote of her Cincinnati appearance: "That a lady of fortune, family, and education, whose youth had been passed in the most refined circles of private life, should present herself to the people as a public lecturer, would naturally excite surprise anywhere . . . but in America where women are guarded by a sevenfold shield of habitual insignificance it has caused an effect which can hardly be described."

Upon her arrival in New York she found herself attacked by several of the city's newspapers. One example from the *Evening Post* followed discovery that the Park Theatre had been leased to Wright for a series of lectures: "We perceive with utter astonishment, and no less alarm than astonishment, that the lessees [*sic*] of this theatre have agreed to let it for six nights to Frances Wright,

Drawing of Wright's center for ideological exchange, where her magazine was published after April 1829

as a place to deliver her lectures in. Have they considered what may be the consequences of the displeasure of the people? Suppose the singular spectacle of a female, publicly and ostentatiously proclaiming doctrines of atheistical fanaticism, and even the most abandoned lewdness, should draw a crowd from a prurient curiosity, and that a riot should ensue, which should end in the demolition of the interior of the building, or even in burning it down, on whom would the loss fall?"

The *New Harmony and Nashoba Gazette, or Free Enquirer* was mailed to the East for its numerous readers, but by early 1829 Wright had decided to move its publishing headquarters to New York. She began publishing a New York edition which generally contained the same material on the same date as the New Harmony edition. She and Robert Jennings, who had followed her to New York from New Harmony, were responsible for the local content of the periodical. Later Robert Dale Owen, son of the New Harmony founder, arrived to handle much of the editorial work.

In the first issue to carry the new, shortened title, the *Free Enquirer*, Wright let loose at the other newspapers of the city: "In the present

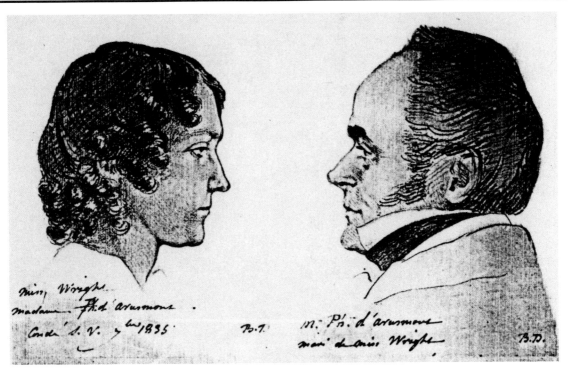

Anonymous pencil drawing of Frances Wright and her husband William Phiquepal D'Arusmont, 1835. The couple divorced in 1851.

state of the American press, it is hard to judge who is on the side of truth. Nay, were we to take the press for an organ of public sentiment, we might conceive that a mental palsy had fallen upon the nation, and that the whole people were engaged in quarrelling about trifles, libeling their public officers, insulting individuals, or sleeping away their intellects under the fumes of tobacco."

After April 1829 the magazine was published in the basement of Wright's new Hall of Science, which contained, upstairs, a lecture hall to seat about twelve hundred persons. The periodical argued theology and urged abolition of capital punishment, an end to imprisonment for debts, political equality for women, including an end to the practice which deprived a woman of her property upon marriage, civil rights for all, universal education free from sectarian teaching, and a forum for the exchange of all manner of views.

The periodical also was used to support a broad range of programs designed to assist the working man, the "mechanic." The *Free Enquirer* movement, which came to be known by its enemies as the Fanny Wright Society, promoted several causes, including a program for more equal distribution of wealth and a state supported health-care system.

Wright could not support, however, another liberal movement of the day, abolition of slavery. She argued both in the *Free Enquirer* and from the lecture platform that a gradual emancipation following her cooperative labor principle attempted at Nashoba was the proper answer, permitting slaves to buy their freedom. Her final step in her own Nashoba experiment came late in 1829 when she traveled back to accompany the few remaining blacks to the new black republic of Haiti. Six months later she was back in New York, the blacks "advantageously and happily settled under the immediate protection of the Haitian president," she wrote in the 1 May 1830 edition of the *Free Enquirer*.

In the summer of 1830, with the *Free Enquirer* group in some disarray and the declining health of her sister apparent, Wright returned to England, although an editorial in the 10 July 1830 edition of the journal noted that Wright had left behind "a variety of articles for the *Free Enquirer*. . . ." Despite her intentions to return promptly to the United States, the death of Camilla in France on 8 February 1831 made Wright realize how alone she was. William Phiquepal D'Arusmont, who had worked with Wright at New Harmony, had followed her to France and assisted her in the considerable details involved with her sister's death. With the impending birth of their child, they legalized their relationship, although they may have planned on marriage even before Wright left the United States. That child's early death was followed by the birth of a daughter, Frances Sylva, in 1832. In this period of her life, Wright appears to have resigned from her role of reformer, lecturer, and writer, although she did deliver a series of lectures on educational reform in England in the spring of 1834.

In November 1835 the D'Arusmonts sailed back to the United States, leaving behind their daughter, he to attempt to recover debts owed Wright and she to reenter a life she had given up for five years. They traveled immediately to Cincinnati, where many of Wright's investments were centered. There she entered into political life again on the lecture and writing circuit; many lectures and articles were built on her belief that the answer to slavery lay in the slow process of education, gradual emancipation, the removal of former slaves to a colony outside the United States, and their replacement in the South by white workers from the North. To further her arguments she published, apparently single-handedly, a newspaper, *Manual of American Principles*, printed while she was in Philadelphia during 1836-1837. She also contributed articles to a liberal Boston newspaper, the *Boston Investigator*.

Wright continued to make Cincinnati her home base, spending much of the spring of 1838 there recovering from a breakdown in her health. Then it was on to New York and on to Europe in June 1839. During most of this time, she and her husband were separated, he more often than not with their daughter. Wright's 1839 trip to Europe was the first of seven more Atlantic crossings she was to make, none of them with her husband. Only briefly in the intervening years were they together. During this later period of her life, Wright largely retired from the lecture platform, seemed uninterested in many issues of the day (for example, she had nothing to do with the developing woman suffrage movement), but seemed to spend most of her time enlarging upon lectures which were to form the basis of *England the Civilizer*, published in 1848 in London.

The D'Arusmonts finally were divorced in 1851 following a long dispute about finances and the care of their daughter. Divorce actions in both Tennessee and Ohio were completed with daughter Sylva firmly estranged from her mother at the end. Shortly thereafter Wright fell while at home in Cincinnati, breaking her hip. She never fully recovered and died on 13 December 1852 at the age of fifty-seven. Her death appears to have attracted little notice at the time.

For Frances Wright her writings were a central vehicle for expression of her far advanced social and philosophical beliefs. In addition to the lecture platform, her writing allowed her to do what few women of her time could accomplish: debating with her contemporaries the issues which concerned her and laying out, although not necessarily in an organized fashion, her theories of how life ought to be ordered.

Biographies:

Amos Gilbert, *Memoir of Frances Wright, the Pioneer Woman in the Cause of Human Rights* (Cincinnati: Longley Brothers, 1855);

William Randall Waterman, *Frances Wright* (New York: Columbia University Press, 1924);

Alice J. G. Perkins and Theresa Wolfson, *Frances Wright, Free Enquirer: The Study of a Temperament* (New York & London: Harper, 1939);

Margaret Lane, *Frances Wright and the "Great Experiment"* (Totowa, N.J.: Rowman & Littlefield, 1972).

Checklist of Further Readings

Allen, Frederick Lewis, William L. Chenery, and Fulton Oursler. "American Magazines, 1741-1941," *Bulletin of the New York Public Library*, 45 (June 1941): 439-456.

Beer, William. *Checklist of American Periodicals 1741-1800*. Worcester, Mass.: American Antiquarian Society, 1923.

Bullock, Penelope L. *The Anglo-American Periodical Press, 1838-1909*. Baton Rouge: Louisiana State University Press, 1981.

Cairns, William B. *On the Development of American Literature from 1815 to 1833; with especial Reference to Periodicals*. Madison: University of Wisconsin, 1898.

Chielens, Edward E. *American Literary Magazines: The Eighteenth and Nineteenth Centuries*. Westport, Conn.: Greenwood Press, 1986.

Chielens. *The Literary Journal in America to 1900*. Detroit: Gale Research Company, 1975.

Ditzion, Sidney. "History of Periodical Literature in the United States," *Bulletin of Bibliography*, 15 (January/April 1935): 110; (May/August 1935): 129-133.

Douglas, Ann. *The Feminization of American Culture*. New York: Knopf, 1977, pp. 227-256.

Drewry, John Eldridge. *Some Magazines and Magazine Makers*. Boston: Stradford, 1924.

Ellison, Rhoda Coleman. *Early American Publications: A Study in Literary Interests*. University: University of Alabama Press, 1947.

Felker, Clay S. "Life Cycles in the Age of Magazines," *Anitoch Review*, 29 (Spring 1969): 7-13.

Ferguson, Marjorie. *Forever Feminine: Women's Magazines and the Cult of Femininity*. Portsmouth, N.H.: Heinemann, 1983.

Ford, P. L. *Checklist of American Magazines Printed in the Eighteenth Century*. Brooklyn: Privately printed, 1889.

Garnsey, Caroline John. "Ladies' Magazines to 1850; the Beginnings of an Industry," *New York Public Library Bulletin*, 58 (February 1954): 74-88.

Gilmer, Gertrude C. *Checklist of Southern Periodicals to 1861*. Boston: F. W. Faxon, 1934.

Gohdes, Clarence. *The Periodicals of American Transcendentalism*. Durham: Duke University Press, 1931.

Hewett, Daniel. "Daniel Hewett's List of Newspapers and Periodicals in the United States in 1828," *American Antiquarian Society, Proceedings*, new series 44 (1935): 365-398.

Hubbell, Jay B. "Southern Magazines," in *Culture in the South*, by W. T. Couch. Chapel Hill: University of North Carolina Press, 1934, pp. 159-182.

Lewis, Benjamin M. *A Register of Editors, Printers, and Publishers of American Magazines, 1741-1810*. New York: New York Public Library, 1957.

Matthews, Brander. "American Magazines," *Bookman*, 49 (July 1919): 533-541.

Moore, John W. *Moore's Historical, Biographical, and Miscellaneous Gatherings*. Concord, N.H.: Republican Press Association, 1886.

Mott, Frank Luther. *A History of American Magazines*, 5 volumes. Cambridge, Mass.: Harvard University Press, 1938-1968.

Neal, Edgar L. *A History and Bibliography of American Magazines, 1810-1820*. Metuchen, N.J.: Scarecrow Press, 1975.

Pullar, Elizabeth. "Illustrated Magazines of the 19th Century," *Antiques Journal*, 34 (November 1979): 25-27.

Repplier, Agnes. "American Magazines," *Yale Review*, 16 (1926-1927): 261-274.

Richardson, Lyon N. *A History of Early American Magazines 1741-1789*. New York: Thomas Nelson, 1931.

Riley, Sam G. *Index to Southern Periodicals*. Westport, Conn.: Greenwood Press, 1986.

Riley. *Magazines of the American South*. Westport, Conn.: Greenwood Press, 1986.

Riley, Susan B. "The Hazards of Periodical Publishing in the South During the Nineteenth Century," *Tennessee Historical Quarterly*, 21 (1962): 365-376.

Riley. "The Southern Literary Magazine of the Mid-Nineteenth Century," *Tennessee Historical Quarterly*, 23 (1964): 221-236.

Schacht, J. H. *A Bibliography for the Study of Magazines*, 4th ed. Urbana, Ill.: College of Communications, 1979.

Smyth, Albert Henry. *The Philadelphia Magazines and Their Contributors, 1741-1850*. Philadelphia: Robert M. Lindsay, 1892.

Stearns, Bertha Monica. "Before Godey's," *American Literature*, 2 (November 1930): 248-255.

Stearns. "Early New England Magazines for Ladies," *New England Quarterly*, 2 (July 1929): 420-457.

Stearns. "Early Philadelphia Magazines for Ladies," *Pennsylvania Magazine of History and Biography*, 64 (October 1940): 479-491.

Stearns. "Southern Magazines for Ladies," *South Atlantic Quarterly*, 31 (January 1932): 70-87.

Stephens, Ethel. "American Popular Magazines, A Bibliography," *Bulletin of Bibliography Pamphlets*, No. 23, 1916.

Tassin, Algernon de Vivier. *The Magazine in America*. New York: Dodd, Mead, 1916.

Tebbel, John. *The American Magazine: A Compact History*. New York: Hawthorne Books, 1969.

Wolseley, Roland E. *The Changing Magazine*. New York: Hastings House, 1983.

Wood, James Playsted. *Magazines in the United States, Their Social and Economic Influence*. New York: Ronald Press Co., 1971.

Contributors

June N. Adamson ....*University of Tennessee*
Donald R. Avery ....*University of Southern Mississippi*
Nora Baker ....*Southern Illinois University at Edwardsville*
Maurine H. Beasley ....*University of Maryland*
Jack W. Berryman ....*University of Washington*
Dorothy A. Bowles ....*University of Tennessee*
James Boylan ....*University of Massachusetts–Amherst*
Patricia Bradley ....*Temple University*
Lloyd E. Chiasson ....*Loyola University in New Orleans*
Earl L. Conn ....*Ball State University*
James S. Featherston ....*Louisiana State University*
Jean Folkerts ....*Mount Vernon College*
Elizabeth M. Fraas ....*Eastern Kentucky University*
James N. Green ....*Library Company of Philadelphia*
Carol Sue Humphrey ....*Oklahoma Baptist University*
William E. Huntzicker ....*Minneapolis, Minnesota*
Ernest C. Hynds ....*University of Georgia*
Terry Hynes ....*California State University, Fullerton*
Kathleen Kearney Keeshen ....*College of Notre Dame, Belmont, California*
James Everett Kibler, Jr. ....*University of Georgia*
John A. Lent ....*Third World Media Associates*
Mary S. Mander ....*Pennsylvania State University*
David E. Matchen ....*Auburn University*
John Nerone ....*University of Illinois*
John J. Pauly ....*University of Tulsa*
Alf Pratte ....*Brigham Young University*
Sam G. Riley ....*Virginia Polytechnic Institute and State University*
Patt Foster Roberson ....*Southern University*
Mark J. Schaefermeyer ....*Virginia Polytechnic Institute and State University*
Judith Serrin ....*Columbia University*
Edward H. Sewell, Jr. ....*Virginia Polytechnic Institute and State University*
George Green Shackelford ....*Virginia Polytechnic Institute and State University*
Jacqueline Steck ....*Temple University*
James Glen Stovall ....*University of Alabama*
Edward Sumter ....*Columbia, South Carolina*
Edward L. Tucker ....*Virginia Polytechnic Institute and State University*
Ada Van Gastel ....*Auburn University*

Cumulative Index

Dictionary of Literary Biography, Volumes 1-73
Dictionary of Literary Biography Yearbook, 1980-1987
Dictionary of Literary Biography Documentary Series, Volumes 1-4

Cumulative Index

DLB before number: *Dictionary of Literary Biography*, Volumes 1-73
Y before number: *Dictionary of Literary Biography Yearbook*, 1980-1987
DS before number: *Dictionary of Literary Biography Documentary Series*, Volumes 1-4

A

Abbey Press DLB-49

The Abbey Theatre and Irish
Drama, 1900-1945 .... DLB-10

Abbot, Willis J. 1863-1934.................... DLB-29

Abbott, Jacob 1803-1879 ....DLB-1

Abbott, Robert S. 1868-1940 .... DLB-29

Abelard-Schuman DLB-46

Abell, Arunah S. 1806-1888 .... DLB-43

Abercrombie, Lascelles 1881-1938............. DLB-19

Abrams, M. H. 1912- DLB-67

Abse, Dannie 1923- DLB-27

Academy Chicago Publishers DLB-46

Ace Books.................................. DLB-46

Acorn, Milton 1923-1986..................... DLB-53

Actors Theatre of Louisville....................DLB-7

Adair, James 1709?-1783? DLB-30

Adamic, Louis 1898-1951......................DLB-9

Adams, Alice 1926- Y-86

Adams, Brooks 1848-1927..................... DLB-47

Adams, Charles Francis, Jr. 1835-1915 .... DLB-47

Adams, Douglas 1952- Y-83

Adams, Franklin P. 1881-1960 .... DLB-29

Adams, Henry 1838-1918 ....DLB-12, 47

Adams, Herbert Baxter 1850-1901 .... DLB-47

Adams, J. S. and C. [publishing house]........ DLB-49

Adams, James Truslow 1878-1949............. DLB-17

Adams, John 1735-1826...................... DLB-31

Adams, John Quincy 1767-1848............... DLB-37

Adams, Léonie 1899- DLB-48

Adams, Samuel 1722-1803 ....DLB-31, 43

Adams, William Taylor 1822-1897 .... DLB-42

Adcock, Fleur 1934- DLB-40

Ade, George 1866-1944 ....DLB-11, 25

Adeler, Max (see Clark, Charles Heber)

Advance Publishing Company................. DLB-49

AE 1867-1935 .... DLB-19

Aesthetic Poetry (1873), by Walter Pater DLB-35

Afro-American Literary Critics:
An Introduction DLB-33

Agassiz, Jean Louis Rodolphe 1807-1873........DLB-1

Agee, James 1909-1955......................DLB-2, 26

Aiken, Conrad 1889-1973 ....DLB-9, 45

Ainsworth, William Harrison 1805-1882....... DLB-21

Aitken, Robert [publishing house]............. DLB-49

Akins, Zoë 1886-1958 .... DLB-26

Alain-Fournier 1886-1914 .... DLB-65

Alba, Nanina 1915-1968...................... DLB-41

Albee, Edward 1928- DLB-7

Alcott, Amos Bronson 1799-1888...............DLB-1

Alcott, Louisa May 1832-1888 ....DLB-1, 42

Alcott, William Andrus 1798-1859...............DLB-1

Alden, Isabella 1841-1930 .... DLB-42

Alden, John B. [publishing house]............. DLB-49

Alden, Beardsley and Company DLB-49

Aldington, Richard 1892-1962.............DLB-20, 36

Aldis, Dorothy 1896-1966 .... DLB-22

Aldiss, Brian W. 1925- DLB-14

Aldrich, Thomas Bailey 1836-1907........DLB-42, 71

Alexander, Charles Wesley
[publishing house] DLB-49

Alexander, James 1691-1756 .... DLB-24

Alexander, Lloyd 1924- DLB-52

Alger, Horatio, Jr. 1832-1899 .... DLB-42

Algonquin Books of Chapel Hill.............. DLB-46

Algren, Nelson 1909-1981............ DLB-9; Y-81, 82

Allan, Ted 1916- DLB-68

Alldritt, Keith 1935- DLB-14

Allen, Ethan 1738-1789 .... DLB-31

Allen, George 1808-1876.................... DLB-59

Allen, Grant 1848-1899..................... DLB-70

Allen, Henry W. 1912- Y-85

Allen, Hervey 1889-1949 ....DLB-9, 45

Allen, James 1739-1808 .... DLB-31

Allen, James Lane 1849-1925................. DLB-71

Allen, Jay Presson 1922- DLB-26

Allen, John, and Company DLB-49

Allen, Samuel W. 1917- DLB-41

Allen, Woody 1935- DLB-44

Allingham, William 1824-1889 .... DLB-35

Allison, W. L. [publishing house]............. DLB-49

Allott, Kenneth 1912-1973 .... DLB-20

Allston, Washington 1779-1843.................DLB-1

Alsop, George 1636-post 1673................ DLB-24

Alsop, Richard 1761-1815 .... DLB-37

Altemus, Henry, and Company............... DLB-49

Alvarez, A. 1929- DLB-14, 40

*America: or, a Poem on the Settlement of the
British Colonies* (1780?), by Timothy
Dwight DLB-37

American Conservatory Theatre.................DLB-7

American Fiction and the 1930s................DLB-9

American Humor: A Historical Survey
East and Northeast
South and Southwest
Midwest
West DLB-11

American News Company DLB-49

The American Poets' Corner: The First
Three Years (1983-1986)......................Y-86

American Publishing Company............... DLB-49

American Stationers' Company DLB-49

American Sunday-School Union.............. DLB-49

American Temperance Union................ DLB-49

American Tract Society..................... DLB-49

The American Writers Congress
(9-12 October 1981)........................Y-81

The American Writers Congress: A Report
on Continuing Business......................Y-81

Ames, Fisher 1758-1808 .... DLB-37

Ames, Mary Clemmer 1831-1884.............. DLB-23

Amini, Johari M. 1935- DLB-41

Amis, Kingsley 1922- DLB-15, 27

Amis, Martin 1949- DLB-14

Ammons, A. R. 1926- DLB-5

Amory, Thomas 1691?-1788................... DLB-39

Andersch, Alfred 1914-1980 .... DLB-69

Anderson, Margaret 1886-1973 ....DLB-4

Anderson, Maxwell 1888-1959 ....DLB-7

Anderson, Patrick 1915-1979................. DLB-68

Anderson, Paul Y. 1893-1938 .... DLB-29

Anderson, Poul 1926- DLB-8

Anderson, Robert 1917- DLB-7

Anderson, Sherwood 1876-1941........DLB-4, 9; DS-1

Andreas-Salomé, Lou 1861-1937 .... DLB-66

Andres, Stefan 1906-1970 .... DLB-69

Andrews, Charles M. 1863-1943.............. DLB-17

Andrieux, Louis (see Aragon, Louis)

Andrus, Silas, and Son DLB-49

Angell, James Burrill 1829-1916............... DLB-64

Angelou, Maya 1928- DLB-38

The "Angry Young Men" DLB-15

Anhalt, Edward 1914- DLB-26

Anners, Henry F. [publishing house].......... DLB-49

Anthony, Piers 1934- DLB-8

Anthony Burgess's *99 Novels*: An Opinion Poll Y-84

Antin, Mary 1881-1949.........................Y-84

Antschel, Paul (see Celan, Paul)

Appleton, D., and Company.................. DLB-49

Appleton-Century-Crofts DLB-46

Apple-wood Books DLB-46

Aquin, Hubert 1929-1977 .... DLB-53

Aragon, Louis 1897-1982..................... DLB-72

Arbor House Publishing Company DLB-46

Arcadia House............................. DLB-46

Archer, William 1856-1924.................. DLB-10

Arden, John 1930- DLB-13

Arden of Faversham DLB-62

The Arena Publishing Company DLB-49

Arena Stage DLB-7

Arensberg, Ann 1937- Y-82

Arland, Marcel 1899-1986..................... DLB-72

Arlen, Michael 1895-1956 .... DLB-36

Armed Services Editions...................... DLB-46

Arno Press..................................... DLB-46

Arnold, Edwin 1832-1904 .... DLB-35

Arnold, Matthew 1822-1888...............DLB-32, 57

Arnold, Thomas 1795-1842 .... DLB-55

Arnow, Harriette Simpson 1908-1986..........DLB-6

Arp, Bill (see Smith, Charles Henry)

Arthur, Timothy Shay 1809-1885 ....DLB-3, 42

As I See It, by Carolyn Cassady DLB-16

Asch, Nathan 1902-1964 ....DLB-4, 28

Ash, John 1948- DLB-40

Ashbery, John 1927- DLB-5; Y-81

Asher, Sandy 1942- Y-83

Ashton, Winifred (see Dane, Clemence)

Asimov, Isaac 1920- DLB-8

Atheneum Publishers......................... DLB-46

Atherton, Gertrude 1857-1948 ....DLB-9

Atkins, Josiah circa 1755-1781................. DLB-31

Atkins, Russell 1926- DLB-41

The Atlantic Monthly Press................... DLB-46

Atwood, Margaret 1939- DLB-53

Aubert, Alvin 1930- DLB-41

Aubin, Penelope 1685-circa, 1731 .... DLB-39

Auchincloss, Louis 1917- DLB-2; Y-80

Auden, W. H. 1907-1973...................DLB-10, 20

Audio Art in America: A Personal
    Memoir Y-85

Austin, Alfred 1835-1913..................... DLB-35

Austin, Mary 1868-1934......................DLB-9

The Author's Apology for His Book
    (1684), by John Bunyan.................. DLB-39

An Author's Response, by Ronald Sukenick.......Y-82

Authors and Newspapers Association......... DLB-46

Authors' Publishing Company................ DLB-49

Avalon Books................................. DLB-46

Avison, Margaret 1918- DLB-53

Avon Books DLB-46

Ayckbourn, Alan 1939- DLB-13

Aymé, Marcel 1902-1967..................... DLB-72

Aytoun, William Edmondstoune 1813-1865 ... DLB-32

B

Babbitt, Irving 1865-1933 .... DLB-63

Babbitt, Natalie 1932- DLB-52

Babcock, John [publishing house] DLB-49

Bache, Benjamin Franklin 1769-1798 .... DLB-43

Bacon, Delia 1811-1859 ....DLB-1

Bacon, Thomas circa 1700-1768.............. DLB-31

Badger, Richard G., and Company............ DLB-49

Bage, Robert 1728-1801....................... DLB-39

Bagehot, Walter 1826-1877.................... DLB-55

Bagnold, Enid 1889-1981..................... DLB-13

Bailey, Alfred Goldsworthy 1905- DLB-68

Bailey, Francis [publishing house] DLB-49

Bailey, Paul 1937- DLB-14

Bailey, Philip James 1816-1902............... DLB-32

Baillie, Hugh 1890-1966...................... DLB-29

Bailyn, Bernard 1922- DLB-17

Bainbridge, Beryl 1933- DLB-14

Baird, Irene 1901-1981....................... DLB-68

The Baker and Taylor Company............. DLB-49

Baker, Houston A., Jr. 1943- DLB-67

Baker, Walter H., Company
    ("Baker's Plays")......................... DLB-49

Bald, Wambly 1902- DLB-4

Balderston, John 1889-1954.................. DLB-26

Baldwin, James 1924-1987.........DLB-2, 7, 33; Y-87

Baldwin, Joseph Glover 1815-1864 ....DLB-3, 11

Ballantine Books.............................. DLB-46

Ballard, J. G. 1930- DLB-14

Ballou, Robert O. [publishing house].......... DLB-46

Bambara, Toni Cade 1939- DLB-38

Bancroft, A. L., and Company DLB-49

Bancroft, George 1800-1891............DLB-1, 30, 59

Bancroft, Hubert Howe 1832-1918............ DLB-47

Bangs, John Kendrick 1862-1922............. DLB-11

Bantam Books................................ DLB-46

Banville, John 1945- DLB-14

Baraka, Amiri 1934- DLB-5, 7, 16, 38

Barber, John Warner 1798-1885 .... DLB-30

Barbour, Ralph Henry 1870-1944............ DLB-22

Barbusse, Henri 1873-1935.................. DLB-65

Barclay, E. E., and Company DLB-49

Bardeen, C. W. [publishing house] DLB-49

Baring, Maurice 1874-1945.................. DLB-34

Barker, A. L. 1918- DLB-14

Barker, George 1913- DLB-20

Barker, Harley Granville 1877-1946.......... DLB-10

Barker, Howard 1946- DLB-13

Barker, James Nelson 1784-1858............. DLB-37

Barker, Jane 1652-1727? DLB-39

Barks, Coleman 1937- DLB-5

Barlach, Ernst 1870-1938.................... DLB-56

Barlow, Joel 1754-1812...................... DLB-37

Barnard, John 1681-1770 .... DLB-24

Barnes, A. S., and Company................. DLB-49

Barnes, Djuna 1892-1982................ DLB-4, 9, 45

Barnes, Margaret Ayer 1886-1967............. DLB-9

Barnes, Peter 1931- DLB-13

Barnes, William 1801-1886 .... DLB-32

Barnes and Noble Books DLB-46

Barney, Natalie 1876-1972 .... DLB-4

Baron, Richard W., Publishing Company...... DLB-46

Barr, Robert 1850-1912 .... DLB-70

Barrax, Gerald William 1933- DLB-41

Barrie, James M. 1860-1937.................. DLB-10

Barry, Philip 1896-1949...................... DLB-7

Barse and Hopkins........................... DLB-46

Barstow, Stan 1928- DLB-14

Barth, John 1930- DLB-2

Barthelme, Donald 1931- DLB-2; Y-80

Barthelme, Frederick 1943- Y-85

Bartlett, John 1820-1905 .... DLB-1

Bartol, Cyrus Augustus 1813-1900 .... DLB-1

Bartram, John 1699-1777 .... DLB-31

Bartram, William 1739-1823.................. DLB-37

Basic Books................................. DLB-46

Bass, T. J. 1932- Y-81

Bassett, John Spencer 1867-1928............. DLB-17

Bassler, Thomas Joseph (see Bass, T. J.)

Bate, Walter Jackson 1918- DLB-67

Bates, Katharine Lee 1859-1929.............. DLB-71

Baum, L. Frank 1856-1919................... DLB-22

Baumbach, Jonathan 1933- Y-80

Bawden, Nina 1925- DLB-14

Bax, Clifford 1886-1962..................... DLB-10

Bayer, Eleanor (see Perry, Eleanor)

Beach, Sylvia 1887-1962...................... DLB-4

Beacon Press DLB-49

Beadle and Adams DLB-49

Beagle, Peter S. 1939- Y-80

Beal, M. F. 1937- Y-81

Beale, Howard K. 1899-1959................. DLB-17

Beard, Charles A. 1874-1948................. DLB-17

A Beat Chronology: The First Twenty-five
    Years, 1944-1969....................... DLB-16

Beattie, Ann 1947- Y-82

Beauchemin, Yves 1941- DLB-60

Beaulieu, Victor-Lévy 1945- DLB-53

Beaumont, Francis circa 1584-1616
    and Fletcher, John 1579-1625............ DLB-58

Beauvoir, Simone de 1908-1986........ Y-86, DLB-72

Becher, Ulrich 1910- DLB-69

Becker, Carl 1873-1945...................... DLB-17

Beckett, Samuel 1906- DLB-13, 15

Beckford, William 1760-1844................. DLB-39

Beckham, Barry 1944- DLB-33

Beecher, Catharine Esther 1800-1878.......... DLB-1

Beecher, Henry Ward 1813-1887............ DLB-3, 43

Beer, George L. 1872-1920................... DLB-47

Beer, Patricia 1919- DLB-40

Beerbohm, Max 1872-1956................... DLB-34

Beers, Henry A. 1847-1926................... DLB-71

Behan, Brendan 1923-1964 .... DLB-13

Behn, Aphra 1640?-1689..................... DLB-39

Behn, Harry 1898-1973 .... DLB-61

Behrman, S. N. 1893-1973 ....DLB-7, 44

Belasco, David 1853-1931 ....DLB-7

Belford, Clarke and Company................. DLB-49

Belitt, Ben 1911- DLB-5

Belknap, Jeremy 1744-1798 ....DLB-30, 37

Bell, James Madison 1826-1902 .... DLB-50

Bell, Marvin 1937- DLB-5

Bell, Robert [publishing house]............... DLB-49

Bellamy, Edward 1850-1898................... DLB-12

Bellamy, Joseph 1719-1790................... DLB-31

Belloc, Hilaire 1870-1953..................... DLB-19

Bellow, Saul 1915- DLB-2, 28; Y-82; DS-3

Belmont Productions DLB-46

Bemelmans, Ludwig 1898-1962 .... DLB-22

Bemis, Samuel Flagg 1891-1973............... DLB-17

Benchley, Robert 1889-1945................... DLB-11

Benedictus, David 1938- DLB-14

Benedikt, Michael 1935- DLB-5

Benét, Stephen Vincent 1898-1943..........DLB-4, 48

Benét, William Rose 1886-1950............... DLB-45

Benford, Gregory 1941- Y-82

Benjamin, Park 1809-1864 ....DLB-3, 59, 73

Benn, Gottfried 1886-1956 .... DLB-56

Bennett, Arnold 1867-1931.................DLB-10, 34

Bennett, Charles 1899- DLB-44

Bennett, Gwendolyn 1902- DLB-51

Bennett, Hal 1930- DLB-33

Bennett, James Gordon 1795-1872 .... DLB-43

Bennett, James Gordon, Jr. 1841-1918 .... DLB-23

Bennett, John 1865-1956..................... DLB-42

Benoit, Jacques 1941- DLB-60

Benson, Stella 1892-1933..................... DLB-36

Bentley, E. C. 1875-1956 .... DLB-70

Benton, Robert 1932- and Newman,
    David 1937- DLB-44

Benziger Brothers DLB-49

Beresford, Anne 1929- DLB-40

Berford, R. G., Company..................... DLB-49

Berg, Stephen 1934- DLB-5

Bergengruen, Werner 1892-1964............. DLB-56

Berger, John 1926- DLB-14

Berger, Meyer 1898-1959 .... DLB-29

Berger, Thomas 1924- DLB-2; Y-80

Berkeley, George 1685-1753................... DLB-31

The Berkley Publishing Corporation DLB-46

Bernanos, Georges 1888-1948................. DLB-72

Bernard, John 1756-1828 .... DLB-37

Berrigan, Daniel 1921- DLB-5

Berrigan, Ted 1934-1983........................DLB-5

Berry, Wendell 1934- DLB-5, 6

Berryman, John 1914-1972.................... DLB-48

Bersianik, Louky 1930- DLB-60

Berton, Pierre 1920- DLB-68

Bessette, Gerard 1920- DLB-53

Bessie, Alvah 1904-1985...................... DLB-26

Bester, Alfred 1913- DLB-8

The Bestseller Lists: An Assessment...............Y-84

Betjeman, John 1906-1984 .... DLB-20; Y-84

Betts, Doris 1932- Y-82

Beveridge, Albert J. 1862-1927................ DLB-17

Beverley, Robert circa 1673-1722...........DLB-24, 30

Biddle, Drexel [publishing house] DLB-49

Bierbaum, Otto Julius 1865-1910.............. DLB-66

Bierce, Ambrose 1842-1914? DLB-11, 12, 23, 71

Biggle, Lloyd, Jr. 1923- DLB-8

Biglow, Hosea (see Lowell, James Russell)

Billings, Josh (see Shaw, Henry Wheeler)

Binding, Rudolf G. 1867-1938................. DLB-66

Bingham, Caleb 1757-1817.................... DLB-42

Binyon, Laurence 1869-1943 .... DLB-19

Biographical Documents I.........................Y-84

Biographical Documents II........................Y-85

Bioren, John [publishing house]............... DLB-49

Bird, William 1888-1963........................DLB-4

Bishop, Elizabeth 1911-1979....................DLB-5

Bishop, John Peale 1892-1944............DLB-4, 9, 45

Bissett, Bill 1939- DLB-53

Black, David (D. M.) 1941- DLB-40

Black, Walter J. [publishing house] DLB-46

Black, Winifred 1863-1936 . . . . DLB-25

The Black Arts Movement, by Larry Neal DLB-38

Black Theaters and Theater Organizations in
    America, 1961-1982: A Research List DLB-38

Black Theatre: A Forum [excerpts] DLB-38

Blackamore, Arthur 1679-? DLB-24, 39

Blackburn, Alexander L. 1929- Y-85

Blackburn, Paul 1926-1971 . . . . DLB-16; Y-81

Blackburn, Thomas 1916-1977 . . . . DLB-27

Blackmore, R. D. 1825-1900 . . . . DLB-18

Blackmur, R. P. 1904-1965 . . . . DLB-63

Blackwood, Caroline 1931- DLB-14

Blair, Eric Arthur (see Orwell, George)

Blair, Francis Preston 1791-1876 . . . . DLB-43

Blair, James circa 1655-1743 . . . . DLB-24

Blair, John Durburrow 1759-1823 . . . . DLB-37

Blais, Marie-Claire 1939- DLB-53

Blaise, Clark 1940- DLB-53

The Blakiston Company DLB-49

Blanchot, Maurice 1907- DLB-72

Bledsoe, Albert Taylor 1809-1877 . . . . DLB-3

Blelock and Company DLB-49

Blish, James 1921-1975 . . . . DLB-8

Bliss, E., and E. White [publishing house] DLB-49

Bloch, Robert 1917- DLB-44

Block, Rudolph (see Lessing, Bruno)

Bloom, Harold 1930- DLB-67

Blume, Judy 1938- DLB-52

Blunck, Hans Friedrich 1888-1961 . . . . DLB-66

Blunden, Edmund 1896-1974 . . . . DLB-20

Blunt, Wilfrid Scawen 1840-1922 . . . . DLB-19

Bly, Nellie (see Cochrane, Elizabeth)

Bly, Robert 1926- DLB-5

The Bobbs-Merrill Company DLB-46

Bodenheim, Maxwell 1892-1954 . . . . DLB-9, 45

Bodkin, M. McDonnell 1850-1933 . . . . DLB-70

Bodsworth, Fred 1918- DLB-68

Boehm, Sydney 1908- DLB-44

Boer, Charles 1939- DLB-5

Bogan, Louise 1897-1970 . . . . DLB-45

Bogarde, Dirk 1921- DLB-14

Boland, Eavan 1944- DLB-40

Böll, Heinrich 1917-1985 . . . . Y-85, DLB-69

Bolling, Robert 1738-1775 . . . . DLB-31

Bolt, Carol 1941- DLB-60

Bolt, Robert 1924- DLB-13

Bolton, Herbert E. 1870-1953 . . . . DLB-17

Bond, Edward 1934- DLB-13

Boni, Albert and Charles [publishing house] . . DLB-46

Boni and Liveright DLB-46

Robert Bonner's Sons DLB-49

Bontemps, Arna 1902-1973 . . . . DLB-48, 51

The Book League of America DLB-46

Book Reviewing in America: I Y-87

Book Supply Company DLB-49

The Booker Prize
    Address by Anthony Thwaite, Chairman
      of the Booker Prize Judges
    Comments from Former Booker Prize
      Winners Y-86

Boorstin, Daniel J. 1914- DLB-17

Booth, Philip 1925- Y-82

Booth, Wayne C. 1921- DLB-67

Borchardt, Rudolf 1877-1945 . . . . DLB-66

Borchert, Wolfgang 1921-1947 . . . . DLB-69

Borges, Jorge Luis 1899-1986 . . . . Y-86

Borrow, George 1803-1881 . . . . DLB-21, 55

Bosco, Henri 1888-1976 . . . . DLB-72

Bosco, Monique 1927- DLB-53

Botta, Anne C. Lynch 1815-1891 . . . . DLB-3

Bottomley, Gordon 1874-1948 . . . . DLB-10

Bottoms, David 1949- Y-83

Bottrall, Ronald 1906- DLB-20

Boucher, Anthony 1911-1968 . . . . DLB-8

Boucher, Jonathan 1738-1804 . . . . DLB-31

Bourjaily, Vance Nye 1922- DLB-2

Bourne, Edward Gaylord 1860-1908 . . . . DLB-47

Bourne, Randolph 1886-1918 . . . . DLB-63

Bousquet, Joë 1897-1950 . . . . DLB-72

Bova, Ben 1932- Y-81

Bove, Emmanuel 1898-1945 . . . . DLB-72

Bovard, Oliver K. 1872-1945 .... DLB-25

Bowen, Elizabeth 1899-1973 .... DLB-15

Bowen, Francis 1811-1890 .... DLB-1, 59

Bowen, John 1924- DLB-13

Bowen-Merrill Company DLB-49

Bowering, George 1935- DLB-53

Bowers, Claude G. 1878-1958 .... DLB-17

Bowers, Edgar 1924- DLB-5

Bowles, Paul 1910- DLB-5, 6

Bowles, Samuel III 1826-1878 .... DLB-43

Bowman, Louise Morey 1882-1944 .... DLB-68

Boyd, James 1888-1944 .... DLB-9

Boyd, John 1919- DLB-8

Boyd, Thomas 1898-1935 .... DLB-9

Boyesen, Hjalmar Hjorth 1848-1895 .... DLB-12, 71

Boyle, Kay 1902- DLB-4, 9, 48

Boyle, T. Coraghessan 1948- Y-86

Brackenbury, Alison 1953- DLB-40

Brackenridge, Hugh Henry 1748-1816 ..... DLB-11, 37

Brackett, Charles 1892-1969 .... DLB-26

Brackett, Leigh 1915-1978 .... DLB-8, 26

Bradburn, John [publishing house] DLB-49

Bradbury, Malcolm 1932- DLB-14

Bradbury, Ray 1920- DLB-2, 8

Braddon, Mary Elizabeth 1835-1915 .... DLB-18, 70

Bradford, Andrew 1686-1742 .... DLB-43, 73

Bradford, Gamaliel 1863-1932 .... DLB-17

Bradford, John 1749-1830 .... DLB-43

Bradford, William 1590-1657 .... DLB-24, 30

Bradford, William III 1719-1791 .... DLB-43, 73

Bradlaugh, Charles 1833-1891 .... DLB-57

Bradley, David 1950- DLB-33

Bradley, Ira, and Company DLB-49

Bradley, J. W., and Company DLB-49

Bradley, Marion Zimmer 1930- DLB-8

Bradley, William Aspenwall 1878-1939 .... DLB-4

Bradstreet, Anne 1612 or 1613-1672 .... DLB-24

Brady, Frederic A. [publishing house] DLB-49

Bragg, Melvyn 1939- DLB-14

Brainard, Charles H. [publishing house] DLB-49

Braine, John 1922-1986 .... DLB-15; Y-86

Braithwaite, William Stanley
  1878-1962 .... DLB-50, 54

Bramah, Ernest 1868-1942 .... DLB-70

Branagan, Thomas 1774-1843 .... DLB-37

Branden Press DLB-46

Brault, Jacques 1933- DLB-53

Brautigan, Richard 1935-1984 ...... DLB-2, 5; Y-80, 84

Braxton, Joanne M. 1950- DLB-41

Bray, Thomas 1656-1730 .... DLB-24

Braziller, George [publishing house] DLB-46

The Bread Loaf Writers' Conference 1983 .... Y-84

The Break-Up of the Novel (1922),
  by John Middleton Murry DLB-36

Breasted, James Henry 1865-1935 .... DLB-47

Brecht, Bertolt 1898-1956 .... DLB-56

Bredel, Willi 1901-1964 .... DLB-56

Bremser, Bonnie 1939- DLB-16

Bremser, Ray 1934- DLB-16

Brentano, Bernard von 1901-1964 .... DLB-56

Brentano's DLB-49

Brenton, Howard 1942- DLB-13

Breton, André 1896-1966 .... DLB-65

Brewer, Warren and Putnam DLB-46

Brewster, Elizabeth 1922- DLB-60

Bridgers, Sue Ellen 1942- DLB-52

Bridges, Robert 1844-1930 .... DLB-19

Bridie, James 1888-1951 .... DLB-10

Briggs, Charles Frederick 1804-1877 .... DLB-3

Brighouse, Harold 1882-1958 .... DLB-10

Brimmer, B. J., Company DLB-46

Brinnin, John Malcolm 1916- DLB-48

Brisbane, Albert 1809-1890 .... DLB-3

Brisbane, Arthur 1864-1936 .... DLB-25

Broadway Publishing Company DLB-46

Brochu, André 1942- DLB-53

Brock, Edwin 1927- DLB-40

Brodhead, John R. 1814-1873 .... DLB-30

Brome, Richard circa 1590-1652 .... DLB-58

Bromfield, Louis 1896-1956 .... DLB-4, 9

Broner, E. M. 1930- DLB-28

Brontë, Anne 1820-1849 .... DLB-21

Brontë, Charlotte 1816-1855 .... DLB-21

Brontë, Emily 1818-1848 ....DLB-21, 32

Brooke, Frances 1724-1789................... DLB-39

Brooke, Henry 1703?-1783................... DLB-39

Brooke, Rupert 1887-1915 .... DLB-19

Brooke-Rose, Christine 1926- DLB-14

Brookner, Anita 1928- Y-87

Brooks, Charles Timothy 1813-1883 ....DLB-1

Brooks, Cleanth 1906- DLB-63

Brooks, Gwendolyn 1917- DLB-5

Brooks, Jeremy 1926- DLB-14

Brooks, Mel 1926- DLB-26

Brooks, Noah 1830-1903 .... DLB-42

Brooks, Richard 1912- DLB-44

Brooks, Van Wyck 1886-1963 ....DLB-45, 63

Brophy, Brigid 1929- DLB-14

Brossard, Chandler 1922- DLB-16

Brossard, Nicole 1943- DLB-53

Brother Antoninus (see Everson, William)

Brougham, John 1810-1880 .... DLB-11

Broughton, James 1913- DLB-5

Broughton, Rhoda 1840-1920 .... DLB-18

Broun, Heywood 1888-1939............ DLB-29

Brown, Bob 1886-1959 ....DLB-4, 45

Brown, Cecil 1943- DLB-33

Brown, Charles Brockden 1771-1810...DLB-37, 59, 73

Brown, Christy 1932-1981.................... DLB-14

Brown, Dee 1908- Y-80

Brown, Fredric 1906-1972.....................DLB-8

Brown, George Mackay 1921- DLB-14, 27

Brown, Harry 1917-1986.................... DLB-26

Brown, Marcia 1918- DLB-61

Brown, Margaret Wise 1910-1952 .... DLB-22

Brown, Oliver Madox 1855-1874 .... DLB-21

Brown, Sterling 1901- DLB-48, 51, 63

Brown, T. E. 1830-1897 .... DLB-35

Brown, William Hill 1765-1793................ DLB-37

Brown, William Wells 1814-1884 ....DLB-3, 50

Browne, Charles Farrar 1834-1867 .... DLB-11

Browne, Michael Dennis 1940- DLB-40

Browne, Wynyard 1911-1964................. DLB-13

Brownell, W. C. 1851-1928................... DLB-71

Browning, Elizabeth Barrett 1806-1861 .... DLB-32

Browning, Robert 1812-1889................. DLB-32

Brownjohn, Allan 1931- DLB-40

Brownson, Orestes Augustus
       1803-1876.........................DLB-1, 59, 73

Bruce, Charles 1906-1971 .... DLB-68

Bruce, Philip Alexander 1856-1933 .... DLB-47

Bruce Humphries [publishing house] DLB-46

Bruckman, Clyde 1894-1955 .... DLB-26

Brundage, John Herbert (see Herbert, John)

Bryant, William Cullen 1794-1878.......DLB-3, 43, 59

Buchan, John 1875-1940 ....DLB-34, 70

Buchanan, Robert 1841-1901.............DLB-18, 35

Buchman, Sidney 1902-1975 .... DLB-26

Buck, Pearl S. 1892-1973.....................DLB-9

Buckingham, Joseph Tinker 1779-1861 and
       Buckingham, Edwin 1810-1833 .... DLB-73

Buckler, Ernest 1908-1984 .... DLB-68

Buckley, William F., Jr. 1925- Y-80

Buckminster, Joseph Stevens 1784-1812....... DLB-37

Buckner, Robert 1906- DLB-26

Budd, Thomas ?-1698..................... DLB-24

Budrys, A. J. 1931- DLB-8

Buechner, Frederick 1926- Y-80

Buell, John 1927- DLB-53

Buffum, Job [publishing house] DLB-49

Bukowski, Charles 1920- DLB-5

Bullins, Ed 1935- DLB-7, 38

Bulwer-Lytton, Edward (also Edward Bulwer)
       1803-1873............................... DLB-21

Bumpus, Jerry 1937- Y-81

Bunce and Brother......................... DLB-49

Bunting, Basil 1900-1985..................... DLB-20

Bunyan, John 1628-1688 .... DLB-39

Burch, Robert 1925- DLB-52

Burgess, Anthony 1917- DLB-14

Burgess, Gelett 1866-1951.................... DLB-11

Burgess, John W. 1844-1931 .... DLB-47

Burgess, Thornton W. 1874-1965 .... DLB-22

Burgess, Stringer and Company DLB-49

Burk, John Daly circa 1772-1808 .... DLB-37

Burke, Kenneth 1897- DLB-45, 63

Burnett, Frances Hodgson 1849-1924 .... DLB-42

Burnett, W. R. 1899-1982 .... DLB-9

Burney, Fanny 1752-1840 .... DLB-39

Burns, Alan 1929- DLB-14

Burns, John Horne 1916-1953 .... Y-85

Burnshaw, Stanley 1906- DLB-48

Burroughs, Edgar Rice 1875-1950 .... DLB-8

Burroughs, John 1837-1921 .... DLB-64

Burroughs, Margaret T. G. 1917- DLB-41

Burroughs, William S., Jr. 1947-1981 .... DLB-16

Burroughs, William Seward 1914-
.... DLB-2, 8, 16; Y-81

Burroway, Janet 1936- DLB-6

Burt, A. L., and Company DLB-49

Burton, Richard F. 1821-1890 .... DLB-55

Burton, Virginia Lee 1909-1968 .... DLB-22

Burton, William Evans 1804-1860 .... DLB-73

Busch, Frederick 1941- DLB-6

Busch, Niven 1903- DLB-44

Butler, E. H., and Company DLB-49

Butler, Juan 1942-1981 .... DLB-53

Butler, Octavia E. 1947- DLB-33

Butler, Samuel 1835-1902 .... DLB-18, 57

Butterworth, Hezekiah 1839-1905 .... DLB-42

B. V. (see Thomson, James)

Byars, Betsy 1928- DLB-52

Byatt, A. S. 1936- DLB-14

Byles, Mather 1707-1788 .... DLB-24

Bynner, Witter 1881-1968 .... DLB-54

Byrd, William II 1674-1744 .... DLB-24

Byrne, John Keyes (see Leonard, Hugh)

C

Cabell, James Branch 1879-1958 .... DLB-9

Cable, George Washington 1844-1925 .... DLB-12

Cahan, Abraham 1860-1951 .... DLB-9, 25, 28

Cain, George 1943- DLB-33

Caldwell, Ben 1937- DLB-38

Caldwell, Erskine 1903-1987 .... DLB-9

Caldwell, H. M., Company DLB-49

Calhoun, John C. 1782-1850 .... DLB-3

Calisher, Hortense 1911- DLB-2

Callaghan, Morley 1903- DLB-68

Callaloo Y-87

Calmer, Edgar 1907- DLB-4

Calverley, C. S. 1831-1884 .... DLB-35

Calvert, George Henry 1803-1889 .... DLB-1, 64

Cambridge Press DLB-49

Cameron, Eleanor 1912- DLB-52

Camm, John 1718-1778 .... DLB-31

Campbell, Gabrielle Margaret Vere
    (see Shearing, Joseph)

Campbell, James Edwin 1867-1896 .... DLB-50

Campbell, John 1653-1728 .... DLB-43

Campbell, John W., Jr. 1910-1971 .... DLB-8

Campbell, Roy 1901-1957 .... DLB-20

Campion, Thomas 1567-1620 .... DLB-58

Camus, Albert 1913-1960 .... DLB-72

Candour in English Fiction (1890),
    by Thomas Hardy DLB-18

Cannan, Gilbert 1884-1955 .... DLB-10

Cannell, Kathleen 1891-1974 .... DLB-4

Cannell, Skipwith 1887-1957 .... DLB-45

Cantwell, Robert 1908-1978 .... DLB-9

Cape, Jonathan, and Harrison Smith
    [publishing house] DLB-46

Capen, Joseph 1658-1725 .... DLB-24

Capote, Truman 1924-1984 .... DLB-2; Y-80, 84

Carey, M., and Company DLB-49

Carey, Mathew 1760-1839 .... DLB-37, 73

Carey and Hart DLB-49

Carlell, Lodowick 1602-1675 .... DLB-58

Carleton, G. W. [publishing house]............ DLB-49

Carossa, Hans 1878-1956..................... DLB-66

Carr, Emily 1871-1945 .... DLB-68

Carrier, Roch 1937- DLB-53

Carlyle, Jane Welsh 1801-1866 .... DLB-55

Carlyle, Thomas 1795-1881 .... DLB-55

Carpenter, Stephen Cullen ?-1820?........... DLB-73

Carroll, Gladys Hasty 1904- DLB-9

Carroll, John 1735-1815..................... DLB-37

Carroll, Lewis 1832-1898 .... DLB-18

Carroll, Paul 1927- DLB-16

Carroll, Paul Vincent 1900-1968.............. DLB-10

Carroll and Graf Publishers DLB-46

Carruth, Hayden 1921- DLB-5

Carryl, Charles E. 1841-1920................ DLB-42

Carswell, Catherine 1879-1946 .... DLB-36

Carter, Angela 1940- DLB-14

Carter, Henry (see Leslie, Frank)

Carter, Landon 1710-1778 .... DLB-31

Carter, Lin 1930- Y-81

Carter, Robert, and Brothers................. DLB-49

Carter and Hendee.......................... DLB-49

Caruthers, William Alexander 1802-1846 ....DLB-3

Carver, Jonathan 1710-1780................. DLB-31

Carver, Raymond 1938- Y-84

Cary, Joyce 1888-1957...................... DLB-15

Casey, Juanita 1925- DLB-14

Casey, Michael 1947- DLB-5

Cassady, Carolyn 1923- DLB-16

Cassady, Neal 1926-1968 .... DLB-16

Cassell Publishing Company................. DLB-49

Cassill, R. V. 1919- DLB-6

Castlemon, Harry (see Fosdick, Charles Austin)

Caswall, Edward 1814-1878 .... DLB-32

Cather, Willa 1873-1947............. DLB-9, 54; DS-1

Catton, Bruce 1899-1978..................... DLB-17

Causley, Charles 1917- DLB-27

Caute, David 1936- DLB-14

Cawein, Madison 1865-1914.................. DLB-54

The Caxton Printers, Limited DLB-46

Celan, Paul 1920-1970........................ DLB-69

Céline, Louis-Ferdinand 1894-1961 .... DLB-72

Center for the Book Research.....................Y-84

The Century Company........................ DLB-49

Challans, Eileen Mary (see Renault, Mary)

Chalmers, George 1742-1825.................. DLB-30

Chamberlain, Samuel S. 1851-1916........... DLB-25

Chamberland, Paul 1939- DLB-60

Chamberlin, William Henry 1897-1969........ DLB-29

Chambers, Charles Haddon 1860-1921........ DLB-10

Chandler, Harry 1864-1944 .... DLB-29

Channing, Edward 1856-1931 .... DLB-17

Channing, Edward Tyrrell 1790-1856.......DLB-1, 59

Channing, William Ellery 1780-1842 ....DLB-1, 59

Channing, William Ellery II 1817-1901.........DLB-1

Channing, William Henry 1810-1884.......DLB-1, 59

Chaplin, Charlie 1889-1977 .... DLB-44

Chapman, George 1559 or 1560-1634......... DLB-62

Chappell, Fred 1936- DLB-6

Charbonneau, Robert 1911-1967.............. DLB-68

Charles, Gerda 1914- DLB-14

Charles, William [publishing house] DLB-49

The Charles Wood Affair:
   A Playwright Revived Y-83

Charlotte Forten: Pages from her Diary....... DLB-50

Charyn, Jerome 1937- Y-83

Chase, Borden 1900-1971 .... DLB-26

Chase-Riboud, Barbara 1936- DLB-33

Chauncy, Charles 1705-1787 .... DLB-24

Chayefsky, Paddy 1923-1981 .... DLB-7, 44; Y-81

Cheever, Ezekiel 1615-1708 .... DLB-24

Cheever, George Barrell 1807-1890 .... DLB-59

Cheever, John 1912-1982............ DLB-2; Y-80, 82

Cheever, Susan 1943- Y-82

Chelsea House.................................. DLB-46

Cheney, Ednah Dow (Littlehale) 1824-1904 .....DLB-1

Cherry, Kelly 1940 ....Y-83

Cherryh, C. J. 1942- Y-80

Chesnutt, Charles Waddell 1858-1932......DLB-12, 50

Chesterton, G. K. 1874-1936 ....DLB-10, 19, 34, 70

Cheyney, Edward P. 1861-1947 .... DLB-47

Child, Francis James 1825-1896 ....DLB-1, 64

Child, Lydia Maria 1802-1880..................DLB-1

Child, Philip 1898-1978 .... DLB-68

Childers, Erskine 1870-1922.................. DLB-70

Children's Book Awards and Prizes DLB-61

Childress, Alice 1920- DLB-7, 38

Childs, George W. 1829-1894 .... DLB-23

Chilton Book Company........................ DLB-46

Chittenden, Hiram Martin 1858-1917 .... DLB-47

Chivers, Thomas Holley 1809-1858 ....DLB-3

Chopin, Kate 1850 or 1851-1904.............. DLB-12

Choquette, Adrienne 1915-1973.............. DLB-68

Choquette, Robert 1905- DLB-68

The Christian Publishing Company DLB-49

Christie, Agatha 1890-1976................... DLB-13

Church, Benjamin 1734-1778 .... DLB-31

Churchill, Caryl 1938- DLB-13

Ciardi, John 1916-1986.................. DLB-5; Y-86

City Lights Books............................ DLB-46

Clapper, Raymond 1892-1944................ DLB-29

Clare, John 1793-1864....................... DLB-55

Clark, Ann Nolan 1896- DLB-52

Clark, C. M., Publishing Company DLB-46

Clark, Catherine Anthony 1892-1977......... DLB-68

Clark, Charles Heber 1841-1915 .... DLB-11

Clark, Eleanor 1913- DLB-6

Clark, Lewis Gaylord 1808-1873........ DLB-3, 64, 73

Clark, Walter Van Tilburg 1909-1971...........DLB-9

Clarke, Austin 1896-1974...................DLB-10, 20

Clarke, Austin C. 1934- DLB-53

Clarke, Gillian 1937- DLB-40

Clarke, James Freeman 1810-1888 ....DLB-1, 59

Clarke, Rebecca Sophia 1833-1906 .... DLB-42

Clarke, Robert, and Company................ DLB-49

Clausen, Andy 1943- DLB-16

Claxton, Remsen and Haffelfinger DLB-49

Clay, Cassius Marcellus 1810-1903............ DLB-43

Cleary, Beverly 1916- DLB-52

Cleaver, Vera 1919-   and
    Cleaver, Bill 1920-1981 .... DLB-52

Cleland, John 1710-1789 .... DLB-39

Clemens, Samuel Langhorne
    1835-1910....................DLB-11, 12, 23, 64

Clement, Hal 1922- DLB-8

Clemo, Jack 1916- DLB-27

Clifton, Lucille 1936- DLB-5, 41

Clode, Edward J. [publishing house] DLB-46

Clough, Arthur Hugh 1819-1861.............. DLB-32

Cloutier, Cécile 1930- DLB-60

Coates, Robert M. 1897-1973.................DLB-4, 9

Coatsworth, Elizabeth 1893- DLB-22

Cobb, Jr., Charles E. 1943- DLB-41

Cobb, Frank I. 1869-1923 .... DLB-25

Cobb, Irvin S. 1876-1944....................DLB-11, 25

Cobbett, William 1762-1835 .... DLB-43

Cochran, Thomas C. 1902- DLB-17

Cochrane, Elizabeth 1867-1922................ DLB-25

Cockerill, John A. 1845-1896.................. DLB-23

Cocteau, Jean 1889-1963 .... DLB-65

Coffee, Lenore J. 1900?-1984 .... DLB-44

Coffin, Robert P. Tristram 1892-1955......... DLB-45

Cogswell, Fred 1917- DLB-60

Cogswell, Mason Fitch 1761-1830 .... DLB-37

Cohen, Arthur A. 1928-1986.................. DLB-28

Cohen, Leonard 1934- DLB-53

Cohen, Matt 1942- DLB-53

Colden, Cadwallader 1688-1776............DLB-24, 30

Cole, Barry 1936- DLB-14

Colegate, Isabel 1931- DLB-14

Coleman, Emily Holmes 1899-1974 ....DLB-4

Coleridge, Mary 1861-1907.................... DLB-19

Colette 1873-1954 .... DLB-65

Colette, Sidonie Gabrielle (see Colette)

Collier, P. F. [publishing house] DLB-49

Collin and Small............................. DLB-49

Collins, Isaac [publishing house]............... DLB-49

Collins, Mortimer 1827-1876 ....DLB-21, 35

Collins, Wilkie 1824-1889.................DLB-18, 70

Collyer, Mary 1716?-1763? DLB-39

Colman, Benjamin 1673-1747 .... DLB-24

Colman, S. [publishing house] DLB-49

Colombo, John Robert 1936- DLB-53

Colter, Cyrus 1910- DLB-33

Colum, Padraic 1881-1972 .... DLB-19

Colwin, Laurie 1944- Y-80

Comden, Betty 1919- and Green,
    Adolph 1918- DLB-44

The Comic Tradition Continued
    [in the British Novel] DLB-15

Commager, Henry Steele 1902- DLB-17

The Commercialization of the Image of
    Revolt, by Kenneth Rexroth DLB-16

Community and Commentators: Black
    Theatre and Its Critics DLB-38

Compton-Burnett, Ivy 1884?-1969 .... DLB-36

Conference on Modern Biography Y-85

Congreve, William 1670-1729 .... DLB-39

Conkey, W. B., Company DLB-49

Connell, Evan S., Jr. 1924- DLB-2; Y-81

Connelly, Marc 1890-1980 .... DLB-7; Y-80

Connor, Tony 1930- DLB-40

Conquest, Robert 1917- DLB-27

Conrad, John, and Company DLB-49

Conrad, Joseph 1857-1924 ....DLB-10, 34

Conroy, Jack 1899- Y-81

Conroy, Pat 1945- DLB-6

The Consolidation of Opinion: Critical
    Responses to the Modernists DLB-36

Constantine, David 1944- DLB-40

Contempo Caravan: Kites in a Windstorm Y-85

A Contemporary Flourescence of Chicano
    Literature Y-84

The Continental Publishing Company DLB-49

A Conversation with Chaim Potok Y-84

Conversations with Publishers I: An Interview
    with Patrick O'Connor Y-84

Conway, Moncure Daniel 1832-1907 ....DLB-1

Cook, David C., Publishing Company DLB-49

Cook, Ebenezer circa 1667-circa 1732 .... DLB-24

Cook, Michael 1933- DLB-53

Cooke, George Willis 1848-1923 .... DLB-71

Cooke, Increase, and Company DLB-49

Cooke, John Esten 1830-1886 ....DLB-3

Cooke, Philip Pendleton 1816-1850 ....DLB-3, 59

Cooke, Rose Terry 1827-1892 .... DLB-12

Coolbrith, Ina 1841-1928 .... DLB-54

Coolidge, George [publishing house] DLB-49

Coolidge, Susan (see Woolsey, Sarah Chauncy)

Cooper, Giles 1918-1966 .... DLB-13

Cooper, James Fenimore 1789-1851 ....DLB-3

Cooper, Kent 1880-1965 .... DLB-29

Coover, Robert 1932- DLB-2; Y-81

Copeland and Day DLB-49

Coppel, Alfred 1921- Y-83

Coppola, Francis Ford 1939- DLB-44

Corcoran, Barbara 1911- DLB-52

Corelli, Marie 1855-1924 .... DLB-34

Corle, Edwin 1906-1956 ....Y-85

Corman, Cid 1924- DLB-5

Cormier, Robert 1925- DLB-52

Corn, Alfred 1943- Y-80

Cornish, Sam 1935- DLB-41

Corrington, John William 1932- DLB-6

Corrothers, James D. 1869-1917 .... DLB-50

Corso, Gregory 1930- DLB-5, 16

Cortez, Jayne 1936- DLB-41

Corvo, Baron (see Rolfe, Frederick William)

Cory, William Johnson 1823-1892 .... DLB-35

Cosmopolitan Book Corporation DLB-46

Costain, Thomas B. 1885-1965 ....DLB-9

Cotter, Joseph Seamon, Sr.
    1861-1949 .... DLB-50

Cotter, Joseph Seamon, Jr.
    1895-1919 .... DLB-50

Cotton, John 1584-1652 .... DLB-24

Coulter, John 1888-1980 .... DLB-68

Cournos, John 1881-1966 .... DLB-54

Coventry, Francis 1725-1754 .... DLB-39

Coverly, N. [publishing house] DLB-49

Covici-Friede DLB-46

Coward, Noel 1899-1973 .... DLB-10

Coward, McCann and Geoghegan DLB-46

Cowles, Gardner 1861-1946 .... DLB-29

Cowley, Malcolm 1898- DLB-4, 48; Y-81

Cox, Palmer 1840-1924...................... DLB-42

Coxe, Louis 1918- DLB-5

Coxe, Tench 1755-1824 .... DLB-37

Cozzens, James Gould 1903-1978...DLB-9; Y-84; DS-2

Craddock, Charles Egbert (see Murfree, Mary N.)

Cradock, Thomas 1718-1770 .... DLB-31

Craig, Daniel H. 1811-1895 .... DLB-43

Craik, Dinah Maria 1826-1887 .... DLB-35

Cranch, Christopher Pearse 1813-1892......DLB-1, 42

Crane, Hart 1899-1932.....................DLB-4, 48

Crane, R. S. 1886-1967...................... DLB-63

Crane, Stephen 1871-1900 ....DLB-12, 54

Crapsey, Adelaide 1878-1914................. DLB-54

Craven, Avery 1885-1980..................... DLB-17

Crawford, Charles 1752-circa 1815............ DLB-31

Crawford, F. Marion 1854-1909.............. DLB-71

Crawley, Alan 1887-1975.................... DLB-68

Crayon, Geoffrey (see Irving, Washington)

Creative Age Press........................... DLB-46

Creel, George 1876-1953 .... DLB-25

Creeley, Robert 1926- DLB-5, 16

Creelman, James 1859-1915.................. DLB-23

Cregan, David 1931- DLB-13

Crèvecoeur, Michel Guillaume Jean de
    1735-1813............................... DLB-37

Crews, Harry 1935- DLB-6

Crichton, Michael 1942- Y-81

A Crisis of Culture: The Changing Role
    of Religion in the New Republic DLB-37

Cristofer, Michael 1946- DLB-7

"The Critic as Artist" (1891), by Oscar Wilde.. DLB-57

Criticism In Relation To Novels (1863),
    by G. H. Lewes........................... DLB-21

Crockett, David (Davy) 1786-1836...........DLB-3, 11

Croly, Jane Cunningham 1829-1901........... DLB-23

Crosby, Caresse 1892-1970 .... DLB-48

Crosby, Caresse 1892-1970 and Crosby,
    Harry 1898-1929........................DLB-4

Crosby, Harry 1898-1929.................... DLB-48

Crossley-Holland, Kevin 1941- DLB-40

Crothers, Rachel 1878-1958 ....DLB-7

Crowell, Thomas Y., Company DLB-49

Crowley, John 1942- Y-82

Crowley, Mart 1935- DLB-7

Crown Publishers............................. DLB-46

Croy, Homer 1883-1965.......................DLB-4

Crumley, James 1939- Y-84

Cruz, Victor Hernández 1949- DLB-41

Cullen, Countee 1903-1946.............DLB-4, 48, 51

Culler, Jonathan D. 1944- DLB-67

The Cult of Biography
    Excerpts from the Second Folio Debate:
      "Biographies are generally a disease of
      English Literature"—Germaine Greer,
      Victoria Glendinning, Auberon Waugh,
      and Richard Holmes Y-86

Cummings, E. E. 1894-1962.................DLB-4, 48

Cummings, Ray 1887-1957.....................DLB-8

Cummings and Hilliard DLB-49

Cummins, Maria Susanna 1827-1866......... DLB-42

Cuney, Waring 1906-1976.................... DLB-51

Cuney-Hare, Maude 1874-1936 .... DLB-52

Cunningham, J. V. 1911- DLB-5

Cunningham, Peter F. [publishing house] DLB-49

Cuomo, George 1929- Y-80

Cupples and Leon............................ DLB-46

Cupples, Upham and Company DLB-49

Cuppy, Will 1884-1949....................... DLB-11

Currie, Mary Montgomerie Lamb Singleton,
    Lady Currie (see Fane, Violet)

Curti, Merle E. 1897- DLB-17

Curtis, George William 1824-1892...........DLB-1, 43

D

D. M. Thomas: The Plagiarism Controversy.......Y-82

Dabit, Eugène 1898-1936..................... DLB-65

Daborne, Robert circa 1580-1628.............. DLB-58

Dahlberg, Edward 1900-1977.................. DLB-48

Dale, Peter 1938- DLB-40

Dall, Caroline Wells (Healey) 1822-1912........DLB-1

Dallas, E. S. 1828-1879 .... DLB-55

The Dallas Theater Center DLB-7

D'Alton, Louis 1900-1951 .... DLB-10

Daly, T. A. 1871-1948........................ DLB-11

Damon, S. Foster 1893-1971.................. DLB-45

Damrell, William S. [publishing house]........ DLB-49

Dana, Charles A. 1819-1897................DLB-3, 23

Dana, Richard Henry, Jr. 1815-1882 ....DLB-1

Dandridge, Ray Garfield...................... DLB-51

Dane, Clemence 1887-1965.................... DLB-10

Danforth, John 1660-1730.................... DLB-24

Danforth, Samuel I 1626-1674 .... DLB-24

Danforth, Samuel II 1666-1727 .... DLB-24

Dangerous Years: London Theater,
    1939-1945................................. DLB-10

Daniel, John M. 1825-1865................... DLB-43

Daniel, Samuel 1562 or 1563-1619 .... DLB-62

Daniells, Roy 1902-1979..................... DLB-68

Daniels, Josephus 1862-1948 .... DLB-29

Danner, Margaret Esse 1915- DLB-41

Darwin, Charles 1809-1882.................. DLB-57

Daryush, Elizabeth 1887-1977 .... DLB-20

Dashwood, Edmée Elizabeth Monica
    de la Pasture (see Delafield, E. M.)

d'Aulaire, Edgar Parin 1898-   and
    d'Aulaire, Ingri 1904- DLB-22

Davenant, Sir William 1606-1668.............. DLB-58

Davenport, Robert ?-? DLB-58

Daves, Delmer 1904-1977 .... DLB-26

Davey, Frank 1940- DLB-53

Davidson, Avram 1923- DLB-8

Davidson, Donald 1893-1968 .... DLB-45

Davidson, John 1857-1909.................... DLB-19

Davidson, Lionel 1922- DLB-14

Davie, Donald 1922- DLB-27

Davies, Robertson 1913- DLB-68

Davies, Samuel 1723-1761 .... DLB-31

Davies, W. H. 1871-1940 .... DLB-19

Daviot, Gordon 1896-1952 .... DLB-10

Davis, Charles A. 1795-1867................. DLB-11

Davis, Clyde Brion 1894-1962 ....DLB-9

Davis, Dick 1945- DLB-40

Davis, Frank Marshall 1905-?................. DLB-51

Davis, H. L. 1894-1960 ....DLB-9

Davis, John 1774-1854........................ DLB-37

Davis, Margaret Thomson 1926- DLB-14

Davis, Ossie 1917- DLB-7, 38

Davis, Richard Harding 1864-1916........DLB-12, 23

Davis, Samuel Cole 1764-1809................. DLB-37

Davison, Peter 1928- DLB-5

Davys, Mary 1674-1732...................... DLB-39

DAW Books DLB-46

Dawson, William 1704-1752 .... DLB-31

Day, Benjamin Henry 1810-1889.............. DLB-43

Day, Clarence 1874-1935 .... DLB-11

Day, Dorothy 1897-1980...................... DLB-29

Day, John circa 1574-circa 1640 .... DLB-62

Day, The John, Company DLB-46

Day Lewis, C. 1904-1972 ....DLB-15, 20

Day, Mahlon [publishing house].............. DLB-49

Day, Thomas 1748-1789...................... DLB-39

Deacon, William Arthur 1890-1977........... DLB-68

Deal, Borden 1922-1985.......................DLB-6

de Angeli, Marguerite 1889-1987............. DLB-22

De Bow, James D. B. 1820-1867................DLB-3

de Camp, L. Sprague 1907- DLB-8

The Decay of Lying (1889),
    by Oscar Wilde [excerpt]................. DLB-18

Dedication, *Ferdinand Count Fathom* (1753),
    by Tobias Smollett DLB-39

Dedication, *Lasselia* (1723), by Eliza
    Haywood [excerpt]....................... DLB-39

Dedication, *The History of Pompey the
    Little* (1751), by Francis Coventry DLB-39

Dedication, *The Wanderer* (1814),
    by Fanny Burney.......................... DLB-39

Defense of *Amelia* (1752), by Henry Fielding .. DLB-39

Defoe, Daniel 1660-1731 .... DLB-39

de Fontaińe, Felix Gregory 1834-1896........ DLB-43

De Forest, John William 1826-1906 .... DLB-12

de Graff, Robert 1895-1981 ....Y-81

DeJong, Meindert 1906- DLB-52

Dekker, Thomas circa 1572-1632............. DLB-62

Delafield, E. M. 1890-1943 .... DLB-34

de la Mare, Walter 1873-1956 .... DLB-19

de la Roche, Mazo 1879-1961 .... DLB-68

Delaney, Shelagh 1939- DLB-13

Delany, Martin Robinson 1812-1885.......... DLB-50

Delany, Samuel R. 1942- DLB-8, 33

Delbanco, Nicholas 1942- DLB-6

DeLillo, Don 1936- DLB-6

Dell, Floyd 1887-1969 .... DLB-9

Dell Publishing Company..................... DLB-46

del Rey, Lester 1915- DLB-8

de Man, Paul 1919-1983..................... DLB-67

Demby, William 1922- DLB-33

Denham, Sir John 1615-1669................. DLB-58

Denison, T. S., and Company DLB-49

Dennie, Joseph 1768-1812.........DLB-37, 43, 59, 73

Dennis, Nigel 1912- DLB-13, 15

Dent, Tom 1932- DLB-38

Denton, Daniel circa 1626-1703 .... DLB-24

DePaola, Tomie 1934- DLB-61

Derby, George Horatio 1823-1861............. DLB-11

Derby, J. C., and Company.................. DLB-49

Derby and Miller DLB-49

Derleth, August 1909-1971.................... DLB-9

The Derrydale Press......................... DLB-46

Desbiens, Jean-Paul 1927- DLB-53

DesRochers, Alfred 1901-1978 .... DLB-68

Desrosiers, Léo-Paul 1896-1967 .... DLB-68

Destouches, Louis-Ferdinand (see Céline, Louis-Ferdinand)

De Tabley, Lord 1835-1895 .... DLB-35

Deutsch, Babette 1895-1982 .... DLB-45

Deveaux, Alexis 1948- DLB-38

The Development of Lighting in the Staging
　　of Drama, 1900-1945 [in Great Britain]... DLB-10

de Vere, Aubrey 1814-1902 .... DLB-35

The Devin-Adair Company................... DLB-46

De Voto, Bernard 1897-1955.................. DLB-9

De Vries, Peter 1910- DLB-6; Y-82

Dewdney, Christopher 1951- DLB-60

Dewdney, Selwyn 1909-1979 .... DLB-68

DeWitt, Robert M., Publisher................ DLB-49

DeWolfe, Fiske and Company DLB-49

de Young, M. H. 1849-1925.................. DLB-25

The Dial Press.............................. DLB-46

Diamond, I. A. L. 1920- DLB-26

Di Cicco, Pier Giorgio 1949- DLB-60

Dick, Philip K. 1928- DLB-8

Dick and Fitzgerald.......................... DLB-49

Dickens, Charles 1812-1870 ....DLB-21, 55, 70

Dickey, James 1923- DLB-5; Y-82

Dickey, William 1928- DLB-5

Dickinson, Emily 1830-1886................... DLB-1

Dickinson, John 1732-1808................... DLB-31

Dickinson, Jonathan 1688-1747............... DLB-24

Dickinson, Patric 1914- DLB-27

Dickson, Gordon R. 1923- DLB-8

Didion, Joan 1934- DLB-2; Y-81, 86

Di Donato, Pietro 1911- DLB-9

Dillard, Annie 1945- Y-80

Dillard, R. H. W. 1937- DLB-5

Dillingham, Charles T., Company DLB-49

The G. W. Dillingham Company DLB-49

Dintenfass, Mark 1941- Y-84

Diogenes, Jr. (see Brougham, John)

DiPrima, Diane 1934- DLB-5, 16

Disch, Thomas M. 1940- DLB-8

Disney, Walt 1901-1966 .... DLB-22

Disraeli, Benjamin 1804-1881 ....DLB-21, 55

Ditzen, Rudolf (see Fallada, Hans)

Dix, Dorothea Lynde 1802-1887................ DLB-1

Dix, Dorothy (see Gilmer, Elizabeth Meriwether)

Dix, Edwards and Company.................. DLB-49

Dixon, Paige (see Corcoran, Barbara)

Dixon, Richard Watson 1833-1900 .... DLB-19

Dobell, Sydney 1824-1874 .... DLB-32

Döblin, Alfred 1878-1957 .... DLB-66

Dobson, Austin 1840-1921................... DLB-35

Doctorow, E. L. 1931- DLB-2, 28; Y-80

Dodd, William E. 1869-1940................. DLB-17

Dodd, Mead and Company................... DLB-49

Dodge, B. W., and Company................ DLB-46

Dodge, Mary Mapes 1831?-1905.............. DLB-42

Dodge Publishing Company................. DLB-49

Dodgson, Charles Lutwidge (see Carroll, Lewis)

Doesticks, Q. K. Philander, P. B. (see Thomson, Mortimer)

Donahoe, Patrick [publishing house] DLB-49

Donald, David H. 1920- DLB-17

Donleavy, J. P. 1926- DLB-6

Donnelley, R. R., and Sons Company......... DLB-49

Donnelly, Ignatius 1831-1901 .... DLB-12

Donohue and Henneberry.................... DLB-49

Doolady, M. [publishing house]............... DLB-49

Dooley, Ebon (see Ebon)

Doolittle, Hilda 1886-1961...................DLB-4, 45

Doran, George H., Company................. DLB-46

Dorgelès, Roland 1886-1973.................. DLB-65

Dorn, Edward 1929- DLB-5

Dorr, Rheta Childe 1866-1948................. DLB-25

Dos Passos, John 1896-1970...........DLB-4, 9; DS-1

Doubleday and Company..................... DLB-49

Doughty, Charles M. 1843-1926............DLB-19, 57

Douglas, Keith 1920-1944 .... DLB-27

Douglas, Norman 1868-1952 .... DLB-34

Douglass, Frederick 1817?-1895.........DLB-1, 43, 50

Douglass, William circa 1691-1752............. DLB-24

Dover Publications........................... DLB-46

Dowden, Edward 1843-1913................. DLB-35

Downing, J., Major (see Davis, Charles A.)

Downing, Major Jack (see Smith, Seba)

Dowson, Ernest 1867-1900 .... DLB-19

Doxey, William [publishing house] DLB-49

Doyle, Sir Arthur Conan 1859-1930.......DLB-18, 70

Doyle, Kirby 1932- DLB-16

Drabble, Margaret 1939- DLB-14

The Dramatic Publishing Company DLB-49

Dramatists Play Service...................... DLB-46

Draper, John W. 1811-1882 .... DLB-30

Draper, Lyman C. 1815-1891................. DLB-30

Dreiser, Theodore 1871-1945 .... DLB-9, 12; DS-1

Drieu La Rochelle, Pierre 1893-1945 .... DLB-72

Drinkwater, John 1882-1937 ....DLB-10, 19

The Drue Heinz Literature Prize
Excerpt from "Excerpts from a Report
of the Commission," in David
Bosworth's *The Death of Descartes*
An Interview with David Bosworth Y-82

Duane, William 1760-1835 .... DLB-43

Dubé, Marcel 1930- DLB-53

Dubé, Rodolphe (see Hertel, François)

Du Bois, W. E. B. 1868-1963 ....DLB-47, 50

Du Bois, William Pène 1916- DLB-61

Ducharme, Réjean 1941- DLB-60

Duell, Sloan and Pearce DLB-46

Duffield and Green.......................... DLB-46

Duffy, Maureen 1933- DLB-14

Dugan, Alan 1923- DLB-5

Duhamel, Georges 1884-1966 .... DLB-65

Dukes, Ashley 1885-1959..................... DLB-10

Dumas, Henry 1934-1968 .... DLB-41

Dunbar, Paul Laurence 1872-1906 ....DLB-50, 54

Duncan, Robert 1919- DLB-5, 16

Duncan, Ronald 1914-1982.................... DLB-13

Dunigan, Edward, and Brother............... DLB-49

Dunlap, John 1747-1812 .... DLB-43

Dunlap, William 1766-1839............DLB-30, 37, 59

Dunn, Douglas 1942- DLB-40

Dunne, Finley Peter 1867-1936............DLB-11, 23

Dunne, John Gregory 1932- Y-80

Dunne, Philip 1908- DLB-26

Dunning, Ralph Cheever 1878-1930............DLB-4

Dunning, William A. 1857-1922.............. DLB-17

Plunkett, Edward John Moreton Drax,
Lord Dunsany 1878-1957 .... DLB-10

Durand, Lucile (see Bersianik, Louky)

Duranty, Walter 1884-1957................... DLB-29

Durrell, Lawrence 1912- DLB-15, 27

Durrell, William [publishing house] DLB-49

Dürrenmatt, Friedrich 1921- DLB-69

Dutton, E. P., and Company.................. DLB-49

Duvoisin, Roger 1904-1980................... DLB-61

Duyckinck, Evert Augustus 1816-1878 ......DLB-3, 64

Duyckinck, George L. 1823-1863...............DLB-3

Duyckinck and Company..................... DLB-49

Dwight, John Sullivan 1813-1893...............DLB-1

Dwight, Timothy 1752-1817.................. DLB-37

Dyer, Charles 1928- DLB-13

Dylan, Bob 1941- DLB-16

E

Eager, Edward 1911-1964.................... DLB-22

Earle, James H., and Company................ DLB-49

Early American Book Illustration,
       by Sinclair Hamilton DLB-49

Eastlake, William 1917- DLB-6

Eastman, Carol ?- DLB-44

Eberhart, Richard 1904- DLB-48

Ebon 1942- DLB-41

Ecco Press DLB-46

Edes, Benjamin 1732-1803 .... DLB-43

Edgar, David 1948- DLB-13

The Editor Publishing Company DLB-49

Edmonds, Randolph 1900- DLB-51

Edmonds, Walter D. 1903- DLB-9

Edschmid, Kasimir 1890-1966................ DLB-56

Edwards, Jonathan 1703-1758................ DLB-24

Edwards, Jonathan, Jr. 1745-1801............. DLB-37

Edwards, Junius 1929- DLB-33

Edwards, Richard 1524-1566 .... DLB-62

Effinger, George Alec 1947- DLB-8

Eggleston, Edward 1837-1902 .... DLB-12

Eich, Günter 1907-1972 .... DLB-69

1873 Publishers' Catalogues DLB-49

Eighteenth-Century Aesthetic Theories........ DLB-31

Eighteenth-Century Philosophical
       Background............................ DLB-31

Eigner, Larry 1927- DLB-5

Eisner, Kurt 1867-1919..................... DLB-66

Eklund, Gordon 1945- Y-83

Elder, Lonne III 1931- DLB-7, 38, 44

Elder, Paul, and Company..................... DLB-49

Elements of Rhetoric (1828; revised, 1846),
       by Richard Whately [excerpt] DLB-57

Eliot, George 1819-1880...............DLB-21, 35, 55

Eliot, John 1604-1690 .... DLB-24

Eliot, T. S. 1888-1965 ....DLB-7, 10, 45, 63

Elkin, Stanley 1930- DLB-2, 28; Y-80

Ellet, Elizabeth F. 1818?-1877 .... DLB-30

Elliott, George 1923- DLB-68

Elliott, Janice 1931- DLB-14

Elliott, William 1788-1863 ....DLB-3

Elliott, Thomes and Talbot.................... DLB-49

Ellis, Edward S. 1840-1916 .... DLB-42

The George H. Ellis Company DLB-49

Ellison, Harlan 1934- DLB-8

Ellison, Ralph 1914- DLB-2

Ellmann, Richard 1918-1987 ....Y-87

The Elmer Holmes Bobst Awards
       in Arts and Letters..........................Y-87

Emanuel, James Andrew 1921- DLB-41

Emerson, Ralph Waldo 1803-1882 ......DLB-1, 59, 73

Emerson, William 1769-1811 .... DLB-37

Empson, William 1906-1984.................. DLB-20

The End of English Stage Censorship,
       1945-1968............................... DLB-13

Engel, Marian 1933-1985..................... DLB-53

Engle, Paul 1908- DLB-48

English Composition and Rhetoric (1866),
       by Alexander Bain [excerpt] DLB-57

The English Renaissance of Art (1908),
       by Oscar Wilde.......................... DLB-35

Enright, D. J. 1920- DLB-27

Enright, Elizabeth 1909-1968.................. DLB-22

L'Envoi (1882), by Oscar Wilde................ DLB-35

Epps, Bernard 1936- DLB-53

Epstein, Julius 1909- and
       Epstein, Philip 1909-1952................. DLB-26

Equiano, Olaudah circa 1745-1797 ....DLB-37, 50

Ernst, Paul 1866-1933......................... DLB-66

Erskine, John 1879-1951 ....DLB-9

Ervine, St. John Greer 1883-1971 .... DLB-10

Eshleman, Clayton 1935- DLB-5

Ess Ess Publishing Company.................. DLB-49

Essay on Chatterton (1842),
    by Robert Browning DLB-32

Estes, Eleanor 1906- DLB-22

Estes and Lauriat............................ DLB-49

Ets, Marie Hall 1893- DLB-22

Eudora Welty: Eye of the Storyteller Y-87

Eugene O'Neill Memorial Theater Center.......DLB-7

Evans, Donald 1884-1921..................... DLB-54

Evans, George Henry 1805-1856 .... DLB-43

Evans, M., and Company..................... DLB-46

Evans, Mari 1923- DLB-41

Evans, Mary Ann (see Eliot, George)

Evans, Nathaniel 1742-1767 .... DLB-31

Evans, Sebastian 1830-1909................... DLB-35

Everett, Alexander Hill 1790-1847 .... DLB-59

Everett, Edward 1794-1865..................DLB-1, 59

Everson, William 1912- DLB-5, 16

Every Man His Own Poet; or, The
    Inspired Singer's Recipe Book (1877),
    by W. H. Mallock DLB-35

Ewart, Gavin 1916- DLB-40

Ewing, Juliana Horatia 1841-1885............. DLB-21

Exley, Frederick 1929- Y-81

Experiment in the Novel (1929),
    by John D. Beresford DLB-36

F

"F. Scott Fitzgerald: St. Paul's Native Son
    and Distinguished American Writer":
    University of Minnesota Conference,
    29-31 October 1982..........................Y-82

Faber, Frederick William 1814-1863.......... DLB-32

Fair, Ronald L. 1932- DLB-33

Fairfax, Beatrice (see Manning, Marie)

Fallada, Hans 1893-1947 .... DLB-56

Fancher, Betsy 1928- Y-83

Fane, Violet 1843-1905...................... DLB-35

Fantasy Press Publishers..................... DLB-46

Fante, John 1909-1983 ....Y-83

Farber, Norma 1909-1984..................... DLB-61

Farigoule, Louis (see Romains, Jules)

Farley, Walter 1920- DLB-22

Farmer, Philip José 1918- DLB-8

Farquharson, Martha (see Finley, Martha)

Farrar and Rinehart.......................... DLB-46

Farrar, Straus and Giroux.................... DLB-46

Farrell, James T. 1904-1979...........DLB-4, 9; DS-2

Farrell, J. G. 1935-1979...................... DLB-14

Fast, Howard 1914- DLB-9

Faulkner, William 1897-1962
    ....DLB-9, 11, 44; DS-2; Y-86

Fauset, Jessie Redmon 1882-1961 .... DLB-51

Faust, Irvin 1924- DLB-2, 28; Y-80

Fawcett Books DLB-46

Fearing, Kenneth 1902-1961 ....DLB-9

Federal Writers' Project DLB-46

Federman, Raymond 1928- Y-80

Feiffer, Jules 1929- DLB-7, 44

Feinstein, Elaine 1930- DLB-14, 40

Fell, Frederick, Publishers DLB-46

Felton, Cornelius Conway 1807-1862...........DLB-1

Fennario, David 1947- DLB-60

Fenno, John 1751-1798....................... DLB-43

Fenno, R. F., and Company DLB-49

Fenton, James 1949- DLB-40

Ferber, Edna 1885-1968.....................DLB-9, 28

Ferdinand, Vallery III (see Salaam, Kalamu ya)

Ferguson, Sir Samuel 1810-1886 .... DLB-32

Ferguson, William Scott 1875-1954............ DLB-47

Ferlinghetti, Lawrence 1919- DLB-5, 16

Fern, Fanny (see Parton, Sara
    Payson Willis)

Ferret, E., and Company DLB-49

Ferrini, Vincent 1913- DLB-48

Ferron, Jacques 1921-1985 .... DLB-60

Ferron, Madeleine 1922- DLB-53

Fetridge and Company DLB-49

Feuchtwanger, Lion 1884-1958............... DLB-66

Ficke, Arthur Davison 1883-1945.............. DLB-54

Fiction Best-Sellers, 1910-1945 ....DLB-9

Fiction into Film, 1928-1975: A List of Movies Based on the Works of Authors in *British Novelists, 1930-1959* DLB-15

Fiedler, Leslie A. 1917- DLB-28, 67

Field, Eugene 1850-1895 ....DLB-23, 42

Field, Nathan 1587-1619 or 1620............. DLB-58

Field, Rachel 1894-1942 ....DLB-9, 22

A Field Guide to Recent Schools of American Poetry............................Y-86

Fielding, Henry 1707-1754 .... DLB-39

Fielding, Sarah 1710-1768.................... DLB-39

Fields, James Thomas 1817-1881...............DLB-1

Fields, Julia 1938- DLB-41

Fields, W. C. 1880-1946 .... DLB-44

Fields, Osgood and Company DLB-49

Fifty Penguin Years Y-85

Figes, Eva 1932- DLB-14

Filson, John circa 1753-1788 .... DLB-37

Findley, Timothy 1930- DLB-53

Finlay, Ian Hamilton 1925- DLB-40

Finley, Martha 1828-1909 .... DLB-42

Finney, Jack 1911- DLB-8

Finney, Walter Braden (see Finney, Jack)

Firbank, Ronald 1886-1926................... DLB-36

Firmin, Giles 1615-1697 .... DLB-24

First Strauss "Livings" Awarded to Cynthia Ozick and Raymond Carver An Interview with Cynthia Ozick An Interview with Raymond Carver Y-83

Fish, Stanley 1938- DLB-67

Fisher, Clay (see Allen, Henry W.)

Fisher, Dorothy Canfield 1879-1958............DLB-9

Fisher, Leonard Everett 1924- DLB-61

Fisher, Roy 1930- DLB-40

Fisher, Rudolph 1897-1934................... DLB-51

Fisher, Sydney George 1856-1927 .... DLB-47

Fisher, Vardis 1895-1968......................DLB-9

Fiske, John 1608-1677........................ DLB-24

Fiske, John 1842-1901.....................DLB-47, 64

Fitch, Thomas circa 1700-1774 .... DLB-31

Fitch, William Clyde 1865-1909 ....DLB-7

FitzGerald, Edward 1809-1883 .... DLB-32

Fitzgerald, F. Scott 1896-1940 ... DLB-4, 9; Y-81; DS-1

Fitzgerald, Penelope 1916- DLB-14

Fitzgerald, Robert 1910-1985.....................Y-80

Fitzgerald, Thomas 1819-1891 .... DLB-23

Fitzgerald, Zelda Sayre 1900-1948.................Y-84

Fitzhugh, Louise 1928-1974 .... DLB-52

Fitzhugh, William circa 1651-1701............. DLB-24

Flanagan, Thomas 1923- Y-80

Flanner, Hildegarde 1899-1987 .... DLB-48

Flanner, Janet 1892-1978.......................DLB-4

Flavin, Martin 1883-1967.......................DLB-9

Flecker, James Elroy 1884-1915 ....DLB-10, 19

Fleeson, Doris 1901-1970..................... DLB-29

Fleißer, Marieluise 1901-1974 .... DLB-56

The Fleshly School of Poetry and Other Phenomena of the Day (1872), by Robert Buchanan............................... DLB-35

The Fleshly School of Poetry: Mr. D. G. Rossetti (1871), by Thomas Maitland (Robert Buchanan)....................... DLB-35

Fletcher, J. S. 1863-1935 .... DLB-70

Fletcher, John (see Beaumont, Francis)

Fletcher, John Gould 1886-1950.............DLB-4, 45

Flieg, Helmut (see Heym, Stefan)

Flint, F. S. 1885-1960......................... DLB-19

Flint, Timothy 1780-1840 .... DLB-73

Follen, Eliza Lee (Cabot) 1787-1860 ....DLB-1

Follett, Ken 1949- Y-81

Follett Publishing Company DLB-46

Folsom, John West [publishing house]......... DLB-49

Foote, Horton 1916- DLB-26

Foote, Shelby 1916- DLB-2, 17

Forbes, Calvin 1945- DLB-41

Forbes, Ester 1891-1967..................... DLB-22

Forbes and Company........................... DLB-49

Force, Peter 1790-1868....................... DLB-30

Forché, Carolyn 1950- DLB-5

Ford, Charles Henri 1913- DLB-4, 48

Ford, Corey 1902-1969....................... DLB-11

Ford, Ford Madox 1873-1939 .... DLB-34

Ford, J. B., and Company DLB-49

Ford, Jesse Hill 1928- DLB-6

Ford, John 1586-? DLB-58

Ford, Worthington C. 1858-1941............. DLB-47

Fords, Howard, and Hulbert DLB-49

Foreman, Carl 1914-1984 .... DLB-26

Forester, Frank (see Herbert, Henry William)

Fornés, María Irene 1930- DLB-7

Forrest, Leon 1937- DLB-33

Forster, E. M. 1879-1970 .... DLB-34

Forten, Charlotte L. 1837-1914.............. DLB-50

Fortune, T. Thomas 1856-1928 .... DLB-23

Fosdick, Charles Austin 1842-1915........... DLB-42

Foster, Genevieve 1893-1979 .... DLB-61

Foster, Hannah Webster 1758-1840 .... DLB-37

Foster, John 1648-1681...................... DLB-24

Foster, Michael 1904-1956....................DLB-9

Four Essays on the Beat Generation,
     by John Clellon Holmes.................. DLB-16

Four Seas Company DLB-46

Four Winds Press............................ DLB-46

Fournier, Henri Alban (see Alain-Fournier)

Fowler and Wells Company DLB-49

Fowles, John 1926- DLB-14

Fox, John, Jr. 1862 or 1863-1919 ....DLB-9

Fox, Paula 1923- DLB-52

Fox, Richard K. [publishing house]........... DLB-49

Fox, William Price 1926- DLB-2; Y-81

Fraenkel, Michael 1896-1957 ....DLB-4

France, Richard 1938- DLB-7

Francis, C. S. [publishing house].............. DLB-49

Francis, Convers 1795-1863 ....DLB-1

Francke, Kuno 1855-1930 .... DLB-71

Frank, Leonhard 1882-1961.................. DLB-56

Frank, Melvin (see Panama, Norman)

Frank, Waldo 1889-1967 ....DLB-9, 63

Franken, Rose 1895?- Y-84

Franklin, Benjamin 1706-1790 ....DLB-24, 43, 73

Franklin, James 1697-1735 .... DLB-43

Franklin Library............................ DLB-46

Frantz, Ralph Jules 1902-1979.................DLB-4

Fraser, G. S. 1915-1980...................... DLB-27

Frayn, Michael 1933- DLB-13, 14

Frederic, Harold 1856-1898 ....DLB-12, 23

Freeman, Douglas Southall 1886-1953........ DLB-17

Freeman, Legh Richmond 1842-1915 .... DLB-23

Freeman, Mary Wilkins 1852-1930 .... DLB-12

Freeman, R. Austin 1862-1943 .... DLB-70

French, David 1939- DLB-53

French, James [publishing house] DLB-49

French, Samuel [publishing house]........... DLB-49

Freneau, Philip 1752-1832..................DLB-37, 43

Friedman, Bruce Jay 1930- DLB-2, 28

Friel, Brian 1929- DLB-13

Friend, Krebs 1895?-1967? DLB-4

Fringe and Alternative Theater
     in Great Britain DLB-13

Frisch, Max 1911- DLB-69

Fritz, Jean 1915- DLB-52

Frost, Robert 1874-1963...................... DLB-54

Frothingham, Octavius Brooks 1822-1895.......DLB-1

Froude, James Anthony 1818-1894........DLB-18, 57

Fry, Christopher 1907- DLB-13

Frye, Northrop 1912- DLB-67, 68

Fuchs, Daniel 1909- DLB-9, 26, 28

The Fugitives and the Agrarians:
     The First Exhibition Y-85

Fuller, Charles H., Jr. 1939- DLB-38

Fuller, Henry Blake 1857-1929................ DLB-12

Fuller, John 1937- DLB-40

Fuller, Roy 1912- DLB-15, 20

Fuller, Samuel 1912- DLB-26

Fuller, Sarah Margaret, Marchesa
     D'Ossoli 1810-1850..............DLB-1, 59, 73

Fulton, Len 1934- Y-86

Fulton, Robin 1937- DLB-40

Furman, Laura 1945- Y-86

Furness, Horace Howard 1833-1912 .... DLB-64

Furness, William Henry 1802-1896.............DLB-1

Furthman, Jules 1888-1966.................. DLB-26

The Future of the Novel (1899),
   by Henry James.......................... DLB-18

G

Gaddis, William 1922- DLB-2

Gág, Wanda 1893-1946...................... DLB-22

Gagnon, Madeleine 1938- DLB-60

Gaine, Hugh 1726-1807 .... DLB-43

Gaine, Hugh [publishing house].............. DLB-49

Gaines, Ernest J. 1933- DLB-2, 33; Y-80

Gaiser, Gerd 1908-1976 .... DLB-69

Galaxy Science Fiction Novels DLB-46

Gale, Zona 1874-1938 ....DLB-9

Gallagher, William Davis 1808-1894.......... DLB-73

Gallant, Mavis 1922- DLB-53

Gallico, Paul 1897-1976.......................DLB-9

Galsworthy, John 1867-1933...............DLB-10, 34

Galvin, Brendan 1938- DLB-5

Gambit DLB-46

Gammer Gurton's Needle........................ DLB-62

Gannett, Frank E. 1876-1957................. DLB-29

Gardam, Jane 1928- DLB-14

Garden, Alexander circa 1685-1756.......... DLB-31

Gardner, John 1933-1982 .... DLB-2; Y-82

Garis, Howard R. 1873-1962 .... DLB-22

Garland, Hamlin 1860-1940................DLB-12, 71

Garneau, Michel 1939- DLB-53

Garner, Hugh 1913-1979..................... DLB-68

Garnett, David 1892-1981 .... DLB-34

Garraty, John A. 1920- DLB-17

Garrett, George 1929- DLB-2, 5; Y-83

Garrison, William Lloyd 1805-1879..........DLB-1, 43

Gascoyne, David 1916- DLB-20

Gaskell, Elizabeth Cleghorn 1810-1865........ DLB-21

Gass, William Howard 1924- DLB-2

Gates, Doris 1901- DLB-22

Gates, Henry Louis, Jr. 1950- DLB-67

Gates, Lewis E. 1860-1924.................... DLB-71

Gay, Ebenezer 1696-1787..................... DLB-24

The Gay Science (1866),
   by E. S. Dallas [excerpt].................. DLB-21

Gayarré, Charles E. A. 1805-1895 .... DLB-30

Gaylord, Charles [publishing house].......... DLB-49

Geddes, Gary 1940- DLB-60

Geddes, Virgil 1897- DLB-4

Geis, Bernard, Associates...................... DLB-46

Geisel, Theodor Seuss 1904- DLB-61

Gelber, Jack 1932- DLB-7

Gellhorn, Martha 1908- Y-82

Gems, Pam 1925- DLB-13

A General Idea of the College of Mirania (1753),
   by William Smith [excerpts]................ DLB-31

Genet, Jean 1910-1986 .... Y-86, DLB-72

Genevoix, Maurice 1890-1980.................. DLB-65

Genovese, Eugene D. 1930- DLB-17

Gent, Peter 1942- Y-82

George, Henry 1839-1897...................... DLB-23

George, Jean Craighead 1919- DLB-52

Gerhardie, William 1895-1977.................. DLB-36

Gernsback, Hugo 1884-1967 ....DLB-8

Gerrish, Samuel [publishing house]........... DLB-49

Gerrold, David 1944- DLB-8

Geston, Mark S. 1946- DLB-8

Gibbon, Lewis Grassic (see Mitchell, James Leslie)

Gibbons, Floyd 1887-1939...................... DLB-25

Gibbons, William ?-?........................... DLB-73

Gibson, Graeme 1934- DLB-53

Gibson, Wilfrid 1878-1962..................... DLB-19

Gibson, William 1914- DLB-7

Gide, André 1869-1951........................ DLB-65

Giguère, Diane 1937- DLB-53

Giguère, Roland 1929- DLB-60

Gilder, Richard Watson 1844-1909........... DLB-64

Gildersleeve, Basil 1831-1924.................. DLB-71

Giles, Henry 1809-1882 .... DLB-64

Gill, William F., Company DLB-49

Gillespie, A. Lincoln, Jr. 1895-1950 ....DLB-4

Gilliam, Florence ?-?...........................DLB-4

Gilliatt, Penelope 1932- DLB-14

Gillott, Jacky 1939-1980 .... DLB-14

Gilman, Caroline H. 1794-1888 ....DLB-3, 73

Gilman, W. and J. [publishing house] DLB-49

Gilmer, Elizabeth Meriwether 1861-1951 ...... DLB-29

Gilmer, Francis Walker 1790-1826 .... DLB-37

Gilroy, Frank D. 1925- DLB-7

Ginsberg, Allen 1926- DLB-5, 16

Giono, Jean 1895-1970 .... DLB-72

Giovanni, Nikki 1943- DLB-5, 41

Gipson, Lawrence Henry 1880-1971.......... DLB-17

Giraudoux, Jean 1882-1944 .... DLB-65

Gissing, George 1857-1903 .... DLB-18

Gladstone, William Ewart 1809-1898 .... DLB-57

Glaeser, Ernst 1902-1963 .... DLB-69

Glanville, Brian 1931- DLB-15

Glapthorne, Henry 1610-1643? DLB-58

Glasgow, Ellen 1873-1945 .... DLB-9, 12

Glaspell, Susan 1882-1948 .... DLB-7, 9

Glass, Montague 1877-1934 .... DLB-11

Glassco, John 1909-1981..................... DLB-68

Glauser, Friedrich 1896-1938.................. DLB-56

F. Gleason's Publishing Hall DLB-49

Glück, Louise 1943- DLB-5

Godbout, Jacques 1933- DLB-53

Goddard, Morrill 1865-1937.................. DLB-25

Goddard, William 1740-1817.................. DLB-43

Godey, Louis A. 1804-1878................... DLB-73

Godey and McMichael........................ DLB-49

Godfrey, Dave 1938- DLB-60

Godfrey, Thomas 1736-1763 .... DLB-31

Godine, David R., Publisher DLB-46

Godwin, Gail 1937- DLB-6

Godwin, Parke 1816-1904 ....DLB-3, 64

Godwin, William 1756-1836 .... DLB-39

Goes, Albrecht 1908- DLB-69

Goffe, Thomas circa 1592-1629 .... DLB-58

Goffstein, M. B. 1940- DLB-61

Gogarty, Oliver St. John 1878-1957 ....DLB-15, 19

Goines, Donald 1937-1974.................... DLB-33

Gold, Herbert 1924- DLB-2; Y-81

Gold, Michael 1893-1967 ....DLB-9, 28

Goldberg, Dick 1947- DLB-7

Golding, William 1911- DLB-15

Goldman, William 1931- DLB-44

Goldsmith, Oliver 1730 or 1731-1774 .... DLB-39

Goldsmith Publishing Company DLB-46

Gomme, Laurence James
      [publishing house] DLB-46

The Goodman Theatre........................DLB-7

Goodrich, Frances 1891-1984 and
      Hackett, Albert 1900- DLB-26

Goodrich, S. G. [publishing house] DLB-49

Goodrich, Samuel Griswold 1793-1860 .. DLB-1, 42, 73

Goodspeed, C. E., and Company DLB-49

Goodwin, Stephen 1943- Y-82

Gookin, Daniel 1612-1687 .... DLB-24

Gordon, Caroline 1895-1981 ....DLB-4, 9; Y-81

Gordon, Giles 1940- DLB-14

Gordon, Mary 1949- DLB-6; Y-81

Gordone, Charles 1925- DLB-7

Gorey, Edward 1925- DLB-61

Gosse, Edmund 1849-1928 .... DLB-57

Gould, Wallace 1882-1940.................... DLB-54

Goyen, William 1915-1983............... DLB-2; Y-83

Grady, Henry W. 1850-1889 .... DLB-23

Graf, Oskar Maria 1894-1967 .... DLB-56

Graham, George Rex 1813-1894 .... DLB-73

Graham, W. S. 1918- DLB-20

Graham, William H. [publishing house] DLB-49

Grahame, Kenneth 1859-1932................. DLB-34

Gramatky, Hardie 1907-1979.................. DLB-22

Granich, Irwin (see Gold, Michael)

Grant, Harry J. 1881-1963 .... DLB-29

Grant, James Edward 1905-1966 .... DLB-26

Grasty, Charles H. 1863-1924 .... DLB-25

Grau, Shirley Ann 1929- DLB-2

Graves, John 1920- Y-83

Graves, Richard 1715-1804.................... DLB-39

Graves, Robert 1895-1985 ....DLB-20; Y-85

Gray, Asa 1810-1888 ....DLB-1

Gray, David 1838-1861 .... DLB-32

Gray, Simon 1936- DLB-13

Grayson, William J. 1788-1863 ....DLB-3, 64

The Great War and the Theater, 1914-1918
[Great Britain] DLB-10

Greeley, Horace 1811-1872................DLB-3, 43

Green, Adolph (see Comden, Betty)

Green, Duff 1791-1875...................... DLB-43

Green, Gerald 1922- DLB-28

Green, Henry 1905-1973 .... DLB-15

Green, Jonas 1712-1767 .... DLB-31

Green, Joseph 1706-1780..................... DLB-31

Green, Julien 1900- DLB-4, 72

Green, Paul 1894-1981 ....DLB-7, 9; Y-81

Green, T. and S. [publishing house].......... DLB-49

Green, Timothy [publishing house]........... DLB-49

Greenberg: Publisher...................... DLB-46

Green Tiger Press.......................... DLB-46

Greene, Asa 1789-1838..................... DLB-11

Greene, Benjamin H. [publishing house]...... DLB-49

Greene, Graham 1904- DLB-13, 15; Y-85

Greene, Robert 1558-1592.................... DLB-62

Greenhow, Robert 1800-1854 .... DLB-30

Greenough, Horatio 1805-1852 ....DLB-1

Greenwell, Dora 1821-1882.................. DLB-35

Greenwillow Books DLB-46

Greenwood, Grace (see Lippincott, Sara Jane Clarke)

Greenwood, Walter 1903-1974 .... DLB-10

Greer, Ben 1948- DLB-6

Greg, W. R. 1809-1881 .... DLB-55

Gregg Press................................ DLB-46

Persse, Isabella Augusta,
Lady Gregory 1852-1932.................. DLB-10

Gregory, Horace 1898-1982 .... DLB-48

Greville, Fulke, First Lord Brooke
1554-1628.............................. DLB-62

Grey, Zane 1872-1939 ....DLB-9

Grieve, C. M. (see MacDiarmid, Hugh)

Griffith, Elizabeth 1727?-1793................ DLB-39

Griffiths, Trevor 1935- DLB-13

Griggs, S. C., and Company DLB-49

Griggs, Sutton Elbert 1872-1930.............. DLB-50

Grignon, Claude-Henri 1894-1976 .... DLB-68

Grigson, Geoffrey 1905- DLB-27

Grimké, Angelina Weld 1880-1958.........DLB-50, 54

Grimm, Hans 1875-1959 .... DLB-66

Griswold, Rufus Wilmot 1815-1857.........DLB-3, 59

Gross, Milt 1895-1953 .... DLB-11

Grosset and Dunlap DLB-49

Grossman Publishers DLB-46

Groulx, Lionel 1878-1967 .... DLB-68

Grove Press................................. DLB-46

Grubb, Davis 1919-1980.......................DLB-6

Gruelle, Johnny 1880-1938.................... DLB-22

Guare, John 1938- DLB-7

Guest, Barbara 1920- DLB-5

Guèvremont, Germaine 1893-1968 .... DLB-68

Guilloux, Louis 1899-1980.................... DLB-72

Guiney, Louise Imogen 1861-1920 .... DLB-54

Guiterman, Arthur 1871-1943................. DLB-11

Gunn, Bill 1934- DLB-38

Gunn, James E. 1923- DLB-8

Gunn, Neil M. 1891-1973 .... DLB-15

Gunn, Thom 1929- DLB-27

Gunnars, Kristjana 1948- DLB-60

Gurik, Robert 1932- DLB-60

Guthrie, A. B., Jr. 1901- DLB-6

Guthrie, Ramon 1896-1973.....................DLB-4

The Guthrie Theater..........................DLB-7

Guy, Ray 1939- DLB-60

Guy, Rosa 1925- DLB-33

Gwynne, Erskine 1898-1948.....................DLB-4

Gysin, Brion 1916- DLB-16

H

H. D. (see Doolittle, Hilda)

Hackett, Albert (see Goodrich, Frances)

Hagelstange, Rudolf 1912-1984 .... DLB-69

Haggard, H. Rider 1856-1925................. DLB-70

Hailey, Arthur 1920- Y-82

Haines, John 1924- DLB-5

Hake, Thomas Gordon 1809-1895 .... DLB-32

Haldeman, Joe 1943- DLB-8

Haldeman-Julius Company.................... DLB-46

Hale, E. J., and Son DLB-49

Hale, Edward Everett 1822-1909 ....DLB-1, 42

Hale, Leo Thomas (see Ebon)

Hale, Lucretia Peabody 1820-1900 .... DLB-42

Hale, Nancy 1908- Y-80

Hale, Sarah Josepha (Buell) 1788-1879..DLB-1, 42, 73

Haley, Alex 1921- DLB-38

Haliburton, Thomas Chandler 1796-1865..... DLB-11

Hall, Donald 1928- DLB-5

Hall, James 1793-1868........................ DLB-73

Hall, Samuel [publishing house]............... DLB-49

Hallam, Arthur Henry 1811-1833............ DLB-32

Halleck, Fitz-Greene 1790-1867 ....DLB-3

Hallmark Editions........................... DLB-46

Halper, Albert 1904-1984 ....DLB-9

Halstead, Murat 1829-1908.................... DLB-23

Hamburger, Michael 1924- DLB-27

Hamilton, Alexander 1712-1756.............. DLB-31

Hamilton, Alexander 1755?-1804.............. DLB-37

Hamilton, Cicely 1872-1952 .... DLB-10

Hamilton, Edmond 1904-1977 ....DLB-8

Hamilton, Gail (see Corcoran, Barbara)

Hamilton, Ian 1938- DLB-40

Hamilton, Patrick 1904-1962 .... DLB-10

Hamilton, Virginia 1936- DLB-33, 52

Hammon, Jupiter 1711-died between
    1790 and 1806 ....DLB-31, 50

Hammond, John ?-1663...................... DLB-24

Hamner, Earl 1923- DLB-6

Hampton, Christopher 1946- DLB-13

Handlin, Oscar 1915- DLB-17

Hankin, St. John 1869-1909.................. DLB-10

Hanley, Clifford 1922- DLB-14

Hannah, Barry 1942- DLB-6

Hannay, James 1827-1873..................... DLB-21

Hansberry, Lorraine 1930-1965 ....DLB-7, 38

Harcourt Brace Jovanovich.................... DLB-46

Hardwick, Elizabeth 1916- DLB-6

Hardy, Thomas 1840-1928 ....DLB-18, 19

Hare, David 1947- DLB-13

Hargrove, Marion 1919- DLB-11

Harlow, Robert 1923- DLB-60

Harness, Charles L. 1915- DLB-8

Harper, Frances Ellen Watkins
    1825-1911................................ DLB-50

Harper, Michael S. 1938- DLB-41

Harper and Brothers......................... DLB-49

Harris, Benjamin ?-circa 1720 ....DLB-42, 43

Harris, George Washington 1814-1869......DLB-3, 11

Harris, Joel Chandler 1848-1908 ....DLB-11, 23, 42

Harris, Mark 1922- DLB-2; Y-80

Harrison, Charles Yale 1898-1954............. DLB-68

Harrison, Frederic 1831-1923 .... DLB-57

Harrison, Harry 1925- DLB-8

Harrison, James P., Company DLB-49

Harrison, Jim 1937- Y-82

Harrison, Paul Carter 1936- DLB-38

Harrison, Tony 1937- DLB-40

Harrisse, Henry 1829-1910.................... DLB-47

Harsent, David 1942- DLB-40

Hart, Albert Bushnell 1854-1943.............. DLB-17

Hart, Moss 1904-1961 ....DLB-7

Hart, Oliver 1723-1795........................ DLB-31

Harte, Bret 1836-1902.....................DLB-12, 64

Hartlaub, Felix 1913-1945.................... DLB-56

Hartley, L. P. 1895-1972 .... DLB-15

Hartley, Marsden 1877-1943 .... DLB-54

Hartman, Geoffrey H. 1929- DLB-67

Hartmann, Sadakichi 1867-1944.............. DLB-54

Harwood, Lee 1939- DLB-40

Harwood, Ronald 1934- DLB-13

Haskins, Charles Homer 1870-1937 .... DLB-47

A Haughty and Proud Generation (1922),
    by Ford Madox Hueffer DLB-36

Hauptmann, Carl 1858-1921 .... DLB-66

Hauptmann, Gerhart 1862-1946 .... DLB-66

Hauser, Marianne 1910- Y-83

Hawker, Robert Stephen 1803-1875........... DLB-32

Hawkes, John 1925- DLB-2, 7; Y-80

Hawkins, Walter Everette 1883-? DLB-50

Hawthorne, Nathaniel 1804-1864 ....DLB-1

Hay, John 1838-1905......................DLB-12, 47

Hayden, Robert 1913-1980.....................DLB-5

Hayes, John Michael 1919- DLB-26

Hayne, Paul Hamilton 1830-1886 ....DLB-3, 64

Haywood, Eliza 1693?-1756 .... DLB-39

Hazard, Willis P. [publishing house].......... DLB-49

Hazzard, Shirley 1931- Y-82

Headley, Joel T. 1813-1897 .... DLB-30

Heaney, Seamus 1939- DLB-40

Heard, Nathan C. 1936- DLB-33

Hearn, Lafcadio 1850-1904................. DLB-12

Hearst, William Randolph 1863-1951 .... DLB-25

Heath, Catherine 1924- DLB-14

Heath-Stubbs, John 1918- DLB-27

Hébert, Anne 1916- DLB-68

Hébert, Jacques 1923- DLB-53

Hecht, Anthony 1923- DLB-5

Hecht, Ben 1894-1964........... DLB-7, 9, 25, 26, 28

Hecker, Isaac Thomas 1819-1888 ....DLB-1

Hedge, Frederic Henry 1805-1890 ....DLB-1, 59

Heidish, Marcy 1947- Y-82

Heinlein, Robert A. 1907- DLB-8

Heller, Joseph 1923- DLB-2, 28; Y-80

Hellman, Lillian 1906-1984................ DLB-7; Y-84

Helprin, Mark 1947- Y-85

Helwig, David 1938- DLB-60

Hemingway, Ernest
    1899-1961.............. DLB-4, 9; Y-81, 87; DS-1

Hemingway: Twenty-Five Years Later.............Y-85

Hemphill, Paul 1936- Y-87

Henchman, Daniel 1689-1761 .... DLB-24

Henderson, Alice Corbin 1881-1949........... DLB-54

Henderson, David 1942- DLB-41

Henderson, George Wylie 1904- DLB-51

Henderson, Zenna 1917- DLB-8

Henley, Beth 1952- Y-86

Henley, William Ernest 1849-1903 .... DLB-19

Henry, Buck 1930- DLB-26

Henry, Marguerite 1902- DLB-22

Henry, Robert Selph 1889-1970.............. DLB-17

Henry, Will (see Allen, Henry W.)

Henschke, Alfred (see Klabund)

Henty, G. A. 1832-1902 .... DLB-18

Hentz, Caroline Lee 1800-1856.................DLB-3

Herbert, Alan Patrick 1890-1971 .... DLB-10

Herbert, Frank 1920-1986.....................DLB-8

Herbert, Henry William 1807-1858..........DLB-3, 73

Herbert, John 1926- DLB-53

Herbst, Josephine 1892-1969....................DLB-9

Hercules, Frank E. M. 1917- DLB-33

Herder, B., Book Company DLB-49

Hergesheimer, Joseph 1880-1954 ....DLB-9

Heritage Press................................ DLB-46

Hermlin, Stephan 1915- DLB-69

Hernton, Calvin C. 1932- DLB-38

"The Hero as Man of Letters: Johnson,
    Rousseau, Burns" (1841), by Thomas
    Carlyle [excerpt] DLB-57

The Hero as Poet. Dante; Shakspeare (1841),
    by Thomas Carlyle........................ DLB-32

Herrick, E. R., and Company.................. DLB-49

Herrick, Robert 1868-1938.................DLB-9, 12

Herrick, William 1915- Y-83

Herrmann, John 1900-1959.....................DLB-4

Hersey, John 1914- DLB-6

Hertel, François 1905-1985.................... DLB-68

Herzog, Emile Salomon Wilhelm (see Maurois, André)

Hesse, Hermann 1877-1962................... DLB-66

Hewat, Alexander circa 1743-circa 1824....... DLB-30

Hewitt, John 1907- DLB-27

Hewlett, Maurice 1861-1923................... DLB-34

Heyen, William 1940- DLB-5

Heym, Stefan 1913- DLB-69

Heyward, Dorothy 1890-1961 and
    Heyward, DuBose 1885-1940 ....DLB-7

Heyward, DuBose 1885-1940............. DLB-7, 9, 45

Heywood, Thomas 1573 or 1574-1641 .... DLB-62

Hiebert, Paul 1892-1987...................... DLB-68

Higgins, Aidan 1927- DLB-14

Higgins, Colin 1941- DLB-26

Higgins, George V. 1939- DLB-2; Y-81

Higginson, Thomas Wentworth 1823-1911 . . DLB-1, 64

Highwater, Jamake 1942?- DLB-52; Y-85

Hildesheimer, Wolfgang 1916- DLB-69

Hildreth, Richard 1807-1865 .... DLB-1, 30, 59

Hill, Geoffrey 1932- DLB-40

Hill, George M., Company DLB-49

Hill, "Sir" John 1714?-1775 .... DLB-39

Hill, Lawrence, and Company, Publishers DLB-46

Hill, Leslie 1880-1960 .... DLB-51

Hill, Susan 1942- DLB-14

Hill, Walter 1942- DLB-44

Hill and Wang DLB-46

Hilliard, Gray and Company DLB-49

Hillyer, Robert 1895-1961 .... DLB-54

Hilton, James 1900-1954 .... DLB-34

Hilton and Company DLB-49

Himes, Chester 1909-1984 .... DLB-2

Hine, Daryl 1936- DLB-60

The History of the Adventures of Joseph Andrews
(1742), by Henry Fielding [excerpt] DLB-39

Hirsch, E. D., Jr. 1928- DLB-67

Hoagland, Edward 1932- DLB-6

Hoagland, Everett H. III 1942- DLB-41

Hoban, Russell 1925- DLB-52

Hobsbaum, Philip 1932- DLB-40

Hobson, Laura Z. 1900- DLB-28

Hochman, Sandra 1936- DLB-5

Hodgins, Jack 1938- DLB-60

Hodgman, Helen 1945- DLB-14

Hodgson, Ralph 1871-1962 .... DLB-19

Hodgson, William Hope 1877-1918 .... DLB-70

Hoffenstein, Samuel 1890-1947 .... DLB-11

Hoffman, Charles Fenno 1806-1884 .... DLB-3

Hoffman, Daniel 1923- DLB-5

Hofmann, Michael 1957- DLB-40

Hofstadter, Richard 1916-1970 .... DLB-17

Hogan, Desmond 1950- DLB-14

Hogan and Thompson DLB-49

Hohl, Ludwig 1904-1980 .... DLB-56

Holbrook, David 1923- DLB-14, 40

Holcroft, Thomas 1745-1809 .... DLB-39

Holden, Molly 1927-1981 .... DLB-40

Holiday House DLB-46

Holland, Norman N. 1927- DLB-67

Hollander, John 1929- DLB-5

Holley, Marietta 1836-1926 .... DLB-11

Hollingsworth, Margaret 1940- DLB-60

Hollo, Anselm 1934- DLB-40

Holloway, John 1920- DLB-27

Holloway House Publishing Company DLB-46

Holme, Constance 1880-1955 .... DLB-34

Holmes, Oliver Wendell 1809-1894 .... DLB-1

Holmes, John Clellon 1926- DLB-16

Holst, Hermann E. von 1841-1904 .... DLB-47

Holt, Henry, and Company DLB-49

Holt, John 1721-1784 .... DLB-43

Holt, Rinehart and Winston DLB-46

Holthusen, Hans Egon 1913- DLB-69

Home, Henry, Lord Kames 1696-1782 .... DLB-31

Home Publishing Company DLB-49

Home, William Douglas 1912- DLB-13

Homes, Geoffrey (see Mainwaring, Daniel)

Honig, Edwin 1919- DLB-5

Hood, Hugh 1928- DLB-53

Hooker, Jeremy 1941- DLB-40

Hooker, Thomas 1586-1647 .... DLB-24

Hooper, Johnson Jones 1815-1862 .... DLB-3, 11

Hopkins, Gerard Manley 1844-1889 .... DLB-35, 57

Hopkins, John H., and Son DLB-46

Hopkins, Lemuel 1750-1801 .... DLB-37

Hopkins, Pauline Elizabeth 1859-1930 .... DLB-50

Hopkins, Samuel 1721-1803 .... DLB-31

Hopkinson, Francis 1737-1791 .... DLB-31

Horgan, Paul 1903- Y-85

Horizon Press DLB-46

Horne, Frank 1899-1974 .... DLB-51

Horne, Richard Henry (Hengist) 1802
or 1803-1884 .... DLB-32

Hornung, E. W. 1866-1921 .... DLB-70

Horovitz, Israel 1939- DLB-7

Horton, George Moses 1797?-1883?.......... DLB-50

Horwood, Harold 1923- DLB-60

Hosford, E. and E. [publishing house]........ DLB-49

Hotchkiss and Company..................... DLB-49

Hough, Emerson 1857-1923....................DLB-9

Houghton Mifflin Company.................. DLB-49

Houghton, Stanley 1881-1913 .... DLB-10

Housman, A. E. 1859-1936................... DLB-19

Housman, Laurence 1865-1959 .... DLB-10

Hovey, Richard 1864-1900 .... DLB-54

Howard, Maureen 1930- Y-83

Howard, Richard 1929- DLB-5

Howard, Roy W. 1883-1964 .... DLB-29

Howard, Sidney 1891-1939.................DLB-7, 26

Howe, E. W. 1853-1937 ....DLB-12, 25

Howe, Henry 1816-1893 .... DLB-30

Howe, Irving 1920- DLB-67

Howe, Julia Ward 1819-1910...................DLB-1

Howell, Clark, Sr. 1863-1936................. DLB-25

Howell, Evan P. 1839-1905.................... DLB-23

Howell, Soskin and Company DLB-46

Howells, William Dean 1837-1920.........DLB-12, 64

Hoyem, Andrew 1935- DLB-5

Hoyt, Henry [publishing house].............. DLB-49

Hubbard, Kin 1868-1930..................... DLB-11

Hubbard, William circa 1621-1704 .... DLB-24

Huch, Friedrich 1873-1913................... DLB-66

Huch, Ricarda 1864-1947 .... DLB-66

Huck at 100: How Old Is
  Huckleberry Finn? Y-85

Hudson, Henry Norman 1814-1886........... DLB-64

Hudson and Goodwin DLB-49

Huebsch, B. W. [publishing house]........... DLB-46

Hughes, David 1930- DLB-14

Hughes, Langston 1902-1967........ DLB-4, 7, 48, 51

Hughes, Richard 1900-1976................. DLB-15

Hughes, Ted 1930- DLB-40

Hughes, Thomas 1822-1896.................. DLB-18

Hugo, Richard 1923-1982.....................DLB-5

Hugo Awards and Nebula Awards DLB-8

Hulme, T. E. 1883-1917..................... DLB-19

Hume, Fergus 1859-1932..................... DLB-70

Humorous Book Illustration.................. DLB-11

Humphrey, William 1924- DLB-6

Humphreys, David 1752-1818................ DLB-37

Humphreys, Emyr 1919- DLB-15

Huncke, Herbert 1915- DLB-16

Huneker, James Gibbons 1857-1921........... DLB-71

Hunt, Irene 1907- DLB-52

Hunt, William Gibbes 1791-1833 .... DLB-73

Hunter, Evan 1926- Y-82

Hunter, Jim 1939- DLB-14

Hunter, Kristin 1931- DLB-33

Hunter, N. C. 1908-1971..................... DLB-10

Hurd and Houghton DLB-49

Hurst and Company.......................... DLB-49

Hurston, Zora Neale 1891-1960.............. DLB-51

Huston, John 1906- DLB-26

Hutcheson, Francis 1694-1746................ DLB-31

Hutchinson, Thomas 1711-1780...........DLB-30, 31

Hutton, Richard Holt 1826-1897 .... DLB-57

Huxley, Aldous 1894-1963 .... DLB-36

Huxley, T. H. 1825-1895..................... DLB-57

Hyman, Trina Schart 1939- DLB-61

I

The Iconography of Science-Fiction Art.........DLB-8

Ignatow, David 1914- DLB-5

Imbs, Bravig 1904-1946 ....DLB-4

Inchbald, Elizabeth 1753-1821................. DLB-39

Inge, William 1913-1973 ....DLB-7

Ingelow, Jean 1820-1897 .... DLB-35

The Ingersoll Prizes Y-84

Ingraham, Joseph Holt 1809-1860 ....DLB-3

Inman, John 1805-1850 .... DLB-73

International Publishers Company............ DLB-46

An Interview with Peter S. Prescott..............Y-86

An Interview with Tom Jenks...................Y-86

Introduction to Paul Laurence Dunbar,
    Lyrics of Lowly Life (1896),
    by William Dean Howells DLB-50

Introductory Essay: *Letters of Percy Bysshe
    Shelley* (1852), by Robert Browning ...., DLB-32

Introductory Letters from the Second Edition
    of *Pamela* (1741), by Samuel Richardson .. DLB-39

Irving, John 1942- DLB-6; Y-82

Irving, Washington 1783-1859 .. DLB-3, 11, 30, 59, 73

Irwin, Grace 1907- DLB-68

Irwin, Will 1873-1948 .... DLB-25

Isherwood, Christopher 1904-1986 ...... DLB-15; Y-86

The Island Trees Case: A Symposium on School
        Library Censorship
    An Interview with Judith Krug
    An Interview with Phyllis Schlafly
    An Interview with Edward B. Jenkinson
    An Interview with Lamarr Mooneyham
    An Interview with Harriet Bernstein Y-82

Ivers, M. J., and Company DLB-49

J

Jackmon, Marvin E. (see Marvin X)

Jackson, Angela 1951- DLB-41

Jackson, Helen Hunt 1830-1885 .... DLB-42, 47

Jackson, Laura Riding 1901- DLB-48

Jackson, Shirley 1919-1965 .... DLB-6

Jacob, Piers Anthony Dillingham (see Anthony,
    Piers)

Jacobs, George W., and Company DLB-49

Jacobson, Dan 1929- DLB-14

Jahnn, Hans Henny 1894-1959 .... DLB-56

Jakes, John 1932- Y-83

James, Henry 1843-1916 .... DLB-12, 71

James, John circa 1633-1729 .... DLB-24

James Joyce Centenary: Dublin, 1982 .... Y-82

James Joyce Conference Y-85

James, U. P. [publishing house] DLB-49

Jameson, Fredric 1934- DLB-67

Jameson, J. Franklin 1859-1937 .... DLB-17

Jameson, Storm 1891-1986 .... DLB-36

Jarrell, Randall 1914-1965 .... DLB-48, 52

Jasmin, Claude 1930- DLB-60

Jay, John 1745-1829 .... DLB-31

Jeffers, Lance 1919-1985 .... DLB-41

Jeffers, Robinson 1887-1962 .... DLB-45

Jefferson, Thomas 1743-1826 .... DLB-31

Jellicoe, Ann 1927- DLB-13

Jenkins, Robin 1912- DLB-14

Jenkins, William Fitzgerald (see Leinster, Murray)

Jennings, Elizabeth 1926- DLB-27

Jens, Walter 1923- DLB-69

Jensen, Merrill 1905-1980 .... DLB-17

Jerome, Jerome K. 1859-1927 .... DLB-10, 34

Jewett, John P., and Company DLB-49

Jewett, Sarah Orne 1849-1909 .... DLB-12

The Jewish Publication Society DLB-49

Jewsbury, Geraldine 1812-1880 .... DLB-21

Joans, Ted 1928- DLB-16, 41

John Edward Bruce: Three Documents DLB-50

John Steinbeck Research Center Y-85

John Webster: The Melbourne Manuscript Y-86

Johnson, B. S. 1933-1973 .... DLB-14, 40

Johnson, Benjamin [publishing house] DLB-49

Johnson, Benjamin, Jacob, and
    Robert [publishing house] DLB-49

Johnson, Charles R. 1948- DLB-33

Johnson, Charles S. 1893-1956 .... DLB-51

Johnson, Diane 1934- Y-80

Johnson, Edward 1598-1672 .... DLB-24

Johnson, Fenton 1888-1958 .... DLB-45, 50

Johnson, Georgia Douglas 1886-1966 .... DLB-51

Johnson, Gerald W. 1890-1980 .... DLB-29

Johnson, Helene 1907- DLB-51

Johnson, Jacob, and Company DLB-49

Johnson, James Weldon 1871-1938 .... DLB-51

Johnson, Lionel 1867-1902 .... DLB-19

Johnson, Nunnally 1897-1977 .... DLB-26

Johnson, Owen 1878-1952 .... Y-87

Johnson, Pamela Hansford 1912- DLB-15

Johnson, Samuel 1696-1772 .... DLB-24

Johnson, Samuel 1709-1784 .... DLB-39

Johnson, Samuel 1822-1882 .... DLB-1

Johnston, Annie Fellows 1863-1931 .... DLB-42

Johnston, Basil H. 1929- DLB-60

Johnston, Denis 1901-1984 .... DLB-10

Johnston, Jennifer 1930- DLB-14

Johnston, Mary 1870-1936 .... DLB-9

Johnstone, Charles 1719?-1800? DLB-39

Jolas, Eugene 1894-1952 .... DLB-4, 45

Jones, Charles C., Jr. 1831-1893.............. DLB-30

Jones, D. G. 1929- DLB-53

Jones, David 1895-1974 .... DLB-20

Jones, Ebenezer 1820-1860.................... DLB-32

Jones, Ernest 1819-1868..................... DLB-32

Jones, Gayl 1949- DLB-33

Jones, Glyn 1905- DLB-15

Jones, Gwyn 1907- DLB-15

Jones, Henry Arthur 1851-1929.............. DLB-10

Jones, Hugh circa 1692-1760................. DLB-24

Jones, James 1921-1977 .... DLB-2

Jones, LeRoi (see Baraka, Amiri)

Jones, Lewis 1897-1939...................... DLB-15

Jones, Major Joseph (see Thompson, William Tappan)

Jones, Preston 1936-1979..................... DLB-7

Jones, William Alfred 1817-1900 .... DLB-59

Jones's Publishing House DLB-49

Jong, Erica 1942- DLB-2, 5, 28

Jonson, Ben 1572?-1637..................... DLB-62

Jordan, June 1936- DLB-38

Joseph, Jenny 1932- DLB-40

Josephson, Matthew 1899-1978................. DLB-4

Josiah Allen's Wife (see Holley, Marietta)

Josipovici, Gabriel 1940- DLB-14

Josselyn, John ?-1675....................... DLB-24

Joyce, Adrien (see Eastman, Carol)

Joyce, James 1882-1941 .... DLB-10, 19, 36

Judd, Orange, Publishing Company.......... DLB-49

Judd, Sylvester 1813-1853.................... DLB-1

June, Jennie (see Croly, Jane Cunningham)

Jünger, Ernst 1895- DLB-56

Justice, Donald 1925- Y-83

K

Kalechofsky, Roberta 1931- DLB-28

Kaler, James Otis 1848-1912 .... DLB-12

Kandel, Lenore 1932- DLB-16

Kanin, Garson 1912- DLB-7

Kantor, Mackinlay 1904-1977 .... DLB-9

Kaplan, Johanna 1942- DLB-28

Kasack, Hermann 1896-1966.................. DLB-69

Kaschnitz, Marie Luise 1901-1974............ DLB-69

Kästner, Erich 1899-1974.................... DLB-56

Kattan, Naim 1928- DLB-53

Katz, Steve 1935- Y-83

Kauffman, Janet 1945- Y-86

Kaufman, Bob 1925- DLB-16, 41

Kaufman, George S. 1889-1961 .... DLB-7

Kavanagh, Patrick 1904-1967.............. DLB-15, 20

Kavanagh, P. J. 1931- DLB-40

Kaye-Smith, Sheila 1887-1956................. DLB-36

Kazin, Alfred 1915- DLB-67

Keane, John B. 1928- DLB-13

Keats, Ezra Jack 1916-1983................... DLB-61

Keble, John 1792-1866 .... DLB-32, 55

Keeble, John 1944- Y-83

Keeffe, Barrie 1945- DLB-13

Keeley, James 1867-1934 .... DLB-25

W. B. Keen, Cooke and Company............. DLB-49

Keillor, Garrison 1942- Y-87

Kelley, Edith Summers 1884-1956.............. DLB-9

Kelley, William Melvin 1937- DLB-33

Kellogg, Ansel Nash 1832-1886 .... DLB-23

Kellogg, Steven 1941- DLB-61

Kelly, George 1887-1974 .... DLB-7

Kelly, Piet and Company DLB-49

Kelly, Robert 1935- DLB-5

Kemble, Fanny 1809-1893..................... DLB-32

Kemelman, Harry 1908- DLB-28

Kendall, Claude [publishing company] DLB-46

Kendell, George 1809-1867.................... DLB-43

Kenedy, P. J., and Sons....................... DLB-49

Kennedy, Adrienne 1931- DLB-38

Kennedy, John Pendleton 1795-1870...........DLB-3

Kennedy, Margaret 1896-1967 .... DLB-36

Kennedy, William 1928- Y-85

Kennedy, X. J. 1929- DLB-5

Kennelly, Brendan 1936- DLB-40

Kenner, Hugh 1923- DLB-67

Kennerley, Mitchell [publishing house]........ DLB-46

Kent, Frank R. 1877-1958.................... DLB-29

Keppler and Schwartzmann DLB-49

Kerouac, Jack 1922-1969 .... DLB-2, 16; DS-3

Kerouac, Jan 1952- DLB-16

Kerr, Charles H., and Company.............. DLB-49

Kerr, Orpheus C. (see Newell, Robert Henry)

Kesey, Ken 1935- DLB-2, 16

Kessel, Joseph 1898-1979..................... DLB-72

Kessel, Martin 1901- DLB-56

Kesten, Hermann 1900- DLB-56

Keun, Irmgard 1905-1982.................... DLB-69

Key and Biddle............................. DLB-49

Keyserling, Eduard von 1855-1918........... DLB-66

Kiely, Benedict 1919- DLB-15

Kiggins and Kellogg.......................... DLB-49

Kiley, Jed 1889-1962 ....DLB-4

Killens, John Oliver 1916- DLB-33

Killigrew, Thomas 1612-1683 .... DLB-58

Kilmer, Joyce 1886-1918 .... DLB-45

King, Clarence 1842-1901 .... DLB-12

King, Florence 1936...........................Y-85

King, Francis 1923- DLB-15

King, Grace 1852-1932 .... DLB-12

King, Solomon [publishing house]............. DLB-49

King, Stephen 1947- Y-80

King, Woodie, Jr. 1937- DLB-38

Kinglake, Alexander William 1809-1891....... DLB-55

Kingsley, Charles 1819-1875...............DLB-21, 32

Kingsley, Henry 1830-1876................... DLB-21

Kingsley, Sidney 1906- DLB-7

Kingston, Maxine Hong 1940- Y-80

Kinnell, Galway 1927- DLB-5; Y-87

Kinsella, Thomas 1928- DLB-27

Kipling, Rudyard 1865-1936 ....DLB-19, 34

Kirkconnell, Watson 1895-1977 .... DLB-68

Kirkland, Caroline M. 1801-1864...........DLB-3, 73

Kirkland, Joseph 1830-1893................... DLB-12

Kirkup, James 1918- DLB-27

Kirst, Hans Hellmut 1914- DLB-69

Kizer, Carolyn 1925- DLB-5

Klabund 1890-1928.......................... DLB-66

Klappert, Peter 1942- DLB-5

Klass, Philip (see Tenn, William)

Klein, A. M. 1909-1972....................... DLB-68

Knapp, Samuel Lorenzo 1783-1838 .... DLB-59

Knickerbocker, Diedrich (see Irving, Washington)

Knight, Damon 1922- DLB-8

Knight, Etheridge 1931- DLB-41

Knight, John S. 1894-1981 .... DLB-29

Knight, Sarah Kemble 1666-1727 .... DLB-24

Knister, Raymond 1899-1932.................. DLB-68

Knoblock, Edward 1874-1945 .... DLB-10

Knopf, Alfred A. 1892-1984.....................Y-84

Knopf, Alfred A. [publishing house] DLB-46

Knowles, John 1926- DLB-6

Knox, Frank 1874-1944 .... DLB-29

Knox, John Armoy 1850-1906................. DLB-23

Kober, Arthur 1900-1975 .... DLB-11

Koch, Howard 1902- DLB-26

Koch, Kenneth 1925- DLB-5

Koenigsberg, Moses 1879-1945............... DLB-25

Koeppen, Wolfgang 1906- DLB-69

Koestler, Arthur 1905-1983 ....Y-83

Kolb, Annette 1870-1967..................... DLB-66

Kolbenheyer, Erwin Guido 1878-1962......... DLB-66

Kolodny, Annette 1941- DLB-67

Komroff, Manuel 1890-1974 ....DLB-4

Konigsburg, E. L. 1930- DLB-52

Kopit, Arthur 1937- DLB-7

Kops, Bernard 1926?- DLB-13

Kornbluth, C. M. 1923-1958...................DLB-8

Kosinski, Jerzy 1933- DLB-2; Y-82

Kraf, Elaine 1946- Y-81

Krasna, Norman 1909-1984 .... DLB-26

Krauss, Ruth 1911- DLB-52

Kreuder, Ernst 1903-1972................... DLB-69

Kreymborg, Alfred 1883-1966..............DLB-4, 54

Krieger, Murray 1923- DLB-67

Krim, Seymour 1922- DLB-16

Krock, Arthur 1886-1974.................... DLB-29

Kroetsch, Robert 1927- DLB-53

Krutch, Joseph Wood 1893-1970............. DLB-63

Kubrick, Stanley 1928- DLB-26

Kumin, Maxine 1925- DLB-5

Kunitz, Stanley 1905- DLB-48

Kunjufu, Johari M. (see Amini, Johari M.)

Kupferberg, Tuli 1923- DLB-16

Kurz, Isolde 1853-1944....................... DLB-66

Kusenberg, Kurt 1904-1983 .... DLB-69

Kuttner, Henry 1915-1958 ....DLB-8

Kyd, Thomas 1558-1594 .... DLB-62

Kyger, Joanne 1934- DLB-16

L

Laberge, Albert 1871-1960 .... DLB-68

Laberge, Marie 1950- DLB-60

Lacretelle, Jacques de 1888-1985 .... DLB-65

Ladd, Joseph Brown 1764-1786 .... DLB-37

La Farge, Oliver 1901-1963 ....DLB-9

Lafferty, R. A. 1914- DLB-8

Laird, Carobeth 1895- Y-82

Laird and Lee DLB-49

Lalonde, Michèle 1937- DLB-60

Lamantia, Philip 1927- DLB-16

Lambert, Betty 1933-1983 .... DLB-60

L'Amour, Louis 1908?- Y-80

Lamson, Wolffe and Company DLB-49

Lancer Books................................ DLB-46

Landesman, Jay 1919- and
Landesman, Fran 1927- DLB-16

Lane, Charles 1800-1870 ....DLB-1

The John Lane Company DLB-49

Lane, M. Travis 1934- DLB-60

Lane, Patrick 1939- DLB-53

Lane, Pinkie Gordon 1923- DLB-41

Laney, Al 1896- DLB-4

Langevin, André 1927- DLB-60

Langgässer, Elisabeth 1899-1950 .... DLB-69

Lanham, Edwin 1904-1979......................DLB-4

Lanier, Sidney 1842-1881 .... DLB-64

Lardner, Ring 1885-1933...................DLB-11, 25

Lardner, Ring, Jr. 1915- DLB-26

Lardner 100: Ring Lardner
Centennial Symposium........................Y-85

Larkin, Philip 1922-1985 .... DLB-27

La Rocque, Gilbert 1943-1984................. DLB-60

Laroque de Roquebrune, Robert
(see Roquebrune, Robert de)

Larrick, Nancy 1910- DLB-61

Larsen, Nella 1893-1964....................... DLB-51

Lasker-Schüler, Else 1869-1945................ DLB-66

Lathrop, Dorothy P. 1891-1980 .... DLB-22

Lathrop, George Parsons 1851-1898.......... DLB-71

Lathrop, John, Jr. 1772-1820................. DLB-37

Latimore, Jewel Christine McLawler (see Amini,
Johari M.)

Laughlin, James 1914- DLB-48

Laumer, Keith 1925- DLB-8

Laurence, Margaret 1926-1987................ DLB-53

Laurents, Arthur 1918- DLB-26

Laurie, Annie (see Black, Winifred)

Lavin, Mary 1912- DLB-15

Lawrence, David 1888-1973 .... DLB-29

Lawrence, D. H. 1885-1930 ....DLB-10, 19, 36

Lawson, John ?-1711 .... DLB-24

Lawson, Robert 1892-1957 .... DLB-22

Lawson, Victor F. 1850-1925 .... DLB-25

Lea, Henry Charles 1825-1909 .... DLB-47

Lea, Tom 1907- DLB-6

Leacock, John 1729-1802 .... DLB-31

Lear, Edward 1812-1888 .... DLB-32

Leary, Timothy 1920- DLB-16

Leary, W. A., and Company DLB-49

Léautaud, Paul 1872-1956 .... DLB-65

Leavitt and Allen DLB-49

Lécavelé, Roland (see Dorgelès, Roland)

Lechlitner, Ruth 1901- DLB-48

Leclerc, Félix 1914- DLB-60

Lectures on Rhetoric and Belles Lettres (1783),
    by Hugh Blair [excerpts] DLB-31

Leder, Rudolf (see Hermlin, Stephan)

Lederer, Charles 1910-1976 .... DLB-26

Ledwidge, Francis 1887-1917 .... DLB-20

Lee, Dennis 1939- DLB-53

Lee, Don L. (see Madhubuti, Haki R.)

Lee, George W. 1894-1976 .... DLB-51

Lee, Harper 1926- DLB-6

Lee, Harriet (1757-1851) and
    Lee, Sophia (1750-1824) DLB-39

Lee, Laurie 1914- DLB-27

Lee, Vernon 1856-1935 .... DLB-57

Lee and Shepard DLB-49

Le Fanu, Joseph Sheridan 1814-1873 ......DLB-21, 70

Leffland, Ella 1931- Y-84

le Fort, Gertrud von 1876-1971 .... DLB-66

Le Gallienne, Richard 1866-1947 ....DLB-4

Legaré, Hugh Swinton 1797-1843 ....DLB-3, 59, 73

Legaré, James M. 1823-1859 ....DLB-3

Le Guin, Ursula K. 1929- DLB-8, 52

Lehman, Ernest 1920- DLB-44

Lehmann, John 1907- DLB-27

Lehmann, Rosamond 1901- DLB-15

Lehmann, Wilhelm 1882-1968 .... DLB-56

Leiber, Fritz 1910- DLB-8

Leinster, Murray 1896-1975 ....DLB-8

Leitch, Maurice 1933- DLB-14

Leland, Charles G. 1824-1903 .... DLB-11

L'Engle, Madeleine 1918- DLB-52

Lennart, Isobel 1915-1971 .... DLB-44

Lennox, Charlotte 1729 or 1730-1804 .... DLB-39

Lenski, Lois 1893-1974 .... DLB-22

Lenz, Hermann 1913- DLB-69

Leonard, Hugh 1926- DLB-13

Leonard, William Ellery 1876-1944 .... DLB-54

Le Queux, William 1864-1927 .... DLB-70

Lerner, Max 1902- DLB-29

LeSieg, Theo. (see Geisel, Theodor Seuss)

Leslie, Frank 1821-1880 .... DLB-43

The Frank Leslie Publishing House DLB-49

Lessing, Bruno 1870-1940 .... DLB-28

Lessing, Doris 1919- DLB-15; Y-85

Letter to [Samuel] Richardson on *Clarissa*
    (1748), by Henry Fielding DLB-39

Lever, Charles 1806-1872 .... DLB-21

Levertov, Denise 1923- DLB-5

Levi, Peter 1931- DLB-40

Levien, Sonya 1888-1960 .... DLB-44

Levin, Meyer 1905-1981 .... DLB-9, 28; Y-81

Levine, Philip 1928- DLB-5

Levy, Benn Wolfe 1900-1973 .... DLB-13; Y-81

Lewes, George Henry 1817-1878 .... DLB-55

Lewis, Alfred H. 1857-1914 .... DLB-25

Lewis, Alun 1915-1944 .... DLB-20

Lewis, C. Day (see Day Lewis, C.)

Lewis, Charles B. 1842-1924 .... DLB-11

Lewis, C. S. 1898-1963 .... DLB-15

Lewis, Henry Clay 1825-1850 ....DLB-3

Lewis, Janet 1899- Y-87

Lewis, Matthew Gregory 1775-1818 .... DLB-39

Lewis, Richard circa 1700-1734 .... DLB-24

Lewis, Sinclair 1885-1951 .... DLB-9; DS-1

Lewis, Wyndham 1882-1957 .... DLB-15

Lewisohn, Ludwig 1882-1955 .... DLB-4, 9, 28

The Library of America DLB-46

Liebling, A. J. 1904-1963 ....DLB-4

Lilly, Wait and Company DLB-49

Limited Editions Club DLB-46

Lincoln and Edmands DLB-49

Lindsay, Jack 1900- Y-84

Lindsay, Vachel 1879-1931 .... DLB-54

Linebarger, Paul Myron Anthony (see
    Smith, Cordwainer)

Link, Arthur S. 1920- DLB-17

Linn, John Blair 1777-1804 .... DLB-37

Linton, Eliza Lynn 1822-1898 .... DLB-18

Linton, William James 1812-1897 .... DLB-32

Lion Books DLB-46

Lionni, Leo 1910- DLB-61

Lippincott, J. B., Company DLB-49

Lippincott, Sara Jane Clarke 1823-1904 .... DLB-43

Lippmann, Walter 1889-1974 .... DLB-29

Lipton, Lawrence 1898-1975 .... DLB-16

Literary Documents: William Faulkner
    and the People-to-People Program Y-86

Literary Documents II: *Library Journal—*
    Statements and Questionnaires from
    First Novelists Y-87

Literary Effects of World War II
    [British novel] DLB-15

Literary Prizes [British] DLB-15

Literary Research Archives: The Humanities
    Research Center, University of Texas Y-82

Literary Research Archives II: Berg
    Collection of English and American Literature
    of the New York Public Library Y-83

Literary Research Archives III:
    The Lilly Library Y-84

Literary Research Archives IV:
    The John Carter Brown Library Y-85

Literary Research Archives V:
    Kent State Special Collections Y-86

Literary Research Archives VI: The Modern
    Literary Manuscripts Collection in the
    Special Collections of the Washington
    University Libraries Y-87

"Literary Style" (1857), by William
    Forsyth [excerpt] DLB-57

Literature at Nurse, or Circulating Morals (1885),
    by George Moore DLB-18

Little, Brown and Company DLB-49

Littlewood, Joan 1914- DLB-13

Lively, Penelope 1933- DLB-14

Livesay, Dorothy 1909- DLB-68

Livings, Henry 1929- DLB-13

Livingston, Anne Howe 1763-1841 .... DLB-37

Livingston, Myra Cohn 1926- DLB-61

Livingston, William 1723-1790 .... DLB-31

Llewellyn, Richard 1906-1983 .... DLB-15

Lobel, Arnold 1933- DLB-61

Lochridge, Betsy Hopkins (see Fancher, Betsy)

Locke, David Ross 1833-1888 .... DLB-11, 23

Locke, John 1632-1704 .... DLB-31

Locke, Richard Adams 1800-1871 .... DLB-43

Locker-Lampson, Frederick 1821-1895 .... DLB-35

Lockridge, Ross, Jr. 1914-1948 .... Y-80

Locrine and *Selimus* DLB-62

Lodge, David 1935- DLB-14

Lodge, George Cabot 1873-1909 .... DLB-54

Lodge, Henry Cabot 1850-1924 .... DLB-47

Loeb, Harold 1891-1974 .... DLB-4

Logan, James 1674-1751 .... DLB-24

Logan, John 1923- DLB-5

Logue, Christopher 1926- DLB-27

London, Jack 1876-1916 .... DLB-8, 12

Long, H., and Brother DLB-49

Long, Haniel 1888-1956 .... DLB-45

Longfellow, Henry Wadsworth 1807-1882 ... DLB-1, 59

Longfellow, Samuel 1819-1892 .... DLB-1

Longley, Michael 1939- DLB-40

Longmans, Green and Company DLB-49

Longstreet, Augustus Baldwin 1790-1870 ... DLB-3, 11

Longworth, D. [publishing house] DLB-49

Lonsdale, Frederick 1881-1954 .... DLB-10

A Look at the Contemporary Black Theatre
    Movement DLB-38

Loos, Anita 1893-1981 .... DLB-11, 26; Y-81

Lopate, Phillip 1943- Y-80

The Lord Chamberlain's Office and Stage
    Censorship in England DLB-10

Lorde, Audre 1934- DLB-41

Loring, A. K. [publishing house] DLB-49

Loring and Mussey DLB-46

Lossing, Benson J. 1813-1891 .... DLB-30

Lothrop, D., and Company DLB-49

Lothrop, Harriet M. 1844-1924 .... DLB-42

The Lounger, no. 20 (1785), by Henry
    Mackenzie................................ DLB-39

Lounsbury, Thomas R. 1838-1915............ DLB-71

Lovell, John W., Company DLB-49

Lovell, Coryell and Company................. DLB-49

Lovingood, Sut (see Harris, George Washington)

Low, Samuel 1765-? DLB-37

Lowell, Amy 1874-1925 .... DLB-54

Lowell, James Russell 1819-1891 ....DLB-1, 11, 64

Lowell, Robert 1917-1977 ....DLB-5

Lowenfels, Walter 1897-1976...................DLB-4

Lowndes, Marie Belloc 1868-1947............ DLB-70

Lowry, Lois 1937- DLB-52

Lowry, Malcolm 1909-1957.................... DLB-15

Lowther, Pat 1935-1975 .... DLB-53

Loy, Mina 1882-1966.......................DLB-4, 54

Lucas, Fielding, Jr. [publishing house]........ DLB-49

Luce, John W., and Company DLB-46

Lucie-Smith, Edward 1933- DLB-40

Ludlum, Robert 1927- Y-82

Ludwig, Jack 1922- DLB-60

Luke, Peter 1919- DLB-13

The F. M. Lupton Publishing Company....... DLB-49

Lurie, Alison 1926- DLB-2

Lyly, John circa 1554-1606 .... DLB-62

Lyon, Matthew 1749-1822.................... DLB-43

Lytle, Andrew 1902- DLB-6

Lytton, Edward (see Bulwer-Lytton, Edward)

Lytton, Edward Robert Bulwer 1831-1891 .... DLB-32

M

Maass, Joachim 1901-1972.................... DLB-69

Mabie, Hamilton Wright 1845-1916.......... DLB-71

Mac A'Ghobhainn, Iain (see Smith, Iain Crichton)

MacArthur, Charles 1895-1956.........DLB-7, 25, 44

Macaulay, David 1945- DLB-61

Macaulay, Rose 1881-1958.................... DLB-36

Macaulay, Thomas Babington 1800-1859...DLB-32, 55

Macaulay Company........................... DLB-46

MacBeth, George 1932- DLB-40

MacCaig, Norman 1910- DLB-27

MacDiarmid, Hugh 1892-1978 .... DLB-20

MacDonald, George 1824-1905............... DLB-18

MacDonald, John D. 1916-1986 .... DLB-8; Y-86

MacEwen, Gwendolyn 1941- DLB-53

Macfadden, Bernarr 1868-1955 .... DLB-25

Machen, Arthur Llewelyn Jones 1863-1947 ... DLB-36

MacInnes, Colin 1914-1976.................... DLB-14

MacKaye, Percy 1875-1956 .... DLB-54

Macken, Walter 1915-1967 .... DLB-13

Mackenzie, Compton 1883-1972.............. DLB-34

Mackenzie, Henry 1745-1831.................. DLB-39

Mackey, William Wellington 1937- DLB-38

MacLean, Katherine Anne 1925- DLB-8

MacLeish, Archibald 1892-1982 ....DLB-4, 7, 45; Y-82

MacLennan, Hugh 1907- DLB-68

MacLeod, Alistair 1936- DLB-60

Macleod, Norman 1906- DLB-4

The Macmillan Company...................... DLB-49

MacNamara, Brinsley 1890-1963 .... DLB-10

MacNeice, Louis 1907-1963 ....DLB-10, 20

Macpherson, Jay 1931- DLB-53

Macpherson, Jeanie 1884-1946 .... DLB-44

Macrae Smith Company DLB-46

Macy-Masius................................. DLB-46

Madden, David 1933- DLB-6

Maddow, Ben 1909- DLB-44

Madhubuti, Haki R. 1942- DLB-5, 41

Madison, James 1751-1836 .... DLB-37

Mahan, Alfred Thayer 1840-1914............. DLB-47

Maheux-Forcier, Louise 1929- DLB-60

Mahin, John Lee 1902-1984................... DLB-44

Mahon, Derek 1941- DLB-40

Mailer, Norman 1923-
    .... DLB-2, 16, 28; Y-80, 83; DS-3

Maillet, Adrienne 1885-1963 .... DLB-68

Maillet, Antonine 1929- DLB-60

Main Selections of the Book-of-the-Month Club,
    1926-1945................................DLB-9

Main Trends in Twentieth-Century
    Book Clubs............................. DLB-46

Mainwaring, Daniel 1902-1977 .... DLB-44

Major, André 1942- DLB-60

Major, Clarence 1936- DLB-33

Major, Kevin 1949- DLB-60

Major Books.................................. DLB-46

Makemie, Francis circa 1658-1708............ DLB-24

Malamud, Bernard 1914-1986.....DLB-2, 28; Y-80, 86

Mallock, W. H. 1849-1923.................DLB-18, 57

Malone, Dumas 1892-1986 .... DLB-17

Malraux, André 1901-1976................... DLB-72

Malzberg, Barry N. 1939- DLB-8

Mamet, David 1947- DLB-7

Mandel, Eli 1922- DLB-53

Manfred, Frederick 1912- DLB-6

Mangan, Sherry 1904-1961....................DLB-4

Mankiewicz, Herman 1897-1953.............. DLB-26

Mankiewicz, Joseph L. 1909- DLB-44

Mankowitz, Wolf 1924- DLB-15

Manley, Delarivière 1672?-1724 .... DLB-39

Mann, Abby 1927- DLB-44

Mann, Heinrich 1871-1950................... DLB-66

Mann, Horace 1796-1859......................DLB-1

Mann, Klaus 1906-1949 .... DLB-56

Mann, Thomas 1875-1955.................... DLB-66

Manning, Marie 1873?-1945.................. DLB-29

Manning and Loring DLB-49

Mano, D. Keith 1942- DLB-6

Manor Books................................. DLB-46

March, William 1893-1954.....................DLB-9

Marchessault, Jovette 1938- DLB-60

Marcus, Frank 1928- DLB-13

Marek, Richard, Books DLB-46

Marion, Frances 1886-1973.................. DLB-44

Marius, Richard C. 1933- Y-85

The Mark Taper Forum.......................DLB-7

Markfield, Wallace 1926- DLB-2, 28

Markham, Edwin 1852-1940.................. DLB-54

Markle, Fletcher 1921- DLB-68

Marlatt, Daphne 1942- DLB-60

Marlowe, Christopher 1564-1593............. DLB-62

Marmion, Shakerley 1603-1639............... DLB-58

Marquand, John P. 1893-1960..................DLB-9

Marquis, Don 1878-1937 ....DLB-11, 25

Marriott, Anne 1913- DLB-68

Marryat, Frederick 1792-1848................. DLB-21

Marsh, George Perkins 1801-1882..........DLB-1, 64

Marsh, James 1794-1842 ....DLB-1, 59

Marsh, Capen, Lyon and Webb............... DLB-49

Marshall, Edward 1932- DLB-16

Marshall, James 1942- DLB-61

Marshall, Paule 1929- DLB-33

Marshall, Tom 1938- DLB-60

Marston, John 1576-1634.................... DLB-58

Marston, Philip Bourke 1850-1887 .... DLB-35

Martens, Kurt 1870-1945.................... DLB-66

Martien, William S. [publishing house]....... DLB-49

Martin, Abe (see Hubbard, Kin)

Martin, Claire 1914- DLB-60

Martin du Gard, Roger 1881-1958 .... DLB-65

Martineau, Harriet 1802-1876.............DLB-21, 55

Martyn, Edward 1859-1923................... DLB-10

Marvin X 1944- DLB-38

Marzials, Theo 1850-1920................... DLB-35

Masefield, John 1878-1967 ....DLB-10, 19

Mason, A. E. W. 1865-1948 .... DLB-70

Mason, Bobbie Ann 1940- Y-87

Mason Brothers DLB-49

Massey, Gerald 1828-1907................... DLB-32

Massinger, Philip 1583-1640................. DLB-58

Masters, Edgar Lee 1868-1950 .... DLB-54

Mather, Cotton 1663-1728.................DLB-24, 30

Mather, Increase 1639-1723................. DLB-24

Mather, Richard 1596-1669 .... DLB-24

Matheson, Richard 1926- DLB-8, 44

Matheus, John F. 1887- DLB-51

Mathews, Cornelius 1817?-1889 ....DLB-3, 64

Mathias, Roland 1915- DLB-27

Mathis, June 1892-1927 .... DLB-44

Mathis, Sharon Bell 1937- DLB-33

Matthews, Brander 1852-1929................ DLB-71

Matthews, Jack 1925- DLB-6

Matthews, William 1942- DLB-5

Matthiessen, F. O. 1902-1950.................. DLB-63

Matthiessen, Peter 1927- DLB-6

Maugham, W. Somerset 1874-1965........DLB-10, 36

Mauriac, François 1885-1970 .... DLB-65

Maurice, Frederick Denison 1805-1872....... DLB-55

Maurois, André 1885-1967 .... DLB-65

Maury, James 1718-1769 .... DLB-31

Mavor, Elizabeth 1927- DLB-14

Mavor, Osborne Henry (see Bridie, James)

Maxwell, H. [publishing house]............... DLB-49

Maxwell, William 1908- Y-80

May, Elaine 1932- DLB-44

May, Thomas 1595 or 1596-1650............. DLB-58

Mayer, Mercer 1943- DLB-61

Mayer, O. B. 1818-1891 ....DLB-3

Mayes, Wendell 1919- DLB-26

Mayfield, Julian 1928-1984 .... DLB-33; Y-84

Mayhew, Henry 1812-1887 ....DLB-18, 55

Mayhew, Jonathan 1720-1766 .... DLB-31

Mayne, Seymour 1944- DLB-60

Mayor, Flora Macdonald 1872-1932.......... DLB-36

Mazursky, Paul 1930- DLB-44

McAlmon, Robert 1896-1956............... DLB-4, 45

McBride, Robert M., and Company DLB-46

McCaffrey, Anne 1926- DLB-8

McCarthy, Cormac 1933- DLB-6

McCarthy, Mary 1912- DLB-2; Y-81

McCay, Winsor 1871-1934..................... DLB-22

McClatchy, C. K. 1858-1936.................. DLB-25

McClellan, George Marion 1860-1934........ DLB-50

McCloskey, Robert 1914- DLB-22

McClure, Joanna 1930- DLB-16

McClure, Michael 1932- DLB-16

McClure, Phillips and Company.............. DLB-46

McClurg, A. C., and Company DLB-49

McCluskey, John A., Jr. 1944- DLB-33

McCollum, Michael A. 1946 ....Y-87

McCord, David 1897- DLB-61

McCorkle, Jill 1958- Y-87

McCorkle, Samuel Eusebius 1746-1811....... DLB-37

McCormick, Anne O'Hare 1880-1954 .... DLB-29

McCormick, Robert R. 1880-1955 .... DLB-29

McCoy, Horace 1897-1955 ....DLB-9

McCullagh, Joseph B. 1842-1896.............. DLB-23

McCullers, Carson 1917-1967 .... DLB-2, 7

McDonald, Forrest 1927- DLB-17

McDougall, Colin 1917-1984 .... DLB-68

McDowell, Obolensky.......................... DLB-46

McEwan, Ian 1948- DLB-14

McFadden, David 1940- DLB-60

McGahern, John 1934- DLB-14

McGeehan, W. O. 1879-1933 .... DLB-25

McGill, Ralph 1898-1969 .... DLB-29

McGinley, Phyllis 1905-1978...............DLB-11, 48

McGirt, James E. 1874-1930................... DLB-50

McGough, Roger 1937- DLB-40

McGraw-Hill................................... DLB-46

McGuane, Thomas 1939- DLB-2; Y-80

McGuckian, Medbh 1950- DLB-40

McGuffey, William Holmes 1800-1873 .... DLB-42

McIlvanney, William 1936- DLB-14

McIntyre, O. O. 1884-1938.................... DLB-25

McKay, Claude 1889-1948..............DLB-4, 45, 51

The David McKay Company DLB-49

McKean, William V. 1820-1903............... DLB-23

McKinley, Robin 1952- DLB-52

McLaren, Floris Clark 1904-1978.............. DLB-68

McLaverty, Michael 1907- DLB-15

McLean, John R. 1848-1916.................. DLB-23

McLean, William L. 1852-1931 .... DLB-25

McLoughlin Brothers.......................... DLB-49

McMaster, John Bach 1852-1932 .... DLB-47

McMurtry, Larry 1936- DLB-2; Y-80, 87

McNally, Terrence 1939- DLB-7

McNeil, Florence 1937- DLB-60

McPherson, James Alan 1943- DLB-38

McPherson, Sandra 1943- Y-86

McWhirter, George 1939- DLB-60

Mead, Matthew 1924- DLB-40

Mead, Taylor ?- DLB-16

Medill, Joseph 1823-1899.................... DLB-43

Medoff, Mark 1940- DLB-7

Meek, Alexander Beaufort 1814-1865...........DLB-3

Meinke, Peter 1932- DLB-5

Melançon, Robert 1947- DLB-60

Meltzer, David 1937- DLB-16

Meltzer, Milton 1915- DLB-61

Melville, Herman 1819-1891 ....DLB-3

Memoirs of Life and Literature (1920),
    by W. H. Mallock [excerpt]................ DLB-57

Mencken, H. L. 1880-1956 ....DLB-11, 29, 63

Mercer, David 1928-1980..................... DLB-13

Mercer, John 1704-1768..................... DLB-31

Meredith, George 1828-1909...........DLB-18, 35, 57

Meredith, Owen (see Lytton, Edward Robert Bulwer)

Meredith, William 1919- DLB-5

Meriwether, Louise 1923- DLB-33

Merriam, Eve 1916- DLB-61

The Merriam Company DLB-49

Merrill, James 1926- DLB-5; Y-85

Merrill and Baker DLB-49

The Mershon Company DLB-49

Merton, Thomas 1915-1968 .... DLB-48; Y-81

Merwin, W. S. 1927- DLB-5

Messner, Julian [publishing house] DLB-46

Metcalf, J. [publishing house]................. DLB-49

Metcalf, John 1938- DLB-60

The Methodist Book Concern DLB-49

Mew, Charlotte 1869-1928................... DLB-19

Mewshaw, Michael 1943- Y-80

Meyer, Eugene 1875-1959................... DLB-29

Meynell, Alice 1847-1922.................... DLB-19

Micheaux, Oscar 1884-1951 .... DLB-50

Micheline, Jack 1929- DLB-16

Michener, James A. 1907?- DLB-6

Micklejohn, George circa 1717-1818........... DLB-31

Middleton, Christopher 1926- DLB-40

Middleton, Stanley 1919- DLB-14

Middleton, Thomas 1580-1627 .... DLB-58

Miegel, Agnes 1879-1964..................... DLB-56

Miles, Josephine 1911-1985................... DLB-48

Milius, John 1944- DLB-44

Mill, John Stuart 1806-1873 .... DLB-55

Millar, Kenneth 1915-1983 .... DLB-2; Y-83

Millay, Edna St. Vincent 1892-1950 .... DLB-45

Miller, Arthur 1915- DLB-7

Miller, Caroline 1903- DLB-9

Miller, Eugene Ethelbert 1950- DLB-41

Miller, Henry 1891-1980 ....DLB-4, 9; Y-80

Miller, J. Hillis 1928- DLB-67

Miller, James [publishing house].............. DLB-49

Miller, Jason 1939- DLB-7

Miller, May 1899- DLB-41

Miller, Perry 1905-1963 ....DLB-17, 63

Miller, Walter M., Jr. 1923- DLB-8

Miller, Webb 1892-1940 .... DLB-29

Millhauser, Steven 1943- DLB-2

Millican, Arthenia J. Bates 1920- DLB-38

Milne, A. A. 1882-1956...................... DLB-10

Milner, Ron 1938- DLB-38

Milnes, Richard Monckton (Lord Houghton)
    1809-1885............................... DLB-32

Minton, Balch and Company DLB-46

Miron, Gaston 1928- DLB-60

Mitchel, Jonathan 1624-1668 .... DLB-24

Mitchell, Adrian 1932- DLB-40

Mitchell, Donald Grant 1822-1908..............DLB-1

Mitchell, James Leslie 1901-1935 .... DLB-15

Mitchell, John (see Slater, Patrick)

Mitchell, Julian 1935- DLB-14

Mitchell, Ken 1940- DLB-60

Mitchell, Langdon 1862-1935...................DLB-7

Mitchell, Loften 1919- DLB-38

Mitchell, Margaret 1900-1949 ....DLB-9

Modern Age Books........................... DLB-46

"Modern English Prose" (1876),
    by George Saintsbury DLB-57

The Modern Language Association of America
    Celebrates Its Centennial....................Y-84

The Modern Library DLB-46

Modern Novelists—Great and Small (1855), by
    Margaret Oliphant DLB-21

"Modern Style" (1857), by Cockburn
    Thomson [excerpt]...................... DLB-57

The Modernists (1932), by Joseph Warren
    Beach DLB-36

Moffat, Yard and Company DLB-46

Monkhouse, Allan 1858-1936................. DLB-10

Monro, Harold 1879-1932.................... DLB-19

Monroe, Harriet 1860-1936 .... DLB-54

Monsarrat, Nicholas 1910-1979............... DLB-15

Montague, John 1929- DLB-40

Montgomery, John 1919- DLB-16

Montgomery, Marion 1925- DLB-6

Montherlant, Henry de 1896-1972 .... DLB-72

Moody, Joshua circa 1633-1697 .... DLB-24

Moody, William Vaughn 1869-1910........DLB-7, 54

Moorcock, Michael 1939- DLB-14

Moore, Catherine L. 1911- DLB-8

Moore, Clement Clarke 1779-1863 .... DLB-42

Moore, George 1852-1933.............DLB-10, 18, 57

Moore, Marianne 1887-1972 .... DLB-45

Moore, T. Sturge 1870-1944 .... DLB-19

Moore, Ward 1903-1978.....................DLB-8

Moore, Wilstach, Keys and Company......... DLB-49

Morency, Pierre 1942- DLB-60

Morgan, Berry 1919- DLB-6

Morgan, Charles 1894-1958 .... DLB-34

Morgan, Edmund S. 1916- DLB-17

Morgan, Edwin 1920- DLB-27

Morison, Samuel Eliot 1887-1976............. DLB-17

Morley, Christopher 1890-1957 ....DLB-9

Morley, John 1838-1923..................... DLB-57

Morris, George Pope 1802-1864.............. DLB-73

Morris, Lewis 1833-1907 .... DLB-35

Morris, Richard B. 1904- DLB-17

Morris, William 1834-1896 ....DLB-18, 35, 57

Morris, Willie 1934- Y-80

Morris, Wright 1910- DLB-2; Y-81

Morrison, Arthur 1863-1945 .... DLB-70

Morrison, Toni 1931- DLB-6, 33; Y-81

Morrow, William, and Company.............. DLB-46

Morse, James Herbert 1841-1923.............. DLB-71

Morse, Jedidiah 1761-1826 .... DLB-37

Morse, John T., Jr. 1840-1937................ DLB-47

Mortimer, John 1923- DLB-13

Morton, John P., and Company DLB-49

Morton, Nathaniel 1613-1685 .... DLB-24

Morton, Sarah Wentworth 1759-1846 .... DLB-37

Morton, Thomas circa 1579-circa 1647........ DLB-24

Mosley, Nicholas 1923- DLB-14

Moss, Arthur 1889-1969.......................DLB-4

Moss, Howard 1922- DLB-5

The Most Powerful Book Review in America
    [*New York Times Book Review*] Y-82

Motion, Andrew 1952- DLB-40

Motley, John Lothrop 1814-1877........DLB-1, 30, 59

Mottram, R. H. 1883-1971.................... DLB-36

Mouré, Erin 1955- DLB-60

Movies from Books, 1920-1974..................DLB-9

Mowat, Farley 1921- DLB-68

Mowrer, Edgar Ansel 1892-1977 .... DLB-29

Mowrer, Paul Scott 1887-1971................ DLB-29

Mucedorus................................ DLB-62

Muhajir, El (see Marvin X)

Muhajir, Nazzam Al Fitnah (see Marvin X)

Muir, Edwin 1887-1959 .... DLB-20

Muir, Helen 1937- DLB-14

Mukherjee, Bharati 1940- DLB-60

Muldoon, Paul 1951- DLB-40

Mumford, Lewis 1895- DLB-63

Munby, Arthur Joseph 1828-1910............. DLB-35

Munday, Anthony 1560-1633.................. DLB-62

Munford, Robert circa 1737-1783 .... DLB-31

Munro, Alice 1931- DLB-53

Munro, George [publishing house] DLB-49

Munro, H. H. 1870-1916 .... DLB-34

Munro, Norman L. [publishing house] DLB-49

Munroe, James, and Company DLB-49

Munroe, Kirk 1850-1930 .... DLB-42

Munroe and Francis DLB-49

Munsell, Joel [publishing house] DLB-49

Munsey, Frank A. 1854-1925 . . . . DLB-25

Munsey, Frank A., and Company DLB-49

Murdoch, Iris 1919- DLB-14

Murfree, Mary N. 1850-1922 . . . . DLB-12

Murphy, John, and Company DLB-49

Murphy, Richard 1927- DLB-40

Murray, Albert L. 1916- DLB-38

Murray, Gilbert 1866-1957 . . . . DLB-10

Murray, Judith Sargent 1751-1820 . . . . DLB-37

Murray, Pauli 1910-1985 . . . . DLB-41

Mussey, Benjamin B., and Company DLB-49

Myers, Gustavus 1872-1942 . . . . DLB-47

Myers, L. H. 1881-1944 . . . . DLB-15

Myers, Walter Dean 1937- DLB-33

N

Nabbes, Thomas circa 1605-1641 . . . . DLB-58

Nabokov, Vladimir 1899-1977 . . . . . . DLB-2; Y-80; DS-3

Nabokov Festival at Cornell Y-83

Nafis and Cornish DLB-49

Naipaul, Shiva 1945-1985 . . . . Y-85

Naipaul, V. S. 1932- Y-85

Nancrede, Joseph [publishing house] DLB-49

Nasby, Petroleum Vesuvius (see Locke, David Ross)

Nash, Ogden 1902-1971 . . . . DLB-11

Nathan, Robert 1894-1985 . . . . DLB-9

The National Jewish Book Awards Y-85

The National Theatre and the Royal Shakespeare
    Company: The National Companies DLB-13

Naughton, Bill 1910- DLB-13

Neagoe, Peter 1881-1960 . . . . DLB-4

Neal, John 1793-1876 . . . . DLB-1, 59

Neal, Joseph C. 1807-1847 . . . . DLB-11

Neal, Larry 1937-1981 . . . . DLB-38

The Neale Publishing Company DLB-49

Neely, F. Tennyson [publishing house] DLB-49

"The Negro as a Writer," by
    G. M. McClellan DLB-50

"Negro Poets and Their Poetry," by
    Wallace Thurman DLB-50

Neihardt, John G. 1881-1973 . . . . DLB-9, 54

Nelson, Alice Moore Dunbar
    1875-1935 . . . . DLB-50

Nelson, Thomas, and Sons DLB-49

Nelson, William Rockhill 1841-1915 . . . . DLB-23

Nemerov, Howard 1920- DLB-5, 6; Y-83

Ness, Evaline 1911-1986 . . . . DLB-61

Neugeboren, Jay 1938- DLB-28

Neumann, Alfred 1895-1952 . . . . DLB-56

Nevins, Allan 1890-1971 . . . . DLB-17

The New American Library DLB-46

New Directions Publishing Corporation DLB-46

A New Edition of *Huck Finn* Y-85

New Forces at Work in the American Theatre:
    1915-1925 . . . . DLB-7

New Literary Periodicals: A Report
    for 1987 . . . . Y-87

The New *Ulysses* Y-84

The New Variorum Shakespeare Y-85

A New Voice: The Center for the Book's First
    Five Years Y-83

The New Wave [Science Fiction] DLB-8

Newbolt, Henry 1862-1938 . . . . DLB-19

Newbound, Bernard Slade (see Slade, Bernard)

Newby, P. H. 1918- DLB-15

Newcomb, Charles King 1820-1894 . . . . DLB-1

Newell, Peter 1862-1924 . . . . DLB-42

Newell, Robert Henry 1836-1901 . . . . DLB-11

Newman, David (see Benton, Robert)

Newman, Frances 1883-1928 . . . . Y-80

Newman, John Henry 1801-1890 . . . . . . DLB-18, 32, 55

Newman, Mark [publishing house] DLB-49

Newspaper Syndication of American Humor . . DLB-11

Nichol, B. P. 1944- DLB-53

Nichols, Dudley 1895-1960 . . . . DLB-26

Nichols, John 1940- Y-82

Nichols, Mary Sargeant (Neal) Gove
    1810-1884 . . . . DLB-1

Nichols, Peter 1927- DLB-13

Nichols, Roy F. 1896-1973 . . . . DLB-17

Nichols, Ruth 1948- DLB-60

Nicholson, Norman 1914- DLB-27

Ní Chuilleanáin, Eiléan 1942- DLB-40

Nicol, Eric 1919- DLB-68

Nicolay, John G. 1832-1901 and
    Hay, John 1838-1905 .... DLB-47

Niebuhr, Reinhold 1892-1971 .... DLB-17

Niedecker, Lorine 1903-1970................. DLB-48

Nieman, Lucius W. 1857-1935................ DLB-25

Niggli, Josefina 1910- Y-80

Niles, Hezekiah 1777-1839 .... DLB-43

Nims, John Frederick 1913- DLB-5

Nin, Anaïs 1903-1977 .... DLB-2, 4

1985: The Year of the Mystery:
    A Symposium Y-85

Nissenson, Hugh 1933- DLB-28

Niven, Larry 1938- DLB-8

Nizan, Paul 1905-1940...................... DLB-72

Nobel Peace Prize
    The 1986 Nobel Peace Prize
        Nobel Lecture 1986: Hope, Despair
        and Memory
        Tributes from Abraham Bernstein,
        Norman Lamm, and John R. Silber Y-86

Nobel Prize in Literature
    The 1982 Nobel Prize in Literature
        Announcement by the Swedish Academy
        of the Nobel Prize
        Nobel Lecture 1982: The Solitude of Latin
        America
        Excerpt from *One Hundred Years*
        of Solitude
        The Magical World of Macondo
        A Tribute to Gabriel García Márquez Y-82
    The 1983 Nobel Prize in Literature
        Announcement by the Swedish
        Academy
        Nobel Lecture 1983
        The Stature of William Golding Y-83
    The 1984 Nobel Prize in Literature
        Announcement by the Swedish
        Academy
        Jaroslav Seifert Through the Eyes of the
        English-Speaking Reader
        Three Poems by Jaroslav Seifert Y-84
    The 1985 Nobel Prize in Literature
        Announcement by the Swedish
        Academy
        Nobel Lecture 1985 ....Y-85

The 1986 Nobel Prize in Literature
    Nobel Lecture 1986: This Past Must
        Address Its Present....................Y-86
The 1987 Nobel Prize in Literature
    Nobel Lecture 1987 ....Y-87

Noel, Roden 1834-1894 .... DLB-35

Nolan, William F. 1928- DLB-8

Noland, C. F. M. 1810?-1858 .... DLB-11

Noonday Press............................... DLB-46

Noone, John 1936- DLB-14

Nordhoff, Charles 1887-1947 ....DLB-9

Norman, Marsha 1947- Y-84

Norris, Charles G. 1881-1945...................DLB-9

Norris, Frank 1870-1902 .... DLB-12

Norris, Leslie 1921- DLB-27

Norse, Harold 1916- DLB-16

North Point Press............................ DLB-46

Norton, Alice Mary (see Norton, Andre)

Norton, Andre 1912- DLB-8, 52

Norton, Andrews 1786-1853 ....DLB-1

Norton, Caroline 1808-1877................... DLB-21

Norton, Charles Eliot 1827-1908 ....DLB-1, 64

Norton, John 1606-1663...................... DLB-24

Norton, Thomas (see Sackville, Thomas)

Norton, W. W., and Company................. DLB-46

Nossack, Hans Erich 1901-1977 .... DLB-69

A Note on Technique (1926), by Elizabeth
    A. Drew [excerpts] DLB-36

Nourse, Alan E. 1928- DLB-8

The Novel in [Robert Browning's] "The Ring
    and the Book" (1912), by Henry James ... DLB-32

Novel-Reading: *The Works of Charles Dickens*,
    The Works of W. Makepeace Thackeray (1879),
    by Anthony Trollope..................... DLB-21

The Novels of Dorothy Richardson (1918), by
    May Sinclair............................. DLB-36

Novels with a Purpose (1864),
    by Justin M'Carthy....................... DLB-21

Nowlan, Alden 1933-1983.................... DLB-53

Noyes, Alfred 1880-1958 .... DLB-20

Noyes, Crosby S. 1825-1908 .... DLB-23

Noyes, Nicholas 1647-1717 .... DLB-24

Noyes, Theodore W. 1858-1946 .... DLB-29

Nugent, Frank 1908-1965 .... DLB-44

Nye, Edgar Wilson (Bill) 1850-1896 ....DLB-11, 23

Nye, Robert 1939- DLB-14

O

Oakes, Urian circa 1631-1681 .... DLB-24

Oates, Joyce Carol 1938- DLB-2, 5; Y-81

Oberholtzer, Ellis Paxson 1868-1936 .... DLB-47

O'Brien, Edna 1932- DLB-14

O'Brien, Kate 1897-1974 .... DLB-15

O'Brien, Tim 1946- Y-80

O'Casey, Sean 1880-1964.................... DLB-10

Ochs, Adolph S. 1858-1935................... DLB-25

O'Connor, Flannery 1925-1964.......... DLB-2; Y-80

O'Dell, Scott 1903- DLB-52

Odell, Jonathan 1737-1818 .... DLB-31

Odets, Clifford 1906-1963..................DLB-7, 26

O'Faolain, Julia 1932- DLB-14

O'Faolain, Sean 1900- DLB-15

O'Flaherty, Liam 1896-1984 .... DLB-36; Y-84

Off Broadway and Off-Off-Broadway..........DLB-7

Off-Loop Theatres DLB-7

Ogilvie, J. S., and Company DLB-49

O'Grady, Desmond 1935- DLB-40

O'Hagan, Howard 1902-1982 .... DLB-68

O'Hara, Frank 1926-1966 ....DLB-5, 16

O'Hara, John 1905-1970 .... DLB-9; DS-2

O. Henry (see Porter, William S.)

Old Franklin Publishing House................ DLB-49

Older, Fremont 1856-1935 .... DLB-25

Oliphant, Laurence 1829?-1888 .... DLB-18

Oliphant, Margaret 1828-1897 .... DLB-18

Oliver, Chad 1928- DLB-8

Oliver, Mary 1935- DLB-5

Olsen, Tillie 1913?- DLB-28; Y-80

Olson, Charles 1910-1970 ....DLB-5, 16

Olson, Elder 1909- DLB-48, 63

On Art in Fiction (1838), by
    Edward Bulwer DLB-21

On Some of the Characteristics of Modern
    Poetry and On the Lyrical Poems of Alfred
    Tennyson (1831), by Arthur Henry
    Hallam DLB-32

"On Style in English Prose" (1898), by Frederic
    Harrison DLB-57

"On Style in Literature: Its Technical Elements"
    (1885), by Robert Louis Stevenson DLB-57

"On the Writing of Essays" (1862),
    by Alexander Smith...................... DLB-57

Ondaatje, Michael 1943- DLB-60

O'Neill, Eugene 1888-1953 ....DLB-7

Oppen, George 1908-1984 ....DLB-5

Oppenheim, E. Phillips 1866-1946 .... DLB-70

Oppenheim, James 1882-1932................. DLB-28

Oppenheimer, Joel 1930- DLB-5

Optic, Oliver (see Adams, William Taylor)

Orczy, Emma, Baroness 1865-1947............ DLB-70

Orlovitz, Gil 1918-1973......................DLB-2, 5

Orlovsky, Peter 1933- DLB-16

Ormond, John 1923- DLB-27

Ornitz, Samuel 1890-1957..................DLB-28, 44

Orton, Joe 1933-1967 .... DLB-13

Orwell, George 1903-1950.................... DLB-15

The Orwell Year Y-84

Osbon, B. S. 1827-1912...................... DLB-43

Osborne, John 1929- DLB-13

Osgood, Herbert L. 1855-1918 .... DLB-47

Osgood, James R., and Company............. DLB-49

O'Shaughnessy, Arthur 1844-1881 .... DLB-35

O'Shea, Patrick [publishing house] DLB-49

Oswald, Eleazer 1755-1795 .... DLB-43

Otis, James (see Kaler, James Otis)

Otis, James, Jr. 1725-1783................... DLB-31

Otis, Broaders and Company.................. DLB-49

Ottendorfer, Oswald 1826-1900 .... DLB-23

Ouellette, Fernand 1930- DLB-60

Ouida 1839-1908 .... DLB-18

Outing Publishing Company................... DLB-46

Outlaw Days, by Joyce Johnson.............. DLB-16

The Overlook Press DLB-46

Overview of U.S. Book Publishing, 1910-1945...DLB-9

Owen, Guy 1925- DLB-5

Owen, John [publishing house]............... DLB-49

Owen, Wilfred 1893-1918 .... DLB-20

Owsley, Frank L. 1890-1956.................. DLB-17

Ozick, Cynthia 1928- DLB-28; Y-82

P

Pack, Robert 1929- DLB-5

Packaging Papa: *The Garden of Eden* Y-86

Padell Publishing Company................... DLB-46

Padgett, Ron 1942- DLB-5

Page, L. C., and Company.................... DLB-49

Page, P. K. 1916- DLB-68

Page, Thomas Nelson 1853-1922.............. DLB-12

Page, Walter Hines 1855-1918................ DLB-71

Paget, Violet (see Lee, Vernon)

Pain, Philip ?-circa 1666 .... DLB-24

Paine, Robert Treat, Jr. 1773-1811 .... DLB-37

Paine, Thomas 1737-1809.............DLB-31, 43, 73

Paley, Grace 1922- DLB-28

Palfrey, John Gorham 1796-1881...........DLB-1, 30

Palgrave, Francis Turner 1824-1897.......... DLB-35

Paltock, Robert 1697-1767.................... DLB-39

Panama, Norman 1914-   and
  Frank, Melvin 1913- DLB-26

Pangborn, Edgar 1909-1976...................DLB-8

"Panic Among the Philistines": A Postscript,
  An Interview with Bryan Griffin.............Y-81

Panneton, Philippe (see Ringuet)

Panshin, Alexei 1940- DLB-8

Pansy (see Alden, Isabella)

Pantheon Books DLB-46

Paperback Library.......................... DLB-46

Paperback Science Fiction DLB-8

Paquet, Alfons 1881-1944 .... DLB-66

Paradis, Suzanne 1936- DLB-53

Parents' Magazine Press DLB-46

Parisian Theater, Fall 1984: Toward
  A New Baroque....................... Y-85

Parizeau, Alice 1930- DLB-60

Parke, John 1754-1789 .... DLB-31

Parker, Dorothy 1893-1967.................DLB-11, 45

Parker, James 1714-1770 .... DLB-43

Parker, Theodore 1810-1860...................DLB-1

Parkman, Francis, Jr. 1823-1893 ....DLB-1, 30

Parks, Gordon 1912- DLB-33

Parks, William 1698-1750.................... DLB-43

Parks, William [publishing house] DLB-49

Parley, Peter (see Goodrich, Samuel Griswold)

Parrington, Vernon L. 1871-1929 ....DLB-17, 63

Parton, James 1822-1891 .... DLB-30

Parton, Sara Payson Willis 1811-1872 .... DLB-43

Pastan, Linda 1932- DLB-5

Pastorius, Francis Daniel 1651-circa 1720...... DLB-24

Patchen, Kenneth 1911-1972 ....DLB-16, 48

Pater, Walter 1839-1894..................... DLB-57

Paterson, Katherine 1932- DLB-52

Patmore, Coventry 1823-1896 .... DLB-35

Paton, Joseph Noel 1821-1901................ DLB-35

Patrick, John 1906- DLB-7

Pattee, Fred Lewis 1863-1950 .... DLB-71

Patterson, Eleanor Medill 1881-1948 .... DLB-29

Patterson, Joseph Medill 1879-1946 .... DLB-29

Pattillo, Henry 1726-1801 .... DLB-37

Paul, Elliot 1891-1958 ....DLB-4

Paul, Peter, Book Company DLB-49

Paulding, James Kirke 1778-1860 ....DLB-3, 59

Paulin, Tom 1949- DLB-40

Pauper, Peter, Press......................... DLB-46

Paxton, John 1911-1985..................... DLB-44

Payn, James 1830-1898..................... DLB-18

Payne, John 1842-1916..................... DLB-35

Payne, John Howard 1791-1852.............. DLB-37

Payson and Clarke........................... DLB-46

Peabody, Elizabeth Palmer 1804-1894..........DLB-1

Peabody, Elizabeth Palmer [publishing
  house]................................ DLB-49

Peabody, Oliver William Bourn 1799-1848.... DLB-59

Peachtree Publishers, Limited DLB-46

Pead, Deuel ?-1727 .... DLB-24

Peake, Mervyn 1911-1968 .... DLB-15

Pearson, H. B. [publishing house] DLB-49

Peck, George W. 1840-1916 ....DLB-23, 42

Peck, H. C., and Theo. Bliss [publishing
    house]................................... DLB-49

Peck, Harry Thurston 1856-1914.............. DLB-71

Peele, George 1556-1596 .... DLB-62

Pellegrini and Cudahy........................ DLB-46

Pemberton, Sir Max 1863-1950................ DLB-70

Penguin Books DLB-46

Penn Publishing Company.................... DLB-49

Penn, William 1644-1718..................... DLB-24

Penner, Jonathan 1940- Y-83

Pennington, Lee 1939- Y-82

Percy, Walker 1916- DLB-2; Y-80

Perelman, S. J. 1904-1979 ....DLB-11, 44

Periodicals of the Beat Generation DLB-16

Perkins, Eugene 1932- DLB-41

Perkoff, Stuart Z. 1930-1974 .... DLB-16

Permabooks DLB-46

Perry, Bliss 1860-1954........................ DLB-71

Perry, Eleanor 1915-1981 .... DLB-44

"Personal Style" (1890), by John Addington
    Symonds DLB-57

Peter, Laurence J. 1919- DLB-53

Peterkin, Julia 1880-1961......................DLB-9

Petersham, Maud 1889-1971 and
    Petersham, Miska 1888-1960.............. DLB-22

Peterson, T. B., and Brothers DLB-49

Pharr, Robert Deane 1916- DLB-33

Philippe, Charles-Louis 1874-1909 .... DLB-65

Phillips, David Graham 1867-1911 ....DLB-9, 12

Phillips, Jayne Anne 1952- Y-80

Phillips, Stephen 1864-1915 .... DLB-10

Phillips, Ulrich B. 1877-1934 .... DLB-17

Phillips, Willard 1784-1873................... DLB-59

Phillips, Sampson and Company.............. DLB-49

Phillpotts, Eden 1862-1960 ....DLB-10, 70

Philosophical Library........................ DLB-46

"The Philosophy of Style" (1852), by
    Herbert Spencer DLB-57

Phinney, Elihu [publishing house]............ DLB-49

Phoenix, John (see Derby, George Horatio)

Pickard, Tom 1946- DLB-40

Pictorial Printing Company................... DLB-49

Pilon, Jean-Guy 1930- DLB-60

Pinckney, Josephine 1895-1957.................DLB-6

Pinero, Arthur Wing 1855-1934............... DLB-10

Pinnacle Books DLB-46

Pinsky, Robert 1940- Y-82

Pinter, Harold 1930- DLB-13

Piper, H. Beam 1904-1964 ....DLB-8

Piper, Watty DLB-22

Pisar, Samuel 1929- Y-83

Pitkin, Timothy 1766-1847 .... DLB-30

The Pitt Poetry Series: Poetry
    Publishing Today Y-85

Pitter, Ruth 1897- DLB-20

The Place of Realism in Fiction (1895), by
    George Gissing........................... DLB-18

Plante, David 1940- Y-83

Plath, Sylvia 1932-1963......................DLB-5, 6

Platt and Munk Company DLB-46

Playboy Press................................ DLB-46

Playwrights and Professors, by Tom
    Stoppard DLB-13

Plievier, Theodor 1892-1955 .... DLB-69

Plomer, William 1903-1973................... DLB-20

Plumly, Stanley 1939- DLB-5

Plumpp, Sterling D. 1940- DLB-41

Plunkett, James 1920- DLB-14

Plymell, Charles 1935- DLB-16

Pocket Books DLB-46

Poe, Edgar Allan 1809-1849.............DLB-3, 59, 73

Poe, James 1921-1980 .... DLB-44

The Poet Laureate of the United States
    Statements from Former Consultants
    in Poetry Y-86

Pohl, Frederik 1919- DLB-8

Poliakoff, Stephen 1952- DLB-13

Polite, Carlene Hatcher 1932- DLB-33

Pollard, Edward A. 1832-1872................. DLB-30

Pollard, Percival 1869-1911................... DLB-71

Pollard and Moss............................ DLB-49

Pollock, Sharon 1936- DLB-60

Polonsky, Abraham 1910- DLB-26

Poole, Ernest 1880-1950.......................DLB-9

Poore, Benjamin Perley 1820-1887........... DLB-23

Popular Library DLB-46

Porter, Eleanor H. 1868-1920 ....DLB-9

Porter, Henry ?-?........................... DLB-62

Porter, Katherine Anne 1890-1980.....DLB-4, 9; Y-80

Porter, Peter 1929- DLB-40

Porter, William S. 1862-1910................. DLB-12

Porter, William T. 1809-1858...............DLB-3, 43

Porter and Coates DLB-49

Portis, Charles 1933- DLB-6

Poston, Ted 1906-1974...................... DLB-51

Postscript to [the Third Edition of] *Clarissa*
(1751), by Samuel Richardson............ DLB-39

Potok, Chaim 1929- DLB-28; Y-84

Potter, David M. 1910-1971 .... DLB-17

Potter, John E., and Company............... DLB-49

Pottle, Frederick A. 1897-1987 ....Y-87

Poulin, Jacques 1937- DLB-60

Pound, Ezra 1885-1972.................DLB-4, 45, 63

Powell, Anthony 1905- DLB-15

Pownall, David 1938- DLB-14

Powys, John Cowper 1872-1963 .... DLB-15

Powys, T. F. 1875-1953...................... DLB-36

The Practice of Biography: An Interview with
Stanley Weintraub Y-82

The Practice of Biography II: An Interview with
B. L. Reid...................................Y-83

The Practice of Biography III: An Interview with
Humphrey Carpenter.......................Y-84

The Practice of Biography IV: An Interview with
William Manchester.......................Y-85

The Practice of Biography V: An Interview with
Justin Kaplan Y-86

The Practice of Biography VI: An Interview with
David Herbert Donald Y-87

Praeger Publishers........................... DLB-46

Pratt, Samuel Jackson 1749-1814............. DLB-39

Preface to *Alwyn* (1780), by Thomas
Holcroft.................................... DLB-39

Preface to *Colonel Jack* (1722), by Daniel
Defoe DLB-39

Preface to *Evelina* (1778), by Fanny Burney ... DLB-39

Preface to *Ferdinand Count Fathom* (1753), by
Tobias Smollett DLB-39

Preface to *Incognita* (1692), by William
Congreve.................................. DLB-39

Preface to *Joseph Andrews* (1742), by
Henry Fielding............................ DLB-39

Preface to *Moll Flanders* (1722), by Daniel
Defoe DLB-39

Preface to *Poems* (1853), by Matthew
Arnold DLB-32

Preface to *Robinson Crusoe* (1719), by Daniel
Defoe DLB-39

Preface to *Roderick Random* (1748), by Tobias
Smollett DLB-39

Preface to *Roxana* (1724), by Daniel Defoe DLB-39

Preface to *St. Leon* (1799),
by William Godwin........................ DLB-39

Preface to Sarah Fielding's *Familiar Letters*
(1747), by Henry Fielding [excerpt]....... DLB-39

Preface to Sarah Fielding's *The Adventures of
David Simple* (1744), by Henry Fielding ... DLB-39

Preface to *The Cry* (1754), by Sarah Fielding... DLB-39

Preface to *The Delicate Distress* (1769), by
Elizabeth Griffin DLB-39

Preface to *The Disguis'd Prince* (1733), by Eliza
Haywood [excerpt]........................ DLB-39

Preface to *The Farther Adventures of Robinson
Crusoe* (1719), by Daniel Defoe............ DLB-39

Preface to the First Edition of *Pamela* (1740), by
Samuel Richardson........................ DLB-39

Preface to the First Edition of *The Castle of
Otranto* (1764), by Horace Walpole........ DLB-39

Preface to *The History of Romances* (1715), by
Pierre Daniel Huet [excerpts]............. DLB-39

Preface to *The Life of Charlotta du Pont* (1723),
by Penelope Aubin......................... DLB-39

Preface to *The Old English Baron* (1778), by
Clara Reeve DLB-39

Preface to the Second Edition of *The Castle of
Otranto* (1765), by Horace Walpole........ DLB-39

Preface to *The Secret History, of Queen Zarah, and the Zarazians* (1705), by Delarivière Manley DLB-39

Preface to the Third Edition of *Clarissa* (1751), by Samuel Richardson [excerpt] DLB-39

Preface to *The Works of Mrs. Davys* (1725), by Mary Davys DLB-39

Preface to Volume 1 of *Clarissa* (1747), by Samuel Richardson DLB-39

Preface to Volume 3 of *Clarissa* (1748), by Samuel Richardson DLB-39

Préfontaine, Yves 1937- DLB-53

Prelutsky, Jack 1940- DLB-61

Prentice, George D. 1802-1870 .... DLB-43

Prentice-Hall DLB-46

Prescott, William Hickling 1796-1859.... DLB-1, 30, 59

The Present State of the English Novel (1892), by George Saintsbury DLB-18

Preston, Thomas 1537-1598 .... DLB-62

Price, Reynolds 1933- DLB-2

Price, Richard 1949- Y-81

Priest, Christopher 1943- DLB-14

Priestley, J. B. 1894-1984 .... DLB-10, 34; Y-84

Prime, Benjamin Young 1733-1791 .... DLB-31

Prince, F. T. 1912- DLB-20

Prince, Thomas 1687-1758 .... DLB-24

The Principles of Success in Literature (1865), by George Henry Lewes [excerpt]........... DLB-57

Pritchett, V. S. 1900- DLB-15

Procter, Adelaide Anne 1825-1864 .... DLB-32

The Progress of Romance (1785), by Clara Reeve [excerpt] DLB-39

Prokosch, Frederic 1906- DLB-48

The Proletarian Novel.........................DLB-9

Propper, Dan 1937- DLB-16

The Prospect of Peace (1778), by Joel Barlow.... DLB-37

Proud, Robert 1728-1813..................... DLB-30

Proust, Marcel 1871-1922 .... DLB-65

Prynne, J. H. 1936- DLB-40

Przybyszewski, Stanislaw 1868-1927 .... DLB-66

The Public Lending Right in America
     Statement by Sen. Charles McC. Mathias, Jr.

PLR and the Meaning of Literary Property
     Statements on PLR by American Writers Y-83

The Public Lending Right in the United Kingdom
     Public Lending Right: The First Year in the
         United Kingdom...........................Y-83

The Publication of English Renaissance Plays DLB-62

Publications and Social Movements [Transcendentalism] DLB-1

Publishers and Agents: The Columbia Connection...................................Y-87

Publishing Fiction at LSU Press Y-87

Pugin, A. Welby 1812-1852.................... DLB-55

Pulitzer, Joseph 1847-1911 .... DLB-23

Pulitzer, Joseph, Jr. 1885-1955 .... DLB-29

Pulitzer Prizes for the Novel, 1917-1945.........DLB-9

Purdy, James 1923- DLB-2

Pusey, Edward Bouverie 1800-1882 .... DLB-55

Putnam, George Palmer 1814-1872.............DLB-3

Putnam, Samuel 1892-1950.....................DLB-4

G. P. Putnam's Sons DLB-49

Puzo, Mario 1920- DLB-6

Pyle, Ernie 1900-1945 .... DLB-29

Pyle, Howard 1853-1911 .... DLB-42

Pym, Barbara 1913-1980 .... DLB-14; Y-87

Pynchon, Thomas 1937- DLB-2

Pyramid Books DLB-46

Pyrnelle, Louise-Clarke 1850-1907 .... DLB-42

Q

Quad, M. (see Lewis, Charles B.)

The Queen City Publishing House DLB-49

Queneau, Raymond 1903-1976................ DLB-72

The Question of American Copyright
     in the Nineteenth Century
         Headnote
         Preface, by George Haven Putnam
         The Evolution of Copyright, by Brander
            Matthews
         Summary of Copyright Legislation in the
            United States, by R. R. Bowker
         Analysis of the Provisions of the Copyright
            Law of 1891, by George Haven Putnam

The Contest for International Copyright,
  by George Haven Putnam
Cheap Books and Good Books,
  by Brander Matthews DLB-49

Quin, Ann 1936-1973 .... DLB-14

Quincy, Samuel of Georgia ?-? DLB-31

Quincy, Samuel of Massachusetts 1734-1789 .. DLB-31

Quist, Harlin, Books.......................... DLB-46

R

Rabe, David 1940- DLB-7

Radcliffe, Ann 1764-1823 .... DLB-39

Raddall, Thomas 1903- DLB-68

Radiguet, Raymond 1903-1923............... DLB-65

Radványi, Netty Reiling (see Seghers, Anna)

Raine, Craig 1944- DLB-40

Raine, Kathleen 1908- DLB-20

Ralph, Julian 1853-1903..................... DLB-23

Ralph Waldo Emerson in 1982 ....Y-82

Rambler, no. 4 (1750), by Samuel Johnson
  [excerpt] DLB-39

Ramée, Marie Louise de la (see Ouida)

Ramsay, David 1749-1815 .... DLB-30

Rand, Avery and Company................... DLB-49

Rand McNally and Company................... DLB-49

Randall, Dudley 1914- DLB-41

Randall, Henry S. 1811-1876................. DLB-30

Randall, James G. 1881-1953................. DLB-17

The Randall Jarrell Symposium: A Small
  Collection of Randall Jarrells
  Excerpts From Papers Delivered at
  the Randall Jarrell Symposium Y-86

Randolph, Anson D. F. [publishing house] DLB-49

Randolph, Thomas 1605-1635................. DLB-58

Random House............................... DLB-46

Ranlet, Henry [publishing house].............. DLB-49

Ransom, John Crowe 1888-1974 ....DLB-45, 63

Raphael, Frederic 1931- DLB-14

Raphaelson, Samson 1896-1983 .... DLB-44

Raskin, Ellen 1928-1984..................... DLB-52

Rattigan, Terence 1911-1977 .... DLB-13

Rawlings, Marjorie Kinnan 1896-1953.......DLB-9, 22

Raworth, Tom 1938- DLB-40

Ray, David 1932- DLB-5

Ray, Henrietta Cordelia 1849-1916........... DLB-50

Raymond, Henry 1820-1869.................. DLB-43

Reach, Angus 1821-1856 .... DLB-70

Read, Herbert 1893-1968.................... DLB-20

Read, Opie 1852-1939....................... DLB-23

Read, Piers Paul 1941- DLB-14

Reade, Charles 1814-1884.................... DLB-21

Reader's Digest Condensed Books............. DLB-46

Reading, Peter 1946- DLB-40

Reaney, James 1926- DLB-68

Rechy, John 1934- Y-82

Redding, J. Saunders 1906- DLB-63

Redfield, J. S. [publishing house]............. DLB-49

Redgrove, Peter 1932- DLB-40

Redmon, Anne 1943- Y-86

Redmond, Eugene B. 1937- DLB-41

Redpath, James [publishing house]........... DLB-49

Reed, Henry 1808-1854 .... DLB-59

Reed, Henry 1914- DLB-27

Reed, Ishmael 1938- DLB-2, 5, 33

Reed, Sampson 1800-1880......................DLB-1

Reese, Lizette Woodworth 1856-1935 .... DLB-54

Reese, Thomas 1742-1796.................... DLB-37

Reeve, Clara 1729-1807 .... DLB-39

Regnery, Henry, Company DLB-46

Reid, Alastair 1926- DLB-27

Reid, Christopher 1949- DLB-40

Reid, Helen Rogers 1882-1970 .... DLB-29

Reid, James ?-? DLB-31

Reid, Mayne 1818-1883 .... DLB-21

Reid, Thomas 1710-1796.................... DLB-31

Reid, Whitelaw 1837-1912................... DLB-23

Reilly and Lee Publishing Company.......... DLB-46

Reisch, Walter 1903-1983.................... DLB-44

Remarque, Erich Maria 1898-1970 .... DLB-56

"Re-meeting of Old Friends": The Jack Kerouac
  Conference.................................Y-82

Remington, Frederic 1861-1909 .... DLB-12

Renaud, Jacques 1943- DLB-60

Renault, Mary 1905-1983......................Y-83

Representative Men and Women: A Historical
    Perspective on the British Novel,
    1930-1960................................ DLB-15

(Re-)Publishing Orwell...........................Y-86

Reuter, Gabriele 1859-1941 .... DLB-66

Revell, Fleming H., Company DLB-49

Reventlow, Franziska Gräfin zu
    1871-1918............................... DLB-66

Review of [Samuel Richardson's] *Clarissa* (1748),
    by Henry Fielding....................... DLB-39

The Revolt (1937), by Mary
    Colum [excerpts]........................ DLB-36

Rexroth, Kenneth 1905-1982........ DLB-16, 48; Y-82

Rey, H. A. 1898-1977........................ DLB-22

Reynal and Hitchcock DLB-46

Reynolds, G. W. M. 1814-1879 .... DLB-21

Reynolds, Mack 1917- DLB-8

Reznikoff, Charles 1894-1976 ....DLB-28, 45

"Rhetoric" (1828; revised, 1859), by
    Thomas de Quincey [excerpt]............ DLB-57

Rhett, Robert Barnwell 1800-1876............ DLB-43

Rhodes, James Ford 1848-1927............... DLB-47

Rhys, Jean 1890-1979 .... DLB-36

Rice, Elmer 1892-1967 ....DLB-4, 7

Rice, Grantland 1880-1954 .... DLB-29

Rich, Adrienne 1929- DLB-5, 67

Richards, David Adams 1950- DLB-53

Richards, George circa 1760-1814 .... DLB-37

Richards, I. A. 1893-1979 .... DLB-27

Richards, Laura E. 1850-1943 .... DLB-42

Richards, William Carey 1818-1892 .... DLB-73

Richardson, Charles F. 1851-1913............ DLB-71

Richardson, Dorothy M. 1873-1957 .... DLB-36

Richardson, Jack 1935- DLB-7

Richardson, Samuel 1689-1761 .... DLB-39

Richardson, Willis 1889-1977................ DLB-51

Richler, Mordecai 1931- DLB-53

Richter, Conrad 1890-1968....................DLB-9

Richter, Hans Werner 1908- DLB-69

Rickword, Edgell 1898-1982.................. DLB-20

Riddell, John (see Ford, Corey)

Ridge, Lola 1873-1941........................ DLB-54

Ridler, Anne 1912- DLB-27

Riffaterre, Michael 1924- DLB-67

Riis, Jacob 1849-1914........................ DLB-23

Riker, John C. [publishing house] DLB-49

Riley, John 1938-1978........................ DLB-40

Rinehart and Company....................... DLB-46

Ringuet 1895-1960 .... DLB-68

Rinser, Luise 1911- DLB-69

Ripley, Arthur 1895-1961 .... DLB-44

Ripley, George 1802-1880 .... DLB-1, 64, 73

The Rising Glory of America: Three Poems... DLB-37

The Rising Glory of America: Written in 1771
    (1786), by Hugh Henry Brackenridge and
    Philip Freneau DLB-37

Riskin, Robert 1897-1955..................... DLB-26

Risse, Heinz 1898- DLB-69

Ritchie, Anna Mowatt 1819-1870...............DLB-3

Ritchie, Anne Thackeray 1837-1919.......... DLB-18

Ritchie, Thomas 1778-1854................... DLB-43

Rites of Passage [on William Saroyan].............Y-83

The Ritz Paris Hemingway Award.................Y-85

Rivers, Conrad Kent 1933-1968 .... DLB-41

Riverside Press DLB-49

Rivington, James circa 1724-1802 .... DLB-43

Rivkin, Allen 1903- DLB-26

Robbins, Tom 1936- Y-80

Roberts, Elizabeth Madox 1881-1941........DLB-9, 54

Roberts, Kenneth 1885-1957 ....DLB-9

Roberts Brothers DLB-49

Robertson, A. M., and Company DLB-49

Robinson, Casey 1903-1979.................... DLB-44

Robinson, Edwin Arlington 1869-1935 .... DLB-54

Robinson, James Harvey 1863-1936........... DLB-47

Robinson, Lennox 1886-1958.................. DLB-10

Robinson, Mabel Louise 1874-1962............ DLB-22

Robinson, Therese 1797-1870 .... DLB-59

Rodgers, Carolyn M. 1945- DLB-41

Rodgers, W. R. 1909-1969.................... DLB-20

Roethke, Theodore 1908-1963 ....DLB-5

Rogers, Will 1879-1935......................DLB-11

Rohmer, Sax 1883-1959.....................DLB-70

Roiphe, Anne 1935- Y-80

Rolfe, Frederick William 1860-1913..........DLB-34

Rolland, Romain 1866-1944..................DLB-65

Rolvaag, O. E. 1876-1931.....................DLB-9

Romains, Jules 1885-1972....................DLB-65

Roman, A., and Company....................DLB-49

Roosevelt, Theodore 1858-1919..............DLB-47

Root, Waverley 1903-1982....................DLB-4

Roquebrune, Robert de 1889-1978...........DLB-68

Rose, Reginald 1920- DLB-26

Rosen, Norma 1925- DLB-28

Rosenberg, Isaac 1890-1918..................DLB-20

Rosenfeld, Isaac 1918-1956...................DLB-28

Rosenthal, M. L. 1917- DLB-5

Ross, Leonard Q. (see Rosten, Leo)

Rossen, Robert 1908-1966....................DLB-26

Rossetti, Christina 1830-1894.................DLB-35

Rossetti, Dante Gabriel 1828-1882............DLB-35

Rossner, Judith 1935- DLB-6

Rosten, Leo 1908- DLB-11

Roth, Henry 1906?- DLB-28

Roth, Philip 1933- DLB-2, 28; Y-82

Rothenberg, Jerome 1931- DLB-5

Rowe, Elizabeth 1674-1737...................DLB-39

Rowlandson, Mary circa 1635-circa 1678......DLB-24

Rowley, William circa 1585-1626..............DLB-58

Rowson, Susanna Haswell circa 1762-1824....DLB-37

Roy, Gabrielle 1909-1983....................DLB-68

The Royal Court Theatre and the English
    Stage Company.........................DLB-13

The Royal Court Theatre and the New
    Drama................................DLB-10

Royall, Anne 1769-1854......................DLB-43

The Roycroft Printing Shop..................DLB-49

Rubens, Bernice 1928- DLB-14

Rudd and Carleton..........................DLB-49

Rudkin, David 1936- DLB-13

Ruggles, Henry Joseph 1813-1906.............DLB-64

Rukeyser, Muriel 1913-1980..................DLB-48

Rule, Jane 1931- DLB-60

Rumaker, Michael 1932- DLB-16

Rumens, Carol 1944- DLB-40

Runyon, Damon 1880-1946...................DLB-11

Rush, Benjamin 1746-1813...................DLB-37

Ruskin, John 1819-1900......................DLB-55

Russ, Joanna 1937- DLB-8

Russell, B. B., and Company..................DLB-49

Russell, Benjamin 1761-1845.................DLB-43

Russell, Charles Edward 1860-1941...........DLB-25

Russell, George William (see AE)

Russell, R. H., and Son......................DLB-49

Rutherford, Mark 1831-1913..................DLB-18

Ryan, Michael 1946- Y-82

Ryan, Oscar 1904- DLB-68

Ryga, George 1932- DLB-60

Ryskind, Morrie 1895-1985...................DLB-26

S

The Saalfield Publishing Company............DLB-46

Saberhagen, Fred 1930- DLB-8

Sackler, Howard 1929-1982..................DLB-7

Sackville, Thomas 1536-1608
    and Norton, Thomas 1532-1584..........DLB-62

Sackville-West, V. 1892-1962.................DLB-34

Sadlier, D. and J., and Company..............DLB-49

Saffin, John circa 1626-1710..................DLB-24

Sage, Robert 1899-1962......................DLB-4

Sahkomaapii, Piitai (see Highwater, Jamake)

Sahl, Hans 1902- DLB-69

Said, Edward W. 1935- DLB-67

St. Johns, Adela Rogers 1894- DLB-29

St. Martin's Press............................DLB-46

Saint-Exupéry, Antoine de 1900-1944.........DLB-72

Saintsbury, George 1845-1933................DLB-57

Saki (see Munro, H. H.)

Salaam, Kalamu ya 1947- DLB-38

Salemson, Harold J. 1910- DLB-4

Salinger, J. D. 1919- DLB-2

Salt, Waldo 1914- DLB-44

Sanborn, Franklin Benjamin 1831-1917 ....DLB-1

Sanchez, Sonia 1934- DLB-41

Sandburg, Carl 1878-1967.................DLB-17, 54

Sanders, Ed 1939- DLB-16

Sandoz, Mari 1896-1966.......................DLB-9

Sandys, George 1578-1644 .... DLB-24

Santayana, George 1863-1952 ....DLB-54, 71

Santmyer, Helen Hooven 1895-1986 ....Y-84

Sargent, Pamela 1948- DLB-8

Saroyan, William 1908-1981...........DLB-7, 9; Y-81

Sarton, May 1912- DLB-48; Y-81

Sartre, Jean-Paul 1905-1980.................. DLB-72

Sassoon, Siegfried 1886-1967................. DLB-20

Saturday Review Press........................ DLB-46

Saunders, James 1925- DLB-13

Saunders, John Monk 1897-1940.............. DLB-26

Savage, James 1784-1873..................... DLB-30

Savage, Marmion W. 1803?-1872.............. DLB-21

Savard, Félix-Antoine 1896-1982 .... DLB-68

Sawyer, Ruth 1880-1970...................... DLB-22

Sayers, Dorothy L. 1893-1957 ....DLB-10, 36

Sayles, John Thomas 1950- DLB-44

Scannell, Vernon 1922- DLB-27

Scarry, Richard 1919- DLB-61

Schaeffer, Albrecht 1885-1950 .... DLB-66

Schaeffer, Susan Fromberg 1941- DLB-28

Schaper, Edzard 1908-1984 .... DLB-69

Scharf, J. Thomas 1843-1898................. DLB-47

Schickele, René 1883-1940 .... DLB-66

Schlesinger, Arthur M., Jr. 1917- DLB-17

Schlumberger, Jean 1877-1968................ DLB-65

Schmid, Eduard Hermann Wilhelm
    (see Edschmid, Kasimir)

Schmidt, Arno 1914-1979 .... DLB-69

Schmidt, Michael 1947- DLB-40

Schmitz, James H. 1911- DLB-8

Schnurre, Wolfdietrich 1920- DLB-69

Schocken Books DLB-46

Schouler, James 1839-1920.................... DLB-47

Schrader, Paul 1946- DLB-44

Schreiner, Olive 1855-1920................... DLB-18

Schroeder, Andreas 1946- DLB-53

Schulberg, Budd 1914- DLB-6, 26, 28; Y-81

Schulte, F. J., and Company.................. DLB-49

Schurz, Carl 1829-1906....................... DLB-23

Schuyler, George S. 1895-1977 ....DLB-29, 51

Schuyler, James 1923- DLB-5

Schwartz, Delmore 1913-1966..............DLB-28, 48

Schwartz, Jonathan 1938- Y-82

Science Fantasy...............................DLB-8

Science-Fiction Fandom and Conventions DLB-8

Science-Fiction Fanzines: The Time Binders DLB-8

Science-Fiction Films DLB-8

Science Fiction Writers of America and the
    Nebula Awards.............................DLB-8

Scott, Evelyn 1893-1963 ....DLB-9, 48

Scott, Harvey W. 1838-1910.................. DLB-23

Scott, Paul 1920-1978........................ DLB-14

Scott, Sarah 1723-1795 .... DLB-39

Scott, Tom 1918- DLB-27

Scott, William Bell 1811-1890 .... DLB-32

Scott, William R. [publishing house].......... DLB-46

Scott-Heron, Gil 1949- DLB-41

Charles Scribner's Sons...................... DLB-49

Scripps, E. W. 1854-1926..................... DLB-25

Scudder, Horace Elisha 1838-1902 ....DLB-42, 71

Scudder, Vida Dutton 1861-1954.............. DLB-71

Scupham, Peter 1933- DLB-40

Seabrook, William 1886-1945..................DLB-4

Seabury, Samuel 1729-1796 .... DLB-31

Sears Publishing Company DLB-46

Seaton, George 1911-1979.................... DLB-44

Seaton, William Winston 1785-1866 .... DLB-43

Sedgwick, Arthur George 1844-1915.......... DLB-64

Sedgwick, Catharine Maria 1789-1867..........DLB-1

Seeger, Alan 1888-1916 .... DLB-45

Segal, Erich 1937- Y-86

Seghers, Anna 1900-1983 .... DLB-69

Seid, Ruth (see Sinclair, Jo)

Seidel, Frederick Lewis 1936- Y-84

Seidel, Ina 1885-1974 .... DLB-56

Séjour, Victor 1817-1874 .... DLB-50

Séjour Marcou et Ferrand,
    Juan Victor (see Séjour, Victor)

Selby, Hubert, Jr. 1928- DLB-2

Selden, George 1929- DLB-52

Selected English-Language Little Magazines and
    Newspapers [France, 1920-1939]...........DLB-4

Selected Humorous Magazines (1820-1950) ... DLB-11

Selected Science-Fiction Magazines and
    Anthologies DLB-8

Seligman, Edwin R. A. 1861-1939 .... DLB-47

Seltzer, Thomas [publishing house]........... DLB-46

Sendak, Maurice 1928- DLB-61

Sensation Novels (1863), by H. L. Manse DLB-21

Seredy, Kate 1899-1975 .... DLB-22

Serling, Rod 1924-1975....................... DLB-26

Settle, Mary Lee 1918- DLB-6

Seuss, Dr. (see Geisel, Theodor Seuss)

Sewall, Joseph 1688-1769..................... DLB-24

Sewell, Samuel 1652-1730 .... DLB-24

Sex, Class, Politics, and Religion [in the British
    Novel, 1930-1959]........................ DLB-15

Sexton, Anne 1928-1974 ....DLB-5

Shaara, Michael 1929- Y-83

Shaffer, Anthony 1926- DLB-13

Shaffer, Peter 1926- DLB-13

Shairp, Mordaunt 1887-1939................. DLB-10

Shakespeare, William 1564-1616 .... DLB-62

Shange, Ntozake 1948- DLB-38

Shapiro, Karl 1913- DLB-48

Sharon Publications......................... DLB-46

Sharpe, Tom 1928- DLB-14

Shaw, Bernard 1856-1950 ....DLB-10, 57

Shaw, Henry Wheeler 1818-1885............. DLB-11

Shaw, Irwin 1913-1984 .... DLB-6; Y-84

Shaw, Robert 1927-1978...................DLB-13, 14

Shay, Frank [publishing house]............... DLB-46

Shea, John Gilmary 1824-1892 .... DLB-30

Shearing, Joseph 1886-1952 .... DLB-70

Shebbeare, John 1709-1788 .... DLB-39

Sheckley, Robert 1928- DLB-8

Shedd, William G. T. 1820-1894 .... DLB-64

Sheed, Wilfred 1930- DLB-6

Sheed and Ward............................ DLB-46

Sheldon, Alice B. (see Tiptree, James, Jr.)

Sheldon, Edward 1886-1946...................DLB-7

Sheldon and Company DLB-49

Shepard, Sam 1943- DLB-7

Shepard, Thomas I 1604 or 1605-1649........ DLB-24

Shepard, Thomas II 1635-1677 .... DLB-24

Shepard, Clark and Brown DLB-49

Sheridan, Frances 1724-1766................. DLB-39

Sherriff, R. C. 1896-1975.................... DLB-10

Sherwood, Robert 1896-1955.............DLB-7, 26

Shiels, George 1886-1949.................... DLB-10

Shillaber, B.[enjamin] P.[enhallow]
    1814-1890...........................DLB-1, 11

Shine, Ted 1931- DLB-38

Shirer, William L. 1904- DLB-4

Shirley, James 1596-1666.................... DLB-58

Shockley, Ann Allen 1927- DLB-33

Shorthouse, Joseph Henry 1834-1903 .... DLB-18

Showalter, Elaine 1941- DLB-67

Shulevitz, Uri 1935- DLB-61

Shulman, Max 1919- DLB-11

Shute, Henry A. 1856-1943 ....DLB-9

Shuttle, Penelope 1947- DLB-14, 40

Sidney, Margaret (see Lothrop, Harriet M.)

Sidney's Press................................ DLB-49

Siegfried Loraine Sassoon: A Centenary Essay
    Tributes from Vivien F. Clarke and
      Michael Thorpe Y-86

Sierra Club Books DLB-49

Sigourney, Lydia Howard (Huntley)
    1791-1865.........................DLB-1, 42, 73

Silkin, Jon 1930- DLB-27

Silliphant, Stirling 1918- DLB-26

Sillitoe, Alan 1928- DLB-14

Silman, Roberta 1934- DLB-28

Silverberg, Robert 1935- DLB-8

Simak, Clifford D. 1904- DLB-8

Simcox, George Augustus 1841-1905.......... DLB-35

Simenon, Georges 1903- DLB-72

Simmel, Johannes Mario 1924- DLB-69

Simmons, Herbert Alfred 1930- DLB-33

Simmons, James 1933- DLB-40

Simms, William Gilmore
1806-1870..................... DLB-3, 30, 59, 73

Simon, Neil 1927- DLB-7

Simon and Schuster DLB-46

Simons, Katherine Drayton Mayrant 1890-1969...Y-83

Simpson, Louis 1923- DLB-5

Simpson, N. F. 1919- DLB-13

Sims, George R. 1847-1922................DLB-35, 70

Sinclair, Andrew 1935- DLB-14

Sinclair, Jo 1913- DLB-28

Sinclair Lewis Centennial Conference Y-85

Sinclair, May 1863-1946...................... DLB-36

Sinclair, Upton 1878-1968....................DLB-9

Sinclair, Upton [publishing house]............ DLB-46

Singer, Isaac Bashevis 1904- DLB-6, 28, 52

Singmaster, Elsie 1879-1958...................DLB-9

Siodmak, Curt 1902- DLB-44

Sissman, L. E. 1928-1976.....................DLB-5

Sisson, C. H. 1914- DLB-27

Sitwell, Edith 1887-1964...................... DLB-20

Skelton, Robin 1925- DLB-27, 53

Skinner, John Stuart 1788-1851 .... DLB-73

Skipsey, Joseph 1832-1903 .... DLB-35

Slade, Bernard 1930- DLB-53

Slater, Patrick 1880-1951 .... DLB-68

Slavitt, David 1935- DLB-5, 6

A Slender Thread of Hope: The Kennedy
Center Black Theatre Project DLB-38

Slick, Sam (see Haliburton, Thomas Chandler)

Sloane, William, Associates DLB-46

Small, Maynard and Company DLB-49

Small Presses in Great Britain and Ireland,
1960-1985................................ DLB-40

Small Presses I: Jargon Society Y-84

Small Presses II: The Spirit That
Moves Us Press Y-85

Small Presses III: Pushcart Press Y-87

Smiles, Samuel 1812-1904..................... DLB-55

Smith, Alexander 1829-1867 ....DLB-32, 55

Smith, Betty 1896-1972..........................Y-82

Smith, Carol Sturm 1938- Y-81

Smith, Charles Henry 1826-1903.............. DLB-11

Smith, Charlotte 1749-1806 .... DLB-39

Smith, Cordwainer 1913-1966....................DLB-8

Smith, Dave 1942- DLB-5

Smith, Dodie 1896- DLB-10

Smith, Doris Buchanan 1934- DLB-52

Smith, E. E. 1890-1965 ....DLB-8

Smith, Elihu Hubbard 1771-1798 .... DLB-37

Smith, Elizabeth Oakes (Prince) 1806-1893......DLB-1

Smith, George O. 1911-1981 ....DLB-8

Smith, H. Allen 1907-1976 ....DLB-11, 29

Smith, Harrison, and Robert Haas
[publishing house] DLB-46

Smith, Iain Crichten 1928- DLB-40

Smith, J. Allen 1860-1924 .... DLB-47

Smith, J. Stilman, and Company............... DLB-49

Smith, John 1580-1631 ....DLB-24, 30

Smith, Josiah 1704-1781...................... DLB-24

Smith, Ken 1938- DLB-40

Smith, Lee 1944- Y-83

Smith, Mark 1935- Y-82

Smith, Michael 1698-circa 1771................ DLB-31

Smith, Red 1905-1982........................ DLB-29

Smith, Samuel Harrison 1772-1845............ DLB-43

Smith, Samuel Stanhope 1751-1819 .... DLB-37

Smith, Seba 1792-1868 ....DLB-1, 11

Smith, Stevie 1902-1971 .... DLB-20

Smith, Sydney Goodsir 1915-1975............. DLB-27

Smith, W. B., and Company................... DLB-49

Smith, William 1727-1803 .... DLB-31

Smith, William 1728-1793 .... DLB-30

Smith, William Jay 1918- DLB-5

Smollett, Tobias 1721-1771.................... DLB-39

Snellings, Rolland (see Touré, Askia Muhammad)

Snodgrass, W. D. 1926- DLB-5

Snow, C. P. 1905-1980........................ DLB-15

Snyder, Gary 1930- DLB-5, 16

Sobiloff, Hy 1912-1970...................... DLB-48

The Society for Textual Scholarship
    and *TEXT*....................................Y-87

Solano, Solita 1888-1975........................DLB-4

Solomon, Carl 1928- DLB-16

Solway, David 1941- DLB-53

Solzhenitsyn and America Y-85

Sontag, Susan 1933- DLB-2, 67

Sorrentino, Gilbert 1929- DLB-5; Y-80

Sources for the Study of Tudor
    and Stuart Drama...................... DLB-62

Southerland, Ellease 1943- DLB-33

Southern, Terry 1924- DLB-2

Southern Writers Between the Wars............DLB-9

Spark, Muriel 1918- DLB-15

Sparks, Jared 1789-1866.....................DLB-1, 30

Sparshott, Francis 1926- DLB-60

Spellman, A. B. 1935- DLB-41

Spencer, Anne 1882-1975 ....DLB-51, 54

Spencer, Elizabeth 1921- DLB-6

Spencer, Herbert 1820-1903.................. DLB-57

Spencer, Scott 1945- Y-86

Spender, Stephen 1909-...................... DLB-20

Spicer, Jack 1925-1965 ....DLB-5, 16

Spielberg, Peter 1929- Y-81

Spier, Peter 1927- DLB-61

Spinrad, Norman 1940- DLB-8

Squibob (see Derby, George Horatio)

Stafford, Jean 1915-1979.......................DLB-2

Stafford, William 1914- DLB-5

Stage Censorship: "The Rejected Statement"
    (1911), by Bernard Shaw [excerpts]....... DLB-10

Stallings, Laurence 1894-1968...............DLB-7, 44

Stallworthy, Jon 1935- DLB-40

Stampp, Kenneth M. 1912- DLB-17

Stanford, Ann 1916- DLB-5

Stanton, Frank L. 1857-1927 .... DLB-25

Stapledon, Olaf 1886-1950 .... DLB-15

Star Spangled Banner Office DLB-49

Starkweather, David 1935- DLB-7

Statements on the Art of Poetry............... DLB-54

Steadman, Mark 1930- DLB-6

The Stealthy School of Criticism (1871), by
    Dante Gabriel Rossetti DLB-35

Stearns, Harold E. 1891-1943 ....DLB-4

Stedman, Edmund Clarence 1833-1908 .... DLB-64

Steele, Max 1922- Y-80

Steere, Richard circa 1643-1721 .... DLB-24

Stegner, Wallace 1909- DLB-9

Stehr, Hermann 1864-1940.................... DLB-66

Steig, William 1907- DLB-61

Stein, Gertrude 1874-1946...................DLB-4, 54

Stein, Leo 1872-1947...........................DLB-4

Stein and Day Publishers DLB-46

Steinbeck, John 1902-1968 ....DLB-7, 9; DS-2

Steiner, George 1929- DLB-67

Stephen, Leslie 1832-1904..................... DLB-57

Stephens, Alexander H. 1812-1883........... DLB-47

Stephens, Ann 1810-1886 ....DLB-3, 73

Stephens, Charles Asbury 1844?-1931........ DLB-42

Stephens, James 1882?-1950................... DLB-19

Sterling, George 1869-1926.................... DLB-54

Sterling, James 1701-1763 .... DLB-24

Stern, Richard 1928- Y-87

Stern, Stewart 1922- DLB-26

Sterne, Laurence 1713-1768................... DLB-39

Sternheim, Carl 1878-1942 .... DLB-56

Stevens, Wallace 1879-1955.................... DLB-54

Stevenson, Anne 1933- DLB-40

Stevenson, Robert Louis 1850-1894 ....DLB-18, 57

Stewart, Donald Ogden 1894-1980 ......DLB-4, 11, 26

Stewart, Dugald 1753-1828.................... DLB-31

Stewart, George R. 1895-1980...................DLB-8

Stewart and Kidd Company DLB-46

Stickney, Trumbull 1874-1904................. DLB-54

Stiles, Ezra 1727-1795 .... DLB-31

Still, James 1906- DLB-9

Stith, William 1707-1755 .... DLB-31

Stockton, Frank R. 1834-1902 .... DLB-42

Stoddard, Ashbel [publishing house] DLB-49

Stoddard, Richard Henry 1825-1903 ....DLB-3, 64

Stoddard, Solomon 1643-1729................ DLB-24

Stoker, Bram 1847-1912....................DLB-36, 70

Stokes, Frederick A., Company............... DLB-49

Stokes, Thomas L. 1898-1958 .... DLB-29

Stone, Herbert S., and Company DLB-49

Stone, Melville 1848-1929 .... DLB-25

Stone, Samuel 1602-1663..................... DLB-24

Stone and Kimball............................ DLB-49

Stoppard, Tom 1937- DLB-13; Y-85

Storey, Anthony 1928- DLB-14

Storey, David 1933- DLB-13, 14

Story, Thomas circa 1670-1742................ DLB-31

Story, William Wetmore 1819-1895.............DLB-1

Storytelling: A Contemporary Renaissance Y-84

Stoughton, William 1631-1701................ DLB-24

Stowe, Harriet Beecher 1811-1896 ......DLB-1, 12, 42

Stowe, Leland 1899- DLB-29

Strand, Mark 1934- DLB-5

Stratemeyer, Edward 1862-1930.............. DLB-42

Stratton and Barnard........................ DLB-49

Straub, Peter 1943- Y-84

Street and Smith............................ DLB-49

Streeter, Edward 1891-1976.................. DLB-11

Stribling, T. S. 1881-1965 ....DLB-9

Stringer and Townsend DLB-49

Strittmatter, Erwin 1912- DLB-69

Strother, David Hunter 1816-1888 ....DLB-3

Stuart, Jesse 1906-1984.............. DLB-9, 48; Y-84

Stuart, Lyle [publishing house] DLB-46

Stubbs, Harry Clement (see Clement, Hal)

The Study of Poetry (1880), by Matthew
       Arnold DLB-35

Sturgeon, Theodore 1918-1985 .... DLB-8; Y-85

Sturges, Preston 1898-1959.................... DLB-26

"Style" (1840; revised, 1859), by Thomas
       de Quincey [excerpt]..................... DLB-57

"Style" (1888), by Walter Pater DLB-57

Style (1897), by Walter Raleigh [excerpt]....... DLB-57

"Style" (1877), by T. H. Wright [excerpt]...... DLB-57

"Le Style c'est l'homme" (1892),
       by W. H. Mallock DLB-57

Styron, William 1925- DLB-2; Y-80

Such, Peter 1939- DLB-60

Suckling, Sir John 1609-1642................... DLB-58

Suckow, Ruth 1892-1960 ....DLB-9

Suggs, Simon (see Hooper, Johnson Jones)

Sukenick, Ronald 1932- Y-81

Suknaski, Andrew 1942- DLB-53

Sullivan, C. Gardner 1886-1965 .... DLB-26

Sullivan, Frank 1892-1976.................... DLB-11

Summers, Hollis 1916- DLB-6

Sumner, Henry A. [publishing house]........ DLB-49

Surtees, Robert Smith 1803-1864.............. DLB-21

A Survey of Poetry
       Anthologies, 1879-1960 .... DLB-54

Surveys of the Year's Biography
       A Transit of Poets and Others: American
              Biography in 1982 ....Y-82
       The Year in Literary Biography Y-83
       The Year in Literary Biography Y-84
       The Year in Literary Biography Y-85
       The Year in Literary Biography Y-86
       The Year in Literary Biography Y-87

Surveys of the Year's Book Publishing
       The Year in Book Publishing................Y-86

Surveys of the Year's Drama
       The Year in Drama Y-82
       The Year in Drama Y-83
       The Year in Drama Y-84
       The Year in Drama Y-85
       The Year in Drama Y-87

Surveys of the Year's Fiction
       The Year's Work in Fiction: A Survey Y-82
       The Year in Fiction: A Biased View Y-83
       The Year in Fiction Y-84
       The Year in Fiction Y-85
       The Year in Fiction Y-86
       The Year in the Novel Y-87
       The Year in Short Stories....................Y-87

Surveys of the Year's Poetry
       The Year's Work in American Poetry.........Y-82
       The Year in Poetry Y-83
       The Year in Poetry Y-84
       The Year in Poetry Y-85
       The Year in Poetry Y-86

The Year in Poetry Y-87

Sutherland, John 1919-1956 .... DLB-68

Sutro, Alfred 1863-1933 .... DLB-10

Swados, Harvey 1920-1972 .... DLB-2

Swain, Charles 1801-1874 .... DLB-32

Swallow Press DLB-46

Swenson, May 1919- DLB-5

Swerling, Jo 1897- DLB-44

Swift, Jonathan 1667-1745 .... DLB-39

Swinburne, A. C. 1837-1909 .... DLB-35, 57

Swinnerton, Frank 1884-1982 .... DLB-34

Swisshelm, Jane Grey 1815-1884 .... DLB-43

Swope, Herbert Bayard 1882-1958 .... DLB-25

Swords, T. and J., and Company DLB-49

Swords, Thomas 1763-1843 and
    Swords, James ?-1844 .... DLB-73

Symonds, John Addington 1840-1893 .... DLB-57

Symons, Arthur 1865-1945 .... DLB-19, 57

Symons, Scott 1933- DLB-53

Synge, John Millington 1871-1909 .... DLB-10, 19

T

Taggard, Genevieve 1894-1948 .... DLB-45

Tait, J. Selwin, and Sons DLB-49

Talvj or Talvi (see Robinson, Therese)

Taradash, Daniel 1913- DLB-44

Tarbell, Ida M. 1857-1944 .... DLB-47

Tarkington, Booth 1869-1946 .... DLB-9

Tashlin, Frank 1913-1972 .... DLB-44

Tate, Allen 1899-1979 .... DLB-4, 45, 63

Tate, James 1943- DLB-5

Taylor, Bayard 1825-1878 .... DLB-3

Taylor, Bert Leston 1866-1921 .... DLB-25

Taylor, Charles H. 1846-1921 .... DLB-25

Taylor, Edward circa 1642-1729 .... DLB-24

Taylor, Henry 1942- DLB-5

Taylor, Sir Henry 1800-1886 .... DLB-32

Taylor, Mildred D. ?- DLB-52

Taylor, Peter 1917- Y-81

Taylor, William, and Company DLB-49

Taylor-Made Shakespeare? Or Is
    "Shall I Die?" the Long-Lost Text
    of Bottom's Dream? Y-85

Teasdale, Sara 1884-1933 .... DLB-45

The Tea-Table (1725), by Eliza Haywood
    [excerpt] DLB-39

Tenn, William 1919- DLB-8

Tennant, Emma 1937- DLB-14

Tenney, Tabitha Gilman 1762-1837 .... DLB-37

Tennyson, Alfred 1809-1892 .... DLB-32

Tennyson, Frederick 1807-1898 .... DLB-32

Terhune, Albert Payson 1872-1942 .... DLB-9

Terry, Megan 1932- DLB-7

Terson, Peter 1932- DLB-13

Tesich, Steve 1943- Y-83

Thacher, James 1754-1844 .... DLB-37

Thackeray, William Makepeace
    1811-1863 .... DLB-21, 55

The Theater in Shakespeare's Time DLB-62

The Theatre Guild DLB-7

Thério, Adrien 1925- DLB-53

Theroux, Paul 1941- DLB-2

Thoma, Ludwig 1867-1921 .... DLB-66

Thoma, Richard 1902- DLB-4

Thomas, Audrey 1935- DLB-60

Thomas, D. M. 1935- DLB-40

Thomas, Dylan 1914-1953 .... DLB-13, 20

Thomas, Edward 1878-1917 .... DLB-19

Thomas, Gwyn 1913-1981 .... DLB-15

Thomas, Isaiah 1750-1831 .... DLB-43, 73

Thomas, Isaiah [publishing house] DLB-49

Thomas, John 1900-1932 .... DLB-4

Thomas, Joyce Carol 1938- DLB-33

Thomas, Lorenzo 1944- DLB-41

Thomas, R. S. 1915- DLB-27

Thompson, Dorothy 1893-1961 .... DLB-29

Thompson, Francis 1859-1907 .... DLB-19

Thompson, George Selden (see Selden, George)

Thompson, John 1938-1976 .... DLB-60

Thompson, John R. 1823-1873 .... DLB-3, 73

Thompson, Maurice 1844-1901 .... DLB-71

Thompson, Ruth Plumly 1891-1976 .... DLB-22

Thompson, William Tappan 1812-1882 ..... DLB-3, 11

Thomson, James 1834-1882 .... DLB-35

Thomson, Mortimer 1831-1875 .... DLB-11

Thoreau, Henry David 1817-1862 .... DLB-1

Thorpe, Thomas Bangs 1815-1878 .... DLB-3, 11

Thoughts on Poetry and Its Varieties (1833),
    by John Stuart Mill DLB-32

Thurber, James 1894-1961 .... DLB-4, 11, 22

Thurman, Wallace 1902-1934 .... DLB-51

Thwaite, Anthony 1930- DLB-40

Thwaites, Reuben Gold 1853-1913 .... DLB-47

Ticknor, George 1791-1871 .... DLB-1, 59

Ticknor and Fields DLB-49

Ticknor and Fields (revived) DLB-46

Tietjens, Eunice 1884-1944 .... DLB-54

Tilton, J. E., and Company DLB-49

Time and Western Man (1927), by Wyndham
    Lewis [excerpts] DLB-36

Time-Life Books DLB-46

Times Books DLB-46

Timothy, Peter circa 1725-1782 .... DLB-43

Timrod, Henry 1828-1867 .... DLB-3

Tiptree, James, Jr. 1915- DLB-8

Titus, Edward William 1870-1952 .... DLB-4

Toklas, Alice B. 1877-1967 .... DLB-4

Tolkien, J. R. R. 1892-1973 .... DLB-15

Tolson, Melvin B. 1898-1966 .... DLB-48

Tom Jones (1749), by Henry
    Fielding [excerpt] DLB-39

Tomlinson, Charles 1927- DLB-40

Tomlinson, Henry Major 1873-1958 .... DLB-36

Tompkins, Abel [publishing house] DLB-49

Tompson, Benjamin 1642-1714 .... DLB-24

Tonks, Rosemary 1932- DLB-14

Toole, John Kennedy 1937-1969 .... Y-81

Toomer, Jean 1894-1967 .... DLB-45, 51

Tor Books DLB-46

Torrence, Ridgely 1874-1950 .... DLB-54

Toth, Susan Allen 1940- Y-86

Tough-Guy Literature DLB-9

Touré, Askia Muhammad 1938- DLB-41

Tourneur, Cyril circa 1580-1626 .... DLB-58

Tousey, Frank [publishing house] DLB-49

Tower Publications DLB-46

Towne, Benjamin circa 1740-1793 .... DLB-43

Towne, Robert 1936- DLB-44

Tracy, Honor 1913- DLB-15

The Transatlantic Publishing Company DLB-49

Traven, B. 1882? or 1890?-1969? DLB-9, 56

Travers, Ben 1886-1980 .... DLB-10

Tremain, Rose 1943- DLB-14

Tremblay, Michel 1942- DLB-60

Trends in Twentieth-Century
    Mass Market Publishing DLB-46

Trent, William P. 1862-1939 .... DLB-47

Trescot, William Henry 1822-1898 .... DLB-30

Trevor, William 1928- DLB-14

Trilling, Lionel 1905-1975 .... DLB-28, 63

Triolet, Elsa 1896-1970 .... DLB-72

Tripp, John 1927- DLB-40

Trocchi, Alexander 1925- DLB-15

Trollope, Anthony 1815-1882 .... DLB-21, 57

Trollope, Frances 1779-1863 .... DLB-21

Troop, Elizabeth 1931- DLB-14

Trotti, Lamar 1898-1952 .... DLB-44

Trottier, Pierre 1925- DLB-60

Troupe, Quincy Thomas, Jr. 1943- DLB-41

Trow, John F., and Company DLB-49

Trumbo, Dalton 1905-1976 .... DLB-26

Trumbull, Benjamin 1735-1820 .... DLB-30

Trumbull, John 1750-1831 .... DLB-31

Tucholsky, Kurt 1890-1935 .... DLB-56

Tucker, George 1775-1861 .... DLB-3, 30

Tucker, Nathaniel Beverley 1784-1851 .... DLB-3

Tucker, St. George 1752-1827 .... DLB-37

Tuckerman, Henry Theodore 1813-1871 ..... DLB-64

Tunis, John R. 1889-1975 .... DLB-22

Tuohy, Frank 1925- DLB-14

Tupper, Martin F. 1810-1889 .... DLB-32

Turbyfill, Mark 1896- DLB-45

Turco, Lewis 1934- Y-84

Turnbull, Gael 1928- DLB-40

Turner, Charles (Tennyson) 1808-1879 .... DLB-32

Turner, Frederick 1943- DLB-40

Turner, Frederick Jackson 1861-1932........ DLB-17

Turpin, Waters Edward 1910-1968............ DLB-51

Twain, Mark (see Clemens, Samuel Langhorne)

Tyler, Anne 1941- DLB-6; Y-82

Tyler, Moses Coit 1835-1900 ....DLB-47, 64

Tyler, Royall 1757-1826 .... DLB-37

Tylor, Edward Burnett 1832-1917............ DLB-57

U

Udall, Nicholas 1504-1556.................... DLB-62

Uhse, Bodo 1904-1963 .... DLB-69

Under the Microscope (1872), by A. C.
    Swinburne DLB-35

United States Book Company DLB-49

Universal Publishing and Distributing
    Corporation............................ DLB-46

The University of Iowa Writers'
    Workshop Golden Jubilee....................Y-86

"The Unknown Public" (1858), by
    Wilkie Collins [excerpt] DLB-57

Unruh, Fritz von 1885-1970.................. DLB-56

Upchurch, Boyd B. (see Boyd, John)

Updike, John 1932- DLB-2, 5; Y-80, 82; DS-3

Upton, Charles 1948- DLB-16

Upward, Allen 1863-1926 .... DLB-36

Ustinov, Peter 1921- DLB-13

V

Vail, Laurence 1891-1968 ....DLB-4

Vajda, Ernest 1887-1954 .... DLB-44

Valgardson, W. D. 1939- DLB-60

Van Allsburg, Chris 1949- DLB-61

Van Anda, Carr 1864-1945.................... DLB-25

Vance, Jack 1916?- DLB-8

Van Doran, Mark 1894-1972 .... DLB-45

van Druten, John 1901-1957 .... DLB-10

Van Duyn, Mona 1921- DLB-5

Van Dyke, Henry 1852-1933 .... DLB-71

Van Dyke, Henry 1928- DLB-33

Vane, Sutton 1888-1963...................... DLB-10

Vanguard Press.............................. DLB-46

van Itallie, Jean-Claude 1936- DLB-7

Vann, Robert L. 1879-1940................... DLB-29

Van Rensselaer, Mariana Griswold
    1851-1934............................... DLB-47

Van Rensselaer, Mrs. Schuyler (see Van
    Rensselaer, Mariana Griswold)

Van Vechten, Carl 1880-1964 .... DLB-4, 9

van Vogt, A. E. 1912- DLB-8

Varley, John 1947- Y-81

Vassa, Gustavus (see Equiano, Olaudah)

Vega, Janine Pommy 1942- DLB-16

Veiller, Anthony 1903-1965 .... DLB-44

Verplanck, Gulian C. 1786-1870.............. DLB-59

Very, Jones 1813-1880 ....DLB-1

Vian, Boris 1920-1959 .... DLB-72

Victoria 1819-1901 .... DLB-55

Vidal, Gore 1925- DLB-6

Viebig, Clara 1860-1952...................... DLB-66

Viereck, George Sylvester 1884-1962.......... DLB-54

Viereck, Peter 1916- DLB-5

Viewpoint: Politics and Performance, by David
    Edgar DLB-13

Vigneault, Gilles 1928- DLB-60

The Viking Press........................... DLB-46

Villard, Henry 1835-1900 .... DLB-23

Villard, Oswald Garrison 1872-1949.......... DLB-25

Villemaire, Yolande 1949- DLB-60

Viorst, Judith ?- DLB-52

Volland, P. F., Company DLB-46

Vonnegut, Kurt 1922- DLB-2, 8; Y-80; DS-3

Vroman, Mary Elizabeth circa 1924-1967...... DLB-33

W

Waddington, Miriam 1917- DLB-68

Wagoner, David 1926- DLB-5

Wah, Fred 1939- DLB-60

Wain, John 1925- DLB-15, 27

Wainwright, Jeffrey 1944- DLB-40

Waite, Peirce and Company DLB-49

Wakoski, Diane 1937- DLB-5

Walck, Henry Z. DLB-46

Walcott, Derek 1930- Y-81

Waldman, Anne 1945- DLB-16

Walker, Alice 1944- DLB-6, 33

Walker, George F. 1947- DLB-60

Walker, Joseph A. 1935- DLB-38

Walker, Ted 1934- DLB-40

Walker and Company DLB-49

Walker, Evans and Cogswell Company DLB-49

Wallace, Edgar 1875-1932 .... DLB-70

Wallant, Edward Lewis 1926-1962 .... DLB-2, 28

Walpole, Horace 1717-1797 .... DLB-39

Walpole, Hugh 1884-1941 .... DLB-34

Walrond, Eric 1898-1966 .... DLB-51

Walser, Robert 1878-1956 .... DLB-66

Walsh, Ernest 1895-1926 .... DLB-4, 45

Walsh, Robert 1784-1859 .... DLB-59

Wambaugh, Joseph 1937- DLB-6; Y-83

Ward, Artemus (see Browne, Charles Farrar)

Ward, Arthur Henry Sarsfield
    (see Rohmer, Sax)

Ward, Douglas Turner 1930- DLB-7, 38

Ward, Lynd 1905-1985 .... DLB-22

Ward, Mrs. Humphry 1851-1920 .... DLB-18

Ward, Nathaniel circa 1578-1652 .... DLB-24

Ware, William 1797-1852 .... DLB-1

Warne, Frederick, and Company DLB-49

Warner, Charles Dudley 1829-1900 .... DLB-64

Warner, Rex 1905- DLB-15

Warner, Susan Bogert 1819-1885 .... DLB-3, 42

Warner, Sylvia Townsend 1893-1978 .... DLB-34

Warner Books DLB-46

Warren, John Byrne Leicester (see De Tabley, Lord)

Warren, Lella 1899-1982 .... Y-83

Warren, Mercy Otis 1728-1814 .... DLB-31

Warren, Robert Penn 1905- DLB-2, 48; Y-80

Washington, George 1732-1799 .... DLB-31

Wassermann, Jakob 1873-1934 .... DLB-66

Wasson, David Atwood 1823-1887 .... DLB-1

Waterhouse, Keith 1929- DLB-13, 15

Waterman, Andrew 1940- DLB-40

Waters, Frank 1902- Y-86

Watkins, Tobias 1780-1855 .... DLB-73

Watkins, Vernon 1906-1967 .... DLB-20

Watmough, David 1926- DLB-53

Watson, Sheila 1909- DLB-60

Watson, Wilfred 1911- DLB-60

Watt, W. J., and Company DLB-46

Watterson, Henry 1840-1921 .... DLB-25

Watts, Alan 1915-1973 .... DLB-16

Watts, Franklin [publishing house] DLB-46

Waugh, Auberon 1939- DLB-14

Waugh, Evelyn 1903-1966 .... DLB-15

Way and Williams DLB-49

Wayman, Tom 1945- DLB-53

Weatherly, Tom 1942- DLB-41

Webb, Frank J. ?-? DLB-50

Webb, James Watson 1802-1884 .... DLB-43

Webb, Mary 1881-1927 .... DLB-34

Webb, Phyllis 1927- DLB-53

Webb, Walter Prescott 1888-1963 .... DLB-17

Webster, Augusta 1837-1894 .... DLB-35

Webster, Charles L., and Company DLB-49

Webster, John 1579 or 1580-1634? DLB-58

Webster, Noah 1758-1843 .... DLB-1, 37, 42, 43, 73

Weems, Mason Locke 1759-1825 .... DLB-30, 37, 42

Weidman, Jerome 1913- DLB-28

Weinbaum, Stanley Grauman 1902-1935 .... DLB-8

Weisenborn, Günther 1902-1969 .... DLB-69

Weiss, John 1818-1879 .... DLB-1

Weiss, Peter 1916-1982 . . . . DLB-69

Weiss, Theodore 1916- DLB-5

Welch, Lew 1926-1971? DLB-16

Weldon, Fay 1931- DLB-14

Wellek, René 1903- DLB-63

Wells, Carolyn 1862-1942 . . . . DLB-11

Wells, Charles Jeremiah circa 1800-1879 . . . . . DLB-32

Wells, H. G. 1866-1946 . . . . DLB-34, 70

Wells, Robert 1947- DLB-40

Wells-Barnett, Ida B. 1862-1931 . . . . DLB-23

Welty, Eudora 1909- DLB-2; Y-87

Wendell, Barrett 1855-1921 . . . . DLB-71

The Werner Company DLB-49

Wersba, Barbara 1932- DLB-52

Wescott, Glenway 1901- DLB-4, 9

Wesker, Arnold 1932- DLB-13

Wesley, Richard 1945- DLB-38

Wessels, A., and Company DLB-46

West, Anthony 1914- DLB-15

West, Jessamyn 1902-1984 . . . . DLB-6; Y-84

West, Mae 1892-1980 . . . . DLB-44

West, Nathanael 1903-1940 . . . . DLB-4, 9, 28

West, Paul 1930- DLB-14

West, Rebecca 1892-1983 . . . . DLB-36; Y-83

West and Johnson DLB-49

Western Publishing Company DLB-46

Wetherell, Elizabeth (see Warner, Susan Bogert)

Whalen, Philip 1923- DLB-16

Wharton, Edith 1862-1937 . . . . DLB-4, 9, 12

Wharton, William 1920s?- Y-80

What's Really Wrong With Bestseller Lists Y-84

Wheatley, Phillis circa 1754-1784 . . . . DLB-31, 50

Wheeler, Charles Stearns 1816-1843 . . . . DLB-1

Wheeler, Monroe 1900- DLB-4

Wheelock, John Hall 1886-1978 . . . . DLB-45

Wheelwright, John circa 1592-1679 . . . . DLB-24

Wheelwright, J. B. 1897-1940 . . . . DLB-45

Whetstone, Colonel Pete (see Noland, C. F. M.)

Whipple, Edwin Percy 1819-1886 . . . . DLB-1, 64

Whitaker, Alexander 1585-1617 . . . . DLB-24

Whitaker, Daniel K. 1801-1881 . . . . DLB-73

Whitcher, Frances Miriam 1814-1852 . . . . DLB-11

White, Andrew 1579-1656 . . . . DLB-24

White, Andrew Dickson 1832-1918 . . . . DLB-47

White, E. B. 1899-1985 . . . . DLB-11, 22

White, Edgar B. 1947- DLB-38

White, Horace 1834-1916 . . . . DLB-23

White, Richard Grant 1821-1885 . . . . DLB-64

White, Walter 1893-1955 . . . . DLB-51

White, William, and Company DLB-49

White, William Allen 1868-1944 . . . . DLB-9, 25

White, William Anthony Parker (see Boucher, Anthony)

White, William Hale (see Rutherford, Mark)

Whitechurch, Victor L. 1868-1933 . . . . DLB-70

Whitehead, James 1936- Y-81

Whitfield, James Monroe 1822-1871 . . . . DLB-50

Whiting, John 1917-1963 . . . . DLB-13

Whiting, Samuel 1597-1679 . . . . DLB-24

Whitlock, Brand 1869-1934 . . . . DLB-12

Whitman, Albert, and Company DLB-46

Whitman, Albery Allson 1851-1901 . . . . DLB-50

Whitman, Sarah Helen (Power) 1803-1878 . . . . . . DLB-1

Whitman, Walt 1819-1892 . . . . DLB-3, 64

Whitman Publishing Company DLB-46

Whittemore, Reed 1919- DLB-5

Whittier, John Greenleaf 1807-1892 . . . . DLB-1

Whittlesey House DLB-46

Wideman, John Edgar 1941- DLB-33

Wiebe, Rudy 1934- DLB-60

Wiechert, Ernst 1887-1950 . . . . DLB-56

Wieners, John 1934- DLB-16

Wier, Ester 1910- DLB-52

Wiesel, Elie 1928- Y-87

Wiggin, Kate Douglas 1856-1923 . . . . DLB-42

Wigglesworth, Michael 1631-1705 . . . . DLB-24

Wilbur, Richard 1921- DLB-5

Wild, Peter 1940- DLB-5

Wilde, Oscar 1854-1900 . . . . DLB-10, 19, 34, 57

Wilde, Richard Henry 1789-1847 . . . . DLB-3, 59

Wilde, W. A., Company DLB-49

Wilder, Billy 1906- DLB-26

Wilder, Laura Ingalls 1867-1957 .... DLB-22

Wilder, Thornton 1897-1975 .... DLB-4, 7, 9

Wiley, Bell Irvin 1906-1980 .... DLB-17

Wiley, John, and Sons DLB-49

Wilhelm, Kate 1928- DLB-8

Wilkinson, Sylvia 1940- Y-86

Wilkinson, William Cleaver 1833-1920 .... DLB-71

Willard, L. [publishing house] DLB-49

Willard, Nancy 1936- DLB-5, 52

Willard, Samuel 1640-1707 .... DLB-24

Williams, A., and Company DLB-49

Williams, C. K. 1936- DLB-5

Williams, Emlyn 1905- DLB-10

Williams, Garth 1912- DLB-22

Williams, George Washington 1849-1891 ...... DLB-47

Williams, Heathcote 1941- DLB-13

Williams, Hugo 1942- DLB-40

Williams, Isaac 1802-1865 .... DLB-32

Williams, Joan 1928- DLB-6

Williams, John A. 1925- DLB-2, 33

Williams, John E. 1922- DLB-6

Williams, Jonathan 1929- DLB-5

Williams, Raymond 1921- DLB-14

Williams, Roger circa 1603-1683 .... DLB-24

Williams, Samm-Art 1946- DLB-38

Williams, Sherley Anne 1944- DLB-41

Williams, T. Harry 1909-1979 .... DLB-17

Williams, Tennessee 1911-1983 ..... DLB-7; Y-83; DS-4

Williams, William Appleman 1921- DLB-17

Williams, William Carlos 1883-1963 ..... DLB-4, 16, 54

Williams, Wirt 1921- DLB-6

Williams Brothers DLB-49

Williamson, Jack 1908- DLB-8

Willingham, Calder Baynard, Jr. 1922- ... DLB-2, 44

Willis, Nathaniel Parker 1806-1867 ...... DLB-3, 59, 73

Wilmer, Clive 1945- DLB-40

Wilson, A. N. 1950- DLB-14

Wilson, Angus 1913- DLB-15

Wilson, Arthur 1595-1652 .... DLB-58

Wilson, Augusta Jane Evans 1835-1909 .... DLB-42

Wilson, Colin 1931- DLB-14

Wilson, Edmund 1895-1972 .... DLB-63

Wilson, Ethel 1888-1980 .... DLB-68

Wilson, Harriet E. Adams 1828?-1863? DLB-50

Wilson, Harry Leon 1867-1939 .... DLB-9

Wilson, John 1588-1667 .... DLB-24

Wilson, Lanford 1937- DLB-7

Wilson, Margaret 1882-1973 .... DLB-9

Wilson, Michael 1914-1978 .... DLB-44

Wilson, Woodrow 1856-1924 .... DLB-47

Wimsatt, William K., Jr. 1907-1975 .... DLB-63

Winchell, Walter 1897-1972 .... DLB-29

Winchester, J. [publishing house] DLB-49

Windham, Donald 1920- DLB-6

Winsor, Justin 1831-1897 .... DLB-47

John C. Winston Company DLB-49

Winters, Yvor 1900-1968 .... DLB-48

Winthrop, John 1588-1649 .... DLB-24, 30

Winthrop, John, Jr. 1606-1676 .... DLB-24

Wirt, William 1772-1834 .... DLB-37

Wise, John 1652-1725 .... DLB-24

Wisner, George 1812-1849 .... DLB-43

Wister, Owen 1860-1938 .... DLB-9

Witherspoon, John 1723-1794 .... DLB-31

Wodehouse, P. G. 1881-1975 .... DLB-34

Woiwode, Larry 1941- DLB-6

Wolcott, Roger 1679-1767 .... DLB-24

Wolfe, Gene 1931- DLB-8

Wolfe, Thomas 1900-1938 .... DLB-9; DS-2; Y-85

Wollstonecraft, Mary 1759-1797 .... DLB-39

Wood, Benjamin 1820-1900 .... DLB-23

Wood, Charles 1932- DLB-13

Wood, Mrs. Henry 1814-1887 .... DLB-18

Wood, Samuel [publishing house] DLB-49

Wood, William ?-? DLB-24

Woodberry, George Edward 1855-1930 .... DLB-71

Woodbridge, Benjamin 1622-1684 .... DLB-24

Woodmason, Charles circa 1720-? DLB-31

Woodson, Carter G. 1875-1950 .... DLB-17

Woodward, C. Vann 1908- DLB-17

Woolf, David (see Maddow, Ben)

Woolf, Virginia 1882-1941 .... DLB-36

Woollcott, Alexander 1887-1943.............. DLB-29

Woolman, John 1720-1772 .... DLB-31

Woolner, Thomas 1825-1892................. DLB-35

Woolsey, Sarah Chauncy 1835-1905.......... DLB-42

Woolson, Constance Fenimore 1840-1894 ..... DLB-12

Worcester, Joseph Emerson 1784-1865.........DLB-1

The Works of the Rev. John Witherspoon
(1800-1801) [excerpts] DLB-31

A World Chronology of Important Science
Fiction Works (1818-1979) DLB-8

World Publishing Company DLB-46

Worthington, R., and Company DLB-49

Wouk, Herman 1915- Y-82

Wright, Charles 1935- Y-82

Wright, Charles Stevenson 1932- DLB-33

Wright, Frances 1795-1852 .... DLB-73

Wright, Harold Bell 1872-1944.................DLB-9

Wright, James 1927-1980......................DLB-5

Wright, Jay 1935- DLB-41

Wright, Louis B. 1899-1984 .... DLB-17

Wright, Richard 1908-1960......................DS-2

Wright, Richard B. 1937- DLB-53

Wright, Sarah Elizabeth 1928- DLB-33

Writers' Forum Y-85

Writing for the Theatre, by Harold Pinter DLB-13

Wylie, Elinor 1885-1928....................DLB-9, 45

Wylie, Philip 1902-1971 ....DLB-9

Y

Yates, J. Michael 1938- DLB-60

Yates, Richard 1926- DLB-2; Y-81

Yeats, William Butler 1865-1939 ....DLB-10, 19

Yep, Laurence 1948- DLB-52

Yezierska, Anzia 1885-1970 .... DLB-28

Yolen, Jane 1939- DLB-52

Yonge, Charlotte Mary 1823-1901............. DLB-18

A Yorkshire Tragedy......................... DLB-58

Yoseloff, Thomas [publishing house]......... DLB-46

Young, Al 1939- DLB-33

Young, Stark 1881-1963.......................DLB-9

Young, Waldeman 1880-1938 .... DLB-26

Young, William [publishing house]........... DLB-49

Yourcenar, Marguerite 1903-1987............. DLB-72

"You've Never Had It So Good," Gusted by
"Winds of Change": British Fiction in the
1950s, 1960s, and After................... DLB-14

Z

Zangwill, Israel 1864-1926.................... DLB-10

Zebra Books DLB-46

Zebrowski, George 1945- DLB-8

Zech, Paul 1881-1946......................... DLB-56

Zelazny, Roger 1937- DLB-8

Zenger, John Peter 1697-1746.............DLB-24, 43

Zieber, G. B., and Company.................. DLB-49

Zieroth, Dale 1946- DLB-60

Zimmer, Paul 1934- DLB-5

Zindel, Paul 1936- DLB-7, 52

Zolotow, Charlotte 1915- DLB-52

Zubly, John Joachim 1724-1781 .... DLB-31

Zu-Bolton II, Ahmos 1936- DLB-41

Zuckmayer, Carl 1896-1977 .... DLB-56

Zukofsky, Louis 1904-1978....................DLB-5

zur Mühlen, Hermynia 1883-1951............. DLB-56

Zweig, Arnold 1887-1968..................... DLB-66

Dictionary of Literary Biography

1: *The American Renaissance in New England*, edited by Joel Myerson (1978)

2: *American Novelists Since World War II*, edited by Jeffrey Helterman and Richard Layman (1978)

3: *Antebellum Writers in New York and the South*, edited by Joel Myerson (1979)

4: *American Writers in Paris, 1920-1939*, edited by Karen Lane Rood (1980)

5: *American Poets Since World War II*, 2 parts, edited by Donald J. Greiner (1980)

6: *American Novelists Since World War II*, Second Series, edited by James E. Kibler, Jr. (1980)

7: *Twentieth-Century American Dramatists*, 2 parts, edited by John MacNicholas (1981)

8: *Twentieth-Century American Science-Fiction Writers*, 2 parts, edited by David Cowart and Thomas L. Wymer (1981)

9: *American Novelists, 1910-1945*, 3 parts, edited by James J. Martine (1981)

10: *Modern British Dramatists, 1900-1945*, 2 parts, edited by Stanley Weintraub (1982)

11: *American Humorists, 1800-1950*, 2 parts, edited by Stanley Trachtenberg (1982)

12: *American Realists and Naturalists*, edited by Donald Pizer and Earl N. Harbert (1982)

13: *British Dramatists Since World War II*, 2 parts, edited by Stanley Weintraub (1982)

14: *British Novelists Since 1960*, 2 parts, edited by Jay L. Halio (1983)

15: *British Novelists, 1930-1959*, 2 parts, edited by Bernard Oldsey (1983)

16: *The Beats: Literary Bohemians in Postwar America*, 2 parts, edited by Ann Charters (1983)

17: *Twentieth-Century American Historians*, edited by Clyde N. Wilson (1983)

18: *Victorian Novelists After 1885*, edited by Ira B. Nadel and William E. Fredeman (1983)

19: *British Poets, 1880-1914*, edited by Donald E. Stanford (1983)

20: *British Poets, 1914-1945*, edited by Donald E. Stanford (1983)

21: *Victorian Novelists Before 1885*, edited by Ira B. Nadel and William E. Fredeman (1983)

22: *American Writers for Children, 1900-1960*, edited by John Cech (1983)

23: *American Newspaper Journalists, 1873-1900*, edited by Perry J. Ashley (1983)

24: *American Colonial Writers, 1606-1734*, edited by Emory Elliott (1984)

25: *American Newspaper Journalists, 1901-1925*, edited by Perry J. Ashley (1984)

26: *American Screenwriters*, edited by Robert E. Morsberger, Stephen O. Lesser, and Randall Clark (1984)

27: *Poets of Great Britain and Ireland, 1945-1960*, edited by Vincent B. Sherry, Jr. (1984)

28: *Twentieth-Century American-Jewish Fiction Writers*, edited by Daniel Walden (1984)

29: *American Newspaper Journalists, 1926-1950*, edited by Perry J. Ashley (1984)

30: *American Historians, 1607-1865*, edited by Clyde N. Wilson (1984)

31: *American Colonial Writers, 1735-1781*, edited by Emory Elliott (1984)

32: *Victorian Poets Before 1850*, edited by William E. Fredeman and Ira B. Nadel (1984)

33: *Afro-American Fiction Writers After 1955*, edited by Thadious M. Davis and Trudier Harris (1984)

34: *British Novelists, 1890-1929: Traditionalists*, edited by Thomas F. Staley (1985)

35: *Victorian Poets After 1850*, edited by William E. Fredeman and Ira B. Nadel (1985)

36: *British Novelists, 1890-1929: Modernists*, edited by Thomas F. Staley (1985)

37: *American Writers of the Early Republic*, edited by Emory Elliott (1985)

38: *Afro-American Writers After 1955: Dramatists and Prose Writers*, edited by Thadious M. Davis and Trudier Harris (1985)

39: *British Novelists, 1660-1800*, 2 parts, edited by Martin C. Battestin (1985)

40: *Poets of Great Britain and Ireland Since 1960*, 2 parts, edited by Vincent B. Sherry, Jr. (1985)

41: *Afro-American Poets Since 1955*, edited by Trudier Harris and Thadious M. Davis (1985)

42: *American Writers for Children Before 1900*, edited by Glenn E. Estes (1985)

43: *American Newspaper Journalists, 1690-1872*, edited by Perry J. Ashley (1986)

44: *American Screenwriters*, Second Series, edited by Randall Clark, Robert E. Morsberger, and Stephen O. Lesser (1986)

45: *American Poets, 1880-1945*, First Series, edited by Peter Quartermain (1986)

46: *American Literary Publishing Houses, 1900-1980: Trade and Paperback*, edited by Peter Dzwonkoski (1986)

47: *American Historians, 1866-1912*, edited by Clyde N. Wilson (1986)